THE LAIDLAW
SOCIAL SCIENCE PROGRAM

Concepts in Social Science

King • Bracken • Sloan • Rudman • Epperly • Cooke

PEOPLE AND THEIR NEEDS, Study Prints
PEOPLE AT HOME
FAMILIES AND SOCIAL NEEDS
COMMUNITIES AND SOCIAL NEEDS
REGIONS AND SOCIAL NEEDS
USING THE SOCIAL STUDIES
THE SOCIAL STUDIES AND OUR COUNTRY
THE SOCIAL STUDIES AND OUR WORLD

A CONTEMPORARY SOCIAL SCIENCE PROGRAM

THE LAIDLAW SOCIAL SCIENCE PROGRAM is a contemporary program based on current research in the social sciences. The program provides:

- An interdisciplinary approach to content which emphasizes the interrelationships of the social science disciplines—anthropology, economics, geography, history, political science, and sociology.

- An emphasis on developing the values and attitudes which prepare the pupil for effective participation in a democratic society.

- An inductive-inquiry approach in the presentation of content which guides discovery and involves pupils in using the skills of the social scientist.

- Development of the pupil's ability to evaluate and make decisions.

- Cross-cultural studies which enable the pupil to expand his horizons and develop positive attitudes toward people of various cultural backgrounds.

(For further information,
see the Back Flyleaf)

LAIDLAW BROTHERS

A Division of Doubleday

Thatcher and Madison

River Forest, Illinois 60305

The Social Studies and Our World

CONCEPTS IN SOCIAL SCIENCE

FREDERICK M. KING
Director of Instruction
Rochester, Minnesota

HERBERT C. RUDMAN
Professor of Education
Michigan State University
East Lansing, Michigan

HERBERT V. EPPERLY
Principal, Kellar West School
Peoria, Illinois

RALPH J. COOKE
Senior Editor
Laidlaw Social Science Program

LAIDLAW BROTHERS · PUBLISHERS
A Division of Doubleday & Company, Inc.
RIVER FOREST, ILLINOIS

Palo Alto, California   Dallas, Texas   Atlanta, Georgia   Toronto, Canada

The LAIDLAW SOCIAL SCIENCE PROGRAM

PEOPLE AND THEIR NEEDS
Concepts in Social Science

PEOPLE AT HOME
Concepts in Social Science

FAMILIES AND SOCIAL NEEDS
Concepts in Social Science

COMMUNITIES AND SOCIAL NEEDS
Concepts in Social Science

REGIONS AND SOCIAL NEEDS
Concepts in Social Science

USING THE SOCIAL STUDIES
Concepts in Social Science

THE SOCIAL STUDIES AND OUR COUNTRY
Concepts in Social Science

THE SOCIAL STUDIES AND OUR WORLD
Concepts in Social Science

The artwork for this book was done by TOM DUNNINGTON and CHARLES JOSLIN.
Maps were prepared by ART LUTZ; charts and graphs by DONALD T. PITCHER.

Photographs used in this book were supplied by the following:

Alinari: 135 *top right.*
Allied Chemical Corporation: 404.
Courtesy of the American Museum of Natural History: 10, 45 *both,* 53, 61 *bottom center,* 63, 83, 379 *bottom right.*
Authenticated News International: 21 *right,* 322, 332, 345, 383 *right,* 385, 391 *right,* 399 *top.*
Bethlehem Steel Corporation: 382 *top left.*
The Bettmann Archive: 148, 180, 192, 212, 228, 231, 235, 267, 269 *left,* 278 *left,* 278 *center,* 280 *bottom,* 282, 308.
The Boeing Company, Seattle: 370.
Brown Brothers: 250, 387.
J. Allan Cash: 36 *right,* 48, 94 *top,* 111, 125, 133, 159, 163, 326.
Chase Manhattan Bank: 263.
Courtesy Chicago Natural History Museum: 74 *left.*
Tourism Council, Republic of China, Taiwan: 309 *both.*
Communication Satellite Corporation: 370.
Courtesy Corning Museum of Glass: 262.
Culver Pictures, Inc.: 181, 190, 254 *both,* 276, 293, 295 *both.*
Charles Phelps Cushing: 28 *top,* 34 *top,* 36 *left,* 238, 242 *top,* 243.
J. E. Dayton: 65 *both,* 74 *right.*
A. Devaney, Inc.: 17, 144, 155, 189 *bottom left,* 241, 242 *bottom,* 277, 291, 315, 383 *bottom left.*
De Wys, Inc.: 23, 99 *top,* 118 *top,* 187, 196, 248, 304 *top,* 316, 324, 357 *top right,* 358 *right,* 372, 391 *left;* (G. Reitz) 337.
Editions Hoa-Qui, Paris: 245.
Harrison Forman: 32, 94 *bottom,* 100, 115 *top,* 147, 186, 240, 283, 312 *left,* 321, 325 *top,* 328 *both,* 352 *both left,* 386 *left.*
Fox Photos, Ltd.: 317, 333, 402.
Freeport Sulfur Company: 384 *both.*
Courtesy of the French Government Tourist Office: 182, 218.
General Motors Corporation: 314.
Grant Heilman: 109, 110, 357 *top left,* 359, 364, 365, 380, 382 *top right,* 390, 393 *top.*
Hirmer Fotoarchiv München: 84, 101, 102, 114, 116 *bottom.*
Historical Pictures Service, Inc., Chicago: 85, 129, 145, 165 *both,* 183, 185, 189 *top right,* 202, 203, 207, 215, 216, 239, 251, 266, 270, 294, 299, 302, 343.
Michael Holford Library: 174, 204; (British Museum) 224.
International Society for Educational Information Tokyo, Inc.: 393 *bottom.*
Israel Information Service: 157.

Consulate General of Japan: 386.
Jericho Excavation Fund: 69.
A. F. Kersting: 97, 118 *bottom.*
Leon Kofod: 73.
John LaDue: 352 *right.*
Cy LaTour: 9, 13 *top,* 21 *left.*
Metropolitan Museum of Art: 112 *right.*
Monkmeyer Press Photo Service: 198, 361; (Warren Slater) 62.
Musée de l'Homme, Paris: 57, 61 *top left,* 61 *top center,* 61 *right.*
Courtesy, Museum of Fine Arts, Boston: 164.
Museum für Volkerkunde, Berlin: 233, 237.
National Coal Association: 379 *bottom left,* 397.
National Geographic Society: (Robert F. Sisson © 1961) 11 *top.*
Collection of the Newark Museum: 168.
Oriental Institute, University of Chicago: 89 *both,* 91, 106, 112 *left,* 116 *top.*
Oscar & Associates, Inc.: 141.
Carl E. Ostman: 143.
Courtesy of the Pan American Union: 34 *bottom.*
Publix Pictorial Service Corporation: 126; (C. A. Peterson) 312 *center,* 312 *right.*
H. Armstrong Roberts: 16, 22, 81, 99 *bottom,* 146 *both,* 162, 166, 213, 220, 236, 278 *right,* 356, 357 *bottom right,* 368, 383 *center.*
The Rouse Company, Columbia, Maryland: 18.
Royal Ontario Museum, Toronto, Canada: 40 *both.*
Josephine Powell: 95, 104.
Scala, New York/Florence: (Karachi Museum) 115 *bottom;* (Antwerp Museum) 209.
Sovfoto: 305, 340; (Novosti) 319 *top;* (Tass) 319 *bottom;* (Eastfoto) 327.
Three Lions, Inc.: 26, 28 *bottom,* 34 *center,* 35 *left,* 35 *center,* 122, 138, 139, 269 *center,* 269 *right,* 280 *top,* 281; (British Museum, London) 78; (Schiff) 313.
United Press International: 13 *bottom,* 29, 47, 160, 304 *bottom,* 306, 339 *both,* 347 *bottom,* 395.
U.S. Treasury Department, Bureau of the Mint: 12.
University Museum, University of Pennsylvania: 217, 274.
Van Cleve Photography: (Gerhard Reimann) 51.
Water and Power Department, Los Angeles, California: 377.
Wide World Photos: 47 *right,* 346, 347 *top,* 348, 378, 394, 405.
Roger Wood Studio: 67, 88.
Zentrale Farbbild Agentur: 6, 11 *bottom,* 49, 54, 151, 249, 253, 265, 272, 373, 376.

ISBN-0-8445-6626-8

Copyright © 1974, 1972 by Laidlaw Brothers, Publishers

A Division of Doubleday & Company, Inc.

Printed in the United States of America

3456789   321098765

Teacher's Edition ISBN 0-8445-6636-5   23456789   321098765

A Look at the Social Sciences

UNIT 1

Man Before History

UNIT 2

Ancient Civilizations

UNIT 3

Eastern and Western Civilizations

UNIT 4

List of Maps

List of Charts and Graphs

For Teaching Helps, see page T17.

UNIT 1   A LOOK AT THE SOCIAL SCIENCES

Stress:
1. Throughout the world, more and more people are living in cities.
2. Urbanization creates new problems that have to be solved.
3. Overcrowding, as is shown in the picture below, is a serious problem in many modern cities.

Chapters
1. Social Scientists at Work
2. Planning a New City

*4. Why do more people today tend to live in cities than ever before?

Modern Hong Kong

6

Stress:
1. Social scientists study about man and his societies.
2. Modern social scientists tend to specialize in one area--i.e., political science, sociology, history, economics, anthropology, or geography.

Social science is man's search for knowledge about himself—about his past; about his societies; about various systems for providing himself with goods and services. Some evidence indicates that man has changed through the ages. How the changes occurred and how the changes should be interpreted are questions that are still to be answered. In this book, some theories about these changes are mentioned. As you study, keep in mind that these are theories, not facts.

See #1 above.

In order to study the social sciences today, it is necessary to use the findings of many social scientists. Some of these people are historians or geographers. Others are economists or political scientists. Still others are sociologists or anthropologists. These social scientists are concerned with observing people, places, and events in an attempt to answer certain questions about man.

See #2 above.

The social scientist is a person with a great amount of curiosity. He wants to know why and how things are happening. Each social scientist in his particular field searches for new information, or researches past information. From this information, he hopes to gain new insights into today's problems.

See #3 below.

The social sciences are **interrelated**; that is, they depend on one another. The information discovered by the anthropologist is helpful to the historian. The knowledge gained by the economist about prices and wages is of interest to the political scientist.

See #4 below.

As you study this unit, try to find answers to questions such as these:

1. What are the methods of the social scientists?
2. How are the social sciences interrelated?
3. What are the problems faced by social scientists?

3. Social scientists observe man and try to solve some of the problems facing modern societies.
4. Social scientists rely upon each other for information.
*5. How might a social scientist--for example, a political scientist-- help people in your community?

7

For Teaching Helps, see page T17.
Stress:
1. The continuing nature of the class project. See pp. 25 and 37.

CLASS PROJECT—PART 1

2. Social scientists are interested in how people live, work, and relax.

To begin the class project, determine carefully the boundaries of an area your class would like to study as a social scientist might. A six-block area around your school may be one possibility. What kinds of questions would you like to ask about this area? What questions do you think a social scientist would ask about it? Place the questions on a chalkboard. The picture below may give you some ideas concerning questions to ask. As a next step classify the questions under various topics—for example, land, buildings, people of early days, and so on. Select one of the topics for study by the entire class. How might the class organize to explore the topic further? One suggestion would be to divide the class into six groups with each group taking the role of one of the six types of social scientists you will be studying.

As you study Chapter 1, take notes regarding the work and methods employed by the social scientist your group selected. These notes will help you with Part 2 of the class project. Also, be thinking about the topic.

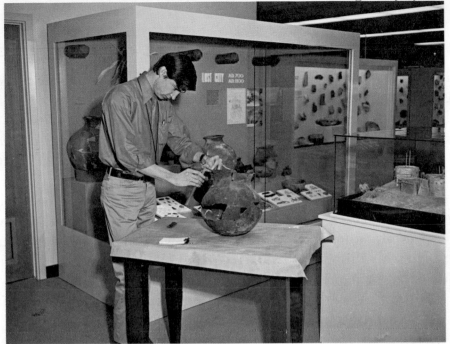

An anthropologist at work rebuilding an artifact

1. Social Scientists at Work

Each social scientist looks for a different type of information about man. Depending on his field of study, the social scientist uses different methods to find needed information.

An anthropologist, like the one in the picture, may rely on observations of man-made objects called artifacts to tell him something about the materials and skills early people had. A sociologist might depend on interviews and observations of a group, such as a labor union, that he was studying.

All social scientists are concerned with the accuracy of their findings. They are careful to try to draw the correct conclusions from their research. They must be willing to accept the findings of others, even though they may disagree with the findings.

In this chapter the work of some social scientists will be discussed.

JUST FOR FUN

Bring an artifact to class. Display it along with a question about man that someone can answer by observing your artifact. Your question should begin with the word *what, when, where,* or *why.*

Stress:
1. Social scientists study about man and his way of life.
*2. Why is accuracy so important to a social scientist?

9

For Teaching Helps, see page T19.
Stress:
1. Anthropologists study about early man—his government, his economy, and his society.

THE ANTHROPOLOGIST AT WORK

The science of anthropology Some anthropologists attempt to find out how early man lived. In their work they have searched for man's oldest ancestors. They want to know how early man looked. In their attempts to answer their questions, anthropologists have located and uncovered buried cities.

See #1 above.

Anthropologists are interested in all aspects of early man's life. They want to know how early man organized his society, his government, and his economy. What other social scientists would be able to help the anthropologist in answering these questions? All others.

The work of Dr. Leakey One of the well-known anthropologists of our times is Dr. Louis Leakey. He was born in Kenya, Africa, in 1903. His parents were English missionaries, and he was educated in England.

Reconstruction of Zinjanthropus

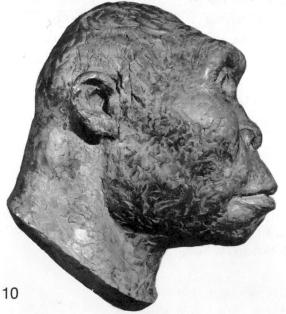

Louis then returned to Africa as an anthropologist trying to find information about man's early ancestors. He and his wife Mary, who was also an anthropologist, did most of their **excavating,** or digging, in the country of Tanzania. After thirty years of research and excavations, they were rewarded with a great discovery. In 1959 they found a skull that had been in the ground a long time. From analyzing the bone structure of the skull, the Leakeys felt that the skull was that of a young man sixteen to eighteen years old when he died. The Leakeys called their discovery *Zinjanthropus* (zin′jan thrō′pəs). "Zinj" was an early name for Africa and "anthropus" means man. The Leakeys asked themselves this question: Was this an ancestor of early man? Study the picture. What do you think?

However, in the early 1960's the Leakeys made new discoveries in the same area. They found the remains of an early man they called *Homo habilis* (hō′mō hab′ə ləs), which means handy man, or man with ability. As a result, Dr. Leakey decided that *Zinjanthropus* was not a true man, but instead only a "near-man." Thus, Dr. Leakey now places *Homo habilis* as the earliest known type of man who lived at least 1,750,000 years ago. *Homo habilis* was, according to Dr. Leakey, the first known man who made and used tools.

See #2 below.

2. Recent discoveries indicate that early man may have lived over 1,750,000 years ago.

An early culture Along with the skeletal bones of some of the earliest people on earth, Dr. Leakey also found tools made of bone. The picture shows him using tools patterned after them. Dr. Leakey showed that bone tools would have most likely been used for smoothing and polishing animal skins into usable leather. Dr. Leakey believed that the animal skins were then used for mats, clothes, and covers for dwellings.

See #1 below.

The remains of the early culture indicated that the people probably depended for food on animals that could be easily caught. For example, although remains of tortoises (giant turtles), catfish, and water birds were found, very few bones of large animals were found. Then Dr. Leakey asked himself this question: If *Homo habilis* was not mainly a hunter of big game, then where did he get the skins? Although he had little evidence to help him answer his question, Dr. Leakey believed that this early man was not yet hunting large animals for food. However, if an animal died a natural death, or was killed by another animal, early man arrived at the scene, had a feast, and then took the skins. Why do you think this early man did not hunt large animals for food? Lacked weapons.

Problems of the anthropologist In the account you have read, you have seen some of the problems of the anthropologist. He may have very little evidence to use in answering his questions. His conclusions may have to be "educated guesses" until more proof is found.

See #2 below.

Work of the archaeologist The people shown in the picture are seeking remains of an early culture. These social

Stress:
1. Early man had crude tools made from bone and stone.
2. Anthropologists reach conclusions based on the evidence they find.

11

Stress:
1. Artifacts are evidence used by archaeologists to learn about other cultures.
*2. In what ways could other social scientists use the findings of archaeologists?

which might have been a coin. Assuming you were able to determine the language, you would observe that among other things the piece of metal was engraved with the words, "United States of America," "quarter dollar," and the date "1970." If you were to study this piece of metal, a quarter, you might first list some questions you would be trying to answer. Here are some examples of questions you might ask.

1. Did the people know more than one language?
2. Who might the picture represent?
3. Is the artifact all the same type of metal? If not, what might this indicate about the culture of the people?
4. What conclusions might you draw about the civilization?
5. Are your conclusions correct?

See #1 above.
scientists are archaeologists. Archaeologists are interested in studying such things as pottery, ruins of buildings, and coins which were left behind by people of early cultures. From these artifacts, the archaeologist tries to draw conclusions about the society that produced and used them.

A ↔

To discover how archaeologists work, imagine you and some friends are archaeologists 2,000 years in the future. You are conducting an archaeological dig at a site in North America. One of the objects you find is a piece of metal

A ←

Think for Yourself

What can a real archaeologist do to check his conclusions about a society that produced an artifact that he is studying? Do research and ask questions.

For Teaching Helps, see page T20.

THE HISTORIAN AT WORK

For a class activity, see #2 on page 25.

The study of history Man has always been curious about what happened before he was born. He sees the world today and wonders how and why it became this way. A historian studies the people and events of the past trying to recon-

H ↔

struct what took place. He asks the question: Why did things happen this way instead of another way? He wants to know why people lived as they did.

In his study of the past, the historian has many problems. If he is

Stress:
1. Historians often work with the
   written records of the past.

searching for the story of the earliest man, there are no written records for him to use. He might turn to other social scientists to help him answer his questions. Who might be able to help the historian?

See #1 above.

In some cases the historian can find only **fragments**, or parts, of written records. There are gaps in his knowledge of the past. The historian may find several accounts of the same event which disagree. He must ask and then answer the question: Which is accurate? How might a historian find the answer to his question?

See #2 below.

Sources of information In order to find information about the past, the historian may rely on accounts that were written by eyewitnesses or people who were alive at the time. He uses diaries, newspapers, letters, and any other records he can find. These are called **primary sources.** He must ask whether these sources could or would give an accurate picture. The historian may also use accounts that were written after an event took place. These works would be called **secondary sources.** Which of the two kinds of sources is the historian shown above using?

Checking information The historian must examine his sources carefully. Some people have deliberately produced false evidence which at first appeared to be true. One example is the famous Piltdown fraud. In a gravel pit at Pilt-

Historian at work with an old newspaper

down in Sussex, England, an amateur archaeologist named Charles Dawson discovered some interesting bones in 1911. He found part of a skull and, nearby, a jawbone. Dawson and researchers from the British Museum pieced together the fragments, making a model called Piltdown Man. The picture shows a model of what the Piltdown Man might have looked like. Although the skull was that of a human, the jawbone seemed more like that of an ape. However, since few other bones were found

Reconstruction of Piltdown Man

2. Historians use primary and secondary
   sources.
3. Historians must be careful to make
   sure the records they use are accurate.

13

For Teaching Helps, see page T20.
Stress:
1. Scientific tests can be used to verify some historical information.

in the area, the scientists believed that the two did belong together.

At first, scientists believed the bones were those of a man who had lived about 1,000,000 years ago. It was a tremendous discovery! Museums made copies of the skull. However, the Piltdown Man was not accepted as genuine by some social scientists. Many were puzzled by the apelike jawbone of this man. It didn't seem to go along with other findings and studies of prehistoric man that had been made. Not wanting to injure the bones, the scientists did no further experiments at that time.

Exposing a fraud For over forty years, the Piltdown Man was considered genuine, although suspicion remained. In 1953 scientists ran other experiments which proved that this human skull was only 50,000 years old. The tests that were done on the jawbone proved that it had belonged to a modern ape. In addition, the jawbone had been treated with chemicals to make it look older than it was. Someone had tried to make historians and scientists believe that the skull and jawbone were those of a prehistoric man. Since Charles Dawson and the other researchers were dead, it was difficult to find out who had done this. Historians were not able to find the answer to their question: Who was responsible for the Piltdown fraud?

Historians and other social scientists often face this problem: Something is

believed to be true, but new information proves it to be false. Great care is taken to avoid this situation. What are some things social scientists might do to avoid these problems? What must they do when they discover that their information is no longer true?

A problem with sources To discover how historians work, imagine you are a historian studying the American Revolution. On the facing page there are several selections from primary and secondary sources. They all tell about the colonists' being warned of the advancing British troops. As you read these selections, try to answer the following questions.

1. In what details do the selections agree? The colonists were forewarned.
2. What differences do you find in the selections? No mention of Paul Revere in some.
3. Why do you think Paul Revere's name is mentioned in the sources written after 1863? Longfellow's poem used as a source.
4. Who had the greatest influence in making Paul Revere's name live in history? Longfellow.
5. Which problems that are presented to the historian are shown by these selections? Different sources tell different stories.

Think for Yourself

Name some primary and secondary sources you could check for information about a space flight. Diaries, letters, newspapers, and accounts written after the flight.

See #1 above.

14 2. Historians often compare different sources to ensure accuracy.
  *3. Why might some historians interpret facts one way and other historians interpret the same facts in another way?

Source (1775): *The London Gazette* (English version).

Lieutenant-Colonel Smith finding, after he had advanced some miles on his march, that the country had been alarmed by the firing of guns and ringing of bells. . . .

Source (1857): An American history text written in 1857.

The men arrived there (Lexington) at seven. The inhabitants had received news of the intended movement about midnight.

Source (1863): *Tales of a Wayside Inn*, Henry Wadsworth Longfellow.

Paul Revere's Ride

Listen, my children, and you
　　shall hear
Of the midnight ride of Paul
　　Revere,
On the eighteenth of April,
　　in seventy-five;
Hardly a man is now alive
Who remembers that famous
　　day and year.

. . . .

So through the night rode
　　Paul Revere;
And so through the night
　　went his cry of alarm
To every Middlesex village
　　and farm, . . .

Source (1905): Historian George Elliott Howard.

[General] Gage now determined to send a secret expedition to destroy the magazines at Concord, a village eighteen miles northwest of Boston. . . . [T]he secret was not well kept, and William Dawes and Paul Revere were dispatched to give the alarm.

Source (1917): *An American History*, David Muzzey. Ginn and Company.*

On the night of the eighteenth of April, Gage sent troops to seize the powder the provincials had collected at Concord. . . . But the ardent Boston patriot, Paul Revere, had learned of the expedition, and galloping ahead of the British troops, he roused the farmers on the way and warned the refugees.

Source (1945): *Paul Revere*, Esther Forbes. Houghton Mifflin Company.**

The idea that Paul Revere was the only rider out that night was so picturesquely implanted in the American mind by Longfellow that there was a natural reaction when it was learned that he was by no means out alone. Although Joseph Warren officially sent out from Boston two men —William Dawes and Paul Revere— at least three others noticed that something was afoot that day in town and in a mild way did spread the alarm.

Source (1966): *History of Our United States*, Eibling, King, Harlow. Laidlaw Brothers, Publishers.

The rebels in Boston, however, were not asleep. On the night of April 18, 1775, when about 800 British troops moved out of Boston toward Concord, two horsemen sped out of Boston, each in a different direction. One was William Dawes, the other Paul Revere; their mission, to arouse the countryside and warn the people of the British move.

*From *An American History,* by David Saville Muzzey. Copyright © 1917 by Ginn and Company. Reprinted by permission.
**From *Paul Revere and the World He Lived In,* by Esther Forbes. Copyright © 1945 by Houghton Mifflin. Reprinted by permission.

Stress:
1. Most people belong to some type of a group.

THE SOCIOLOGIST AT WORK

2. Cooperating groups of people make up a society.

The study of society Most people spend their entire lives as members of one group or another. A child is born into a family group. He becomes part of a school group. He may become part of a church group or a youth group. As he grows older, man becomes part of a business group and then may begin his own family group. When people live together in cooperating groups, we call this a society. Social scientists called sociologists study societies. They are looking at man in his groups. Sociologists ask the questions: How do various groups affect man? Do these groups cause man to change his way of behaving? Sociologists also want to know how man in his groups affects society.

See #1 and #2 above.

Sociologists are interested in the surrounding conditions and influences that affect man. These conditions and influences are called **environment** (en vĭ′rən mənt). A special type of sociologist is interested in groups that live in a city environment. These sociologists are called **urban** sociologists. They want to know how city life affects man. Urban sociologists study the many differences between living in a country environment and living in a city environment. Man responds differently to city life than to country life and may form different types of groups.

See #3 below.

Problems of the cities The large cities of the United States are great centers of industry, trade, and cultural activities. It is estimated that about 30 per cent of the American people live in cities having over 100,000 people. Our large cities provide many opportunities for people, but they also present many problems.

3. Urban sociologists study how man is affected by life in cities.

Family studying plans for their new home

Smog in Chicago

Many urban sociologists are becoming very concerned about the city. They see its "bigness" as a source of many problems for man. The overcrowded conditions and the heavy pollution as shown in this picture can be harmful to man. One well-known American urban sociologist is Lewis Mumford. He has done much research on the problems of the ever-growing cities and their effects on man in the twentieth century.

S/E →

S ←

Cities of the past Lewis Mumford studied the growth of cities in the past. He used information that the archaeologist and the historian had discovered. But Mumford felt that he had to go beyond their findings. As an urban sociologist, Mumford was interested in discovering how city life affected man in the past and how it affects him today.

S/G →

A/H ←

See #1
below.

In his study, Mumford found that most large cities grew without much advance planning. Cities developed as commercial and manufacturing centers. As industries grew, more people left the country areas to come to the cities. Mumford found that while the cities were growing rapidly, plans for meeting the people's needs were not being made as rapidly.

See #2
below.

Groups of people living together in a city have certain needs. There is a need for government, an educational system, and for social services, such as hospitals and police protection. Mumford defines these as **social needs.** In cities that expanded rapidly, these services were often inadequate. As a result, man found many problems to face in these large cities.

Stress:
1. Other social scientists provide information used by sociologists.
2. Throughout history, most cities have developed without advance planning.

For Teaching Helps, see page T21.
Stress:
1. Some sociologists feel that future cities should be planned.

Cities for the future To overcome some of these problems, Mumford believes that the cities of the future must be planned. The social needs of the people must become the most important part of city planning. The structure of the city—the location of its industries, the traffic routes, the housing areas—must be planned to serve the people.

The cities of the future, as seen by Mumford, may be what he calls **regional cities.** Regional cities would be planned communities with their own industries, trade, and social life. These communities would be linked to a large city. The picture on this page shows an example of a regional city called Columbia, located in Maryland. Its aim is to combine the friendliness of a small town with the advantages and opportunities of a large modern city.

Aerial view of Columbia, Md.

Columbia, Maryland In the diagram on page 19, each orange patch represents a village of 9,000 to 12,000 people. The village center contains junior and senior high schools, a shopping mall, a library, a swimming pool, and community buildings. Each of the five areas within each village consists of neighborhoods of 500 to 600 families. Each neighborhood center contains an elementary school, a nursery school, parks, and playgrounds.

The villages are arranged around the central city or the town center. Here are found the government offices, museums and theaters, hospitals, office buildings, and a junior college.

Industries are located far enough away from the villages so as not to be disturbing, but close enough to make it easy for people to get to work. Each village depends on the town center and still is small enough to avoid the problems of many large cities. Excellent bus transportation, as shown by the dotted lines, solves many traffic problems. The surrounding countryside is reserved for farming and recreation.

A regional city, such as Columbia, would bring together the neighborhoods, villages, and the central city into one large, well-organized unit. The social needs of the people could be planned for and met in an organized way. This city, which is expected to be completed in 1980, was planned by a group made up

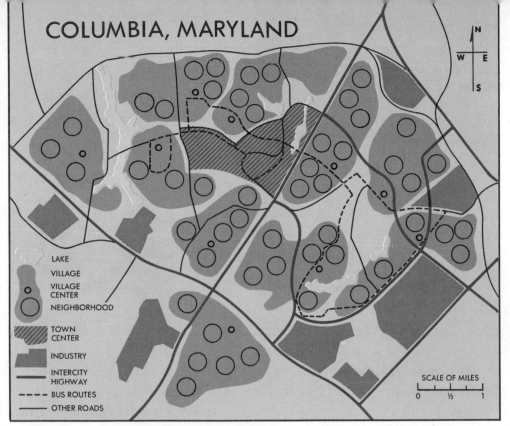

COLUMBIA, MARYLAND

LAKE
VILLAGE
VILLAGE CENTER
NEIGHBORHOOD
TOWN CENTER
INDUSTRY
INTERCITY HIGHWAY
BUS ROUTES
OTHER ROADS

SCALE OF MILES
0   ½   1

Stress:
1. Many social scientists may be involved in planning a city.

of experts in local government, family life, economics, and geography. Do you think you might like to live in a city like this? Why or why not?

Problems of the urban sociologist One of the difficulties facing the urban sociologist is the fact that human society in the city is influenced by so many things. In order to study society, sociologists must consider man's customs, values, beliefs, and way of life. Thus, the sociologist has many different things to consider before he is able to reach any firm conclusions about man's way of life in the city.

See #2 below.

S ↔

S/G →

Study of population One group of sociologists is interested in studying

population. They want to know the number of people living in urban areas and the number in rural areas. They ask the questions: Why do large numbers of people settle in one particular place rather than another? What causes people to move from one area to another? This study of population concentration and movement is called **demography** (di mog′rə fi).

A demographic study Sociologists often use a demographic study in their work. Maps like the one on the following page are very useful to sociologists. As you study the map showing population density, see if you can answer the following questions.

See #3 below.

2. Man's customs, values, beliefs, and way of life must be considered by an urban sociologist.

3. Some sociologists study population and how it is distributed.

19

POPULATION DENSITY
OF THE UNITED STATES

PERSONS PER
SQUARE MILE

25 TO 125	(hatched)
UNDER 2	125 TO 250
2 TO 25	OVER 250

ALASKA

HAWAII

SCALE OF MILES
0 200 400 600

SCALE OF MILES
0 100 200

SCALE OF MILES
0 200 400

For Teaching Helps, see page T21.

1. How does your state compare in population density to a nearby state?

2. Why do some very large states have a lesser population density than some of the smaller states? Climate and geography.

3. Which part of the United States, the northeast, southeast, north-west, or southwest, has the most people? Northeast.

4. Which part of our country has the smallest number of people? Southwest.

S/G
↔

Think for Yourself

How does your city try to provide for the needs of its citizens? Police and fire protection, health services, and so on.

THE ECONOMIST AT WORK

For Teaching Helps, see page T22.

See #1 below.

The study of economics All men have certain basic needs including food, shelter, clothing, and recreation. In addition to these needs, people have unlimited wants. Refer to the first picture on page 21. What wants might these boys have? Could they ever satisfy all of them? Why or why not? No, they are unlimited.

Economists study how people and nations use their limited resources to satisfy their needs and wants. These economists ask the question: How are resources being used? What other social scientists might economists ask for help in answering this question? Geographers.

The economist Many economists work for the government. They might advise the President and Congress on how military spending or highway expenses will affect the country. Other

E
↔

E/G
→

Stress:
1. All people have certain basic needs and unlimited wants.
2. Economists study how limited resources are used by man to satisfy his needs and wants.

Young people in front of a hobby shop

Market researchers using modern equipment

economists study the organization of business. They might advise a company on wages and prices.

A particularly interesting work of some economists is market research. Companies planning to introduce a new product may use market research to determine if it will sell. They may pass out samples and then ask people's opinions about them. Economists may then use computers to determine how best to sell the products. Has your family ever been a part of such a study? If so, what were some of the questions asked?

Market researchers also study the reasons why people are attracted to the products they buy. The results of one study on new cars are shown on this page. After reading the survey, decide how this survey would be of value to automobile manufacturers.

See #1 below.

E ←

Think for Yourself

How does your family decide how to use its resources? By determining its needs and wants.

E ←

MARKET RESEARCH

A study was made of 10,000 people to find out their reasons for selecting one type of new car. The answers given, in order of importance, were:

1. "Family loyalty"—25% of the people would buy the same make of car they had before.
2. Turn-in value
3. Styling, exterior appearance
4. Price
5. Handling ease
6. Performance
7. Cost of operation
8. Engineering

Stress:
1. Some economists try to find out why people buy the things they do.
*2. Why might an economist be interested in the information provided by a sociologist?

For Teaching Helps, see page T23.
Stress:
1. Geographers are interested in man and the earth and how they affect one
   another.

THE GEOGRAPHER AT WORK

The study of geography The earth is continually changing. Some of these changes are natural, as a river washing away the soil on its banks. Other changes are man-made, as men clearing land to build a city or building a dam to provide water power. Geographers are interested in the changing earth as man's home. They ask these questions: How do the earth's changes affect man? How do man-made changes affect the earth?

The geographer Geographers have a wide range of interests. Some may be especially interested in a region such as northern Europe. They would be geographers with a **regional specialty.** Other geographers might be interested in a topic such as climate or minerals. They would be geographers with a **topical specialty.** How might the work of geographers with regional or topical specialties be useful to the government or industries? How might they be useful to tourists? Provide information about a region.

Some geographers are mapmakers. They are called **cartographers** (kär tog′ rə fərz). Cartographers may produce maps used for navigation. They may make a map showing the location of minerals and other natural resources in an area. Cartographers may draw a map showing population density. Can you name some other maps that they might produce? Who would be likely to use them?

See #2 below.

Men changing the nature of the earth by clearing land for new homes

22

Modern housing development

Using our natural resources Man is a major cause of changes on the earth's surface. Some of these changes are good and for the benefit of man. Others are not. Forests have been cleared to provide land for building homes as shown in the picture. Other times, man has carelessly destroyed forests through fires. Rivers have been made wider and deeper for better transportation. However, at the same time, many of our rivers and lakes have been polluted by waste materials. Many of our natural resources such as coal, iron, and oil are being used up at a rapid rate.

G
↔

Geographers, as well as others, are very concerned about the problem of using our natural resources wisely. Some of our resources can be replaced over a long period of time, such as replanting a forest. However, some of our resources cannot be replaced. For example, coal and iron which are mined cannot be replaced. What do you think man can do to stop the waste of our natural resources? Conserve present resources and find new resources.

Think for Yourself

How has your state tried to conserve its natural resources?

23

For Teaching Helps, see page T24.
Stress:
1. Political scientists study man and his government.

THE POLITICAL SCIENTIST AT WORK

The study of government There are many different types of governments in the world. Some countries have a king and parliament, some have a president and congress, others have military leaders. In some countries, the people are directly involved in their government. The people are able to vote for their leaders. In other countries, the leaders are not chosen by the people and may hold power by force. Political scientists are interested in man's relationship to his government. They study different types of government and ask the following questions: Why and how does one government differ from another? What effects does this government have on the people?

See #1 and #2 above.

Political scientists study the operation of government and its agencies. Many political scientists work for the government as advisers on government programs. A number of others work as aides to public officials.

Studying public opinion Political scientists are interested in knowing how and why man has developed his political views. To study this, they may refer to a public opinion poll. In a poll a carefully selected group of people, called a **sample,** are asked certain questions. The people who are taking the poll try to get a sample that includes people of many different religions, races, and occupations. They hope that this sample will be a good guide as to what most people believe.

The questions shown on this page were asked of a sample of 3,215 people. Political scientists would study the results of such a poll. What conclusions might they draw from this study? Can you give some reasons why a poll may not give an accurate picture of what most people believe?

Think for Yourself

See if you can find out how your city is governed.

POLL QUESTIONS *

1. In politics as of today, do you consider yourself a Republican, Democrat, or Independent?

Republican	24%
Democrat	49%
Independent	24%
Other or don't know	3%

2. As you remember it, for which party did your father usually vote in Presidential elections when you were too young to vote?

Republican	26%
Democratic	47%
Other	1%
Sometimes Republican	6%
Sometimes Democratic Don't know	20%

*From *The Political Beliefs of Americans: A Study of Public Opinion*, by L. A. Free and H. Cantril. Copyright © 1967 by Rutgers University Press. Reprinted by permission.

*3. Why do the values and beliefs of people affect the type of government a society has?

Things to Do

See page 16.

1. Pretend you are the chairman of a group making plans to develop a new city. The first year this city is developed it will have a population of 10,000 people. Make a drawing of your plan for this city showing main streets, housing areas, factories, schools, churches, recreational areas, and so on. Think! Dream!

See page 12.

2. If you were a historian doing research on the early history of your school, would you try to locate primary source materials, secondary source materials, or both? Tell why. See if you can locate some newspaper clippings telling about the history of your school to share with the class.

CLASS PROJECT—PART 2

Do you have your notes regarding the work and methods employed by one of the social scientists? Your group may want to discuss and clarify this work.

It is now important to begin to gather information for your study. One way to begin is to make a list of questions the social scientist represented by your group would ask about the topic. For example, suppose the class chose to study the topic, Early Settlement of the Area. The historian might ask the following questions: When was the area first settled? What was the homeland of the first people who came? Why did the people settle here? The anthropologist might ask: What tools did these early people use in building their homes? Could we learn about the construction of the first school in this area by looking at the foundation?

As you study Chapter 2, see if you can find information that will help you. You may want to make a list of places where you may find materials. Could talking with people in the area be of help to you?

It might be well to keep your notes in a notebook as you do your research. Get started soon!

Stores and shops   Government buildings   Apartments

Brasília, capital of Brazil

2. Planning a New City

For Teaching Helps, see page T25.

Social scientists are interested in how people live. They are interested in what is happening to cities today. Some new cities have been planned with the help of social scientists. It is possible that social scientists will have much to do with the planning of new cities in the future.

Most cities just grew up. Some have been planned, but they are the exceptions. Cities that grew with little planning have many problems today. Usually

For a class activity, see #3 on page 37.

cities that were planned were able to avoid some of these problems.

An aerial view of a planned city is shown on this page. As you observe the picture, decide how the land is being used. Try to determine where people probably live and where they work.

The city shown in the picture is Brasília, the capital of Brazil since 1960. In this chapter you will discover some of the things the people of Brazil did to create Brasília.

JUST FOR FUN

See if you can find out how far you would have to travel to reach Brasília.

Stress:

26

1. Brasília is a planned city in Brazil.

*2. What examples can you think of that show city planning in your community?

COMPARISON OF BRAZIL'S SIZE

U.S.S.R.

CANADA

CHINA

UNITED STATES

Stress:

1. Brazil is smaller than China, Canada, or the United States, and less than one-half as large as the U.S.S.R.

BRAZIL

The land of Brazil Brazil is the largest country in South America. Its coastline makes up almost one-fourth of South America's entire coastline. As you study the pictures above, what can you determine about the size of Brazil as compared with some other countries in the world? Using a globe or a world map, determine in which hemisphere, the Northern or the Southern, each of the countries shown is located.

See #1 above.

Having such a large area gives Brazil much variety. It has different climates and a wide range of physical features. Study the map at the right. What resources and crops are shown? Where do you notice the greatest population concentration in Brazil? What reasons can you give for the uneven distribution of population in Brazil? Which area needs to be further developed?

See #2 below.

See #3 below.

2. Brazil is most heavily populated along its seacoast where the land is fertile.

3. Much of western Brazil is still undeveloped.

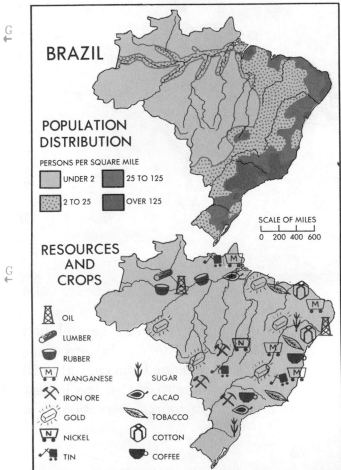

BRAZIL

POPULATION DISTRIBUTION

PERSONS PER SQUARE MILE

UNDER 2   25 TO 125

2 TO 25   OVER 125

SCALE OF MILES
0 200 400 600

RESOURCES AND CROPS

OIL

LUMBER

RUBBER

MANGANESE   SUGAR

IRON ORE   CACAO

GOLD   TOBACCO

NICKEL   COTTON

TIN   COFFEE

For Teaching Helps, see page T26.
For a class activity, see #1 on page 37.

Rio de Janeiro

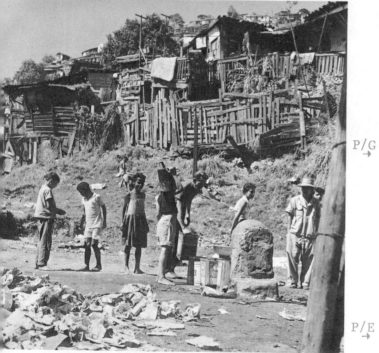

Public pump in Rio de Janeiro slum

Rio de Janeiro Brazil's capital had been located at Rio de Janeiro since the 1700's. It remained the capital until 1960. Rio de Janeiro is still the largest city and a major tourist attraction. It is today a very overcrowded city. From observing this picture, see if you can give reasons why it would be difficult for Rio de Janeiro to expand.

S→ In contrast to the beautiful buildings of the city are the **favelas,** or shacks, which make up Rio de Janeiro's slum areas. These shacks have been built on the hills surrounding Rio de Janeiro. Over 1,000,000 people now live in the *favelas.* Slum areas, like the one at the left, have no modern sewage disposal or running water. Social scientists, especially sociologists, are very concerned about problems created by slum housing. What might some of these problems be? *See #1 below.*

P/G→ One of the questions that interest a political scientist studying the government of a country is this: How did the government choose its capital city? According to historians, for many years leaders of the Brazilian government had talked about building a new capital city farther inland. But Brazil has had many other expenses to face throughout the years. Much of the tax money that was collected had to be spent on solving the problems of the cities. Economists advised the government leaders that the cost of building a new capital city would be very high. Brazilians asked themselves this question: Would the money be better spent on solving problems in the cities that already existed rather than on building a new capital? The government decided to build a new capital, *See #2 below.*

P/E→

P/G←

Stress:

28 1. Overcrowded slum areas can lead to health and housing problems.
2. Based on information from social scientists, the government of Brazil decided to build a new capital.

Stress:
1. The Brazilian government decided
   that a new capital in the west would
   help that area develop.

President Juscelino Kubitschek

A new capital is planned In studying the history of Brazil's choice of a capital city, political scientists discovered that many years before the decision to build a new capital was made, the land for it had been set aside. An area called the Federal District, located in the west, was to be the site of a new capital which would be called Brasília. Why do you suppose they chose a western site? See #1 above.

In 1955 Juscelino Kubitschek (kü bē′ chek) was elected President of Brazil. One campaign promise was to build a new capital. He hoped to see it completed by the time he left office. The President of Brazil can only serve one five-year term. This did not allow President Kubitschek much time to make the new capital become a reality.

choosing a site far to the west. By doing so, the government hoped to encourage more people to move away from the coast and develop the resources of the west. This would surely help solve some of Brazil's major problems.

*2. Why do you think that some areas in the United States are not fully developed?

Think for Yourself

What examples can you give to show how your state or country has had to make a choice of how to spend its tax money?

For Teaching Helps, see page T27.

PLANNING THE NEW CAPITAL

For a class activity, see #2 on page 37.

Selecting the site A study of Brasília's history shows that geographers were called upon to help select the best site for Brazil's new capital city. To guide themselves in making the selection, geographers would ask themselves such questions as these: Is the climate suitable? Is there a good water supply?

Can the land support the buildings?

A New York firm was hired by the Brazilian government to make a survey of the Federal District. This group of geologists and engineers began by making an aerial survey of the land. From there, they proceeded to study the land in greater detail. The geologists and

Stress:
1. Brazil used expert help to select the site for the new capital.

29

For Teaching Helps, see page T27.
Stress:
1. Geography was important in determining the site of Brasília.

engineers marked the area off in squares. Then they mapped each square again and again on the basis of various factors: climate, landforms, water, type of soil, and present land use.

In time the work was done. The New York firm said that any one of five places within the Federal District would be fine for a new capital.

See #1
above.

The government leaders chose a committee to make the choice. This committee chose the present location as the best of the five. The area they picked is on a plateau 3,000 feet above sea level. The temperature is pleasant for most of the year, and the humidity is low. It was a good site for Brasília.

Novacap An economist making a study of the history of a city created by a government would want to know how the government got the money to pay for it. Economists tell us that one of the big problems facing the Brazilian government was how to provide the money for the new capital. Economists and financial experts estimated that the cost of Brasília would be as high as $400,000,000. In order to raise the necessary money, the government set up a corporation. It was called **Novacap.** This is a short word for the Portuguese words for "new capital."

See #2
below.

Novacap set about the job of getting money to pay for Brasília. The corporation was able to borrow money from people of Brazil. It borrowed money

from nations, too. The United States gave a credit of $10,000,000 for equipment and materials to be bought in the United States. How would this help both countries?

According to historians, in order to select the design for the city, Novacap set up a contest open to all architects in Brazil. A large cash prize was offered. More than sixty plans were sent in to the selection committee. Novacap had set up a selection committee made up of famous architects and city planners from the United States, England, France, and Brazil.

The committee agreed to award the prize to Lúcio Costa, one of Brazil's leading architects. His plan was the one followed in the construction of Brasília. The Brazilian architect, Oscar Niemeyer, was selected to design the buildings for the city planned by Costa.

Costa's plan Cities need residential areas, business districts, schools, hospitals, recreational areas, and so on. In addition, since Brasília was to be the capital of Brazil, the government buildings were to be located there. Costa's plan for Brasília was quite simple. Look at the picture of the layout of the city on the facing page. Some people have said it looks like an airplane. What resemblance can you see? The "wings" make up the residential area. The "body" is the five-mile-long main street called Monumental Avenue. At the

2. Economists helped the Brazilian government estimate the cost of the new capital.

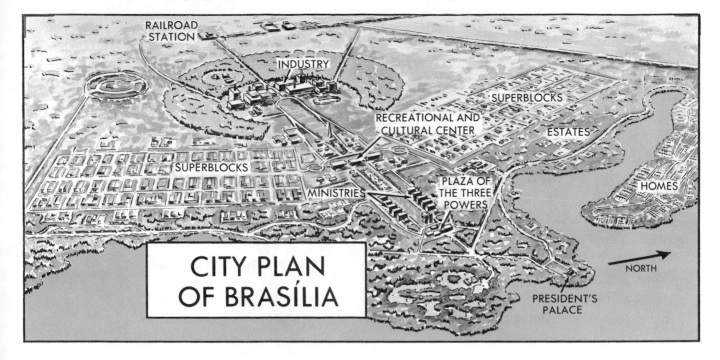

CITY PLAN OF BRASÍLIA

point where the two areas cross are found the recreational and cultural centers. The government buildings are located at the end of Monumental Avenue.

See #1 above.

Mr. Costa, the city planner, and Mr. Niemeyer, the architect, worked together to plan a city that would meet the needs of the people. They were able to call upon experts in many fields for help. They talked to many social scientists, especially sociologists and geographers. All wanted to help. They wanted to see if man could plan and build a city that would avoid many of the problems faced by today's large cities. What kind of help might the city planners ask sociologists to give? What help might they seek from geographers?

2. Transportation to Brasília was a major problem that had to be solved.

Problems along the way Geographers tell us that the job of building a city in a rather isolated area presented many problems. Judging by the map on this page, what can you see as one of the problems?

See #2 below.

Site of Brasília

BRAZIL - TRANSPORTATION ROUTES BEFORE 1961

----- RAILROADS
——— ROADS

SCALE OF MILES
0   200   400   600

Stress:
1. Workers and materials had to be transported to the new site.
*2. Could Brasília have been built without government help? Why?

See #1 above.

Few people lived in the place chosen for Brasília. For this reason getting enough workers to build the city was a problem. G/E The government leaders had to find answers to questions such as these: How can we make workers want to go to the place chosen for Brazília? How will we transport them there? Where will the workers be housed?

Another problem was how to build the city. This problem arose because all building materials and equipment had to be hauled to the site.

Time was also a problem. President Kubitschek was determined to see the new capital finished before he left office in 1961. He felt that Brazil had waited long enough for a new capital. If the new capital was not built during his time in office, Kubitschek was afraid that it might never be built. The next president might want to build something else. Why might a new president want to build something that he had thought of by himself?

Lack of interest, too expensive.

Think for Yourself

How do you think the site for your town or city might have been selected?

BUILDING A NEW CITY

For Teaching Helps, see page T28.

The workers Historians tell us that at one time over 60,000 people were working to build Brasília. Many of the H/S workers were skilled laborers from the large cities of Brazil. Others were unskilled laborers or farmers who had never seen a modern building—much less helped to build one. In order to encourage workers, Novacap offered good P/E wages. In many cases, enough jobs were not available in the other cities, and so workers were willing to go to Brasília.

Free Town One problem was to provide a place for the workers to live while they were building Brasília. The solution was **Cidade Livre** (sē dä′dä lē′vrä) which is Portuguese for Free Town. Free Town, shown here, is several miles outside of Brasília. It was originally supposed to be called Pioneer Center. But

Stress:
1. Large numbers of workers were needed to build Brasília.

Stress:
1. The Brazilian government offered a
   tax-free town to attract workers.

See #1
above.

the government announced that the people who lived there while building Brasília would not have to pay taxes. So the name Free Town was adopted by the residents. Why do you suppose the government decided not to collect taxes in Free Town?

P/E

Free Town was to be a temporary community for the people who were building Brasília. All stores and shacks for housing were built of wood. A historian would say that it looked like a frontier town of the American West in its pioneer days. What other evidence can you see in the picture that leads you to believe that Free Town was not meant to last? Free Town has lasted longer than its planned four years. It still attracts settlers.

S

H

Free Town was as unplanned as Brasília was planned. Within ten miles of each other stand the two towns. One is a splendidly planned, beautiful community—the other, a relatively crude settlement.

Transportation to Brasília One of the major obstacles to the building of Brasília was the lack of transportation. There were no roads or railroads leading to the area. The first requirement was an airport so that necessary workers, materials, and equipment could be flown to the site. However, even the materials to build the airport runway had to be transported by planes. Where do you suppose these first planes landed?

G

S

BRAZIL - TRANSPORTATION ROUTES AFTER 1961

RAILROADS
ROADS
SCALE OF MILES
0   200   400   600

Roads and railroads linking Brasília to the other major cities have since been built. As you study the map on this page, determine the distance between Brasília and the major cities.

G

The superblocks A major concern of the city planner and the architect of Brasília was to provide for housing. The residential areas are divided into **superblocks**—arrangements of ten to sixteen apartment buildings. Hundreds of families live here. Each superblock has its own elementary school.

In addition to the apartment buildings in the superblocks, many individual homes have been built in Brasília. Many of the important government officials and the wealthy people of Brasília live on large estates along the lake.

2. Brasília was joined to the other major cities of Brazil by roads, railroads, and airlines.

33

Offices   Supreme Court   Congress

Plaza of the Three Powers

The first picture above shows a super-block. The shafts, like those marked by arrows, are for stairways and elevators. Why is this a good place for them?

Government buildings The chief business of Brasília was to be the government of Brazil. The government buildings were placed along the strip of land that makes up the "body" of the "plane."

Political scientists tell us that Brazil's government is set up very much like that

Stress:
1. For convenience, all government buildings in Brasília are located together.

of the United States. They have an elected President who enforces the laws. Their Congress, which has two houses— a Senate and a Chamber of Deputies— makes the laws. Brazil also has a Supreme Court to judge the laws. The buildings for each branch of government are located in the Plaza of the Three Powers shown at the left.

The building with the bowl-like designs is the meeting place of Congress. The tall, narrow buildings behind it are the congressional office buildings. In the background is the Supreme Court, and located nearby are the executive offices where the President works. The buildings on either side of the roadway leading toward the town, as shown on page 31, are the ministries. The President selects a group of people to advise him on various matters, such as foreign affairs, finance, and so on. The Brazilians call these advisers **ministers.** Does the United States government have anything similar to Brazil's ministries?

The President's palace shown here is located on the peninsula which juts out

President's palace

34

For Teaching Helps, see page T28.

Business district of Brasília

into the lake. President Kubitschek spent the last nine months of his term of office in Brasília—the capital he had worked so hard to see completed.

Business districts Each superblock has some small stores which are within walking distance of the apartments. In addition, at the point where the "wings" cross the "body," a large shopping district can be found. Banks and office buildings are also located there. Nearby are found fine restaurants, theaters, and Brasília's cultural center. The business section of Brasília is shown in the picture. Notice how the planners have left much room for future development.

The majority of the hotels in Brasília are situated near this area. Why do you think this is a good location for them?

Brasília does not have too many large industries. However, the few that are located there are found west of the city near the railroad station. What other reasons can you determine for locating industries in this area?

Transportation within Brasília The city planners realized the need for a good transportation network within the city. Brasília is one of the few large cities without many traffic problems. Along with the wide streets there are many parking areas in the center of town.

Community services Sociologists tell us that the very "bigness" of some cities makes some people feel rather isolated. The planners of Brasília have tried to get around this problem. Each superblock, with its surrounding stores and school, makes up a unit.

Hospitals have been kept small to provide more personal service. They are scattered throughout the city. In this sense, a small-town flavor is found in a large city.

Recreation Sociologists are aware of a very important need of the people—the need for recreation. Undoubtedly, the city planners asked sociologists to suggest ways in which this need could be met in Brasília. Historians tell us that

See #2 below.

Stress:
1. Brasília was planned to allow for future growth.
2. Industry in Brasília is located near transportation facilities and away from residential areas.

35

Yacht club on Lake Brasília

Statue honoring pioneers

the city planners have made it easy for the people of Brasília to meet their need for recreation. In addition to the theaters and the cultural center in the heart of town, there is a sports stadium located west of town. Brasília also has a racetrack and golf courses. The people shown in the first picture are enjoying Lake Brasília.

See #1 below.

S ←

Lake Brasília is a man-made lake. The planners of Brasília dammed up streams to give the city a 10,000 acre lake. Besides providing recreation for the city, the lake is also the city's water supply.

The people of Brasília Historians tell us that the men and women who came to Brasília to help build it and the first citizens of Brasília referred to themselves as **candangos.** *Candango* is the Portuguese word for pioneer. Brasília has honored the memory of the *candangos* by displaying the sculpture shown in the second picture on this page. Why might they have done this?

Brasília began as a city of young people. Many older people were not interested in moving to the new city. The young people came to Brasília in hopes of being able to find better jobs with faster advancement.

G/S ←

Since Brasília was dedicated as Brazil's new capital in 1960, it has continued to grow. More industries are locating there, and more people are moving to this planned city—this beautiful Brasília.

H/S ←

Think for Yourself

What cities have you visited that seemed very well planned?

Stress:
1. Recreational and cultural centers were planned in Brasília.
*2. Do you think a city similar to Brasília would be popular in your area? Why?

Test Yourself

On your own paper, write your answer to each question.

Test 1   Social Science Words

Match the words and groups of words given below.

c. 1. environment   a. the study of population and movement

d. 2. primary source   b. having to do with the city

b. 3. urban   c. conditions and influences that affect man

a. 4. demography   d. eyewitness account, diary, letter

Which of these words is needed to complete each sentence below?

cartographer   *favelas*
candangos   ministers
social needs   regional city

5. A __ is a geographer who makes maps. cartographer

6. Hospitals, schools, and government are called __ of the people. social needs

7. People who helped build the capital city of Brazil call themselves __. candangos

8. The __, or shacks, make up Rio de Janeiro's slum areas. favelas

Test 2   Facts and Ideas

Which is the best answer to each question below?

1. Important officials that advise the President of Brazil on various matters are called what?

a. candangos
b. ministers
c. clerks

2. What does a historian call an account that was written after an event took place?

a. a primary source
b. a map
c. a secondary source

3. What would you expect to see an urban sociologist studying in a big city?

a. people
b. machinery
c. laws

4. In studying the history of your school, a historian might be involved in which of the following activities?

a. doing market research
b. looking at old coins
c. talking with people

39

For Teaching Helps, see page T29.

UNIT
2   MAN BEFORE HISTORY

Stress:
1. Field investigations by archaeologists and anthropologists, as shown below, have uncovered many artifacts made by early man.
2. Early man, like modern man, had to find ways to meet his basic needs.
*3. Why might modern sociologists be interested in the way of life of early man?

Chapters

3. Early Man and His World
4. The Beginnings of Civilization

40

Stress: For Teaching Helps, see page T29.
1. Throughout history, man has adjusted to his environment.
2. Man's prehistoric period ended with the development of writing.
3. During prehistoric time, man learned to make and use tools,
   domesticate animals, and to raise crops.

Wherever man has chosen to live, he has had to adjust to his environment. In many cases, these adjustments have led to a new way of life. For example, the way of life of some groups of early men changed when they moved from the forests to the plains. And early man's way of life changed greatly when he gave up hunting for farming.

See #1 above.

A/S ←

The material in Unit 2 deals with a long period of man's progress. It was a period that began well over 1,000,000 years ago. Social scientists usually call this period the **prehistoric period**—the period before writing and written history. Normally, this period is considered to have ended about 3400 B.C. when man developed writing.

See #2 above.

Today, the great achievements of the prehistoric period are accepted as part of modern man's way of life. Seldom does modern man think about how much he owes to his distant ancestors of the past. But when we consider that these prehistoric achievements include such things as producing tools, practicing agriculture, domesticating animals, and so on, the debt becomes clear.

H/A ←

See #3 above.

The story of man's progress from cave man to farmer, during the prehistoric period, is presented in this unit. As you read the material that follows, you will learn the answers to such questions as these:

H/A ←

1. How did man's environment change?
2. How did changes in man's environment affect his way of life?
3. How did man learn to adjust to his environment?

*4. In what ways do you have to adjust your way of life to your environment?

For Teaching Helps, see page T29.
Stress:
1. The continuing nature of the class project. See pp. 58 and 75.
2. Much of what social scientists know about early man comes from the study
   of artifacts.

CLASS PROJECT—PART 1

As a class project for this unit, plan and build a display. The purpose of the display is to provide information on early man —where he lived, his tools, his clothes, his appearance, his homes, his villages, his work. The things you learn about early man as you study this unit will help you decide what should be included in the display.

To begin your project select a place in your classroom for the display on early man. One suggestion is to bring the largest box you can find to your classroom. Stand the box so that one end is open and make your display inside the box. The picture below may give you some ideas about the display area. In studying Chapter 3 and Chapter 4, you will find information about early man. Studying these chapters should help you decide what is important to include in your display. Write the suggestions you have for the display in a notebook. You will need these suggestions to do Part 2 of the class project.

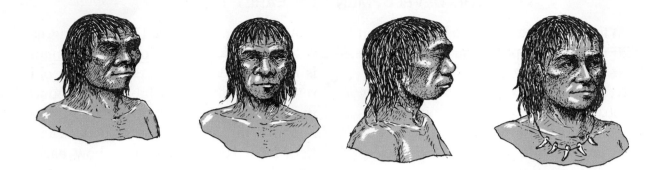

500,000 B.C.		300,000 B.C.		150,000 B.C.		40,000 B.C.		15,000 B.C.
Java man *Homo erectus*		Swanscombe man		Neanderthal man *Homo sapiens*			Cro-Magnon man	

TYPES OF EARLY MAN

Stress: For Teaching Helps, see page T30.
1. Many social scientists have contributed to our knowledge of early man.

3. Early Man and His World

Have you ever seen a time line like the one shown above? What can you learn from such a time line? How many years does the time line cover?

See #1 above.
Social scientists—historians, anthropologists, archaeologists, and others— have all worked together to discover how man first developed. The task has not been an easy one. Nor do we know the full story of man's development today.

The search for the truth about early man has gone on for many, many years. People from all walks of life have contributed to our knowledge.

From the discoveries of social scientists, and others, we are now able to put together the story of early man. It is a story that points out man's continuing ability to adjust to new and challenging conditions.
See #2 below.

2. Early man developed as he adjusted to new conditions.

JUST FOR FUN

Make a time line covering one week. On the time line, show important events that happened to you during the period. How does this help you to understand how things change?

*3. What type of new conditions might have faced early man?

For Teaching Helps, see page T31.
Stress:
1. Social scientists disagree about when man first appeared on earth.
2. The study of early man can help social scientists understand modern man.

THE DEVELOPMENT OF EARLY MAN

What archaeologists tell us When did man first appear on earth? This question still puzzles social scientists today. Some experts believe man is nearly 1,750,000 years old. Other social scientists are not so sure that man goes back that far. Why do you think social scientists disagree about this?

See #1 above.

Much of what we know about early man comes from anthropologists and archaeologists. These social scientists have made many interesting discoveries. Dr. Louis Leakey, for example, found what he believed were the remains of an early man. These remains—part of a skull and other bones—are thought to be nearly 1,750,000 years old. Dr. Leakey feels these remains are what is left of an early man which he has called *Homo habilis*.

3. Many social scientists believe man originated in Africa.

Although not all social scientists agree with Dr. Leakey, they do agree that man is at least 1,000,000 years old. Very old remains of early men have been found in many parts of the world. From these remains, and from artifacts, social scientists have tried to discover how early man developed. Why do historians and other social scientists want to know how early man developed?

The forerunners of modern man Where did man first appear on earth? No one is quite sure where the human race first began. Much of the evidence points to Africa. Certainly the remains found in Africa show that man lived there long ago. It is possible that early types of man moved from Africa to other continents. What might have caused this movement? Change in environment.

See #3 and #4 below.

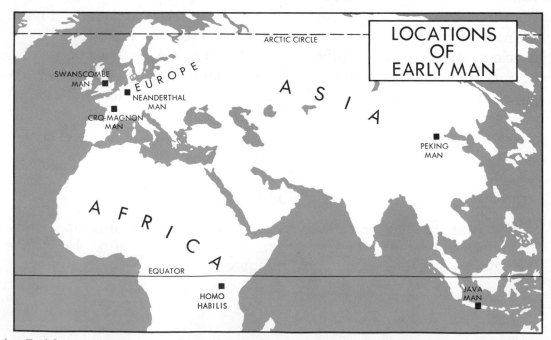

LOCATIONS OF EARLY MAN

ARCTIC CIRCLE

EUROPE
SWANSCOMBE MAN
NEANDERTHAL MAN
CRO-MAGNON MAN

ASIA

PEKING MAN

AFRICA

EQUATOR

HOMO HABILIS

JAVA MAN

44

4. Evidence seems to show that early man moved from continent to continent.

Neanderthal man

Cro-Magnon man (see page 56)

Remains of early men we call Peking man and Java man have been found. These early men are thought to be at least 500,000 years old. The map on page 44 shows us where the remains were found. On, or near, what continent did Peking man and Java man live? Would you guess that they lived in a place having a warm or a cool climate? Why?

These early men were not what we consider to be modern man. But they were one step in the development of modern man. Those early men are called *Homo erectus* (hō′mō i rect′əs), or erect man.

Homo sapiens All modern men are part of the species we call *Homo sapiens* (hō′mō sā′pi enz), or thinking man. Many early types of *Homo sapiens* have been found. One type, Swanscombe (swonz′kəm) man lived in Europe, probably about 300,000 years ago. A more

highly developed human, Neanderthal (ni an′dər thôl) man, appeared a bit later. Most experts think Neanderthal man lived about 150,000 years ago. Remains of Neanderthal man have been found in Europe, Asia, and Africa. Then, for some unknown reason, about 35,000 years ago Neanderthal man disappeared.

See #1 below.

A more modern man then replaced the Neanderthals. The picture shows what we think the Neanderthal man and one type of more modern man looked like. What differences between the two can you discover? Why might the more modern type of man have survived while Neanderthal man did not?

See #2 below.

Some social scientists think Neanderthal man was killed off by the more modern type of man. But others think that Neanderthal man intermixed with his more modern neighbors and disappeared as a separate group.

Stress:
1. Some types of early man have disappeared.
2. Modern man survived because he was better able to adjust to new and changing conditions.

A group of early people in search of food

For Teaching Helps, see page T31.

Whatever happened, it is clear that highly developed types of *Homo sapiens* lived about 40,000 years ago. Most authorities believe that these people originated in southwestern Asia or Africa and then moved throughout the world. But exactly where they came from no one is quite sure.

Movements of early man Early man lived very simply. He relied upon hunting and food gathering as his means of staying alive. Because of this, groups of people moved from one place to another in search of food. The picture shows how such a group might have looked.

Because early man had to move about, he usually had no permanent home. And what shelter he did have was usually provided by nature. In some areas, early man lived in caves. In other areas, he made crude shelters of tree limbs. In still other areas he merely lived without shelter at all if it was warm enough.

Even today, some hunting and food-gathering people live as early man probably did thousands of years ago. The Arunta (ə run′tə) people of Australia are examples. The Arunta are thought by some social scientists to live as Neanderthal man did 40,000 years ago. Where these people came from is not clear. But their isolated life in Australia has left the Arunta with a highly primitive way of life.

The Arunta live by hunting and gathering of food. However, contacts with other people are changing the Arunta's way of life. Studies of their older way of life tells us how man may have lived many thousands of years ago.

Stress:
1. Early man had to move about in search of food.
2. Some primitive people living today have a way of life similar to that of early man.

46

Stress: For a class activity, see #1 on page 58.

1. The various races of man developed about 30,000 years ago.
2. All human beings are of the same species, Homo sapiens.

Races of man As man migrated throughout the world, groups of people intermixed. As a result of this—and other factors—groups in certain areas began to be physically alike.

The races of mankind are not very old. Most social scientists feel that races originated about 30,000 years ago.

See #2 above.

We do know that all men are basically alike. And we also know that all men are *Homo sapiens*. But there are some differences. Some people have dark skin and others have light skin. Some people differ in other ways, such as types of hair, color of eyes, and types of eyelids. Based on such things as these, some social scientists speak of three races—the Negroid (nē′groid), the Caucasoid (kô′kə soid), and the Mongoloid (mong′ gə loid). Each of these three races has produced leaders, scientists, and scholars. In the pictures below are three famous leaders. Which race does each of these famous leaders represent?

See #3 below.

When we look at these pictures we must remember that they show only one type of features found in each race. We also must remember that not all members of a race are alike. For example, a member of the Caucasoid race is usually thought of as having light skin. However, the people of India are also members of the Caucasoid race and their skin is dark. And while both the Chinese and the American Indians are Mongoloids, they may not look alike.

Martin Luther King, Jr.

Winston Churchill

Emperor Hirohito

3. Throughout history, each race has provided outstanding leaders.

Bedouin tribesman of North Africa

Stress:
1. Certain racial characteristics may help man to adjust to his environment.

For example, a dark skin is an advantage in areas where the rays of the sun are more direct. Thus dark-skinned people are better able to live near the equator where the rays of the sun are more direct. People with lighter skins tend to be found in places away from the equator where the sun rays are not as direct.

A/G See #1 above.

The Bedouin (bed'ů in) tribesman in the picture has adjusted to his environment. He lives in a desert region. What physical features help him to survive? How else has he adjusted? Clothing and way of life.

S/G

What appears to be true, is that races developed as man moved into new areas. As early man—*Homo sapiens*—moved from Asia and Africa to all parts of the world, he met new conditions. In each area, groups intermixed, changes occurred, and new types of man developed.

A

For these and other reasons, social scientists do not always agree on what are the races of man. Many anthropologists feel that man cannot be put into specific groups. The important thing, social scientists point out, is the similarities among men, not the differences. And what differences do exist are thought by some to be, in part, a result of man's adjustment to different climates and geographic conditions.

*2. Why do you think some social scientists believe there are really many different races of man and not just three?

Think for Yourself

What factors other than environment and intermixing may have influenced the development of races? Why?

EARLY MAN'S ENVIRONMENT

For Teaching Helps, see page T32.

Environment Scientists who study the earth—tell us the earth is probably about 4,000,000,000 years old. In this study of the earth, geologists have divided its history into time periods. Today we live in what is called the Recent Epoch, which began about 10,000 years ago. Before this period man lived in an epoch called the Ice Age or the Pleistocene (plĭs'tə sēn) Epoch. The Pleistocene Epoch lasted about 1,000,000 years. It was the period in which great

Stress: For a class activity, see #2 on page 58.
1. Climates of the earth have gone through a series of changes.
2. Early man had to adjust to changing climates.

glaciers (glā'shərz) covered part of the earth. A few of these glaciers remain today. One of these is shown in the picture. Do you think people live in this area? Why or why not? Why might social scientists be interested in glaciers and where they covered the earth?

As you study the map of the glaciers, you should notice that they covered almost 30 per cent of the earth. What continents did the glaciers partially cover? Which continents were left untouched by the glaciers?

See #1 above. Before the glaciers, the climate of the earth was warm. Then the glaciers began to form and move slowly over the land. From what direction did the glaciers come? In which direction did they move? How do you think this affected the earth's climate?

There were four glacial (glā'shəl) periods. Then between each glacial period, the glaciers withdrew. Each of these periods covered about 100,000 years. The last retreat of the glaciers began 10,000 years ago, and it is still continuing.

Effects of glacial periods Glaciers affected the earth's surface as well as plant and animal life. Because much of the earth's water was frozen into glaciers, the levels of our oceans, rivers, and lakes fell. Some experts estimate that the level of the oceans fell nearly 400 feet. New land appeared as the water level fell. Regions of the world that had

Glacier in Switzerland

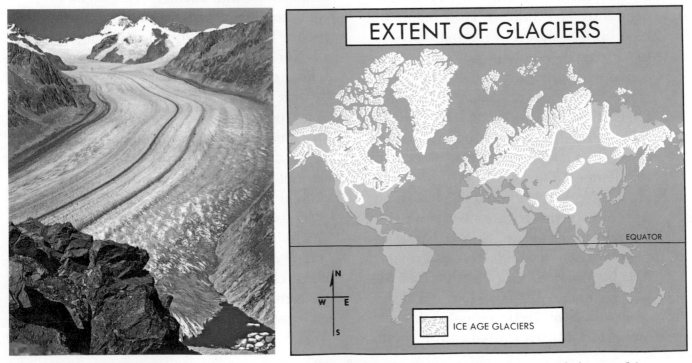

EXTENT OF GLACIERS

EQUATOR

N
W   E
S

ICE AGE GLACIERS

3. As the map shows, the continents of Africa, South America, and Australia were free from glaciers.

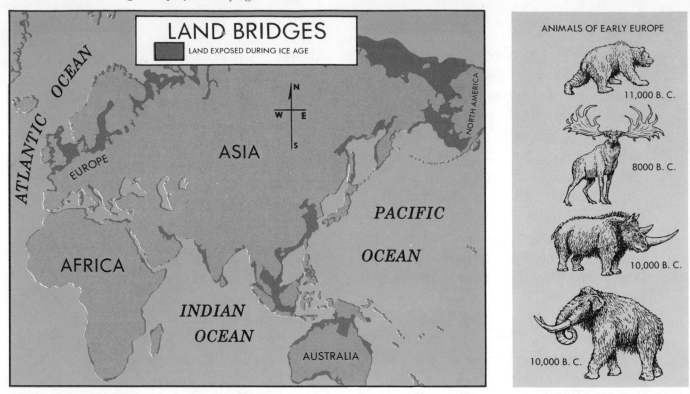

LAND BRIDGES

LAND EXPOSED DURING ICE AGE

ATLANTIC OCEAN

EUROPE

ASIA

AFRICA

INDIAN OCEAN

PACIFIC OCEAN

AUSTRALIA

NORTH AMERICA

ANIMALS OF EARLY EUROPE

11,000 B. C.

8000 B. C.

10,000 B. C.

10,000 B. C.

See #1 below.

See #2 below.

See #3 below.

been separated by water were then connected by land bridges. How might the land bridges shown in the map have affected man? What do you think happened when the glaciers melted?

As glaciers advanced over the land, the earth's climate changed. Rainfall, for example, shifted toward the equator and changed some areas from deserts or woodlands to grassy plains. As areas grew cold, men and animals had to adjust. Before the Ice Age early types of crocodiles existed in Europe, and elephants, horses, and camels roamed North America. During the Ice Age woolly mammoths emerged in Europe, and remains of Arctic animals have been found in southern United States. Many

animals became **extinct** (ek stingkt′)— died out—or disappeared from certain areas. The elephant, horse, and camel of North America are good examples. These animals disappeared from North America during the glacial period. This was true in Europe as well. For example, the illustration shows some of Europe's early animals and when they became extinct. Why do we say that man and animal must adjust or perish?

Thus, as glaciers advanced and retreated, plant and animal life changed in many areas of the world. How might these changes result in a change in the pattern of man's life? Could these changes have affected where man lived? Why?

Stress:

50

1. Early man migrated over land bridges that once joined continents together.
2. The land bridges disappeared as glaciers melted and water levels rose.
3. Changes in environments sometimes led to the adjustment, migration, or death of man and animals.

Stress: For Teaching Helps, see page T32.
1. Environment can limit man's choices in his way of life.
2. Man, unlike plants and animals, is better able to adjust to changes in his
   environment.

The impact of climate on man. Man's environment is an important factor in See #1 his way of life. This does not mean that above. environment alone will produce a certain way of life. But it does mean that environment can limit man's choices.

For example, several thousands of years ago man learned to live in some very cold regions. The Eskimos were one such group. In cold regions, early man found that he could live in several different ways. That is, he could live in different types of houses, and he could live in small groups or in large groups. He also used different types of tools, had different religions, and so on. But all people living in cold areas were also limited in their way of life. For instance, they could not raise crops, and they had to hunt animals for food. How did this affect the size of early communities?

Even today, living in a cold region may affect a group's way of life. Does the Eskimo dwelling in the picture reflect the environment? Does the igloo (ig′lü) look like a permanent home? Do you think people who live in cold regions tend to move about more than farmers do? Why might this be true?

Man adjusts to new conditions Climate and other factors of environment affect man's way of life today. Thus it should be clear that they also affected man in the past. During the Ice Age, early man had to adjust to new conditions. He could do this in several ways.

First, early man could move, or migrate, to new areas if his environment changed. Early man did this as his climate changed and became colder. Early man also moved as his source of food—animals and plants—migrated or died. Much of early man's migrations occurred during the Ice Age. Why do most people migrate today?

Second, early man could stay where he was and adjust to new conditions. To do this, he had to develop new skills and See #2 tools which helped him to survive under above. the new conditions. Neanderthal man, for example, used fire, lived in caves, and developed new tools and weapons. Using

Eskimos and an igloo they have built

Neanderthals
making
clothing
from animal
skins

Awl to make holes   Needle and thongs

these skills and techniques, he could remain in colder regions as the glaciers
advanced. The Neanderthals in the picture are shown using a new skill they
developed. What is this skill? What new
tools did Neanderthal man need for this
skill? Sewing clothing--awl and needle.

Third, man could die out and become
extinct. Some types of animals did this.
And perhaps some early men who failed

to adjust did this as well. But normally
man was able to survive changes where
many animals could not. Why was this
possible? Is it still true of man today?
Why or why not? Man was better able
to develop new ways of life. This is
still true today.

Think for Yourself

*How does the climate in your area affect
your way of life? Why?*

*2. Why did some types of early man survive while others did not survive?

EARLY MAN AND HIS CULTURES

For Teaching Helps, see page T33.   For a class activity, see #3 on page 58.

The nature of culture Every person
has certain basic needs. These needs include water, food, sleep, shelter, and
physical comfort. The way each person
goes about taking care of his needs depends upon his culture. Culture is a
group's way of life; that is, it is the way
in which a group of people go about

satisfying their needs and wants. Culture also includes the basic beliefs and
attitudes of the group.

Each child learns how to satisfy his
needs and wants from his family and his
group. In this way the group's culture
is passed from one generation to the next
with only some changes to meet new

See #1 below.

See #2 below.

Stress:
52
1. The way people go about satisfying their basic needs is influenced by their
   culture.
2. Children normally first learn about their group's way of life from their
   family.

Children learning the use of a bone tool

same environment are the same. Man has found many ways to meet his needs. And while environment may influence these ways, it does not determine them. For example, the North American Eskimos worked out ways of life that helped them to adapt to a harsh environment. They developed the igloo, sled, snow goggles, and the kayak (kī'ak). In Arctic Asia, people who were similar to Eskimos lived in a similar environment. But these people did not live the same way as the Eskimos. One of this group's dwellings is shown in the picture. How does it differ from an Eskimo's igloo? What does this difference tell us about culture and environment? See #2 below.

Chuckchi winter house in Siberia

conditions. How are the children in the picture learning about their group's way of life? Who is doing the teaching? Why? How do you learn your way of life?

Culture, then, is how people live in groups—it is their way of life. Culture includes all the ideas, customs, beliefs, tools, clothes, houses, and other things of life. When social scientists study a culture they study all these things. In this way they can discover how people live and act. How do the things we use every day reflect our way of life?

Culture and environment Since all men must live in their particular environment, their culture must adjust to the environment. And since culture is man's way of being comfortable and meeting his needs, every culture is influenced by the environment. This does not mean, however, that all cultures in the

Stress:
1. Every culture is, to some extent, influenced by the environment.
2. Cultures, even in the same environment, often differ.

Australian aborigines making a musical instrument and a hat for a celebration. These nomadic people live in a warm climate.

can get an idea of how early man may have lived. Hunting and food-gathering people live in small groups. The picture shows two Australian aborigines (ab'ə rij'ə nēz). They are hunters and food gatherers. From the picture can you tell in what type of climate these people live? How does their way of life differ from that of a farmer?

See caption above.

See #1 below.

Some hunters and food gatherers build temporary homes as they travel. But in some areas where food is plentiful, they may settle in one place. This was as true in very early times as it is today. However, this did not happen very often. Most early men continued to move about in their search for food.

Types of early cultures Cultures are, as we have said, all the things that make up a group's way of life. Unfortunately, what we know about early man's way of life depends upon the remains we have found. Why might we know very little about some early cultures?

From the remains that have been found, at least two things are clear. One is that early man knew how to use fire

The cultures of early man Until about 11,000 years ago, the cultures of early man were similar in a few general ways. They were, for example, all food-gathering or hunting cultures. It was not until about 8000 B.C. that man first learned to grow and harvest food. Why might this skill have led to differences in cultures? Why do you think all cultures throughout the world did not become farming cultures?

If we look at some people today who are still food gatherers and hunters we

METHODS OF STARTING FIRES

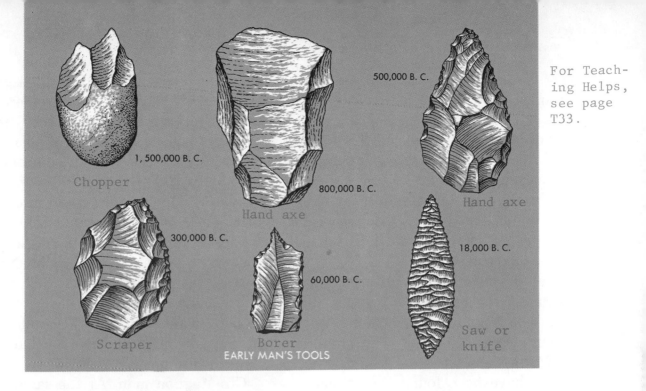

1,500,000 B. C.
Chopper

800,000 B. C.
Hand axe

500,000 B. C.

Hand axe

300,000 B. C.
Scraper

60,000 B. C.
Borer

18,000 B. C.

Saw or knife

EARLY MAN'S TOOLS

For Teaching Helps, see page T33.

over 500,000 years ago. At that time early man may not have known how to start a fire, but he did know how to keep a fire going if he found one burning.

At some time in history, man learned to make fire. Exactly when this happened we may never know. It is clear that thousands of years ago, an early genius learned a method of starting a fire. Probably one of the methods shown on page 54 was used. These methods are still used by some primitive people today. Each of these methods requires a skill. What are these skills? How might early man first have learned these skills?

A second fact we know from remains is that early man used tools. He also learned to develop new tools. These tools then helped him to develop new ways of life.

Early man's tools Early man in his development had to adjust to his environment. Since he did not know how to raise food, he had to hunt or gather food where it was available. For some of these tasks he needed tools. Some of the tools used by man nearly 1,000,000 years ago have been found. For what purpose do you think the tools that are shown in the picture were used?

The remains of man's earliest tools have been found in Africa, Asia, and Europe. These tools were remarkably alike. However, just because many early men used similar tools does not mean they all lived the same way. Early cultures must have varied from place to place just as they do today. What are some of the reasons for the differences in cultures from one place to another?

See #1 below.

A →
A ←
A/G →
A ←

See #2 below.

Stress:
1. Man's ability to make tools and start fires helped him to adjust to his environment.
2. Similar tools were used in widely different cultures.

Stress:
1. Neanderthal man's burial practices seem to show that there was a belief in life after death.

For Teaching Helps, see page T33.

The types of tools changed as man developed. The illustration on page 55 shows how the types of tools changed. Most of these tools were made of stone.

The methods early man used to make tools are shown below. You may want to make stone tools yourself. If you do, you will find that these methods require certain skills. How do you think early man learned these skills?

Later development of cultures Unfortunately the remains of many early cultures have not as yet been found. But in some areas of Europe—and around the Mediterranean Sea—Neanderthal remains have been found. These show that Neanderthal groups buried their dead. In the graves, the Neanderthals placed various tools and other items with the bodies. What might this indicate about the beliefs of these people?

See #1 above.

Neanderthal men, who lived up until about 35,000 years ago, could also start fires. They lived in caves in colder climates, but they also built primitive shelters in some areas. Usually, Neanderthal man moved about to find the animals he hunted. However, where game was abundant, he lived all year in one area. Did all Neanderthal men have the same culture? Why?

Cro-Magnon man At the same time that Neanderthal man lived, so did the ancestors of modern man. One of these more highly developed people was Cro-Magnon (krō mag′non) man.

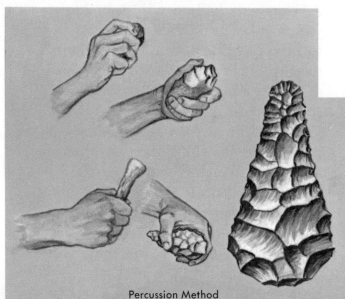

Percussion Method
A stone or a piece of bone was struck against the surface of a rock to remove a chip which left a sharp, jagged edge.

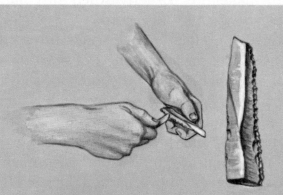

Pressure-Flaking Method
A pointed piece of wood, bone, or stone was used to flake off a chip of rock and produce a sharp cutting edge.

METHODS OF EARLY TOOL MAKING

2. Cro-Magnon man was the ancestor of modern man.

Wall painting from cave in France

See #1 above.

The Cro-Magnons entered Europe, either from southwestern Asia or from Africa. They brought with them their advanced cultures. They were hunters and food gatherers who had developed improved tools and weapons. These people lived in larger groups than did other early men, and they were skilled artists. Cave paintings have given us clues to their ways of life. These paintings are often found in dark, isolated areas of the caves. These paintings, such as the one on this page, were probably used for magical or religious purposes. Why do you think these paintings may have been used for religious purposes?

A/S

See #2 below.

Cro-Magnon man also lived in caves as did Neanderthal man. In some areas, however, evidence has been found of homes built by Cro-Magnon men in which they used animal skins. Once again man showed his ability to adjust to his environment through his culture and the development of new skills and techniques. And the nature of this adjustment varied as cultures differed from one group of people to the next.

Think for Yourself

How would you describe your culture to a visitor from another country? What features of your culture would you stress? Why?

2. Evidence shows that some groups of Cro-Magnon men built houses of animal skins.
*3. Why might Cro-Magnon man's ability to build houses have helped him to adjust and survive?

Things to Do

See
pages 47-48.
1. On a world map or globe, locate a country that is inhabited largely by people of the Negroid race. Locate a country that is inhabited largely by people of the Caucasoid race. Locate a country that is inhabited largely by people of the Mongoloid race.

See
page 49.
2. Find a picture of a glacier today. Look at the surrounding land area in the picture and see if it shows some effect of glacial action that took place long ago.

See
page 52.
3. Construct a small display showing early man's attempt to adjust to his environment. One example would be a display showing a shelter being constructed. Another example would be a display showing man's attempt to raise crops.

CLASS PROJECT—PART 2

Do you have your suggestions for what to include in the display about early man? The class may want to make a list of these suggestions. It might help you to decide on what to include in the display on early man if you will do the following: (1) Decide what materials or objects you have in your classroom, or that members of the class may bring from home, that could be a part of the display on early man. For example, an artifact might be an important object for your display. (2) Decide what materials or objects members of the class will need to build for the display about early man. For example, you may want to build a model of a shelter used by early man.

It might be well to establish two committees at this time. One committee would include pupils who have agreed to bring materials for the display on early man. A second committee would include pupils who are going to build things for the display on early man. Start both committees working. As materials and objects are assembled for the display on early man, decide where you will keep these materials until work on putting the display together begins.

4. The Beginnings of Civilization

Stress:

1. The development of agriculture was a major step toward civilization.

The study of man, from earliest times to the present, is a wonderful story of achievement. The path of man from a primitive hunter to a modern civilized individual has been a long one. Along this path man has developed new skills and techniques. These have helped him to adjust to his environment.

A/S →

See #1 above.

A major step toward the society that we now have was taken many years ago. The step was the development of agri-culture. Agriculture, in turn, led man to a more settled community life. In the Danube River Valley of Europe, villages looked something like the one shown in the picture. Compared with earlier hunting and food-gathering societies, what new achievements are shown in the picture? Which of these achievements are still used by man today? How have these achievements improved man's way of life?

See #2 below.

2. During Neolithic times man learned how to farm, domesticate animals, build houses, live in settled villages, and use new tools.

JUST FOR FUN

Make a map of your community. Show on your map how the land in and around your community is being used. What achievements of man have led to these types of land usage?

*3. In what ways would the development of agriculture help man to adjust to his environment?

59

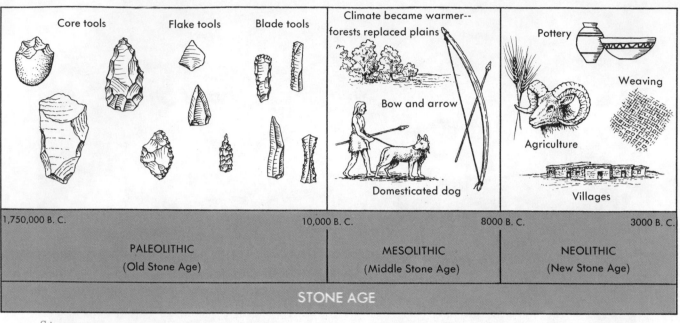

Stress:
1. Periods shown on the time line are approximate, and developments varied in time from one culture to another.

MAN'S PROGRESS IN THE STONE AGE

2. Man's development in the Stone Age took almost 1,750,000 years.

The Old Stone Age Before man learned to use metals, he made his tools from stone. Social scientists refer to this period of man's development as the Stone Age. As you study the time line, you can see that the Stone Age lasted a long time. About how many years did the Stone Age last?

See #2 above.

You can also see from the time line that the Stone Age is divided into smaller periods of time. Each of these periods is based on the type of stone tools used at the time. What are the three periods called?

The oldest period in the Stone Age is called the Paleolithic (pā′li ə lith′ik) period, or the Old Stone Age. This pe-riod began when man first made simple stone tools more than 1,500,000 years ago. These rather crude tools were an important step in the development of the skills of early man.

Old Stone Age achievements During the Old Stone Age, man made progress in developing new skills and in control-ling his environment. But this progress was very slow. At first man used **pebble tools**, which were stones that were worn down by water. Early man broke off one end of these stones and used the jagged edge for cutting and scraping. Later man learned to chip off pieces of stones and thus produce a sharper cutting edge. By about 30,000 B.C. early man was making

3. Man has made relatively rapid progress since 10,000 B.C.
*4. What connection can you see between the end of the Ice Age and Stone Age developments?

60

Stress: For Teaching Helps, see page T35.
1. Early man's ability to use fire, make clothing, and build shelters
   helped him to survive in nearly every type of environment.

blade tools, which were sharp pieces of flint. In the picture you can see a comparison of pebble and blade tools. How are they different. Why are blade tools an improvement? They are sharper.

See #1 above.

Also during the Old Stone Age, early man learned to use and control fire. This knowledge, plus early man's ability to sew skins together to make clothing and to build shelters, helped man to adjust to his environment. In addition, man's ability to develop new tools enabled him to hunt larger animals. And his skill in building shelters made it possible for early man to move about and to live in

various climates. How do you think man's ability to think, to remember, and to teach helped him to survive in his environment?

The Middle Stone Age The second Stone Age period is called the Middle Stone Age, or Mesolithic (mes′ə lith′ik) period. This period began about 10,000 B.C., and it lasted until about 8000 B.C.

During the Middle Stone Age it appears that man learned to tame animals. Also in this period man probably invented the bow and arrow.

The Middle Stone Age began when the Ice Age ended. After the Ice Age

Stone chopper

Hand axe   Hand axe

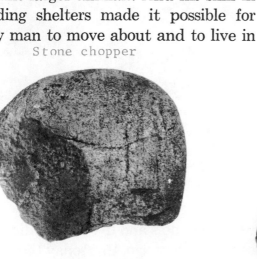

Pebble Tools

Stone chopper

Blade Tools

2. Improved tools helped to increase early man's supply of food.

Stress:
1. When the Ice Age ended, climates became warmer.
2. During the Middle Stone Age, early man migrated to new regions.

ended, large forests began to replace grassy plains. And as the earth's climate became warmer, man moved into new regions in search of food.

Today we look upon the Middle Stone Age as the period that bridged the gap between the Old Stone Age and the New Stone Age. It was a period in which the large herds of mammoths and other animals became smaller. As a result, hunting became more difficult for Mesolithic man. Mesolithic man's ability to tame dogs and make better tools helped him to adjust to new conditions. How did these abilities aid man in adjusting to his changing environment?

The New Stone Age In the Neolithic (nē'ə lith'ik) period—the New Stone Age—new achievements changed man's way of life. These achievements are part of what social scientists call the Neolithic Revolution.

In the Neolithic period—from about 8000 B.C. to 3000 B.C.—man made rapid progress in controlling his environments. However, this progress did not occur at the same time in every place throughout the world. Instead, it first began in several areas and then spread to others. As a result, during the New Stone Age the way of life changed in nearly every part of the world.

Today, some people still live in a New Stone Age culture. Some of these people are shown in the picture. They are the Pygmies of southern Africa. They still

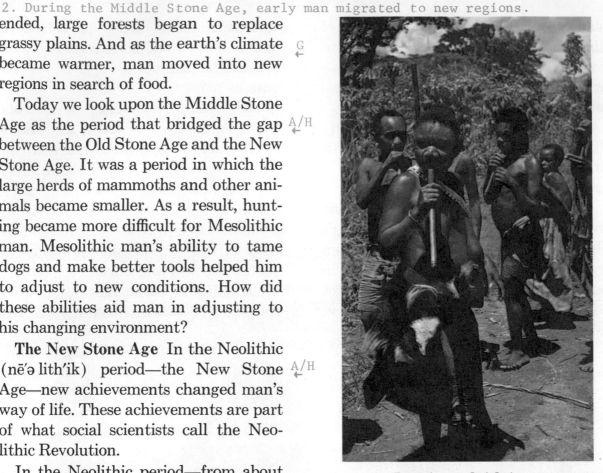

Pygmies of Africa

use stone tools and live as man did thousands of years ago. But today these New Stone Age cultures are rare and almost all people, throughout the world, live in civilized societies. These civilized societies are possible because of man's achievements during the Neolithic period.

Think for Yourself

Why do you think man has made faster progress in one period of time than in others? See #3 below.

62

Stress:
1. Tools were improved during the New Stone Age.
2. Agriculture was developed in the New Stone Age.

For Teaching Helps, see page T36.

THE NEOLITHIC REVOLUTION

A new era The great achievements of the Neolithic period were agriculture and the domestication of certain animals as a source of food. Also during this time man learned how to make pottery and to weave. Stone tools were still used, but these were now highly polished. These polished stone tools remained in use until man learned to make and to use tools made of metal.

See #1 above.

The New Stone Age tools included many of the tools we use today. Some of these tools are shown in the picture. For what purposes were these tools used? How have these tools been improved today?

The development of agriculture Social scientists are not yet able to tell exactly where or when farming first be-

gan. It is known that at some time between 8000 B.C. and 6000 B.C., man began to raise crops.

Some social scientists believe farming began in southwestern Asia about 8000 B.C. They think agriculture then spread to western Europe and eastern Asia over a period of about 3,000 or 4,000 years. Other social scientists believe that agriculture began in several areas at about the same time. As yet, there is not enough evidence to answer this question to everyone's satisfaction. However, evidence has been discovered that indicates that farming did develop in the Americas about 6500 B.C. It appears, at least in the Americas, that farming developed independently and was not learned from other people in Asia.

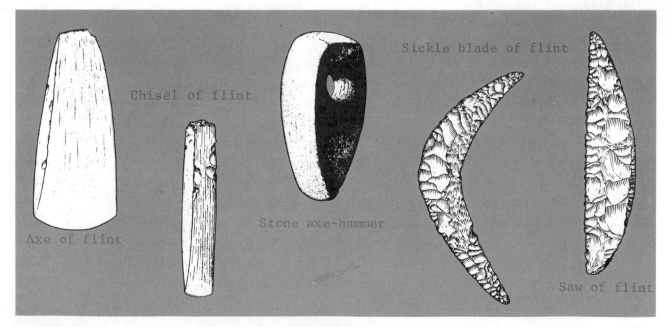

Chisel of flint

Sickle blade of flint

Stone axe-hammer

Axe of flint

Saw of flint

3. Social scientists believe that agriculture began in several different regions at approximately the same time.

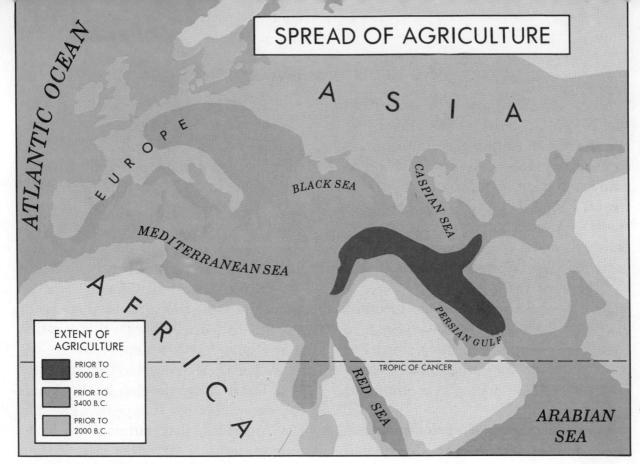

SPREAD OF AGRICULTURE

ATLANTIC OCEAN

ASIA

EUROPE

BLACK SEA

CASPIAN SEA

MEDITERRANEAN SEA

AFRICA

PERSIAN GULF

TROPIC OF CANCER

RED SEA

ARABIAN SEA

EXTENT OF
AGRICULTURE

PRIOR TO
5000 B.C.

PRIOR TO
3400 B.C.

PRIOR TO
2000 B.C.

Stress:

1. Migration and trade helped to spread the knowledge of agriculture.

The map shows the use of agriculture in parts of Africa, Asia, and Europe. Decide whether or not the areas where people farmed before 3400 B.C. have any features in common. After you study the map, try to answer these questions:

G
←

A/G
→

1. Where does the map show that agriculture probably began? Southwest Asia.

See #1 above.
2. How do you think the knowledge of farming might have been spread?

See #2 below.
3. Why did some areas of the world learn about farming later than others?

See #3 below.
4. Why were some areas shown on the map not used for farming?

Exactly how man first learned to plant and raise crops is unknown. In all likelihood, farming was developed by accident. Some anthropologists believe that when food was scarce, people may have been forced to gather wild plants to eat. Since wheat and barley are known to have grown wild, these were probably gathered. Then it is believed that an early genius must have tried to plant seeds from these plants. The next step was taken when man learned, that with care and a proper climate, these plants could be raised and harvested. At this point, farming began.

2. People living in areas farther away from farming areas or trade routes learned about farming later than people in other areas where contact with farming cultures was more common.

3. In some areas, geographic conditions worked against the development of agriculture.

For a class activity, see #3 on page 75.   For Teaching Helps, see page T36.
Stress:
1. The domestication of animals enabled man to raise livestock for food.

The domestication of animals Evidence seems to show that dogs were first taken into man's villages and allowed to live in them during the Middle Stone Age. These were probably wild dogs which became pets. But the domestication of other animals, which were used as a source of food, probably came later. Once again no exact date for this is known. Nor is it known which animal was first domesticated for use as food. However, evidence does show that early in the New Stone Age, man domesticated goats, sheep, pigs, cattle, horses, and donkeys. Some social scientists believe that cattle, horses, and donkeys were the last to be domesticated. They think that these were probably domesticated after the discovery of agriculture. See #2 below. How might Neolithic man have used horses? See #3 below. Why do you think horses might have been domesticated after the discovery of agriculture?

Pottery and weaving Another of man's achievements during the Neolithic period was the making of pots. This achievement apparently was not limited to only one area of the world, for the remains of Neolithic pots have been found in America as well as in Asia.

The pots in the illustration are from southwest Asia, and they are about 6,000 years old. What material was probably used to make these pots? What was the most likely source of this material? These pots served a number of purposes.

What might some of these purposes have been? To carry and store food or water.

Some anthropologists believe that pottery probably was made only after people learned to farm. This was because farming made it possible for people to settle in one place for a long period of time and to live in communities. Pottery was more important to settled people and less desired by nomadic people. Why do you think this was true?

Weaving also came after agriculture. Evidence shows that the art of weaving dates back at least to 5000 B.C.

Stress:
1. The discovery and spread of Neolithic developments helped man, throughout
   the world, adjust to changing conditions.

Once the art of weaving was learned, people began to sew pieces of woven material together to fashion clothing. How might weaving and the ability to use cloth in making clothing have affected man's way of life?

The spread of Neolithic achievements Today, much of what occurred in the New Stone Age is still a mystery. Archaeological studies in many parts of the world are still being made. In time, however, new discoveries by social scientists will undoubtedly increase our knowledge of this period.

On the basis of the evidence that has been discovered, many social scientists believe that the great achievements of the Neolithic period may have originated in several places. These achievements were then spread in all directions to other people. This is called **cultural diffusion.**

Geography and climate seem to have had some influence upon cultural diffusion during the Neolithic period. In Africa, for example, people were farming well before 3000 B.C. But this was mainly along the coast of the Mediterranean

Sea. To the south, near the equator, there were abundant forests, food was plentiful, and the climate was hot and wet. In this area of Africa, agriculture was not quickly adopted, and many people continued their old ways of life as hunters and food gatherers.

Thus, for several reasons, Neolithic societies throughout the world developed in different ways and at different rates of speed. But at some point during the Neolithic period many people, in all parts of the world, began to develop a new way of life. For these people, it was a culture in which people began to settle in communities, to farm, and to raise livestock. This new way of life was typical of what social scientists call Neolithic society. What old ways of life do you think were changed? Why do you think these changes in the ways of life occurred?

Think for Yourself

Compared to agriculture, do you think any other discoveries have so completely changed man's way of life? Why or why not?

NEOLITHIC COMMUNITIES

Location of Neolithic settlements Because the people in most Neolithic settlements depended upon farming and livestock raising, the land that was available for farming and grazing was important. Therefore, geography played a large part in determining where a Neolithic settlement was located. Usually, villages were near a supply of water—an oasis, a lake, or a river. As the climate

66

Nile River Valley

changed in some areas, or as population grew, or as the land became worn out, people moved. Often they settled near springs or in river valleys such as the A/G Nile River Valley in the picture. Why were river valleys good places for villages to develop? Are river valleys still considered to be good areas for settlements today? Why or why not?

See #1 above.

Neolithic houses When man was a hunter, he was almost always moving about in search of food. Often small groups of hunters slept wherever their search for food left them. Usually they had no shelter at night except an overhanging cliff or a cave. And only in rare cases was there enough food for a group of people to settle in one area for any length of time.

But with the discovery of farming, people began to live in settlements. At that time, during the New Stone Age, permanent houses were built and a step toward community life was taken.

See #2 below.

Stress:
1. Neolithic houses were usually built from materials found in each area.

See #1 above.

The picture shows how one type of Neolithic house was constructed. What materials were used in constructing these houses? Why might this type of house be suitable in some climates and not in others? Mud blocks broke up in wet climates.

Early villages When Neolithic farmers built their houses close together, they formed a village. Archaeologists have found the remains of some of these early villages. Neolithic villages usually contained between eight and thirty houses in each village. The people living in these villages were almost entirely dependent upon the surrounding land for their food. How might this have affected the size of a village?

Because of the more settled life and better supply of food, population in most Neolithic villages grew. When the population of a village became too large, some people had to move. These people then found, and settled on, new land and started a new village. Do you think this movement of people may have helped to spread the knowledge of agriculture? Why? Yes, through cultural diffusion.

The first town Not far from the Dead Sea there was a spring. This spring provided water for an oasis at which the

A/G

Mixing straw with mud or clay

Straw and mud or clay block

2. The amount of food Neolithic farmers were able to raise often limited the size of their villages.

Stress:
1. One of the world's earliest towns was Jericho in southwest Asia.

See #1 above. oldest known town—Jericho (jer'ə kō) —was founded. At first it was a small settlement, but by about 7000 B.C. it had grown into a town of about 3,000 people.

The first Neolithic farmers of Jericho built permanent round homes. Later these were replaced by rectangular houses which were closely grouped together inside a stone wall. Observe the picture of the remains of Jericho. The picture shows part of the wall that was built around the ancient town of Jericho. What material was used by the people to build the wall? Stones.

The wall around Jericho seems to indicate the need for defense. This is unusual, since wars were not common among Neolithic people. Many Neolithic villages, for example, had no walls. And Neolithic villages in Europe often had walls only to keep out animals. Why do you think the people of Jericho might have needed a wall when other villages did not? Good supply of water in a very dry area.

Social scientists often wonder why towns such as Jericho develop and grow, while others do not. One reason may have been Jericho's excellent supply of water which enabled the people to farm and raise livestock. The people of Jericho were among the first to develop a system of irrigation which enabled them to fully use their supply of water.

Another reason might have been that the people learned to cooperate and to

Remains of the wall at Jericho

respect the laws of the community. Some authorities feel that this cooperation and respect for the law came from the need for irrigation. Why do you think irrigation led to cooperation and to respect for the law? See #2 below.

Jarmo   In 1948 Dr. Robert Braidwood, an anthropologist, began a study of a site in northern Iraq, where he found the remains of an early farming

2. People living in early towns developed laws to regulate the use of such things as water and land.

69

Clay blocks

Thatched roof

Oven

Type of house built in Jarmo

Stress:
1. Evidence indicates that Jarmo was a farming community.

community. This community—Jarmo— is believed to be over 8,000 years old. It probably began not long after Jericho, probably about 6000 B.C.

Although smaller in size than Jericho, Jarmo was also a permanent Neolithic community. The people of Jarmo lived in houses much like the one shown in the picture. What does the picture tell us about the climate? What does the picture tell us about the culture of the people? Warm, dry climate, settled way of life.

In the remains of Jarmo, archaeologists have found seeds, sickles, and bits of pottery. From this evidence, social scientists have gained some idea about how the people lived. What can you tell about the people of Jarmo from this evidence?

See #1 above.

Think for Yourself

How has your community been affected by changes in population?

*2. Why did the earliest towns first develop in southwest Asia?

NEOLITHIC SOCIETY

For Teaching Helps, see page T38.

Neolithic cultures Agriculture, domesticated animals, pottery, weaving, and polished stone tools were commonly found in most Neolithic cultures. But not every group of people living during the Neolithic period adopted all these

things. And for those that did, they often did so at different times. In England, for example, men did not begin to farm until about 3000 B.C. This was 4,000 years after the people of Jericho had begun raising crops.

Stress:
1. Neolithic cultures varied from one area to another.

70

Unfortunately, it is difficult today to know exactly what life was like 10,000 years ago. However, anthropologists and historians have studied the remains of Neolithic settlements. From these studies, social scientists have developed some ideas about how Neolithic people may have lived. Based on this evidence, many of the changes that occurred as man progressed from the Middle Stone Age to the Neolithic period can be determined.

Economic and social changes During the Neolithic period, man's economic and social way of life changed. Before Neolithic times, in the Old and Middle Stone ages, man's way of life was simpler. Small nomadic hunting groups moved about in search of food. In most cases each small group lived independently, and contacts between groups were not common. As a result of this way of life, man before the Neolithic period had little knowledge of such things as community life, land ownership, and organized government.

However, after the development of farming, many changes occurred. First, people settled down and communities were formed. Although these communities were quite small, they still brought people into close contact with one another. And this contact, in turn, led to increased cooperation among the people as they worked to develop permanent farming communities.

See #2 below.

A second change during the time was that the number of people in the world increased. Study the graph showing this increase and answer these questions:

1. About how many people were alive in Neolithic times? 88,000,000.
2. How great an increase was this from earlier times? Seventeen times greater than in 25,000 B.C.
3. What may have caused this increase? More food and better environment.
4. How might these increases have affected community life? Larger communities.

Other changes also occurred. For example, the idea of owning land developed. In most early villages the farmland probably was owned by the village as a whole. Sections of this land were then distributed, in some way, among the villagers. Who might have been in charge of distributing land in early times? Who might distribute land to people today?

See #3 below.

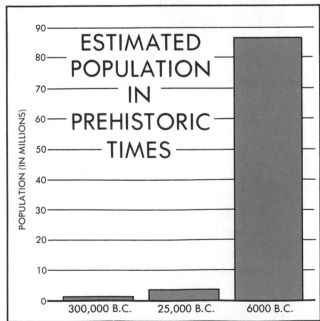

ESTIMATED POPULATION IN PREHISTORIC TIMES

POPULATION (IN MILLIONS)

| | 300,000 B.C. | 25,000 B.C. | 6000 B.C. |

2. Living in larger groups taught people to cooperate with each other.

3. In many Neolithic villages, farmland was probably owned by the village and then divided among the people by the village government.

For Teaching Helps, see page T38.
Stress:
1. The division of jobs among members of a group is called a division of labor.

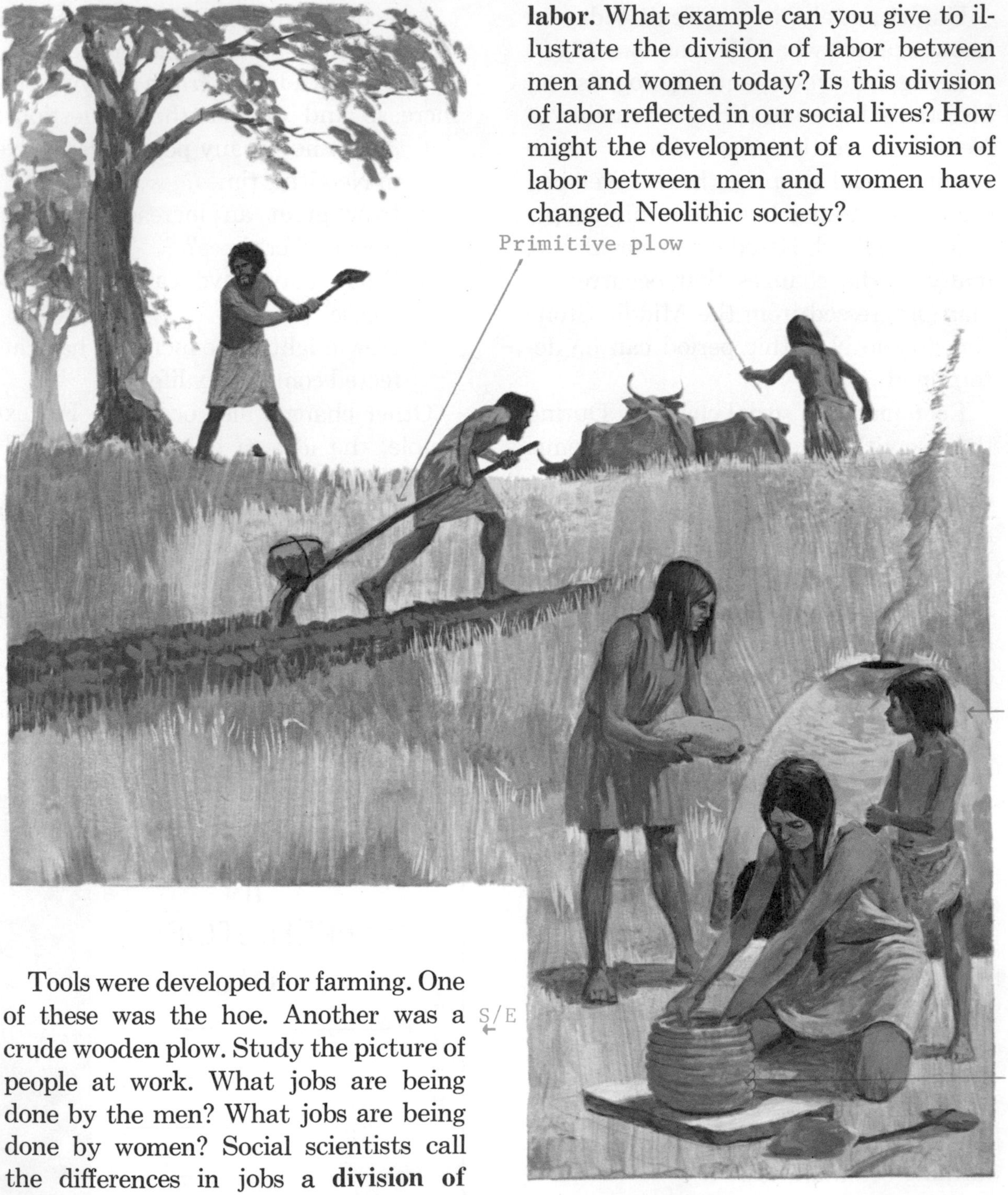
Primitive plow
Oven
Pot being made

Tools were developed for farming. One of these was the hoe. Another was a crude wooden plow. Study the picture of people at work. What jobs are being done by the men? What jobs are being done by women? Social scientists call the differences in jobs a **division of labor.** What example can you give to illustrate the division of labor between men and women today? Is this division of labor reflected in our social lives? How might the development of a division of labor between men and women have changed Neolithic society? S/E

2. As Neolithic men developed additional skills, the division of labor in their societies increased.

Stress: For Teaching Helps, see page T38.
1. Leaders of groups in the Old Stone Age were probably chosen on the basis
   of their strength, courage, and hunting skills.

Changes in political life Social scientists cannot tell for sure how early Neolithic people governed themselves. They can, however, study evidence and reach conclusions.

See #1 above.

One conclusion is that in the Old Stone Age men became leaders of groups because of their strength, courage, and hunting skills. But in Neolithic communities, which depended upon farming, these particular talents were less important. Leaders in Neolithic villages may have been older men who formed a village council or a group of elders. Community problems, such as land ownership, rights to water, and so on, might have been decided by the council or group of elders. The picture shows a village council still in use in India. Why, in a farming community, is knowledge and experience more important than strength and courage? How might a change in the culture have changed the way a group was governed?

See #2 below.

Since every group needs rules, some method is needed to enforce the rules. Thus, in the Old Stone Age, rules were probably enforced by the best hunter who was the leader of the group. But in Neolithic settlements, the older and wiser members of the group probably enforced the community's rules. The enforcement of a society's rules is a function of government. What might happen to your society if there was no government to enforce rules?

See #3 below.

Art and religion Art from the Old Stone Age can be seen in cave paintings. These paintings often were of animals. Early man probably believed his paintings were magical and would aid him in hunting the animals. Thus, early man's art was concerned with magic and possibly religion. What might man have worshiped during the Old Stone Age?

In the New Stone Age, art took a different form. For example, Paleolithic art often took the form of cave paintings, while Neolithic art often was used to decorate pottery. Compare the Old

Village council in modern India

2. Leaders in Neolithic groups were probably chosen on the basis of their
   knowledge and experience.
3. Every society needs some form of rules and regulations.

73

Stress:
1. Art in Neolithic times was often used for decorative purposes.
For Teaching Helps, see page T38.

Stone Age man painting on wall of a cave

Neolithic pot

Stone Age cave painting and the design on the Neolithic clay pot. How does the art differ? How had the change from a hunting society to a farming society changed art? Why?

Religions also changed somewhat in the New Stone Age. Old Stone Age man was concerned with animals, but New Stone Age man was more concerned with the seasons. Neolithic man was also concerned with the force that controlled the seasons. Why were the seasons of the year important to Neolithic man?

Both Paleolithic man and Neolithic man worshiped spirits. These they found in nature—animals, trees, stones,

and so on. Magic was then used in the hopes of forcing these spirits to aid man. At first medicine men were believed to have this magical power. Later, as Neolithic man developed communities, priests became a special social class in the society. And as civilizations began and cities grew, these priests often became leaders in their societies. This development will be discussed in Unit 3 which deals with the growth of civilizations.

Think for Yourself

What talents or skills are desired in the leaders of your community? Why are these important?

2. Early agricultural people developed religions that were concerned with the seasons of the year, the climate, and so on.

74 *3. What similarities can you see between your community and a Neolithic community?

Things to Do

See page 60.
1. Write a few statements telling about the progress made by man during the New Stone Age.

See page 66.
2. Suppose you are in charge of planning and developing a Neolithic village. Prepare to tell how you will carry out this responsibility. Consider such things as location, number of dwellings, utilization of surrounding land area, and so on.

See page 65.
3. Find books in your school library that give information on the domestication of animals. Share these with your class.

See page 68.
4. Pretend that you are in an airplane looking down on the old city of Jericho about 700 B.C. Describe what you see.

CLASS PROJECT—PART 3

All materials and objects for the display on early man should now be collected. Is the display area in your classroom ready to house all the materials? For Part 3 of your class project, decide where to place materials and objects in your display area on early man. Complete this part of the project by placing materials and objects in the display area so that an attractive display on early man is the result of your efforts. When your class project is completed, the class may want to discuss these questions: What lessons did you learn about early man by making this display? If you were to do this project again, what changes would you make to improve the display?

Have the pupils find each of the review words in the unit. For each word, have them answer such questions as these:

Checkup Time
1. How was the word used in the book?
2. How might you use the word yourself?

For question 2 above, encourage the pupils to use each word in a social science context.

Review Words

agriculture	cultural diffusion	economic changes	migrate
blade tools	culture	environment	pebble tools
civilization	division of labor	extinct	prehistoric
climate	domestication	*Homo habilis*	social changes

Review Questions
Typical answers only.

Social Science Facts

1. What are some ways early man chose to adjust to his environment? (44, 46, 51-52, 60-62, 63) Migrate or develop new tools and skills.

2. What are some likenesses and differences among the races? (47-48) See bottom margin.

3. What influence did climate have upon early man's effort to secure food? (50-52, 64-66) Made it easier or more difficult.

4. What were some of the cultures developed by early man? (52-57, 66-70) See bottom margin.

5. What developments by early man assisted him in altering his environment and in moving toward a civilized society? (59, 60-61, 63-66) Tools, agriculture, domesticated animals.

6. What were some of the changes that came about with the development of agriculture? (59, 63, 67, 71-74) See bottom margin.

2. All are <u>Homo sapiens</u> but may differ in skin color, hair, color of eyes, and eyelids.

4. Hunting, food gathering, farming.

5. Settled communities, population increase, political development.

Social Science Ideas

1. What kinds of things do you see in your community that show man's attempt to adjust to his environment? Various answers.

2. How do geography and climate affect the appearance of people who are members of the same race? May influence skin color.

3. Why might it be important today to consider climate when locating and building a new factory? May affect workers and transportation of goods.

4. Why does man sometimes develop different cultures while living in similar surroundings? Man has many choices in determining his way of life.

5. Why is it important for man to alter his environment? To improve living conditions.

6. Why do communities today develop in different ways and at different rates of speed? Better environment, resources, and leadership.

6. Communities, trade, commerce, religious changes, civilization, and so on.

Test Yourself

On your own paper write your answers to each question.

Test 1 Social Science Words

Which groups of words below tell ways early man adjusted to his environment?
1. became extinct
(2.) migrated throughout the world
(3.) used blade and pebble tools
4. changed the climate

Which groups of words below are factors that influenced the development of races?
(5.) many social changes
6. introduction of social scientists
(7.) changes in environment

Which groups of words below tell ways early man attempted to change his environment?
8. began to develop agriculture
(9.) moved to a new area
10. domesticated animals

Which sentences below are true?
T 11. Cultures are all the things that make up a group's way of life.
12. Geography played no part in determining where prehistoric man lived.
T 13. Glaciers affect the earth's climate.

Test 2 Facts and Ideas

Which answers to each question below are true?
1. What are some likenesses among people of different races?
(a.) They must learn to meet new conditions of life.
(b.) They are physically alike.
c. They have different colored skin.
2. What changes in society came about with the development of agriculture?
a. Villages declined in population.
(b.) Economic and social life changed.
(c.) Land ownership developed.
3. Why are customs often different among families living in the same surroundings?
(a.) because of family influence
(b.) because of religious beliefs
c. because of a different climate

Which sentences below are true?
T 4. The prehistoric period came before man developed writing.
T 5. Environment influences culture.
F 6. A division of labor was unknown in the Neolithic society.

UNIT 3 ANCIENT CIVILIZATIONS

Stress:
1. Ancient civilizations usually developed near rivers or lakes.
2. Rivers were important means of transportation in ancient times.
*3. In what way does the picture below show how men learned to cooperate and work together in ancient civilizations?

Chapters

5. Ancient Societies
6. Patterns of Ancient Governments
7. Ancient Economic Systems

Egyptian wall painting (2900 B.C.) showing royal ships going up and down the Nile

Stress:
1. Ways of life in certain regions are referred to as civilizations.
2. The term civilization is often used to describe a society that has developed social, political, and economic systems.
3. Urbanization and writing are also characteristics of civilizations.
*4. Why might ancient civilizations have developed in different places at different times?

Historians often use the word civilization to describe the ways of life in certain regions. Thus, they often refer to Asian civilizations, African civilizations, and American civilizations. But exactly what is meant by the term civilization sometimes differs. In this book the word is used to refer to a group of people who have developed in certain similar ways. These ways include the development of writing, government, and an economic system. The word civilization is also used to refer to the people who have built cities and have at least a part of the population living in cities.

See #1 above.

H/A

See #2 and #3 above.

With this latter definition of civilization in mind, it is possible to see that ancient civilizations occurred in several places. These places are often referred to as the "cradles of civilization." Three of these cradles of civilizations were in Asia; one, in Africa; one, in North America; and one, in South America.

A/G

Each of man's first civilizations developed in different ways. Some of the early civilizations had contacts with one another. But others did not.

Three of the earliest civilizations developed in Mesopotamia, Egypt, and India. The material in this unit discusses these three early civilizations.

A/G

As you study the material that follows, try to answer the following questions.

1. What basic characteristics did each civilization have in common and why?
2. In what ways did each of the civilizations differ and why?
3. How did each civilization affect the ideas, values, and beliefs of the people?

For Teaching Helps, see page T39.
Stress:
1. The continuing nature of the class project. See pp. 96, 108, and 119.

CLASS PROJECT—PART 1

2. Modern man stores information for future use.

Man in his modern world has need for storing information. A good example of a system for storing information is a recipe box. Each recipe card contains information that can be retrieved, or referred to, at will. Together these cards make up the system. We can call a system that stores information a retrieval system.

As your class project for this unit, make plans to build a retrieval system. To begin the project bring a large, square box to your classroom. You may want to paint the box, rule it off, and put labels in place as shown in the picture. The large envelopes glued on each of the rectangular spaces will serve as storage centers for information. Start calling this box a retrieval system.

As you study Chapter 5, you will find information on the topics placed on side 1 of your retrieval system. Part 2 of the class project will help you get started with putting pieces of information in the retrieval system.

Radio tower

Modern buildings

Thatched roof

Traditional market place

Hand-woven baskets

Town in Nigeria, Africa

5. Ancient Societies

See #2 below.

One pattern found in the history of man is the growth of cities which began in about 3400 B.C. This continuous growth and development of cities is called **urbanization.**

As urbanization occurred, ancient people learned to live together and to cooperate. In this way societies developed and different social, political, and economic ways of life were formed. The picture above shows a town in modern

For Teaching Helps, see page T40.

Africa. It shows how old and new ways of life are blending together. This blending of the past and present is a common feature of urbanization throughout many parts of the world. In what ways does the picture illustrate the blending of old and new ways of life? How is the way of life shown in the picture both similar to and different from the way of life found in the cities in your area?

See #3 below.

A/S

P/E

Stress:
1. Cities are larger and more organized than are towns.

JUST FOR FUN

Talk to your parents and other adults and try to find out how the way of life has changed in your area in the last fifty years.

2. Cities began to develop about 3400 B.C.
3. Towns and cities blended old and new ways of life as is shown in the picture above.
*4. Why do most people like to hold on to their old way of life?

For Teaching Helps, see page T41.
Stress:
1. The first known civilization developed in the Tigris-Euphrates river valley.

THE SUMERIAN SOCIETY

The first civilization Study the map of Mesopotamia (mes′ə pə tā′mē ə). The name means "land between the rivers." What two rivers form the area known as Mesopotamia? What is the southernmost area of Mesopotamia called? Sumer.

See #1 above.

G ⇄

G/E →

It was in Sumer (sü′mər) that the world's first civilization developed about 3400 B.C. From this beginning, ideas spread to other people and influenced their development as well. In fact, almost the entire area of Mesopotamia developed civilizations which were, in some ways, influenced by the Sumerians (sü mir′i ənz). Some historians, anthropologists, and economists believe that

G/H ←

G/S →

man's first civilization was helped in its development by two conditions. One of these conditions was an abundance of rich, fertile land which could be easily worked by the people with their simple tools. A second condition was a warm climate. Why would fertile land be an aid to the development of a civilization? Why would a warm climate be more helpful than a very hot or a very cold climate? Conditions are less extreme.

See #2 above.

The Sumerian people During the late Paleolithic period—about 10,000 B.C.—the climate in parts of the world became hot and dry. As a result, groups of people moved from such areas toward the fertile river valleys.

Exactly where the first settlers of Sumer came from is still unknown. Nor do social scientists agree upon the origins of the other groups of people who later moved into Sumer. However, it is clear that the population of Sumer soon became a mixture of many different groups. One of these groups brought an advanced culture. This culture—the Uruk (ü′rük) culture—became, in time, the basis for the Sumerian civilization. This civilization had, by 3400 B.C., progressed to the point where the people had created the world's first system of writing, invented the wheel, and established large cities.

See #3 below.

A/S →

Geographic setting of Sumer Each year the rains and melting snow in the

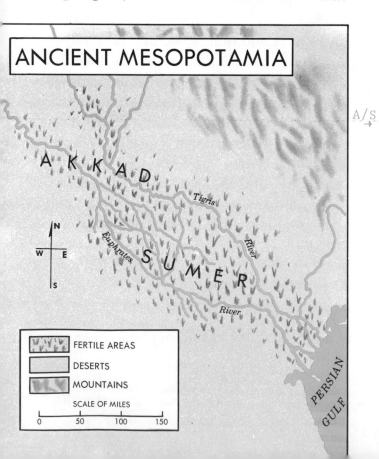

ANCIENT MESOPOTAMIA

AKKAD

Tigris

SUMER

Euphrates

River

River

N
W E
S

FERTILE AREAS

DESERTS

MOUNTAINS

SCALE OF MILES
0   50   100   150

PERSIAN GULF

For a class activity, see #2 on page 96.

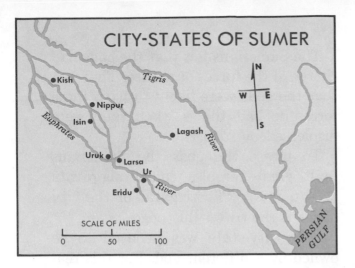

CITY-STATES OF SUMER

Kish

Tigris

Nippur

Isin

Euphrates

Lagash

Uruk

Larsa

Ur

River

Eridu

River

SCALE OF MILES

0   50   100

PERSIAN GULF

Brick walls   Ziggurat

Reconstruction of the city of Ur

north caused the Tigris (tī′grəs) and Euphrates (yu̇ frāt′ēz) rivers to rise. Often they overflowed their banks and flooded the surrounding land. Flooding was particularly dangerous near the Euphrates River since the river bed was higher than the surrounding land.

See #1 above.

Since the annual floods usually occurred during the growing season, the Sumerians had to design a method to control the flood. At the same time it was also necessary to develop an irrigation system to water the land in the dry season. Thus, to protect the land from flooding, high riverbanks had to be built and maintained. To water the land, a series of canals had to be dug to carry the water from the river. How might these activities have influenced the Sumerian way of life? Led to cooperation.

See #2 below.

The cities of Sumer The first basic element of the Sumerian civilization and its society was the **city-state.** Each city-state was made up of an independent city which controlled a certain amount

of the surrounding territory. The major Sumerian city-states are shown on the map. Most of these are near which river? Why do you think this occurred?

See #4 below.

In most ways the cultures of each of the Sumerian city-states were much alike. Each city-state had similar social, political, and economic ways of life and citizens of all the city-states shared the same language, religious beliefs, and outlook on life.

A reconstruction of one Sumerian city-state, the city of Ur (ėr), is shown in the picture. At one time the city of Ur may have had a population of over 200,000 people. Study the picture of the remains of Ur. What material was used to build the houses? Do you think the city was as crowded as a modern city? Do you think the people of Ur had to obey certain rules and laws? Why or why not?

2. Sumerians designed ways to control flooding and irrigate fields.
3. Most early Sumerian cities were built near rivers.
4. The Tigris River was swift and difficult to navigate.

For Teaching Helps, see page T41.
For a class activity, see #1 on page 96.
Stress:
1. The Sumerian religion influenced Sumerian life.

The Sumerian religion A second important element in the Sumerian society was religion. Social scientists say that it influenced nearly every phase of Sumerian life—political, economic, and social.

The Sumerian religion was based upon certain beliefs about the forces of nature and the powers of man. One belief about a force of nature is told in the Sumerian verse given below. What was the force?

The rampant flood which no man can oppose, which shakes the heavens and causes the earth to tremble . . . [and] drowns the harvest in its time for ripeness.

What could floods do to the heavens? To the earth? To plants?

The Sumerians felt that the gods had charge of the forces of nature. They felt that the gods were likely to have these forces do bad things when they were displeased by man.

To please the gods the Sumerians built great temples called **ziggurats** (zig' u rats). The ziggurat of the city of Ur is shown on this page.

Each city-state was believed to be owned by a different god. For this reason each city-state built a ziggurat to honor that god. The ruler of each city-state—the king-priest—was thought to be picked by the city's god.

The Sumerians also believed that the city-state's god had to be provided with food and shelter when he visited his city. Thus, the Sumerians believed that

See #1 above.

See #2 below.

See #3 below.

Brick walls   Steps

Ziggurat of Ur

2. The Sumerians feared the gods and felt helpless before the forces of nature.
3. The rulers of Sumerian city-states were high priests.

life on earth was to be spent working for the gods. In return for their work—and for food and shelter—the Sumerians hoped that the gods would be kind. To help ensure this kindness, special sacrifices and prayers were offered by the ruler and priests of each city-state. What group in the society do you think held political power? Why? Priests.

The average Sumerian was convinced that after his death his spirit passed to another world. This spirit world was described by the Sumerians as a place where

See #1 below.

> Ghosts like bats flutter their wings there; On the gates and gateposts the dust lies undisturbed . . .

Do you think the Sumerians looked forward to life after death? Why?

Sumerian social classes When the Sumerian civilization first began, social classes were probably not important. No doubt, in early times, elders and the heads of families were important. But most citizens were probably considered equal and most performed the same general tasks.

See #2 below.

However, as time passed, different social classes developed. By about 2000 B.C. it seems clear that there were three social classes in most city-states.

The upper social class was composed of the city-state's wealthiest families. Members of this social class usually held important positions in the society. Consider the important elements of the

Sumerian scribe

Sumerian society. What positions do you think the members of the upper class held? Priests, government officials.

The second, or middle, social class in Sumer was the largest. It was made up of the majority of the free citizens of the city-state. In the middle class were the scribes—who could write—craftsmen, merchants, farmers, builders, and so on. The illustration shows a member of the middle class. He was employed as a scribe by the government. Why was he important to the Sumerian society?

See #3 below.

Stress:
1. Sumerians believed that life after death was unpleasant.
2. Sumer had three social classes.
3. Those who were able to write kept records of political and economic events and transactions.

85

Stress:
1. Many historians believe slaves in Sumer were well treated.
*2. How did Sumerian slavery differ from slavery in the United States?

In the third social class in Sumer were the slaves. Since warfare was common among the city-states, many prisoners of war became slaves. But a number of Sumerian slaves had not been prisoners of war. Generally, these slaves were people who owed money. To pay their debts, they sold themselves or their families into slavery.

The role slavery played in the Sumerian society is hard to determine. Authorities tend to disagree about the place of the slave in Sumer. A number of historians, however, feel that the slaves were not too badly treated. In many cases a slave could earn money and buy his freedom. Slaves also appear to have been protected by the law. In part, this may have been because most slaves were Sumerians. Do you think a slave in Sumer might have been more harshly treated if he had not been a Sumerian? Why or why not?

Contributions of the Sumerians The Sumerian society made several important contributions to the progress of man. Although the Sumerians fell under the control of other people after 2000 B.C., these contributions lived on.

The most important contributions of the Sumerians—writing and the invention of the wheel—quickly spread to people in other areas. The Sumerians' way of life influenced other societies for centuries after Sumer's decline.

Think for Yourself

Do you think the life of the average Sumerian was strictly controlled by the ruler of the city-state? Why or why not?

THE EGYPTIAN SOCIETY

For Teaching Helps, see page T42.

Geographic setting At about the same time that villages were starting in Sumer, villages were also being established in Africa. A number of these villages developed in the Nile River Valley.

Geographers believe that at one time most of northern Africa was a large, grassy plain. However, as the climate changed and became hot and dry, the northern area changed. The map of ancient Egypt on page 87 shows the nature of the area about 3400 B.C. What happened to the grassy plains? What areas were fertile and suitable for farming and village life?

The same map can also tell us something about the development of the Egyptian civilization. For example, social scientists know that until about 1650 B.C. Egypt was isolated and free from invasion. This helped the Egyptians to prosper and build their civilization. Study the map. In what area of

See #1 below.

See #2 below.

Stress:
1. Much of North Africa changed to desert except in the Nile River Valley.
2. Much of Egypt was isolated from outside invasion by a desert or a sea.

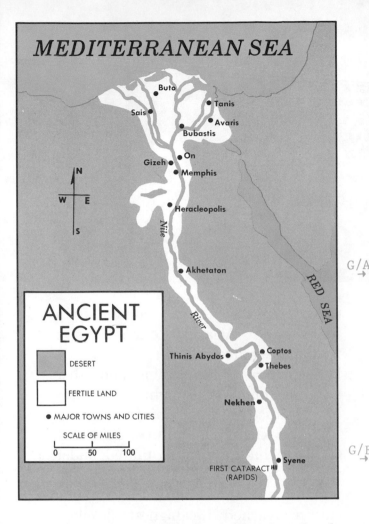

MEDITERRANEAN SEA

ANCIENT EGYPT

- ▨ DESERT
- ☐ FERTILE LAND
- ● MAJOR TOWNS AND CITIES

SCALE OF MILES
0   50   100

Major towns: Buto, Tanis, Sais, Avaris, Bubastis, Gizeh, On, Memphis, Heracleopolis, Akhetaton, Thinis Abydos, Coptos, Thebes, Nekhen, Syene

Nile River

RED SEA

FIRST CATARACT (RAPIDS)

of the Nile River was predictable and less rapid and therefore it was easier to control. How might the nature of these floods have caused the Egyptians and Sumerians to differ in their ideas about the forces of nature? *Egyptians were more optimistic.*

Today, we know that the annual flooding of the Nile—which is shown in the picture on page 88—comes from the rains and melting snow in Central Africa. But the ancient Egyptians believed that the yearly flooding of the Nile was caused by the tears of the goddess Isis (ī'sis). They thought that Isis cried because the people of Egypt had so little rain.

See #2 below.

The Nile flood occurs each year between the middle of August and early October. Thus, the annual flood occurred after the Egyptians had harvested their crops and when the land was dry. How did the time of the floods in Egypt differ from the time of the floods in Sumer? How might this difference have affected attitudes and work in Egypt?

Controlling the annual floods In very early times the settlers moved away from the river during a flood. After the flood had passed, those early farmers moved back along the river and planted their crops in the fertile soil left by the flooding waters. The fertile soil had been carried by the water from the highlands in the south.

A warm climate, and the fertile soil

Egypt do you think civilization developed? Why do you think that area of Egypt was free from invasion? How did the freedom from invasion aid the Egyptians in their development of a civilization?

The Nile floods In at least one way, the environment of ancient Egypt was less harsh than that of Sumer. Both civilizations—the Egyptian and the Sumerian—relied upon the floods that occurred annually. But unlike the flooding of the Euphrates River, the flooding

Stress:
1. Egypt's floods were predictable and easy to control.
2. Egyptians, like the Sumerians, believed the forces of nature were controlled by the gods and goddesses.

Nile River at floodtime

See #2 below.

left by the flood, allowed the early Egyptians to produce a surplus of food. As a result, the population increased and new villages grew. But soon the need for more food created a need for more land. To solve the problem, Egyptians developed a system of irrigation which increased the amount of land available for farming. This required cooperation among the people. But it took less work than was required to control the floods and irrigate the farms in Sumer. Can you think of any reasons why Egypt did not develop city-states? Explain your answer.

G/E

P/H

A/H

The Egyptian people The population of ancient Egypt, like that of Sumer, was a mixture of many people. Generally, three groups of people settled in Egypt in ancient times. One group came from Libya (lib′ē ə), which was to the west of Egypt. A second group came from Nubia (nü′bē ə), which was to the south of Egypt. A third group of people,

S/G

called Semites (sem′īts), arrived from southwestern Asia. Historians believe that the Semites brought with them a knowledge of metal, writing, and other achievements. Where might the Semites have learned of these things?

A slow-changing culture In about 3200 B.C., all Egypt was united under the rule of one king. It was after the unification of the country that Egypt's culture reached its highest development.

The culture that developed early in Egypt's history, between 2800 B.C. and 2200 B.C., remained basically unchanged for a long period of time. During that period, the Egyptians learned to build huge stone monuments, developed art and sculpturing, and established their way of life. Although some changes occurred in the years that followed, the basic way of life of the Egyptians changed very slowly.

One of the reasons that the Egyptian

88

Stress:
1. The Egyptian culture changed very slowly.
2. Early Egyptian society was made up of two basic social classes.

culture did not change very rapidly was because Egypt was isolated from its neighbors. The deserts to the east and west were hard to cross. It was not until about 1650 B.C. that Egypt was conquered by invaders. At that time a people called the Hyksos (hik′sos) conquered Egypt. The picture below shows an Egyptian chariot copied from the Hyksos. How might chariots have enabled the Hyksos to invade Egypt from the east? Could cross the deserts.

Social classes in Egypt Up until the Hyksos invasion, the Egyptian society was made up of two social classes. One was the upper class. This class included the king—called the pharaoh (fãr′ō)— the royal family, and government officials. The government officials were usually wealthy nobles or priests.

The second social class included all the other members of the Egyptian society. Most of these were farmers, but there were also scribes, craftsmen, metal workers, servants, and so on. Most of these workers were employed by the pharaoh or by the wealthy nobles. The Egyptian painting above shows carpenters and other craftsmen who were em-

Man weighing gold

Men carving ornaments

Carpenter   Pottery maker   Sculptor

ployed by one of Egypt's pharaohs. Rarely did a member of this lower social class move into the upper class.

Unlike many other ancient civilizations, Egypt had very few slaves. In part this was because Egypt was rarely at war and therefore took few prisoners of war. Another reason was that Egypt was thickly populated and had no shortage of labor. Still another reason may have been Egypt's religion. Since the pharaoh was believed to be a god, citizens worked on monuments and other projects willingly for the honor and glory of their king. See #3 below.

Religion in ancient Egypt Religion in ancient Egypt influenced almost every

Egyptian cavalry

Enemies of the Egyptians

Egyptian painting showing chariot adopted from the Hyksos

89

Stress:
1. The Egyptian religion influenced all aspects of Egyptian life.

part of the society. In political affairs religion was represented by the pharaoh who was believed to be both a king and a god. Religion also played a role in the economic and social life of the Egyptians. For example, the Egyptians believed that everything, from the flooding of the Nile to the death of a man, was influenced by the gods. Two of the many Egyptian gods are shown on this page. One is Re (rā), the sun god. The other is Osiris (ō sī′ris), king of the land of the dead. Can you tell which of the two gods pictured is the sun god? Explain the reason for your choice.

The Egyptians had a strong belief in life after death. At first it was believed that only the pharaoh lived after death. Why do you think the pharaoh was believed to live after death and not other Egyptians? He was part god.

See #2 below.

2. The Egyptians believed in life after death.

As time passed and the Egyptian society developed, life after death was believed to be possible for all people. However, to obtain this afterlife, the dead body had to be preserved. Wealthy Egyptians were buried in tombs, but the poorer people were buried in simple graves. The warm, dry climate of Egypt helped to preserve the bodies and many mummies have been found.

Life in ancient Egypt Ancient Egypt was primarily an agricultural country. Most of the people were peasant farmers who worked on the land owned by the pharaoh or by other members of the upper class.

In general, the life of the peasants—members of the lower social class—was filled with hard work. Much of their time was spent plowing, planting, watering, and harvesting the crops. Peas-

Symbol of the sun

Symbol of life

90

Re, the sun god   Osiris, god of the dead

Egyptian painting showing crops being harvested and loaded on donkeys

ants received only a small portion of the crops they raised. Most of the crops went to the owners of the land. The Egyptian painting shows peasants at work in the fields. What tasks are the peasants performing? What tool are they using? Sickles.

Other members of the lower social class were usually paid wages for what they produced. These wages usually were some type of produce, such as bread, meat, grain, and so on.

Members of the upper social class

*2. Why were Egyptian workers paid with produce?

lived a much better life than did those in the lower class. Often, the wealthy Egyptians lived a life of leisure and luxury. They lived in large, roomy houses and had an abundance of food to eat. Most wealthy families had servants to take care of the daily tasks.

Think for Yourself

How do you think the social classes in Egypt reflected the importance of religion in Egyptian life? Priests were part of the upper class.

THE INDUS SOCIETY

An almost unknown civilization A third great ancient civilization developed in India about 4,500 years ago. Until very recent times, almost nothing was known about this early civilization. Even today historians have very little

For Teaching Helps, see page T43.
information about what is called the Indus (in′dəs) civilization.

The Indus civilization reached its fullest development in India about 2500 B.C. It lasted for about 1,000 years and then disappeared around 1500 B.C.
See #2 below.

Stress:
1. Historians still have very little information about the Indus civilization.
2. The Indus civilization reached its peak about 2500 B.C.

91

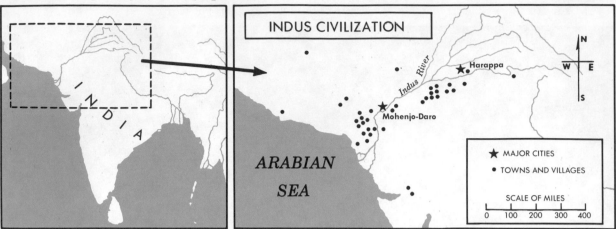

The region in which the Indus civilization developed is shown on the map above. How did the Indus civilization get its name? What geographic factors do you think led to the development of the Indus civilization? Why?

Archaeologists began to unearth the main cities of the Indus civilization in 1922. As yet, not enough evidence has been discovered to tell us the complete story of early life along the Indus River. For example, it is still not known what happened about 1500 B.C. that ended the Indus civilization. Several theories have been proposed, but definite evidence has not been found. Perhaps it never will be known, since no one has as yet learned to read the writing used by the people of the Indus civilization.

A study of India's first civilization shows how social scientists have carefully gathered and used evidence. From the evidence that has been found, geographers, historians, archaeologists, and anthropologists have developed clues to India's past.

The geographic setting The map below shows historic India. What geographic term would you use to describe the shape of India? India is part of what continent? Asia.

On the north, northeast, and northwest mountains separate India from the rest of Asia. These mountains made early India somewhat isolated from its neighbors. How might this have affected

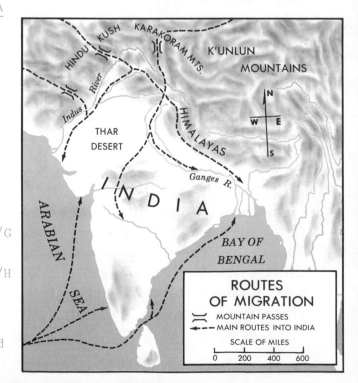

See #1 below.

See #2 below.

A/G

G

A

A/G

A/H

Stress:
1. The Indus civilization developed in the Indus River Valley.
2. Without knowledge of their writing, what ended the Indus civilization is unknown.

Stress:
1. People of all races from Asia, Africa, and Europe settled in India.
2. The Indus River Valley was once fertile and productive.

India's development? These mountains were not impassable. At times groups of people entered India through mountain passes, and a highly mixed population developed in India. Several of the routes used by these people are also shown on the map on page 92. What human races do you think might have come to be part of India's population?

See #1 above.

The Indus River Valley The Indus River Valley is a large plain about 950 miles long and in some places 700 miles wide. Today, part of this area is harsh, unfertile land. But in 3000 B.C. the valley was a fertile area of forests and plains. Rainfall in the area was probably rather light. However, the annual river floods—many of which were unpredictable and severe—occurred between May and August. These floods helped the people to produce enough food to support a large population. How did the flooding of the Indus Valley compare with the flooding in the Nile and Tigris-Euphrates valleys? Similar.

The people Traces of early man in India go back over 100,000 years. Where these early men came from and what happened to them is unknown. Evidence does show, however, that *Homo sapiens* appeared in India during the Old Stone Age.

At first these people were hunters and food gatherers. But sometime before 3000 B.C., the knowledge of agriculture reached India and permanent villages began in the Indus Valley. Pottery from these early villages has been found. But this pottery differs from that found in the remains of the Indus civilization.

Thus, whether the original settlers of India began the Indus civilization is not clear. It is at this point that some historians disagree. Much of the disagreement depends on how other existing evidence is interpreted.

For example, human skulls found in the remains of the Indus cities are of several types. One common type of skull indicates that some people were related to the Australian aborigines. These people had flat noses and thick lips. Nearly one-half of the skulls found were of a second type. These skulls were similar to those found in the remains of the cities in Sumer.

Some social scientists believe these skulls indicate that the Indus civilization was brought to India from the West. However, other historians believe that the Indus civilization developed from earlier Indian cultures. They base their belief upon the differences between life in ancient India and life in the ancient civilizations to the west.

See #3 below.

Early Indus cities On the map on page 92, find the cities of Harappa (hə rap′ə) and Mohenjo-Daro (mō hen′jō där′ō). These were the two most important cities of the Indus civilization. About how far apart were these two cities? 400 miles.

3. Some historians believe the Indus civilization came into India from the West but other historians believe it developed in India.

Ruins of Mohenjo-Daro

See #1 above. The features of the two major cities were remarkably similar. For example, as shown in the picture above, most homes were built of mud bricks. These were hardened by heating in ovens. The bricks were almost exactly alike—in size and shape—in both cities. In addition, both cities were planned and laid out in a similar manner. Some social scientists believe these similarities indicate that both cities were under one central government. If these cities were See #2 below. under one control, why might they have been so far apart? Do you think the two cities could have been built by people who invaded India? Why?

Mohenjo-Daro and Harappa Both Mohenjo-Daro and Harappa were miracles of city planning. The streets of both cities were laid out in a checkerboard pattern. The main streets were wide and crossed one another at right

angles. A main street of Mohenjo-Daro is shown in the picture below.

Throughout the history of these cities, private homes remained unchanged in design for 1,000 years. Does the fact that these buildings remained unchanged for 1,000 years seem unusual? Why?

Most homes in the Indus cities were built around a courtyard. Wealthy citizens had large homes, while workers often lived in small, two-room cottages. Windows and entrances usually opened into alleys rather than into the streets. Most homes had bathrooms. Drains ran from each house to central sewers beneath the main streets.

The overall appearance of the cities must have been rather dull. Homes apparently were built for use, not for appearance. The appearance of the houses, the well-planned street and sewer systems all seem to indicate a

Street in Mohenjo-Daro

2. Some social scientists believe Mohenjo-Daro and Harappa were established as centers of government to rule an area.

Stress: For Teaching Helps, see page T43.
1. The Indus society appears to have been as highly organized as the Sumerian
   society.

Indus
writing

Seals used by people in the Indus civilization

See #1
above.

highly organized, practical people. Do you think the Indus society was more like the Egyptian society than the Sumerian society? Why or why not?

Unfortunately, the way of life in the Indus cities is unknown. Largely this is because no one has found out how to read the Indus writing.

Only a few samples of Indus writing have been found. Most of these samples are on carved seals such as are shown in the illustration. Carved out of stone, these seals were probably used for identification and for religious purposes. Historians believe most merchants carried or wore these seals. Why might merchants have needed these seals? For records.

The end of the Indus society About 1500 B.C. the Indus civilization collapsed. And with its collapse the Indus society disappeared.

H/S →

Exactly what happened in 1500 B.C. is still unknown. In some areas—such as Mohenjo-Daro—skeletons have been found. Some of these were in groups, and it appears that the people may have been killed. But similar evidence has not been found at Harappa.

See #2
below.

Some scholars believe invaders destroyed the Indus civilization. Other scholars believe that the land became less fertile and that this led to the decline of the Indus civilization.

Whatever the cause, the Indus civilization disappeared. But it left behind lasting evidence of how man could and did develop a highly civilized society.

A ←

Think for Yourself

What social classes do you think were present in the Indus society? Why?

2. Many social scientists believe the Indus civilization was destroyed
   by invaders in 1500 B.C.
*3. Why might the decline of land's fertility lead to a decline of a
   civilization?

95

Things to Do

See page 84.

1. Make a picture or a model of a ziggurat. Display your picture, or model, together with a paragraph explaining its importance to the people.

See page 86.

2. Make a working model showing the irrigation of land, using papier-mâché, flour and water, or other materials.

CLASS PROJECT—PART 2

In studying Chapter 5 what pieces of information will you place in the envelopes on side 1 of your retrieval system? A class discussion could help you decide what information to place in the retrieval system. The information could be placed on cards and filed in the proper envelope. Rule off and place labels on another side of the box you will use as a retrieval system. Include the information shown below.

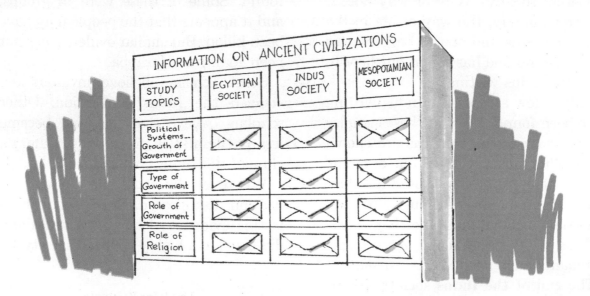

As you study Chapter 6, you will find information to be placed in the second part of the retrieval system.

The Great Sphinx

6. Patterns of Ancient Governments

For Teaching Helps, see page T44.

Perhaps you have watched an artist at work. If so, you know that artists like to work from live models. Anthropologists believe that the sculptor who planned the Great Sphinx (sfingks) shown above worked from a live model —the pharaoh of Egypt at the time.

Study the picture of the Great Sphinx. What does it tell you about the early rulers of Egypt? Vain and powerful.

In early Egypt religion played a major part in how the government operated. The Great Sphinx, for example, represented the sun god. Evidence shows that in Sumer, too, religion helped determine government. It is very likely that religion was also a factor in the way the people of the Indus civilization were ruled.

See #1 below.

Although each civilization—the Egyptian, Sumerian, and Indus—developed differently, all shared some things in common. These general similarities can be seen in their forms of government. The story of these forms of government is told in this chapter.

See #2 below.

JUST FOR FUN

Make a model of the Great Sphinx. See how nearly you can capture its expression.

Stress:
1. Religion played a major role in the government of Egypt.
2. There were similarities between some of the ancient governments.
*3. What are some of the reasons people are loyal to their leaders today?

97

For Teaching Helps, see page T45.
Stress:
1. Every group of people has some rules of behavior.

THE NATURE OF ANCIENT GOVERNMENTS

The development of ancient governments Even when small groups of people live together, they must have rules of behavior. No doubt, in man's early settlements these rules were first enforced by the heads of families—the fathers. Later, when these settlements grew in size, a group of family leaders usually formed a council that enforced the rules, customs, and traditions of the group.

In general, life in the early settlements of Egypt, Sumer, and the Indus Valley went on according to the customs of the past. A village council usually met only when these customs were violated or when a decision affecting the group was needed. Thus, the group's government was not formally organized, nor did the people meet regularly to run the affairs of a settlement.

During times of emergency, however, effective leadership was often needed. Therefore, when a settlement was attacked, a flood occurred, or some other emergency arose a leader was chosen. It seems likely that these early chiefs or kings were also religious leaders. Perhaps they were even the village priest. Based on what you know about early religious beliefs, why do you think the people appointed religious leaders as rulers during emergencies? Why might religious leaders be thought to be more effective as rulers during emergencies than other members of a group? Thought to be able to influence the gods.

In all likelihood these priest-rulers gained more power as the need for a stronger government arose. For example, early irrigation systems often required a great amount of labor. This, in turn, meant that someone had to organize and direct the people. That someone usually formed a type of government ruled by a strong leader—a priest-king. As time passed, the position of priest-king became **hereditary** (hə red′ə ter′i) as the position was passed from father to son. It was only natural that as cities grew and societies became civilized, these priest-kings became powerful rulers. What other reasons might have led to the rise of priest-kings?

Political scientists are often interested in how governments began. Studies of ancient civilizations have provided clues to man's need for government and to how organized governments developed in ancient times.

Organized governments, as we think of them today, did not exist much before 3400 B.C. This was because most of man's first permanent settlements were quite small and the people had little need for a strong, organized government.

Religion and ancient government in Egypt Today, thousands of tourists visit the pyramids shown in the picture. What is the name of the country in which the pyramids are found? What is the name of the nearest city?

2. Leaders of groups often performed religious duties.
3. Prior to 3400 B.C., people had little need for a strong, organized government.

Stress: For a class activity, see #1 on page 108.
1. Political freedom was virtually unknown in most ancient societies.
2. The highest social classes in most ancient societies were made up of high
   political or religious officials.

on this later evidence, what type of government do you think existed in the Indus civilization? Why? Powerful and tied to the religion.

Government and the people The people in most ancient civilizations had almost no idea of political freedom. Because of their beliefs about religion, the people thought that they had to obey their priests and rulers. If they did not obey, the gods were likely to harm them or their families. There were few revolts against ancient governments. The people appear to have accepted their governments without question.

P/A

Do you think the early rulers wanted the people to obey them without asking questions? Why? Do our leaders of government expect the people to ask questions? How do you know?

Social scientists tell us that ancient beliefs in religion and government helped to determine social classes. The upper class in ancient societies was made up of the ruler, the priests, and other government officials. Their religious and political duties were highly valued by the people. They thought that everything in the society depended upon how well these people pleased the gods. For this reason priests and leaders of government held high social positions as well as important political jobs. All the rest of the people were in a lower social class, since their duties were less important. Only rarely could someone of this lower class rise to the upper class.

A/S

Egyptian scribe

This rise could take place only if the king was impressed by a man's abilities or skills. The picture shows a statue of an ancient Egyptian scribe. Sometimes the scribes were made part of the government in ancient Egypt. Why might a scribe's skill and education help him rise to a high position? Scribes were needed to keep records and write reports.

Think for Yourself

What skill or skills might help a person rise to a high position in your society? Why?

3. Craftsmen, scribes, and other workers were members of the lower social
   classes in ancient societies.
*4. Why do people today feel so strongly about political freedom?

101

For Teaching Helps, see page T46.
Stress:
1. Ancient governments performed some of the same functions that modern governments perform today.

THE OPERATION OF ANCIENT GOVERNMENTS

The Sumerian government The Sumerian government was, in some ways, similar to your government today. Like a modern government, the Sumerian government made and enforced laws, built buildings, and protected the people from invasion. For example, the illustration shows one of the activities of the priest-king of Ur (center of top row). What was this activity? Who performs the same duty in your country?

See #1 above.

See caption below.

The President.

The rulers of the independent Sumerian city-states also were like a few modern rulers in another way. They were, for instance, all-powerful and they had the power of life and death over the people. What term do we usually use to describe such all-powerful rulers today? Would you use this term to describe the leader of your country? Why?

See #2 below.

The people who aided a Sumerian priest-king in his duties were usually other priests from the city-state. These priests, under the direction of the ruler, held most of the high offices in the government. They were, in turn, helped by the educated men of the city-state. These educated men—scribes—often held less important government offices and were usually the sons of priests, nobles, or army officers.

Some historians believe that at one time the governments of most city-states controlled almost every phase of life within the city-state. Craftsmen, merchants, and scribes worked in shops built around the ziggurat. The peasants often worked on the land owned or controlled by the priest-king and other officials. Part of what these workers produced was given to the government or to the temple. The workers lived on what was left. Do you think you would have been happy living in Sumer? Why?

Standard of Ur showing Sumerian soldiers and their commander in chief, the king

Sumerian chariot   Soldiers   Priest-king   Prisoners of war

2. Sumerian rulers were all-powerful, just as some dictators are today.
3. Life in a Sumerian city-state was controlled by the government.

The Egyptian government The government of ancient Egypt also did many of the things done by the government in your country today. However, the Egyptian rulers—the god-kings—were also all-powerful just like the priest-kings in Sumer. In fact, the Egyptian pharaohs were often more powerful than most priest-kings because they ruled an entire nation, not just a city-state.

The powerful government of Egypt was first established in about 3200 B.C. At that time, a strong king conquered all Egypt and united all the land and all the people under his rule. Normally the rule of Egypt passed from father to son. A series of rulers, all from one family, is called a **dynasty** (dī′nə sti). The chart on this page shows a number of Egyptian dynasties and the dates during which each dynasty was in power.

The dry climate of Egypt has helped to preserve evidence, and today social scientists know quite a bit about how ancient Egypt was governed. Much of the actual operation of the government was carried out by a deputy—a **vizier** (vi zir′)—appointed by the pharaoh. Through the vizier, the pharaoh controlled all of Egypt's land, taxes, trade, law courts, and so on. Below the vizier were a number of priests and nobles who also held positions in the government.

Just as is done in governments today, Egyptian officials received pay for their services. Normally they were given land

EGYPTIAN DYNASTIES, I-XVII	
Early Period 3200-2686 B.C.	Dynasty I 3200-2890 B.C. Dynasty II 2890-2686 B.C.
Old Kingdom 2686-2181 B.C.	Dynasty III 2686-2613 B.C. Dynasty IV 2613-2494 B.C. Dynasty V 2494-2345 B.C. Dynasty VI 2345-2181 B.C.
First Intermediate Period 2181-2040 B.C.	Dynasty VII 2181-2173 B.C. Dynasty VIII 2173-2160 B.C. Dynasty IX 2160-2130 B.C. Dynasty X 2130-2040 B.C.
Middle Kingdom 2133-1786 B.C.	Dynasty XI 2133-1991 B.C. Dynasty XII 1991-1786 B.C.
Second Intermediate Period 1786-1567 B.C.	Dynasty XIII 1786-1633 B.C. Dynasty XIV 1786-1603 B.C. Dynasty XV 1674-1567 B.C. Dynasty XVI 1684-1567 B.C. Dynasty XVII 1650-1567 B.C.

and certain privileges. One of these privileges was that they did not have to pay taxes. Many of these officials became very wealthy and powerful.

In time, the practice of rewarding the nobles and priests led to trouble for the pharaohs. As the wealth and power of the priests and nobles grew, the power of the pharaohs declined and civil wars occurred. Study the table of Egyptian dynasties. Why do you think there were so many different dynasties during the Intermediate periods? In what period do you think strong pharaohs regained power? Why? Middle Kingdom--fewer dynasties.

2. A series of rulers, all from one family, is called a dynasty.
3. During the First Intermediate Period, many powerful nobles claimed the right to rule.

103

Stress:
1. Many social scientists believe there
   was a strong Indus government.

The Indus government The statue shown in the picture was found in the remains of Mohenjo-Daro. Social scientists are not sure, but some believe that this was a statue of an important official or a ruler. Why might social scientists think this is a statue of a ruler?

See #1
above.

A/S ←

Reviewing the evidence found in Mohenjo-Daro and Harappa, several things are certain. One, each city was carefully planned and built. Two, construction of the homes and buildings in each city was very closely alike. Three, each city had a highly efficient system of drains and sewers. These were built so that they could be inspected through openings in the streets. Four, both cities had the same system of weights and measures.

Added together these facts have led to some conclusions about the type and operation of government in the Indus civilization. Based on these facts and on

Statue believed to be of an Indus ruler

what you know about your community, what would you conclude about the operation of governments in the Indus civilization?

P ←

Think for Yourself

In what ways were ancient governments similar to the government of your country? How were they different? Why?

*2. Why do modern governments perform more functions than did governments in
     ancient times?

LAW IN ANCIENT SOCIETIES

• For Teaching Helps, see page T47.   For a class activity, see #2 on page 108.

See #1
below.

The basis of laws Each of us, in our daily activities, comes into contact with rules. This is true whether we are playing a game, driving a car, or doing anything else that involves other people. Why are rules a necessary part of life?

Sociologists tell us that whenever and wherever people live together in groups they establish rules of behavior. In modern societies many of these rules are

A →

S/P ←

called laws and are enforced by a government. But many rules of behavior—even in modern societies—are not laws. Instead, these rules are customs and traditions, some of which are very old. The picture on page 105 illustrates certain common customs found in a modern society. What are these customs? Are they usually enforced by the government? Why?

See #2
below.

Stress:
104 1. Rules control behavior and help us live in groups.
         2. Some customs and traditions are not enforced as are laws.

Stress:
1. Early men lived in accordance with accepted age-old customs and traditions; later some of these became laws.

Early men, living in very small groups, did not have written laws. These people usually lived in accordance with the age-old customs and traditions of their culture. These customs and traditions were early man's rules of behavior. However, they were not actually laws, since laws are established and enforced by governments. It was not until man became civilized and established organized governments that he changed some of his customs and traditions into laws.

See #1 above.

A/S

A

P

For example, early man in his primitive societies lived according to the customs of his group. Violations of these customs often led to punishments. Thus, if an early man killed a member of his group, he might expect to be killed in return. Sometimes this punishment was

A/S

A/P

Customs of greeting and courtesy

S/P

carried out by the victim's relatives. In other cases, the entire group might carry out the punishment.

The customs and traditions—rules of behavior—in most early societies were designed to protect the welfare of the group. Usually these customs covered most of the group's religious and social activities. A violation of these customs was often thought to threaten the welfare of the group. Thus, the punishment for such things as stealing, offending the gods, and so on ranged from exile from the group to death.

See #2 below.

The development of laws When civilizations were developed by man and governments were established, many of the old customs became laws. That is, they were enforced by the government. Then, as time passed and as cities grew, new ways of life developed. As a result, more and newer rules of behavior were needed. These new rules were needed because some of the old customs no longer could be used.

See #3 below.

Enforcing these new rules of behavior was the responsibility of the society's government and the new rules became laws. Even today, laws are changed to meet the needs of a new way of life in our society. See if you can give an example of a new law and tell why it was needed.

Written laws With the development of writing in ancient times, many laws were written down. These written laws

2. Customs, traditions, and laws usually protect the welfare of the group. **105**
3. New and changing conditions required that some customs be changed and replaced by laws.

Original Code of Hammurabi

The Code of Hammurabi Although Hammurabi's ancient code of laws is the most complete code that has been found, it is not the oldest. For example, many of the laws contained in Hammurabi's code are based on earlier Sumerian laws. And many of these Sumerian laws were, in turn, based upon much older customs and traditions.

Think, for a moment, about the laws of your society. You can tell something about your society from its laws. For example, which crimes are most severely punished in your society? What does this indicate is highly valued in your society? Why? Human life.

were grouped together into what are called **codes of law.**

The most complete ancient code of ancient laws that has been found is the Code of Hammurabi (ham ə räb′ē). The illustration shows this code of laws, which is almost 3,700 years old. A study of these laws provides many clues to the nature of law in at least one ancient civilization.

Historians tell us that Hammurabi was the king of the city of Babylon, which was near the Euphrates River. By 1700 B.C. Hammurabi had conquered Sumer and had his code of laws carved in stone. Why do you think Hammurabi wanted to establish a code of laws? Why did he have them carved on a stone block?

You can also learn about an ancient society by studying its laws. In some societies a basic form of punishment, for example, was "an eye for an eye, a tooth for a tooth." Study the table on page 107. It contains some of the laws found on Hammurabi's code. What do you think "an eye for an eye, a tooth for a tooth" means? How does this differ from the types of legal punishments in your country? Which punishments—those of Hammurabi's or those in your country —are the most "civilized"? Why?

Ancient laws also reflected the society's social system. Thus, in some cases, ancient laws stressed the definite differences in social classes. Where and how does the Code of Hammurabi show the differences among social classes? Why were these differences in the laws?

See #1 below

See #2 below

Stress:

1. A society's laws indicate a great deal about the nature of the society, what the people believed, and how the government operated.
2. Ancient laws sometimes prescribed harshest punishments for those who injured someone of the upper class.

Law courts To handle disputes that arose under their laws, ancient societies set up courts. There, citizens presented their cases before judges.

Most of the judges in the law courts in ancient Sumer were priests. This was because the people believed that their laws represented the wishes of the gods. As a result, the Sumerian law courts were often in or near a temple.

See #1 above.

Egyptian courts were somewhat different from the Sumerian courts. The Egyptian courts were under the direct control of the god-king—the pharaoh. The judges in Egypt were appointed by the pharaoh, and many of the judges were priests. However, the pharaoh's viziers also served as judges. So, too, did a few other men who were appointed as judges by the pharaoh. But on the whole, the courts in Egypt were strongly influenced by the priests and, of course, by the nation's religious beliefs.

See #2 below.

In both the Sumerian and the Egyptian societies, crimes against the government were believed to be the most serious ones of all. Why did these ancient people believe that crimes against the government were so bad? Did this have anything to do with their religion? What makes you think so?

Think for Yourself

Why do you think that the laws of ancient societies reflected the beliefs and values of the people? Is this also true about the laws in your society? Explain your answer.

EXCERPTS—HAMMURABI'S CODE

If a son strike his father, his hands shall be hewn off.

If a man put out the eye of another man, his eye shall be put out.

If he break another man's bone, his bone shall be broken.

If he put out the eye of a man's slave, or break the bone of a man's slave, he shall pay one-half of its [the slave's] value. . . .

If any one strike the body of a man higher in rank than he, he shall receive sixty blows with an ox whip in public.

If a free-born man strike the body of another free-born man of equal rank, he shall pay one gold mina [about one pound]. . . .

If during a quarrel one man strike another and wound him, then he shall swear, "'I did not injure him wittingly,'" and pay the physicians. . . .

If a builder build a house for some one, and does not construct it properly, and the house which he built fall in and kill its owner, then that builder shall be put to death.

If it kill the son of the owner, the son of that builder shall be put to death.

If it kill a slave of the owner, then he shall pay slave for slave to the owner of the house.

If a patrician has stilen [stolen] ox, sheep, ass, pig, or ship, whether from a temple, or a house, he shall pay thirty-fold. If he be a plebeian, he shall return tenfold. If the thief cannot pay, he shall be put to death.

2. Crimes against ancient rulers were often considered to be crimes against the gods since the gods were thought to protect the rulers.

*3. Why is it better for the people to have laws written down for all to read?

107

Things to Do

See page 101.

1. Find books in your school library that have pictures of objects such as jewelry or pottery made by ancient, skilled Egyptian craftsmen. In showing these pictures to your class, tell some interesting information about them.

See page 104.

2. Write down two laws that probably existed in ancient Sumer. Use "Codes of Law" as a heading for your paper.

CLASS PROJECT—PART 3

You have now learned about the patterns of the ancient governments of the early societies of Mesopotamia, Egypt, and India. What pieces of information will you place on cards for filing in the retrieval system? In continuing your class project, rule off and place labels on the third side of your box used as a retrieval system. Include the information pictured below.

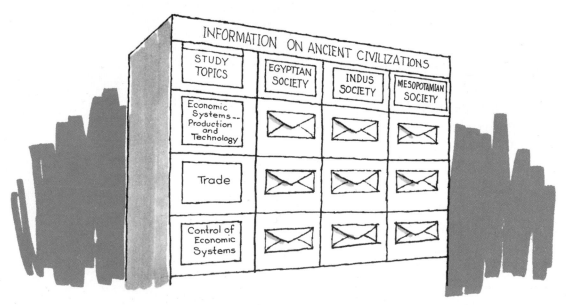

A study of Chapter 7 will help you decide what to place in the third part of the retrieval system.

Industrial plants in Pittsburgh, Pennsylvania

7. Ancient Economic Systems

For Teaching Helps, see page T48.

See #1 below.

See #2 below.

Every civilization—whether modern or ancient—has an economic way of life. The methods and ways a civilization uses to produce and distribute goods is called its **economic system.**

The picture above would help a visitor to the United States understand something about our economic system. One thing the visitor could see is that there are large factories in the United States. What else could the visitor tell about the economic system of the United States from this picture? Many means of transportation.

As you read about how ancient civilizations produced goods, compare their ways with the ways goods are produced in the United States. Also try to compare the ways goods were distributed in the past with the ways goods are distributed today. Do you think you will find that ways of producing and distributing goods have changed? Why?

Stress:
1. All civilizations have an economic way of life.

JUST FOR FUN

Take a survey of your neighborhood and then describe the different types of economic activities that are going on there. In what ways do these activities reflect your country's economic system?

2. Every society must decide what goods will be produced and how these goods will be distributed.

*3. Why must a society produce goods?

109

For Teaching Helps, see page T49.
Stress:
1. Farmers in the Nile, Tigris-Euphrates, and Indus river valleys were able
   to raise surplus crops.
2. Surplus crops could be sold or traded.

PRODUCTION

Modern farm in the United States

Economic surplus As people travel through the United States they can see many farms such as the one shown in the illustration. But today, less than 5 per cent of the workers in the United States make their living as farmers. However, using modern machinery and techniques, this small percentage of the nation's workers are able to raise enough crops to feed the entire nation and still have some left over. When the American farmer raises more food than he needs to feed his family this is called a **surplus.** What does the American farmer do with his surplus crops? Sells it.

G/E → An economist studying ancient civilizations would see that the farmers in Sumer, Egypt, and in the Indus Valley also produced surplus crops. Since these surplus crops could be traded or exchanged for other goods, the crops had value. And since these crops had value, they were a form of **wealth.**

See #1 and #2 above.

E → Economists have a term they use to describe a surplus of wealth. They say that when a society is able to produce more wealth than the people need for survival, the society has an **economic surplus.** This surplus wealth is an economic surplus because it can be used for economic purposes—it can be sold or traded for other goods. Every ancient urban civilization produced economic surpluses. These surpluses were used to feed and to pay those who were not farmers and who lived in the cities. What other things were probably done S/E ← with these economic surpluses? Why?

See #3 below.

The production of economic surpluses Some historians believe that most of the peasants in Sumer and Egypt worked on land that was owned or controlled by the ruler, the priests, or the wealthy S/H → nobles. But unlike many American farmers, ancient farmers did not own all the crops that they produced. Instead, the farmers in ancient civilizations usually kept only a small part of their crops; the rest went to the owners of the

See #4 below.

3. Every ancient civilization was based on the production of surplus crops.
4. Many peasants in ancient Sumer and Egypt did not own the land they
   farmed.

Stress:
1. Landowners in ancient societies used surplus crops to hire craftsmen.
2. Surplus crops made production of other goods possible.

land. In good years, when the harvest was large, the peasants had enough to live on and perhaps a bit left over. What surplus crops the peasants had, they used to trade for other things they needed, such as metal tools, pottery, cloth, and so on.

See #1 above.

The landowners, on the other hand, often had more crops than they needed for themselves and their families. These landowners often hired craftsmen to make other items they wanted and paid them with the surplus goods obtained from the peasants. Surplus crops, and the products made by the craftsmen, were also used in trading with other people for additional goods.

See #2 above.

Thus, the basis for each ancient civilization was the economic surplus of crops. As long as each ancient civilization could produce a surplus of crops, trade and the production of other goods continued. As a result, many people had more goods and their way of life im-

proved. What do you think happened to an ancient civilization when it could not produce a surplus of crops? Would the same thing probably happen to civilizations today? Why or why not?

The use of tools Anthropologists and economists often classify civilizations on the basis of their tools. For example, the tools that are developed by a group of people and the ways the people use these tools are referred to as the society's **technology.** Thus, when a society has only a few crude tools it has a low level of technology. And when a society has many effective tools the society has a high level of technology. Study the picture on this page. The man shown in the picture is a farmer. Usually, he is able to produce only enough food to feed himself and his family. Would you say he has a low level of technology? Why? Does a low level of technology affect production? Why?

At first, ancient farmers had a low

Farmer using wooden plow in India

111

Stress: For Teaching Helps, see page T49.
1. Improved technology usually enables people to produce more goods.
2. People often depend upon others to produce some of the goods they need and want.

level of technology. But when the farmers in ancient Egypt, Sumer, and India learned to irrigate their fields, use plows, and make metal tools, production increased. Through the use of improved tools and methods, ancient farmers soon were able to produce more food than they needed. These tools and methods of irrigation were as valuable to the ancient farmer as the tractor, plow, and other tools are to the modern farmer. In what ways were the ancient civilizations more advanced in their technology than were the people of the Old Stone Age? In what ways is your country more advanced in its technology than it was fifty years ago?

See #1
above.

Interdependence and the specialization of labor It is estimated that today only about one-half of all the adult people in the world are farmers. The rest of the world's adult population make their living in other ways. This means that a large number of people in the world today are producing other things than food. But in producing these other things, these people depend upon farmers for their food. In turn, farmers de-

See #2
above.

pend upon other people to produce the tools, machines, and other goods they need. Thus, people today depend upon each other for the things they need. This is called **interdependence** (in'tər di pen'dəns). In what way is your family dependent upon others for the things they need? Are people in your society interdependent? Why?

G/E

In much the same way, people depended upon one another in ancient societies. This was because there was a **specialization of labor** in ancient civilizations. For example, Egyptian farmers produced surplus crops. These crops were used to hire carpenters, builders, pottery makers, metalworkers, and others who produced goods needed by the society. The pictures on this page show some ancient Egyptian craftsmen at work. What are the jobs they are per-

A/E

S/E

Egyptian pottery maker

Egyptian metalworkers making metal vases

Stress:
1. Specialization of labor occurs when people specialize in doing one type of job.
2. Specialization tends to increase production.
*3. What examples of specialization of labor today can you name?

For Teaching Helps, see page T49.

forming? Do you think each of these craftsmen specializes in one job? How does the picture illustrate the specialization of labor in ancient Egypt?

As people in ancient societies specialized in certain jobs, they produced more goods. Having more goods often led to surpluses in goods other than just crops. As a result, trade among people and civilizations grew. Why might people produce more goods when they specialized in certain jobs? Has specialization given us more goods today than ever before? Why? People tend to become more efficient when they specialize in one type of work.

Think for Yourself

How may the production of economic surpluses lead to a better way of life for a group of people? People can produce other goods.

ECONOMIC ACTIVITY IN ANCIENT CIVILIZATIONS

For a class activity, see #3 on page 119.

The Sumerian economy The Sumerian economic system was the result of two things. One, the land was fertile enough to produce a surplus of crops—an economic surplus. Two, some natural resources were not found in Mesopotamia. For example, Sumer had almost no good timber or stone. And copper, gold, and silver were not found there either. Think for a moment about these two factors. Based upon them, why do you think trade was important to people living in the Sumerian economy?

Much of the economic activity in Sumer was influenced by religious beliefs. The belief that the land belonged to the gods is an example. A very large amount of the land was directly controlled by the priest-kings and the other priests of the temple. Other large pieces of a city-state's land were given to individuals. The people—members of the lower class and the slaves—worked the land. They had to pay rent or taxes on what they produced to the landowners, the priests, or the priest-king.

However, not all economic activity in Sumer was controlled by the king or the priests. Some of the people were merchants. Some of them sold goods and traded within the city-state and with people of other areas. This trade was supervised by the government. It wanted to make sure the merchants were honest. But the merchants were able to trade freely as long as they obeyed the laws of the city-state. Why might the government want trade to be carried on honestly?

Some historians believe that the Sumerian civilization was the result of Sumer's economic surplus and lack of some natural resources. These factors led to the rise of trade—often with areas far from Sumer. It is also believed that the trade with areas far from Sumer

See #1 below.

See #2 below.

G/E

P/E

A/E

S/E

Stress:
1. Geographic factors influenced the nature of the Sumerian economy.
2. A surplus of crops and a shortage of timber and stone made trade an important economic activity in Sumer.

113

Stress:
1. Trade with other nations encouraged the Sumerians to develop new skills, such as metalworking.

Golden vase from Sumer

See #1
above.

caused the Sumerians to become skilled in manufacturing—particularly of items made from metal. See, for example, the skillfully made golden vase shown in the picture. Why might trade with distant areas lead to the production of metal tools and other objects? Does your country export only surplus crops? Why?

The Egyptian economy Unlike Sumer, almost all Egypt's economic activities were controlled by the ruler. All the land was owned by the god-king. The god-king gave some of the land to the priests, nobles, and other people that he favored. In return, those who received the land paid taxes to the pharaoh. The tax money came from the peasants who farmed the land. They had to pay rent to the landowners.

See #2
below.

In most cases, the taxes were based on what was produced on the land and on the amount of livestock. The pharaoh chose people in all parts of Egypt to help decide how much tax the landowners should pay. They also had to collect tax money for the pharaoh.

In Egypt the pharaoh controlled all the trade Egyptians had with people outside the country. He tried to control all the trade within Egypt, too. This was impossible. The pharaoh could not watch everyone all the time. Many people exchanged goods for other things they needed. But the overall economic life of Egypt—both production and trade—was largely controlled by the pharaoh.

Two reasons may account for the way Egypt's economy operated. One reason may have been that Egypt was rather self-sufficient. Much of what the average peasant needed to live on could be produced by the peasant himself. Another reason was the belief that the welfare of the nation depended upon the well-being of the pharaoh—both while he lived and after his death. Thus, pyramids and other tombs had to be built. In

See #3
below.

2. The Egyptian pharaoh controlled almost all of the economic activity in ancient Egypt.
3. Egypt's economic system reflected the country's self-sufficiency and the belief in the divinity of the pharaoh.

114

For a class activity, see #1 on page 119.

Stress:
1. The Egyptian pharaoh controlled all Egyptian trade with other countries.

Reconstruction of Mohenjo-Daro

addition, the pharaoh also had to be supplied with food, shelter, clothing, jewels, and so on. All this required a large amount of labor on the part of nearly every Egyptian. Why might the belief that the welfare of the nation depended on the well-being of the pharaoh limit the economic freedom of the Egyptians?

See #1 above. P/E ← It is interesting to note that no evidence of any Egyptian laws regulating trade have been found. Why might there have been no need for laws regulating trade in Egypt?

The Indus economy The illustration shows how some authorities believe Mohenjo-Daro looked about 2500 B.C. Study the picture. What are the people doing? What can you tell about economic life in Mohenjo-Daro from the picture? Trade and transportation were important.

E/G → From the evidence that has been found in the remains of the Indus civilization, historians have reached certain

H/E → conclusions. Agriculture was probably the basis of economic life, just as it was in other ancient civilizations. The remains of huge buildings for storing grain indicate that surplus crops were not uncommon. Some historians believe the grain was collected and stored so that it could be used for trade, or in case of a famine. What do you think these large granaries tell us about the Indus government? Why? See #2 below.

P/E ← Other items of evidence also provide clues about the Indus economy. Remains of ship docks have been found

Indus writing

Seal used by Indus merchant

along the Arabian seacoast. And seals used by merchants from Mohenjo-Daro, such as the one shown in the picture, have been found in Mesopotamia. Evidence also shows that cotton was first grown in the Indus Valley, but it soon

2. Some historians believe the Indus government stored crops and controlled trade.
3. Evidence indicates that trade with people in other areas was an important economic activity of the Indus civilization.

115

became a product used by other people. What might this evidence indicate about an important economic activity of the Indus civilization?

Think for Yourself

How did economic activity in ancient civilizations differ from economic activity in your society? Government controlled.

For Teaching Helps, see page T51.

TRANSPORTATION AND COMMUNICATION

Wheeled toy from Sumer (c. 3500 B.C.)

Land transportation Most people in modern societies take the wheel and wheeled vehicles for granted. It is hard for us today to imagine how man could have managed to live without the use of the wheel. But as we look at the long history of man, we can see that the wheel is a rather recent invention.

The first wheeled vehicle was invented by the Sumerians sometime around 3000 B.C. Knowledge of the wheel, however, goes back before that date. The wheeled toy shown in the picture was made for a Sumerian child over 5,500 years ago. How long it took man to transfer the wheel from toys to wagons is not known. In fact, some ancient people never made the transfer of the wheel from toys to carts. In ancient Mexico, for example, wheeled toys were built for children, but wheeled carts or wagons were never used for transportation. Do you think the fact that there were no horses or other beasts of burden in ancient Mexico may explain why there were no carts or wagons? Why?

See #1 above.

In time, the knowledge of the wheel spread from the Sumerians to other people. The wheel alone, however, did not immediately answer all man's transportation problems.

The illustration shows what Sumerian war chariots were like. The chariot wheels were made of solid wood, and the chariot was pulled by four donkeys.

The use of wheels on chariots is shown in the Standard of Ur

116

2. The spread of the knowledge of the wheel is an example of <u>cultural diffusion</u>.

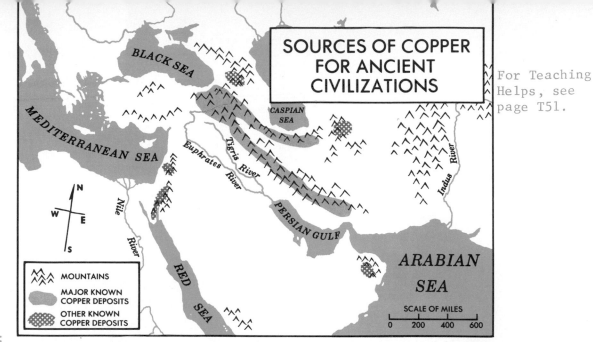

SOURCES OF COPPER FOR ANCIENT CIVILIZATIONS

For Teaching Helps, see page T51.

BLACK SEA

MEDITERRANEAN SEA

CASPIAN SEA

Euphrates River

Tigris River

Indus River

PERSIAN GULF

Nile

River

RED SEA

ARABIAN SEA

SCALE OF MILES
0   200   400   600

MOUNTAINS
MAJOR KNOWN COPPER DEPOSITS
OTHER KNOWN COPPER DEPOSITS

Stress:
1. Lack of roads and bridges limited land travel with heavy loads.

Wagons and carts that were built during the same period had similar wheels and they were usually pulled by two oxen. None of these vehicles were very fast and they were used to carry goods only on short trips. For, even with the wheel, overland travel in the ancient world was slow and difficult. Largely this was because the ancient world lacked one of the things needed for long-distance journeys. To understand what was lacking in the ancient world, imagine you were about to take a trip by wagon across the United States 200 years ago. What would have to be built before such a trip would be possible? Why was overland travel difficult in ancient times?

See #1 above.

G/E →

Water transportation Because long trips by land were slow and difficult, water transportation was important. Each of the major ancient civilizations relied upon water transportation for

G ←

long trips with heavy loads. These trips sometimes carried people across seas to other lands in search of needed raw materials. For example, the use of metal, such as copper, increased the need for water transportation. The map shows the copper deposits used by ancient people. Study the map. How do you think copper was transported? Why?

See #2 below.

Since the Sumerian, Egyptian, and Indus civilizations all developed along rivers, water transportation was also important to the trade carried on within each civilization. For example, the current of the Nile flows northward to the Mediterranean. Winds along the Nile generally blow from the north to the south. How might these conditions have influenced the types of boats built by the ancient Egyptians? Why did these conditions help encourage trade in ancient Egypt?

2. Water transportation was used by most ancient societies to carry heavy loads of such things as copper ore.
3. Rivers were important means of transportation within many ancient civilizations.

117

"Feluccas" are used to carry goods in Egypt today

Similar geographic conditions encourage trade along rivers today. For example, modern Egyptians still rely upon sailboats to carry goods along the Nile, as is shown in the picture.

Writing Today nearly 98 per cent of the people in the United States can read

Hieroglyphics from a tomb in an Egyptian pyramid

For a class activity, see #2 on page 119.
Stress:
1. Writing was developed in about 3500 B.C.

and write. Few people realize when and where man's ability to write was first developed.

A/H → The Sumerians first developed writing about 5,500 years ago. Their writing was done on soft clay tablets with a pointed instrument. Historians call this type of writing **cuneiform** (kūnē′ə fôrm), which means wedge-shaped writing.

See #1 above.

A/H → Quickly, the idea of writing spread to other civilizations which then developed their own styles of writing. The ancient Egyptians developed a type of picture writing called **hieroglyphics** (hī′ər ə glif′iks). An example of Egyptian hieroglyphics is shown in the picture on this page. An example of the Indus writing is shown on the top of the seal on page 115. As yet no one has learned how to read the Indus writing.

G/E ←

E → Much of man's first writing was done by scribes who kept records of business and trade. Later, writing began to be used for recording many kinds of things, including stories and laws. Writing was also used for magical purposes. Why do you think economic activity led to the first development of writing? What examples can you give to show how important writing is to American businessmen and tradesmen today?

See #2 below.

Think for Yourself

How were the developments of the wheel and of writing influenced by the growth of trade?

2. The need for records of business and trade activities led to writing.
*3. Would your way of life be possible without writing? Why?

Things to Do

See
page 115.

1. Find a newspaper or magazine article telling about one of the laws of our society. Show this article to members of your class and tell why you think this law is needed in our society today.

See
page 118.

2. See if you can make a model of a boat similar to those used on the Nile River to transport goods several thousand years ago.

See
page 113.

3. Pretend you are an economist planning to visit a farmer of ancient Sumer. Write three questions you would like to ask the farmer.

CLASS PROJECT—PART 4

What information will you place in your retrieval system on the economic systems of Mesopotamia, Egypt, and India?

You can use the data you have classified in your retrieval system to draw some conclusions about all early civilizations. Some examples of conclusions follow.

1. Early civilizations tended to develop in river valleys.
2. The people of early civilizations were not dependent on trade.
3. The power to rule early civilizations was given to one strong leader.

A good way to make your conclusions a part of your retrieval system is to classify them in envelopes having these labels.

culture   economics   geography   government
technology   trade   urbanization

These envelopes may then be placed on the fourth side of the box used in making your retrieval system.

The building of a retrieval system has been completed. You might invite someone to hear your class tell about this class project—the study of three ancient societies and the building of a retrieval system.

Have the pupils find each of the review words in the unit. For each word, have them answer such questions as these:

Checkup Time

1. How was the word used in the book?
2. How might you use the word yourself?

For question 2 above, encourage the pupils to use each word in a social science context.

Review Words

citadel	dynasty	immortal	technology
city-state	economic surplus	interdependence	urbanization
civilization	economic systems	social changes	vizier
codes of law	hereditary	specialization of labor	wealth
cuneiform	hieroglyphics	surplus	ziggurats

Review Questions

Typical answers only.

Social Science Facts

1. What favorable conditions helped man in developing the Sumerian, Egyptian, and Indus civilizations? (82, 86, 87-88, 93) Fertile land, warm climate, supply of water.

2. What did the ancient Sumerians and Egyptians do to supply water for their land? (83, 88) Built irrigation systems.

3. What social classes of people developed in the Sumerian and Egyptian societies? (85-86, 89) Upper, middle, and lower.

4. What were some of the titles given to leaders of ancient societies? (98, 99, 100, 102, 103, 107) Priest-king, pharaoh, god-king.

5. What was needed to help direct the behavior of people in ancient societies as cities grew and new ways of life developed? (105) Laws.

6. What was one important result of specialization of labor in ancient civilizations? (112-113) Interdependence.

7. What methods of transportation did ancient civilizations use to transport goods? (117) Wheeled vehicles and boats.

Social Science Ideas

1. How have land, water, and climate conditions affected the development of the community in which you are now living? Answers will vary.

2. Why it is very important for man today to make every effort to control his supply of water? For drinking and watering crops.

3. Why do people living in various societies today often develop certain social classes? Social classes reflect the values of the society, i.e., wealth or power.

4. How are the organization and development of a society affected by its leaders? Leaders may influence attitudes and views of the people.

5. Why is it sometimes necessary today for some of the laws governing the behavior of the people of a city to be changed? Conditions change.

6. Why does specialization of labor have an important result upon the economic activities of a country? See bottom margin.

7. Why is the development of new methods of transportation important to our country today? Increase economic activity.

6. May increase production, trade, and interdependence.

Test Yourself

On your own paper, write your answer to each question.

Test 1 Social Science Words

Match the words and groups of words given below.

c. 1. city-state

d. 2. economic system

e. 3. interdependence

a. 4. dynasty

b. 5. urbanization

a. a series of rulers from one family

b. the growth and development of cities

c. an independent city controlling some surrounding territory

d. methods and ways to produce and distribute goods

e. to depend upon one another

Which of these words are needed to complete each sentence below?

hereditary   economic system
technology   surplus
codes of law   dynasty

6. In ancient civilizations the position of priest-king became ___. hereditary

7. Written laws were often grouped together into what were called ___. codes of law

8. A farmer that raises more food than he needs to feed his family is said to have a ___. surplus

9. A society having many effective tools probably has a high level of ___. technology

Test 2 Facts and Ideas

Which is the best answer to each question below?

1. What method of transportation did people of early civilizations use to move heavy loads long distances?
   (a.) water transportation
   b. rail transportation
   c. land transportation

2. What happened to old customs of the people of ancient civilizations as governments were established?
   a. All customs were forgotten.
   (b.) Many old customs became laws.
   c. All old customs became laws.

3. What happened to production as people in ancient societies specialized in certain jobs?
   a. Production decreased.
   (b.) Production increased.
   c. Production was stopped.

Which word or words in ( ) make each sentence below true?

4. Development of the early civilizations ((was,) was not) affected by the flood waters of rivers.

5. There were ((three,) six) social classes of people in most of the early city-states.

6. Rules sometimes replace (ziggurats, (customs)).

For Teaching Helps, see page T52.

UNIT
4 EASTERN AND WESTERN CIVILIZATIONS

Stress:

1. Civilizations in the East differed from those in the West.

Chapters

8. Eastern and Western Societies
9. Eastern and Western Governments
10. Eastern and Western Economies

*2. Would you expect civilizations to develop differently in different parts of the world? Why?

Chinese mandarin on a gondola

Stress:
1. The terms Eastern and Western may have a variety of meanings.
2. In early times, Europe was considered to be the West and India, China, and Japan were considered to be the East.
3. Today West often is used to refer to Europe and the Americas, while East is used to refer to Asia and parts of Africa.

What do the words East and West mean to you? Some people, when hearing these words, might think of a person's name. Some might think of a general direction or a part of a country. To social scientists the terms East or Eastern and West or Western have a further meaning. For example, when geographers use the terms Eastern and Western, they are usually referring to the parts of the world called the Eastern Hemisphere and the Western Hemisphere.

See #1 above.

G
←

During the period from 1500 B.C. to A.D. 500, the people of Europe considered the Eastern Hemisphere the entire world. Although exploration and trade had made Asia, Europe, and parts of Africa known to one another, the Europeans had not yet discovered the continents of North America and South America. The people of Europe referred to India, China, and Japan as the East and referred to their own continent as the West.

G/E
←
See #2 above.

Today many historians and sociologists often use the words West or Western when speaking of social, political, or economic ways of life in Europe or the Americas. They use the words East or Eastern to refer to the ways of life in the countries of Asia and in parts of Africa.

See #3 above.

In this unit you will discover the ways of life developed by people living in two societies often classified as Eastern and in two societies often classified as Western. You will find answers to questions such as these.

1. How was life similar in Eastern and Western civilizations?
2. How was life different in Eastern and Western civilizations?
*4. What reasons can you give to explain why the terms East and West have different meanings today than they did in A.D. 500?

For Teaching Helps, see page T52.
Stress:
1. The continuing nature of the class project. See pp. 140, 156, and 171.

CLASS PROJECT—PART 1

To begin the class project, think of some questions a social scientist might ask in studying about families—their habits, customs, work, rules, houses—in India, China, Greece, and the Roman Empire many years ago. What kinds of questions do you think a social scientist would ask about families? Place these questions on a chalkboard. The picture below may give you some ideas concerning questions to ask.

As you study Chapter 8, take notes regarding family life in India, China, Greece, and the Roman Empire. These notes should help you answer the questions you placed on the chalkboard. The notes will also help you do Part 2 of the class project in which you will be planning some activities—pantomimes, displays, reports—that show what you have discovered about family life.

Family of Indian farmers

8. Eastern and Western Societies

For Teaching Helps, see page T53.

The people shown in the picture live in India. Each person is a member of a family that follows traditions and customs which were set up many years ago. The community where these people live is similar to Indian communities of more than 2,000 years ago.

The rural communities of some countries of the West, such as those in Europe, have changed greatly during the same time that those of the East have changed very little. Social scientists are curious to find out why.

See #1 below.

Social scientists have discovered that many rural communities of the East, including those of India and China, have remained relatively unchanged for many years. They wonder why this is so.

See #2 below.

Over the years, many social scientists have studied Eastern and Western societies. What explanations for the differences among the societies might they have discovered? How do you think they obtained the information?

Stress:
1. Some communities change greatly as years pass, others remain relatively unchanged.

JUST FOR FUN

See if you can find pictures, stories, or poems to illustrate differences between the societies of the East and the West. Be ready to share your findings with your classmates.

2. Social scientists are interested in the differences among societies.

125

For Teaching Helps, see page T54.   For a class activity, see #2 on page 140.

THE CLOSED SOCIETY OF INDIA

A closed society In many ways the India of today is not so different from the India of the past. The type of clothing worn by these women of modern India is similar to the clothing worn by the women of India many hundreds of years ago.

The similarities between the Indian societies of today and of 1500 B.C. go even deeper than similarities in dress. The way many of the Indians live today is based on customs and ways of life which developed long ago. Few changes have been made, for instance, in the rigid social structure of India. Some laws have been passed that would change the structure of society. But the people have followed their old laws and customs for many years. They find it difficult to obey new laws that would change their way of life. What problems do you see in trying to replace customs with laws?

India had in the past, and has today, a rigid social structure. The people are born into a certain social class and they cannot rise out of it. Being born into a particular class in society, or **caste,** decides a complete way of life for the Indian. His diet, clothing, job, duties, and privileges are determined in advance by the customs of the social group. This type of structure is called a **closed society.** How does this differ from societies that you know?

The Hindu family In Hindu society the family, rather than the individual, was the basic unit of society. The Hindu family was very large. In one house, or in a group of houses, would live a man —the absolute head of the family—his wife, his sons, and his sons' wives. Also included in the family would be the brothers of the head of the family and their wives, their sons and their wives, as well as unmarried daughters and various uncles and cousins. This type of family was called a **joint family.** The joint family provided a sense of security and well-being for all its members. The joint family ruled the lives of its members. What advantages and disadvan-

A/S

S

A/H

S

S

See #1 above.

See #2 below.

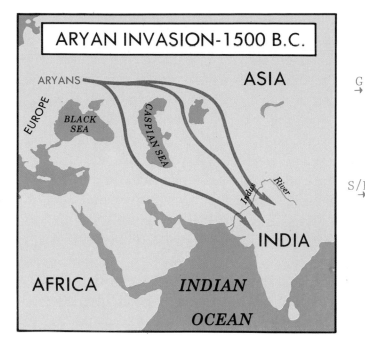

ARYAN INVASION - 1500 B.C.

EUROPE
ASIA
ARYANS
BLACK SEA
CASPIAN SEA
Indus River
INDIA
AFRICA
INDIAN OCEAN

called Dravidians (drə vid'i ənz). The Aryans were tall, lighter-skinned people from an area north of the Black Sea. Find their homeland on the map and follow their routes of invasion.

The conquered people, the Dravidians, had darker skin than the Aryans. At first the Aryans refused to allow intermarriage with the Dravidians. The Aryans were concerned about keeping their own culture and way of life without mixing with any others. What do you suppose is likely to happen to the culture of both groups when two groups live so close together?

The caste system One of the foundations of India's closed society was the caste system. Aryan society was made up of three classes—warriors, priests, and workers, in that order of importance. The Dravidians who were taken into Aryan society were treated as slaves and considered to be the lowest class. In order to keep the Dravidians in the lowest class, the social structure of the Aryans was made very rigid. All classes had their specific jobs and were forbidden to move into other jobs. A son had to follow the profession of his father. People were forbidden to marry someone of another caste. What differences do we find in our society?

The people who developed the caste system later set up four main classes. They were (1) priests, (2) warriors and political leaders, (3) merchants, and

See #1 below.

See #2 below.

tages would members of a joint family have?

The members of a joint family worked together in their business—farming, for example. All the men in the family owned and operated the family business in common. After the death of the head of the family, the land was evenly divided among the sons. But they still worked it together. What problems can you see that could develop from this method of running a farm?

Invasion of India Many changes took place in Indian society as a result of invasions. Warlike nomadic herders called Aryans (ãr'i ənz) invaded India about 1500 B.C. The Aryans conquered the people of northern India who were

Stress:
1. Indian society changed as invasions took place.
2. The caste system set up a rigid social structure.

127

(4) tenant farmers and unskilled workmen. Among these main classes were thousands of subcastes, each with its own duties and privileges.

Beyond the four classes was a group of people, called the **untouchables,** who were not even allowed to live within the community. Their jobs included those which were thought to be unclean, such as cremating the dead or executing criminals. How does a society get people to perform unpleasant jobs? Reward or force.

Power of the caste In some cases the power of the caste was greater than the power of the family. If a person committed a serious offense, he could be excluded from the community by a decision made by his caste. He could be kept out of all social activities and barred from taking part in business. As a result, the person was somewhat isolated. This process of excluding a person from the community was called **ostracism** (os′trə siz əm). If a person was ostracized by his caste, his family was also expected to turn him out. If the family did not, they too would be ostracized. Once this happened members of the entire family were truly social outcasts—forced to live the life of the untouchables. What type of behavior would this develop in members of such a society? Obedient.

Growth of Hinduism The Hindu religion, called Hinduism, also contributed to making India a closed society. Hin-

duism's religious beliefs developed over many centuries. The rigid class system was included as a part of the beliefs. The Hindus believed that each person had a soul, and that each soul was struggling to be reunited with the "world soul." Then his soul would be at rest and perfectly happy. To reach this state of happiness, man had to purify himself. According to Hindu beliefs, if a man did not purify himself in his first life—his soul was reborn in a new form. The rebirth of the soul in a new form was called **reincarnation.** If a person tried to lead a good life, but failed, his second life on earth would be in a lower state. The reverse was also true. A person's soul might go through the process of reincarnation, or rebirth, several times before he reached his goal.

Even today the class or caste system in India is connected to the religious system. A person who belongs to one of the lower classes has the hope of being reborn into a higher class. The upper classes are seen as people who have gone through several stages of rebirth and are closer to being perfect. How would a belief like this help keep peace in a society? Hope of a better life in the future.

See #1 above.

See #2 below.

Think for Yourself

In what ways does the family system of India differ from the family system in the United States?

128

Stress:
1. Traditional societies are those which rely on the past.
2. Members of Chinese families worked very closely together.

THE TRADITIONAL SOCIETY OF CHINA

A traditional society Some societies are based on customs and traditions of the past. A society of this kind is called **a traditional society.**

See #1 above.

China, in many ways, fits the pattern of traditional societies everywhere. Many of the Chinese people still live the way their ancestors did over 2,000 years ago. Today over 80 per cent of the Chinese people still live in rural communities.

In ancient China the majority of the people lived in rural communities. Their farmland was their most important form of wealth. The people had very little contact with the world beyond their community.

In a traditional society a person is born into a particular class. He might find it difficult to rise out of his class—except through education. Education itself was often limited to a few privileged or wealthy members of the community.

A traditional society, in China or elsewhere, which follows this pattern is maintained by many things. Social scientists ask the question: What are some of the things which make a society remain traditional? See if you can suggest answers to their question even before you study the next few pages of your text.

Family life For the Chinese people, family unity was most important to society. The members of the family worked together as a group. Most of the Chinese lived in farming villages like the one shown. A Chinese farming village usually was made up of large family groups. Even though all members of the family might not live in the same house, they would live in the same village.

See #2 above.

Chinese farming village

Tea plants

129

Stress:
1. People in Chinese societies tended to follow earlier customs.
2. Ancestor worship was a very important aspect of Chinese life.

See #1 above.

Respect for all family members, especially the elders, was stressed. The parents' way of doing things was usually followed by their children. Often people were unwilling to change the customs that had been handed down to them.

Many Chinese villages were separated by long distances because of the mountain ranges. What is likely to happen to family groups in a village that does not have contact with other villages?

The Chinese family was ruled absolutely by the father. All family members were subject to his will. A family which had many sons was considered very fortunate. Besides helping to work the land, sons were the only ones allowed to carry out religious ceremonies. A family which had no sons was to be pitied. Daughters worked with their families until they were fourteen or fifteen, at which time they usually married. They would then live and work with their husband's family.

See #2 above.

Ancestor worship The Chinese family felt that both the living and the dead were members of the family. Ancestors who had died were still thought to be able to influence and protect the living members of the family. A family's ancestors were worshiped in religious ceremonies. Only sons could perform these ceremonies. Having many sons ensured that the family's ancestors would be worshiped properly. A family believed that their ancestors would desert them

A/S and disasters would occur if worship was not carried out. How would this belief in ancestor worship help to maintain a traditional society?

G/S The family believed that if a family member did something noble and good, he brought honor to the entire family. If he committed a crime or did something evil, the entire family, including the ancestors, was shamed. What effect would this belief have on members of the family?

S S **Social classes** Social classes in Chinese society were not as rigid as those found in many societies. There were, in general, two dividing lines separating the members of society.

People who owned land or a business were in a higher class than those who did not own property. The educated people were in a higher class than the uneducated. The people who were educated were highly respected and found many jobs open to them. For example, S/P in order to become a government official, a person had to be educated in order to A/S pass the examinations.

See #3 below.

S/E These social classes were not fixed; that is, a person could move from a lower to a higher class. A peasant could save enough money to buy land and move into a higher class. A peasant's son could study and pass the examinations to become a government official and be highly respected. This would bring great honor to the family.

Girls spinning and weaving

Confucianism Chinese society was greatly shaped by the moral teachings of a Chinese scholar named Confucius (kən fū′shəs). Confucius lived from about 551 to 478 B.C. His teachings stressed respect and loyalty to elders and their ways of life. Confucius believed that life would go smoothly if everyone realized his duties in what Confucius called the five basic relationships. These were the relationships between ruler and subject, father and son, husband and wife, older brother and younger brother, and between two friends. Confucius taught that people should develop a sense of responsibility and honesty toward others, especially toward members of one's own family. One of his basic principles was, "What you do not want done to yourself, do not do to others." What is another way to express this idea?

A/H →

See #2 below.

Education in China The instruction that was given by Chinese scholars was based on studies from earlier writings. The emphasis of these writings was on the way things had been done in the past and on what people had believed. These were the customs and ways of life that were followed. How would this style of education aid in maintaining a traditional society?

A/H ←

S/P →

See #1 below.

Education was not free in early China. A family might only be able to educate one or two of its children. It was the sons who received the education. Why do you think this was so? Refer to the picture. What type of education did girls receive?

S ←

The stress that Confucius placed on family loyalty was carried over to the government. Government was seen as an extension of the family. As the ruler had to care for his subjects as a father would, so the subjects were to respect and obey the ruler as children did in a family. What type of attitude would this develop in people?

Think for Yourself

How is the Chinese view of the family different or similar to our view?

Stress:
1. Education in China was based on earlier ways of doing things.
2. The teachings of Confucius stressed respect and responsibility.
*3. Why do some societies have a different type of education for boys than they have for girls?

131

For Teaching Helps, see page T56.
Stress:
1. Trading activities carried on by the Greeks brought them wealth as well as new
   ideas from other countries.
2. Greece was made up of independent city-states.

THE GREEK WAY OF LIFE

Aegean civilizations Many civilizations had risen and fallen in the area of the Aegean (i jē′ən) Sea. On the island of Crete (krēt) and in Mycenae (mī sē′nē), highly developed cultures existed between 1600 B.C. and 1300 B.C. Locate these places on the map. The Greek civilization that reached its peak in the fifth century B.C. had learned much from these earlier civilizations.

G/H

See #1 above.

The Greeks were active in carrying on trade with neighboring countries. As you study the map, what geographical reasons can you give for this? Because of their contacts with other civilizations, the Greeks borrowed many ideas from the eastern civilizations.

E/G

Greece The land of Greece is extremely mountainous, which presented many problems. One of these problems was difficulty in unifying the country. What other problems could develop?

Because of the difficulty of uniting the country, each city tended to act on its own. Some cities even became powerful enough to set up colonies in other lands. Each city-state, as these cities were called, had its own system of government, its own social structure, and its own economic system. The cultures of two of the city-states, Athens and Sparta, show an interesting contrast.

P

See #2 above.

Athens By 500 B.C., the city-state of Athens was the most highly developed area in Greece. Although many of its buildings are in ruins today, the picture on the facing page of the Parthenon on the Acropolis still gives us a good idea of the magnificence of the city.

See #3 below.

The citizens of Athens enjoyed a political freedom which most other people in the world at that time did not have. Athens had a government in which all citizens took an active part. This type of government will be discussed in a later chapter. The wealth of Athens was based on trade with her colonies and with other nations. Besides wealth, what other benefits would this trade bring Athens?

P

E

AEGEAN CIVILIZATIONS

N
W E
S

GREECE

AEGEAN SEA

• Athens

• Mycenae

• Sparta

MEDITERRANEAN SEA

CRETE

SCALE OF MILES
0 50 100 150

The Parthenon

Social classes The class structure of Athens was not as rigid as in other societies. The dividing lines in Athenian society were drawn between citizens and noncitizens, and between free men and slaves. Only citizens had the right to take part in the government. They could work at any business they wanted. Noncitizens were limited as to where they could work. There was no way for them to become citizens. In order for a person to be a citizen, both of his parents had to be Athenian citizens. All citizens were treated equally. Noncitizens were protected under the laws, but they had no say in helping to make those laws. In addition noncitizens had to pay extra taxes. What effects would these rights given only to citizens have on members of society?

The lowest class in Athenian society were the slaves, who made up one-third of the population. The slaves had no social or political rights. They were people who had been captured in wars or born of slave parents. Some who were educated served as teachers. But most of the slaves worked in the homes or businesses of their masters.

It may seem strange to speak of political freedom in Athens, with every citizen taking part in the government, while at the same time so many people were kept in slavery. These political rights were extended only to citizens. The fact that citizens kept slaves gave the citizens time to take an active part in their government. Some citizens of Athens felt it was wrong to keep slaves. What arguments do you suppose were

See #1 below.

See #2 below.

S ↔

S/P ↔

Stress:
1. Citizens of Athens were granted more rights than noncitizens.
2. Slavery existed at the same time as political freedom in Athens.

133

Agora in Athens

given for and against slavery by the Athenians?

Life in Athens The busiest spot in the city of Athens was the market place, called the **agora** (ag′ər ə). The agora was the public meeting place. What activities took place in the agora, according to this picture?

The men of Athens would meet here after a few hours of work to discuss events of the day. The women of Athens did not have as much freedom as the men. The women were trained to run a house and handle many servants. They did not take much part in public life.

The children of Athens led happy and carefree lives until the age of seven. The girls were then trained in the art of housekeeping. They were taught how to cook and sew, and perhaps how to read

and write. The parents would arrange the marriages for their daughters.

The boys of Athens began their education at the age of seven. The law required that parents educate their sons, but did not require the state to provide schools. Private teachers were hired to instruct boys in reading, writing, arithmetic, poetry, and music.

Greek art The Greeks had a great love for art, drama, and music. Plays for the theater that were written by the early Greeks are still being performed today. Many of the famous works of sculpture that were done have been lost or broken throughout the centuries. However, many museums still have some original Greek sculptures or some Roman copies of them. An example of Greek sculpture is shown by this Roman

See #1 below.

See #2 below.

S/E ←
S/P →
S ←
A →
A/S ←

Stress:
1. Boys were educated differently than girls in Athens.
2. The Greeks were skilled in the arts.

1. Sparta concentrated on creating a
   strong army.

copy of a statue called "Discobolus" (dis kob'ə ləs), which means the discus thrower. How does this Greek statue differ from Egyptian statues that you have seen?

Sparta While the Greeks of Athens were developing a society with much political freedom and freedom of ex- A/S ← pression, the Greeks of Sparta were developing quite differently. Locate Sparta on the map on page 132. About how far is it from Athens to Sparta? 100 miles.

See #1 above.

Rather than building its power and wealth through trade, Sparta gained its wealth from the neighboring states that it had conquered. Sparta was a military state. All energies were turned to creating and maintaining a strong military force.

The government-controlled family S/P → The people of Sparta were rigidly con-

"Discobolus"

trolled by the government from birth to death. In Sparta the family was not the most important unit in society. The army was considered the most important. Children up to the age of seven were raised by their mother. After the age of seven, boys were turned over to the government to be trained as soldiers. Look at the picture at the left. How are these youths being trained for military life?

See #2 below.

Men served in the army full-time until they were thirty. After that they could be called to serve again if necessary. A fine fighting force was developed, but there was very little family life.

Girls were educated differently. They were trained so they could one day man- S/A → age their husband's land while he was away fighting in the army. Girls were expected to become wives and mothers

Spartan military training

2. Education in Sparta emphasized
   military training.

135

and trained to bravely send their husbands and sons off to war.

When children were born, they were taken to the government leaders to be checked. If the child was healthy, he was allowed to live. If the child was sickly or born with a deformity, he was left on a hillside to die. Why would the Spartans see nothing wrong in this practice? S/P

Social classes The social structure of Sparta was very rigid but very simple. Government officials held the highest position, along with military heroes. The soldiers, which included almost all the men, were considered next in importance. Last were the slaves and peas-

See #1 above.

ants who worked the land. Spartan citizens were actually outnumbered by the slaves and peasants. How do you suppose they were able to keep them under control?

The tightly controlled society of Sparta gave people very little chance to express themselves in art and drama. People were locked into their group in society. They knew what was expected of them. What type of attitude might this develop in members of society? S/A

*2. Could a tightly controlled society develop today? Explain.

Think for Yourself

Which city-state of Greece most closely resembles our society?

THE ROMAN WAY OF LIFE

For Teaching Helps, see page T57.   For a class activity, see #1 on page 140.

A great empire Some six centuries after the decline of Athens, the Roman Empire had reached its height. Study the map on this page. What new areas G were brought under Roman control by the second century?

The unity and stability that the Roman Empire brought to that part of

THE GROWTH OF THE ROMAN EMPIRE

ROMAN TERRITORY IN 133 B.C.

ROMAN EMPIRE AT ITS GREATEST EXTENT, 167 A.D.

SCALE OF MILES
0   200   400   600   800   1,000

136

the world allowed a great civilization to flourish. When the Romans conquered a new area, they took what was best in the society and adapted it to their own ways. The ever-changing Roman culture was then carried into other areas. What then would happen as more and more new areas were absorbed into the empire? Changing culture spread.

Social classes All citizens of Rome were equal under the law, but at the same time there were sharp dividing lines drawn in society. There were four main social classes in Roman society. Highest in rank and importance were the government officials and military leaders. These people were called the **patricians** (pə trish′ənz). The businessmen made up the second class in society. The third class, the **plebeians** (pli bē′ənz), was made up of small farmers and craftsmen. The lowest class were the slaves. A Roman's education, his career, and even his clothes reflected his social position. The patricians, for instance, were allowed to have a wide band of purple on the bottom of their loose-flowing garments called **togas.** What other ways can you think of that a society might use to distinguish between classes? Do all societies do this?

Family life The Roman family was set up much like the Athenian family. The father was the unquestioned head of the family. The job of the Roman wife was to run a large household consisting of the family and many servants. The care of the children was turned over to servants or slaves, many of whom were well-educated Greeks.

Children began their education at the age of seven. Boys and girls went to school together until the age of thirteen. The girls continued their education at home with special tutors. The boys continued in school until the age of eighteen or so. Young Romans were taught the basic subjects of reading, writing, and mathematics; as well as history, Greek and Latin, geography, and astronomy. How does this school situation differ from the school situations in other societies?

Religion in Rome The early Romans worshiped many gods. They had gods to protect every aspect of life. There were gods to worship to ensure a good harvest. There were gods to pray to for victory in battle. The emperor was considered a god and public worship was demanded for him.

The Romans came into contact with many other religions among the peoples they conquered. They allowed other religions to exist as long as they did not oppose the Roman religion or the Roman government. The Romans even borrowed some ideas and new gods from these different religions.

Two religions, the Jewish and the Christian, were not tolerated or accepted by the Romans. The Jews in

2. There were sharp social distinctions, but there was equality under the law.
3. The Romans tolerated religions that they felt did not threaten the
   Roman government.   137

Stress: For Teaching Helps, see page T57.
1. The Jews were banished from their homeland by the Romans.
2. The Christians were persecuted by the Romans, but later Christianity was made
   the official religion.

See #1
above.

the state of Palestine had been ruled by the Romans since 63 B.C. The Jews had been united in their belief in one God for 1,300 years. Their government and their laws were based on their religion. The Jews of the empire had refused to accept Roman ways or Roman gods. After several revolts the Romans banished the Jews from Jerusalem and forbade them to re-enter. The Jews no longer had a homeland. This condition lasted until the twentieth century when the country of Israel was created.

See #2
above.

A new religion In Palestine, in the early part of the first century, Jesus of Nazareth preached a way of life which stressed nonviolence and love for one's fellowman. The followers of Jesus came to be known as Christians. This new religion, called Christianity, spread rapidly throughout the Roman world. Christianity became one of the religions not tolerated by the Roman government. The Christians felt that it was wrong to serve in the Roman army or hold political office. They also refused to take part in the public worship of the emperor, saying that they would worship only one God. Many of the Christians were put to death by the Romans.

By the fourth century Christianity was recognized as a legal religion in the Roman Empire. Eventually, it was made the official religion of Rome. How would the unity of the empire help the spread of Christianity?

Roman achievements The uniting of such a large empire, along with the system of government and code of laws, was a great achievement of Rome. This will be discussed in a later chapter.

See #3
below.

Another great achievement of the Romans was their building projects. In order to link an empire the size of Rome, a good network of roads was needed. What reasons can you think of that a large empire would require good roads? Some of the roads built by the Romans over 1,800 years ago are still in use, such as the Appian Way shown in the picture. How does it compare with roads you have seen?

Part of the
Appian Way
still in use

Stress:
1. The aqueducts and other building projects made life better for the Romans.
2. Many modern languages have borrowed from the Latin language.

The Romans also built channels or pipelines to bring water into the cities. These were called **aqueducts** (ak′wə dukts). The aqueducts were well-constructed and impressive. Rome had eleven aqueducts which carried 200,000,000 gallons of water daily into Rome. A picture of an aqueduct is shown. The water was carried along a stone channel thirty to sixty miles in length. In order to cross valleys, arches were built to support the aqueduct. Some Roman aqueducts are still in use today.

See #1 above.

The building projects of Rome helped to create a better life for the people. The roads and services that were provided also brought many people to the cities, which created overcrowded conditions. What problems can you see arising from overcrowded cities?

Latin, the language of the Romans, survived the Roman Empire. Many of the European languages of today are based on Latin. Italian, French, Spanish, and Rumanian are called Romance languages. That is, they are based on the Roman language. Even the English language has borrowed many words from Latin. Our word *urban*, referring to a city, comes from the Latin word *urbs*, meaning "city." See if you can give other examples of English words which came from Latin.

See #2 above.

Breakdown of the empire By the fifth century the Roman Empire was beginning to break down. Eventually it collapsed. Great changes took place in the lives of the people. Many of the ideas and achievements of the Roman Empire lived on in later civilizations. The knowledge that was gained from other areas helped to shape the European civilization that was to follow.

Roman-built aqueduct, the Pont du Gard, in southern France

Think for Yourself

What aspects of Roman society seem similar to society in the United States?

*3. Do you think that our society could break down? Why?

Things to Do

See page 136.
1. Find books or reference materials in your school or public library that give information on the Roman Empire. Try to interest your classmates in examining these materials by telling them briefly what each is about.

See page 126.
2. Pretend you are a sociologist planning to visit a member of the untouchable caste in India. Write two or more questions you would like to ask the person.

CLASS PROJECT—PART 2

Do your notes help you to answer the questions you placed on the chalkboard in Part 1 of the class project? What are some group activities you could plan that would show what you have discovered about family life in India, China, Greece, and the Roman Empire? The following list may give you some ideas.

1. Presenting a pantomime
2. Constructing a bulletin-board display
3. Giving a panel presentation
4. Making models and pictures

After the list of activities is completed, each pupil may select the one he likes best. Those making the same choice may work together. At the first meeting of your group, you will want to answer the following questions.

1. Who will be the chairman of your group?
2. What part of family life will your activity show? The homes families live in? The customs families have?
3. What materials will your group need to carry out its activity? Where will you find and keep these materials?
4. What specific responsibility will each member of your group have?

During your study of the remainder of this unit, make your plans to carry out your group activity.

NBC NEWS

Democratic National Convention--1968

9. Eastern and Western Governments

For Teaching Helps, see page T58.

Stress:

1. In some societies the people held more power than people in other societies.

See #1 above.

The amount of power held by the people in various societies differed. In some societies, the people were ruled by one man or by a group of men. They had very little say in how their political system was organized. In other societies, the people made political decisions together. The people shown in the picture are selecting the leaders who will govern them. As you study this chapter, you will learn which type of government allows people to make this kind of decision.

S/P

See #2 below.

As countries grew larger, it was often difficult for one man to keep control and authority was divided. As communities grew larger in size and in population, the earlier, less complicated forms of government were no longer adequate. A more efficient political system was needed. In this chapter the different views of government found in the Eastern societies of India and China will be compared with those found in the Western societies of Greece and Rome.

2. As communities grew in size and population, governments needed to be more efficient.

JUST FOR FUN

See if you can find out how your city was governed in the past. Determine if the government has changed. If so, why has it?

141

For Teaching Helps, see page T59.   For a class activity, see #3 on page 156.
Stress:
1. People in the villages of India handled many local problems through councils
   called panchayats.

GOVERNMENT AND THE PEOPLE

Indian village councils For several hundred years following the Aryan invasions of 1500 B.C., most of the Indian tribes lived in small villages. Political scientists tell us that each village operated independently of the others. Each tribe had its own government.

As India grew in size and population, a more complex government was needed. Many new areas were conquered and states were formed. As states were conquered, a large empire was formed. The empire was ruled by a strong leader and able advisers. Each village still maintained a great deal of control over its own affairs. Village councils were formed to solve local problems. These councils were called **panchayats** (pun chä′yətz). A panchayat was made up of several villagers who were elected. Women were allowed to be members. This was unusual, for during this time, women were given few political or economic rights.

Power of the panchayat The members of the panchayat were responsible for collecting taxes for the government. As long as the government received its funds, the village was left largely on its own. The panchayat was responsible for enforcing the laws. These included not only the laws regarding property and business, but also the laws of India's caste system. Members of the panchayat could meet to decide whether or not a person should be ostracized, or excluded, from the community for a serious offense against the caste system. See if you can think of any modern groups that operate like a panchayat.

Village councils like the panchayats still exist in many parts of India. A group of villagers are shown on page 143 discussing a problem which would affect all of them. What kind of village problems might they be discussing?

Chinese villages In another Eastern society, China, the people were able to decide on solutions to many of their local problems. Within each village there were some officials who were responsible for taking care of local problems. This group was called a council of elders. The council was made up of the heads of the families in the village. Also included were the highly respected men of the village, such as the scholars and schoolteachers.

Because the village was small and everyone knew everyone else, formal elections were rarely held. Membership in the council of elders was decided through public opinion. People simply knew and agreed on who they wanted. Could this method of selecting leaders be used in your city? Why or why not?

Group responsibility Many local problems in the villages were solved through a sense of group responsibility.

S/P ↔

H/P ←

S/P →

P/E ←

P/S ←

See #1 above.

See #2 below.

See #3 below.

2. Members of the panchayat enforced laws, collected taxes, and made
   decisions on caste violations.
142   3. People in Chinese villages selected a council of elders to take care
   of local problems.

Village council meeting in Nolikeri, India

Private groups carried out many of the jobs which might have been carried out by the government. Each village usually had a volunteer fire department and a group to guard the harvest. Many mutual-aid societies were formed to provide money or food for people who were in need. How are many of these things taken care of today in small towns? In big cities?

Athens Many changes took place over the years in the forms of governments in Western societies. At one time Athens had a king, but by the eighth century B.C. the king had very little power. A council of nobles ruled Athens. As trade and manufacturing grew, a wealthy class developed. The merchants were not nobles, but they demanded and eventually received the same political rights as the nobles. Gradually more and more power was given to the people of Athens.

In Athens' form of government, there were some limitations. Political rights were granted only to male citizens. Women, slaves, and foreigners could not take part in the affairs of government.

Athenian Assembly Laws for the city were passed by the Athenian Assembly. The Assembly was open to all free, male citizens. The Assembly met forty times a year. Any citizen could speak on any subject he wished as long as he could keep an audience. However, the Assembly did have certain policies and possible laws to discuss. These policies had been drawn up by the other governing body of Athens—the Council of 500.

See #1 below.

See #2 below.

S/P

S/P

H/P

S/P

Stress:
1. Political power was slowly granted to all free, male Athenian citizens.
2. An assembly made up of all free, male citizens made the laws for Athens.

143

For Teaching Helps, see page T59.
Stress:
1. In a direct democracy all citizens can help to make the laws.

Members of the Council were chosen by drawing names from a list of volunteers. Council members were paid salaries, and they served in office for one year. Within the Council of 500 was a smaller group, made up of fifty men, which met daily. In effect, this group ran the government. The members of the group were changed ten times a year. Why do you suppose these members were changed so often?

See #1 above.

Democracy in Athens The type of government in which all citizens are allowed to take an active part and meet to make the laws themselves is known as a **direct democracy**. In many areas this was not a practical form of government. Do you think this would be practical for a large country? Why or why not?

The population of the city-state of Athens was small enough so that all citizens could meet and discuss laws. A form of direct democracy can be seen today in many New England town meetings like the one shown here. All citizens of the town can meet to decide solutions to various problems facing their town.

The citizens of Athens had the power to banish anyone they felt was a danger to the city. A public vote was held and if a majority of citizens agreed that a person was dangerous, he was banished from the city for ten years. The voting was done by scratching the accused person's name on a piece of tile or broken pottery called *ostrakon* as shown in the picture on page 145. From this comes the word "ostracize." Do you think ostracism was a good practice? Why?

See #2 below.

New England town meeting

Ostrakon with a vote for banishment

Roman government In the centuries before the Roman Empire was founded, the people of Rome were ruled by a king. The king was elected by an assembly made up of all citizens. He was advised by a council called the Senate. Senators were elected for life and came mainly from the patrician or highest class. The farmers and craftsmen who were members of the plebeian class did not have much influence on their government in these early times.

See #1 above.

Eventually, the plebeians gained in power. A new form of government had been set up in Rome. Instead of electing a king, the people could elect two officials, called consuls. The consuls had to be from the patrician class and could only serve one year.

Besides the consuls and the Senate, two new assemblies were set up. One was limited to land-owning citizens. The other was open to the plebeians. The plebeians' assembly grew to have a powerful influence on Rome. This form of government in which the people elect representatives to carry on the work of government is called a **republic,** or representative government. What advantages and disadvantages can you see in this form of government? How does this form compare with the direct democracy of Athens?

See #2 below.

Plebeians demand reform The plebeians were interested mainly in two things: (1) guarding their basic political rights and (2) increasing their political power. The plebeians felt that the laws of Rome were often used to favor the patricians. The plebeians demanded that laws be classified, written down, and posted in a public place. How would this help ensure fairness?

See #3 below.

The laws were posted in the Roman Forum for all to see. The Forum was the location of the government buildings as

2. In a republic people elect representatives to make the laws.
3. The plebeians of Rome demanded that the laws be classified and posted.

145

Roman Forum today

View of reconstructed Roman Forum

well as a marketplace. Here the citizens of Rome could gather to take part in political discussions, hear news from other parts of the world, and purchase a variety of products. Today the Forum is in ruins as shown in the picture. The other picture shows how the Forum probably looked when the Roman Em-

pire was at its height over 1,800 years ago.

S

*1. How are new laws, or possible new laws, publicized today?

Think for Yourself

Do the people of our country have the power to rule themselves? What evidence can you give to prove your answer?

GOVERNMENT AND STRONG LEADERS

For Teaching Helps, see page T60. For a class activity, see #2 on page 156.

See #1 below.

Indian states As Indian villages grew, they often joined together to form a state. Each state was ruled by a **rajah** (rä′jə), or king. The rajahs of these various states held a great deal of power. They were advised by a royal council made up of trusted men.

Among these states, there was constant warfare to gain land or better trade routes. In order to protect their

P
←

P
→

people, rajahs built walled cities. Besides the wall, what else do you see in the picture on page 147 that would provide protection for the people?

The independent states of India— some ruled by strong rajahs, others by weak rajahs—remained small. None of them achieved great political or economic importance. Warfare and shifting military alliances kept the area in a state

See #2 below.

Stress:
1. The states of India were ruled by rajahs.
2. As independent states, the Indian states never gained much power.

146

Stress:
1. The northern states of India were
   united under one ruler.

of confusion. Unity was needed. A strong leader and a strong central government could provide this unity.

The kings of India The states of northern India were threatened by invasion in the fourth century B.C. The invaders were successfully driven back, mainly by the army of Chandragupta (chən'drə gup'tə), who was rajah of one of the northern states. In twenty-four years Chandragupta had conquered all of northern India. The Maurya (mou' ər ə) Dynasty founded by Chandragupta ruled northern India for over 100 years.

The kings of India were regarded as almost godlike. Judging from this passage from an Indian poem written over 2,000 years ago, why did the people feel a king was so necessary?

The king's role was not seen as that of lawmaking, but rather that of providing protection. His job was not only to protect his people from invasion but also to protect the order in society. The king had to uphold the caste system and ensure that laws were passed that would keep the castes separate.

See #1 above.

A/P

P/S

See #2 below.

2. The role of the king was to maintain the order in society.

EXCERPTS—RAMAYANA

Where the land is kingless the cloud, lightning-wreathed and loud-voiced, gives no rain to the earth.

Where the land is kingless the son does not honour his father, nor the wife her husband.

Where the land is kingless men do not meet in assemblies, nor make lovely gardens and temples.

Where the land is kingless the rich are unprotected, and shepherds and peasants sleep with bolted doors.

A river without water, a forest without grass, a herd of cattle without a herdsman, is the land without a king.

Walled city—Gwalior, India

For Teaching Helps, see page T60.
Stress:
1. The Chinese political system was based on the teachings of Confucius.
2. The Chinese thought the emperor's right to rule came from heaven.

China In their view of the ruler, Chinese society was very similar to Indian society. Confucius, shown here, had stated that the world would run smoothly if everyone followed his duties and responsibilities in the five basic relationships. One of these was the relationship between ruler and subject. Confucius compared this relationship in government with the relationship between father and son. Just as the son owed loyalty and obedience to his father, so the subject owed loyalty and obedience to his ruler. Also, as the father was responsible for the protection and guidance of his sons, so the ruler was to be as a father to his subjects.

See #1 above.

Confucius

Role of the emperor China followed a pattern very similar to India's in organization. For centuries China had been divided into small independent states at war with one another. Eventually a strong leader from one state would conquer neighboring states. A strong country would emerge under a new dynasty, or ruling family.

The rulers of the Chinese were called emperors. The Chinese people believed that their emperor was chosen by heaven to rule. They called this a **Mandate of Heaven.** As long as heaven was pleased with the emperor, he continued to have a **mandate,** that is, a right to rule. If China was hit by hard times— famines or droughts—this was sometimes seen as a sign that heaven was no longer pleased with the emperor. The people could then revolt and overthrow the emperor. What possible dangers can you see in this belief in a Mandate of Heaven?

See #2 above.

Athens In the Western society of Athens, leadership was very different from leadership in Eastern societies. In a direct democracy where full power is in the hands of the people, the role of the leader is mainly to carry out the views of the people. He himself does not have a great deal of power. Before Athens developed its democratic form of government, there were various leaders who controlled the city. These men were called **tyrants,** which at that time meant

See #3 below.

Stress:
1. Reforms were made in Athens by some early leaders.
2. Some Roman leaders tried to limit the power of the people.

"master." See if you can find out what meaning the word tyrant has today.

Two Athenian leaders Some of the tyrants ruled Athens wisely and helped to create the democracy which followed. One of these men was Solon (sō'lən), who lived over 2,500 years ago. One of the political reforms made by Solon was to make wealth, rather than noble birth, a requirement for holding high political office. As Athens increased its trade and commerce, more citizens were able to qualify for public office.

See #1 above.

Under the leadership of Pericles (per'ə klēz'), Athens reached the height of its democracy. The reforms made by Pericles truly put the people in control of their government.

Roman Republic During the time that Rome was a republic, many consuls found ways to become very powerful. At times this resulted in the people having less say in their government. Some consuls increased the size of the Senate by appointing their friends. In this way they could limit the power of the plebeians' assembly. What dangers do you see in leaders appointing their friends to public office? Not necessarily qualified.

See #2 above.

Rise of the emperors As Rome took more and more new areas under its control, a new form of government developed. Power became concentrated more in the hands of one man. Many of the emperors who rose to power had the support of the army. The change took

See #3 below.

place gradually. When Julius Caesar, a powerful military leader, took power he did not really change the form of the government.

P/H ←

The Roman Peace The heir of Julius Caesar, Octavian, took the name of "Augustus" meaning the "revered one." The form of government set up under Augustus was to last for almost 200 years.

Augustus reorganized the government of the empire. By this time the Roman Empire had over 100,000,000 people. People of different races and cultures mixed freely. Large cities were developing. This 200-year period of peace and growth under the emperors was known as the **Pax Romana,** or the Roman Peace.

P/H →

See #4 below.

During the *Pax Romana,* Rome was ruled by many different emperors. Some, such as Augustus, were wise and ruled well. Others were not so wise. Some emperors were often cruel and greedy for power.

P/H ←

By the third century A. D. the *Pax Romana* had started to decline. The Senate and the assemblies had lost most of their power. The emperors remained in power mainly with the support of the army. The government had lost touch with the people.

P/H →

P/H ←

Think for Yourself

How can government leaders of today keep in touch with the people of their country?

P/H ←

3. Many emperors ruled the Roman Empire with the support of the army.
4. The large and varied Roman Empire had a 200-year period of peace and growth.
*5. How does our society's view of its leader compare to that of the society of India?

149

For Teaching Helps, see page T61. For a class activity, see #1 on page 156.
Stress:
1. India's strong central government provided many services for the people.
2. The courts established in India were well organized but harsh in their
   punishments.

GOVERNMENT IN ACTION

India India's government was well organized under the Maurya Dynasty. P/H ← The lives of the people were improved in many ways. Good roads were built to connect the major cities of the empire. A very fine postal system was set up. Besides providing many jobs for the P/H → people, the government looked after the welfare of the people. Commissions were formed to see that there was proper care for orphans and for the aged. The poor were given jobs in state-owned factories. Doctors were limited in the amount they could charge for their P/S ← services. The government searched for and grew plants that could be used as medicines. The government had given all these services. How else could these services have been given?

See #1 above.

Hindu law During the Maurya Dynasty a very good court system was set up. However, many of the punishments P/S ← were very cruel. Some criminals were sentenced to be trampled to death by oxen. Others were killed by starvation. The courts set the punishment for a crime on the basis of a person's caste. A member of a higher caste would be given a much lighter sentence than a member of a lower caste for the very same crime.

See #2 above.

A new policy Many of the harsh laws of the Indian government were relaxed under the rule of Chandragupta's grand-

son, Asoka (ä sō′kä). Asoka made the size of the empire larger by conquering all of India except part of the southern tip.

The forty-year rule of Asoka and his officials was a time of peace and well-being for the people of India. His successors were not as capable as Asoka. In time the Maurya Dynasty lost its power. India was again broken up into small, warring states. The idea of a strong central authority remained, however, and other dynasties in the future would build on these ideas.

See #3 below.

China As the Chinese Empire grew, more people were needed to help rule it. Officials were appointed by the emperor to advise him or to help rule the

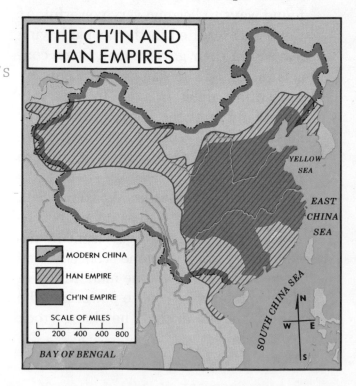

THE CH'IN AND HAN EMPIRES

MODERN CHINA

HAN EMPIRE

CH'IN EMPIRE

SCALE OF MILES
0 200 400 600 800

YELLOW SEA

EAST CHINA SEA

SOUTH CHINA SEA

BAY OF BENGAL

3. When the central government
   collapsed, India was again
   broken up into warring states.

The Great Wall of China

large empire. The actual work of the government was in the hands of these men. This type of government by officials is called a **bureaucracy** (byu rok′rə si). Many countries in the world today have bureaucratic governments. What possible advantages and disadvantages can you see in this form of government?

Although rulers in China always had advisers, it was not until the Ch'in Dynasty that a true bureaucracy developed. The name "China" was taken from the Ch'in Dynasty, which ruled over 2,000 years ago. The Ch'in Dynasty got its power by fighting wars and winning them. Look at the map on page 150. How much of today's China did it control?

See #1 below.

In order to provide greater protection for the empire, fortifications were built. These started at the seacoast and went 1,500 miles into the interior. These fortifications were the Great Wall of China. As you look at the picture on this page, try to decide why the Great Wall was useful to the Chinese.

See #2 below.

Historians tell us that peasants and slaves were forced to build the Great Wall. Many died in the effort to build it. One historian said that every stone placed cost a human life.

Han Dynasty The harsh, rigid rule of the Ch'in Dynasty did not last long. The severe laws and the heavy burden of taxation for public works under the first ruler of the dynasty were part of the

Stress:
1. The actual work of government in China was carried out by a bureaucracy.
2. The Great Wall of China provided protection for the people.

151

reason for revolts against the rulers who followed him.

The Han Dynasty, which came into power over 2,000 years ago, expanded the Ch'in Empire as shown on the map on page 150. A great change in the form of the bureaucracy came under the Han emperor Wu-ti (wū'-di'). Wu-ti decided that public officials should be educated and capable men. He did not agree with the idea of appointing people simply because they were friends. Wu-ti also did not agree with the ignoring of tradition that had taken place during the rule of the Ch'in Dynasty. The rule

of Wu-ti and the emperors to follow was based on Confucianism. A university was established to encourage the study of Confucianism.

In order to become a government official, it was necessary to pass an examination. The examination was based on the writings of Confucius. The rulers were looking for men who would respect and continue the traditions of the past. The picture shows a commission made up of the emperor and some of his officials. They would select officials from among the candidates on the basis of these examinations. Do you think this

See #1 above.

Commission examining candidates for government positions

was a good way of selecting officials? Why or why not?

Athens Although the city-state of Athens had many colonies in the Mediterranean Sea, it never really developed as a strong central authority. Athens was not able to spread a feeling of national unity among the Greeks. Economists tell us that Athenian colonies and certain Greek city-states depended on Athens for trade and protection. However, a strong political bond was never formed.

See #1 above.

With a small population and a direct democracy such as Athens had, a large central government did not develop. The laws were made by the people. There had to be, of course, leaders to carry out the decisions of the people. The leaders of Athens had to handle relationships with other states. Men were chosen by the council to carry out these duties.

Decline of the city-states The independence of the city-states began to decline about thirty years after Athens had reached its peak. Athens and her allies were involved in a war with Sparta and her allies. Sparta, being victorious, took over the government of Athens and replaced democracy with a council of thirty men. These men ruled harshly, and spent most of their time persecuting their enemies. The people of Athens successfully revolted after a year of Sparta's rule. The council was driven out and democracy was restored. However, the people of Athens had a difficult time resuming their way of life, which had been badly upset.

See #2 above.

Sparta at this time had the chance to unify the Greek city-states. However, the rulers that Sparta appointed held all power to themselves. They did not know how to rule people who were used to ruling themselves. The rulers often misused public funds. In addition, there were other forms of corruption in the government. Sparta's control began to break down. The Greek city-states weakened by war were an easy target for a conqueror. Why would this be so?

A strong leader North of Greece in the present-day country of Yugoslavia, a man named Philip II ruled Macedonia (mas′ə dō′ni ə). He and his countrymen were of Greek descent. Philip felt that he could unify the Greek city-states. After a brief war, Philip organized all the city-states except Sparta into a league under his military leadership. Each was allowed to have a measure of local control. Before Philip could carry out his plans for further conquest, he was murdered. His son, Alexander the Great, continued his father's policies.

See #3 below.

Alexander expanded the Macedonian Empire far beyond the Aegean Sea. In his thirty-three years of life, he managed to extend the empire's boundaries as far east as India. Refer to the map on page 154. Compare it with a modern map. What present-day countries were in

153

For Teaching Helps, see page T61.
Stress:
1. Roman leaders established provincial governments for their scattered empire.

Alexander's empire? What was the great extent of the empire from north to south?

Effect on Greece The Greek city-states never again achieved lasting independence and true democracy. Less than 200 years after the breakdown of Alexander's empire, the Greeks were made a part of the Roman Empire.

Rome One of the major problems that the Roman Empire had to solve was the governing of all its territories. With such a large area and so many people, an efficient, loyal group of officials was needed. Under the first emperor, Augustus, the empire was divided into two types of **provinces,** or territories. Some provinces were controlled by the Senate. Every year the Senate would appoint a governor for each area. Other provinces were under the control of the emperor, who

could appoint a governor for each province. In addition, each province had a council made up of representatives from every city and town in the province. These councils met only once a year and reported back to Rome on the activities of the governor. What would be some possible dangers in setting up provincial governments in this way?

Many cities and towns within the empire were allowed to have a large measure of self-government. Some areas even issued their own coins. What problem can you see in this?

Roman code of laws One of the most lasting achievements of the Roman Empire was its code of laws. Under the Roman Republic the Law of the Twelve Tables had been established. This was the basic legal code of Rome for almost 1,000 years. Roman law continued to de-

See #1 above.

See #2 below.

2. Many cities in the Roman Empire acted quite independently.

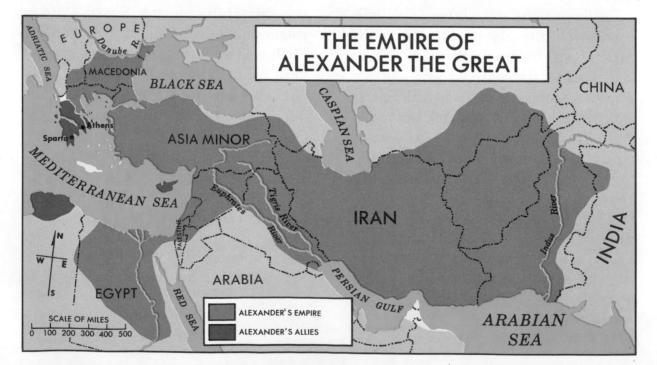

THE EMPIRE OF ALEXANDER THE GREAT

EUROPE

ADRIATIC SEA

Danube R.

MACEDONIA

BLACK SEA

CASPIAN SEA

CHINA

ASIA MINOR

Athens

Sparta

MEDITERRANEAN SEA

Euphrates River

Tigris River

IRAN

Indus River

INDIA

PALESTINE

EGYPT

RED SEA

ARABIA

PERSIAN GULF

ARABIAN SEA

N W E S

SCALE OF MILES
0 100 200 300 400 500

◻ ALEXANDER'S EMPIRE
◼ ALEXANDER'S ALLIES

velop and expand but was not organized into a code of laws until the sixth century A.D.

See #1 above.

By the fourth century A.D., the capital of the Roman Empire had been moved to Constantinople shown here. The Roman Empire in the west was fighting against invaders from the north. In the east, the Roman Empire survived. One of its greatest emperors was Justinian (ju′stin′ē ən). He selected ten men to collect and group all Roman laws into the Code of Civil Law. The code included laws and legal principles. It was illustrated by real cases. Some of Justinian's code is printed here. Do we have laws today that are like those given in the code?

Istanbul, formerly Constantinople

EXCERPTS—JUSTINIAN'S CODE

No one is compelled to defend a cause against his will.

No one suffers a penalty for what he thinks.

No one may be forcibly removed from his own house.

A father is not a competent witness for a son, nor a son for a father.

In inflicting penalties, the age and inexperience of the guilty party must be taken into account.

The Roman code of laws had a great influence on later legal systems that were developed. The Romans' idea of justice and the rights of people influenced the law codes of France and Germany. England's legal system took some ideas from Roman law. The American system in turn was mainly based on England's system.

See #2 below.

Think for Yourself

Why does a country need a code of laws? Why might a country sometimes revise its code of laws?

Things to Do

See
page 150.

1. Find some pictures of people in our country today who earn their living by working for our government. Observe the pictures to see if you can determine what the kind of work is and whether or not workers of India, China, Greece, and the Roman Empire might have had similar jobs.

See
page 146.

2. Make a model or picture of an Indian village of long ago. The picture on page 147 may help you develop your plans.

See
page 142.

3. Pretend that you and your classmates are going to form a council—a panchayat—to govern your class. Prepare a short report telling the rules and regulations you will establish and how you will enforce these regulations.

CLASS PROJECT—PART 3

The activity groups should now be completing their preparations for showing family life in India, China, Greece, or the Roman Empire. Each chairman may want to check to be sure all members of his group have completed particular responsibilities. Some members may need to assist others who are in need of help.

The groups may continue their work by doing the following:

1. Discuss what remains to be done so that your group will be ready to present its activity.
2. Decide if pupils making pictures and models may place them on the bulletin board or on tables.
3. Have each member of the group prepare notes on what he is going to do as part of the group activity.
4. Make plans to rehearse your activity.

It might be fun to share your activities showing family life in India, China, Greece, and the Roman Empire with visitors. How would you plan to do this?

For Teaching Helps, see page T62.

Oranges for export being loaded into a ship in the Israeli port of Ashdod

Stress:
1. The production and distribution of goods occur in all societies.

10. Eastern and Western Economies

2. Societies must solve the problems of producing and distributing goods.

In many of the world's ports, ships like the Israeli ship shown here are a common sight. A visitor to the docks would see some of the goods produced by the farms, mines, and factories of Israel. Many of the goods were produced far from the Israeli port where the ship was loaded. What methods of G/E transportation were probably used in moving the goods from the places they were produced to the port? What part P/E might the government of Israel have played in the production and distribution of these surplus goods?

In every civilization, even those in the period between 1500 B.C. to A.D. 500 covered in this chapter, the people are faced with the problems of developing economic systems for producing and distributing goods. In this chapter you will discover how the Eastern societies of China and India and the Western societies of Greece and the Roman Empire solved these problems.

See #1 and #2 above.

*3. Why is the way goods are distributed important?

JUST FOR FUN

Make a list of the various economic activities that are carried on in your town. Share your findings with your classmates.

157

Stress:
1. Geographic conditions and climate in India vary greatly in different areas.

THE LAND AND ITS USE

2. Climatic conditions affect economic activity in India.

India As you study the map of India, find the chain of mountains that cuts India off from much of the rest of Asia. Then find the plains through which the Ganges (gan'jēz') River flows and the plains of India that border the Arabian Sea. How would you describe the height of the land of much of the rest of India?

In the plains bordering the Ganges and the other great rivers of India, the soil is very fertile. Study the map again. Find the latitude and longitude of the mouth of the Ganges River. Would you expect this area to have a warm or a cold climate? Why?

India has three seasons. In India there is a cool dry season, a hot dry season, and a hot rainy season. The rainy season, during which crops grow rapidly, lasts from June through September. During this time moisture-bearing winds blow from the southwest, as shown on the map. These winds are called the southwest **monsoons.** Where, in India, would you expect these winds to drop their moisture? The southwest monsoons are essential to the farmers of India. If the monsoon rains come too early, the crops will be flooded. If the rains are late, the crops might fail.

Now find the arrows showing the northeast monsoons. Would you expect these winds to carry a great or a small amount of moisture? Why? During the dry season of the year, the farmers have to irrigate their fields if they plan to raise crops. As early as the first century A.D., the government had built artificial lakes for irrigation purposes. What ways can you think of that our government has helped the farmers in our country?

Farming in India The farmers of India have always been able to grow a variety of crops. In the cooler areas, they grow wheat and barley. In the hot, humid areas, farmers grow cotton, rice, sugar, and spices. In early times India produced a surplus of sugar and spices. These were the bases of India's trade with Europe.

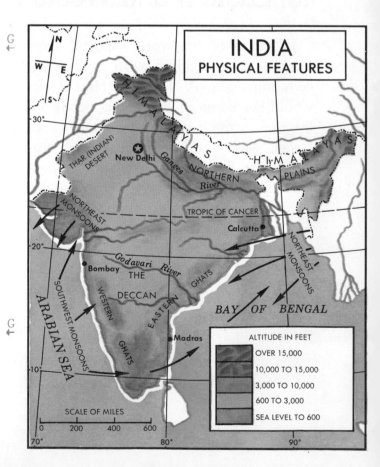

See #1
above.

See #2
above.

See #3
below.

3. Agriculture is a primary
economic activity in India.

158

Stress:
1. Age-old traditional farming practices are still used in parts of India.

Operating a water wheel in India

See #1
above.

Anthropologists tell us that the farming methods used by some of the people of India today are very similar to the methods their ancestors used hundreds of years ago. The people shown in the picture are using an ancient water wheel to irrigate their fields. Do you think that farmers using this method of irrigation would produce a surplus of crops? Why?

China As you study the map of China, compare the amount of mountainous land with the amount of land that is plains. Which amount seems greater to you? Which of the two kinds of land is unsuited to farming?

See #2
below.

Geographers tell us that a total of 70 per cent of the land of China is either too mountainous, too dry, or too cold for agriculture. In earlier times the majority of the people settled in the fertile river valleys. Chinese agriculture began along the Wei (wā) River. On the map find

2. About 11 per cent of the land in
   China is suitable for farming.

the Wei River and the highlands to the north. These helped make the land good for agriculture because they cut off the dry north winds.

Many farmers also settled along the Yangtze (yang'tsē') River and the Hwang Ho (hwäng' hō'). Locate these rivers on the map. Would you expect the climate in the valleys along these rivers to be mild or cold? Why? These river valleys were good places to settle. Why?

Farming in China A major problem for the Chinese farmers in the river valleys has always been water—there is either too little or too much. The farmers' control of water was necessary for agriculture to flourish. During the time when China was divided into warring states over 2,500 years ago, rival princes found that providing ways to control the water supply was a good way to gain

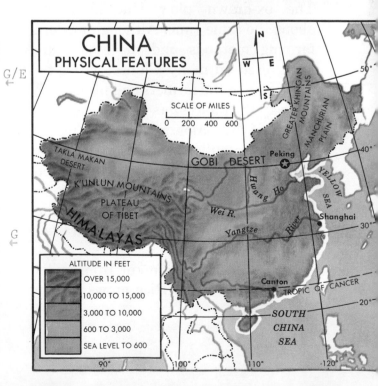

CHINA
PHYSICAL FEATURES

SCALE OF MILES
0   200   400   600

TAKLA MAKAN DESERT

K'UNLUN MOUNTAINS

PLATEAU OF TIBET

HIMALAYAS

GOBI DESERT

GREATER KHINGAN MOUNTAINS

MANCHURIAN PLAIN

Peking

Hwang Ho

Wei R.

Yangtze River

YELLOW SEA

Shanghai

Canton

TROPIC OF CANCER

SOUTH CHINA SEA

ALTITUDE IN FEET
OVER 15,000
10,000 TO 15,000
3,000 TO 10,000
600 TO 3,000
SEA LEVEL TO 600

Terraced farmland in northwestern China

G →

places having a warm climate. Rice needs much water in order to grow, and at times, the rice fields must be flooded. As more and more irrigation systems were built in early times, rice became a major crop.

G/E →

As the Chinese population grew, more land was needed to grow the rice. Because much of China's land is mountainous, the Chinese farmers developed the technique illustrated in the picture. What did they probably have to do to get level land? Why was the technique so important to farmers living in hilly areas? Made land available for farming.

See #1 below.

The technique of getting strips of level land on hillsides is called **terracing.** This technique is used in many countries even today.

A ←

Greece and Italy Find Athens on the map and decide what kind of land— mountains or plains—surround it. Then

support from the people. As a result, the princes built dikes and canals and set up other projects for irrigation.

Chinese farmers began to use iron tools instead of stone tools about 500 B.C. The ox-drawn plow reached China about the same time. Although modern farming methods and machinery are being used on many Chinese farms today, some of the farmers still farm much the way their ancestors did.

Two of the major crops of the Chinese farmers are **millet,** which is a wheatlike grain, and rice. Millet can be grown on many types of soil, including the poorer soil of the plateaus. It even grows well in places that are quite dry and rather cool.

G/E ←

Rice is entirely different from millet in its requirements. Rice grows best in

Stress:
1. China has been faced with the problems of a shortage of land suitable for farming and a rapidly growing population.

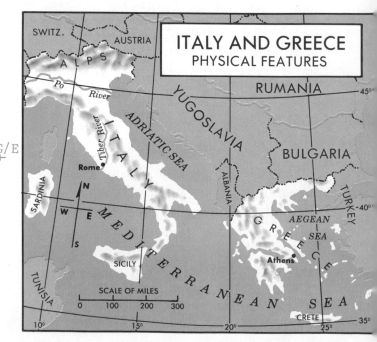

ITALY AND GREECE
PHYSICAL FEATURES

Stress:
1. Both Athens and Rome had a
   shortage of fertile land.

find Rome and make similar decisions about the land surrounding it. Why might it be difficult to farm there?

Although Athens and Rome were centers of early civilization, the nearby farmers could not meet their needs for food. The soil in the surrounding areas was thin and rocky. Furthermore, Greece and the southern part of Italy have very long, hot, dry summers. Except in those places where farmers could irrigate their fields, they produced very little surplus food.

See #1 above. E/G ←

Land-ownership and use In both Greece and the Roman Empire, much of the farmland was divided into large estates owned by wealthy people who did not have to farm for a living. One of the main crops raised on the estates in Greece was olives. These were not raised by the small farmers who had neither the time nor the money to grow olives.

S/E ←
P/E →

The government of Greece wanted to help the small farmers get started in raising olives to sell. For this reason, the government sometimes made loans to farmers in order to encourage the planting of olive trees. They were expected to repay the loans from money earned by selling surplus olives and olive oil. Refer to the picture on this page. What activities are being carried on to prepare olive oil?

S →
See #2 below.
E ↔

In the Roman Empire, which included vast amounts of land, large estates were quite common. As new lands were con-

Ancient Greeks preparing olive oil

quered and added to the empire, the government sold the land to anyone who would farm it and pay a tax by giving the government part of the crops grown on it. Only the wealthy could afford to buy and farm this land.

Some of the work of farming the large estates of both the Greeks and the Romans was done by slaves. Many of the slaves came from Asia Minor and Africa where they were captured when their homelands were conquered.

See #3 below.

Some of the land of both Greece and Rome was owned by farmers who worked their small pieces of land. Farmers in the area around Athens grew grain for food for themselves and their livestock, and grapes for wine. Farmers in Italy produced such fruits as apples, pears, and peaches. They learned vege-

2. Economic growth was encouraged by the government in Greece and in the
   Roman Empire.
3. Slaves were used as laborers in Greece and in the Roman Empire.

161

Stress:
1. Large plantations drove many small farmers out of business in the Roman Empire.

table farming from the people of Egypt and the people from the area once known as Mesopotamia.

Many of the farmers of the Roman Empire could not afford to own even small amounts of land. Often they took jobs offered them by owners of the large estates who needed workers. This need S/E became very great during the time of the *Pax Romana* when few new lands were being conquered and few prisoners were taken to be slaves.

To meet the need for workers, many peasants agreed to work on the estates, giving a part of their crops to the landowners. The peasants were allowed to S/E keep the rest of their crops and sell them as they wished. This system was followed for centuries. What advantages and disadvantages can you see to both landowner and peasant?

Decline of large estates By the third and fourth centuries A.D., many of the large estates of the Roman Empire were broken up and sold to farmers. The farmers who were able to purchase the small pieces of land had neither the money nor the workers to carry on large-scale farming. As a result, Rome could no longer purchase the food it needed without going to far-distant Roman provinces. The demand for their crops helped make the provinces the leading centers of agricultural production. This put a greater strain on the Roman transportation system because products had to be brought long distances to Rome.

See #1 above.

Think for Yourself

What would probably happen to the food supply of your community if all its transportation system broke down at the same time?

*2. In what ways may geography influence social and economic activities?

PRODUCERS OF GOODS AND RAW MATERIALS

Indian craftsmen Have you ever tried to make something out of metal by yourself? If so, you know the importance of having the right materials, of heating them properly, and of being a skillful craftsman. Centuries ago Indian craftsmen worked with brass much as this man is doing. They would expect someone to buy their metal goods so that they could have money to buy other goods. E

The basis of early Indian industry

Stress:
1. Skilled craftsmen in India produced products for sale or trade with other people.

Stress:
1. Craftsmen in India formed social and
   economic groups called guilds.

Iron Column of Delhi, India

guilds also were social groups. See if you can think of any modern groups that operate like a guild.

The craftsmen took great pride in their work. Through the guilds the workers improved their skills and left many lasting monuments. One example is shown in this picture of the Iron Column of Delhi which was built over 1,600 years ago. The column is twenty-four feet high and weighs over six tons. What does an object like this tell us about the skills of the people?

Workers in government-controlled industries Along with goods produced by craftsmen, India had goods produced by groups of workers hired by the government. Their job was to produce certain materials or products. For example, under the Maurya Dynasty the government controlled many of the iron mines and hired workers to mine ore. The government also owned workshops where spinning and weaving were carried on. It hired craftsmen and trained people to work in these workshops. The manufacture of weapons was controlled by the government. It determined the numbers and kinds of weapons to produce and the ways in which they should be distributed. What advantages and disadvantages can you see in the control of certain industries by the government?

See #2 below.

Chinese craftsmen As in India, many of the goods of China were produced by craftsmen. Like the Indian craftsman,

was the individual craftsman. A small village might have had only one craftsman or specialist. The larger towns would have had several.

The craftsman's workshop was also his home. He sold the products in a space in front of his home. The individual craftsman was the producer, the advertiser, and the salesman for his products.

The time spent in selling the products limited the amount of time a craftsman could spend producing them. Soon the task of getting goods from producers to consumers was taken over by traders.

Craftsmen as well as traders formed cooperative groups which were called **guilds.** The pottery makers had their guild, the metalworkers had theirs, and so on. The purpose of the guilds was to set standards for the products and preserve the traditions of the craft. The

See #1 above.

2. The government of India encouraged economic growth and regulated production of certain products.

Stress:
1. Chinese craftsmen were skilled metalworkers over 3,000 years ago.

See #1 above.

the Chinese craftsman took great pride in his work. Many of the Chinese were metalworkers and showed great skill in working with bronze and iron. Bronze, which came into general use in China over 3,000 years ago, was used for weapons, tools, and chariot fittings. Many items had very elaborate designs such as the bronze swords and daggers which are shown in the picture below.

The Chinese were very skilled at woodworking. Wood was used more often for building purposes than were brick or stone, so carpentry skills were highly developed. In addition, furniture making reached great heights during the time that the Han Dynasty was ruling China over 2,000 years ago.

A government-controlled industry in China An industry which was to bring great wealth to China was the silk in-

Bronze daggers and swords from China

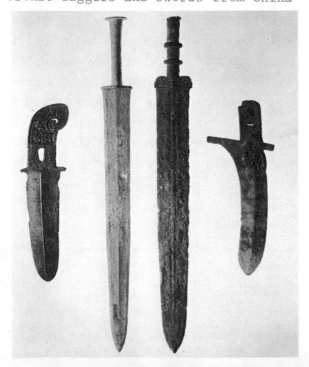

dustry. The exact date when silk was first produced is not known, but it is thought to have been produced in China for over 3,000 years. At that time the silk was considered suitable only to be worn by nobles.

The government controlled the production of silk, possibly to keep the supply somewhat less than the demand. In what way would this policy affect the price of silk? The government also refused to allow anyone to take silkworms or mulberry trees out of the country. This was a crime that was punishable by death. What disadvantages do you see for other countries in this policy?

See #2 below.

Workers of Greece and the Roman Empire As the Western societies of Greece and the Roman Empire expanded their territories and cities grew, there was a greater demand for goods. This demand led to the development of many industries. Many people living in Greece and in the Roman Empire worked in large-scale industries. However, many people also worked as craftsmen. Many industrial methods were borrowed from the Eastern countries that Greece and the Roman Empire had contacted through trade. For example, glassmaking had been learned from the Egyptians and Syrians.

See #3 below.

In Greece crafts such as pottery making, glassmaking, and metalworking were handed down from father to son. Athenian parents were required by law

2. The Chinese government controlled the silk production and trade.
3. Increased demand for goods led to increased production in Greece and Rome.

Stress:
1. Increased production and trade led
   to the specialization of labor.

to teach their sons a trade. What trade is this boy learning from his father? The law stated that children did not have to support their elderly parents if their parents had not taught them a trade.

S
←

In both Greece and the Roman Empire, mining was an important industry and many workers had jobs in the production and distribution of minerals. The mines both of Greece and the Roman Empire were owned by the government and rented to operators who often used slave labor. Some men made their living by buying slaves and renting them out to mine operators. The slaves who worked in the mines had difficult and dangerous jobs. They were often treated very badly by the mine operators.

P/E
←

Boy learning to make pots in ancient times

Roman candleholder made of bronze

Both the Greeks and the Romans had highly developed methods of working with metals. The coins that the Greeks produced were 98 per cent pure silver. The Roman candleholder shown here is an example of their highly developed skills. See if you can decide what some of the skills of the metalworkers must have been.

A
→

See #1
above.

Other workers Since both Greece and Rome had colonies and depended greatly on trade, shipbuilding became an important industry. The designers of ships experimented with different styles trying to improve the ships they built. Much work was done to improve the

E/G
→

2. Increases in trade led to improvements in means of transportation.

165

For Teaching Helps, see page T64.
Stress:
1. Surplus goods were traded for other goods needed by the people.

harbors of the major ports of the Roman Empire. What kinds of jobs were probably required of workers in and around the harbors?

Many workers had jobs in the building trades. Bricklayers and stoneworkers E/S were in demand for the many public buildings that were constructed. Both the Greeks and the Romans used slave labor for many projects, such as the building of aqueducts.

See #1 above. In Greece many of the common textiles, such as those made of wool, were produced in the home. The woman shown in the picture is using one of the methods used by the women in Greece over 2,000 years ago. Many women who produced textiles at home hired helpers or used slaves to produce E/S a surplus of woolen textiles that could then be traded for other goods that were needed.

Slaves and freemen The Athenians felt that the citizens of Athens should have as much free time as possible to take part in government. They also felt S/E that they should devote their time to the arts, music, and drama. In order to achieve this spare time, the Athenians forced slaves to do the hard work required in producing goods.

In Athens there were a number of freemen who were not allowed to be citizens because they had been born in a foreign country. These men often ran the businesses of Greece. S

Greek woman spinning thread

The Roman system of production depended greatly on slave labor. When Greece was taken by the Romans, many of the Greek artists, musicians, and doctors were forced to become the slaves of wealthy Romans. Slaves who were educated were kept as private teachers. The less-educated slaves were forced to work in the mines or on the estates.

Think for Yourself

Would you expect slaves to produce more or less goods in a day than the same number of other workers would produce? Why?

Stress: For Teaching Helps, see page T65.
1. Surplus production was the basis for most trade.
2. Communication and transportation are needed if trade is to grow.

TRADE AND COMMERCE

Trade within a country In the Eastern societies of China and India, the people of different villages carried on trade with one another. One village might have had a surplus of grain but a shortage of salt. A neighboring village might have had a surplus of salt but a shortage of grain. In very early times, a great amount of trade between these two villages went on. The people of each village would be willing to trade their surplus products for products which another village had. What advantages can you see in using the barter system? What disadvantages can you see? In early times, transportation among villages was poor. There was little communication among villages.

See #1 above.

Trade within either China or India did not really grow on a large scale until communication and transportation improved. These improvements were not possible when each local community governed itself. When the villages became united under one strong government, the villages became more closely tied together. Then trade increased. In China, for example, it was not until the early empires grew that trade grew. People who lived in the interior of China learned that people on the coast had salt and iron to trade. Along with communication, how would better transportation help to increase trade within a country?

See #2 above.

Trade with other countries The people of the Eastern societies of India and China began to trade with other countries after the third century B.C. In China, when the Han Dynasty got larger by taking land to the west, trade with Europe grew. The Chinese had silk to sell. They found buyers among the rich people of Europe who wanted this fine material. Traders from Persia, which is present-day Iran, controlled the silk trade. They served as the link between the producers and the consumers of the silk. This control lasted until the sixth century A.D. Then the Roman Emperor Justinian sent two monks to China as spies. They risked their life to smuggle silkworm eggs and some seeds of the mulberry tree out of China and into Europe by hiding them in hollow bamboo canes. The Europeans were then able to raise silkworms, produce raw silk, and make silk textiles on their own without having to depend on the Chinese.

By the second century A.D., China and India were trading many products with other countries in Asia. They were also trading with Western countries in Europe. Besides products being exchanged, what other benefits do you think came out of this trade?

See #3 below.

A money system develops The barter system worked as long as the people doing the bartering could use the prod-

167

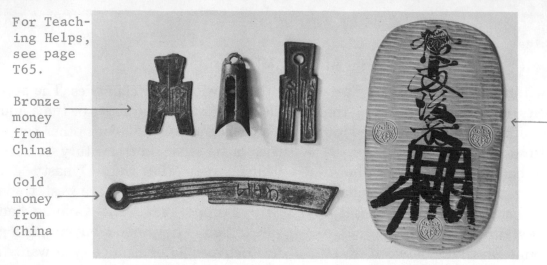

For Teaching Helps, see page T65.

Bronze money from China

Gold money from China

Gold money from Japan

Examples of money used in China and Japan

See #1 below.

ucts that were being traded. However, when a country became involved in foreign trade on a large scale, a more efficient system was needed. This system involved putting a money value on goods. Then a price could be placed on the goods and they could be exchanged for money rather than for other goods. China and India began coining money, as their foreign trade grew. The metallic pieces shown in the picture were used by the Chinese. Do you suppose that any of these coins were ever used in Europe as well as in Asia? Why?

Trade routes Beginning in very early times, camel caravans were used to transport goods between the countries of Europe, Asia, and Africa. These caravans sometimes had as many as 5,000 camels. Following the caravan routes shown on the map at the top of page 169, traders would bring silk, precious stones, cotton, and spices from Asia.

The caravans traveled great distances across several countries. Often the rulers of these countries levied a heavy tax on the products being transported.

On the map at the top of page 169 find Byzantium (bi zan'shi əm), Antioch (an'ti ok), and Damascus (də mas' kəs). Why were these places so well known by the leaders of caravans? Locate the Great Silk Route. Where did the Great Silk Route begin and end?

The caravan leaders had to sell the products to merchants who would then sell these goods to traders from Europe. What do you suppose happened to the prices of these goods when they finally reached the consumers?

As you can see by the map at the top of the next page, part of the trade routes involved travel by sea. Sailors found that if they sailed to the East during the monsoon season, they could take advantage of the monsoon winds which speeded their journey.

Greece trades with its colonies There was a great deal of trade among the villages both in Greece and in the Roman

Stress:
1. The use of money allowed goods to be priced and exchanged.
2. Cities developed along important trade routes.

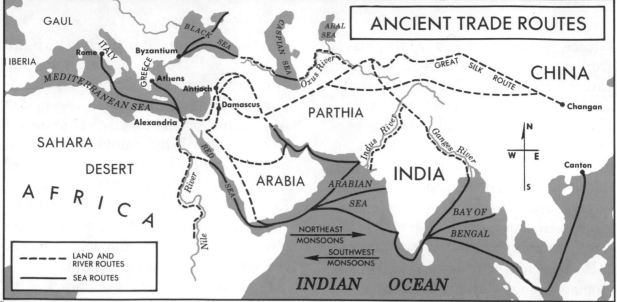

ANCIENT TRADE ROUTES

See #1 above.
See #2 below.
See #3 below.

Stress:

1. Trade among Greek and Roman villages was usually carried on through barter.

Empire. This trade was usually carried on by the barter system. Local villagers would exchange their surplus products for the surplus products of another village.

Over 2,500 years ago the Greeks sent groups of people to settle in different areas of the Mediterranean. Refer to the map at the bottom of this page. Were most of the areas settled by the Greeks near the coast or inland? Why do you suppose they chose to settle there?

The Greek colonies sent raw materials and foods back to Greece. For example, both Asia Minor and Sicily produced a surplus of grain which was shipped to

2. Greek colonies were established near the sea and reached by ship.

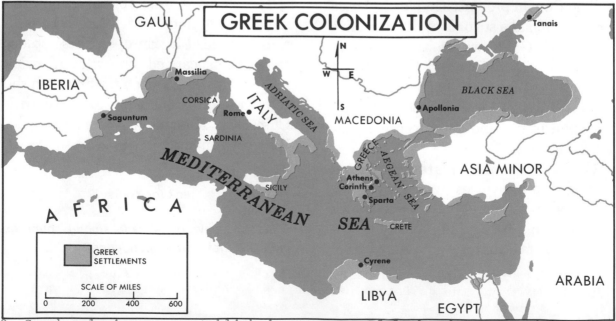

GREEK COLONIZATION

3. Greek colonies were established as sources of food and raw materials.

For Teaching Helps, see page T65.
Stress:
1. Roman provinces supplied the empire with food, raw materials, and other goods.

Greece. Sicily produced a surplus of fruit and of cheese which was also shipped to Greece. The Greek colonies would then buy products from Greece—mostly wine, oil, minerals, and works of art. After buying these products, the colonists would then sell some to people in the interior. These people would then have a desire for more products from Greece. How would this desire affect the Greek economy? Would increase production.

Rome trades with its provinces The Roman Empire depended most heavily on trade with its provinces. Having such a scattered empire gave the Romans a variety of products. Refer to the map on page 136 to locate the Roman provinces. What types of transportation must have been used as links among the provinces? Trade among the provinces centered around three types of products —food and wine, raw materials, and manufactured goods.

See #1 above.

The Roman provinces in North Africa and Spain had a surplus of figs and olive oil to sell. Gaul—which is present-day France—Asia Minor, and Syria had a surplus of wine. And Spain, Egypt, and the provinces of the Black Sea area had a surplus of fish and meat to use in carrying on trade.

One of the raw materials traded among the provinces was timber for building purposes. This was available from North Africa, Gaul, and Asia Minor. Other raw materials obtained from

trees included tar and pitch, which are called **naval stores.** Naval stores are used in shipbuilding. Forests growing in the land along the Danube River and in Asia Minor produced great amounts of naval stores. Why would timber and naval stores be so important to Rome?

The third type of products that the Romans purchased was manufactured goods. In the cities of the Roman Empire were produced fine metal goods, pottery, textiles, and perfumes.

Foreign trade Besides trading with their own colonies and provinces, both Greece and the Roman Empire carried on trade with other countries. They purchased silk, cotton, precious stones, and spices from India and China.

See #2 below.

The Romans also traded with the Germanic tribes to the north. The Germanic people were willing to trade animal hides and slaves in return for iron weapons and tools.

The Romans were able to trade their metal goods and fabrics for raw materials produced in Europe. These trades were often carried on without using money. However, when trading with the countries of the East, especially with China, the Romans had to pay in gold. Why do you suppose this was so?

Think for Yourself

In what ways does trade among countries increase their interdependence?

Things to Do

See
page 158.
1. Make a modern map of India today using papier-mâché, flour and water, or other materials. On your map include major land features such as mountain ranges, plains, rivers, cities, and so on. It is suggested that you paint your map, using a different color to show the different land and water features.

See
page 160.
2. Construct a small display showing the terracing of land as carried on by farmers in China.

CLASS PROJECT—PART 4

Each group should now be prepared to present an activity showing information discovered about family life.

The class may want to take time, after all the activities have been presented, to summarize what it has learned about family life in India, China, Greece, and the Roman Empire. This question may guide you in making the summary: What new information did you learn about a nation's family life from observing and listening to the various group activities? As a final step in the class project, your class may evaluate the group activities by answering this question: If the group activities were to be presented again, what suggestions do members of the class have to improve the presentations?

(This page is a review of Unit 4.)

Have the pupils find each of the review words in the unit. For each word, have them answer such questions as these:

Checkup Time

1. How was the word used in the book?
2. How might you use the word yourself?

For question 2 above, encourage the pupils to use each word in a social science context.

Review Words

aqueducts	joint family	patricians	reincarnation
bureaucracy	mandate	*Pax Romana*	republic
caste	monsoons	plebeians	terracing
closed society	ostracism	provinces	tyrants
direct democracy	panchayats	rajah	untouchables

Review Questions

Typical answers only.

Social Science Facts

1. What are some similarities among Indian societies of today and of the past? (126, 128) Caste system, Hinduism.

2. What religion helped to continue the rigid class system of India? (128) Hinduism.

3. What was a major difference in the way the city-states of Athens and Sparta attained their wealth? (135) See bottom margin.

4. What change came about in Roman government due to the influence of the farmers and craftsmen? (145) Plebeian's assembly.

5. What did government leaders of India do to help improve the lives of their people? (150-158) See bottom margin.

6. What people produced goods and raw materials in China, India, Greece, and the Roman Empire? (162, 163, 166) See bottom margin.

7. As foreign trade developed, what system of placing a value on goods replaced the barter system? (167-168) Money system.

Social Science Ideas

1. Why are some American customs today very similar to American customs of the past? Traditions handed down.

2. How can religion affect the social classes that people form? See bottom margin.

3. Why do countries often develop different methods and ways to attain economic wealth? Based on their resources.

4. How do people of our country work together to bring changes to our system of government? Protests, voting, lobbying.

5. Why do the people of our country today often need certain kinds of government services? No longer self-sufficient.

6. Why does producing goods and raw materials depend upon people with many different skills and abilities? See bottom margin.

7. Why is it necessary for our country, in carrying on trade activities, to determine a money value for its goods? More efficient than barter system.

3. Athens-trade; Sparta-conquest.
5. Care for orphans and aged, postal system, jobs, irrigation projects, roads.
6. Craftsmen and slaves.

2. Religion can enforce class system.
6. Different jobs necessary to produce greater variety.

Test Yourself

On your own paper, write your answer to each question.

Test 1 Social Science Words

Which words below name social classes in Roman society?

1. patricians
2. rajah
3. plebeians
4. tyrants

Which words below name types of governments?

5. direct democracy
6. panchayats
7. republic
8. mandate

Which words below name a social structure of India?

9. caste
10. closed society
11. joint family
12. bureaucracy

Which word names a technique for leveling land on hillsides?

13. province
14. terracing
15. erosion
16. flooding

Which word or words in ( ) make each sentence below true?

17. A (caste, *Pax Romana*, tyrant) is a certain social class of people in the country of India.

18. Another word for king is (untouchable, rajah, plebeian).

19. Moisture-bearing winds are called (aqueducts, provinces, monsoons).

20. In Indian society the (joint family, untouchables, patricians) ruled the lives of its family members.

Test 2 Facts and Ideas

Which answer to each question below is best?

1. Which of the following names a Hindu religious belief?

   a. belief in a democracy
   b. belief in an open society
   c. belief in a class system

2. How were the city-states of Athens and Sparta similar?

   a. Each developed its own government.
   b. Each had a strong army.
   c. Each rigidly controlled its people.

3. What was the government of Rome just before the Roman Empire called?

   a. bureaucracy
   b. republic
   c. province

Which word in ( ) makes each sentence below true?

4. People of our country (never, seldom, often) need government services.

5. Early craftsmen were very (industrialized, skilled, unskilled).

6. People form (provinces, groups, customs) to help themselves get the things they want.

173

UNIT
5 MAN IN THE MIDDLE AGES

Stress:
1. The Middle Ages was a period of social, political, and economic changes in many parts of the world.
2. During the early part of the Middle Ages, civilizations in Asia were more advanced than were the civilizations in Europe.

Chapters
11. Social Development in the Middle Ages
12. Political Development in the Middle Ages
13. Economic Development in the Middle Ages

3. Europe suffered from invasions and warfare which hindered its development during the first part of the Middle Ages.
4. The Bayeux Tapestry, part of which is shown in the picture, shows events pertaining to the invasion of England in 1066.
*5. In what ways does the picture below show the specialization of labor?

Normans building ships for the invasion of England

Stress:
1. The Middle Ages is a historical term used to apply to a period of time that lasted from A.D. 500 to A.D. 1500.
2. Societies usually change as the result of internal and external forces.
3. Ways of life during the Middle Ages varied from one society to another.
*4. Why do you think historians use the term Middle Ages?

The history of man is a long story of change and development. The period from A.D. 500 to A.D. 1500 provides good examples of how man and his societies have changed to meet challenges.

See #1 above.

Changes in societies have often occurred because of two principal reasons. One reason has been that problems or new conditions have arisen within a society. The second reason has been that a society has been influenced by people with a different way of life.

See #2 above. A/S ←

During the 1,000 years of history covered in this unit, societies in Europe, Asia, Africa, and America changed and developed. Some of these societies, such as those in Asia, reached a high level of learning and accomplishment early in this period. Then, these societies began to decline. Other societies, such as those in Europe, began to reach a higher level of development after A.D. 1000.

A/S ←

There is no way to describe all the changing societies throughout the world. Each had somewhat different social, political, and economic ways of life. These different ways of life were the result of different conditions in each area. Thus, for example, European societies during this period were just beginning to develop strong governments. But in Latin America, some societies had already developed a powerful central government.

See #3 above.

A/G ←

As you study the material in this unit, try to answer these questions.

1. What outside forces caused each society to develop differently?
2. In what ways were various societies similar? Why?
3. In what ways did conditions within each society affect its development?

175

For Teaching Helps, see page T66.
Stress:
1. The continuing nature of the class project. See pp. 193, 208, and 221.

CLASS PROJECT—PART 1

For this class project, develop a panel show like those you have seen on television. The guests on the panel show will answer questions and discuss life in the Middle Ages.

The first step is to divide your class into three groups. One group will be responsible for presenting information about European society. The second group will be responsible for Japanese society, and the third group will be responsible for the Aztec society. Then divide each of the three large groups into three smaller groups as is shown in the picture below. Each of the smaller groups should be ready to talk about the social, the political, or the economic life of its society in the Middle Ages.

As you study Chapter 11, write some questions you want to ask the guests when they appear on the panel show. Questions about the social way of life in each society should be developed first.

2. To understand a society, it is necessary to study its social, political, and economic systems.

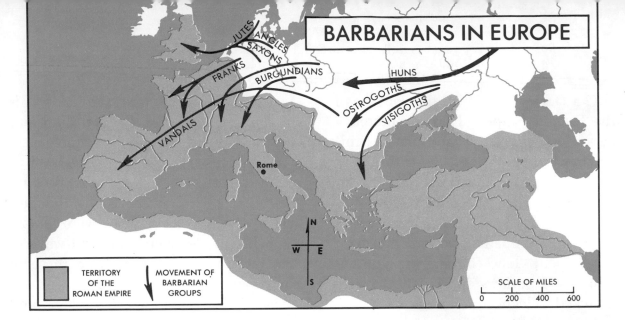

For Teaching Helps, see page T67.

11. Social Development in the Middle Ages

See #1 below.

The map shows the movement of people in Europe after A.D. 350. These people had not, as yet, become civilized and the Romans called them **barbarians** (bär bãr′i əns). As you can see on the map, the Huns came from Asia and invaded Europe. What does the map show the barbarian tribes living in Europe did when the Huns began to invade their territory? Forced their way into the Roman Empire.

At first, the Roman Empire was able to fight off the barbarians. But the Roman Empire was finally conquered. Europe then entered a period of change as a new way of life developed. Historians call this period of change the Middle Ages. It lasted from about A.D. 500 to A.D. 1500.

See #2 below.

H/G

As life in Europe was changing, civilizations were growing in Asia, Africa, and the Americas. In this chapter you will study how some of these civilizations developed and changed during the Middle Ages.

JUST FOR FUN

Make a time line beginning with the birth of Christ and ending at A.D. 2000. Color the portion of the time line that represents the Middle Ages. As you read this chapter, mark the important events of the Middle Ages on your time line.

Stress:
1. Barbarians roamed through much of Europe after A.D. 350.
2. Less civilized barbarians destroyed much of the Roman civilization in Europe.
*3. Why did the civilized way of life decline in Europe after A.D. 350?

177

For Teaching Helps, see page T68.
Stress:
1. The Dark Ages was a period of lawlessness and confusion in Europe.
2. Population declined in Europe during the Dark Ages.

SOCIAL ORDER IN EUROPE

The Dark Ages With the collapse of the Roman Empire, Europe entered a period of confusion. Historians call this first part of the Middle Ages the Dark Ages in Europe. The Dark Ages in Europe lasted from the fall of Rome until about A.D. 800. During this period, people in Europe had no strong central government. Laws often were not enforced and outlaws and invaders freely attacked villages and towns.

See #2 above. As a result of these attacks many farms were destroyed and food became scarce. Disease, hunger, and death were common in many parts of Europe during the Dark Ages and the population of Europe declined. Travel and trade also declined since outlaws often at-

Medieval robbers attacking travelers

tacked anyone who used the roads as is shown in the picture. Do you think our country might face similar problems if our government was destroyed? Why?

Most of these problems arose because many of the German tribes that invaded the Roman Empire were almost uncivilized. Their customs and ways of life were quite different from those of the Romans. At first, powerful German chiefs tried to establish kingdoms and restore peace to Europe. But none of these kingdoms lasted for long. As a result, about 500 years passed after the fall of the Roman Empire before the people of Europe began to enjoy a stable and secure way of life.

A new social order Faced with new problems, the people in Europe had to develop a new way of life. Part of this new way of life was a new social system. This new social system had three social classes. The upper class was made up of the nobility who were primarily warriors and the rulers. The lower class was made up of the peasants who produced the food and other goods for the society. A third class of people were the churchmen—the clergy (klėr′ji). These churchmen took care of the religious needs of the society. Why was there no middle class of merchants and traders?

The development of these three social classes—the nobles, the clergy, and the peasants—happened slowly. But by

Stress:
1. The common people of Europe traded
   their land and freedom for protection.

the twelfth century (A.D. 1100) these social classes were firmly established. It was this type of social system that helped to restore order in Europe.

The nature of the new social system

The large majority of people in Europe were farmers and craftsmen. These people were not warriors nor did most of them own weapons. To get protection from outlaws and invaders, these people turned to powerful warriors for help. In return for this protection, the people gave up their land and their freedom. The warriors became the fighters, the rulers, and the owners of the land. The rest of the people became peasants. They worked the land and did the other jobs needed by the society.

See #1 above.

See #2 below.

See #3 below.

A person's place in the social system of Europe usually depended upon birth. If he was born into a noble family, he was a noble. If he was born into a peasant family, he usually remained a peasant until he died. In a few ways peasants could escape the lower class. One way was by becoming a priest. The second way was by being a brave and successful fighter for a noble. Such a fighter might—through some courageous deed—be made a knight (nīt), the lowest ranking noble.

The life of a noble Almost every nobleman was trained at an early age to be a warrior—a knight. Even many of the nobles who became churchmen were first trained as knights.

Squire training to be a knight

Usually a noble's training was in three stages. At seven years of age, he became a page. During this period the young noble was taught to ride, how to take care of weapons and armor, and to be polite. At fourteen, he became a squire and learned how to fight. The squire also served a knight by taking care of his weapons and by aiding the knight if he was injured. The picture shows a squire learning to use a lance.

When the young noble was twenty-one-years old, he usually became a knight. From then until he died, the knight took his place in the society as a warrior. Brave and skillful knights often gained power and land through wars. In this way a knight might become a higher ranking noble—a count, a duke, or even a king, for example.

2. The warriors in Europe gained wealth and power during the Middle Ages.
3. Usually, a European's social position was hereditary.
4. Most nobles were trained to be warriors (knights).

179

Knights jousting at a tournament

For Teaching Helps, see page T68.
For a class activity, see #1 on page 193.

Many knights also inherited a higher position when their fathers died.

But whatever his rank, every noble was expected to follow the knight's code of life. This code of life was called **chivalry** (shiv′əl ri).

The code of chivalry. Chivalry was a code of behavior for the nobles of Europe. Unfortunately not all nobles followed the code as they were expected to do.

The code of chivalry called for the knight to be loyal, generous, brave, and strong. A true knight was to be a defender of Christianity. He was also expected to defend the poor, the weak, and, of course, women. In addition, a true knight was expected to fight for justice and to defend his country against all enemies.

By about A.D. 1300, the code of chivalry was a strong influence upon the warlike nobles. But it was never a strong enough influence to end their fighting among themselves. Noblemen of all ranks often fought each other in small wars. And when wars were not being fought, nobles sharpened their skills in contests called **tournaments** (tėr′ nə mənts). Such a tournament is shown in the picture. Heavily armored knights often fought each other in these tournaments, and deaths or serious injuries were not uncommon.

Life of the peasants The life of the peasants was quite unlike that of the nobility in Europe. Many peasants were farmers and they were bound for life to the land which they farmed. Most peasants could not leave the land.

Stress:
1. Most nobles in medieval Europe followed a code of behavior called chivalry.
2. Life in medieval Europe was based upon agriculture, and most peasants were farmers who worked for the nobles.

Stress:
1. Most peasants in Europe were bound to the land and under the control of the noble who owned the land.
2. Semifree peasants in Europe were called serfs.

Nor were they free to change jobs, marry, or do many other things without the permission of their lord who owned the land. Usually a lord had control over the peasants who farmed his land. But the lord did not own the peasants and, therefore, the peasants could not be sold to another lord. These semifree peasants were called **serfs** (sėrfs). In what way was a serf different from a slave?

Life in most villages was hard for the serfs. Most of them worked from sunrise to sunset in the fields. A few serfs were skilled in certain crafts and were not farmers. But nearly all serfs were farmers who worked for their lord raising food for the lord and the village. Only on special occasions—such as weddings or holidays—was the serf able to relax. The painting shows some serfs enjoying themselves on a religious holiday. What were some of their ways of enjoying themselves? What are some of these same things that people do today?

See caption below.

The influence of religion After the fall of Rome, Christianity spread throughout much of Europe. The Roman Catholic Church became a powerful force in western Europe under the leadership of the bishop of Rome, the Pope.

To many Europeans who faced the troubles of the Middle Ages, the Roman Catholic Church offered hope of a better life. For example, many Christians believed that life after death in heaven depended upon their being members of

Peasants enjoying a holiday with dancing, eating, and playing a bagpipe

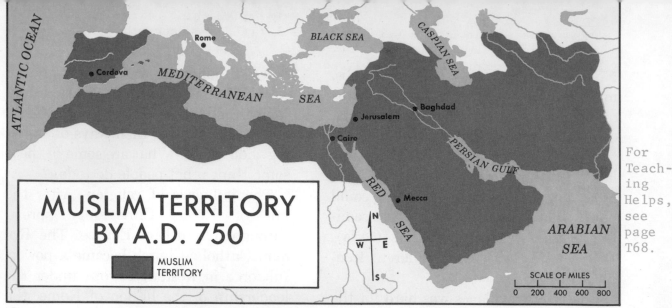

MUSLIM TERRITORY BY A.D. 750

■ MUSLIM TERRITORY

ATLANTIC OCEAN

Rome

BLACK SEA

CASPIAN SEA

Cordova

MEDITERRANEAN SEA

Baghdad

Jerusalem

Cairo

PERSIAN GULF

RED SEA

Mecca

ARABIAN SEA

SCALE OF MILES
0 200 400 600 800

For Teaching Helps, see page T68.

See #1 and #2 above.

See #3 below.

Stress:
1. People in Europe during the Middle Ages were highly religious.
2. All Christians in medieval Europe belonged to the Roman Catholic Church.

the Roman Catholic Church. As a result, many people in Europe during the Middle Ages were deeply religious and tried to lead peaceful lives.

The Roman Catholic Church also helped the people learn new things. For example, some of the clergy in Europe decided to live away from others in religious communities called **monasteries** (mon'ə ster'iz). One of these monasteries is shown in the picture. In these monasteries, the clergy ran schools and produced books. Monasteries also offered medical care for the people. And in some places, the clergy developed new methods of farming which helped the peasants to produce more food. Thus, the monasteries provided many needed services for the society. Why did the monasteries have to provide these services for the people? In your society, who provides the same services as the

monasteries did for Europe in the Middle Ages? Why? Usually the government. Because the nation is large.

A holy war In about A.D. 570 a man named Mohammed was born in what today is Saudi Arabia. During his lifetime he established a new religion— Islam. The followers of Islam—called Muslims (muz'ləms)—believe in one god called Allah.

By 750 Islam had spread from India

A
→

A/S
←

E
←

Monastery at Mont-Saint-Michel

3. The Roman Catholic Church influenced the social system in Europe during the Middle Ages.

Stress: For a class activity, see #2 on page 193.
1. A crusade was organized in 1096 to free Jerusalem from the Muslims.
2. The crusaders came into contact with the more civilized way of life of the
    Muslims.

to Spain. The map on page 182 shows the territory controlled by the Muslims. The city of Jerusalem, which was a holy city to Christians, Jews, and Muslims, was in this territory.

See #1 above.

In 1096, the head of the Roman Catholic Church—Pope Urban II—called for a holy war—a **crusade** (krü sād′). The goal of the Crusade was to free Jerusalem from Muslim control. Thousands of Europeans answered the Pope's call. Many of these crusaders—as they were called—were powerful nobles. The picture shows the crusaders in one of the battles against the Muslims.

Although the first crusaders captured Jerusalem, they were unable to hold it very long. Later crusaders were even less successful and Jerusalem remained in the hands of the Muslims.

However, the various crusaders had an effect upon life in Europe. When the crusaders got to southwest Asia, they learned about the more civilized way of life of the Muslims. They also learned of new foods, textiles, and other goods. What effect do you think this new knowledge had upon the trade between Europe and Asia? Why?

See #2 above.
See #3 below.

After the Crusades, a new social class began to develop in Europe. This new social class was made up of traders, merchants, and craftsmen. As time passed, this new social class—called the middle class—gained wealth and power. By about 1500 a new and more modern way of life had developed in Europe. This new way of life will be discussed in the next unit.

See #4 below.

Think for Yourself

In what ways did the social system help to restore order in Europe during the Middle Ages? Brought stability and rules of behavior.

3. The crusaders learned about new products from the Muslims and this led to an increase in trade with the people in Asia.
4. Increases in trade led to a new social class in Europe.
*5. Why might people trade freedom for protection today?

Members of the Third Crusade landing at Jaffa and battling a Muslim army

For Teaching Helps, see page T69.
Stress:
1. During the Middle Ages, civilizations in Asia were more advanced than were
    those in Europe.

SOCIETIES OF ASIA

Civilization in India In about A.D. 320, shortly before the beginning of the Dark Ages in Europe, a new dynasty gained power in India. This dynasty was called the Gupta (gup'tə) Dynasty after its first ruler Chandragupta I. The Gupta Dynasty lasted for over 150 years. During this time India reached a high level of civilization—a **golden age** —as wise and powerful rulers brought peace to the country. Why might wise and powerful rulers help to bring about a better way of life for their people?

H/P

Knowledge of science and mathematics developed rapidly during India's golden age. For example, the numerals and the decimal system used in our country today were first developed in India. Cement and soap were also discovered by Indians in the Gupta period. These discoveries, and others, were soon adopted by the Arabs who lived in southwest Asia. How might these discoveries have later reached Europe? Trade.

See #2 below.

A

Muslim invasions Unlike Europe, India's way of life changed very little during the Middle Ages. Both Hinduism and the caste system grew stronger under the Gupta and other dynasties. However, many years ago the Muslims began to invade India.

S

Slowly the Muslims conquered most of India. The map on this page shows the Muslim advance. About how many years did it take for the Muslims to con-

H/P

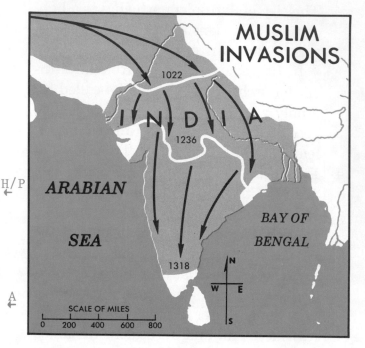

MUSLIM INVASIONS

INDIA

1022

1236

1318

ARABIAN SEA

BAY OF BENGAL

N W E S

SCALE OF MILES
0   200   400   600   800

quer most of India? Why do you think India's civilization declined during this period? Invasions brought warfare and destruction.

The golden age of China The Han Dynasty fell in A.D. 220 and China suffered through a period of confusion for more than 300 years. During this period, various tribes of barbarians—Turks, Huns, and Mongols—entered China and raided the countryside. Finally, in 618, a new ruling group, the T'ang (täng) Dynasty, restored peace in China. Thus, as Europe was going through its Dark Ages, China began to develop a highly advanced civilization.

See #4 below.

Under the T'ang Dynasty—and the

2. Cultural diffusion helped to spread knowledge from Asia to Europe.
3. Civilized life in India changed very little until the Muslim invasions.
4. China developed a highly advanced civilization while Europe was in its
    Dark Ages.

Stress:
1. Chinese achievements spread to Europe and helped Europe's development.

Sung (sŭng) Dynasty which followed— the Chinese entered their golden age. New developments in art and science took place. The few Europeans who reached China during the Middle Ages found a way of life more civilized than the way of life in Europe at the time. Printing, gunpowder, the compass, and relief maps were a few of the Chinese discoveries later used by the Europeans. In what ways did some of these discoveries help the Europeans to expand into the Americas?

Unfortunately, the advanced civilization of China did not last. Mongol invaders from the north overran China about 800 years ago. The constant warfare that followed ended much of China's progress.

Thus, as Europe began to develop a more stable way of life after A.D. 1000, China and India did not. Attacked by invaders, China and India both entered periods of invasion, warfare, and confusion. Europe, on the other hand, was free from serious outside invasion during the last part of the Middle Ages.

Civilization in Japan At about the same time that China was invaded by the Mongols, Japan began to develop. At first, Japanese culture was strongly influenced by the culture of China. But the Japanese culture soon became a mixture of Chinese and Japanese ways of life. The result was a society and a civilization that was similar in some ways to that of Europe during the Middle Ages.

The people of Japan The first people in Japan were a mixture of several types. One type of these early people— the Ainu (ī′nü)—are shown in the picture. No one knows where the Ainu came from originally. They are probably of the Caucasoid race who came to Japan thousands of years ago. Today, only a few of them are left in Japan. They live in several areas set aside for them on the island of Hokkaido (hō′

See #1 above.

See #2 below.

See #3 below.

See #4 below.

Ainu man and wife in nineteenth-century Japan

2. Invasion and warfare led to a decline of the Chinese civilization.
3. At first, culture in Japan was strongly influenced by the Chinese.
4. People of different races settled in Japan.

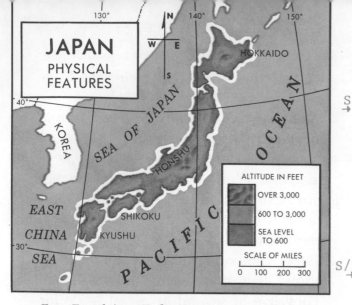

JAPAN
PHYSICAL
FEATURES

130° 140° 150°

HOKKAIDO

SEA OF JAPAN

KOREA

HONSHU

EAST
CHINA
SEA

SHIKOKU

KYUSHU

PACIFIC OCEAN

ALTITUDE IN FEET

OVER 3,000

600 TO 3,000

SEA LEVEL
TO 600

SCALE OF MILES
0 100 200 300

For Teaching Helps, see page T69.

kī′dō). See if you can find Hokkaido on the map of Japan.

See #1
above.

The Ainus were, in time, driven from their land by new people who came to Japan. These new people probably came from Korea and China. They were members of the Mongoloid race, and they were more civilized than the Ainu. These people were the ancestors of the modern Japanese. In what way is the history of the American Indian similar to the history of the Ainu? Both driven from their lands.

The Japanese way of life At first, the Japanese people lived in tribes ruled by powerful chiefs. As these tribes learned to farm and settled in communities, powerful families developed.

See #2
below.

Members of these powerful families became the rulers and warrior-nobles. Members of other families were the workers—the farmers, fishermen, and craftsmen of Japan. In what way was the Japanese society similar to the society of Europe in the Middle Ages?

2. As in Europe, powerful warriors ruled Japan.

186 3. The Japanese believed their emperor was related to the sun goddess.

Stress:
1. Mongoloids came to Japan from Korea and China.

At the top of the Japanese society was the royal family. Every emperor came from this family. The Japanese believed that their emperor was related to the sun goddess. Directly below the royal family were the nobles. These nobles came from a few powerful families who owned most of the land in Japan.

See #3
below.

All the rest of the people in Japan were peasants. Some of the peasants owned their own land and paid taxes. But most of the peasants worked on the land owned by the nobles. These peasants paid rent and were often bound to the land. In what way were the peasants of Japan similar to the peasants of Europe? Did not own land, worked for nobles bound to land like serfs in Europe.

The samurai The picture shows a samurai warrior of Japan. These warriors were nobles who were trained as fighting men from an early age. Study the picture, notice especially the armor.

Samurai warrior in full armor

Buddhist shrine in Japan

How was the samurai's armor different from the armor used by the knight shown on page 180?

See #1 below.
The samurai lived by a code that was, in some ways, similar to the European knight's code of chivalry. For example, a samurai was expected to be brave, loyal, and warlike. The samurai code was called *bushido* (bü′shi dō′).

Unlike the code of the European knight, the samurai's code did not stress romantic love and devotion to women. Instead, the samurai was only expected to be a highly skilled and well-equipped fighting man. His major goal in life was to live and die with his sword in his hand.

Religion in Japan Two major religions were important to the Japanese. One was Shintoism (shin′tō iz əm). The other was Buddhism (bùd′iz əm).

Shinto, which means the way of the gods, was an early religion of Japan. The gods of Shintoism were the gods of nature. Some of the gods and goddesses were the god of the sky, the god of the water, and most important, the sun goddess. Why would the belief that the emperor was related to the sun goddess make the royal family important in the society?

Buddhism was a religion that first began in India. However, Buddhism became most popular in China and Japan. The Japanese saw Buddhism as another way to get good crops and other help from the gods.

Both Shintoism and Buddhism are still practiced in modern Japan. The Buddhist shrine shown in the picture, for example, is still in use today.

Think for Yourself

Why do you think that today some countries of Europe are more advanced than are some countries of Asia?

Stress:
1. Japanese samurai warriors lived by a code of behavior called bushido.
2. Shintoism and Buddhism became the two major religions in Japan.
*3. Why did the religious beliefs of the Japanese make them loyal to their emperor?

187

Stress:
1. Man first came to the Americas over 20,000 years ago.

SOCIETIES OF LATIN AMERICA

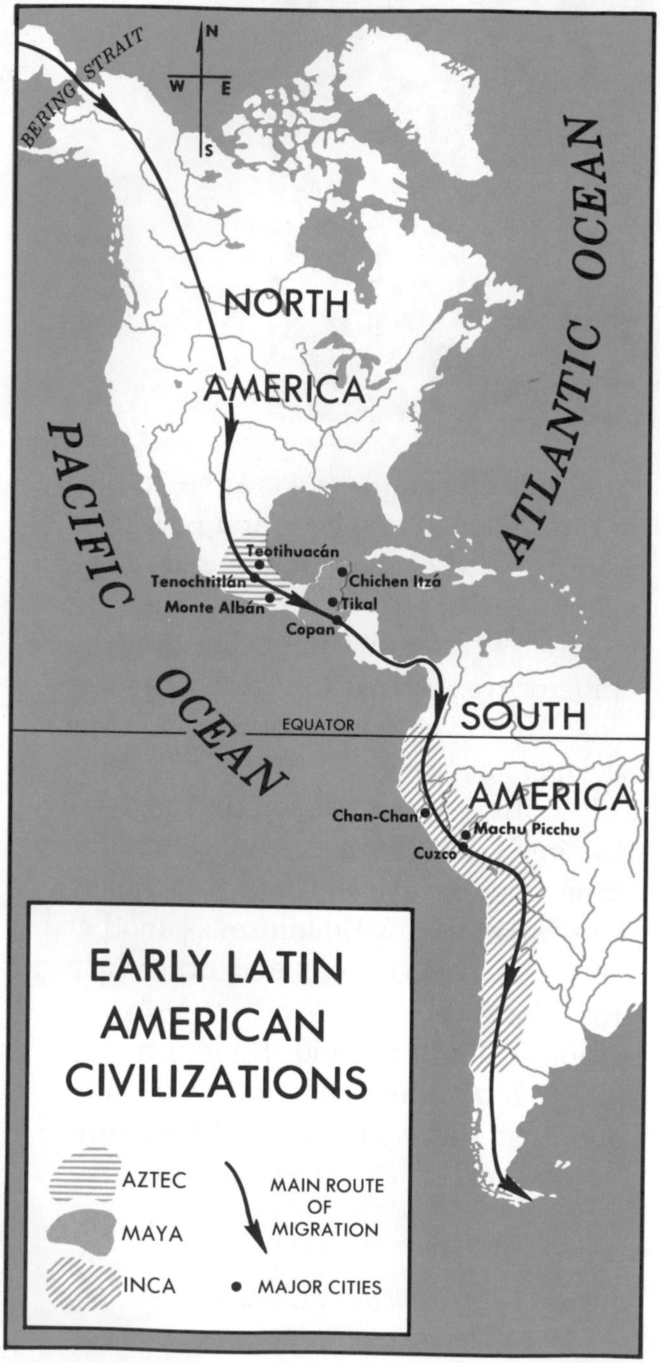

The people of Latin America Study the map on this page. On the map you can see the main route used by early G/A man when he came to the Americas. You can also see the locations of the first major civilizations in the Americas. If you were an archaeologist, to which modern countries would you probably go to locate the remains of some of these early civilizations? Mexico, Guatemala, Peru, and Chile.

The first men may have come to America over 20,000 years ago. Anthropologists believe that these people came A from another continent. Which continent do you think these early settlers came from? Why? Asia--across the Bering Strait.

See #1 above.

These early settlers were nomads who spread out through North and South A America. At first, these people were hunters and food gatherers. But sometime, over 5,000 years ago, a group of these people learned to plant and raise maize (corn). Historians believe that agriculture began first in Mexico. The knowledge of agriculture then is believed to have spread to other people in the Americas.

See #3 below.

The development of agriculture led to the growth of small villages in Latin A America. At first, these villages made slow progress. But not long before the Roman Empire collapsed an advanced civilization had developed.

The Mayan civilization The Mayan (mä′yən) civilization reached its high-

EARLY LATIN AMERICAN CIVILIZATIONS

AZTEC

MAYA

INCA

MAIN ROUTE OF MIGRATION

● MAJOR CITIES

NORTH AMERICA

SOUTH AMERICA

PACIFIC OCEAN

ATLANTIC OCEAN

BERING STRAIT

EQUATOR

Teotihuacán
Tenochtitlán
Monte Albán
Chichen Itzá
Tikal
Copan
Chan-Chan
Machu Picchu
Cuzco

2. America's first civilizations developed in Latin America.

188 3. Agriculture was first developed in America about 5,000 years ago in what today is Mexico.

Stress:
1. The Mayan civilization was America's first civilization.
2. Social scientists have as yet not been able to read all the Mayan writing.

est level between A.D. 300 and A.D. 900. What happened to end the civilization is still unknown.

Archaeologists have discovered the remains of the cities and the religious centers of the Mayan civilization. In their religious centers the Mayan people built great pyramids. One of these pyramids is shown in the picture. What materials were used to build the pyramid? In what way do you think the building at the top of the pyramid was used? Why?

See #2 above.

Unfortunately, social scientists have not learned how to read much of the writing used by the Mayan people. As a result, social scientists do not know all there is to know about the Mayan civilization. Much of what is known about the Mayan civilization comes from artifacts such as the wall painting shown on this page. What can you tell

A

Mayan wall painting of a fishing village

about the Mayan people from this wall painting? Lived in houses, wore clothes, had boats, fished, used fire, had pots.

The Mayan society Social scientists believe that the Mayan society had several social classes. At the top of the society were the rulers, the priests, and the nobles. Below this class were the merchants, traders, and craftsmen. The lower class was made up of farmers.

See #3 below.

Evidence seems to show that the Mayan people were strongly religious. Their gods were gods of nature. The priests, through rituals and sacrifices, tried to please these gods. Apparently some humans were killed—sacrificed—to please the gods. But humans were usually sacrificed only on certain special occasions. As an agricultural people, what nature gods do you think the Mayan people worshiped? Why?

Mayan pyramid temple at Chichén Itzá (in Mexico)

189

For Teaching Helps, see page T70.
Stress:
1. Differences between social classes in the Mayan society may not have been great.

It is not clear whether a Mayan of the lower class could move up into a higher class. Normally, the knowledge of writing was controlled by the priests. But it may have been possible for some members of the lower class to learn to write. If so, they may have been able to rise to a higher class.

A/S ←

See #1 above.

The remains of Mayan houses seem to show that many members of the lower class lived rather comfortably. Therefore, the differences in social classes may not have been too great. Does the way people live in our society reflect their social position? Why?

The Aztec civilization Two other early civilizations also developed in Latin America. The Inca (ing′kə) civilization in Peru was one of these. The other, and most unusual, was the Aztec (az′tek) civilization.

A ←

See #2 below.

Unlike the Mayas, the Aztecs were very warlike and cruel. Almost no other society in history matches the Aztec society for its cruelty.

The Aztec city of Tenochtitlán (tä nach′tē tlän′) was the capital of the Aztec Empire. The picture on this page shows what part of this city may have looked like. Notice the religious pyramids. In what way are the Aztec pyramids similiar to those of the Mayas?

A ←

Tenochtitlán was built where Mexico City stands today. It was an amazing city of homes, temples, and farms built in a shallow part of Lake Texcoco

(tä skō′kō′). Roads and bridges joined the city to the shore.

When Spanish explorers first saw Tenochtitlán they could hardly believe their eyes. One of the Spaniards wrote that some of the soldiers wondered if they were dreaming when they saw the great city. But for all its greatness, Tenochtitlán and the Aztec Empire were still conquered by less than 400 Spanish soldiers and their native allies.

S ←

One reason for the Aztec defeat was the guns used by the Europeans. Another reason was the nature of the Aztecs themselves. For the Aztecs, through their warlike activities, had made many enemies throughout Mexico. In the 1500's these enemies joined the Spanish and helped to destroy the Aztec civilization.

See #3 below.

Reconstruction of "Temple of Papantla" in Tenochtitlán

2. The Aztec civilization was based on warfare and human sacrifice.

3. The Aztec civilization was destroyed by invaders in the sixteenth century A.D.

Woodcutter   Stonecutter   Feather worker

Fisherman   Farm worker

Stress:
1. The Aztec society and social system were government controlled.

Aztec society The society of the Aztecs was strictly controlled by the government. The society was also divided into several definite social classes.

At the top of the society was the ruling class. The Aztec emperors were, in theory, elected by a group of nobles. But, in fact, all the Aztec emperors generally came from the same family. The position, therefore, usually passed from father to son or to some other close relative. All the other members of the ruling class were usually chosen from certain leading families. These officials held the high offices in the government and in the army.

Priests were also members of the upper class in the Aztec society. But within the priesthood there were several ranks. The priests of the highest rank also held a high position in the social system.

Merchants and traders formed a middle class in the Aztec society. Since these people often worked for the government, they often had special privileges.

The lower class was made up of craftsmen and farmers. This lower class contained most of the people. It is unlikely that members of this class were ever able to rise to a higher position. However, members of the lower class could choose different jobs. The painting at the top of the page shows some of these jobs. Study the picture. What are some of the jobs shown in the picture? See captions.

At the very bottom of the Aztec society were the slaves. Some of these slaves were prisoners of war who had not been sacrificed to the gods. Other slaves were Aztecs who had committed crimes and had been sentenced to slavery. And still other people became slaves because they were in debt or sold themselves for a price.

The life of the slave in the Aztec society was not too harsh. Often the

See #2 below.

P/S ←

S/P ←

S →

S ↔

S ↔

2. Members of the upper social class held the high positions in the Aztec government, priesthood, and army.
3. Middle-class Aztecs were merchants and traders, and the lower-class Aztecs were workers.

191

Mictantecutli, the Aztec god of death

The Aztec religion The chief god of the Aztecs was Huitzilopochtli (wē tsē loh pōhch'tlē) the god of war and the sun. It was believed by the Aztecs that Huitzilopochtli needed human sacrifices to please him. The Aztecs believed that unless the sun god received human blood each day the sun would not rise. As a result, the Aztecs sacrificed many human beings every year. Some of these victims were Aztecs. But many of them were prisoners from other areas who were captured in wars. Why might the religious practices of the Aztecs have made them hated by other people?

The Aztecs also believed in life after death. For those who died in battle, there was a special heaven. Others who were chosen by the gods might also go to heaven. The rest of the people went to a gloomy underworld when they died. The Aztec god of the underworld is shown in the picture.

In general, the world was seen by the Aztecs as a place where disaster could strike at any moment. They believed that demons and spirits always threatened men. Do you think the outlook on life by the average Aztec was a happy or an unhappy one? Why?

See #1 above.

slaves were treated as members of the family. In many cases slaves were able to buy their freedom, while others married free persons and became heads of households. Thus, slavery in the Aztec society was not like the slavery once found in the United States. Instead it was more like a temporary condition where freedom could be earned. Often Aztec slaves were freed when their master died.

Unlike European and most Asian societies in the Middle Ages, the Aztecs had a strong central government. In addition, the Aztecs had also developed a strong middle class of merchants and traders. As a result, the Aztec society was very stable and fighting among nobles was not, as in Europe, very common.

Think for Yourself

Why do you think the Aztec society was different from European society in the Middle Ages?

Things to Do

See
page 180.

1. The code of chivalry stressed politeness and kindness toward women. See if you can find pictures in newspapers and magazines of men being polite toward women today. Prepare a bulletin-board display of these pictures.

See
page 183.

2. Using encyclopedias or world history books, draw a map showing the routes of the crusaders during the Middle Ages. Show the map to your class, telling when each of the routes was used.

CLASS PROJECT—PART 2

Now that you have finished Chapter 11, you are ready to begin your first panel discussion. One of your smaller groups is prepared to talk about the social life of the Aztecs during the Middle Ages. The members of this group will be the guests on the panel, and they will answer questions from the class. Members of the smaller groups responsible for the social life in Europe and Japan will also appear on the panel.

It may be more fun if each panel guest is given a part to play. For example, one guest may be chosen to play the part of an Aztec noble. Another guest may be asked to be an Aztec farmer. Models, pictures, and posters may be used by each guest to help to explain his subject.

While studying Chapter 12, members of the class should be developing questions on political life for use in the next panel discussion.

Charlemagne

Yoritomo

Montezuma

Stress:
1. Each civilization during the Middle Ages produced strong and gifted leaders.

12. Political Development in the Middle Ages

See #1 above.

The picture on this page shows some of the important political leaders of the Middle Ages. These were the men who had the power to rule over large numbers of people living in such widely separated areas as Europe, Asia, and Latin America. These men had the power to make laws and to see that they were obeyed. Often they had the right to judge suspected wrongdoers and to punish them if they were found guilty.

See #2 below.

See #3 below.

Like governments of today, governments of early times provided needed services for the people they ruled. What services do governments provide? How are they able to provide them?

In this chapter you will study some of man's attempts to govern himself during the Middle Ages. You will discover some of the likenesses and differences among the types of governments formed by man.

JUST FOR FUN

See if you can find out who the political leaders are of France, Japan, and Mexico today.

2. Governments of every civilization provide services for the people.
3. Governments usually provide such services as protection, justice, laws, system of money, and so on by using their power and money from taxes.
*4. Why do systems of government differ from one country to another?

194

For a class activity, see #1 on page 208.   For Teaching Helps, see page T72.

EARLY LEADERS OF GOVERNMENT

See #1
above.

Unrest in Europe The Roman Empire had been able to absorb gradual barbarian invasions during the third century. However, from the fourth century on, the Roman system of government had begun to break down. The army was no longer a strong fighting force. When new waves of barbarians struck at the Roman Empire, it collapsed.

See #2
below.

With the breakdown of the Roman system of government, far-reaching changes took place. Without one strong government, the empire broke into thousands of small communities. Communication became poor because the Roman postal system no longer operated. Trade slowed as the very fine system of Roman-built roads was no longer kept in repair. Bands of robbers made travel and trade very dangerous. Many traders were killed. What other effects can you think of that might take place with the breakdown of a government?

With the loss of a strong government for the whole empire, local communities had to set up governments of their own. Often the power to govern was given to a chief. Many of the chiefs took large areas of land. They ruled them by choosing officials who they felt could be trusted.

The power and effectiveness of the ruler depended on his skill. Some chiefs, or kings as they called themselves, became very powerful and ruled their land well. Others were weak and their kingdoms were easily destroyed.

A strong leader arises In the eighth century a king named Charlemagne (shär′lə mān) extended his rule throughout what is present-day France, parts of Germany, Austria, and Italy. Look at the map. How far would you have to travel from east to west in Charlemagne's Empire? From north to south?

See #3
below.

Charlemagne's Empire was well organized and efficiently run as long as he lived. However, he did not have a **standing army**—a permanent army of soldiers; nor did he have a fleet of ships to protect his empire. After Charlemagne's

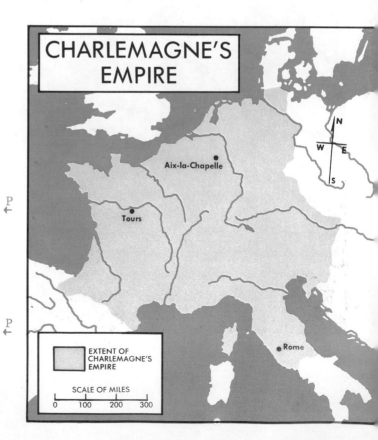

CHARLEMAGNE'S EMPIRE

Aix-la-Chapelle

Tours

Rome

EXTENT OF CHARLEMAGNE'S EMPIRE

SCALE OF MILES

0   100   200   300

2. The breakdown of the Roman government left much of Europe without a central government.
3. Charlemagne controlled much of Europe for a time.

Stress:
1. Charlemagne's Empire collapsed after his death in 814.
2. Confusion and lack of a central government in Europe led to a new political system called feudalism.

Remains of German castle on the Rhine

death in the year 814, his empire collapsed because of weak rulers and the lack of an organized bureaucracy, or group of government officials.

See #1 above.

Parts of Europe had had a short breathing spell during which law and order were maintained. However, by the ninth and tenth centuries, Europe was struck by new invasions. This, along with the breakdown of a large well-run empire, helped bring about a new form of government and a new type of economy. The new political system that developed in Europe was called **feudalism** (fū′də liz əm).

See #2 above.

H/P →

Under feudalism, or the feudal system, political power was held by the nobles who were large landowners. Under the law, all land belonged to the king, but the nobles controlled and ruled the people living on their own pieces of land.

See #3 below.

P/S →

Large castles, like the one shown here, were built by the nobles to give protection against enemies. How would a castle like this keep enemies out?

Unrest in Asia Many of the countries of Asia were going through a period of change in the fifth and sixth centuries. One of the countries in which great political changes occurred was Japan.

See #4 below.

H/P →

In early times Japan was ruled as a tribe is ruled. Certain powerful families controlled various areas. The people who lived on the fertile plain of the region called Yamato (yä′mä tō) eventually

P/S →

196
3. In a feudal system power and land are held by the nobles or the wealthy.
4. Political changes also occurred in Japan.

Stress:
1. During the Taika Reform, Japan developed a government based on the system
   used in China.

HONSHU

SCALE OF MILES
0   100   200

MOUNTAINS

HOKKAIDO

SEA OF JAPAN

HONSHU

JAPANESE ALPS

KANTO PLAIN

Tokyo
Yokohama

Hiroshima

YAMATO PLAIN

Kyoto   Nagoya
Osaka   Nara

SHIKOKU

KYUSHU

PACIFIC OCEAN

tually gained control. The Japanese government at Yamato sent young scholars to China to learn Chinese ways and report back to the government. How does one country learn about another country today?

Japanese bureaucracy In the seventh century, after the death of one of the rulers, a struggle for power took place in the Yamato government. A group of capable young men, aided by the scholars who had studied in China, gained control of the court. These men brought about a great period of change called the Taika (tī kä) Reform. These men hoped to set up a state based on the efficient and well-organized T'ang government in China. See #1 above.

The Taika Reform tried to establish the authority of the Japanese ruler, but the real power to rule was in the hands of a bureaucracy. Although the Japanese borrowed much from the Chinese, they made changes that would fit their own needs. See #2 below.

A strong leader of the Incas The Incas of modern-day Peru were ruled in a very strict fashion. The king, who was called the Inca, inherited his throne and had much control over the lives of the people. The power of the ruler depended on a strong army. Every young man had to go through a period of military training. Do you think this is a good idea? Why or why not? See #3 below.

The Incas conquered new lands and

formed the strongest state. Find the Yamato Plain on the map. Why would it be a good place to settle? Access to water and protected.

Many people from the warring kingdoms of Korea came to Yamato seeking a better way of life. They brought with them their skills in farming and crafts. Why would these people be good additions to the population?

These new people brought with them many new ideas of government which they had learned from the Chinese. These new ideas brought about a sharp division in the Yamato government. There were some people who wished to learn more about the new ways of China. They ran into conflict with the people who did not wish to change. Those who wished to learn more about China even-

2. Political systems, even when copied from that of another country,
   must be adapted to the nature of the society.

3. The Incas were ruled by a powerful king.

197

Stress:
1. The Incas allowed conquered people
   to rule themselves as long as they
   were loyal and obeyed the Incas.

new people came under their control.
The chiefs of the conquered people were
sent to the Inca capital to be trained in
See #1 the ways of the Incas. If they were will-
above. ing to go along with the Incas, they were
allowed to return to their land and continue ruling their people. Why was this
a clever move on the part of the Incas?
What do you suppose would have happened to the chiefs if they had refused
See #2 to go along with the Incas?
below.

The Incas would also send groups of
loyal Incan subjects into the newly conquered areas. They would help rebuild
damaged areas and also teach the people
how to improve their farming methods.

The Incas had many skills to share
with the people they conquered. They
were expert architects. Refer to the picture of the remains of an Incan city
shown on this page. What can you tell
about their skills from this picture?

Rise of the Aztecs By the 1200's a
warlike group of people had moved into
the area around present-day Mexico
City. The Aztecs, as they called themselves, settled first on an island in Lake
Texcoco where they built their capital
city. The Aztecs set out on a program of
military conquest. They built a strong
military force and conquered many surrounding areas.

The Aztecs followed a different policy
toward their conquered people than the
Incas did. The Aztecs believed that in
order to be successful in war their gods

Ruins of Machu Picchu in Peru

demanded human sacrifices. But to get
humans to use in making the sacrifices, it
was necessary to go to war. To win the
war, more human sacrifices were needed.
Eventually, to what would this belief
lead? Constant warfare and human
sacrifices.

A ruler of the Aztecs The Aztec government was controlled by a powerful
emperor. The emperor was advised by a
council made up of representatives from
the leading tribes. The council advised
the emperor on military matters and on
new programs for the country. In addition, the council also had the job of selecting the new ruler. The emperor was
usually selected from one of the powerful families.

Think for Yourself

*Why is a country's policy toward conquered
people so important?*

2. The Incas tried to help and befriend the people they conquered and thus
   reduced the chances of revolts.
3. The Aztecs harshly treated those they conquered, and made many enemies.
*4. Why, in a warlike nation, is the central government powerful?

198

Stress: For Teaching Helps, see page T73.
1. The need for protection and security led to the feudal system in Europe.
2. In return for protection and land, the vassal agreed to aid his lord.

PATTERNS OF GOVERNMENT

The feudal system develops in Europe
The need for protection helped bring about the feudal system in Europe. With the breakdown of Charlemagne's Empire, people had been advised to place themselves under the protection of strong noblemen. However, the people who were being protected had to offer something in return. Kings needed military support, but in return they had to offer something to the nobles.

See #1 above.

A noble would receive a large piece of land called a **fief** (fēf) from the king. In return the noble pledged loyalty and military support to the king. The noble would grant parts of his fief to lesser nobles who would pledge loyalty to him. The king or noble granting the land was called a lord. The noble receiving the land was called a **vassal** (vas'əl). The fief was granted and loyalty was pledged in a sacred and legal ceremony.

See #2 above.

A lord and his vassals had certain duties and privileges. By the feudal agreement a lord was required to protect his vassals. He also agreed to ensure justice for his vassals in the feudal courts. In return the vassal pledged himself to a certain number of days of military service to his lord. A vassal also had to provide payments to his lord when the lord's oldest son became a knight or when his oldest daughter was to be married.

The lord kept a great deal of control over the fief. The lord could control the land until the heir was old enough. If the vassal died without an heir, the lord was free to grant the fief to someone else. What problems can you see arising from this much control of the fief by the lord?

The position of most men in the feudal system was that of both lord and vassal. Refer to the diagram on this page. Whose vassal was Count A? Whose lord was he? To whom did Duke D owe loyalty? What problems might this create for both vassals and lords? Conflicting loyalties.

Feudal courts If a vassal had a complaint or a dispute to be settled, the lord would call all his vassals together. The

Theoretical arrangement of a feudal system

FEUDAL LOYALTIES

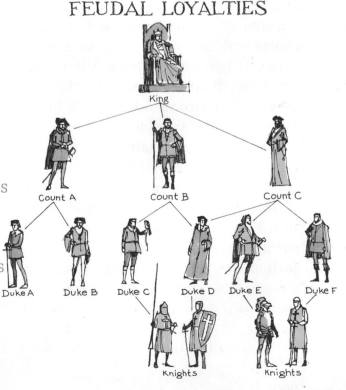

King

Count A   Count B   Count C

Duke A   Duke B   Duke C   Duke D   Duke E   Duke F

Knights   Knights

3. Most nobles in Europe were both lords and vassals.

4. In theory, but not often in practice, the king was at the top of the feudal system and all nobles were his vassals and obeyed the king's orders.

A feudal court in operation

King or lord

Vassals pleading their cases

For a class activity, see page 208.

Stress:

1. Without a central government in Europe to settle disputes, the lords established courts to handle disagreements among their vassals.

See #1 above.

lord would preside over the court and the decisions would be made by the vassals. Refer to the picture on this page. How does this compare with courts in the United States today?

P/S

Some of the customs of the feudal courts did not carry over to modern times. If two vassals had a dispute, the court might order them to a **trial by combat.** The two vassals would fight and the winner was considered to have won his case. Another method used in the feudal courts was **trial by ordeal.** A person accused of a crime was subjected to torture such as having his hand placed in a fire. If the wound started to heal within three days and there was no infection, the person was then judged innocent. The idea behind both of these methods was that if the person was innocent, no harm would come to him. How accurate do you suppose these

See #2 below.

S/P

P/S

E/P

methods were? Why do you suppose these methods are no longer used?

Beginnings of feudalism in Japan

Following the Taika Reform a new capital for Japan was set up at Nara (när′ə). Locate this city on the map on page 197. The leaders attempted to follow the type of government which had been established by the T'ang Dynasty in China. A system of land reform was set up which tried to divide the land more fairly among the people. However, this system did not work because too many exceptions were made. Large grants of land were given to court officials, or nobles, in much the same way as large grants of land were given to nobles in Europe.

The Japanese court officials were freed from having to pay the tax on their land. The laws that increased the wealth and power of the landowners weakened, at

2. Justice in Europe during the Middle Ages was often based on the belief that God would aid the innocent and give them strength.

3. A feudal system developed in Japan.

Stress:
1. Feudal systems weaken or prevent strong central governments because they allow power to be held by various nobles.

the same time, the power and effectiveness of the central government.

Under the rule of a strong emperor in the eighth century, reforms were made in the army. Until that time, the government had forced the peasants to serve in the army. The emperor set up a standing army made up of men skilled in the use of weapons. This was the beginning of a warrior class in Japan which was to achieve power in later times. What advantages and disadvantages can you see in a standing army?

From the eighth to the twelfth centuries, Japan was in the midst of change. The power of the central government was declining. The government was not able to maintain order in the scattered provinces. The large landowners had to look elsewhere for protection and order. Leadership in the provinces came to rest with landowners who were skilled in the use of weapons. These nobles realized the need to organize in some way to pro-

tect their common interests. If the noble was not strong enough he would pledge support and loyalty to one of the stronger military families. How does this system compare with the feudal system that was developing in Europe?

A struggle for power Most nobles of Japan had joined the forces of either of two great military families—the Taira (tä i rä) or the Minamoto (mi nä mō tō). By the twelfth century a full-scale war had developed, involving the warriors of these two families. Refer to the picture on this page. How was warfare carried on in Japan at that time?

At first the Taira family was victorious. Its members married into the emperor's family and took over many court positions. However, the Taira family moved into the capital city and soon lost touch with the provinces. An effective central government was not developed.

The forces of the Minamoto family reorganized under the leadership of Yori-

Japanese warriors in battle used swords, spears, and bows and arrows.

201

For Teaching
Helps, see
page T73.

Yoritomo   Samurai   Yoritomo's brother

Yoritomo meeting with his warriors

tomo (yō ri tō mō). Yoritomo became one of Japan's greatest leaders. His forces defeated the Taira family in a lengthy war. Yoritomo is shown in this picture discussing battle plans with some of his nobles.

Government of the Aztecs The people ruled by the Aztecs were tightly controlled. Aztec cities were divided into smaller areas so they could be more easily ruled. The Aztec council appointed officials for these areas.

See #1
below.

P/S
←

The government supported itself through taxation. Taxes could be paid in food, clothing, animal skins, pottery, or many other items. As the Aztecs took over new areas, they demanded that taxes be paid. The Aztecs kept very careful records of the taxes they received from their provinces. The taxes sent by the provinces provided the Aztecs with

P/E
↔

large amounts of food and materials. One record shows that in one year, the Aztec government received 14,000,000 pounds of corn, 8,000,000 pounds of beans, and 2,000,000 cotton cloaks from its provinces. Besides having been used to feed and clothe the people in the capital city, how else do you suppose these goods were used? For trade.

E
→

See #2
below.

When the Spaniards took over the Aztec Empire, they destroyed many of the written records of the Aztecs. The Spaniards, however, kept the records of the amount of taxes paid to the Aztec rulers. Why do you suppose the Spaniards would be so interested in these records? So that they could also collect taxes.

Think for Yourself

How do governments use their tax money today? To provide services for the people.

Stress:
1. People in the Aztec Empire were strictly controlled by the ruler.
2. Like other governments, the Aztec government was supported by taxes paid by the people.
*3. Why might a conquered people resent paying taxes?

202

Stress:
1. Feudalism helped to create a stable society in Europe.
2. European kings hired professional soldiers and reduced the power of the nobles.
For Teaching Helps, see page T74.

CHANGING GOVERNMENTS FOR CHANGING TIMES

Decline of feudalism in Europe Throughout the time that Europe was without strong central governments, feudalism helped to create a stable society. It brought a type of law and order to Europe. However, feudalism did not last. The kings in many areas of Europe began to gain more power. While many of the nobles were away from Europe fighting in the Crusades, certain kings saw their chance to increase their power through increased taxation of the fiefs.

By the thirteenth century more money was available in Europe. Kings were able to hire soldiers instead of having to depend on nobles who owed them loyalty for their fiefs. In addition, new weapons, such as the longbows and crossbows shown in the picture, helped to create a new type of warfare. The use of gunpowder, which had been developed in China, brought many changes to Europe's methods of warfare.

The knights were no longer as useful as they had been. Instead of depending on knights on horseback, kings now depended on soldiers on foot, armed with new weapons. These soldiers made up the **infantry.** The infantry became a very effective fighting force. What weapons or types of warfare can you think of that have changed methods of fighting?

Kings increase their power The kings of Europe acted in similar ways at different times to make their governments more efficient. In England, for example, a stronger type of government was introduced by William I. Over 900 years ago, William, the ruler of a French area called Normandy, invaded England and was

Painting depicting the Battle of Crécy between the English and French during the Hundred Years' War

Crossbows

Longbows

203

For Teaching
Helps, see
page T74.

Bayeux Tapestry
showing the
Normans con-
quering England

crowned king. The picture at the top shows the invasion force of William the Conqueror. The story of the invasion was woven into the Bayeux Tapestry (bā ū′ tap′ə stri). From this, historians have learned much about the methods and style of warfare in the eleventh century. What can you tell about their weapons and style of warfare from the picture?

See #1 above.

William I was a strong and capable ruler. He made the fiefs smaller so they could be governed more easily. William I also set up a method so he could tax his subjects more fairly. These ideas were used by other kings in Europe as well.

See #2 below.

By the twelfth century the power of the feudal courts in England was weakened. Independent courts were set up. Judges appointed by the king would travel around the country, set up courts, and try cases in them. Trial by jury became an important feature of these courts. In other countries of Europe, courts were set up in a similar way which increased the power of the kings.

Political advances Some kings ruled wisely while others were cruel and harsh. It was during the rule of one such harsh king, King John, that the English were able to make an advance in political freedom. King John had tried to collect illegal feudal payments from his nobles. The nobles revolted and were successful. The picture shows the nobles forcing King John to sign an agreement which gave them certain rights. This docu-

King John signing the Magna Charta

2. During the last part of the
   Middle Ages, European kings
   established strong governments.

204

1. The Magna Charta established certain rights for Englishmen and became part
   of Great Britain's "unwritten" constitution.

ment was known as the Magna Charta (mag′nə kär′tə) or the great charter. The Magna Charta, signed in 1215, provided that taxes could only be levied with the consent of the king's council of advisors. One of the provisions in the Magna Charta was taken to mean that a freeman had the right to a trial by jury.

See #1 above.

By the thirteenth and fourteenth centuries, assemblies that included representatives from many classes appeared in the European countries of France, Spain, and England. The representative assembly that developed in England was called Parliament. Parliament became a very effective force in England. It eventually became the lawmaking body of England. Many countries today have a lawmaking body patterned after the British Parliament. Why do you suppose this is so?

See #2 below.

A new type of leadership in Japan After the war between the two Japanese families, Yoritomo set up a new government in 1192. He was determined not to make the same mistakes that the Taira family had made. An emperor was still on the throne in Japan, but he was not an effective ruler. Yoritomo set up the strongest government that Japan had ever known. He applied the feudal system and loyalty code of the samurai to the entire country. Yoritomo set up military rule for Japan. He took for himself the title of **shogun** (shō′gun), which means commander in chief. The shogun

See #3 below.

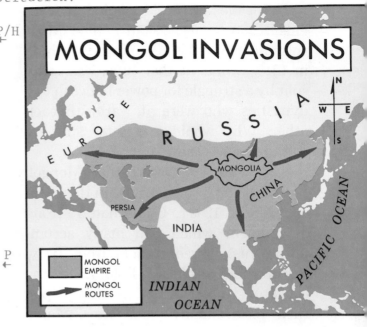

MONGOL INVASIONS

EUROPE · RUSSIA · MONGOLIA · CHINA · PERSIA · INDIA · PACIFIC OCEAN · INDIAN OCEAN

☐ MONGOL EMPIRE
➤ MONGOL ROUTES

had the power to choose government leaders in the provinces. What kind of men would you expect him to choose?

Yoritomo offered large pieces of land and political offices to soldiers in return for their pledge of loyalty. Most soldiers gave their pledge and were well rewarded. Japan had a strong government. Military rule had brought order to Japan, but soon events outside Japan changed this.

Barbarians threaten Asia By the 1200's Asia and parts of Europe were again in danger from invasions. The invaders were called Mongols (mong′gəlz). Look at the map shown on this page. Where did the Mongols come from? What areas of Asia and Europe did they move into?

2. During the fourteenth and fifteenth centuries, a representative legislature--
   called Parliament--developed in England.
3. The emperor of Japan had little power; the actual ruler was the shogun--
   the military commander in chief.

205

Stress:
1. Civil war in China made the country easier to conquer.

See #1
above.

The leader of the Mongols was Genghis Khan (jeng′gə skän′). The Mongols under Genghis Khan invaded China in 1215. China, at that time, was badly split by a struggle for power between two dynasties who were at war with each other. Why would a country split by warfare be easier to conquer?

See #2
below.

Under the rule of another Mongol, Kublai Khan (kū′blī′ kän′), in the latter part of the 1200's, China had a strong government which had many accomplishments. Three traders from Italy, one of whom was Marco Polo, visited the court of Kublai Khan in 1275. Upon their return many years later, Marco Polo wrote of their travels. To Europeans, the writings of Marco Polo were truly amazing. His descriptions of the beautiful cities of China and of the orderly government were quite different from those the Europeans were used to at that time. In what ways might a book such as Marco Polo's affect the people of Europe?

After settling China and Korea, the Mongols looked toward Japan. The Mongols sent fleets to invade Japan in 1274 and again in 1281. Both attempts failed, partly because of the well-prepared defenses. Another factor which helped to defeat the Mongols were the strong coastal winds. The attempted invasion by the Mongols in 1281 was the last time Japan was attacked until modern times in World War II. Why do you think Japan was free from invasion for such a long time?

The feudal system and the power of shoguns in Japan began to decline after the 1300's. Japan continued to have a shogun for many centuries but at times powerful emperors and court officials would gain control.

Europeans invade America As the rulers of Europe became stronger at home, they began to look for ways to increase their wealth and power. One way they could do this was through trade. By sailing west searching for new trade routes to the East, Christopher Columbus discovered the islands of the Caribbean Sea. Because he had been sponsored by the Spanish, Columbus claimed the land for Spain. Other explorers from Spain had reached Latin America by the early 1500's.

See #3
below.

The Spanish **conquistadors** (kon kwis′tə dôrz), or conquerors, led by Hernando Cortes (hər nan′do kôr tez′) landed on the coast of Mexico in 1519. The Aztec leader, Montezuma (mon′tə zü′mə), thinking that Cortes was a god, did not send his soldiers out to do battle. Instead, objects made of gold were sent as gifts to Cortes and he was allowed to enter the capital. The picture on the facing page shows Montezuma receiving Cortes. In what ways do the two leaders seem to be different?

The conquistadors were much impressed by the tremendous wealth of the

2. European travelers found a highly developed civilization in China.
206 3. European kings tried to increase their wealth and power through exploration and trade.

Aztec Empire. Within two years, the small band of Spaniards was able to conquer the Aztecs and send much of this wealth back to Spain. The Incan Empire was conquered in much the same way as was the Aztec Empire. Historians wonder why these wealthy and powerful empires were so easily conquered by the Spaniards.

Collapse of the Aztec Empire The Aztec Empire was not able to withstand the Spanish attack, partly because the people that the Aztecs had conquered chose to fight with the Spanish against their former conquerors. Why do you suppose this was so?

See #1 above.

The Spanish troops were much better prepared for war than were the Aztecs.

They were using guns and cannons while the Aztecs were fighting with bows and arrows.

Perhaps the most important reason for the fall of the Aztecs was their overorganization. Soldiers were trained to take orders, not to give them. When an Aztec leader was killed or captured, no one could come forward to take his place. If the leaders of the government did not make decisions, then no one acted.

E/H

S/P

See #2 below.

See #3 below.

Think for Yourself

Is a democratic society able or unable to avoid problems that occur when a leader is killed or captured? Why?

Montezuma, the Aztec ruler, receiving Hernando Cortes in 1519

Things to Do

See
page 195.
1. From newspapers and magazines, find pictures of political leaders from various countries. For a bulletin-board display, prepare a map of the world. On the map, match the picture of the political leaders with their country.

See
page 200.
2. If possible, interview someone who has served on a jury. Ask him to tell what he was expected to do while on jury duty. Report your findings to the class.

See
page 206.
3. Draw a map showing the route followed by Marco Polo. If you were to follow the same route today, what modern countries would you visit? Show on the map the names of these modern countries.

CLASS PROJECT—PART 3

After you have finished Chapter 12, a second panel discussion can be held. Members of each smaller group dealing with political life in Europe, Japan, or the Aztec society will be the guests.

You and your classmates should once again decide upon the part each guest should play. Since this panel discussion deals with political life in each society, you may want to decide that the guests represent kings, nobles, commoners, and slaves. Each guest should be able to talk about what part he plays in the political life of his society in the Middle Ages. The rest of the class should be ready to ask the guests questions about the political life in each society.

At this point, everyone should begin to develop questions about economic life for use in the last panel discussion.

Medieval peasants in Europe harvesting crops

13. Economic Development in the Middle Ages

For Teaching Helps, see page T75.

See #1 below.

The Middle Ages was a period of economic growth throughout much of the world. However, this economic growth came at different times in different places. S/E →

Asia, for example, enjoyed its best economic growth during the first 500 years of the Middle Ages. Invasions and warfare then reduced this growth. Europe, on the other hand, suffered from invasions and warfare during the first part of the Middle Ages. Then after the E/H ← year 1000, Europe became more peaceful and began to grow economically.

See #2 below.

The picture shows a group of peasants harvesting crops in Europe. It was peasants, such as these, that helped to produce surplus crops which led to the growth of cities in Europe. These cities then led to the development of a new way of life for Europe and, later, for America. Why would the development of a new way of life in Europe affect the development of America? Settled by Europeans.

See #3 below.

JUST FOR FUN

See if you can find out whether or not the people of the Middle Ages used money. If so, see if you can find pictures of some of the coins they used.

Stress:
1. Economic growth in the Middle Ages varied from place to place.
2. Invasions and warfare limited economic growth.
3. The production of surplus crops led to the growth of cities.
*4. Why might warfare today limit a nation's economic growth?

209

For Teaching Helps, see page T76.
Stress:
1. During the Middle Ages, man's primary economic occupation was agriculture.

AGRICULTURE

The importance of agriculture During the period from 500 to 1500, agriculture was man's major economic activity. Civilizations in Asia, Africa, Latin America, and Europe all depended upon farming. In each area, the people developed different crops and methods of farming.

The major crop in Japan and China, for example, was rice. Rice farming in these countries required irrigation. Europeans, on the other hand, raised wheat, rye, and other grains. Irrigation in Europe was far less important because of the type of crops and the climate. In Latin America the Aztecs built their farms upon a lake and developed a different method of farming from those of most other civilizations. The Aztec method of farming is discussed later in this chapter.

In each case, civilizations grew and developed as the people were able to raise surplus crops. The ways in which each civilization went about raising its crops reflected the society.

The manor in Europe Throughout most of the Middle Ages, economic life in Europe was primarily agricultural. By far the vast majority of the people were farmers. Most of the farming was done on land owned by the nobles or by the Roman Catholic Church. The land owned by a noble was called a **manor.** A typical manor normally contained a

manor house where the lord lived. It also had a small village where the common people lived. Most manors also had at least one church. If the manor was owned by a powerful noble, the manor house might be a castle. Why do you think a wealthy noble would need a castle?

The three-field system On many manors in Europe, the farmers planted their crops in three fields. Each year the first field usually was planted in the spring; the second field, in the fall; and the third field was not planted at all. The next year, the first field was not planted. However, the second and third fields were planted. Study the map of a manor on page 211. Notice the three fields which are labeled A, B, and C. Assume that A and B were planted this year and C was not planted at all. Under the three-field system, which fields would be planted next year? Which fields would be planted the year after next?

During the Middle Ages, the peasants in Europe knew very little about how to save or improve the soil. By changing fields each year, the peasants hoped they would not wear out the soil. To make sure that none of the peasants got only poor, worn-out land, each peasant had land in each field.

The fields used for planting were divided into strips. Most of the peasants were assigned certain strips. Often, each

See #2 below.

E/G ←

A/E →

E ←

E/S ←

E/S →

E ←

See #4 below.

2. The ways in which each society produces crops reflects the nature of the society.

210   3. The basic economic unit for production of agricultural goods in Europe was the manor.

4. Farming practices in medieval Europe were often based on custom rather than on scientific knowledge.

For Teaching Helps, see page T76.

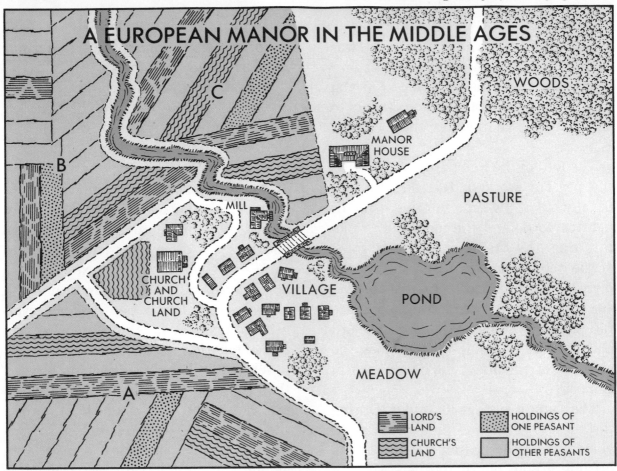

A EUROPEAN MANOR IN THE MIDDLE AGES

WOODS

MANOR HOUSE

PASTURE

C

B

MILL

CHURCH AND CHURCH LAND

VILLAGE

POND

A

MEADOW

LORD'S LAND

CHURCH'S LAND

HOLDINGS OF ONE PEASANT

HOLDINGS OF OTHER PEASANTS

Stress:

1. The three-field system was used on most European manors.

peasant's strip of land was separated from his neighbor's strip of land by a small narrow row of dirt. Every peasant planted the same crop on his strip of land. Thus, for example, all of one field was planted in wheat. The second field might then be planted in rye. Why do you think every peasant had to plant the same crop? Why did every peasant have to harvest the crops at the same time?

See #2 below.

Life on a manor in Europe The life of the average peasant was hard. His workday was usually from sunrise to sunset.

Since most peasants were farmers, they worked in the fields tending the crops. About three days of each week were spent tending the crops on the lord's land or doing other work for the lord. The rest of the time the peasant spent working his land.

See #3 below.

The peasants on a manor paid part of what they produced to the lord. The lord of the manor also owned the mill where grain was ground into flour. He also

E/S ←
E/S →
E/S →

2. Since strips of land adjoined each other, farmers using the three-field system had to plant and harvest the same crops at the same time to avoid traffic in the fields that would damage the crops.

3. Peasants in Europe worked their land and their lord's land.

211

For Teaching Helps, see page T76.
Stress:
1. Nobles in feudal Europe defended their manors from attacks by outlaws and other nobles.

owned the oven where the bread was baked. The peasants had to pay the lord when they used these services. Do you think a lord would allow the peasants to make their own flour in their homes? Why? No--he would lose income.

See #1 above.

The lord of the manor did not work as the peasant worked. Instead, the lord usually spent his time hunting game or fighting to defend the manor. The picture from the Middle Ages shows some of the activities on a manor. Study the picture. What parts of the manor can you identify from the picture? What are the peasants doing? What are the lord and his family doing? What does the picture tell you about life on a manor in Europe?

See captions below.

The manor system in Japan During the T'ang Dynasty in China, land was divided among the peasants. Thus, China became a land of free farmers working their own land. The Japanese tried to adopt the same system, but it did not work as it had in China.

At first, each Japanese family received a certain amount of land. The taxes on this land were heavy and were paid to the government. The noble landowners in Japan did not like having their land given to the peasants. Nor did the nobles want to pay taxes on the land they owned. By bribing government officials, and through other ways, many nobles were able to stop paying taxes on their land. This meant that the peasants who owned small farms had to pay even heavier taxes. Was this Japanese system of taxation fair? Why?

See #2 below.

When the Japanese peasants learned that the land controlled by the nobles was not taxed, many of them turned their land over to the nobles. In this way, the nobles in Japan gained large amounts of land which became manors. In return for having no taxes, the peas-

Fifteenth-century drawing of noble, peasants, and manor in Europe

Manor house→

Tending animals

Mill

Nobles and family hunting

Peasant plowing

2. Taxation forced some farmers in Japan to give up their land to the nobles.

Stress:
1. Japanese nobles formed powerful
   manors and ignored the rules of
   the central government

ants paid rent and did work for the lords of the manors. Usually the peasants' rent and work was less than the peasants paid when they were taxed by the government. The lords of the manors hired warriors and ignored the government. As a result, many manors in Japan became independent areas controlled by powerful nobles.

See #1 above.

Life on a manor in Japan Life on a manor in Japan was different from life on a manor in Europe. The picture shows Japanese farmers at work in their rice fields today. Compare this type of farming with European farming shown on page 212. In what way does rice farming differ from the way farming was done in Europe in the Middle Ages? Why was irrigation so important on Japanese manors? Why would the need for irrigation cause the Japanese farmer to cooperate with his neighbors?

See #2 below.

No two Japanese manors were exactly alike. But most of them were similar in some ways. For example, each manor in Japan had its rice fields. Around these rice fields was dry land. On the dry land there were the houses of the peasants. Beyond the dry land was **wasteland**— land that was not farmed. This wasteland went out as far as the next manor or a natural boundary. As the population of a manor grew, the wasteland slowly was turned into more rice fields.

Some of the rice fields and the dry land were used only by the lord. The

Farmer in Japan farming as his ancestors did in the past

lord's land was farmed by the peasants. The rest of the land was farmed in individual plots by each family. Part of the crop was paid to the lord as rent or taxes. In what way was the Japanese manor similar to manors in Europe? In what way was the Japanese manor different?

Aztec farming Farming in Latin America varied from area to area. But the most unusual, and perhaps the most interesting method of farming, was developed by the Aztecs.

The center of the Aztec civilization was the city of Tenochtitlán. This city was built, as you know, in a shallow area of Lake Texococo. To farm in an area covered by water required new methods. Thus, the Aztecs actually had to build farmland in the lake.

See #3 below.

The method of building and farming land in the water is called the **chinampa**

2. Rice required irrigation systems which, in turn, led to cooperation
   among farmers in Japan in their efforts to conserve and distribute
   water.

3. The Aztecs developed new farming techniques to solve the problems
   presented by their environment.

213

Canal   Chinampa system   Reed wall

(chi nam′pə) **system.** People who go to Mexico City can still see this type of farming in the famous floating gardens.

The *chinampa* system of farming is shown in the picture on this page. Aztecs built the strips of land by first digging canals through the marshland. Walls were built and the reeds and the mud from the canals were piled between the walls. Mud from the lake bottom was then added until strips of land about 300 feet long and about 20 feet wide were completed. In this fertile soil, the Aztec farmers raised their crops. The Aztec farmers then used canoes to reach and farm their land. Study the picture of the *chinampas.* Why do you think the Aztecs planted trees along the strips of land? To hold soil in place.

On their *chinampas*, Aztec peasants were able to raise about seven crops a year. These crops, of maize and vegetables, supported a city of more than 200,000 people. In addition, surplus crops were also used for trade. ⟩ See #1 below.

The *chinampas* were farmed by peasants—the lower class in the Aztec society. Often, each peasant family controlled a certain section of farmland. Taxes on this land were paid to the government. Unlike the Japanese or the European farmers, the Aztec farmers were controlled by the government and not so much by individual nobles. In ⟩ See #2 below. what ways did the economic system of the Aztecs reflect their society? Why?

Think for Yourself

Why do you think the Aztecs did not develop manors similar to those in Europe and Japan?

E →

G/E ←

P/S →

Stress:

214

1. The chinampa system enabled the Aztecs to raise surplus crops to support their cities and for use in trade with other people.

*2. In what ways were the manor systems in Europe and Japan the response to new conditions?

For Teaching Helps, see page T77.
For a class activity, see #2 on page 221.

TRADE AND COMMERCE

Technology During the Middle Ages, Europeans began to use improved tools. E/S The picture shows some peasants with some of the tools they used in farming. What tools are they using? Which, if any, of these tools are still used today?

Improved plows began to make it possible for the peasants to produce more crops. Also, as the peasants learned to E/S use the three-field system, farm production increased. This increase in production helped to support the growing population of Europe. In addition, surplus food meant that more people could do jobs other than farming. Slowly, manors throughout Europe began to produce more crops and other goods. Why did surplus crops lead to more production of other goods? Freed people from farming for other jobs.

See #2 below. As you have learned in Chapter 12, feudalism began to bring peace and a more stable society to Europe after 1100. At the same time, people began to produce more goods. As a result, trade began to increase throughout much of Europe. Why might peace, a stable society, H/E and an increase in population have led to an increase in trade in Europe?

The growth of trade in Europe Even during the Dark Ages, some trade among people in Europe and other areas had continued. But this trade was very limited. Traders and merchants, for protection, often traveled in caravans.

After the Crusades, the people in Eu- E

Medieval print showing tools used by peasants in Europe

rope began to want some of the goods from the East. With their increased production of food and goods, the Europeans had something to trade. Some European goods were traded to the people in Africa. The people of the great African civilizations of Ghana (gä′nə) and Mali (mä′li), for example, traded gold and other goods with the people of Europe and Asia.

Slowly, Europe began to increase its trade. And this trade with the civilizations in other parts of the world helped

Stress:
1. An improved technology increased Europe's economic growth in the Middle Ages.
2. Peace and a stable society also increased economic growth in medieval Europe.
3. Economic growth in Europe led to surpluses which encouraged trade.
4. Europeans traded with people in Asia and Africa during the Middle Ages.

to improve life in Europe. For example, from Asia, Europeans learned about the compass. From Africa and southwest Asia, Europeans learned about new developments in medicine, science, and mathematics. What goods does trade with other areas of the world bring to our country? In what ways do these goods help to improve our way of life? Why?

Trade and commerce in India and China As you know, during the Dark Ages trade and commerce were very limited in Europe. In Asia, on the other hand, trade and commerce flourished during the same period. For example, Indian merchants traveled throughout much of Asia buying and selling goods, and important marketplaces were established in cities in India.

At about the same time in history, products from India and China also reached Europe. However, most of the products from Asia were traded to Europeans living near the Mediterranean Sea. Why were Europeans living near the Mediterranean Sea more likely to have products from the East? The map on page 169 may help you answer this question.

Invasions that occurred in Asia after the year 1000 reduced trade and commerce. India, for example, was invaded by the Muslims in large numbers after A.D. 1000. The warfare that followed for the next several hundred years interfered with India's trade with other countries. China too was invaded. The Mongols, a barbarian people who lived to the north of China, brought a period of confusion to much of Asia. A Mongol village is shown in the picture. From the picture would you say that the Mongols had a high level of civilization? Why?

Medieval Mongol village showing huts and how they were moved

Stress: For Teaching Helps, see page T77.
1. Geographic conditions hindered trade in Japan.
2. Much of Japan's trade was carried on by use of ships.

Trade and commerce in Japan Several islands make up the country of Japan. These islands have many mountains and valleys. In addition, the roads in early Japan were usually in poor condition. As a result, travel and trade within Japan were difficult. However, the Japanese were good sailors and often traveled by ships. Frequently, these sailors traded with people in other countries. Where would you expect to find market-places in Japan? Why? Near the sea.

The Japanese often traded with people in Korea and China. Pots from China, such as the one shown in the picture, were highly prized by the Japanese. Silk, copper coins, books, and paintings were other items the Japanese received through trade with China and Korea. In return, the Japanese traded goods and material they produced. Sulfur—from the volcanoes in Japan—and swords were two common items the Japanese sent to other countries in exchange for the goods they desired. Considering the items that were traded, do you think that the trade with China and Korea affected the Japanese way of life? Why?

Trade in Latin America To some extent, trade in Latin America was limited. Until the Europeans arrived, wheeled carts and wagons were unknown in Latin America. As a result, trade between distant areas was not too common.

Nevertheless, some trade was carried on. The Aztecs in particular sent mer-

Type of Chinese pot used in trade with Japan

chants to various parts of Latin America. But these merchants were sometimes interested in things other than trade.

The Aztec merchants were employed by their government. One of their jobs was to get needed goods for the Aztec people. But the merchants also had another important job. This job was to spy upon other societies and get information for the Aztec government. The Aztecs often used the information to plan their attacks upon other societies. Thus, the Aztec merchants helped to expand the empire and to get prisoners of war who were needed for the sacrifices to the Aztec gods.

Think for Yourself

Why does warfare tend to reduce trade among societies?

3. Japan's trade with Korea and China led to cultural diffusion.
*4. What type of a society is most likely to control economic activity   217
    through the government?

The walled city of Carcassonne in southern France

For Teaching Helps, see page T78.

URBANIZATION

For a class activity, see #1 on page 221.

The nature of cities in the Middle Ages Today, the largest city in the world is in Asia. The city is Tokyo, Japan. During the Middle Ages, the world's largest cities were also in Asia. One of these cities was Hangchow (hang′ chou′) and another was Peking (pē′ king′). Both of these cities were in China and had over 1,000,000 people living in them.

Cities in Europe in the Middle Ages were just beginning to grow and develop. By 1500, none of the cities in Europe had over 400,000 people living in them. London, for example, had a population of only about 35,000 in 1300. Why do you think European cities were rather small during most of the Middle Ages?

It is not surprising that the few Europeans who reached China were amazed by the large cities. Marco Polo reached Hangchow during the thirteenth century. He thought Hangchow was greater than any other city in the world in size and beauty. Compared with the dirty and crowded small cities of Europe, Hangchow was correctly called the "City of Heaven."

The growth of European cities The increase of trade after the Crusades led to the growth of cities in Europe. At first, traders and merchants often offered their goods for sale near castle walls. People came to these places to trade the goods they produced and to buy the goods they needed. In time, permanent shops and homes were built near castles, and walls were built to protect these shops and homes. Walled cities, such as the one shown in the picture, slowly developed.

Many of the other cities that developed in Europe were built along rivers. Others were built near crossroads. Why

See #2 below.

Stress:

1. Cities in Asia during the Middle Ages were larger and more advanced than those in Europe.
2. Cities in Europe declined in the Dark Ages and then grew slowly as Europe's economic growth increased.

218

Stress:
1. Geographic and economic conditions influenced the location of cities in Europe.
2. Urban life in Europe was freer and more progressive than life on the manors.

were many cities located near rivers and near crossroads? For trade and commerce.

See #2 above.

Life in the cities in the Middle Ages was different from life on the manors. The people who lived in the cities were usually free. Some of the city dwellers had been serfs or peasants who had run away to the cities. Many others were people who had gained their freedom from the lords in other ways. As the population increased in Europe after 1100, manors became overcrowded. Those serfs and peasants who were able to flee, or leave the manors, usually left for the cities. The result was a rapid growth of cities throughout Europe.

Because most European cities were built within walls, they often became overcrowded. As more and more people moved to the cities, space became very scarce. As a result, most towns had very narrow streets, and the houses and shops

S ←

E/S →

A/S ←

were crowded closely together to save as much space as was possible. Signs showing what was sold in the various shops were hung along the street.

Within the cities in Europe, craftsmen and merchants made and sold the goods needed by the society. A number of these merchants and craftsmen became wealthy, and a new social class began to develop. This new social class—the middle class—grew larger and more powerful toward the end of the Middle Ages. As a result, in the next few hundred years a new way of social, political, and economic life developed in Europe. This new way of life will be discussed in the next unit.

See #3 above.

Cities in Asia The map below shows several of the major cities of early China and Japan. These cities developed as political centers or as economic centers. For example, Peking was the political

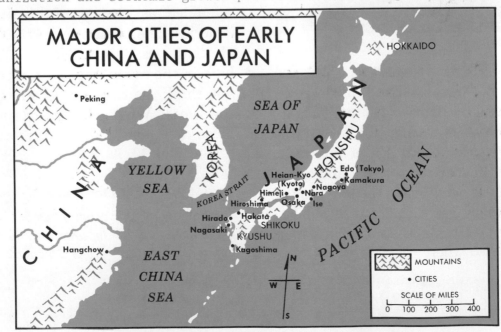

MAJOR CITIES OF EARLY CHINA AND JAPAN

For Teaching Helps, see page T78.
Stress:
1. Cities in Asia developed as political or economic centers.

Ruins of Machu Picchu in what today is Peru

Cities in Latin America Some of the first cities in Latin America were built by the Mayas. At one time the Mayan cities were thriving centers of religion A/H→ and trade. But then, a little more than 1,000 years ago, this ended. What happened to the people in the Mayan cities is still unknown, and perhaps never will be known unless social scientists discover how to read more of the Mayan writings.

When the Spanish arrived in Latin America shortly after 1500, they discovered cities larger than many of those in Europe. Tenochtitlán, the capital of the Aztecs, had a population of at least 200,000 people. And Cuzco (küs′kō), the capital of the Incas, was probably as large as Tenochtitlán.

The map on page 188 shows the location of the major cities in early Latin G/H→ America. The conquest of this area by the Europeans ended most of these cities. And by 1800, none of these cities remained as centers of life in Latin America. The picture shows the remains of what was once an Incan city built high in the mountains. In what way do P/E← you think the terrace land was used by the Incas? What other people also terraced their land? Why? Scarce land was used for farming and was terraced to prevent erosion.

center of China. It was there that the emperor of China lived and ruled. Hangchow was also a political center of China. But much of its wealth and its size was because it was also a center for trade.

Study the map on page 219 and try to determine in what ways the locations of the cities of early Japan are similar. G← Why do you think the cities in Japan were located where they were? For trade.

Think for Yourself

What city in your country has developed as a political center? In what way is this city different from New York or Chicago?

Things to Do

See page 218.

1. Draw a map of your state. Locate the four largest cities in your state on the map. Show the map to your class and explain why the cities are located where they are. See if you can give at least one geographic reason and one economic reason to explain the locations.

See page 215.

2. Make models or artifacts that were once important in the trade among countries during the Middle Ages. Be ready to tell the class where the materials used in making the artifacts were probably obtained.

CLASS PROJECT—PART 4

The last panel discussion of this project deals with economic life in the Middle Ages. The members of each of the smaller groups dealing with economic life in each society are the guests on this final show. The part each of these guests will play is to be decided by the class. Perhaps, one of the guests can be a serf, another a merchant, and a third a craftsman from a European city. The questions and the discussion should center upon the economic way of life in each society.

As a final class activity, have a class discussion to answer questions such as these: What similarities did you see in the three societies? What differences did you see? In which society would you have preferred to live? Why?

Have the pupils find each of the review words in the unit. For each word, have them answer such questions as these:

Checkup Time

1. How was the word used in the book?
2. How might you use the word yourself?

For question 2 above, encourage the pupils to use each word in a social science context.

Review Words

barbarians	Dark Ages	manors	standing army
bushido	feudalism	Middle Ages	three-field system
chivalry	fief	monasteries	tournaments
conquistadors	golden age	serfs	trial by jury
crusade	infantry	shogun	vassal

Review Questions

Typical answers only.

Social Science Facts

1. What happened to Europe when the Roman Empire collapsed? (178, 195) See bottom margin.

2. What were the three new social classes that developed in Europe during the Middle Ages? (178) Nobility, peasants, and clergy.

3. What effect did the Crusades have on Europe? (183) Increased trade, knowledge, and economic activity.

4. How did the Japanese learn about the new government of China? (197) Migration.

5. How did warfare change in Europe during the Middle Ages? (203) New weapons.

6. What did the Magna Charta provide? (205) King could tax only with consent of advisors, and trial by jury.

7. When during the Middle Ages did Europe become more peaceful? (209) A.D. 1000.

8. Why was irrigation more important in Japan than in Europe? (213) Planted rice.

9. With which countries did Japan usually carry on trade? (217) China and Korea.

10. On what continent were the largest cities located during the Middle Ages? (218) Asia.

Social Science Ideas

1. Why do new social classes develop in a society? Conditions change.

2. Why does trade often bring changes to the countries involved? Cultural diffusion.

3. What are some needed services provided by governments? Protection, laws, money.

4. Why do people who are isolated tend to continue doing things the same way they did in the past? No cultural diffusion.

5. Why are political agreements often written down? To make sure they are known and followed.

6. Why did changes in European methods of warfare come about? New discoveries.

7. Why was Europe more peaceful during the last part of the Middle Ages? See bottom margin.

8. Why did farmers in China and Japan have to cooperate with one another? See bottom margin.

9. What influence did geography have upon trade in Japan? Made inland travel hard and travel by sea easier

10. Why were most cities in Europe quite small during the early Middle Ages? Limited surpluses.

1. Breakdown of society.

7. Invasions decreased in number.
8. For irrigation.

Test Yourself

On your own paper, write your answer to each question.

Test 1 Social Science Words

Match the words and groups of words given below.

b .1. feudalism   a. a holy war

c .2. tournaments   b. a political system based on land

e .3. three-field system   c. contests to sharpen knights' skills

a .4. crusade   d. religious communities

d .5. monasteries   e. method of farming

Which words below describe someone who may have control over other people?

6. serf

7. vassal

8. shogun

Which words below could name a permanent military force?

9. standing army

10. crusaders

11. infantry

Which term below describes the early part of the Middle Ages in Europe?

12. Dark Ages

13. crusade

14. golden age

Test 2 Facts and Ideas

Which is the best answer to each question below?

1. Which of the following was, in some way, a result of the Crusades?

    a. barbarian invasions

    b. growth of cities in Europe

    c. decline of trade

    d. fall of Rome

2. Which of the following best describes the Aztec government?

    a. weak central government

    b. no central government

    c. powerful central government

    d. powerful local governments

3. Of the following societies, which had a feudal system?

    a. Japanese

    b. Chinese

    c. Aztec

    d. Mayan

Number the following events in the order in which they occurred. The first event would be numbered 1, the second 2, and so on.

3 .Magna Charta

2 .First Crusade

4 .End of the Aztec civilization

1 .Fall of the Roman Empire

223

For Teaching Helps, see page T79.

UNIT
6 THE WORLD OF 1500 TO 1850

<u>Stress</u>:
1. Many historians call the period after 1500 the period of modern history.
2. From 1500 to 1850 much of the world experienced social, political, and economic changes.
*3. Why are some periods of history, times of more rapid change than are other periods of time?

Chapters
14. How People Thought and Lived
15. Man's Ways of Getting Goods
16. Man's Political Activities

An artist's conception of Queen Elizabeth I riding in the chariot of fame

You have probably heard some older people you know talk about how things were when they were young. Older people often talk about styles of clothing that people wore, the homes in which they lived, the foods they ate, and many other things. Suppose that you could talk to persons who lived in any of the years from 1500 to 1850. You would hear about many interesting things. By asking the right questions, you would learn about things that were similar and things that were different from the world in which you live. And if you could talk to persons who lived in different parts of the world during 1500 to 1850, you would learn about more interesting likenesses and differences in people's ways of thinking and living.

See #1 above.

A/S

See #2 above.

In this unit you will be studying about the world from 1500 to 1850. You will find answers to questions such as the following.

1. What kinds of things did people think about?
2. What was their way of life?
3. How did they make a living?
4. How were they governed?

Stress:
1. The continuing nature of the class project. See pp. 247, 268, and 285.
2. Social attitudes are interrelated with a society's political and economic attitudes.

CLASS PROJECT—PART 1

Your class project for this unit is to write and give a play showing how the people of England lived during the 1600's. To do this you will have to gather information about the people—what they wore, what they ate, what they talked about, and so on.

In this unit you will study about the social, economic, and political activities of people in England during the 1600's. Thus you might group your information according to those activities. Then you might write your play in three acts—one act for each of the above kinds of activities.

You may wish to form committees to work on different things—scenery, costumes, props, and writing the play. Each committee will have many things to do. The picture below shows how one committee might do part of its work for a scene in the first act of the play. Your committees should get some of their ideas about the people's social life as you study Chapter 14. The actual writing of each act will have to be done as you complete your study of each chapter.

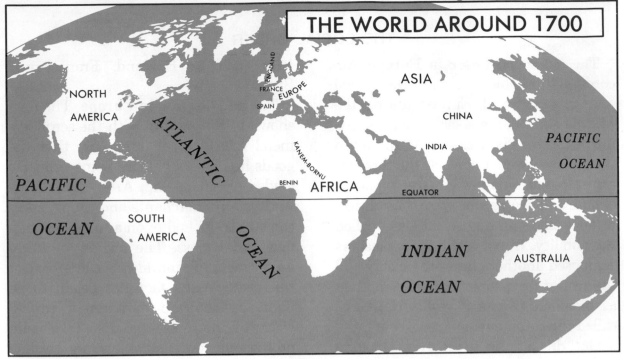

14. How People Thought and Lived

See #1
below.

People in some of the countries of Europe were beginning to change their ways of thinking and living quite rapidly around 1500. But people in some other

See #2
below.

countries of the world at the same time were attempting to preserve the same way of life that they had had for hundreds of years. In this chapter you will be studying the societies of both of the above kinds of countries.

H/G →

S/A ←

Historians are very careful in selecting the places they study. Some of the important places of the world from 1500 to 1850 are shown on the map. These are the places you will study in this chapter and in the following two chapters. Would you expect many or few differences in the societies people developed in these places in the years between 1500 and 1850? Why?

JUST FOR FUN

See if you can find an artifact or a picture of an object that existed after 1500, but earlier than 1850. Be ready to discuss the skills needed to make it.

Stress:

1. People in some areas of Europe had begun to rapidly change their ways of life by 1500.

2. Some societies retained their traditional ways of life during the period from 1500 to 1850 while other societies did not.

*3. Why are some societies quicker to change their ways of life than are other societies?

227

THE SOCIAL ORDER

The old social order in Europe According to sociologists and other social scientists, most of Europe during the Middle Ages had a social order consisting of three social classes. At times the three classes were known as the three estates. People who owned large amounts of land and people who were the political leaders made up one social class, called the nobility. Important religious leaders composed another class—the clergy. All the rest of the people were looked upon as members of the lowest social class, called the commoners.

But during the years from 1500 to 1850, many things were happening in a number of countries of western Europe that brought about changes in the social order. This was especially true in countries such as England, France, and Spain.

Medieval European merchant

The middle class in Europe The man shown in the picture with the scroll is a merchant. He is making sure that the goods he has bought are being properly loaded onto the ship. After the Middle Ages, many merchants and shopkeepers came to be looked upon as members of a new social class. The owners of fairly large tracts of land also became part of this class. When factories began to be built, the factory owners were identified with this new class. People in certain professions, too, such as lawyers, became part of this class. Do you see any relationship between wealth and the rise of this new class in the social order? If so, in what way?

The new social class of which we are speaking is the **middle class.** Eventually, more and more people were considered members of this class. The people in the middle class became very important members of their countries. They became leaders in business and industry. They became the investors and builders in towns and cities. And they became the ones who developed and spread democratic ideas of government.

The upper and lower classes in Europe Above the rising middle class there was a social class called the **upper class.** In this class were many of the men who had been nobles during the Middle Ages.

Indentured servants leaving the ship that carried them to America

These were people who owned huge amounts of land, had great power, or were born into families that once had these things.

Great numbers of people were members of a class just below the middle class. Here were the commoners who had not risen to the ranks of the middle class. Among these people were the rural peasants, the journeymen craft workers, and later on, the factory workers. This class was known as the **lower class**.

The dependent class in Europe There were people who did not work for a profit, a salary, or a wage. Instead, these people worked for their **keep**—food, clothing, and shelter. They also worked to please their master. Some of these people were servants and others were slaves. These people were looked upon as members of the **dependent class**. In this class were the apprentice craftsmen and the household servants.

Social classes in the American colonies In the American colonies the same social classes tended to be found as existed back in the European countries that started the colonies. This was true of the English, the French, and the Spanish colonies. Why do you suppose that this was so? Colonists brought European customs to America.

There were, however, some differences between the social classes in the American colonies and in the countries of western Europe that started the colonies. One difference was that the colonies had **indentured servants**.

Some of the indentured servants were people who came to America of their own free will. In return for their passage across the ocean on ships like the one shown here, they agreed to work for

Stress:
1. In parts of Europe after 1500, there were three social classes--an upper class (the nobility), a middle class (businessmen), and a lower class (workers and peasants).
2. Social classes in America usually followed the social patterns found in Europe.

229

Stress:
1. Indentured servants in America usually agreed to work for the person who paid the expense of their passage from Europe.

someone for a certain number of years, usually seven. If you had lived then, do you think you would have made such an agreement? What reasons can you give for your answer? Other indentured servants were brought to America against their will, but were given their freedom after they had worked for a master a set number of years. In the early days of the American colonies, there were both black indentured servants and white indentured servants.

See #1 above.

Slavery was another difference between the social classes in the American colonies and those in the countries of western Europe. In western Europe there were some household servants who were slaves. But in the American colonies it was not long before nearly all the black people who were brought to America were forced into slavery. Negroes were no longer given their freedom after serving a master a certain number of years. Historians have evidence that Negro slavery in America, particularly in the English colonies, was becoming a permanent part of the social order. Against their will, many of the slaves were forced to work long, hard hours on the plantations. They were treated quite differently from the way household slaves or servants were treated in Europe.

See #2 below.

In the Spanish colonies many of the American natives—the Indians—were brought into society and were made slaves. But when they were made slaves, many Indians lost their will to live. Large numbers of the Indians died. So the Spanish, too, began using Negro slaves to do the work on their plantations. The picture shows a Spanish plantation with Negro slaves. What kind of work are the slaves doing? Cutting sugarcane.

2. Black people were brought to America and forced into slavery.

Slaves at work on a Spanish plantation in America

Stress:
1. Economic conditions affected the use of slaves.

The French were not as interested in agriculture as were the English and the Spanish. They were more involved in fur trapping and trading. Consequently, See #1 above. the French in the American colonies were not very interested in having either Indian slaves or Negro slaves.

The freedom to move from one social class to another In the western European countries and in the American colonies, many people had the freedom to move from one social class to another. We call this **social mobility.** See #2 below.

Naturally, people did not want to move from one social class to a lower one. They wanted to move to a higher social class. Why? Better way of life.

Generally speaking it was easier for people in the lower or middle classes of the American colonies to move to a higher social class than it was for people in the same classes in the countries of western Europe. When the United States gained its independence, it was also easier to move from one social class to another here than it was in Europe. Why do you suppose this was so? Fewer restrictions. See #3 below.

The social order in India By 1500 a very strict class system had been in existence in India for hundreds of years. This was, of course, the caste system that you read about in Chapter 8. The caste system continued to separate the people of India into distinct classes throughout the period from 1500 to 1850.

As has already been discussed in

Member of the Brahman caste of India

Chapter 8, there were four major divisions or classes in this traditional Indian caste system. The man shown in the picture is a priest. He belonged to the highest Indian caste. In what way might his clothes help you know that he belonged to one of the upper rather than one of the lower castes? Highly ornamented and expensive.

Just below the priests were the warriors. The warriors were also known as nobles. Then came the merchants and farmers. The merchants and farmers were also known as the commoners. The last caste consisted of the laborers.

Below the four castes there was a very large group of people who had no official position in society. These people,

2. In western Europe and America, social mobility was usually achieved by gaining wealth.
3. The absence of age-old traditions and customs in America led to freer and easier social mobility in America than in most of Europe.

1. The traditional caste system in India prevented social mobility by restricting caste membership to only those born into each caste.

who made up about one-fifth of the Indian population, were known as the untouchables. Most of the untouchables lived in very great poverty.

See #1 above.

No freedom of movement Sociologists and other social scientists point out that the caste system of India strictly regulated people's lives. It kept each person locked into the caste into which he had been born. There was no social mobility.

See #2 below.

The social order in China People in China were divided into four social classes. The scholars and those who served in governing positions were members of the highest social class. Below them were these classes—the farmers, the craft workers, and the merchants.

Notice that the merchants were lower than the farmers in the Chinese social order. What do you think this says about Chinese society between 1500 and 1850? It did not value trade or commerce very highly.

Importance of the family in China Chinese society, both before and after 1500, was organized mainly around the family. To the Chinese the family was in many ways far more important than any other organization, including the government.

In China the family was more than just a father and mother and their children. It included many kinds of relatives. The oldest living male was the official head of the family.

The family took many responsibilities for its members. It cared for family members who were unemployed, and it supported those who were too old to work. The family also looked after the behavior and reputation of all its members. The family leaders felt a responsibility to discipline any family members who might need it. A Chinese family also felt that it had to pay for any wrongs done by any of its members. Do you think this kind of family structure is good or bad? Why?

As in many other societies of the 1500's to 1800's, there was little social mobility in China. China was a country that was trying very hard to keep things as they were.

See #3 below.

The social order of Benin In the African kingdom of Benin (bə'nin), see the map on page 227, there were both nobles and peasants. The nobles had wealth and power. They became the rulers, warriors, and merchants.

The man shown on page 233 is a noble of Benin. The way that he is dressed shows his social position as a warrior. In what ways does the dress of people in societies today show their social position?

The peasants were less wealthy members of the society in Benin. The peasants did most of the work. They were the hunters, the farmers, and the metalworkers.

The Benin society also had a class of people who were slaves. These were

2. In China, scholars had more social prestige and higher social positions than did merchants.
3. Traditional values and customs were stressed by families, and change and social mobility were discouraged.

Stress:
1. The society of Benin was traditional, and movement upward from one social
   class to another was not one of the customs of the society.
2. Kanem-Bornu had a social order similar to the social order of medieval Europe.

sometimes members of their own society who had been convicted of a crime. Often they were members of other societies who had been captured in war. The people of Benin used slaves as household servants, and apparently even considered them as members of their family.

A/S ←

See #1 above. Because the society of Benin was based upon long-standing tradition, it was difficult for an individual to move from one level of the society to another. People generally tended to remain at the level at which they were born, unless through some misfortune they became slaves.

Noble warrior of the African kingdom of Benin

The social order of Kanem-Bornu

Look again at the map on page 227. Locate the African kingdom of Kanem-Bornu (kä′nem-bôr′nü). Kanem and Bornu are sometimes considered by historians as two separate kingdoms. At other times, as in this book, they are discussed as one kingdom. The kingdom of Kanem-Bornu between 1500 and 1850 had a social structure similar to that of most of Europe during the Middle Ages. There were chiefs or elders who owned and ruled large areas of land. The members of this class corresponded to the nobility of Europe.

A/S ↔ See #2 above.

S →

There were many peasants who lived on the landed estates of the nobles. The peasants worked for and served the owner. In Europe the members of this class would have been called commoners. There were also those in the Kanem-Bornu society who had been taken as prisoners of war. These people served as slaves.

A/S →

As in the European feudal societies of the Middle Ages, it was almost impossible for anyone to change his role in the Kanem-Bornu society. If born an elder, one remained an elder. If born a peasant, one remained a peasant.

Think for Yourself

Why did it become easier for some members of Western societies to move from one class to another than it was for most members of Eastern or African societies to do so? Fewer customs and traditions that restricted social mobility.

233

*3. Why is social mobility so common in the United States?

For Teaching Helps, see page T82.
Stress:
1. Contacts with other civilizations increased knowledge in Europe.
2. By the end of the Middle Ages, Europeans had more time and money to devote to education.

EDUCATION AND LEARNING

Europe becomes highly interested in learning By the end of the Middle Ages, many people in the countries of western Europe were coming into contact with people of other parts of the world. The Crusades, trade, and exploration all contributed to people's increasing contacts with other people. How do you suppose these contacts helped to spread knowledge and ideas? Exposed Europeans to other civilized people.

See #1 above.

G/S →

Historians tell us that much of the new knowledge came to Europe from Constantinople in the East. Locate Constantinople on the map. Also locate Italy, England, France, and Spain. What geographic advantage for trading do coun-

G ←

S/H →

tries such as Italy, England, France, and Spain have? They have seaports.

Much of the learning of the Greek and Roman civilizations had been preserved in books and manuscripts in Constantinople. Now men were taking many of these back to Europe and studying them. The new knowledge spread from Italy into countries such as England, France, and Spain.

A different kind of learning Toward the end of the Middle Ages a new kind of learning was becoming popular in western Europe. This new learning was very much interested in life in this world. Men began asking many questions about the world in which they lived. They wanted to know why things were as they were. They also wanted to know how things came to be this way and what things were like in the past. Do you think these are important questions? Why or why not?

See #3 below.

Men began investigating the world around them. They began making careful observations of what they saw. Men began experimenting with new ideas. They learned many interesting and valuable things from their investigations and experiments. Men were improving upon their old ways of doing things. They invented machines to make life easier. On page 235 you see a picture of a flying machine Leonardo da Vinci (lā′ō när′dō dä vin′chē) designed but

S/H →

See #4 below.

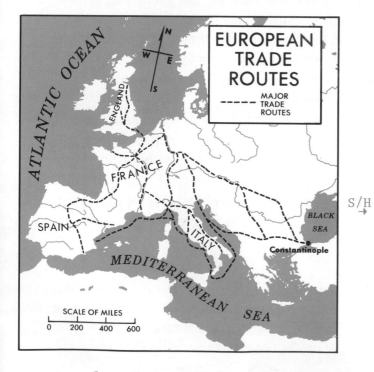

EUROPEAN TRADE ROUTES

MAJOR TRADE ROUTES

ATLANTIC OCEAN

ENGLAND

FRANCE

SPAIN

ITALY

MEDITERRANEAN SEA

BLACK SEA

Constantinople

SCALE OF MILES
0 200 400 600

3. Europeans developed an interest in man's way of life and the world in which man lived.
4. New inventions and discoveries occurred in Europe as knowledge grew and developed.

Stress:
1. The use of the printing press enabled educated people in Europe to learn more about man and about new discoveries.
2. By the end of the Middle Ages, schools had been established in many of the large cities in Europe.

Leonardo da Vinci's design of a flying machine

Early printing press used in England

never built. Men like da Vinci helped to bring the Age of Science.

The picture on the right shows printing in England in the late Middle Ages. The knowledge of printing had been brought to countries of Europe, including England, from China. Europeans during the 1600's began printing books, pamphlets, and newspapers. How do you think printing helped to spread ideas?

See #1 above.

Schools in Europe Many schools began to be organized to help educate the people of western Europe. Some of the schools were still operated by the religious groups, but even these now began teaching much of the new knowledge.

The guilds that were organized to carry on crafts such as making shoes, weaving, and working with metals also developed schools. They were anxious for their members to become educated.

P/S

H/S

S

H/S

S

The governments of the countries of western Europe also helped further education. Sometimes they started schools, and sometimes they helped support schools that others had started.

Learning in the American colonies Many educated people went to the American colonies of England, France, and Spain. Some of these people helped to get learning started in the colonies.

As early as 1536 the Spanish were printing books in America. What does this suggest about their interests in education? Had a high interest in education

The Spanish in America built schools for both the Spanish children and the Indians. They also built universities at Mexico City, Mexico and Lima, Peru.

See #4 below

The University of Lima, also known as the University of San Marcos, is the oldest university in the Americas. This

3. Education in America was developed by the educated colonists from England, France, and Spain.
4. Spanish colonists established schools to educate the natives as well as the settlers of America.

235

For Teaching Helps, see page T82.
Stress:
1. Education in India was often available only to higher-caste children.

University of San Marcos in Lima, Peru

in Indian culture. This cultural learning consisted especially of poetry, music, painting, architecture, and sciences such as mathematics and chemistry. This type of education continued on into the 1600's and 1700's. **See #1 above.**

In the 1800's the English, who were the most successful of the European people in India, took over much of the control of education in that country. The English government established schools to train Indian boys for employment in jobs connected with the government. The English also used the schools as a way to teach Western ideas to the people of India. In what way does this show the importance of education?

Chinese education Education and learning in China were often carried on in the home. The elderly members of the family took the responsibility of educating the children, especially the boys. Often all the families of a village maintained a village primary school. **See #2 below.**

Higher education in China was looked after by the government. This was mainly because higher education in China was to prepare young men for government service.

Chinese learning from 1500 to 1850 was very much like Chinese learning had been before 1500. This learning was based upon the ancient ideas of the great Chinese thinker, Confucius. The Chinese were interested in preserving their ancient culture.

university has been in existence since 1551 and is still used today. The picture shows part of the University of Lima. Obeserve the style of the building.

No newspapers or books were printed in the French colonies in America for over 100 years after the colonies were started. Also, France was very slow to develop schools in its American colonies.

As the English colonies in America became successful, printed books, pamphlets, and newspapers became available. Why was it important for people in the colonies to have reading materials? Various kinds of schools were also started.

Learning in India For hundreds of years before 1500, boys in the higher castes of Indian society were educated

Stress:
1. Education in Benin was largely devoted to teaching practical skills needed to maintain the existing way of life.

Learning and education in Benin Education in Benin was mostly a matter of teaching the children the practical tasks of life. Girls were instructed in how to do A/S such useful things as gathering and preparing foods, making clothing, and helping to take care of the younger children. Boys were taught such things as hunting and farming. They were also trained in warfare.

Some individuals received special training. Those of noble rank were trained in leadership. Other individuals A/S received special training in working with metals, in being traders, or in hunting. The leopard hunters shown in the picture received a special apprenticeship. Hunting animals such as leopards was a special honor among the people of Benin. What reason can you think of why this was so?

Education in Kanem-Bornu The majority of the people of Kanem-Bornu were peasants. Like the people of Benin, they received practical training for the daily tasks of life.

But the noble class of people in Kanem-Bornu received more education than the nobles in Benin. This was because the nobles of Kanem-Bornu benefited from the reading, writing, and learning they got from their contact with the Muslims of Turkey. Turkey A/S was part of the Ottoman Empire. Locate Turkey and Kanem-Bornu on the map. About how far apart are they? But,

Benin art showing men hunting leopards

Muslim culture did not have much effect upon the peasants. They continued to follow their own African traditions.

Think for Yourself

Why is the control of education in a country a very important thing? Because education helps to shape the society.

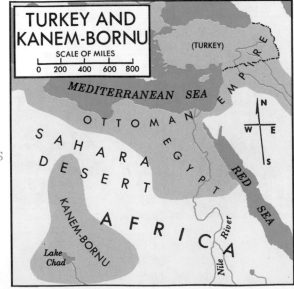

TURKEY AND KANEM-BORNU
SCALE OF MILES
0   200   400   600   800
(TURKEY)
MEDITERRANEAN SEA
OTTOMAN
SAHARA
DESERT
EGYPT
EMPIRE
RED SEA
KANEM-BORNU
AFRICA
Lake Chad
Nile River
N
W   E
S

2. Contacts with other civilizations influenced education in Kanem-Bornu.
*3. Why did some nations encourage education in America while France did not?

For Teaching Helps, see page T83.
Stress:
1. New ideas challenged the traditional European thought about religion in the late Middle Ages.

RELIGION

Religious change in Europe As learning in western Europe by 1500 was changing, so was religion. People began questioning their religious beliefs in the same way they were questioning the world around them.

Cathedral in Laon, France, which was completed in the thirteenth century

A ← The Roman Catholic Church was the church of Europe during the Middle Ages. People gave of their time, energy, and money in order to build beautiful church buildings like the one shown here. What does this say about how important the church was to people?

A/S → But toward the end of the Middle Ages, some men raised questions about both the teachings and practices of the church. They said that the leaders of the church were human and therefore capable of making errors. Some men believed that people should interpret the meaning of the Bible for themselves.

See #1 above.

One of the main critics of the Roman Catholic Church in the 1500's was Martin Luther. He thought that some of the leaders of the church were guilty of certain corrupt practices. Luther thought some of the church leaders, just like some people of his time, had become too interested in worldly wealth and power. He thought their worldly interests interfered with their religious activities and leadership.

See #2 below.

A/H → Martin Luther was not trying to start a new religion or a new church. He was trying to get the Roman Catholic Church to reform itself, to change the things he felt were wrong with it. In criticizing some of the activities of the leaders and the church that they represented, Luther eventually opened the door to questioning the authority of the church.

See #3 below.

Stress:
1. England replaced Roman Catholicism with a national church, the Church of England.
2. Religious dissenters often had to migrate to new lands to find religious freedom.

Many other men later did the same thing, and a number of Protestant religions were formed.

See #1 above.

Religious problems in England In England, the king himself—Henry VIII—did not accept some of the decisions of the Pope. Henry set up his own church in England. The Church of England took the place of the Roman Catholic Church in that country.

See #2 above.

Religious troubles in England did not end with the Church of England. Many people were just as unhappy with this church as they had been with the Roman Catholic Church. One such group was the Puritans. Many of the Puritans finally left England for religious reasons, and went to the English colonies in America. So did other religious groups from England.

Religious troubles in France In the 1500's and after, France also had religious troubles. A number of people in France became Protestants known as Huguenots. Protestant was a term used to refer to those who protested for religious ideas different from those of the Roman Catholic Church.

But France remained mostly a Roman Catholic country. The kings of France, unlike most of the kings and queens of England, were Roman Catholics during this time. The majority of the people in the countries of western Europe followed the same religion as their king or queen.

3. France and Spain remained largely Roman Catholic.

The Roman Catholic Church in Spain Like France, Spain remained a Roman Catholic country. The man shown in the picture is Ignatius Loyola (ig nā′ shəs lôi ō′lə). He was a great leader of the Roman Catholic Church in Spain.

Loyola established a religious order called the Society of Jesus, or Jesuits (jezh′ü its). The Jesuits played an important part in the reform of the Roman Catholic Church. This reform was called the Counter Reformation or the Catholic Reformation.

Religion in the American colonies Political scientists have pointed out that the governments of Spain and France took a very active role in the life of their colonies in America. They kept people who were not Roman Catholics from

Ignatius Loyola who founded the Society of Jesus

Madura Temple which was built in India during the seventeenth century

The religious situation in India Both before and after 1500, India had people S/H of many different religions. Hinduism and Islam were the two most popular Indian religions.

While people in western Europe were fighting over the Roman Catholic and Protestant religions, people in India were quarreling over Hinduism and Islam. Hinduism was a religion with A many gods. Islam was a religion with just one God. Which of these religions do you think would accept the other one? Why?

During the late 1500's Akbar (ak'bar) ruled India. He tried to get the Indian people to honor one another's religious beliefs. Do you think this was a good idea? Why?

Religious differences in India were reflected in the styles of the religious buildings built by the Hindus and the A/S Muslims. The picture on this page shows a Hindu temple. The picture on page 241 shows an Islamic **mosque** (mosk), or place of worship. The dome is one feature by which you can identify the Islamic mosque. More important, however, P/S ever, is the fact that the mosque has no decoration which uses any animal or human forms as the Hindu temple has. Do the pictures shown on these pages make you think that religion was important to the people of India? Why? Yes--elaborate buildings.

Religion in China In the 1500's, as well as before and after that time, China

See #1 below.
going to their colonies. Thus the Spanish and French colonies were basically Roman Catholic like their home countries were.

The English government granted rights to both individuals and groups to begin colonies in America. One of the reasons some of these people started colonies was for religious freedom.

The English colonies thus had many people with religious ideas different from those held by most of the people back in England. How did allowing the people in its colonies to have ideas of their own later affect England?

Stress:
240 1. French and Spanish colonies in America were basically Roman Catholic, but English colonies often differed in religion from that found in England.
2. Islam and Hinduism were the two major religions of India.

Stress:
1. Buddhism and Confucianism were important religions in China.
2. The people of Benin and Kanem-Bornu thought their rulers were gods.

See #1
above.

was a land of many religions. Confucianism and Buddhism were the two most important religions.

The upper classes tended to follow Confucianism while the lower classes often practiced Buddhism. One reason for this was that Confucianism was a scholarly religion. It attempted to educate people to act in certain prescribed ways. Buddhism, on the other hand, was a religion that emphasized faith more than Confucianism did. Buddhism taught a belief in the unimportance of things in this life. Which of these two religions would be easier to follow? Why?

The importance of religion in Benin and in Kanem-Bornu In both the kingdom of Benin and the kingdom of Kanem-Bornu, religion played an important role. Both the people of Benin and the people of Kanem-Bornu looked upon their rulers as some kind of god.

See #2
above.

A
→

A/S
←

A/H
→

A
←

The people of Benin appear to have had many gods, but one was more important to them than the others. They thought that the gods were good, but they also believed there was a devil who was bad and who caused people problems.

The people of Kanem-Bornu actually had more than one religion. The peasants continued to worship the traditional gods of their ancestors. Around 1570 Idris Alooma (id'ris alü'mə) ruled Kanem-Bornu. During his time, the nobles worshiped according to the Islamic religion. Idris encouraged his nobles to make a **pilgrimage,** or religious journey, to the Islamic holy city of Mecca.

Think for Yourself

In what ways can religious beliefs affect the way people treat others?

*3. Why might a society's religious beliefs make the people reluctant to change their ways of life?

Bashahi Mosque, the largest mosque in the world, was built in Lahore, India, in the seventeenth century.

For Teaching Helps, see page T84.
Stress:
1. The rise of a central government can lead to a peaceful and stable society.

PEOPLE AND COMMUNITIES

Nottingham Castle in England

English cottage

Changes in the way people in Europe live Carefully observe the pictures of the two types of English houses shown here. The one at the top, the castle, was lived in by nobles during the Middle A/S Ages. The other house was lived in by Englishmen during the 1500's. Which house looks like it would offer more protection from an invader? How did you decide?

Political scientists point out that the governments of some countries in western Europe, such as England, were becoming strong toward the end of the Middle Ages. These governments could P/S offer their citizens protection. Then people began building homes for comfort and for style rather than mainly for protection.

See #1 above.

The homes of the common people also began to be built for comfort. Cottages A/S and farmhouses that once had been heated with open fires now were built with chimneys. How would this help to make homes more comfortable? Homes also were built with glass windows. In what ways would this improve a home?

See #2 below.

People in western Europe began wearing clothing that was more comfortable and more stylish than people wore in the A/S Middle Ages. Instead of clothes made from coarse woolens, they began wearing clothes made of soft cottons and fine silks. How are these clothes different from the ones you wear? Clothes today are often made of synthetics.

2. Peaceful conditions, stable societies, and new inventions and developments led to a better way of life for many people in Europe.

1. After 1500 cities in Europe began to grow rapidly, and many cities became
   overcrowded as people came to work in the factories.

The people of western Europe also began eating better than they had in the Middle Ages. They now had more food and a greater variety of foods than they had had before. People had more food because they began making better use of the land, using more fertilizers, and using better farming tools. People had a greater variety of foods than before because of increased trade and exploration. Some of the new food varieties that began to be available in Europe were maize, potatoes, chocolate, and tapioca.

E/S

Cities and villages in Europe The picture shows a street in London, England, around 1750. Notice the style of buildings, and the stones used to pave the street. Such a street was called a **cobblestone street.** Cities such as this were being built in the countries of western Europe during the 1700's.

H/S

See #1
above.

Historians have evidence that people soon began crowding into the cities to find jobs in the factories that were being built. Some sections of the cities became very crowded. Most people wanted to live as close as possible to the factories. Why?

E/H

See #2
below.

Soon the overcrowded sections began to become slums. People threw garbage and trash into the streets. The buildings began to need repairing. Do any of these things cause slums in our cities today? What else causes some of today's slums? Poverty and neglect.

S

In the 1700's and 1800's, however, most of the people of western Europe continued to live in rural villages. Life in the villages was, in some ways, similar to city life. But village life was different in at least two important ways. First, people in the villages did not live as crowded together. Second, most of the people in the villages made their living by farming.

See #3
below.

Life in the American colonies In many ways life in the English, French, and Spanish colonies in America was similar to life back in those European countries. What reasons can you give to explain why this was so?

Of course there were some differences in colonial life, especially on the **frontier,** or the most recently settled part, of the colonies. Here people lived a rough

S

Fleet Street in eighteenth-century London

2. Overcrowded cities soon developed new problems such as poor living conditions.
3. Life in villages in Europe during the eighteenth and nineteenth
   centuries remained primarily agricultural, and the people were rarely as overcrowded as they were in the cities.

243

life of carving a community out of the forests.

Even after the United States had gained its independence, the life of the people continued to be similar to life in England. As the years went by, however, the American way of life became more and more a style of its own. Why do you suppose it took a fairly long time for this to happen?

Life in India Huts built of reeds were quite common in India. India is a country with a moderate climate. It is also a country that gets lots of rain sometimes and very little at other times. Why would reed huts offer people enough protection in the type of climate that India has? It did not get very cold in India.

While most people in India in the 1600's and 1700's lived in reed huts, some people lived in very fancy homes. Some of these homes were built of white marble. These homes had many rooms, and were furnished with expensive furniture.

See #1 below.

Just as the homes of people in India varied greatly, so did their dress. The people in the upper castes wore very fine clothes that were artistically decorated. The people of the lower castes wore very plain clothes. Some of the people, especially the untouchables, wore very little, because they had very little to wear.

The food people ate also varied according to caste. Those in the upper castes ate very well. Those in the lower castes ate what they managed to grow for themselves. Many of the untouchables ate very little. Some of them died of starvation.

When the English took over most of India, they tried to prevent starvation. They did things to help the Indians raise more food and to transport the food to where the people lived.

Indian cities and villages. In India, as in western Europe, people lived in cities and villages. Also as in Europe, most of the people lived in villages.

Unlike the cities of Europe, the Indian cities did not have factories. The cities of India were centers of trading, religious, or political activity.

Life in China Like most of the people we are studying, the Chinese built the kind of homes they could afford from the materials they had. If they were prosperous, the Chinese often built homes of many rooms and courtyards so that all the members of their family could live there. Poorer people in China built smaller homes.

See #2 below.

A Chinese gentleman in the 1500's or 1600's might have dressed in a garment that looked like a long skirt or gown. In many ways the people of China had different customs of dress from those that people in Europe had. Both had different customs of dress from what we have today. Do you think one custom or style of dress is any better than another? Why or why not?

Stress:

244

1. The caste system in India often determined how people lived, ate, and dressed.

2. His home and his clothing often reflected the social position and wealth of a person in China.

Village in the Lake Chad region of Africa (formerly Kanem-Bornu)

For a class activity, see #2 on page 247.

The wealthier people of China ate many kinds of food. Most of the people ate more rice than anything else. The Chinese ate their food with chopsticks. This they had been doing for hundreds of years, including the time when the people of Europe were eating with their fingers.

Chinese cities and villages Economists and other social scientists have studied how the people of China made their living in the period from 1500 to 1850. They tell us that some of the people in China made a living by making articles of clay, metal, and silk or cotton. Others made their living by conducting the business of the government. A few made their living by teaching. But most of the people of China made their living by farming.

A/S

S

S/E

G/A

See #1 below.

China was a country of both cities and villages. Do you think most of the Chinese during the time from 1500 to 1850 lived in cities or in villages? What reasons can you give for your answer?

Life in Benin and in Kanem-Bornu
Many people in Benin had small houses. Others had large houses supported by wooden pillars. Do you think the people of high social position in Benin had large or small houses? Why?

Most people of Kanem-Bornu lived in huts made of tall grasses such as reeds or rushes. The picture of a village in the Lake Chad region today shows how such huts may have looked.

Notice the shape of the houses and the type of roofs they have. Do you think this kind of roof would be good in a wet climate? Why or why not?

See #2 below.

Stress:
1. From 1500 to 1850 China remained primarily an agricultural nation and most of the Chinese people lived in rural villages.
2. Most of the people of Kanem-Bornu lived in the type of houses that had been used in the past by their ancestors.

245

Stress:
1. Social position is often shown by the type of homes and clothing people own.

Buildings in the capital city of Benin

See #1 above.

The leading nobles of Kanem-Bornu built houses of red brick. These houses helped them show their social importance.

The people of Benin and of Kanem-Bornu wore clothing and jewelry that reflected their position in society. The people of Benin, especially, wore lots of necklaces and bracelets. They even wore bands, called anklets, around their ankles. Do you think people today use clothing and jewelry to show their position in society? If so, how?

Most people in the lower classes of society in Benin and in Kanem-Bornu got their food from food gathering, hunting, and farming. The nobles had slaves or servants to do these things for them, although many of the nobles did some of their own hunting. The nobles of Benin also got foods such as candied oranges and lemons from their trading activities.

Cities and villages in Benin and Kanem-Bornu The picture shows the capital of Benin. Like the kingdom, it too was named Benin. Do the buildings in the foreground look large or small to you?

People from western Europe were surprised to find such a large and well-built city in Africa in the 1500's. The European merchants described Benin as a clean and well-kept city.

A world of many cultures Certainly the world of 1500 to 1850 was one of many cultures. We have actually only looked at a few of them. In spite of all their differences, a few things seem to have been very similar. They all had social classes. They all had some kind of religion. And they all developed both cities and villages. Do you think these things tell us anything important about people? If so, what?

Think for Yourself

What are some important things about a society that we can learn from studying people's homes? People's clothing? People's food?

2. Different cultures, in all parts of the world, often have a number of things--such as social classes, religion, and urbanization--in common.
*3. Why might urbanization affect the way of life in a traditional society?

Things to Do

See page 232.

1. Look on a recent map of Africa to find out which countries in Africa are now located where the kingdoms of Benin and Kanem-Bornu were located.

See page 245.

2. Draw a picture or make a model of an African village with huts made of reeds or rushes. Use the picture on page 245 or pictures from other books to help you.

See page 244.

3. Look in the library for books on China. Try to find pictures showing how people in China dressed in the 1600's. Also try to find pictures in books, magazines, or newspapers that show how people in China dress today. Compare the pictures.

CLASS PROJECT—PART 2

Each committee should have information to use in developing Act 1 of the play. Now begin working on the scenery, costumes, props, and writing for the first act. Keep the scenery and costumes fairly simple. The first act should be about people's social activities.

It will help the work of each committee if the class decides together what it wants to show about people's social life in England during the 1600's. Here are two suggestions for scenes to use in Act 1.

1. A middle-class family meeting friends on a street.

2. The same middle-class family eating a meal at home.

Your family for the play should have a father, a mother, two boys, and two girls. Add other characters to your play as the acts and scenes require. Keep the same family members throughout the play. Members of the class who are not specific characters in the play can be part of the crowd in some scenes.

As you study Chapter 15, be thinking about the scenes you may want to use in Act 2 of your play.

Imported cheeses on display in a store in the United States

15. Man's Ways of Getting Goods

For Teaching Helps, see page T85.

See #1 below.

Today people in the United States can get goods produced in most of the other nations of the world. The picture shows what some of the goods from other nations are. Which ones are sold in your community?

During the 1500's the nations of the world could only get a small amount of goods from a few places. The 1500's were the years when the nations of Europe that were to become great colonial powers were exploring the world. They were searching for new trade routes. While searching for new routes, they discovered the American continents.

See #2 below.

In this chapter you will learn about many of the economic changes that took place in the world between 1500 and 1850. You will see some of the effects these changes had upon man.

E

E/H

JUST FOR FUN

Look around your home for articles made in other countries. Make a list of four or five things, briefly describing them and telling where they were made.

Stress:

1. Many goods used by people today are imported from other nations.
2. Trade is one way people obtain goods they need or want.
3. The search for trade routes has led to the discovery of new lands.
*4. Why did European nations begin to search for new trade routes after 1500?

248

Stress:
1. The manor system declined in Europe after 1500 and large farms began to develop.

AGRICULTURE

Farming in Europe begins to change The typical manor of the Middle Ages had its farmlands laid out in long, narrow strips. These strips of land were cultivated by the peasants. In return for his labor, a peasant received some of the food crops for his family. Sometimes a peasant owned one or more strips of land that he farmed for himself. Often the strips of land were in different fields.

See #1 above.

Toward the end of the Middle Ages, changes began occurring in European farming, especially in England. Some of the nobles lost their land, and so did some of the peasants. Now many of the narrow strips of land were combined to make larger farms than the farmers used to have. How do you think the larger farms helped to make the work of farmers easier and more efficient?

Some of the large farms of England were used for raising crops. Others were used for raising farm animals such as sheep. Sheep were sometimes raised for food, but often they were raised for their wool. The wool was used in the production of cloth. Many of the sheep farms in England were enclosed. With what is the sheep farm in the picture enclosed? Why do you suppose farms were enclosed?

Improved methods of farming For a long time the farmers of western Europe knew that land used year after year for the same crop no longer produced a good crop. Nor did land so used yield as large a crop as the farmers wanted.

To keep from wearing out the soil by repeated plantings of the same crop, European farmers had learned to let certain fields lie fallow for a while.

See #2 below.

Later the farmers gradually learned more about soils and crops. They learned that it was not necessary to let fields lie fallow. Farmers learned how to **rotate** their crops. This meant that they planted different kinds of crops in a field from the crop they had planted there the year before.

See #3 below.

European farmers began using more fertilizers on their farms than they had used before. The fertilizers made the

Sheep raising in Cornwall, England

2. During the Middle Ages, farmers let some fields lie fallow, or unused.
3. Improved farming methods--the rotation of crops and the use of fertilizers--improved farm production in Europe.

For Teaching Helps, see page T86.
Stress:
1. As farming methods improved, new land was brought under cultivation.
2. The French and Spanish in America were not primarily interested in farming.

soil richer. How do you think this helped the farmers' crops? Improved production.

The farmers of Europe also began specializing in certain crops. They began paying more attention to temperature and rainfall when choosing which crops to grow. They discovered that they got better yields from certain crops in different areas.

See #1 above.

The farmers of western Europe learned to farm lands that they had considered **wastelands,** or lands not suitable for agricultural purposes. Some of the wastelands needed to be irrigated. This suggests that they were what kind of lands? Other wastelands were marshes. They had to be drained before they were suitable for farming. Why?

The importance of agriculture in the American colonies Farming was carried on in the American colonies of Spain, France, and England. The Spanish colonies contained some sugar plantations. There were also many small farms in the Spanish colonies on which the crops to support the colonists and their animals were grown. The French colonies, too, had many small farms for the support of the colonists.

But the Spanish were not very interested in agriculture. They were more interested in getting silver and gold from their American colonies. The French were also more interested in economic activities other than agriculture. The picture shows a French fur trader.

See #2 above.

French fur trader on the American frontier

Stress:
1. In the English colonies in America, agriculture was a major economic activity.
2. Most people of India farmed for a living.

Fur trading was the main economic interest of the French.

See #1 above.

The English were really interested in agricultural activities for economic profit. Most of the **cash crops**—those grown to sell to others—were raised on the plantations of the English colonies. In addition, far more colonists settled in the English colonies and farmed for a living than was true of the Spanish or French colonies.

See #2 above.

Farming in India The majority of people in India from 1500 to 1850 made their living by farming. They farmed the fields around rural villages something like the one shown in the picture. How do you think animals helped the farmer? What do the tools the man has tell you about Indian technology? Low level of technology.

All of India has a temperature that is good for farming, but not all of India receives the same amount of moisture. As was discussed in Chapter 10, the seasonal monsoons bring more moisture to the southern and eastern parts of India than to the northern and western parts.

People in the northern and western parts of India during the time from 1500 to 1850 grew crops such as wheat and **pulses.** Pulses are plants such as peas and beans. In the southern and eastern parts of India, the people grew rice.

Besides the crops mentioned above, the Indians grew some cash crops. Their more important cash crops included sugar cane and pepper.

Nineteenth-century Indian farmer carrying his wooden plow

The Indians also grew poppies which they used in making **opium** (ō'pi əm). Opium is a powerful drug which was traded with other countries. Cotton was also grown in the rich, black soil of some regions of India. The cotton was manufactured into cloth before being traded to other countries.

The English helped improve Indian agriculture After becoming the rulers of large parts of India, the English attempted to improve the productivity of the land. One of the things the English did was to dig a number of irrigation canals. How do you think this helped to make dry lands useful for growing crops?

The English also introduced fertilizers and better tools into India. In addition,

For Teaching Helps, see page T86.
Stress:
1. Geographic conditions affected farming in India and China.

they began research projects to develop varieties of crops for India that would give larger yields.

How the Chinese farmed their land

See #1 above.

Like India, parts of China are affected by the monsoon winds. Therefore, some parts of China get more moisture than other parts. The southern part gets much moisture during the wet, monsoon season.

Rice was the main food crop of the Chinese between 1500 and 1850, just as it was before that time. It was the staff of life for the Chinese, as wheat was for the Europeans.

The picture on page 253 shows Chinese farmers transplanting young rice plants. Observe how the farmers must stand ankle-deep in the soil and water to accomplish this task.

Chinese rice planting took much human labor. The tender, young plants had to be handled very carefully. The Chinese could have avoided some of the labor by sowing their rice seed in big paddies or fields instead of in small seedbeds. But this would have shortened the length of time they could use these same fields for other crops. Why do you think the Chinese wanted to raise more than one crop in their fields? It would also have wasted rice seed, by requiring that the plants be thinned out at a later time.

Other Chinese crops included wheat, millet, tea, and bamboo. Young bamboo sprouts were used for food. Fully grown bamboo was used for building materials and for making coarse cloth.

In the 1700's corn, peanuts, and sweet potatoes were introduced into China by traders from the Americas. These new crops helped the Chinese to feed their growing population. Sweet potatoes were especially valuable because they could be grown in soil that was useless for growing rice.

See #2 below.

Chinese farmers kept animals for food. Pigs, ducks, geese, and chickens were commonly raised on Chinese farms for meat. The chickens also supplied the farmers with eggs.

Fish were also an important source of food for Chinese farmers. Historians have evidence that Chinese farmers raised fish in their irrigation ponds.

Farming in Benin and Kanem-Bornu

The people of both Benin and Kanem-Bornu were food gatherers. But they also grew some of their food.

An especially important food crop was **yams.** Yams are the starchy, solid, thickened root of various vine plants. They are similar to sweet potatoes. Yams provided good food value and could be grown in the hot African climate. The people of both Benin and Kanem-Bornu grew yams.

See #3 below.

Being in the equatorial forests of Africa, Benin was not a very good place for agricultural activities. Many crops could not be easily cultivated there, and many animals could not be safely kept there. The **tsetse** (tset'si) fly—a fly of Africa that causes sleeping sickness and other diseases—was present in most of the equatorial forests. It was deadly to animals such as donkeys and cattle.

Kanem-Bornu was in the **savannas,** or grasslands, of Africa. The people grew millet, beans, and wheat.

The people of Kanem-Bornu also kept animals such as cattle, horses, donkeys, and camels. The tsetse fly was not a problem in the savannas. Thus the people of Kanem-Bornu lived in one of the more desirable parts of Africa for carrying on agricultural activities.

See #1 above.

Think for Yourself

Do you think it is possible for a country to maintain good farmlands year after year? If so, how?

Rice farmers transplanting rice plants

253

Tailor

Hatter

European tradesmen at work

THE MANUFACTURING OF GOODS

Craft guilds in western Europe For hundreds of years after the Middle Ages, goods in the countries of western Europe were made by hand. One person, a craftsman, produced each article all by himself. Most of the time he depended upon muscle power to run any machines he had in his shop.

The craftsmen formed groups called **guilds.** Guild members were trained in the skills needed to produce the goods of one craft. There were different guilds for the making of cloth, shoes, and many other things.

The pictures show two different kinds of craftsmen at work. Observe how each of the kinds of work is done by hand. Do you think that craftsmen could make many goods in a day this way? Why or why not? Only a few items could be made by hand each day.

New sources of power Producing goods by muscle power was a long and slow process. Why? Eventually new sources of power began to be used.

For many years men had been using water power to turn a large water wheel that supplied power needed to turn millstones used in grinding their grain into flour. They also used water power for sawing logs into lumber.

A few men gradually began using water power to run some of the machines they invented. What advantages do you think water power had over muscle power? What disadvantages might there be in depending upon water power?

See #1 below.

See #2 below.

See #3 below.

E/S

S/E

E

Stress:

1. At first, the manufacture of goods was done by hand as shown above.
254 2. In Europe, craftsmen organized into groups called guilds.
3. The use of water power enabled men to run heavy machines, but this required that shops had to be located near rivers and streams.

Stress:
1. During the 1700's, man learned to use steam as a source of power.
2. The invention of certain machines increased production in the 1700's.

Thinking about the geography of a country may help you to decide one disadvantage.

Many men were not satisfied with the amount of goods that they could produce with either muscle power or water power. Some of these men kept searching for new kinds of power that would make greater production possible. Why do you suppose men wanted greater production? To meet needs and wants and for trade.

See #1 above. In the 1700's steam power began to be used. Men were learning to use steam engines for running their machines. What advantages do you think steam power would have over both muscle power and water power?

See #2 above. **The importance of inventions** A number of different kinds of machines for producing goods faster were invented in the 1700's. Many of the first machines invented aided in the production of **textiles,** or cloth. These machines were not very large or complicated. Therefore, they could easily be used in the homes and small shops of the craftsmen. Later on, larger and more complicated textile machines were invented.

Other machines were invented for use in the coal industry and the iron industry. As time went on, machines were invented for many kinds of industry.

Factories develop in Europe When larger and more complicated machines were invented, factories began to be built. Machinery powered by water had to be placed in buildings located near flowing streams of water. Machinery powered by steam was heavy, complicated, and expensive. Why would heavy machinery be better suited to a factory than to a home or small shop? Larger than home or shop.

The use of the new sources of power and machinery to produce more goods is called **industrialization.** As industrialization developed in Europe, the iron industry became important. One reason was because iron was used to make some of the new machinery. Iron was also used to make other kinds of goods.

England as a leader England was the leading nation of Europe in industrialization. There were good reasons for this. Because of its trade, England had money to invest in factories and machines. Also, English inventors showed great skill in applying their new scientific knowledge to machinery.

See #4 below.

England also had the necessary natural resources for industrialization. It had good water resources and excellent supplies of coal and iron. Then too, England had good supplies of **raw materials**—those materials suitable for manufacturing or processing. It got raw wool from its large sheep farms and raw cotton from its American plantations.

France developed textile and iron industries somewhat slower than England did. Spain lagged far behind both England and France in industrialization. Spain did not have very large supplies of

3. The invention of machines to produce goods--the Industrial Revolution--
   led to the development of factories in Europe.
4. Social, economic, and geographic conditions encouraged industrialization
   in England.

255

Stress:
1. Economic growth in Europe led to an increase in trade and in shipbuilding.

natural resources or raw materials. Also, Spain began to lose some of its colonial territories to France and England. Why might this affect Spain's industrialization? Lost natural resources and wealth.

Shipbuilding in the western European countries England, France, and Spain were all interested in developing a shipbuilding industry during the time from 1500 to 1850. Why do you suppose this was so? For trade and exploration. S/E →

Ships at that time were built out of wood, like the one shown in the picture. Lumber was in great demand by shipbuilders. Some of the lumber came from the American colonies. Observe the tall,

straight poles used for the masts of sailing ships. Many of these poles came from American pine trees. Which European country do you think had an advantage in getting materials from America to use in shipbuilding? Why?

The production of goods in the American colonies The colonists of England, France, and Spain in America had to produce for themselves many of the things they needed. As was often true back in Europe, these things were produced in homes or in small craft shops.

It was not too many years, however, before the English colonies in America were producing goods such as textiles and iron products to sell to the people of European countries. England was not very happy about this. It did not want its colonies to sell goods to other countries. Why? England wanted their colonies to trade only with England.

See #2 below.

Neither did France or Spain want their colonies to sell goods to other countries. This was not much of a problem because their colonies produced less manufactured goods than the English colonies. Why was this so?

See #3 below.

When the English colonies in America gained their independence, they increased their production of goods. They no longer had to limit production to please England. E/P →

The United States had many advantages for manufacturing goods. The people of the United States had gained knowledge from England concerning the

Workers building wooden ship in a shipyard E/H →

2. The people in English colonies resented England's restrictions on their manufacturing and trade.
3. Because both France and Spain were slow to industrialize, their colonies lacked machines and thus produced less than the English colonies.

Sorting silkworm cocoons in China

Strands of silk being unraveled from cocoons

use of new sources of power and new kinds of machinery. The United States also had many natural resources and raw materials.

Craft industries in India and China
According to historians and economists, neither India nor China produced goods in factories between 1500 and 1850. But in both countries there were village craftsmen who manufactured goods for local use.

The local village crafts included the making of pottery and the production of various articles of metal or wood. They also included the spinning of yarn and the weaving of cloth.

Besides producing goods for local use, the people of India and China also man-

ufactured some products to sell to others. The Indians were producers of especially fine cotton cloth. This became India's major industry. The production of silk cloth was also an important industry in India, but the raw silk had to be imported from other countries.

The production of silk cloth was, of course, a major Chinese industry. The people of China produced their own raw silk. The pictures on this page show two of the many steps involved in the making of silk. In the picture on the left, silkworm cocoons are being carefully sorted at a table. Notice the trays in the background where the cocoons are kept. In the other picture a woman is unraveling the strands of silk from the cocoons

See #1 below.

E ↔

See #2 below.

H/E ←

E ↔

Stress:
1. Production in India and China from 1500 to 1850 was carried on largely by craftsmen working in homes or small shops.
2. Cotton cloth was exported by India, and silk cloth was exported by China.

257

and collecting the strands on a reel. This is a task that requires slow and careful human labor.

Many other industries of China required much human labor. Among these industries were the production of straw sandals and cloth shoes, the making of leather, the manufacturing of iron pots, and the processing of tea.

The local crafts of Benin and of Kanem-Bornu In the 1700's and 1800's, the people of Benin and Kanem-Bornu did not produce goods by the use of steam power or machinery. But historians and economists do have evidence that some of the people of Benin were lo-

See #1 above.

cal craftsmen. Various articles of bronze and copper appear to have been made in Benin, not brought in by trade. The artistic designs on these articles show activities of the people of Benin. Carvings in ivory suggest that Benin also had ivory craftsmen.

Some people of Kanem-Bornu must have been metal craftsmen. Metal articles that have been found in that area appear to have been made locally.

Think for Yourself

Do you think a demand for goods helped man solve problems of producing more goods? Why or why not?

THE DISTRIBUTION OF GOODS

For Teaching Helps, see page T88.

The rising importance of trade in Europe Toward the end of the Middle Ages, the people of European countries such as Spain, France, and England were no longer satisfied with just what they could produce for themselves in their local communities. They wanted goods produced in other communities. Satisfying these wants led to trade among the communities of each country.

See #1 below.

Trade within Spain was hindered by restrictions on trade and by taxes levied on goods going from one part of the country to another. Trade restrictions and taxes also hindered trade within France. In England there were fewer restrictions and fewer taxes.

The people of Europe also wanted goods produced in other countries—especially countries of the East. Among these goods were spices, cotton cloth, silk cloth, and fine pottery.

The map on page 259 shows some main trade routes in use by Europeans who traded with the East at the end of the Middle Ages. Notice that the trade routes cross both land and water. Also observe that some of the routes go through or near the Ottoman Empire. The people of this empire, called the Ottoman Turks, placed a high tax on the goods going through their lands. This added to the cost of goods from the East when they were sold in Europe.

See #2 below.

Stress:
258 1. The demand for goods led to an increase in trade in Europe.
2. Taxes on goods usually mean that consumers must pay higher prices.

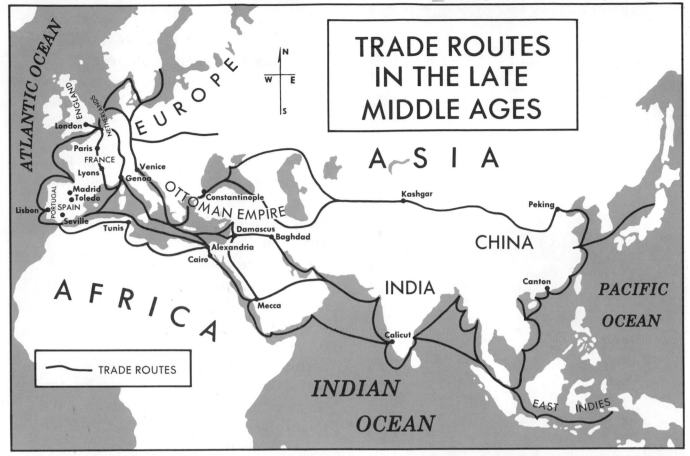

TRADE ROUTES
IN THE LATE
MIDDLE AGES

ATLANTIC OCEAN

EUROPE

ASIA

AFRICA

CHINA

INDIA

PACIFIC OCEAN

INDIAN OCEAN

London · Paris · Lyons · Madrid · Toledo · Lisbon · Seville · Tunis · Venice · Genoa · Constantinople · Damascus · Baghdad · Alexandria · Cairo · Mecca · Kashgar · Peking · Canton · Calicut

ENGLAND · FRANCE · PORTUGAL · SPAIN · NETHERLANDS · OTTOMAN EMPIRE · EAST INDIES

—— TRADE ROUTES

The countries of western Europe go exploring In the late 1400's and early 1500's, many European countries became interested in exploration. They wanted to get goods from places in the East without paying a tax to the Ottoman Turks. They also wanted to find an all-water route to the East.

The sailors of many countries began exploring for new routes to the East. Among the successful exploring countries were Portugal, the Netherlands, Spain, France, and England. Locate these countries on the map. All the Netherlands belonged to Spain until 1579. Explorers tried to go to the East by sailing south and east. They got to India and China by sailing around the southern tip of Africa.

Some explorers tried to reach the East by sailing west because they thought the world was round. These men were right, but the continents of North America and South America blocked their path.

The European countries that discovered different parts of the American continents explored them. They also

See #1 below.

H/G →

E/P ←

G →

See #2 below.

Stress:
1. Economic factors led to an increase in exploration.
2. The search for new trade routes led to the discovery of new lands.

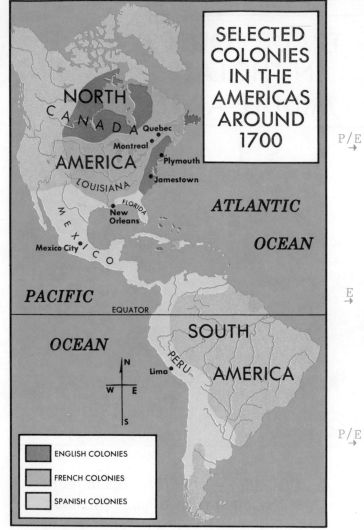

SELECTED
COLONIES
IN THE
AMERICAS
AROUND
1700

NORTH
CANADA
AMERICA
Quebec
Montreal
Plymouth
LOUISIANA
Jamestown
FLORIDA
New
Orleans
MEXICO
Mexico City

ATLANTIC
OCEAN

PACIFIC
OCEAN
EQUATOR

SOUTH
AMERICA
PERU
Lima

N
W E
S

☐ ENGLISH COLONIES
☐ FRENCH COLONIES
☐ SPANISH COLONIES

Stress:
1. Spain, France, and England claimed
   land in the Americas.

Which route to the East do you think the European traders preferred? Why?

The colonial policies of western European countries Spain, France, and England all felt that their colonies should benefit the home country. In their opinion, the main reason for having colonies was to make a profit from them. This way of dealing with the colonies came to be known as **mercantilism** (mėr′kən ti liz′ əm).

P/E →

Under mercantilism the home country expected to get raw materials from its colonies. The home country also expected to sell any of its surplus goods to its colonies.

E →

See #2
below.

How American colonial trade was affected by mercantilism Some of the colonies in America wanted to have their own trade. They wanted to trade with one another, and they wanted to trade with European countries other than their home country. The home country, however, wanted the colonial goods or wanted to make a profit by transporting them. The home country restricted the trade of its colonies.

P/E →

See #3
below.

The trade restrictions on the colonies sometimes kept their economy from growing as fast as it otherwise might have grown. Do you think mercantilism was a fair or unfair way of treating the colonies? Why?

G/H ←

Commercial rivalry There was much rivalry among the countries of western Europe in their trading activities. Each

G ←

started colonies in America. The map on this page shows what parts of the American continents were claimed by Spain, France, and England around 1700. Observe the parts of the Americas that each country claimed.

See #1
above.

Some explorers who sailed west did get all the way to India and China. But they discovered that such a route was much longer than an easterly route.

2. Colonies in North and South America were established to help the growth
   and development of the home countries' economic systems.
3. Trade restrictions hindered economic growth in America and made the
   colonists angry.

country engaged in trade to make a profit. To make a profit, each country thought that its **exports** had to be greater than its **imports.** Exports are goods sent out of a country. Imports are goods brought into a country. When its exports were greater than its imports, a country had a **favorable balance of trade.**

At first Spain gained more wealth from its trade than either France or England did from theirs. Spain got silver and gold from its American colonies.

France also gained wealth from its trading activities. Much of this wealth came from its fur-trading activities in America. As France slowly industrialized, its wealth from its commercial activities increased. Why?

The European nation that gained the most from its colonial and commercial activities was England. England's American colonies developed a more productive system of agriculture and industry than did the colonies of Spain or France. England's own superiority in industrialization gave it great advantages in trade with other countries. Why?

See #1 above.

The commercial activities of India Commercial activities within India were hindered by poor means of transportation. But there were many small market towns scattered throughout the country. At these towns the people exchanged their surplus agricultural crops and their locally produced craft goods.

India had trade with other countries before the arrival of European traders. It carried on a small amount of trade with a few places in Africa and with countries in Asia such as China.

European trade with India Among the European countries competing for trade with India were Portugal, the Netherlands, France, and England. The English finally succeeded in getting most of this trade.

The English established **trading factories,** or posts, at a number of places along the coast of India. The map shows the location of the most important English trading factories. What advantages do you think the distribution of these trading factories gave England? Reduced the distance goods had to be transported.

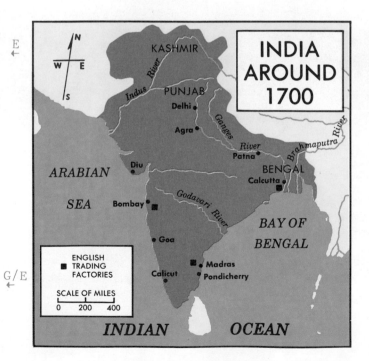

2. Poor means of transportation limited trade in India.
3. European control of lands and people was extended into Asia after 1600.
261

Stress:
1. Industrialization increased England's export of certain goods.

Some of the products that European countries such as England imported from India were cotton goods, sugar, pepper, and **indigo** (in′də gō). Indigo is a plant from which a blue dye can be obtained. European exports to India included wines, novelty items, and silver. After industrialization of its textile industry, England began exporting cotton goods to India. Turning the trade of cotton goods in its favor helped England's balance of trade with India.

See #1 above.

Chinese commercial activities The Chinese conducted much trade within their own country. Agricultural products and goods manufactured by local craftsmen were transported from one village to another. This domestic trading was centered in a village trade fair.

Porcelain vase seen from both sides

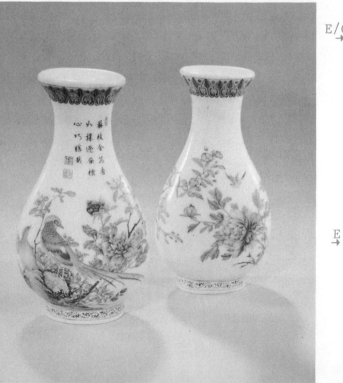

Trade fairs were held at many Chinese villages every ten days. Most of the trade was carried on by the direct exchange of one kind of goods for another.

Some goods which were the special products of certain regions of China were distributed to other regions by peddlers and traveling merchants. Among such goods were articles made of **porcelain** (pôr′sə lin), pottery, and certain kinds of metal goods. Articles of porcelain have a superior whiteness and hardness to the outside finish.

See #2 below.

The porcelain vase shown here was made in China in the early 1800's. Observe the beautiful shape of the vase and its artistic decoration. What do these things tell you about the skills of Chinese craftsmen? Were of a high level.

European countries and trade with China Before European nations came to China for trade, the Chinese engaged in a limited trade with some countries in Asia and certain places along the east coast of Africa. Why would China be more likely to trade along the east coast rather than the west coast of Africa? Looking at a world map or at a globe will help you decide.

From the 1500's on, some European countries tried to increase their trade with China. The people of Europe wanted many of the Chinese goods. Among the goods which were highly desired were tea, silk cloth, and articles of porcelain.

2. Specialization in the manufacture of certain items can improve quality and can lead to an increase in trade.

See #1
above.

Unfortunately for the Europeans, the Chinese did not desire European goods. The Chinese felt that their civilization was superior to that of the Europeans. The Chinese were inclined to look down on Europeans and their goods.

A/E

One thing that the Chinese would accept for their goods was silver. Thus the Chinese exported many goods, but imported mostly silver. Do you think the Europeans or the Chinese had the favorable balance of trade? Why?

E

The Europeans later found a product other than silver which the Chinese merchants would accept. This was opium. This drug had bad effects upon many of the people of China, and the Chinese rulers objected to the opium trade. But the Europeans continued trading opium because it helped the European balance of trade.

E

See #2
below.

A war was finally fought between England and China over the opium trade and many other things. One of the things that England did not like about its trade with China was the many restrictions that China placed upon trade with England. China only allowed European countries to trade at a few places. China did not want contacts with European countries. Do you think a nation should have a right not to have contacts with other nations? Why or why not?

H/E

Benin's commercial activities Dutch traders from the Netherlands were the first Europeans to trade with the mer-

Rings of metal (at top) and shells (at bottom) were used as money in Benin.

chants of Benin. Later came the Portuguese, and still later the English.

Among the goods Dutch traders imported from Benin were pepper, leopard skins, and **jasper stones.** Jasper stones are a variety of quartz that may be red, brown, green, or yellow in color. They also imported female slaves.

The Dutch exported many kinds of goods to Benin, including cloth of cotton, linen, velvet, silk, and flannel. They also exported items such as candied oranges and lemons, mirrors, brass bracelets, and bars of iron.

E

For money, the people of Benin used the articles shown in the picture. The crescent-shaped rings of metal were called **manillas** (mə nil'əz). The shells were **cowrie** (kou'ri) **shells.** A cowrie is

2. Conflicts, mainly over economic policies and trade, led to a war between England and China.

263

3. Europeans tended to export manufactured goods to people in Africa in return for natural resources.

Warrior of Kanem-Bornu

a small, snail-like animal, with a brightly colored shell.

The merchants of Benin traded items to the Portuguese and the English that were similar to those that they traded to the Dutch. Later on, however, the trade in slaves became more important than anything else. The slave trade began including males and children.

See #1 below.

In the end, the slave trade had a bad effect upon Benin. It led the people of Benin to raid other tribes for slaves to sell. It led to warfare, destruction, and finally the downfall of Benin.

The commercial activities of Kanem-Bornu The merchants of Kanem-Bornu controlled the trade of the entire area around Lake Chad. Lake Chad was at the southern end of some of the northern trade routes. These northern trade routes began in the cities along the coasts of the Mediterranean Sea and the Nile River. Therefore, most of the trade of Kanem-Bornu was with merchants of the Ottoman Empire.

The imports of Kanem-Bornu included salt, copper, cotton cloth, wood products, glassware, beads, swords, **chain mail,** and horses. Chain mail was a type of armor made of metal rings linked together. The people of Kanem-Bornu wanted swords, chain mail, and horses for use by warriors like the one shown here.

Kanem-Bornu exported ivory, gold, ostrich feathers, **kola nuts,** and slaves. Kola nuts are the seeds of a variety of African tree. Today the juice of kola nuts is used in making many kinds of cola beverages. What cola beverages have you had?

See #2 below.

The kingdom of Kanem-Bornu maintained a prosperous trade for many, many years. Its fine location around Lake Chad was mainly responsible for this.

Think for Yourself

Do you think location is important in maintaining good trade today? Why or why not?

Stress:
1. The slave trade led to the downfall of the kingdom of Benin.
2. Geographic conditions can influence a society's trade with other societies.
*3. In what ways can trade benefit industrialized and nonindustrialized nations?

TRANSPORTATION

The importance of water transportation in Europe From the 1500's to the 1800's, water transportation was important in most European countries. One reason for this was the lack of good roads. The rivers and streams of England, France, and Spain served as highways for transporting goods and people.

One disadvantage of water transportation is the fact that rivers and streams do not always go where people want to go. To help overcome this problem, many canals were built.

Streets and roads are improved For many years the countries of Europe had streets and roads of dirt. These roads were dusty in dry weather and muddy in wet weather. Almost always, they had deep ruts in them. Frequently, dirt roads washed out altogether.

As countries of Europe such as England, France, and Spain increased their trading activities, they began to improve their roads. Some of the roads were paved with crushed rock so they would not be as muddy as before or wash out easily. Why did trading help to further the building of good roads?

The picture shows a man in a cart crossing a bridge in Spain. Bridges such

265

Spanish peasant crossing a bridge in his cart

For Teaching Helps, see page T89.
Stress:
1. Railroads helped to increase economic activity in Europe and America.

as the one shown in the picture made it much easier for people to cross rivers and streams. How do you suppose people crossed bodies of water before bridges were built?

In the 1800's railroads were being built in European countries. This new form of land transportation helped to transport both goods and people.

See #1 above.

Transportation in the American colonies People in the American colonies transported their goods and traveled very much as the people did in Europe. Rivers and streams became their first highways. Later on, canals were built to link many of the important rivers.

As time went by, dirt paths and trails were widened into roads. Some of the

Chinese "coolie" transporting goods

roads were even paved, and bridges were built over many rivers and streams.

In the 1800's railroads began to be built in the United States. Many parts of the east coast of the United States were linked by railroads to towns on the Mississippi River.

See #1 above.

Transportation in India Rivers and streams were important for transportation in India, just as they were in Europe. Wherever it was possible, both goods and people were transported by water.

India had some very poor roads. Wagons pulled by bulls or carts pulled by camels traveled these roads. Pack horses were also used.

See #2 below.

When the English took over much of India, they helped to improve transportation. The English widened the old roads and built many news ones. They also began building a railway system in India.

China's transportation China, like India and the countries of Europe, also used water transportation. In addition to using the rivers and streams, the Chinese built some canals.

Roads in China were very narrow, dirt paths or trails. The Chinese transported goods over them in carts and wheelbarrows. In the northern parts of China, people also used animals such as donkeys and camels for transporting goods.

See #2 below.

The picture shows a method that was

Stress:
1. The size of a nation's population can influence the nation's economic
   activities, trade, and transportation.

commonly used for transporting goods in the southern parts of China. Observe the pole, called a **carrying pole,** that the man has balanced on his shoulders. Notice the goods attached to each end of the pole. What advantages do you think there would be to this method of transportation in a country with poor roads and many people? More economical than building roads.

G/E
←

Walking was a common means of travel among the people of all countries. But people in countries that were beginning to build good roads naturally began to use methods of travel that were both faster and easier than walking. In China, however, the roads continued to be narrow, dirt paths. Thus the Chinese relied very heavily upon walking as a means of travel.

Wealthy Chinese might travel in a **sedan chair.** The picture shows a Chinese gentleman being carried in this kind of chair. Why might a country with plenty of human labor be more likely to use this method of transportation than a country where human labor was scarce? Economical.

See #1 above.

Transportation in Benin and in Kanem-Bornu Some transportation in Benin was by water, but much of it was by land. The people walked along the narrow, winding paths, that they had been able to make through the forests. Instead of carrying goods on a pole, as the Chinese did, the people of Benin carried goods on their head. Many

slaves in Benin were used as head carriers. Why would someone have better success carrying things on his head than with a carrying pole in the forests of Benin?

On the rivers of Kanem-Bornu, both goods and people were transported by canoe. The people of Kanem-Bornu also transported goods and traveled by using horses, donkeys, and camels. This was possible because their kingdom was located in the savannas. Thus, the people of Kanem-Bornu had rather good means of transportation compared with much of Africa in the 1600's and 1700's.

E/G
↔

Think for Yourself

How are good means of transportation important to a country and its people?

2. Means of transportation in Benin and Kanem-Bornu were influenced by
   custom, tradition, geography, and available animals.
*3. Why might a nation's transportation system affect the prices of goods?

267

Things to Do

See page 256.

1. Make a model of a ship like the ones that the English used during the years when they were exploring the world. You might use cardboard or heavy construction paper for the body of the ship and paper or lightweight cloth for the sails.

See page 262.

2. Make a list of articles in your home or that you have seen in other places that are made of bamboo. If possible bring an article or a picture of an article made of bamboo to class. Be prepared to tell your class about the article and how it is used.

CLASS PROJECT—PART 3

You should now have everything done for Act 1 of your play. If not, finish Act 1 now. Then you will want to start on Act 2. The second act of your play should be about people's economic activities.

As a class, decide which economic activities of the English people in the 1600's you want to use for scenes in Act 2. Here are two ideas of places your family for the play might use as scenes for such activities.

1. A rural scene with people working on a farm.
2. A small group of people working in a textile shop.

Once a decision has been made, the committees should begin work on the scenery, costumes, props, and the writing for Act 2. Information from studying Chapter 15 should help you.

As you study Chapter 16, be thinking about the scenes you may want to use in Act 3 of your play.

Philip II   Elizabeth I   Louis XIV

16. Man's Political Activities

For Teaching Helps, see page T90.

See #1 below.

If you think about the countries in today's world, you will probably recall certain leaders who have helped to make their country successful. You may also recall some of their important political activities. For example, the President of the United States signs many bills into law and explains important policies of our country to the people.

Between 1500 and 1850 there were many great leaders in Europe. A few of these important leaders are shown here. Philip II of Spain, Louis XIV of France, and Elizabeth I of England were each a strong leader of his individual country. Their political activities helped to make their country important. For example, these strong leaders brought order to the country they ruled. They also promoted their country's exploration, trade, and colonization.

See #2 below.

As you study this chapter, you will learn about many of the world's leaders who lived between 1500 and 1850. You will also learn about many of their political activities.

JUST FOR FUN

Look in newspapers and magazines for pictures of important leaders in the world today. Bring the pictures to class and be ready to identify each person and tell what he does.

Stress:
1. Good leaders can help a nation grow and develop.
2. Strong leadership can provide a stable government and promote economic growth.
*3. In what way does the strong leadership of your political officials help your country remain successful?

For Teaching Helps, see page T91.   For a class activity, see #1 on page 285.
Stress:
1. European monarchs gained strength and power as feudalism declined.

STRONG CENTRAL GOVERNMENTS

See #1 above.

European kings and queens By the end of the Middle Ages, many European **monarchs**—kings and queens who usually inherit their throne—had succeeded in gaining much of the governing power in their country. They did this by reducing the power of the nobles and enforcing their own laws throughout their country.

The monarchs of countries such as Spain, France, and England continued to increase their power in the 1500's and 1600's. The monarchs of these countries became powerful enough to affect many of the historical events of the world during their time.

The monarchs of Spain Among the monarchs who helped to make Spain an important country were Ferdinand and Isabella, who are remembered for their efforts to help make Spain a more unified country. Charles I—who as Charles V, was also emperor of the Holy Roman Empire—was a powerful ruler, but he was too busy with problems in the Germanies and the Netherlands to spend much of his time ruling Spain.

P/H

The picture shows Charles in his armor with his sword. According to the picture, what activity might have kept Charles busy? Warfare.

Perhaps Philip II, who ruled Spain from 1556 to 1598, was more powerful than any of the other monarchs who sat on the throne of Spain. He took steps to assert his authority throughout all the provinces of Spain and to make the country more united. He **recodified,** or reorganized into a uniform system, the laws of Spain. This was done so that the same laws would apply to people living in all parts of the country. Why would this be important to the king and the people? Unified the nation.

P

See #2 below.

The legislative body of Spain was known as the Cortes (kôr′tiz). Its members discussed a number of issues but had little power.

Because many of the important clergymen and nobles were members of the Cortes, Philip II did not want to directly interfere with it. Philip did not care how many issues the Cortes dis-

P/S

Charles I, King of Spain

Stress:
1. Powerful monarchs often ruled without consulting the people.
2. Louis XIV of France was an example of an __absolute__ ruler.

See #1 above.

cussed so long as he did not have to do what the Cortes said. He managed to rule without paying much attention to the Cortes by making and enforcing his own laws.

He managed to control all Spain by appointing loyal officials from among the rising middle class. Not wanting to risk the loss of their job, these officials did what the king asked them to do. King Philip even asserted his claim to the throne of Portugal. He felt free to do so because both his mother and one of his four wives had been Portuguese princesses.

Spain's influence in Europe declined after the reign of Philip II. The monarchs who came after him were generally not so capable as Philip had been. Also, other countries of Europe, such as France and England, were becoming stronger countries than they had been during Philip's reign.

The monarchs of France Some of the earlier French kings, such as Louis XI, Francis I, and Henry IV, helped to increase the power of the monarch over the nobles. But it was Louis XIV—the French king from 1643 to 1715—who stands out as the most important French monarch.

See #2 above.

Louis XIV took much of the ruling power of France into his own hands. He distrusted the nobles, and thus chose his officials from among the middle-class lawyers and businessmen. He gave the nobles social busywork to keep them occupied. But he did not give them any political rights. Why was this a smart move on the part of Louis?

To increase the power of both France and himself, Louis built a standing army of 350,000 men. It was the largest and best-equipped army in all Europe. To make France strong and independent economically, Louis supported many of its industries with financial bonuses and protective tariffs. Why would it be important to the strength of a country to be economically independent?

During the reign of Louis XIV and for many years after, the French legislative body—the Estates General—was never called into session. Strong French kings ruled without a legislative body by making the laws themselves. Louis XIV strengthened his lawmaking authority by forcing the **parlements** (pär′ lə mənts)—the highest courts in France —to accept his laws without question. Do you think this was good or bad? Why?

See #3 below.

The monarchs of England Like the people of Spain and France, the people of England looked to a monarch as their leader. But the people gave some of the power of government to the lawmaking body called Parliament. One of the kings, Henry VII, tried to rule independently of Parliament. He did this by reducing his expenses so he would not have to call Parliament into session to

See #4 below.

271

Stress:
1. Powerful kings in England have tried to control the Parliament.

King Henry VIII of England

vote him more taxes. Do you think the ability to vote taxes is very important? Why? Henry VII also established his own court—the Court of Star Chamber —as the highest court in the land. Why was this an important move on his part?

The picture shows Henry VIII. He was one of England's strongest kings. How does the way he is dressed help to show that he was an important person?

See #1 above. Henry VIII cooperated with Parliament, but his Parliament was made up of people he helped to choose. He attempted to influence elections and thus get king's men elected to the lower house of Parliament—the House of Commons. The upper house of Parliament—the House of Lords—was made up of the clergy and the nobles. Henry VIII also worked to get men of his choice into positions of leadership in the House of Commons. Why would he do this? To control Parliament and increase royal power.

P/S → Another way that Henry VIII used to increase his royal power in England was by appointing many of his officials from among the middle-class professional men and businessmen. Why do you suppose monarchs trusted middle-class men more than they did the nobles? Henry VIII also became powerful as head of the Church of England and as a strong supporter of English industries.

P/E ↔ Elizabeth—the daughter of Henry VIII—who ruled England from 1558 to 1603, also supported England's industries. She encouraged England's commerce and exploration, and she greatly strengthened England's navy. But neither Henry nor Elizabeth kept a standing army like the French king did. Why would a strong navy rather than a strong army be more important to England? See #2 below. See #3 below.

The American colonies and European governments The colonies that European countries established in America were naturally affected by the governments of the European countries that established them. The colonies of a country were expected to fit into the mercantile system of the home country P/E → and help make the home country rich and powerful.

2. Powerful rulers frequently encourage economic development to increase their power.
3. As an island, England relied upon her navy to protect her from invasion and to maintain her overseas colonies.

Stress:
1. Even capable rulers were unable to restore unity to India after 1500.
2. Lack of unity in India helped the Europeans to take over Indian territory.

Spain, France, and England had varying kinds of success with their American colonies. In the end the English had the most success. This was so even though thirteen of its colonies declared their independence and became the United States of America.

Personal lines of rulers in India Like the European countries of Spain, France, and England, India was a land ruled by strong persons during some of the years from 1500 to 1850. One of these was Akbar. He wisely enlisted the support of the Hindus during his reign. Why would this be a wise thing for a Muslim ruler of India to do? Reduced opposition to his rule.

A lack of unity in India In spite of the fact that India had a number of capable rulers who passed the reins of government on to the next ruler, it never had a government that was able to unify the country. Various groups in India maintained different religious and cultural ideas. And, in turn, these differences often led to political and military conflicts among the groups. P ← S/A ←

The lack of unity in India helped European countries to take over important parts of that country. The English were finally the most successful.

Chinese emperors During the 1500's and the first fifty years of the 1600's, emperors of the Ming Dynasty continued to rule China. Historians tell us that Ming emperors ruled China for almost 300 years—from 1368 to 1644. P/H ←

3. The Manchus conquered China and established a new dynasty in 1644.

After the Mings, came the Manchu (man'chü) rulers. K'ang-hsi (käng'-shē'), and Ch'ien-lung (chē en'-lùng'), a grandson of K'ang-hsi, were the two most important Manchu emperors. See #3 below.

The picture shows K'ang-hsi in a robe with many designs. Such designs were commonly used by the Chinese. How does the picture show that K'ang-hsi was an important person?

Together K'ang-hsi and Ch'ien-lung

K'ang-hsi, a Manchu emperor of China

ruled China for 121 years. Do you think the long rule of these two emperors helped to bring stability to China or not? Why?

The Chinese central government
Like some of the Chinese dynasties, the central government of China went on year after year. In fact, much of the organization of the Chinese central government was passed on from one dynasty to the next for hundreds of years. How do you suppose strong, central-government structures helped to bring stability to China? Maintained law and order.

See #1 below.

P/H ←

The ruler of Benin The ruler of Benin had complete power over the people in his kingdom. But he appointed many officials to handle the military, commercial, and economic business of the kingdom.

P/E ←

The ruler took part in the many ceremonies that were part of the political and religious life of the kingdom. He was crowned king in a grand ceremony. He was prepared for kingship by the queen mother of Benin, who was then forced to live a few miles from the city of Benin so she could not interfere in political matters. Do you think this was a wise plan or not? Why?

A ←

The picture shows a bronze sculpture of the queen mother of Benin. Observe her tall, beaded headdress and many necklaces. These are marks of the important position she held in her society. What were some of the marks of polit-

Sculpture of queen mother of Benin

ical importance used in European societies in the period from 1500 to 1850? What kinds of things are used to show the political importance of people in our society today?

A ←

The rulers of Kanem-Bornu Thousands of years ago Kanem-Bornu was ruled by the heads of families. But political scientists have evidence that long before 1500 the people of Kanem-Bornu were ruled by kings.

P/H →

The king of Kanem-Bornu inherited his position from the previous king. How was this like some of the ruling dynasties of Europe during the 1600's?

A ←

Idris Alooma was one of the most fa-

Stress:
1. Trained civil servants maintained the traditional Chinese government even when rulers changed.
2. The king of Benin had absolute and complete power over the people.

Stress:
1. New weapons helped the king of Kanem-Bornu to increase his power.
*2. Why did people in Europe, Asia, and Africa obey their kings?

See #1
above.

mous kings of Kanem-Bornu. He introduced firearms into his kingdom and brought instructors from Turkey to Kanem-Bornu to teach his warriors how to use them. With such weapons Idris attacked many of the kingdoms in the areas around Kanem-Bornu and forced those kingdoms to pay him **tribute**—money or something else of value paid for peace or protection. How was this like a fief or fee paid by people in Europe in the Middle Ages to various nobles?

Think for Yourself

P/E *Is a strong central government good or bad for a country? Why? Are strong rulers good or bad? Why?*

For Teaching Helps, see page T92.

DEMOCRATIC TRENDS

For a class activity, see #3 on page 285.

See #1
below.

Steps toward democratic government in England In democracies people keep much of the power of government for themselves. In the past they have often had to fight to get the power away from monarchs who used it unwisely.

For example, in the early 1200's King John did not rule England wisely. For one thing, he forced the people to pay very high taxes. The king's unjust acts caused the people to unite. By doing so, the people became powerful enough to force the king to agree to give them certain rights. These rights were written into an important document called the Magna Charta. The Magna Charta was one step forward in the people's fight for a democratic government.

Four hundred years passed before another important step toward a democratic government was taken in England. In the early 1600's the English king, Charles I, was ignoring the people's rights concerning taxation. Charles

P/E

was not living up to the provisions of the Magna Charta, but was taxing the people without their consent.

P/E Parliament, because of the support of the people, took action against the king. It developed a document called the Petition of Right. This document told the rights the people demanded for themselves—rights the king had assumed to be his.

E/S

King Charles was forced to give the people the rights they demanded in the Petition of Right. These rights included getting Parliament's permission before the king could collect certain taxes. They also included restrictions on the king's right to imprison people, to force people to keep soldiers in their home, and to declare **martial law**—military law—in times of peace. Do you think the king liked or disliked giving up power to Parliament? Why?

See #2
below.

P/S

The question of who was really to hold the power in England—the people,

P/E

Stress:
1. In a democratic political system, the people control the government.   275
2. Powerful kings usually were opposed to the idea of democracy since democracy reduced the king's power.

For Teaching Helps, see page T92.

Painting showing leaders of Parliament giving the crown to William and Mary

through Parliament, or the king—was not actually settled by either the Magna Charta or the Petition of Right. For example, toward the end of the 1600's James II stubbornly ruled England for three years without regard for the wishes of his subjects. Through the action of Parliament, King James was forced to flee the country.

Parliament was then faced with the task of getting a monarch who would respect the rights of the people. The picture shows Parliament offering the English crown to William III of the Netherlands and his wife Mary, who was the daughter of James II of England. What does the crown stand for? William and Mary accepted the offer and became the new English monarchs.

The Parliament that placed William

P/E →

P/S →

See #1 below.

and Mary on the throne took steps to make sure that in the future a king would be under the law instead of above it. A group of provisions that became known as the Bill of Rights was made the law of the land in England in 1689. Among the provisions of the Bill of Rights were the following points.

1. The king could not set aside laws.
2. The king could not levy taxes without the consent of Parliament.
3. Parliament should meet frequently and have the right to free speech.
4. Parliamentary consent should be necessary to raise a standing army in times of peace.

In what way is each of these provisions important?

Changes that Parliament made placed it above the monarch. In the future, laws

See #2 below.

Stress:
1. The people of England overthrew their king and established the idea that England would be ruled by Parliament and the laws of the land.
2. England's Bill of Rights limited the king's power and strengthened the power of the legislature.

276

were to be made by Parliament, not by the king. They were to be interpreted by judges, not by soldiers. The outcome of these changes became known as the Glorious Revolution, or the Revolution of 1689. Do you think the changes were good or bad? Why?

Thirteen colonies of England in America declare their independence Many things prompted the thirteen English colonies that finally became the United States of America to declare their independence from England. Certainly the colonists were upset by the taxes that England placed upon goods traded between itself and the colonies. The colonists declared that this was illegal and unfair because they had no representatives in the English Parliament where the tax laws were being passed. This idea became a famous slogan in the American Revolution, expressed in the words "no taxation without representation."

The colonists came to believe that the English King, George III, no longer had a right to rule them. They held that through the restrictive actions of his governors and his soldiers, the king had abused his legal rights with his subjects in the colonies.

The colonists finally decided that they had both a right and a duty to be rid of a bad government and to bring about a new and better one. Their ideas were then written into the Declaration of Independence.

The picture shows a number of the leading colonists gathered to sign the Declaration of Independence. Thomas

See #1 above.

P/E

P

P

E/P

See #2 below.

Painting by John Trumbull showing the signing of the Declaration of Independence

277

For Teaching Helps, see page T92.
Stress:
1. The first government of the United States was formed by the Articles of Confederation.

Jefferson, its chief author, is the man with the red vest who is standing in front of the desk.

After declaring their independence from England, the colonists had to fight to gain it. Some of England's old enemies, such as Spain and France, made war on England. France also gave direct support to the cause of the colonists. When the war ended, England recognized the independence of the thirteen colonies.

The government of the United States It was one thing for the thirteen colonies to have won their independence. It became quite a different thing for thirteen separate colonies to form a workable government that was agreeable to all of them as independent states. Their first attempt, under the Articles of Con-

See #1
above.

federation, was not very successful. After just nine years, representatives from the states met and wrote the Constitution.

The federal government established by the Constitution has been quite successful. Our federal government today still functions under this same Constitution that was written back in 1787. The men who wrote this great document did a very fine job. Some of the important authors of the Constitution are shown in the pictures. See if you can tell at least one important position each of these men later held in our federal government.

P/H
←

P
→

See #2
below.

P
←

Attempts at gaining independence in Latin America As in the thirteen English colonies of North America, the people of the Spanish and Portuguese

James Madison

Alexander Hamilton

George Washington

For a class activity, see #2 on page 285.

Stress:
1. Latin-American people won their
   independence during the 1800's.

See #1
above.

colonies of Latin America wanted to govern themselves. These people were able to win their independence in the early 1800's.

While many brave men aided the cause of Latin-American independence, two men in particular were outstanding leaders. One of these men was José de San Martín (hō zā′ de san′ mär tēn′). The other great leader of Latin-American independence is sometimes thought of as the George Washington of Latin America. This was Simón Bolívar (sē mōn′ bə lē′vär′).

See #2
below.

Study the map carefully. Observe the date when each Latin-American country gained its independence. How would you explain the fact that so many of the Latin-American countries gained their independence around the same time?

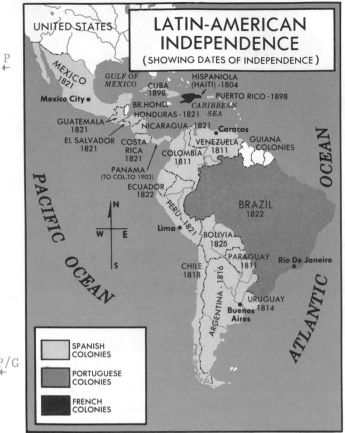

LATIN-AMERICAN INDEPENDENCE
(SHOWING DATES OF INDEPENDENCE)

SPANISH COLONIES

PORTUGUESE COLONIES

FRENCH COLONIES

Struggles for independence in France

See #3
below.

French kings before and after Louis XIV ruled without calling the Estates General into session. Strong French monarchs were successful at making France into one of the great nations of Europe. But around 95 per cent of the French people did not benefit from France's greatness. These people were burdened with high taxes and with high prices for the goods they had to buy. Many were poor, many were hungry, and many were unemployed.

Under Louis XVI the financial condition of France became very bad. France had spent much money fighting

wars. Louis XVI finally called the Estates General into session in 1789 to vote new taxes.

When the Estates General met, the members had more on their mind than just new taxes. They came with lists of complaints that the people of France wanted them to discuss. After 175 years of having no meetings of the Estates General, the people now wanted the government to be reformed.

For six weeks the members of the first two estates debated issues with the members of the third estate. Finally the members of the third estate withdrew

2. The example of the English colonies' successful revolt against England
   and the weakness of Spain led, in part, to the struggles for
   independence in Latin America.
3. Poor economic conditions led to unrest in France.

279

Stress:
1. After the king of France was overthrown, the legislature ruled the country.

Parisians storming the Bastille, July 14, 1789

from the Estates General and declared themselves the National Assembly.

The king tried to prevent the National Assembly from meeting as a separate body. He threatened to use force against it. But on July 14, 1789, a crowd P/S in the streets of Paris showed the king that the people of France were serious about reforming the government and restricting the power of the king.

The picture at the top shows the Paris crowd storming the Bastille (bas tēl')—a prison that had become a symbol of the king's power. Bastille Day is still celebrated as national independence day in France. What similar national A/H holiday do we celebrate in the United States? Fourth of July.

See #1 above. **A new leader for France** Although the National Assembly passed more than 2,000 laws to reform the French government, many people were not

pleased. Riots took place and thousands of people were killed. French attempts at a more democratic government seemed to be failing.

When the people of France failed to form a democratic government that could keep order, they lost some of the rights they had been fighting to gain. See #2 below. The people allowed a strong new leader —Napoleon Bonaparte (nə pō'li ən bō' nə pärt)—to take over the government. The picture at the bottom shows Napoleon being crowned as France's emperor. Do you think people in any of the democratic countries today could lose any of their rights to some powerful leader? If so, how?

Think for Yourself

Why have people usually had to fight for their independence and for democratic forms of government?

Napoleon being crowned as emperor of France

2. The failure of the new democratic government to keep order, caused the people to turn to Napoleon Bonapart.

280

*3. Why do many people want to live in a democratic society?

Stress:
For Teaching Helps, see page T93.
1. In Europe unified nations often became powerful.

RELATIONS AMONG COUNTRIES

A balance of power in Europe Many European monarchs gained power by unifying the various provinces of their country under a strong central government. This resulted in the growth of strong countries as well as strong monarchs. As their country and rulers grew in power, they also tended to grow in importance in the eyes of the people. People began to develop a spirit of **nationalism**—patriotic feelings or devotion toward the interests of one's own country. Both the rulers and the people wanted their country to have the most land, the most power, and the most prestige in the world.

English fleet attacking the Spanish Armada

Strong countries that had people with a spirit of nationalism were in competition for many of the same things—for example, land, gold, trade routes, raw materials, and markets. Competition among the countries of Europe often led to wars. Countries fought one another by both land and sea.

A famous sea battle is shown in the picture. It is the battle in 1588 between the Spanish Armada, or large fleet of warships, and the smaller English fleet. The smaller English ships were able to move about more quickly than the larger Spanish ships. Also the English sailors were more experienced than the Spanish sailors. These circumstances helped the English to defeat the Spanish Armada.

The English victory showed other countries that England had the strongest navy in the world. Because of its navy, England gained control of the seas and held control for hundreds of years afterward. How do you think this battle affected the national pride of Spain? The national pride of England?

Other European countries began to feel that it would be dangerous for the rest of them if any one country, such as England, was to become too strong. They felt that one way that weaker countries could compete with a stronger country was to join forces. The combined power of the weaker countries would balance that of a strong country. Thus a **balance of power** was created in Europe.

2. As nations in Europe became powerful, people developed loyalties to their nation and a spirit of nationalism grew.
281
3. Competition among European nations for power, prestige, and economic gain led to conflicts and warfare.

For Teaching Helps, see page T93.
Stress:
1. A balance of power was maintained in Europe with treaties and alliances.
2. The United States before 1900 tried to keep out of disagreements in Europe.

See #1 above.

Under a balance of power, various countries joined with different countries at different times. For example, sometimes England grouped itself with France and sometimes with Spain, depending upon which country seemed stronger at any given time.

Countries today try to keep a balance of power among the countries of the world. See if you can give a few examples of countries that have done this.

Early foreign policy of the United States The first President of the United States—George Washington—tried to keep our country out of conflict with other countries. When he left office, Washington advised our country to keep free from any agreements that might involve us in the affairs of other countries. Do you think this was wise or unwise advice for a young country? Why?

See #2 above.

The United States was not able to keep completely out of conflict with other countries. It got into disagreements and conflicts with a few of the European countries over some of the land in North America. But the United States did manage to keep out of the affairs of European countries in Europe.

In 1823 President James Monroe delivered a message to Congress concerning the independent countries in Latin America. Among the things he said was that all European countries should keep out of the affairs of the countries on the American continents. This message came to be known as the Monroe Doctrine.

The Monroe Doctrine clearly showed other countries that the United States had interests that went beyond its own borders. The future was to reveal the fact that those interests could not be confined to the American continents. Why do you suppose this was so?

See #3 below.

India's relations with other countries The picture shows Akbar—one of the great Muslim rulers of India—receiving representatives of other countries at his court. Observe Akbar's throne and the objects around it. Many objects in the court of Akbar were obtained through India's contacts with other countries.

Akbar receiving gifts from foreign representatives

3. The United States interest in Latin America was expressed in the Monroe Doctrine.

Stress:
1. China's power enabled the Chinese to dominate some countries in Asia.

India had contacts with European countries such as Portugal, the Netherlands, France, and England. These contacts with the countries of Europe resulted in conflicts between the people of India and Europe. Why?

See #1 above.

China's relations in Asia For many years, China was a more powerful country than its neighbors. Under the Ming emperors, Chinese **junks,** or sailing ships like the one shown here, sailed to a number of small countries in Asia. The Chinese forced these countries to pay tribute to them. Observe the sails of the junk. They were made out of coarse cloth with sticks of bamboo to help keep them rigid.

The sailing expeditions of the Chinese brought them wealth. What else do you think these expeditions brought the Chinese? How might these expeditions have affected the feelings of other people toward China?

In time the Chinese discontinued their sailing expeditions. The Chinese rulers were very uninterested in having contacts with other countries. Many Chinese merchants, however, felt differently. Why? Some of the merchants carried on an illegal trade with other countries.

China's relations with Europe The Chinese rulers were even less anxious for contacts with people from European countries than they were with people from the other countries of Asia. For a

See #2 below.

Chinese "junk"

long time the Chinese tried very hard to keep all Europeans out of their country.

At first the Chinese rulers placed a number of restrictions on the Europeans. Europeans could only come to a few carefully chosen places in China.

Sometime later, China and England fought a war called the Opium War. One result of this war was that a number of other places in China were opened up to Europeans. The five most important ports in China that had been forced open to Europeans and the United

See #3 below.

2. China tried to exclude Europeans from China.
3. The desire of nations to trade in, and to control, parts of China led to conficts and warfare with China.

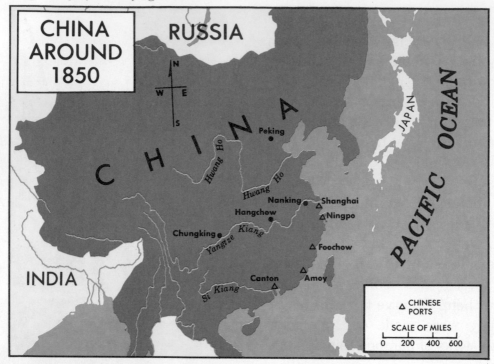

CHINA AROUND 1850

RUSSIA

CHINA

Peking

Hwang Ho

Hwang Ho

Nanking ● ● Shanghai
Hangchow △ Ningpo

Chungking ● Kiang

Yangtze Kiang

△ Foochow

Canton △ ● Amoy

Si Kiang

JAPAN

PACIFIC OCEAN

INDIA

△ CHINESE PORTS

SCALE OF MILES
0   200   400   600

Stress:
1. Map key helps to show the five important ports opened to Europeans and Americans.

States by 1850 are shown on the map. How would you explain their location?

The relations of Benin and of Kanem-Bornu with other countries Being located on the coast of Africa, the kingdom of Benin soon came into contact with the European countries that began exploring Africa. The Portuguese made contacts with the people of Benin shortly before 1500. The king of Benin sent an official representative to Portugal. Later both the Dutch and the English made contacts with Benin.

The African kingdom of Kanem-Bornu had a number of contacts with Islamic countries in the northern part of Africa and around the Mediterranean Sea. The people of Kanem-Bornu engaged in political, religious, and economic activities with some of the foreign countries in those areas.

Kanem-Bornu was located farther in the interior of Africa than Benin. Thus Europeans made contacts with Kanem-Bornu later than they did with Benin.

Some of the countries you have been studying had many contacts with other people. A few of the countries had only a few contacts with others. But none of the countries were isolated from the rest of the world. When it tried to isolate itself from other countries, China failed. Why?

See #2 below.

Think for Yourself

Do you think any country today could isolate itself from the rest of the countries in the world? Why or why not?

G/S ←

A/E ←

 2. By 1850 many countries were in contact with other countries of the world.
*3. Under what conditions might a country want to isolate itself from the rest of the world?

Things to Do

See page 270.
1. Pretend that you are the king or the queen of one of the European countries back in the 1500's or 1600's. Write a paragraph or two telling how you would treat the people of the different classes in your kingdom. You might begin something like this: "Today when I meet..."

See page 279.
2. Read a biography of José de San Martín or Simón Bolívar. Share its story with the members of your class and discuss the person's life.

See page 275.
3. Make a list of changes or reforms that people in the United States today would like to have their government make. You might get such information from articles in newspapers or magazines or from programs on radio or television. Share your list with the members of your class.

CLASS PROJECT—PART 4

You should now have both Act 1 and Act 2 of your class play completed. Now the class should choose political activities of the English people during the 1600's to show in the third act of the play. Two ideas of places your "play" family might use as scenes for political activities are given below.

1. The king and queen holding court.
2. A session of Parliament.

The committees should begin working on the scenery, costumes, props, and writing of Act 3 after a decision has been made by the class. Information from studying Chapter 16 should help you.

As a final step in your class project, you may give your play. You might invite guests to see it. At the end of the play you might discuss what you have learned about the way the people of England lived in the 1600's and how this differs from the way people in the United States live today.

Have the pupils find each of the review words in the unit. For each word, have them answer such questions as these:

Checkup Time

1. How was the word used in the book?
2. How might you use the word yourself?

For question 2 above, encourage the pupils to use each word in a social science context.

Review Words

balance of power	indentured servant	middle class	savanna
balance of trade	lower class	monarch	social mobility
export	martial law	nationalism	tribute
import	mercantilism	raw material	upper class

Review Questions

Typical answers only.

Social Science Facts

1. What kinds of questions did men begin asking about the world toward the end of the Middle Ages? (234) See bottom margin.

2. How did village life differ from city life in western Europe during the 1700's? (243) Less crowded and most people were farmers.

3. What kind of houses did the nobles of Kanem-Bornu build? (246) Red brick.

4. What made agricultural activities in Benin somewhat difficult? (252) Equatorial forests.

5. Why did England lead Europe in industrialization? (255) Had money, skills, and raw materials.

6. What hindered commercial activities within India? (261) Poor means of transportation.

7. How did the English Parliament try to make sure that a king would be under the law of England? (276) Bill of Rights.

8. What happened when the people of France failed to form a democratic government? (280) Napoleon Bonaparte gained power.

9. What did competition among the countries of Europe often cause? (281) Conflicts and warfare.

Social Science Ideas

1. How might the interests of people affect the kind of education they desire or get? Traditional ideas may restrict education.

2. How might the type of community in which a person lives affect his way of life? Urban areas have different life styles than do rural areas.

3. How does a person's house tend to show his social position? Show his wealth and power.

4. How can the geography of an area affect its agricultural activities? Limit opportunities.

5. What things might give a country an advantage in industrialization? Raw materials resources, and so on.

6. How can transportation affect the trade of a country? Poor transportation can hinder trade.

7. Why is it important that the ruler of a country be under the law of that country? To ensure that he does not violate the rights of the people.

8. What effect could people's failure to maintain a democratic government have upon their rights? They could lose their rights.

9. How might competition among countries lead to undesirable results? Could cause a war.

1. Why things were as they were, and how things came to be as they were.

Test Yourself

On your own paper, write your answer to each question.

Test 1 Social Science Words

Which word or words below refer to bringing goods into a country?
1. import   3. indentured servant
2. export   4. middle class

Which word or words below express the idea of being able to move from one social class to another?
5. rotate   7. lower class
6. indigo   8. social mobility

Which word or words below name a type of hereditary ruler?
9. balance of power   11. monarch
10. balance of trade   12. upper class

Which of these words is needed to complete each sentence below?

martial law   nationalism   savanna
mercantilism   raw material   tribute

13. A material suitable for manufacturing is called a __. raw material
14. — is a region of grassland. savanna
15. — is a home country's policy for dealing with colonies. mercantilism
16. Something of value paid for peace or protection is known as __. tribute
17. __ means military law. martial law
18. __ is a patriotic feeling or devotion toward one's own country. nationalism

Test 2 Facts and Ideas

Which is the best answer to each question below?

1. A good supply of which thing is needed for industrialization?
   a. raw materials   c. animals
   b. houses   d. villages
2. What might hinder the commercial activities of a country?
   a. an abundance of raw materials
   b. a large population
   c. poor transportation facilities
3. What is one big difference between life in a village and life in a city?
   a. how much people know
   b. how crowded people are
   c. what religion people have

Write the word or words in ( ) that make each sentence below true.

4. To help prevent wars, countries should engage in more (competition, cooperation).
5. Besides providing shelter, people's houses may show their (social position, educational interests).
6. The ruler of a country is usually (under the law, above the law).
7. Political rights of people in democratic countries have (always existed, been won over many years).

287

For Teaching Helps, see page T194.

UNIT
7 THE WORLD SINCE 1850

Stress:
1. As shown below, all societies have not achieved the same level of economic
   development.

Chapters
17. Modern Societies
18. Major Economic Systems
19. Governments of Modern Times

Indian women at work

Japanese television factory

*2. Which of these pictures most closely resembles life in America?

Stress:
1. Machines have changed people's
   living patterns.

17. Modern Societies

Man invented and used tools and machinery in order to improve his way of life. In many ways, machines have made S/E life simpler for people in the industrial societies. Name the objects shown in this picture which have made life easier for many. At the same time, machinery and industry have greatly changed people's living habits.

See #1 above.

People have had to find new ways of organizing their societies. Some societies were reorganized through violent revolutions. Other societies changed more peacefully.

See #2 below.

The people of every continent have been affected to some extent by the modern industrial world of western Europe and North America. African, Asian, and Latin-American countries are in the process of developing their own industrial societies. These countries are finding that social changes are necessary in S/E order to successfully industrialize. At the same time, social changes are being forced on these people as they come in contact with industry and modern farming techniques.

Refrigerator

Toaster

Electric iron   Stove

In this chapter you will see how European and American societies developed as a result of the changes brought about by industrialization. You will also see how people in some other parts of the world are trying to remake their societies.

See #3 below.

2. Sometimes changes within a society are brought about violently.

JUST FOR FUN

If you can, talk to a retired worker asking him to tell you the number of hours he worked on his first job and on his last job. Be ready to share your information with your classmates.

3. Industrialization brought about a reordering of societies in Europe and North America.

For Teaching Helps, see page T96.   For a class activity, see #1 on page 311.
Stress:
1. As industrialization progressed, the middle class increased in size and
   strength.

INDUSTRIALIZATION CHANGES SOCIETY

See #1 above.

Social classes Several changes took place in social classes in western Europe as societies became more industrialized. The members of one class—the middle class—became more numerous and more powerful. The new businessmen came largely from the middle class.

The middle class was further expanded as the factory owners sought people to manage the factories. These managers usually had some education. As more factories were built, more people were needed to act as managers. As a result, the middle class grew even larger. Those men who were in charge of the running of the factories did not usually own them, but their jobs were very important. These people were paid **salaries,** or fixed sums of money, each week or month.

See #2 below.

Some of the factory owners and bankers made great fortunes. People who own part of or all of an industrial concern are called **capitalists.** As some of these capitalists made great fortunes, they moved out of the middle class and into the upper class.

Some of the original members of the upper class became interested in business and invested their money in industry. Others refused to take part in industrial activities. Do you think these people kept or lost their standing as members of the upper class. Why?

A new class which resulted from the growth of industry was the working class. The men, women, and children who labored in the factories, mines, and on construction projects were all part of this class. At first the working class was made up of landless peasants. But as industrialization increased, many left their farms to work in the factories. What might have caused people to leave their farms? What effect would their leaving have on the societies they left?

See #3 below.

Increasing urbanization People who flocked into the cities found themselves faced with problems unlike anything they had ever experienced before. Housing shortages were common. Often families of five or six shared a one-room apartment. Slums, crooked streets, unpleasant odors, and crowded conditions were all part of the cities.

See #4 below.

Most factory workers lived in the cities in order to be near their jobs. On page 293 there is a scene of a New York neighborhood in the late 1800's. How would you describe what you see there?

In the United States the size and number of cities increased rapidly in the late 1800's. Part of this immense growth was a result of the flood of immigrants who arrived in America looking for factory work. One such immigrant was Michael Gold. Read the following passages which were taken from a book he

2. Soon the wealthiest members of society were successful capitalists.
3. The growth of industry led to the creation of a working class.
4. Industrialization caused the rapid growth of unplanned, overcrowded,
   unsanitary cities.

Tenements

Pushcart peddlers

East Side New York about 1900

wrote about his life in East Side New York. The time is about 1900. What were some problems faced by the working classes living in the cities? Housing shortages, poor sanitation, crime.

Always these faces at the tenement [a house divided into separate rooms occupied by many families] windows. The street never failed them. It was an immense excitement. It never slept. It roared like a sea. It exploded like fireworks.

People pushed and wrangled in the street. There were armies of howling pushcart peddlers. Women screamed. Dogs barked. . . . Babies cried.

The plaster was always falling down, the stairs were broken and dirty. Five times that winter the water pipes froze, and floods spurted from the plumbing, and dropped from the ceilings.

There was no drinking water in

Stress:
1. American cities grew rapidly.

*From *Jews Without Money*, by Michael Gold. Published, 1930, by Horace Liveright, Inc.

the tenement for days. The women had to put on their shawls and hunt in the street for water. Up and down the stairs they groaned, lugging pails of water.*

Urban centers sprang up almost overnight in some societies. Study the chart of urban growth in America. Which city grew the fastest? What kinds of problems can such rapid growth of a city bring to the people living there?

See #1 below.

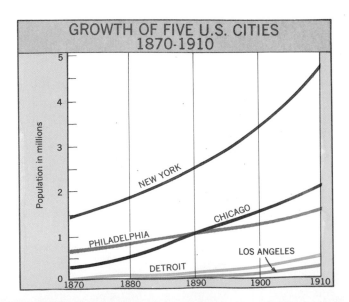

GROWTH OF FIVE U.S. CITIES
1870-1910

Population in millions

NEW YORK
CHICAGO
PHILADELPHIA
DETROIT
LOS ANGELES

Young man leaving the farm, about 1900

Breakdown of the family Sociologists are interested in studying the changes in family structure brought about by industrialization. Why is the family an important organization in most societies? Basic economic and social unit.

As families moved from the farms into the cities, they had to adjust to a whole new way of life. One worker living in a factory town described his life this way.

> The green grass and the healthful hayfield are shut out from our path. The whistling of the birds is not for us—our melody is the deafening noise of the engine. We eat the worst food, drink the worst drink; our clothes, our houses, our everything, shows our poverty.

Another change in the family came in its size. In agricultural societies families were often large. Usually all the relatives lived close to one another. But as people moved to cities, the number of children in each family usually decreased.

As families moved about from city to city in search of jobs, the closeness within families was further destroyed. Grandparents were seen less often by the grandchildren. For some people, there was less contact with cousins and aunts and uncles.

The city was a lonely and frightening place. People felt cut off from familiar people and safe surroundings. Look at this young man in the picture. He is leaving his family to find work in the city. In what ways will life in the city probably be different for him?

See #1 below.

See #2 below.

Stress:
1. Urban families are smaller and more mobile than agricultural families.
2. Adjusting to city life was lonely and difficult for many people.

1. Low wages and fear of losing their
   jobs were the chief concerns of
   working people for many years.

Plight of the workers Historians who write about the working people in the 1800's generally tell a story of struggle— a struggle to overcome the problems caused by industry. The chief concerns See #1 above. of most unskilled laborers were low pay and fear of unemployment. The hourly S/E wage or pay in some industries was often too small for a man to support his family. In many cases all members of the family were required to work. Look at the picture of these coal miners in Scranton, Pennsylvania. Some of them are just young boys. What effect did this work probably have on their health?

The fear of losing his job haunted the workingman. Often industries slowed S/E production because of loss of markets or for other reasons. Without warning, a man could be left with no income. Because his wages were low, he could not save money for such an emergency.

As a society became more highly industrialized, the people became more

Pennsylvania coal miners

removed from farming or fishing or other means of support. No longer could an unemployed worker turn to his farm to keep him alive until the next job came along. Many workers were now city people, completely dependent on the factories for a living. When his job was See #2 below. gone, the laborer had no other way of supporting himself. The people in the picture are lined up for food. What has probably happened to their jobs?

A breadline for unemployed workers

Stress:
1. Division of labor within factories caused work to become monotonous and uncreative.
2. Factory owners and managers often had little regard for the workers' welfare.

Loss of skills There was little room for craftsmen and skilled workmen in a highly industrialized society. Machines were replacing the artistry and skill of the workmen. A man could no longer claim credit for the product which he made.

As the methods of manufacturing changed, the problem became even worse for the workers, skilled and unskilled alike. The manufacturing of products was broken down into a number of separate, simple jobs. Each worker was assigned a small task to do. Dividing the work in this way is known as division of labor. As a result of division of labor, many workers lost the feeling of satis-

faction which comes from creating a product. They could expect no choice in the work assigned to them. But they could expect to repeat the same simple task over and over for twelve or fourteen hours a day, six days a week. A worker found it impossible to take pride in his work or to feel responsible for its quality. What was the only way in which a man was rewarded for doing work?

See #1 above.

Boredom with the job became a real problem for the factory worker. The factories were often managed with little or no regard for the worker. He was allowed few breaks in the routine. There were many rules and regulations. In some cases a worker could be fined for whistling at work or for being as little as five minutes late. But workers could not look forward to vacations or to any time off with pay.

See #2 above.

The unskilled worker had many of the same problems as the skilled worker. In addition he had to worry about low pay and fear of unemployment. All workers felt some measure of unhappiness and dissatisfaction over their conditions. Study the picture and describe the working conditions that you see.

See #3 above.

A sweatshop scene

Think for Yourself

If you had been a factory worker in the 1800's in England, France, or another industrial society, what would you have done to solve your problems?

*4. Why do you suppose that so few factory owners took an interest in the welfare of their employees?

Cooperative society of New Harmony, Indiana

For Teaching Helps, see page T97.

NEW IDEAS ABOUT SOCIETY

Help for the workers Factory workers and small farmers faced poor living and working conditions, unemployment and starvation. The small farmer found that he could not afford the new farm machines. In many cases he gave up his farm to take a factory job in the city.

See #1 below. Most people saw the evils that industrial change had brought. But people disagreed on how the problems should be solved. Many people believed that industry and farming should be left alone, and that the problems would be solved without any interference by the government or any other group. Other people felt that action had to be taken. One of these people was Robert Owen, an English cotton manufacturer. He lived before 1850, but his influence lasted past that date.

In 1800 Owen became the head of textile mills in New Lanark, Scotland. These mills employed 5,000 people, 500 of whom were children. Conditions in the mill town were horrible.

Owen increased workers' pay and improved working conditions. Schools and new houses were built. The worst evils of the town were removed. The factory owners, as well as the factory workers, earned more money. What do you think was the reason why profits from the mills increased? People worked better. See #2 below.

A model society Because the New Lanark community was so successful, Owen tried to build another similar society at New Harmony, Indiana. He established a social order based on community ownership. The property and the profits were shared by all the people living there. Study the picture and tell who did the work at New Harmony.

Stress:
1. Some people did not believe that the government should interfere with industry.
2. Robert Owen believed in people cooperating and sharing for the common good.

Stress:
1. Socialists believe that the government should own the means of production.
2. Many Europeans believed that socialism might solve the problems of industrialization.

Everyone was to do as much work as he was capable of doing. Owen thought that cooperation was the key to a successful society. No one should be poor or rich.

A social system like the one just described is called **socialism.** Owen and others who believed in this system were called **socialists.** Socialists expect the government to own the means of production—farms, factories, mines, and railroads. They expect the government to run these means of production for the benefit of all the people.

See #1 above.

Despite Owen's determination to build a model community, the experiment failed. The people of New Harmony were not truly willing to make the effort necessary for a successful society. But Owen was not alone in his failure. Others who believed as he did set up socialistic societies. They were also unable to make their ideal communities work. Do you think that anyone could make such a socialistic society work? Why or why not?

The spread of socialism In France, Germany, and Russia, many people began to see socialism as a solution to the problems caused by industrialization. Some believed, as Owen did, that the way to achieve socialism was through gradual and peaceful change. They dreamed of whole communities being built which would eventually change the way of life of an entire country.

See #2 above.

In 1848 a Frenchman, Louis Blanc, urged the French government to provide work for the unemployed. Although Blanc was not looking for a perfect society, he could also be called a socialist. Why?

Socialists and revolution There were other socialists who also saw evils in the industrial society. They too believed in common ownership of property and in the welfare of the workers. But unlike Owen and other socialists, some were not content to wait for gradual change. They believed that a socialistic society could only come about through the violent overthrow of existing governments. This form of socialism is called **communism.** Many people of the upper classes feared communism. Why?

See #3 below.

Communist thinkers Karl Marx, a German writer and social thinker, established the ideas and theories of present-day communism. Because of the influence of communism in today's world, Karl Marx is a most important historical figure.

See #4 below.

Marx came from a well-to-do family. He was given an excellent education, studying law, history, and philosophy. Marx could not become a university teacher because he was considered a **radical,** or one who favors extreme social changes. Marx's radical ideas caused him to lose his position on a newspaper. He left Germany and lived for some time in France and later in Belgium and England.

Stress:
1. Marx and Friedrich Engels wrote about the social and economic conditions of Europe.
2. Marx and Engels wrote the Communist Manifesto.

See #1
above.

In 1844 Marx met a factory manager, Friedrich Engels. The two men formed a lifelong friendship. Marx, the student with great mental power, provided the ideas; Engels knew factory conditions. Together, they studied the economic and social conditions of the 1840's. What kinds of things would they have seen?

See #2
above.

In 1848 they wrote a pamphlet which is still regarded as a blueprint for violent revolution. This pamphlet, first printed in German, was called the *Communist Manifesto* (man'ə fes'tō). It was the first statement of the principles of modern communism. Can you read any words on its cover?

E/S

The *Communist Manifesto* was written at a time when workers had no defenses against the evils of unregulated industry. Women everywhere lacked legal rights of any kind. In democratic America millions of slaves labored on southern farms.

Read the last section of the *Communist Manifesto*, keeping in mind the social problems of the middle 1800's.

P/S

The Communists disdain [refuse] to conceal their views and aims. They openly declare that their ends can be attained [reached] only by the forcible overthrow of all existing social conditions. Let the ruling classes tremble at a Communistic revolution. The proletarians [laboring class] have nothing to lose but their chains. They have a world to win.

Working men of all countries unite!

H/S

Why would this kind of writing appeal to so many workers of the 1800's? Present-day historians of nonsocialistic countries can find fault with the *Communist Manifesto*. They can criticize it for its failure to predict how social conditions could be changed without violent revolution. But despite the errors in much of Marx's thinking, even today the *Communist Manifesto* is accepted as the absolute truth by millions of workers throughout the world. See if you can tell why.

See #3
below.

3. The Communist Manifesto is still
   an important document because many
   people accept it as truth.

Communist Manifesto

Stress:
1. Marx predicted that the middle class in the industrial societies would disappear.
2. According to Marx, the workers would revolt and take control of industrial
   societies.

Marx and the working class Marx believed that as the society became more highly industrialized, almost everyone would become a **proletarian**—a member of the working class. According to Marx, the middle class would lose its money and disappear. There would eventually be only two classes in society. One class would control all the wealth—the businessmen who owned the banks and factories. Who would make up the other class?

See #1
above.

Marx believed that the owning class would become richer and the working class poorer. He predicted that businesses would finally fail in every industrial society. Factories would produce more goods than the workers could afford to buy. Factories would then close and millions of people would lose their jobs. At that point the workers would rise up and take over the control of the government. Under this system who would own the factories, farms, and other means of production? The workers.

See #2
above.

Think for Yourself

The communist revolution first took place in Russia, an agricultural society. Why would Marx have been surprised at this event?

*3. What has happened to the middle class in most industrial societies?

DEMOCRACIES AND SOCIAL CHANGE

For Teaching Helps, see page T98.   For a class activity, see #4 on page 311.

Threat of class war As the poverty of the people worsened in the 1800's, the predictions of Karl Marx seemed more likely to come true. It looked as though war might come between the workers and the business class. In Paris in 1871 a violent struggle took place between the workers and the business-controlled government. The workers actually managed to gain control of Paris for a few weeks. When the government did defeat the workers, some were immediately executed and others were put in prisons.

See #1
below.

In the United States there were a few clashes between the workers and the police. In 1892 a serious gun battle took place between protesting workers and private detectives hired by the Carnegie Steel Company. Most middle-class Americans opposed any organizations of workers. Why? Feared their power.

Lengthy class warfare did not take place in the industrial societies of western Europe or the United States. In the late 1800's and early 1900's some social changes helped prevent violence.

Good effects of industrialization The living conditions of the working classes improved as a result of the general benefits of industry. As a society became more industrialized, life improved to some degree for everyone. For example, lack of food was a constant fear in non-industrialized societies. The use of scientific methods and machines in farming reduced the threat of starvation.

See #2
below.

Stress:
1. Sometimes violence erupted when laborers clashed with their employers
   or with the police.
2. Improved living conditions helped western societies to avoid violence.

Stress:
1. The working class did not immediately
   gain any benefits from industrialization.

Advances in medicine made possible longer, healthier lives for most people in industrial societies. Study the chart and tell how much longer the average American is expected to live now as compared to 1850. What reasons can you give for these changes?

See #1 above. But these good results of industrialization did not immediately affect the workers. Other changes had to take place first.

Growing awareness of the need for change Writers, social workers, and church leaders helped to make the evils See #2 below. of industrialization known to the middle and upper classes. In England a famous writer, Charles Dickens, wrote novels in which he told about the hard lives led by the poor.

In the United States there was a whole group of writers who attacked the shameful conditions which resulted from unregulated businesses. One such author was Upton Sinclair. The American people were horrified by his description of the condition of unskilled workers in the meat-packing industry. Because of his book, *The Jungle*, the United States government began to inspect meat. You have probably noticed the "Government Inspected" seals on meat in the stores. What else do these government seals tell you?

See #3 below. **Workers join together** In the 1800's workers in industrial societies tried to form organizations or **labor unions.**

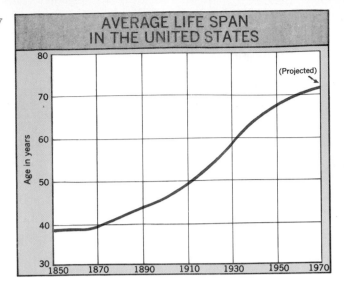

AVERAGE LIFE SPAN IN THE UNITED STATES

They hoped the unions could force factory owners to increase wages and to improve working conditions. Why would labor unions have more power to bring change than individuals acting alone?

For a long time workers were forbidden by law to form unions. See if you can tell why. Gradually labor unions were recognized as legal. They won protection through laws. In the 1870's unions in England were granted the See #4 below. right to **strike.** This meant that workers could leave work until the employer listened to their complaints. Why was the right to strike an important gain for the workingman? What are some other ways that unions might be able to peacefully reach their goals?

Throughout the late 1800's and early 1900's, serious strikes had taken place in the industrial societies. The governments began to realize the necessity of providing for the workers' needs.

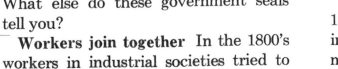

2. Many people helped to make the plight of the workers known to the upper
   classes.
3. Workers organized unions to make themselves better able to bargain with
   employers.
4. The right to strike became a powerful weapon for the unions.

301

1. Becoming politically active helped the British workers achieve government sponsored social welfare programs.

See #1 above. In the early 1900's British workers organized a political party. Their elected representatives spoke for the workers in Parliament. Before the outbreak of World War I in 1914, Great Britain started a social welfare program. Its laws made provisions for slum-clearance programs, government employment agencies for the people, and a **minimum wage** law for some industries. In other words, the factory owner would have to pay at least a certain amount of money to the workers.

By 1914 workers had made important advances in the democratic societies of Europe. Social laws came more slowly in the United States. Because of America's growing economy and many opportunities, people were not very aware of See #2 below. the evils of industrialization. Then millions of immigrants flocked to America in the late 1800's. Cities became more overcrowded. Slums and poverty were more noticeable. Individuals like Jane Addams of Chicago began bringing the problems of the cities to the attention of the American people. She opened a settlement house in a poor neighborhood of Chicago. There the immigrants sought help and advice. Jane Addams is pictured here. How does the picture show evidence of her concern for people? Partly as a result of the labor unions and the work of people like Jane Addams, the American government began responding to the needs of the workers.

P/S

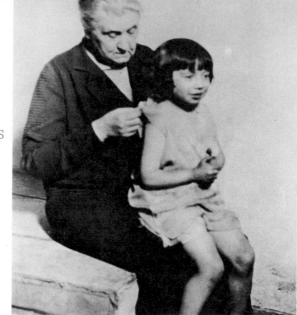

Jane Addams, social worker

Education Before the 1800's there was little or no effort on the part of governments to educate all the people. S/E Most Europeans were unable to read or write. Education was the privilege of the upper classes. Historians believe that as See #3 below. the right to vote was extended to more H/S people, governments concluded that the people must be educated in order to vote wisely.

As the result of an education bill passed in England in 1870, school attendance soon jumped from 1,000,000 to P/S 4,000,000 students. Other western European countries also began providing the people with free schooling. By 1900 most western European countries had laws requiring elementary schooling for all. Before 1920, however, a high-school education was still unusual.

2. The arrival of millions of immigrants helped Americans to become aware of the plight of the workers.

3. As more people in democratic societies got the right to vote, more public schools were provided to educate the citizens.

See #1
above.

People living in the United States had free public schooling long before people living in other societies had it. By 1860 most northern and western states had free public schooling. By the middle of the 1920's, the United States was spending as much money on schools as the rest of the world put together. Study the chart below. What are some of the changes that have taken place since 1900?

The growth of public education aided in bringing about more social equality. Explain how education helps to make more equal opportunity for all people.

Other social progress Slavery was one of the worst things about some democratic societies. The slave trade was slowly being stopped in the 1800's. Parliament put an end to slavery in the British colonies in 1833. It took a Civil War and a constitutional amendment to end slavery in the United States. By 1900 slavery had ended in most parts of the world.

See #2
below.

During World War II (1939–1945), the Germans made slaves of some of the people they conquered. And there still are reports of "slave-labor" camps in the Soviet Union.

In the democracies women worked for many years to win the rights and privileges which men have long enjoyed. Women had been used to having little or no schooling, few chances to get good jobs, and no legal rights.

As societies became more highly industrialized, more women joined the work force. Soon they were demanding equal pay, schooling, and the right to vote.

See #3
below.

The first women's college was opened in Massachusetts in 1836. The first women doctors were graduated from schools in Sweden.

The right to vote for women was first won in Australia. American women were granted voting rights in 1919. Other democratic societies extended the vote to women throughout the 1900's. In

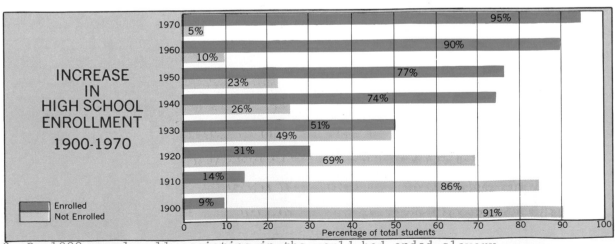

INCREASE
IN
HIGH SCHOOL
ENROLLMENT
1900-1970

Enrolled
Not Enrolled

Year	Enrolled	Not Enrolled
1970	5%	95%
1960	10%	90%
1950	23%	77%
1940	26%	74%
1930	49%	51%
1920	31%	69%
1910	14%	86%
1900	9%	91%

Percentage of total students

Slum scene in an American city

Continuing need for social change

Since the end of World War II in 1945, democracies of Europe, North America, and Japan have enjoyed economic **prosperity,** or good times. The United States especially has reached unequaled prosperity. Yet there are still unsolved social E/S problems in all these societies. Study the pictures and describe the social problems you see.

Why is it so important for democracies to find answers to these problems? If you were a sociologist, what social problems might you want to study? Why?

Think for Yourself

Name some social problems in today's society. How are they related to the rise of industry?

France women have been permitted to vote only since 1945.

Women gradually won some degree of economic independence. Married women were permitted to own property and to participate in the conduct of business. Women's struggle to reach equality with men still continues. In some less modern P/S societies, women are still not permitted out of the home. In the more highly See #1 industrialized and democratic societies, above. women have the same political and legal rights as men. Can you tell some ways in which American women of today still are not equal to men?

*2. What books or movies have been popular recently which tell about a social problem?

304

Pickets at General Electric

For Teaching Helps, see page T99.

Stress: For class activities, see #2 and #3 on page 311.
1. A new kind of society was established in Russia following the revolution
    of 1917.

EXAMPLES OF SOCIAL SYSTEMS

A communist society The Russian revolution of 1917 produced a new kind of society. The Soviet Union is an example of a society seeking new answers to the major problems of industrialization. Under communist leadership, this agricultural society became a modern industrial power. Because of the world power and influence which the Soviet Union possesses today, it is important to know something about the working of its social system. Why do leaders of less developed countries often study the successes of the Soviet Union?

See #1 above.

Before 1917 Study the picture of these Russian peasants taken before the revolution of 1917. On the basis of what you see here, try to describe the kind of life these people probably led. Before 1917 Russia was chiefly an agricultural society. The peasants worked the land which was owned by the rich, ruling class. There was almost no middle class in Russia.

Throughout the early 1900's many Russians wanted social change. Although the government freed the peasants in 1861, the people still had little opportunity to rise out of their poverty. The people had no land; and they often had little food. Industry was growing slowly, but it had already produced urban centers and a restless working class. The laborers were united enough

See #2 below.

Hungry Russian peasants during time of Czar.

to be an important force in demanding social change and in overthrowing the government.

Within a few years after the overthrow of the Russian government in 1917, the communists came to power. The communists hoped to completely reorganize the society of the Soviet Union. In some ways they have radically changed the society. In other ways Soviet society is much as it was before 1917.

See #3 below.

See #4 below.

Private property was done away with under the communists. Private industry

2. Before 1917 the Russian government did not respond to the needs of the
    Russian people.
3. The communists took power in Russia after the revolution.
4. In some ways the communists have radically changed the society of the
    Soviet Union.

305

was taken over by the government. Small farms were joined together to form government-owned farms or **collective farms.** People worked in groups on collective farms. The produce of the farmers was given to the government and then distributed among the people. How was this system similar to Robert Owen's New Harmony experiment?

See #1 above.

Many of the peasants resisted life on the collective farms. Poor planning by the government and lack of cooperation among the farmers led to millions of deaths from starvation. What do you

See #2 above.

think the Soviet government might have done before forcing the people onto the collective farms? What kinds of questions might a sociologist want to ask about life on collective farms?

P/E

A new way of life Industrialization has brought some important changes in the Russian society. People have more money to spend and more goods to buy. Workers have more free time. The picture shows a department store in Moscow. Can you identify any of the products for sale?

S/E

See #3 below.

P/S

Communism has brought a better life

A busy department store in Moscow, U.S.S.R

3. As a result of industrialization, Soviet people have more money and more free time.

Stress:
1. It is the Communist party, not the people, which governs the Soviet Union.
2. Many European societies were badly disorganized following World War I.

See #1 above.

to the working people of Russia. But Marx had predicted that there would be no need for a government in a communist society. However, Soviet society is strictly regulated by the government. The people are permitted few freedoms. The people have no power, while the leaders have absolute power. Would Karl Marx see the Soviet Union as an ideal communist society? Why or why not?

See #2 above.

Another undemocratic social system World War I ended in 1918. European societies were all changed by the war. Some of the greatest changes took place in Italy. As a result of the war, both its government and business were weakened.

The soldiers returning from the war could find no work. There was too little food. Workers rioted in the streets. People had to have solutions to their problems. Some saw a communist revolution as the answer. However, most of the people did not want it. They did not want the system of communism.

The Italians chose another system of government called **fascism.** Under fascism, the government has control of industry and labor. Although private property and private business were allowed, the government closely regulated business. The government made believe it was protecting the interests of all the people. But it made the divisions among the social classes greater than ever.

The rich classes were favored by the government.

Italian fascism made some good social changes. New schools were built. Crime decreased. People who had been out of work could now find jobs.

But by the 1930's Italian society was no longer democratic in any way. Workers' strikes were made illegal. The citizens lost most of their rights. People had to obey the government without question.

See #3 below.

Think about communism and fascism as ways to organize society. In what ways are the two systems alike? How are they different? Would you choose to live in either society? Why or why not?

Germany and fascism Following World War I defeated Germany was in turmoil. People were uncertain about Germany's future and about the way its society should be organized. Many groups did not want the new democratic society. In 1929 business almost stopped, and many Germans lost their jobs. There was great unrest and fear. Poverty and hunger led many Germans to think that communism might be a way out of their problems. The chance of having a communist revolution led the people to accept fascism.

See #4 below.

The fascist group which gained control of Germany was called the **Nazi party.** Led by Adolf Hitler, the Nazis built a society similar to that of Italy. But the fascism of Nazi Germany was

See #5 below.

3. Italian society adopted fascism which robbed people of their civil rights.
4. Poverty and hunger led the German people to adopt a fascist social system.
5. The Nazi party, led by Adolf Hitler, created the fascist society in Germany.

307

Stress:
1. German fascism permitted no opposition to the government.
2. Many Germans, particularly the Jews, were deliberately murdered by the Nazis.

See #1 above.

even more undemocratic and more cruel than Italian fascism. All those believed to be opponents of the Nazis were imprisoned. Newspapers, schools, and the churches were controlled by the government. Many of Germany's leading thinkers, scientists, and writers left the country. Why? The Nazis wanted a perfect society. This society should only include people having Germanic ancestors. They believed that all others, especially Jews, were inferior people. As a result millions of Jews were killed by the Nazis.

See #2 above.

P/S ↔

German society became more prosperous under the Nazis. But the price of better economic times was high—the loss of all concern for people. How does this picture of Jews in a Nazi prison camp prove this disregard for human life? Would you want to live under a society like that of the Nazis? Why or why not?

Decline of fascism A third society which adopted fascism was Japan. Italy, Germany, and Japan joined together to make war on countries that had not adopted fascism. This gigantic struggle was known as World War II. By August of 1945 these three fascist powers had been defeated.

See #3 below.

Today the three major social systems in the world are communism, socialism, and democracy. However, fascist societies still exist in Spain and in some Latin-American countries. Which social system does America have?

See #4 below.

Prisoners of a Nazi concentration camp

P/S →

Think for Yourself

What were some of the causes of social change in Italy and Germany? Political disorganization, economic failures.

A communist society in China Since about 1920 there has been a communist movement in China. The Russian revolution had a great impact on China. Some Chinese students studied in the Soviet Union. They returned to China armed with ideas of a communist society.

See #5 below.

3. Japan became fascist, joining with Germany and Italy to make war on the world.

308
4. The major fascist powers were defeated in World War II.
5. Following the Russian revolution of 1917, the Chinese started a Communist party.

The Nationalist party had been most powerful in China before 1949. When the communists took control of the country, the Nationalists fled to Formosa. It is an island about 100 miles east of China. The people of Formosa have set up a society that is independent of Communist China.

E/S → Economic aid given by the United States has made it possible for the Formosans to build a strong society. Formosa has big factories like the one shown in the picture on this page. However, most of the Formosans make their living by working on farms. The people now have more food, better clothes, and better houses than in the early 1950's. Why might the Chinese in China itself hope that the society on Formosa might fail?

The rulers of China are trying to make it a strong industrial nation. In order to do so, the leaders are attacking the traditions of an ancient society. No one knows whether the Chinese Communists will be able to build a strong new society that will last.

See #2 below.

See #3 below.

P/S → Probably the peasants of China have been the most affected by the communists. There has been a revolution in farm life. All farm workers were forced to move to huge **communes,** similar to Russian collective farms. Their lives were so controlled that many people rebelled or refused to work. As a result, the communists have had to soften their

See #4 below.

See #1 above.

In the late 1930's Japan tried expanding its power in China. After the defeat of the Japanese in 1945, China faced great problems. Its industries were destroyed, many families had been broken up, and jobs were hard to find. The Chinese people were short of food. People had lost faith in the government of China. The communists were well organized. They told the Chinese people that they could make things better. People believed the communists. By 1949 the communists had taken over control of China. When do societies seem most eager to accept communism? During political and economic crises.

P/H ←

2. Some Chinese fled from the communists to the island of Formosa.
3. The communists in China are attempting to create a new society.
4. The Chinese peasants have been most affected by social changes.

309

Stress:
1. The communists are trying to destroy most of China's old social institutions.
2. A social system is always changed by the society adopting it.

program. The following passage is a description of life on a commune.

In the Three Joss Sticks commune, the work whistles started sounding at 4:30 A.M. Breakfast was at 5 A.M. Twenty minutes later, men and women marched to the fields. At 11:30 A.M. two sweet potatoes were distributed to each worker. A double-time march to the dining room got the work brigades back just in time for a 6 P.M. meal of rice and vegetables. After that, there was work in the fields under flood lights, or political sessions in camp. The whistles signaled everybody to bed at midnight.*

Why would people probably resent this way of life?

See #1 above.

The communists are educating the Chinese people to accept a whole new way of life. They are no longer to worship ancestors. Their family loyalties are being swept away. And the teachings of Confucius are being replaced by the teachings of Mao Tse-tung (mou′ tse′-tung). Mao has been the leader of China since 1949. The people have been taught to worship him, especially the young people. Why might the communists encourage such worship of the Chinese leader? Schools are concentrating on scientific learning, rather than on memorizing age-old writings. Women, once quiet and ignored, are now working

in the fields and factories with the men. They are productive members of the society.

Think for Yourself

Chinese children are often brought up in nurseries, rather than by the once-honored old people. How will this practice change Chinese society? The family will exert less control over the children.

Spread of social systems As you have just seen, China is one example of a society affected by a more modern, industrialized society. What nation has served as a model for recent social changes in China? The Soviet Union.

In large measure, socialism, communism, fascism, and democracy were developed by societies in order to respond to the problems of industrialization. Which of these social systems a society chooses depends on its history, its culture, and its particular problems. Each society will fit a new system to its own needs. What are some reasons why many Chinese favored communism?

See #2 above.

As the less developed areas of the world try to "catch up," they will experiment with the already tried social systems. It cannot be predicted now which systems will gain the most followers.

Think for Yourself

What are ways in which less developed societies learn about industrialized nations?

Sending young people abroad to study.

*From the copyrighted article "Life in a Red Commune—," in *U.S. News & World Report*, April 6, 1959.

*3. Why might it be possible for fascism to again become a powerful force in the world?

Things to Do

See
page 292.

1. Make believe you are a coal miner in Pennsylvania in about 1900. Write a short story about a day in your life. Be ready to read your story to the class.

2. Draw a picture or cartoon which shows one of the evils of the fascist society established in Germany by Hitler.

See
page 305.

3. Cut out pictures from magazines and newspapers which show any aspect of life in the Soviet Union. Mount a few of the pictures you like best on a bulletin board together with a short paragraph telling why you chose each picture.

See
page 300.

4. If possible, interview someone who belongs to some kind of union. Ask the person the questions below. Your class may wish to discuss your findings.
   a. Why did he join the union?
   b. In what ways does the union help him?
   c. How does he support the union?

CLASS PROJECT—PART 2

Now you should have the societies located on the world map. You should also have a number of markers ready for use.

The committee members should pretend that they are sociologists. They may review Chapter 17 and list some facts and ideas about the societies they have chosen to study. Further research about these societies could be done in the library. Remember that your list should be of special interest to sociologists. Choose what you believe are the most important items on your list and place them on a marker. Put the markers on the display and connect them to the proper society.

Auto factory--
Calcutta, India

Woodcarvers in a Kenyan village

Camera manufacturing in Sweden

18. Solving Economic Problems

For Teaching Helps, see page T100.

The people shown in the pictures are producing goods which will be sold. The money they receive for their work will be spent for goods and services produced by other workers. Ways of producing and distributing goods and services are different for each of the countries shown here. Each of the countries has its own economic system.

See #1 below.

E ←

E/S →

Economic systems are devised by societies to solve these economic problems —what goods to produce, how to produce goods, how to distribute the goods to the people. Each society develops a system that will best fit its own culture. As the society develops and changes, so will its economic system.

See #2 below.

This chapter helps you discover some of the economic systems man has developed. Also, you will better understand why there are different economic systems.

JUST FOR FUN

Talk to a person who was once a jobholder in a foreign country. Ask him to tell ways in which its stores differed from those in your community. Share the information you get with your classmates.

Stress:
312 1. Each society has developed its own economic system.
2. A society will develop an economic system which best suits its needs.

For Teaching Helps, see page T101.

Stress: For class activities, see #2 and #3 on page 331.
1. Under capitalism, manufacturers produce goods for profits.

MODERN ECONOMIC SYSTEMS

Free enterprise One way of organizing an economy is for individuals within a society to cooperate to produce and distribute goods. Manufacturers decide what to produce. Their decisions are based on what is demanded by the **consumers,** or people buying the goods. However, the manufacturers also try to persuade the consumers to buy their products. They try to persuade people by advertising. Tell about an advertisement which you have seen that does this kind of thing.

The kind of economic system just described is called a free enterprise system or **capitalism.** Under capitalism the manufacturers make goods which they believe that people will want to buy. The goods are sold at prices which the buyer will pay and which will provide profits for the manufacturers.

See #1 above.

The distribution of goods in a capitalistic economy depends largely on their price. People can decide what goods they will buy. But what limits how much a person can buy?

Most people cannot have all the goods that they want. They must select what they can afford, and must choose the items which are most important to them.

The picture shows a characteristic of capitalism—people making free choices. What are these people deciding? Be-

3. Today the American economy is the leading capitalistic economy in the world.

cause individual choices are necessary in a capitalistic economy, capitalism would not work well in all kinds of societies. The capitalistic system is almost always found in democratic societies. Why?

See #2 above.

American capitalism in the late 1800's The United States is probably the best example of a capitalistic economy in the world today. American capitalism has undergone many changes. But the American economy still has more of the characteristics of capitalism than any other of the world's economies. During the late 1800's in America there was little government regulation of the economy. This time is sometimes called a **laissez-faire** (les′ā fãr′) period, meaning that the economy was largely allowed to run itself. However, the government aided the growth of the economy.

See #3 below.

Stockholders' meeting

It gave land to railroads, for example. But the government did not often interfere in the operation of the economic system. There were few laws regulating businesses or business practices.

See #1 above.

Between 1870 and 1900 America's economy expanded rapidly. The output of manufactured goods increased fourfold. It was during this period that today's most important form of business organization was created, the **corporation.** A corporation is owned by **stockholders,** or people who have bought shares in the business. The stockholders share in the profits. The picture shows a meeting of stockholders and corporation leaders. What might they be discussing? Because so many people invest their money in the shares of large corporations, a great amount of capital can be raised by them. Huge amounts of capital make it possible for a corporation to hire the best managers and pay good wages to attract the workers. The corporation can afford to buy raw materials and high-quality machinery. Under such circumstances, a business can produce a greater quantity of goods and sell them at lower prices than can smaller businesses.

American capitalism in more recent times During the late 1800's the corporations steadily grew in size and importance in America's economy. But early in the 1900's many people in the United States became concerned about the great power of these giant businesses. In some industries one corporation alone controlled all the production. By 1880 John D. Rockefeller's Standard Oil Company controlled 90 per cent of the oil-refining business in the United States. Rockefeller had deliberately destroyed many competing oil companies. Since competition is an important part of the capitalistic system, these practices were considered harmful. Why is competition an important feature of capitalism?

See #2 below.

Gradually the government began playing a larger part in the American economy. Laws were passed making certain business practices illegal. During the economic depression of the 1930's the government became even more active in the operation of the economy. It began investing in public projects like the construction of dams, buildings, and highways. Aid was given by the government to agriculture, housing construction, and people's welfare.

See #3 below.

Stress:
1. Americans continue to debate about how much power the government should
   exercise in the economy.

American capitalism today In America today, debate continues over how much power the government should have in the economy. Some believe that the government already has too much control of the economy. Certainly the laissez-faire period is ended. But the economic system in America is not controlled by the government. Businessmen and consumers continue to determine what will be produced and how it will be produced. The distribution of goods has been affected by the government. Taxation, for example, brings about a more equal distribution of wealth. People who earn more money pay more money in taxes. How is this an attempt to bring about more economic equality? The picture shows one place where tax money is spent. How does money spent on weapons affect our economy? Try to explain some other way in which government spending affects the economy. For example, how can the government create jobs for people?

See #1 above.

The continued growth of the American economy is an important sign that our capitalistic system is working. Today, with little more than 6 per cent of the world's population, the United States produces and consumes more than 33 per cent of the world's output of goods and services.

Think for Yourself

Could capitalism exist if people were not allowed to own property? Why? Capitalism is based on the ownership of private property.

Democratic societies with planned economies Some people make a living in countries where there is government ownership and control of the means of production. Banks, factories, farms, and transportation systems are owned by the government and are run for the benefit of all the people. The name given to an economic system such as that described above is **socialism.**

There is no country that has a fully so-

See #2 below.

315

Stress:
1. There is no fully socialized economy in the world today.
2. The economy of Great Britain is only partly socialized.

See #1
above.

cialized economy in the world today. In most countries this economic system is a mixture of socialism and capitalism.

Socialism in Great Britain Great Britain's economy was the first to reach a stage of high development. By 1850 Great Britain was highly industrialized, and standards of living had risen considerably. Great Britain became the world's first industrial power.

For a long time the British economy operated under laissez-faire capitalism. But in the 1900's the government has played an increasingly bigger part in the economy. Despite the increase in government control of the economy, three-fourths of the businesses in Great Britain are privately owned.

See #2
above.

The British government has also taken control of some of the businesses that are necessary to an industrial economy—coal mines, banks, railroads, airlines, and power companies. The picture shows some of the publicly owned planes of British European Airways. Why might the government take control of the airlines? Serve all the people.

There are a number of reasons why these industries were taken over by the government. It was hoped that government control might make these industries more efficient. Another reason was to increase workers' wages and benefits. And it seemed that better use might be made of natural and human resources through government planning.

See #3
below.

In Great Britain, the government paid private owners for property taken from them. Do you think this was fair? Why?

The British people were determined to keep personal freedoms. Therefore, economic planning was only limited. How could an economy planned by the government interfere with the rights of the people? Take away economic choice.

See #4
below.

E/H

P/E

P/E

P/E

Great Britain ranks high among nations in providing economic security for its people. The government provides money for the old and the sick, public housing, health clinics, education, and full employment or jobs for everyone. A nation which provides such services for its citizens is called a **welfare state**. In a welfare state the government takes re-

See #5
below.

3. The British hoped that the government might help the economy.
4. The British have limited economic planning to preserve personal freedoms.
5. The government of Great Britain guarantees the people many social services.

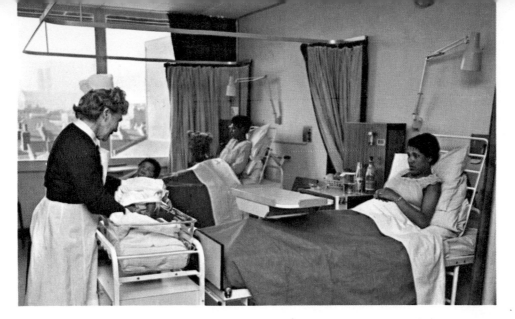

sponsibility for the basic welfare of the people.

The people shown in the picture are receiving medical attention in a government clinic. Is the medical care actually free? How is it paid for? Taxation.

See #1 above. The British economy is not growing very rapidly. The standard of living is not rising as quickly as the British people would like. The economic question facing Great Britain is to decide whether there needs to be more or less socialism. Some in Great Britain favor more government control of the economy—more socialism—even if certain freedoms must be lost. Others believe that the key to future prosperity in Great Britain lies in a free economy.

Think for Yourself

Does the United States have any of the characteristics of a welfare state? If so, what are they? Social security, Medicare, welfare payments.

Other socialistic economies Certain socialistic ideas have been adopted by societies in many parts of the world. P/E Sweden and New Zealand are two countries in which limited socialism exists.

However, socialist economies differ from society to society. Socialism in Sweden, for example, is not quite the same as socialism in Great Britain. The See #2 below. original ideas of socialism have been changed to fit the culture and economic P/E needs of each society.

But private ownership of property is an accepted part of all these economies. In all cases there is a mixture of socialism and capitalism.

The growth of socialism in western Europe was first the result of bad economic conditions in the 1930's. Then World War II speeded the growth of socialism. The war nearly ruined the See #3 below. European economies. Many Europeans called for quick changes.

Stress:
1. Socialism often becomes less popular as societies prosper.
2. In most European countries socialism has improved the general welfare.

In order to rapidly change economic conditions, governments in western Europe began taking control of the means of production and distribution of goods. The socialists could not agree among themselves how much government ownership of industry would be desirable. But they did agree that the government should own enough of the economy to be able to plan production. But in most societies the move toward socialism slowed, as the economies became more prosperous.

See #1 above.

Generally, the results of socialism have been more government services for the people. Many European nations are now welfare states.

See #2 above.

Think for Yourself

Why has socialism never been popular in the United States? Capitalism has worked so successfully.

Nondemocratic societies with government-owned economies The government has almost complete control over every phase of some economies. The government assigns people to jobs, and tells them how much they can earn. The government owns all the resources and decides how much of each kind can be used each year. It controls the railroads, waterways, airlines, and means of communication. Only those goods are produced that the government says can be produced.

See #3 below.

P/E

An economic system like the one described above is called **communism.** Do you think communism would be popular in countries with prosperous economies? Why?

Communism in the Soviet Union All communist economies are not alike. Yugoslavia, for example, has a communist economy; but its economic system is organized differently from the economy of the Soviet Union. In Yugoslavia there are far more privately owned businesses and farms than there are in the Soviet Union.

See #4 below.

The Soviet Union is a most important example of a communist economy. In 1920 it had a poorly developed economy, based mostly upon agriculture. Today the Soviet Union has one of the most highly developed economies in the world. The Soviet economy modernized rapidly. The methods it used to achieve industrialization had not been used before by any other society.

See #5 below.

Beginning in the late 1920's the communist leaders took absolute control of agriculture in the Soviet Union. The farms were taken from the people and run by the government. The government used the profits from farm production to provide the money for building industry. Agriculture in the Soviet Union suffered. Production was low and the farmers were unhappy. But industries grew rapidly with the money gained from agriculture.

3. The government has nearly total control of communist economies.
318 4. Communist economies work differently in different societies.
5. The Soviet Union used communism to rapidly achieve industrialization.

Today the Soviet Union still has problems in feeding its people because agriculture cannot produce enough of the various kinds of foods the people require. Its agriculture is less developed than its industry. Wheat is the chief crop. More wheat is produced in the Soviet Union than in any other nation. The picture of a wheat field shown above was taken in the Soviet Union. Does this picture remind you of other parts of the world? If so, which ones? Despite its huge wheat production, Russia sometimes has to buy wheat from other countries.

The Soviet economy is tightly organized in order to provide particular goods. Almost all the economy is government owned—factories, mines, railroads, construction firms, and stores.

See #1 above.

The goals of the Soviet economy are decided by **Gosplan,** the Soviet central planning board. Each year this central board decides what is to be produced. Gosplan then issues orders to the managers of factories and farms to produce what that year's plan requires. How do factory owners in America decide what to produce?

See #2 below.

In the past the Soviet economic planners have paid little attention to the production of **consumer goods**—radios, washing machines, clothes. Production has been directed toward **heavy industry,** industries producing machinery, machine tools, coal, chemicals, and ships.

2. Consumer goods have not had priority
   in Soviet production.
3. Controls over the Soviet economy
   have been somewhat relaxed.

Harvesting wheat in the Soviet Union

Examples of Soviet goods are shown in the picture below. Why do the Soviets produce so many of these goods?

E/P

After its economy reached a high level of development, the Soviet government relaxed control over it. The government is permitting some degree of planning to be done by individual factories. The

See #3 below.

Soviet factory

P/E

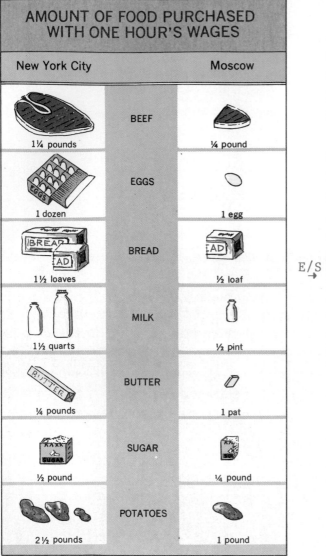

AMOUNT OF FOOD PURCHASED WITH ONE HOUR'S WAGES

New York City		Moscow
1¼ pounds	BEEF	¼ pound
1 dozen	EGGS	1 egg
1½ loaves	BREAD	½ loaf
1½ quarts	MILK	½ pint
¼ pounds	BUTTER	1 pat
½ pound	SUGAR	¼ pound
2½ pounds	POTATOES	1 pound

Although the standard of living in Russia is not as high as the American standard of living, most Soviet people live far better than most of the people in the world live.

Communism in the Soviet Union has not equaled the performance of capitalism in the United States. The chart compares the cost of food for workers in America with the cost of food for workers in the Soviet Union. It shows what an hour's wages will buy in Moscow and in New York City. Study the chart. Which workers spend less on food? Does this mean that the American laborer probably lives better than the Russian laborer? Explain.

See #1 above.

E/S →

Many Russians paid a high price for the Soviet Union's economic progress. People who opposed the government often lost their lives. Many Russian peasants were killed because they refused to live on collective farms.

Economic freedom in the Soviet Union is limited. The people can choose freely among the available goods and services. But they have little influence over what goods and services will be provided. People can pursue many careers, but only if they serve the interests of the nation. The Soviet rulers determine the national interests.

See #2 below.

Russian people are now looking for more production of consumer goods. Since the people are living better now, they are asking for better-quality shoes, clothing, and household goods. However, changes in the Soviet economy are taking place slowly.

The economic system of the Soviet Union has performed well in many ways.

S/E ↔

Think for Yourself

Why would a communist economy not work in our country? It would mean the loss of economic freedoms.

Stress: For Teaching Helps, see page T102.
1. The most technologically advanced societies have highly developed economies.
2. A partly developed economy is still largely dependent on agriculture.

ECONOMIC DEVELOPMENT

Stages of development Societies possess different amounts of wealth. A few are rich, while many are poor. And some societies fall between these extremes.

Economists often disagree on how to describe the type of economy a society has. One way is to decide how well it uses its natural and human resources. Many African societies, for example, are rich in minerals. But the people are not using them. On the other hand, the United States has recently had to import some valuable minerals because of shortages of certain kinds. Although lacking in many kinds of minerals, the United States has reached a stage of economic development which is far beyond that of any African society.

See #1 above.
There are three terms which might be used to describe the types of economies in the world. Those societies which have developed the technology needed to make good use of their resources have **highly developed** economies.

Most people in the highly developed economies of such countries as West Germany or Britain work in industry or trade. Machines powered by coal, oil, or gas make possible the production of large amounts of goods. The workers are able to buy these goods because the great quantity produced lowers their price.

Those societies which are well on their

way toward a high level of technology have economies which might be called **partly developed.** In the partly developed economies of countries like Spain and Italy there are mixtures of farming and industry. However, farming is still the chief occupation. See #2 above.

Economies in societies which are not yet making use of their resources can be described as **newly developing.** Newly developing economies in countries like China and India are chiefly agricultural. But the agriculture is not very productive.

More than two-thirds of the world's population live in societies with newly developing economies. Most of the economies in the societies of Africa, Asia, and Latin America can be considered newly developing. With few exceptions, the people in these areas of the world live in poverty. How might the conditions shown in the picture affect the health of these people? See #3 below.

Shantytown in Cape Town, South Africa

Shoppers in a department store in Tokyo, Japan

Importance of economic growth Especially since World War II, countries have become more dependent on one another, partly as a result of closer economic ties. But despite the economic ties among nations, countries are not all equally wealthy. The people in North America, western Europe, Japan, Australia, and New Zealand live far more comfortably than most other people of the world. Study the picture of shoppers in a Tokyo, Japan, department store. Do the people appear to have a wide choice of goods to buy?

Social scientists generally agree that these economic differences among nations present a serious problem for the world. The question is how to encourage economic growth in the poorer nations. What might the richer nations do to help the poorer nations?

Barriers to economic growth The poorer countries have some similar economic problems. Rapidly increasing populations and lack of food are problems common to most of them. Why are these two problems closely related?

It seems that the economic growth of most of the world does not keep far enough ahead of population growth. Production in India is growing slowly. It increases about 3 per cent each year. But India's population is increasing about 2.5 per cent each year. What is the problem in this case?

All the poorer nations have agricultural economies. Generally, the people raise only enough to feed themselves. As a result, incomes are very low. For what kinds of goods do you suppose people spend most of their income in a poorer nation. Why? Food, shelter.

It seems that nations are poor because they have no industry. Yet, they have no industry because they are too poor to industrialize. What kinds of

E/H ←

E/G →

See #1 below.

See #2 below.

Stress:
1. A few societies in the world are prospering, while many societies are poor.
2. Economic growth in poor societies is often hampered by underfed populations.

322

Stress:
1. Industrialization is China's major economic goal.
2. It appears that feeding its people is China's major economic problem.

avy-duty trucks manufactured in China

A major goal of the economic planners is to industrialize China. Metal production has gone up. New industries have been started. China now has set up Soviet style five-year plans whose chief aim is to get more heavy goods. What heavy goods are shown in the picture? Most Chinese money invested in manufacturing went into heavy industry. Why?

See #1 above.

Difficulties in agriculture caused a drop in the production of goods in factories. Industry relies greatly on raw materials produced by the farmers. It seems that agriculture is the key to economic growth in China. Why? What ways might the Chinese use to get more

See #2 above.

3. Nigeria, in western Africa, became independent of Britain in 1960.
4. A recent civil war in Nigeria has economically and socially disadvantaged the nation.

farm products? If the food problem can be solved, China's industrial growth is likely to increase rapidly. China has enough good resources for industry.

Think for Yourself

Other poor countries are watching China and India carefully. What kinds of lessons can be learned from their experiences?

Nigeria In 1960 this African nation won its independence from Britain. Use the map to locate Nigeria. What is the capital city of Nigeria? This city is also the biggest in Nigeria. What might have caused it to grow? Recently, Nigeria was torn by a civil war. One of the tribes, the Ibo, broke away from Nigeria. The Ibo tried to set up an independent coun-

See #3 below.

See #4 below.

G/H

Stress:
1. Nigeria has agricultural and mineral resources and a good transportation system.
2. The Nigerian economy is primarily agricultural.

try called Biafra. Although the war has ended, the cost of the fighting did great damage to the Nigerian economy. How H/E can wars cause economic problems for nations with newly developing economies? War goods are costly.

Before the civil war, Nigeria was considered to be one African nation which was likely to achieve rapid economic growth. The Nigerians can produce enough food to feed themselves. Nigeria also has mineral resources—tin, coal, G/E See #1 above. iron ore. In addition there are timber supplies and fisheries. The major Nigerian cities are linked by rail and air. There is a fairly good system of highways, P/E and there are two major rivers. Refer again to the map of Nigeria. Which of the major cities are linked by land, air, and water transportation? Why is a good transportation system necessary for economic growth? Transport raw materials and finished products.

The economy of Nigeria is mostly agricultural. Much of its farm production is sold overseas. The picture shows sacks of peanuts being prepared for shipment to processing plants where oil will be extracted. The extracted oils will be exported. Try to think of some products derived from peanuts. Peanut oil.

See #2 above.

Nigeria has tried to develop a capitalistic economic system. Its leaders have said that private enterprise can best accomplish economic growth. But in truth, Nigerian economy is a mixture of capitalism and socialism. The government owns the radio stations, railroads, airlines, and coal mines. The picture shows a Nigerian disc jockey at work. Who is his employer? Local Nigerian governments own parts of hotels, stores, and industries.

See #3 below.

The Nigerian economy has grown steadily. The growth in industry is par-

Peanuts, a major Nigerian export

Nigerian disc jockey

Stress:
1. Nigeria's population is expanding more rapidly than its economy.
2. Economic freedom has been preserved in Nigeria.

ticularly striking. Petroleum production has increased steadily, and Nigeria has petroleum to export. New industries have been established—a towel factory, an automobile-battery plant, textile-print mills, and others. Agriculture, which is still the most important part of the economy, has grown more slowly.

P/E

See #1 above.

Like most other countries with newly developing economies, Nigeria has a population problem. Its population has been increasing at a rate of about 2 per cent each year. The economy is not expanding rapidly enough to keep up with the population. As a result, the standard of living is not rising very much. Only recently, the average Nigerian peasant earned an income of about $14 a year. Try to imagine yourself living on such an income in the United States!

E/S

See #2 above.

The economic future of Nigeria is uncertain. There are many problems to be solved, political as well as economic. But Nigeria has done well in providing for economic freedom. There is job choice and the freedom to buy what one can afford. Nigeria is trying to develop rapidly with a minimum of control by the government. Do you think that the poorer nations should be willing to give up freedoms for economic progress? Why?

G/E

S/E

Mexico In 1910 revolution broke out in Mexico. Its undemocratic government was overthrown. After some years of confusion, a constitution was written.

This Constitution of 1917 planned for a socialist society and economy. Since that time, the Mexican people have attempted to carry out this plan.

The revolution of 1910 led to some important economic changes in Mexico. The feudal-like system of agriculture was ended. The land was divided among poor families that had none. Often the land was turned over to groups of families. These lands, held in common by the people of a village, are called **ejidos** (e hē′ᴛнōs). The people work the lands cooperatively. Not all the *ejidos* have been successful. There has been some movement toward individual ownership of the land. What advantages would there be in groups' owning and working the land? What disadvantages might there be in such a system of landholding?

See #3 below.

Agriculture in Mexico has not been very productive. Nearly 90 per cent of the country's farmland requires irrigation in order to be used. The government has spent a great deal of money on irrigation projects. At the same time, government money has been spent on roads, electric power, drinking water, and schools. The *ejidos* received most of the irrigated land. Why do you suppose the government gave them the better land?

See #4 below.

The irrigation of farmland helped increase the production of crops. Other things have helped, too. For example, new farming methods have been adopted, and different kinds of crops are

329

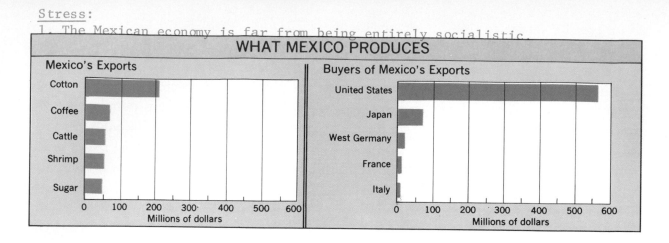

WHAT MEXICO PRODUCES

Mexico's Exports — Cotton, Coffee, Cattle, Shrimp, Sugar; Millions of dollars (0–600)

Buyers of Mexico's Exports — United States, Japan, West Germany, France, Italy; Millions of dollars (0–600)

being raised. Now Mexico is able to export farm production. Study the graphs above showing Mexican exports. What is Mexico's chief export? Which country is Mexico's best customer? What Mexican products do you suppose that the United States buys? Despite increasing farm production many farmers in Mexico are still poor.

Mexico's transportation and communication systems are largely government owned. However, radio and television stations are privately owned. The petroleum industry in Mexico is owned by the government. But the manufacturing of other products from petroleum is done by private businesses. How would you describe the Mexican economic system?

Study the two graphs below. How many millions of Mexicans earn their living in agriculture, forestry, and fishing? How many work in manufacturing? Now compare the value of farm and factory products. What problem do you see here? This problem is common among the countries in Asia, Africa, and Latin America that have newly developing economies.

Think for Yourself

If you were an economist, what kind of economic program would you plan for Mexico?

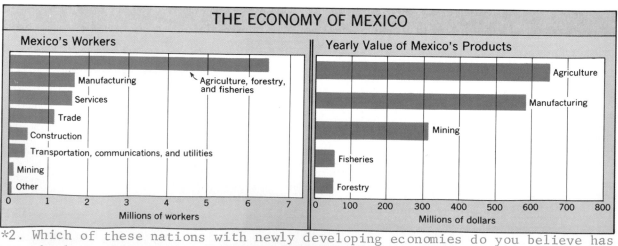

THE ECONOMY OF MEXICO

Mexico's Workers — Agriculture, forestry, and fisheries; Manufacturing; Services; Trade; Construction; Transportation, communications, and utilities; Mining; Other; Millions of workers (0–7)

Yearly Value of Mexico's Products — Agriculture; Manufacturing; Mining; Fisheries; Forestry; Millions of dollars (0–800)

Things to Do

See
page 323.

1. Imagine that you have joined the Peace Corps and that you are working in India. What are some ways in which you might help the Indian farmers? List your ideas on paper and be ready to discuss them in class.

See
page 313.

2. Make a scrapbook or bulletin-board display of pictures of consumer goods and heavy industrial goods. Cut these pictures from magazines and newspapers and place them under the suitable heading. Which pictures could you more easily find? Why?

See
page 313.

3. Pretend that you are a stockholder of one of the large automobile corporations. Write a letter to the president of the corporation and make suggestions about the kinds of cars that you would like to see the corporation manufacture.

CLASS PROJECT—PART 3

Does the world map now have markers with sociological ideas placed around it? If not, you should complete that work.

Next you might review Chapter 18, and do some more library research on your society looking for facts and ideas which would be of special interest to economists. Follow the same directions found in Part 2 of the class project—that is, make and display markers.

Now you may have a class discussion about the display, answering questions such as these.

1. Which societies seem to be most alike?
2. Which societies seem to have changed the most over the last 100 years? How?

19. Governments of Modern Times

Man has developed different political systems or ways of governing himself. In modern democratic political systems, the people choose representatives to govern them. Democratic governments do not all work alike. But they all get their powers from the people.

See #1 above.

Democratic political systems developed gradually in European and North American societies. Entire social classes often had to struggle to win certain political rights. Sometimes they used methods like the one the people shown here used. What political right were these people seeking? What action were they taking to get it?

S/P

Some modern political systems are not democratic. Undemocratic political systems also vary from one society to another. One man or a small group might have power. However, in all undemocratic political systems, power is held mostly by the government, not by the people. The people have only those rights allowed them by their government.

P/S

See #2 above.

In this chapter you will look at the rise of modern political systems, democratic and undemocratic. In order to do so, it will be necessary to study some political changes which took place in the early 1800's. You will see in this chapter how the political systems developed in Europe and North America have been copied by societies in all parts of the world.

P/H

See #3 below.

New York Suffragists Parade, 1912

JUST FOR FUN

See if you can find and bring to class a copy of the constitution of some organization. You and your classmates might compare constitutions and look for ways in which they are alike.

3. Political systems developed in Europe and North America have been copied all over the world.

332

An opening session of a British Parliament

DEMOCRATIC POLITICAL SYSTEMS

How the British government works
Modern Great Britain offers a good example of a democratic political system. A queen or a king no longer has any real power in the British government. Instead, the House of Commons has the governing power. The British system of government is called a **parliamentary** system. Under the parliamentary system, the voters elect the members of the most important house of Parliament, the House of Commons. The members of the other house of Parliament, the House of Lords, are not elected. The British queen is shown here at an opening session of Parliament. Why would she attend the meeting if she had no governing power?

See #1 above.

Parliament selects the **chief executive** or leader of the government. In Great Britain the chief executive, who must be a member of Parliament, is the prime minister. For what reasons is the British political system considered democratic?

See #2 below.

In a parliamentary system of democracy, the prime minister and the lawmakers work closely together. The political party which has the most members in the House of Commons elects the prime minister. The prime minister depends on his fellow party members to support any laws he suggests. If the members of the House of Commons lose confidence in the prime minister, he must either resign or call for an election.

See #3 below.

Stress:
1. British government was quite undemocratic in the early 1800's.
2. Democratic reform came peacefully in Britain through laws.

The prime minister does not serve for a fixed number of years.

As in most democratic political systems, the courts in Great Britain work separately from the rest of the government. At the same time, the courts have no power over Parliament.

Peaceful democratic reform in Great Britain If you were able to go back in time and visit Great Britain in the early 1800's, you would find its government to be quite undemocratic. Few people owned property in Great Britain. But only those who owned property could vote.

See #1 above.

Many in Great Britain believed that political changes were necessary. The growing middle class, the factory workers, farm workers, and women all demanded the right to vote. But the wealthy landowners opposed extending the right to vote to other people. Why?

The Reform Bill of 1832 made some important changes in the British political system. These changes amounted to a kind of revolution—a peaceful revolution, however. The power to govern was taken away from the landed nobles and given to the people, especially to members of the middle class. If you had been a factory worker at that time, and not a member of the middle class, how would you have felt about the Reform Bill of 1832? Why?

See #2 above.

More democracy for Great Britain Gradually the right to vote was granted to all British adults over the age of twenty-one. Another reform bill, passed in 1867, allowed factory workers to vote. About twenty years later the agricultural workers won the right to vote. Women finally got to vote in 1918.

Of the two houses in the British Parliament—the House of Lords and the House of Commons—only the members of the House of Commons are elected by the people. But until the 1900's both houses had equal governing powers. Why was it undemocratic for the House of Lords to have so much governing power in Great Britain? Gradually the House of Commons took over control of the government. Today the British House of Lords has practically no law-making power.

How the American government works The systems of government in the United States and Great Britain are alike in many ways. Both are democracies. By using their right to vote, the people control the representatives who make the political decisions.

See #3 below.

The differences between the British and American governments lie in their organization. The American political system is called a **presidential** system. The chief executive of this system—the President—is elected by the people. In Great Britain the prime minister is elected by members of Parliament.

See #4 below.

In the United States, Congress makes the laws and the President sees that the

3. Both the British and American political systems are representative democracies.
4. Under the American presidential system, the people elect the chief executive.

Stress:
1. Democracy advanced in America throughout the 1800's.
2. Recent federal laws have ensured the political rights of black Americans.

laws are carried out. The Supreme Court has the power to decide whether laws are in accordance with the Constitution.

Slow growth of American democracy Throughout the 1800's the right to vote was extended to more people in the United States. By 1860 most white adult males had the privilege of voting in national elections. After the American Civil War, black men were included in those who could vote. In 1920 American women won the voting privilege.

See #1 above.

But in the United States many of the people having the right to vote were not allowed to use that right. As recently as the 1960's the United States Congress passed laws protecting the voting rights of black people. Do you believe that all Americans today have equal voting rights? Why?

See #2 above.

Democracy spreads through Europe Following the defeat of Napoleon in 1815, European rulers tried to establish strict control over their people. The monarchs wanted to prevent the spread of democracy. Why would they be opposed to democratic governments? For a while it seemed that the monarchs had succeeded in crushing democracy in Europe. Only a few European nations had constitutions. Only a few people had the right to vote.

P/H

But beginning in the 1820's, revolutions broke out all over Europe. In many cases people were seeking a stronger

See #3 below.

P/H

3. Revolutions in Europe brought democratic governments to many societies.

voice in their government. The revolutions proved that most Europeans were unhappy with the governments which then existed.

Study the three maps on this page. Did the number of European revolutions increase or decrease between 1820 and 1848? What possible reasons can you give for the increase in revolutions?

P/H

Democratic ideas were spreading.

S/P

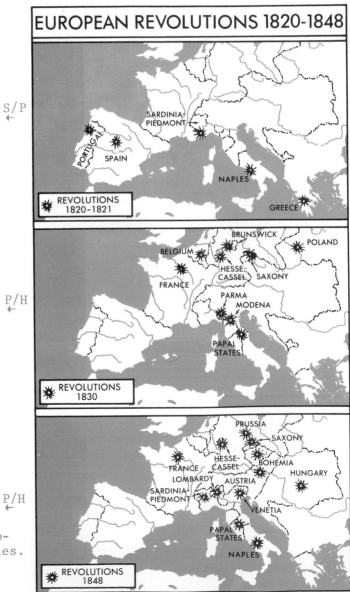

EUROPEAN REVOLUTIONS 1820-1848

REVOLUTIONS 1820-1821

PORTUGAL SPAIN SARDINIA-PIEDMONT NAPLES GREECE

REVOLUTIONS 1830

BELGIUM FRANCE HESSE-CASSEL SAXONY BRUNSWICK POLAND PARMA MODENA PAPAL STATES

REVOLUTIONS 1848

FRANCE SARDINIA-PIEDMONT LOMBARDY HESSE-CASSEL AUSTRIA PRUSSIA SAXONY BOHEMIA HUNGARY VENETIA PAPAL STATES NAPLES

In the years following 1848, the governments of western Europe—such as Switzerland, the Netherlands, Belgium, Denmark—slowly became democratic. For example, in 1848 the king of the Netherlands granted his people a constitution. But he kept many powers for himself. The government of the Netherlands did not become completely democratic until the 1920's.

By the early 1900's France had become the most important democratic P/H country on the European continent. After 100 years of struggle, wars, and revolutions, democracy had been won there. Frenchmen finally had the right to vote. They also enjoyed other rights such as freedom of the press and equality before the law.

Think for Yourself

What rights do you think people of a country must have before its government can be considered democratic?

SPREAD OF WESTERN POLITICAL IDEAS

For Teaching Helps, see page T100. For a class activity, see #3 on page 349.

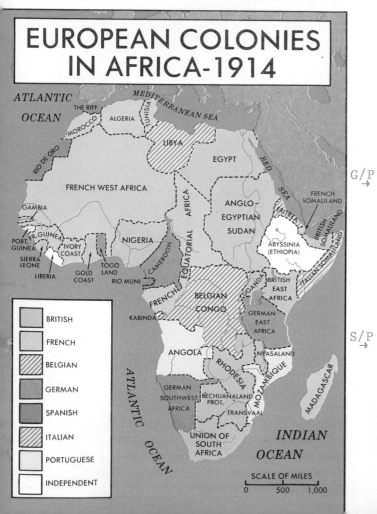

EUROPEAN COLONIES IN AFRICA—1914

ATLANTIC OCEAN

MEDITERRANEAN SEA

THE RIFF
MOROCCO   ALGERIA   TUNISIA
RIO DE ORO
LIBYA
EGYPT
FRENCH WEST AFRICA
RED SEA
GAMBIA
FR. GUINEA
PORT. GUINEA   IVORY COAST
SIERRA LEONE
LIBERIA   GOLD COAST   TOGO LAND   RIO MUNI
NIGERIA
CAMEROON
FRENCH EQUATORIAL AFRICA
ANGLO-EGYPTIAN SUDAN
ERITREA
FRENCH SOMALILAND
BRITISH SOMALILAND
ITALIAN SOMALILAND
ABYSSINIA (ETHIOPIA)
BELGIAN CONGO
KABINDA
UGANDA
BRITISH EAST AFRICA
GERMAN EAST AFRICA
ANGOLA
RHODESIA
NYASALAND
MOZAMBIQUE
MADAGASCAR
ATLANTIC OCEAN
GERMAN SOUTHWEST AFRICA
BECHUANALAND PROT.
TRANSVAAL
UNION OF SOUTH AFRICA
INDIAN OCEAN

BRITISH
FRENCH
BELGIAN
GERMAN
SPANISH
ITALIAN
PORTUGUESE
INDEPENDENT

SCALE OF MILES
0   500   1,000

Empire building in the 1800's Between 1815 and the beginning of World War I in 1914, some countries, especially those of Europe, scrambled for land in many parts of the world. Almost the entire African continent was carved into colonies. Much Asian land was also controlled by Europeans. The map G/P shows colonial Africa in 1914. Study the map to discover which European countries established colonies in Africa. Which two European powers controlled the most land in Africa? Britain, France.

Desire for independence Western ideas were spread by the Europeans to their colonies. A number of young Africans and Asians were educated in Euro- S/P pean schools and universities. They learned about democratic political systems developed by Europeans. Nationalism, democracy, and parliamentary

See #1 below.

See #2 below.

Stress:
1. European colonization reached its peak in 1914.
2. Western political ideas were carried by the Europeans to their African and Asian colonies.

government were some Western ideas which were adopted by non-Western people. When the students began returning to their native homes, the Europeans faced a struggle to keep their colonies. Why?

See #1 above. Following the end of World War II in 1945, the European colonial empires began to fall apart. The colonies demanded independence and self-government.

Today there are only a few colonies in the world. Dozens of new nations have been created in Africa and Asia. These newly independent nations together include over 1,000,000,000 people. Most of these nations are facing tremendous social, economic, and political problems.

Democracy in India India is one of See #2 below. the new nations which has a strong democratic government. The British educational system had taught Western ideas to India. The Magna Charta, the Glorious Revolution, and the Bill of Rights were familiar to many Indian students. The students began asking for political freedoms. How had their education given them a desire for freedom?

India struggled a long time to win self-government. In 1947 it became independent. A constitution created a democratic political system in India. Its government has a president, a prime minister, and a two-house legislature. How is the Indian government organized like the British government? India has a parliamentary system of government.

Prime Minister Ghandi of India

Pictured here is India's prime minister, Mrs. Indira Gandhi (gän'di). She is the daughter of India's first prime minister. Why is Mrs. Gandhi one of the most powerful women in the world?

One reason for the stable Indian government is the Congress party. This political party has ruled India since its See #3 below. independence. The Congress party has been committed to national unity and democracy for India. It has been opposed to the Indian caste system. How is the caste system undemocratic?

If the Congress party can survive, democracy has an excellent chance of succeeding in India. But economic failures could cause the collapse of the

Stress:
1. Japanese society was traditionally authoritarian which helped prevent it from establishing a democratic government.

Congress party. Other groups might then have a chance to gain power in India. In that case, what might happen to the stability of India's government?

Japanese democracy During the 1800's Japan industrialized rapidly and became one of the leading industrial nations of the world. It seemed that Japan might soon develop a democratic government. Its population was educated. And the country was unified. In the late 1800's Japan began taking steps toward developing a parliamentary government.

E/P

But Japan did not develop a democratic political system. The Japanese people were used to obeying authority. Obedience was an important part of their social structure. The military classes in Japan became very powerful. The government became fascist. Finally Japan went to war with the Western powers.

P/S

See #1 above.

Japan was defeated in World War II. The United States occupied the country and helped to establish a new political system there. A democratic constitution was written. Textbooks were rewritten to teach democratic ideas. Land reforms led to the creation of a stronger middle class. How would each change help to build a more democratic government?

H/P

S/P

See #2 below.

The Japanese rapidly adopted the new democratic forms of government. Strong political parties developed. Freedom of speech and press were encouraged, and a parliamentary government began to operate. There have been some violent clashes among groups of people in the parliament and on the streets. But real progress has been made toward democratic government in Japan.

A strong economy and an educated population are two reasons to expect democracy to continue in Japan. But how well the Japanese have actually learned democratic ideas will be found out in the future.

Think for Yourself

There is a possibility that Japan might someday be threatened by invasion from China. How might such a threat cause problems for a democratic government in Japan? The military might gain power again.

Other new governments Many new nations have been created in Africa since World War II. Developing a system of government that most of the people like is proving very difficult. A problem common to some of these nations is tribal loyalty. Many Africans have far closer ties to their tribe than to their national government. Rival tribes speaking different languages often live under the same government. When the African nations were created, not much consideration was given to this problem.

See #3 below.

Most African nations are forming one-party governments with strong, popular

2. The United States helped Japan establish a democratic government following Japan's defeat in World War II.
3. Many of the new African nations are finding that tribal ties of their people are far stronger than national ties.

Stress:
1. Africans face many problems in
   setting up governments.

leaders. The bearded man in the center of the picture is Jomo Kenyatta, the first prime minister of the African nation of Kenya. He had led movements for African independence for over thirty years. Why would this make him popular with most Africans? He fought for their rights.

See #1 above. It is difficult to predict what Africa's political future will be. Political changes are taking place rapidly. There are all kinds of barriers to the development of free government. But the Africans are searching for the political system which will best suit their cultures and needs. It is unlikely that Africans will exactly copy Western political systems. However, this does not mean that there will never be democratic governments in Africa.

P/S

Israel Another of the world's new nations is Israel, located on the eastern shore of the Mediterranean Sea. Israel was created in 1948 as a homeland for Jews from all parts of the world. How had the Nazi party helped to make Jews very anxious to have their own country? Since Israel's birth, it has been almost constantly at war with its Arab neighbors. The Arab nations believe that Israel's land rightfully belongs to the Arabs.

G/H

See #2 below. Israel has a democratic political system. Its elected parliament holds the most governing power. The parliament elects a president whose powers are limited. The head of Israel's government is

P

Jomo Kenyatta of Kenya

the prime minister, appointed by the president. Shown here is Israel's prime minister, Mrs. Golda Meir. As prime minister, what is one serious problem she will have to try and solve?

Think for Yourself

Of what importance is a stable government to a new nation? Helps economic progress.

Mrs. Golda Meir of Israel

2. The newly created nation of Israel has
   a democratic government.
*3. How does the tribal loyalty of Africans
    make it difficult for leaders to create
    unified nations?

Stress:
For Teaching Helps, see page T107.
1. Russia had a long history of undemocratic government.
2. A revolution in 1917 brought the Communist party to power in the Soviet Union.

UNDEMOCRATIC POLITICAL SYSTEMS

Russia's long history of undemocratic government Until the early 1900's Russia was ruled by czars. The people had few political freedoms. In the 1800's, during the reign of Nicholas I, the government held tight control of people's lives. Democratic ideas were forbidden in books, music, and plays. Schools could only use texts approved by the government. Foreigners were feared and were questioned and searched in Russia. Why did the government fear foreigners? Secret police spied on the citizens. Thousands of Russians were imprisoned because they were believed to hold democratic ideas.

In 1917 the Russians revolted against their czar. The leaders of the revolt were members of the Communist party. Within a few years the Communist party won absolute power in Russia.

See #1 above.

See #2 above.

When the communists took control of the Russian government, these undemocratic practices already described, were continued. Although the communists set up a constitution that promised rule by the people, political power came to rest solely in the hands of the Communist party. In 1936 a bill of rights was added to the Soviet constitution. But secret police, a government-controlled press, and suspicion of democratic ideas are still part of the people's daily life.

See #3 above.

How government works in the Soviet Union Pictured here is the Kremlin in Moscow, the capital of the Soviet Union. Many of the offices of the Soviet government are located in the Kremlin. The wall was built before the communists came to power. Why do you suppose a wall was needed?

The government of the Soviet Union

The Kremlin in Moscow

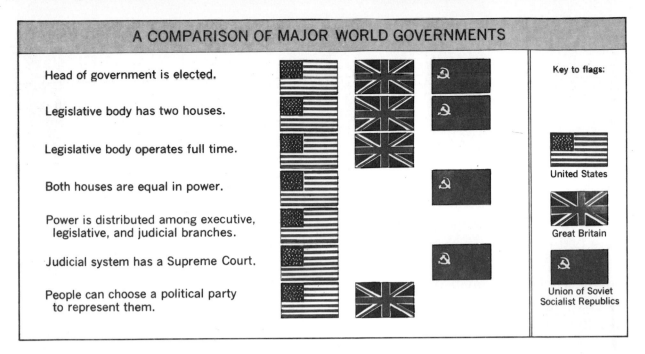

A COMPARISON OF MAJOR WORLD GOVERNMENTS

Head of government is elected.

Legislative body has two houses.

Legislative body operates full time.

Both houses are equal in power.

Power is distributed among executive, legislative, and judicial branches.

Judicial system has a Supreme Court.

People can choose a political party to represent them.

Key to flags:

United States

Great Britain

Union of Soviet Socialist Republics

includes a legislative body called the **Supreme Soviet.** But the Supreme Soviet has no real power. The function of the legislative and most other government bodies is to carry out the decisions of the Communist party.

See #1 below.

The Communist party controls the Soviet Union. Why is the head of the Communist party a very powerful person in Russia? Although the head of the Communist party has great influence, he does not have absolute power. He cannot act without the support of the powerful **Politburo** (pə lit′byur′ō). The politburo is the policy-making body of the Communist party. This committee is also known as the **Presidium** (pri sid′i əm). It sets up economic programs and controls foreign relations for the Soviet Union.

Since the Soviet government is con-

trolled by the Communist party, no opposition parties are allowed. When a Russian citizen enters a voting booth, what kind of choice does he have? Why is the Soviet political system considered undemocratic?

Not all Russians can join the Communist party. Only about 5 per cent of the population holds membership in the Communist party. How do you suppose one might be selected for membership in the Communist party?

See #2 below.

The kind of government adopted by the Soviets has some similarities to the governments of the United States and Great Britain. By studying the chart above you will discover some of the similarities and differences among all these governments. The last item in the table is probably the most important. See if you can tell why.

Stress:
1. The Communist party holds all the power in the Soviet Union.
2. Only a small percentage of the Soviet people belong to the Communist party.

341

Think for Yourself

Why do you suppose the Communist party wrote a constitution that promised rule by the people?

Why democracy failed in Germany The desire for democracy was not strong among the German people in the 1800's. They had long been used to the rule of a strong government in which they had little voice. The German public schools trained children to obey authority, especially the government's authority. The German government took the responsibility for providing its citizens with such social benefits as health insurance and free education. How do these facts help explain why Germany did not establish a democratic government?

However, a strong democratic movement began in Germany in the late 1890's and early 1900's. But before the forces for democracy could gather much strength, Germany became involved in a world war which it lost.

In 1919 a parliamentary system of democratic government was set up in Germany. This government had too many weaknesses to last very long. For one thing, there were many separate political parties which did not agree on how to govern.

For a while times were good and democratic government worked in Germany. But in the late 1920's there were world-wide economic failures which caused hunger and poverty in Germany. The German people quickly lost faith in the ability of a democratic government to solve the problems of their nation.

The Nazi party takes power As economic conditions grew worse in Germany, one of the political parties, the Nazi party, gained strength. Adolf Hitler, the leader of the Nazi party, took advantage of the frightened German population. He convinced the people that Germany could be great again under his leadership. Study the picture of Hitler speaking to the German people. What might he be telling them?

Adolf Hitler

By 1932 Hitler's Nazi party had a larger membership than any other political party in Germany. By threatening their opponents and refusing to allow them to speak, the Nazis helped themselves to win the election of 1933. Hitler then took all governmental power into his own hands.

How the fascist government worked in Germany Hitler became a **dictator,** a leader with absolute governing powers. After gaining control of the German government, he allowed no more free elections. Under a fascist political system, the people are taught to serve the government.

The Nazi party was the only political party allowed to exist in Germany. All its opponents were arrested by the Nazi secret police. Thousands of Germans were imprisoned and killed for speaking out against the Nazis. The most persecuted of the Germans were the Jews. The Jews were blamed for all that was wrong in Germany. They were prevented from owning businesses and working for the government. Their citizenship was taken away from them. Finally Hitler ordered that all Jews be killed. Special camps were built where hundreds of thousands of European Jews were murdered. Some of these Nazi prison camps have not been destroyed. What purpose might there be in preserving them forever?

The fascist political system destroyed democracy in Germany. The courts no longer tried to hold fair trials. Nazi party members were placed as leaders in local German governments.

Very young German children received military training. The picture shows some German boys already prepared to fight. How can such an emphasis on military training threaten world peace?

Military preparation of German youth

A fascist government continued in Germany until the end of World War II in 1945. At that time Germany was defeated, and Adolf Hitler took his own life.

Following World War II the defeated German nation was divided into two

S →

P/S ←

P/H ←

P/S ←

See #1 above.

See #2 below.

See #3 below.

343

separate countries, each having its own government. A democratic government was established in West Germany. The East German government is communist.

Think for Yourself

Why do you suppose that the citizens of West Germany have supported their democratic government so well?

CONFLICTS AMONG GOVERNMENTS

For Teaching Helps, see page T108. For a class activity, see #1 on page 349.

A struggle for power Throughout much of the 1800's there were few wars in Europe. Those few wars were small in size as most nations were eager to keep peace.

But as nations became stronger, they became jealous of other countries. Between 1895 and 1914, the nations of Europe were near war or at war many times. Nations competed with one another for power and colonies. Germany, Italy, and Japan industrialized later than some European countries. Germany hoped to become as strong and powerful as Britain. It wanted to own as many colonies as Britain. Italy, too, hoped to build an empire. Japan was trying to increase its power in Asia. Why was this race for colonies a dangerous situation for world peace?

See #1 below.

E/H

P/G

Each of the European nations became concerned only with its own interests. Love of one's country is not bad. But extreme nationalism can lead to hatred and envy of other nations. How can extreme nationalism make wars more likely to happen?

Since each nation was suspicious of its neighbors, the Europeans began building bigger armies and making more weapons. Soon all Europe was ready to fight on a moment's notice.

The First World War, 1914-1918 War finally came as a result of an incident in southeastern Europe. The future king of Austria was murdered by a young nationalist from the tiny country of Serbia (Sėr′bi ə). Today Serbia is a part of Yugoslavia. Austria declared war on Serbia on July 28, 1914. Soon all the big powers in Europe had taken sides. Gradually, one nation after another was involved in the fighting. Finally twenty-seven countries, including the United States, entered the war.

See #2 below.

Study the map on page 345 which shows the parts of the world involved in World War I. Why do you suppose that much of Latin America did not go to war?

Peace did not come until November 11, 1918. More than 10,000,000 young men had been killed. Millions more were wounded. Men had invented all kinds of new ways of killing one another. They developed tanks, airplanes, machine guns, cannons, and submarines to help destroy their enemies. Study this pic-

See #3 below.

Stress:
1. In the early 1900's the European countries were competing for power.
2. An assassination was the immediate cause of World War I.
3. World War I lasted four years, ending in 1918.

Things to Do

See page 344.

1. For one week keep a record of the names of those political leaders that you hear on the television and radio. Find out what country each leader represents. Which leaders are mentioned most often? Decide with your class why some leaders are in the news so much.

See page 333.

2. Think of some pictures you might draw showing people using rights guaranteed to them under a democratic government. For example, you might show citizens in a voting booth. What are some other possible pictures? List the possibilities. If you wish, draw one of the pictures and share it with the class.

See page 336.

3. Locate Israel on a world map. Make your own map of Israel and include the nations which border it. See if you can find out if any of these nations are friends with Israel. If so, mark them with a special symbol. Display your completed map.

CLASS PROJECT—PART 4

Complete your display by doing the necessary research to find facts and ideas of special interest to political scientists. Then make and display markers about your societies with this information.

Your class should now be prepared to have a discussion of all its findings. The discussion might begin with each committee offering a brief description of the societies it has studied.

Then all the class should try to answer these questions.

1. In what ways are all these societies alike?
2. How have the societies of the world influenced one another?

Have the pupils find each of the review words in the unit. For each word have them answer such questions as these:

Checkup Time

1. How was the word used in the book?
2. How might you use the word yourself?

For question 2 above, encourage the pupils to use each word in a social science context.

Review Words

capitalism	communism	fascism	socialism
chief executive	consumers	labor unions	stockholder
collective farms	corporation	Nazi party	strike
communes	dictator	Presidium	welfare state

Review Questions

Typical answers only.

Social Science Facts

1. Which social system became popular among Europeans in the 1800's (298) *Socialism.*

2. Why did workers in some industrial societies begin forming labor unions in the 1800's? (301) *To gain higher wages and better working conditions.*

3. What were some reasons why radicals gained control of Russia in 1917 and Germany in the 1930's? (305, 307) *Poverty and hunger.*

4. In a capitalistic economy who decides what is to be produced? (313) *Manufacturers.*

5. In partly socialized economies what kinds of businesses or industries will the government usually control? (316) *See bottom margin.*

6. In what two or three areas of the world has economic growth been especially slow? (321) *Africa, Asia, and Latin America.*

7. How is the chief executive chosen in a parliamentary system of government? (333) *By the majority party of the lower house of Parliament.*

8. Where did many colonial people learn Western political ideas? (336) *From Europeans.*

9. What kind of political system did all the defeated nations of World War II have? (347) *Fascist.*

5. Those providing raw materials, money, transportation, and power.

Social Science Ideas

1. Why did socialistic ideas appeal to many Europeans during the 1800's? *See bottom margin.*

2. Why do people often get more accomplished working in groups rather than working alone? *There is strength in numbers.*

3. What steps were taken by those societies which avoided revolution and conflicts between social classes? *Reducing poverty and improving conditions.*

4. Why is a capitalistic economy best suited to a democratic society? *It allows freedom of choice.*

5. Why is some measure of socialism being adopted by most newly developing economies? *Hope that the government can speed economic growth.*

6. Why have all areas of the world not reached the same level of economic growth? *Because of different levels of technology.*

7. What are some of the most important characteristics of a democratic political system? *Free elections, limited power, and a separate court system.*

8. How have Western political ideas affected other areas of the world? *See bottom margin.*

9. Why do nations with different political systems often become enemies of one another? *Their ideas and methods often conflict.*

1. They thought socialism could solve problems caused by industrialization.

8. Many have adopted Western ideas.

Test Yourself

On your own paper, write your answer to each question.

Test 1 Social Science Words

Choose the word or words in ( ) which make each sentence below true.

1. The most important form of business organization in the United States today is the ((corporation), Presidium).

2. Workers in the United States organize into (communes, (labor unions)) in order to gain better wages.

3. The ((Nazi), Communist) party established a fascist political system in Germany.

Answer the following questions with the correct words from the list of Review Words.

4. What are government-owned farms in the Soviet Union? Collective farms.

5. What is a government leader called who has absolute governing power? Dictator.

6. What is the ruling committee of the Soviet Union's Communist party? Presidium.

Match the words with the groups of words given below.

b 7. chief executive   a. government ownership of property

c 8. stockholder   b. head of a government

d 9. strike   c. part owner of a corporation

a 10. socialism   d. stopping work

Test 2 Facts and Ideas

Choose the word or words in ( ) that make each sentence below true.

1. ((Socialism), Fascism) became popular among Europeans in the late 1800's.

2. The chief executive in a parliamentary system of government is the (president, (prime minister)).

3. Under a ((capitalistic), communistic) system the businessmen decide what will be produced.

4. The British government owns (all, (some)) of its country's industries.

Which answer or answers to each question below are correct?

5. Which two of the following statements are true about democratic political systems?

(a.) The lawmakers are freely elected by the people.

(b.) Many political parties are allowed.

c. The government owns all the newspapers.

d. The political party controls the government entirely.

6. Which of these nations was once ruled by the Nazi party?

(a.) Germany

b. Italy

c. Great Britain

UNIT 8   MAN IN A CHANGING WORLD

<u>Stress:</u>
1. Social scientists are interested in the changes in the ways in which man uses the resources of the earth.
2. Social scientists study the ways man meets the challenges of the changing world.

Chapters

20. Recent Trends
21. Challenges Facing Modern Man
22. Meeting the Challenges

Central Asian boarding commercial plane

Electrical power station in India

A Lapp family on a main street of Narvik, Norway

Stress:
1. Man is successful in solving some, but not all, of his problems.
2. Man has learned both from experience and from the special work of social scientists how to solve many of his problems.

Today man is successfully meeting the challenge of solving some of his economic, social, and political problems. For example, he is producing more goods, more food, and more houses than ever before. However, man is unsuccessful in meeting other challenges. Each day the news tells of such things as war, slums, poverty, and crime.

E/S
←
See #1 above.

Throughout his long history man has been faced with the challenge of solving difficult economic, social, and political problems. To help solve these problems, man draws upon experiences gained from earlier successes and failures. He uses the best information that social scientists and many others can provide. Then he lays out plans of action which may or may not be successful.

S/P
←
See #2 above.

A writer of long ago expressed the idea of possible failure when he wrote these lines.

> The best laid plans o' mice and men
> Gang aft a-gley [often go astray];
> An' lea'e us nought but grief and pain,
> For promis'd joy.

See #3 below.

What evidence can you give to prove that the author of these lines was right?

In this unit you will discover some of the trends discovered by social scientists as they study man and society. You will discover some of the things man has done and is doing to help solve society's problems. Here are questions you will be able to answer after studying this unit.

1. What trends are social scientists discovering as they study man and society?
2. What are some of the major challenges modern man must meet? How is man meeting these challenges?
3. Man cannot be sure of the outcome of his plans.
*4. Is experience always the best teacher? Explain.

For Teaching Helps, see page T109.
Stress:
1. The continuing nature of the class project. See pp. 371, 389, and 406.

CLASS PROJECT—PART 1

As your class project for this unit, your class may plan and make a model landscape showing wise use of an area of the earth's surface. The information you will learn from studying this unit will assist you in doing some parts of this project.

To begin the project build a model landscape of the map shown on this page. A suggestion is to build the landscape on a large tabletop, using papier-mâché, texture paint, flour and water, or modeling clay. Some of you may have done modeling of this kind while building a model-railroad layout. You may want to paint your landscape, using different colors to show the different land and water features. Be sure your landscape shows the land and water features shown in the picture. This will be important as you continue your class project.

Part 2 of the class project will give you further directions in developing your model showing the wise use of an area of the earth's surface.

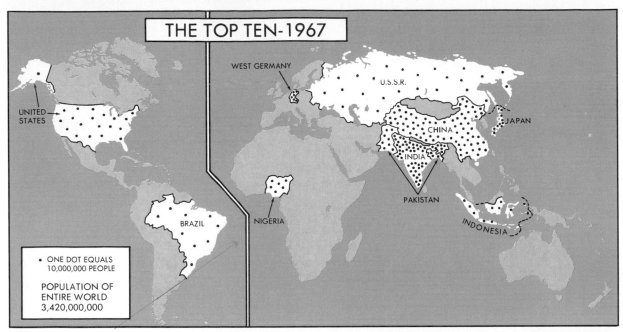

THE TOP TEN-1967

ONE DOT EQUALS
10,000,000 PEOPLE

POPULATION OF
ENTIRE WORLD
3,420,000,000

Vertical line indicates deletion of Atlantic Ocean area.

20. Recent Trends

For Teaching Helps, see page T110.

In every society today there are people who study man's future needs for housing, food supplies, highways, airports, and jobs. They study the ways man uses the earth's land and water. They study population changes. And they often consult with social scientists about trends—population trends, for example.

See #1 below.

Look at the map above. A social scientist might compare the population data on it with data given on an older population map and with data on a more recent one. By comparing the three maps, he might discover population trends for various countries. If the population trend for a country was upward, he might estimate that the upward trend would continue. What estimate would he make if the population trend was downward? Could he be certain that he was right? Why?

See #2 below.

What kinds of trends do social scientists observe? How do they discover trends? This chapter will help you answer both questions.

JUST FOR FUN

Plan a way to discover whether the trend is toward larger or smaller families in some community you know. Then see if you can discover the trend.

Stress:
1. Man must be aware of trends.
2. Social scientists help man prepare for the future.
*3. In what ways might the importance of the social sciences be related to an increase in the world's population?

355

For Teaching Helps, see page T111. For a class activity, see #1 on page 371.
Stress:
1. Most of the earth's surface is covered with water.

LAND USE AND POPULATION TRENDS

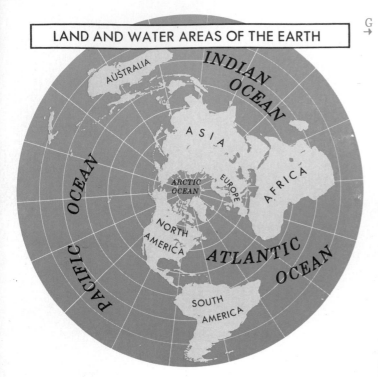

LAND AND WATER AREAS OF THE EARTH

The earth's land and water A space traveler coming near the earth in a space ship sees the cloud cover that hides his view of much of the earth's surface. However, in many places he sees the surface of the earth. Some parts are a mixture of browns, greens, and yellows. These are the land areas of the earth. The brown and green areas are fields, cities, and forests. The yellowish areas are deserts. Other parts of the earth's surface, especially at the North Pole and the South Pole, are white. These are the icecaps that cover the polar regions.

Still other parts of the earth's surface probably look green or blue. These are the parts that are water. Study the map on this page. Notice that the continents look something like islands in a large body of water. Which of the continents appears to have the most land?

See #1 above.

The total area of the earth is about 200,000,000 square miles. Of this area nearly 140,000,000 square miles, or nearly three-fourths of it, are covered by water.

See #1 above.

Land use Coming very close to the earth, a space traveler might see places similar to those shown in the pictures on

View from "Going to the Sun" road, Glacier National Park, Montana

Great Sand Dunes, National Monument, Colorado

Tropical forest

Rocky Mountain National Park, Colorado

these pages. What is there about each of these places that makes it unsuited for homes and cities? Of all the nearly 60,000,000 square miles of land on earth, only about one-eighth of it is suited for making homes, for producing crops, and for developing towns and cities. Geographers tell us that almost seven-eighths of the earth's land area is too dry or too cold for raising crops. Would you expect large cities to develop in these dry or cold places? Why or why not?

See #1 above.

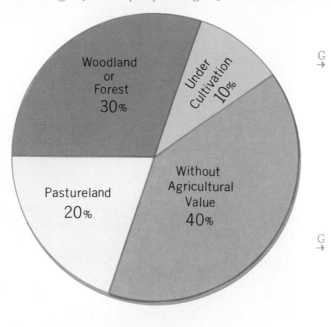

USE OF THE EARTH'S LAND

The process by which rock or soil is removed from a given place by natural forces is called **erosion.** Have you ever seen a place affected by erosion? What kinds of things caused it? Erosion of the earth's surface is likely to increase. And the rate of increase seems likely to be greatest in the heavily populated countries. Why?

Geographers study erosion and its effects on man. What might some of these effects be? Geographers also study the ways in which man causes erosion to occur. You have already discovered that plowing pastureland and removing trees from the land are two of the ways. See if you can think of some others.

Geographers tell us that in addition to causing erosion, man is also reducing in other ways the amount of land now

See #1 above. The graph will help you understand how the land of the earth is being used. Which of the kinds of land named on the graph would people most likely select for their homes? Why?

Some of the land that is now used for pastureland or that is covered by trees could be made into cropland. However, most of this land should never be plowed for farms. The picture will help you decide what sometimes happens to such land when people try to farm it. Find the place where the land seems to have been carried away. This type of place is called a **gully.** A gully is a small, steep valley, or narrow gorge. What might have caused the gully shown in the picture?

See #2 below.

2. Man sometimes misuses his land.

3. Vegetation and erosion are factors affecting man's choice of a place to live.

See #3 below.

Erosion

Strip mining--coal

used for raising food and for living space. He is using large amounts of it for his buildings, highways, dumps, strip mines, and so on. Strip mines like the one shown in the picture ruin thousands of acres of land each year. A recent White House study predicts that 5,000,000 acres of our country's land will be ruined by strip mines by 1980. Do you think that land left behind by strip miners would be good for raising food? Would it be good for building homes or for farming? Why?

G
←

G/H
→

See #1
below.

Think for Yourself

What other things is man doing to spoil land now used to raise food? Is he likely to spoil more land in the future? Why?

A crowded planet Locate Japan on the map on page 355. Using your fingers, trace a belt westward to the nearest ocean. What crowded countries are within this belt?

This belt of land has always had over half of the population of the world. Historians tell us that the density of population has always varied from country to country. It has also varied from continent to continent. For example, Asia and parts of western Europe already had a large population in the middle 1700's. Yet at that time only about 20,000,000 of the 700,000,000 people on earth lived in the Western Hemisphere and in Oceania—the islands of the central and southwestern Pacific which are north, northeast, and east of Australia.

See #2
below.

Stress:
1. Man has used some of his land in such a way as to leave it totally useless as a place to live.
2. Certain areas of the world are much more heavily populated than others.

359

For Teaching Helps, see page T111.
Stress:
1. The populations of the continents have changed at uneven rates.

THE PEOPLE ON EARTH—MILLIONS					
Year	Asia	Africa	Europe incl. USSR	Western Hemisphere and Oceania	World
A.D.1	150	50	45	5	250
1650	300	100	90	10	500
1750	450	100	130	20	700
1850	660	100	290	50	1100
1900	900	120	380	200	1600
1950	1350	200	600	350	2500
2000*	3900	500	1000	900	6300

*A conservative estimate

Uneven rates of growth Study the table on this page. What is the first year shown on the table? Which two continents had the most people in the year A.D. 1? Are the same two continents also expected to have the most people in the year 2000?

Notice that in the years between 1650 and 1900 the population of Africa increased very slowly. One reason for this slow increase may have been the slave trade, which ended in the 1800's.

Referring to the table again, find the answers to these questions.

1. How many people were added to the population of Africa between the years 1900 and 1950?

2. How many people will probably be living in Africa by 2000?

3. Is the population of Asia expected to grow more or less rapidly than the population of Africa?

4. Is the world population expected to double or to more than double during the last half of the 1900's?

Although the population of the earth is increasing rapidly, the growth rates are uneven. In western Europe and in Japan they are low. In the United States and the Soviet Union they are medium. In Latin America, Africa, and in most of Asia the growth rates are highest. Where growth rates are highest, hunger and poverty tend to be greatest. Why?

See #1 above.

See #2 below.

Migrations of people Between 1750 and 1950 millions of people from Europe **migrated**—left their homelands for other lands. Many migrated to the Americas and Australia, which were sparsely populated until about 1850.

Because of their good means of transportation, large numbers of Europeans could migrate to other continents to live. For their new homes they tended to migrate to the uncrowded continents which had land and climate similar to those of their homelands. These continents were North America and Australia. Because they had better weapons the Europeans could take land away from the people already living on these uncrowded continents.

Today, largely because of such migrations, the Americas and Australia have a culture patterned after that of the Europeans. This type of culture is called a **western culture**. The traditional cul-

2. Sometimes a country's population grows so rapidly that its economy cannot meet the people's needs for goods and services.
3. The change in the population size of a particular area has sometimes been brought about by migration.

Stress: For Teaching Helps, see page T111.
1. Land constantly covered by ice and snow is unsuitable as a place to live.
2. Population tends to shift from rural areas to urban centers.

tures of the people of Asia and Africa differ from western cultures. Why? Does the world now have more people with a western culture or with other types of cultures? What evidence can you give to prove your answer?

Except for Antarctica there are no almost empty continents today. Is Antarctica a suitable place for migrations of large numbers of people? Using the picture below, see how much evidence you can find to prove your answer. As you may have guessed by now, the rapidly increasing populations must find places to live on their own continents. In their own homelands they must find ways to feed more people.

In our own times more and more people on all continents are moving away from farms. They are moving to large cities on their own continent—most often in their own country. For example, in Asia between 1900 and 1950 the number of people living in cities over 100,000 went from 19,000,000 to 106,000,000. In the same amount of time

in Africa, the city population went from about 1,400,000 to 10,000,000. How did the change in the city populations of Asia and of Africa compare with the change in the total populations of those continents? See the table on page 360 to help you decide. In the world as a whole, the migration to the cities was not as great between 1900 and 1950 as it was in Asia and Africa. This is true for many reasons. One reason is that the movement started about 150 years sooner on the other continents than in Asia and in Africa.

Social scientists who study population trends believe that the migration to large cities will increase. And this increased migration will cause changes in such things as family life, jobs, and governments. What might some of these changes be?

Think for Yourself

What kinds of things could change the upward population trends in Asia and Africa?

See #1 above.

G/S

See #2 above.

S/G

S/G

*3. Why are social scientists interested in migration patterns?

Antarctica

Weddell
seal
and pup

For Teaching Helps, see page T112.
Stress:
1. Economists are interested in the trend of a country's total production of goods
   and services.

ECONOMIC TRENDS

More goods and services The social scientist most likely to study the production of goods and services is the economist. In his studies of a nation's economy, the economist wants to know what its population is. He also wants to know the total amount of goods and services its people produce. This amount of goods and services is called the **Gross National Product** or **GNP.** In the abbreviation GNP, what word is represented by each letter?

See #1 above.

Suppose that two countries, A and B, have the same GNP. However, country A has twice as many people as country B. In which of the countries, A or B, is the average amount per person of the GNP greater?

Within each country the average amount per person of the Gross National Product is called the **per capita GNP.**

COUNTRY	ESTIMATED POPULATION IN MILLIONS	PER CAPITA GNP (U.S. $) 1967
United States	199	$4,037
West Germany	60	2,021
Japan	100	1,158
Brazil	86	333
Pakistan	107	*125
Indonesia	110	*99
India	511	*88
Nigeria	61	*77

*1966

In their attempt to peer into the future, economists often study the per capita GNP of a country. By turning to the *Statistical Yearbook* of the United Nations, they can find information to use in making tables like the one shown here. As you study the table, answer these questions.

See #2 below.

1. What countries are named in the table?
2. Which country has the most people?
3. Which country has the highest per capita GNP?
4. Which country has the lowest per capita GNP?
5. In which of the countries would you expect the problem of poverty to be greatest?

When this GNP table was prepared, the average per capita GNP for the world as a whole was estimated to be about $600. Which of the countries named in the table fall below the average? By comparing GNP tables like this one with both recent and earlier tables, economists have discovered a trend in per capita GNP for the whole world. They now estimate that by the year 2000 it will average about $1600.

See #3 below.

If the economists are right in estimating economic growth, the average per capita GNP will increase by about two and one-half times during the last thirty years of the 1900's. This increase would seem to show that everyone will have many more goods and services in the near future. Unfortunately this is not true, because the economic growth is not likely to be uniform.

Uneven economic growth Economists tell us that countries with rapidly increasing populations have great difficulty in increasing the per capita GNP. India is such a country. Its population is growing at the rate of 1,000,000 persons each month. It must have a big increase in goods and services just to keep up with the population growth.

See #1 above.

Countries in which the population grows more slowly usually have the highest per capita GNP. Why?

See #2 below.

Many economists believe that the increase in average per capita GNP in the United States will be very great in the future. They point out that the flow of products from American factories has more than doubled every twenty years since 1900. They estimate that in the 1970's alone the production of goods and services in the United States will almost double.

See #3 below.

Think for Yourself

Do you think that everyone in our country will get the same share of the increased amounts of goods and services our country will produce in the future? Why?

Sources of power Anthropologists tell us that man learned of the great power of the forces of nature at about

COMMON SOURCES OF POWER		
Type	Early Development	Source of Mechanical Power
Wood	pre-Neolithic	A.D. 1650-1700
Animal	6000-8000 B.C.	before 500 B.C.
Wind	2000-3000 B.C.	A.D. 600-700
Water	1000-2000 B.C.	before 500 B.C.
Coal	1000-2000 B.C.	A.D. 1650-1700
Petroleum	before 1000 B.C.	A.D. 1860-1870
Electrical	A.D. 1650-1750	A.D. 1750-1880
Atomic	1905-1945	after 1945

the same time he learned to herd animals, to plant and harvest crops, and to make tools and weapons. Information gotten from anthropologists and historians was used in making the table on this page. What are the common types of power used by man? Which type is oldest and which is most recent?

Notice the heading of the third column of the table. The dates named in this column are the dates when man began to use each type of power to turn the wheels of his machines. Which two types of power were first used by man for this purpose? Which type was used most recently?

Energy released by burning Today much of the mechanical power used by man comes from the energy released by the burning of coal, oil, and gas. These fuels are often called **fossil fuels.** The effect of the sun on decaying plant and animal life is one of the factors involved in the formation of coal and petroleum.

2. A low rate of population growth may lead to a greater GNP per person.
3. Economists find indications that the American economy will continue to grow rapidly.

363

Norris Dam, Tennessee

See #1 below.

As man produces more goods, he requires more and more coal, petroleum, and gas for power. In time these sources of power will be gone. In what ways could a shortage of coal, petroleum, and other sources of power affect the economic growth of a nation?

See #2 below.

Water power In many parts of the world, man is making use of the energy in moving water. This energy is used to turn generators that produce electricity, which is used as a source of power. Such power is called **hydroelectric power**. The picture on this page shows the Norris Dam in Tennessee. Find the rectangular building near the base of the dam and the transformer station behind it. Within the building there are huge generators turned by water pouring from the large body of water created behind the dam. Study the picture of the dam. What evidence can you find to prove that the dam is very wide at the top? That it is very high? Suppose that you were a geographer who had been asked to choose a site for a dam and a powerhouse. What questions would you need to ask and answer before making your choice?

A great number of dams and powerhouses are being built in Asia, Africa, and South America. Today there is a trend toward greater use of water power to produce electricity. How would you explain this trend?

One of the very great dams of the world is the Aswan High Dam in Egypt. Water stored behind this dam is used to irrigate many acres of land in Egypt as well as to produce electricity. How,

364

Stress:
1. The economic growth of a nation is related to the amount and sources of its power.
2. Water is a very important source of power.

Stress:
1. The atom is one of man's most important sources of power.

do you think, do dams like the Aswan High Dam affect the number of people who can make a living in Egypt? How can such dams affect the amount of goods a country can produce?

Power from atoms The picture you see here is still a rather uncommon sight in the world today. The buildings contain huge generators that are turned by steam power made by using energy released from atoms of uranium.

See #1 above.

Today power from the atom is used to generate electricity in Great Britain, the United States, Canada, Japan, the Soviet Union, India, and in some other nations. Economists believe that the trend toward using atomic power will increase.

Power from the sun In some nations, especially in India, man is using the sun itself as a direct source of power. Scientists have developed thousands of small solar furnaces which get their heat from the sun. This heat can be used to run solar engines which produce small amounts of electricity at a high cost. Do you think man will learn to build bigger and better solar furnaces that produce electricity for less cost? Why?

Scientists are still searching for new and inexpensive ways to produce power. Why? A country's economic progress is related to the country's means of producing power.

Nuclear power plant, Pennsylvania

Stress:
1. Man has an ever-growing need for more power.

WORLD ELECTRIC POWER PRODUCTION		
Region	Total Electric Power*	Hydroelectric Power*
(a) North America	1,301	314
(b) Western Europe	806	288
(c) Eastern Europe & USSR	692	99
(d) Asia	323	99
(e) Latin America	97	50
(f) Africa & the Middle East	61	10
(g) Australia & New Zealand	46	16
* Billions of kilowatt hours		

2. Some areas of the world produce far more electric power than other areas produce.

Uneven production of electricity
Study the table on this page and answer these questions.

1. What is the title of the table?
2. What regions of the world are named in the table?
3. Which region produces the largest amount of electric power?
4. Which region produces the smallest amount of electric power?
5. Which three regions of the world are most in need of more electric power?

See #1 above. The trend toward a need for more and more power is likely to continue. For that reason economists believe that man must soon find new and inexpensive sources of power.

Think for Yourself

The countries named in the table are arranged in order with the country producing the largest amount of electricity first. What would be another good way of arranging the countries? Why?

G/E

Number of workers and hours worked Throughout the world there is a trend toward using machines in producing goods. Social scientists have wondered whether this trend has reduced the number of hours that people work at their jobs—especially those outside the home. If this has happened workers have more free time than ever before. The question is not an easy one to an-

See #3 below.

3. Industry is making greater and greater use of machines.

Stress:
1. Social scientists have found that since World War II, the workweek has
   been slightly shortened.

See #1 above.

swer and can be answered only after a careful study of many records. A recent study of the number of hours worked shows that in the United States the workweek fell by about two and one-half hours in the years between 1947 and 1969. Some workers have a longer workweek than others, as shown in the graph below.

The workers of our country in all jobs other than agriculture work an average of thirty-eight hours a week. What groups of workers named on the graph work fewer hours than the average number of hours?

Economists have discovered that full-time work schedules in this country have changed very little since World War II. Although workers seem to want more paid holidays and longer vacations, they seem satisfied with the workweek as it is. Most workers seem to want more income instead of more hours of leisure time. See if you can tell why.

See #2 below.

The trend in industry is to use more and more labor-saving devices which are run by computers. These labor-saving devices produce great amounts of goods with the smallest possible amount of labor. As a result, fewer workers are needed and unemployment is on the increase. Increasing unemployment leads to more poverty, and those who live in poverty cannot afford to buy the goods that factories produce. What happens to factories that cannot sell the goods they produce? Are people better off or worse off when factories have to shut down? Why?

See #3 below.

Think for Yourself

How does unemployment affect the amount of goods that the people of a society purchase? It decreases the amount of goods that the people of a society purchase.

2. Workers are more interested in higher incomes than in more free time.

THE WORKWEEK
IN THE UNITED STATES—1970

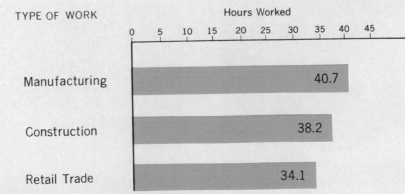

TYPE OF WORK	Hours Worked
Manufacturing	40.7
Construction	38.2
Retail Trade	34.1

3. Labor-saving devices are increasing unemployment.
*4. Why has the length of the workweek remained so stable over the past
   two decades?

367

For Teaching Helps, see page T113.
Stress:
1. In the past two decades the number and average size of nations have grown.

POLITICAL TRENDS

More nations In 1945 when the United Nations was formed, only fifty-one flags were on the plaza of the United Nations shown here. Each flag was a symbol for one of the nations on earth. At the beginning of 1967, 122 flags were on the plaza. Again, each flag represented a different nation. What had happened to the number of nations during the period between 1945 and 1967? What had probably happened to the average size of the nations?

See #1 above.

Many of the new nations of the world are in Africa. Study the map of Africa. How many nations are named on the map? How does this number of nations compare with the number of nations in North America?

United Nations Building, New York City

Flags of member nations

Notice that the boundary lines of countries are sometimes drawn across land once controlled by African tribes. For example, the boundary between Niger and Nigeria cuts across the land of the Hausa tribe. What are some other boundaries that cut across land owned by the same tribe?

See #2 below.

Do you think that it is easy or hard to form stable governments in new nations whose boundaries divide members of a tribe? Why? What problems might the rulers of such new nations face?

Groups for economic cooperation Every nation is interested in preserving itself. Today, however, some of the nations of the world are banding together in groups. Within each group the nations are learning to work together for the benefit of all the members. Sometimes the member nations of a group agree to lower tariff barriers. They may also agree to cut down the amount of economic competition among the nations. One of the most successful groups is the European Economic Community, usually called the Common Market. When the Common Market was formed in 1957, it included six nations—Belgium, France, Italy, Luxembourg, the Netherlands, and West Germany. At the time the Common Market was formed, economists predicted that the countries joining it would have faster economic growth than would other European nations.

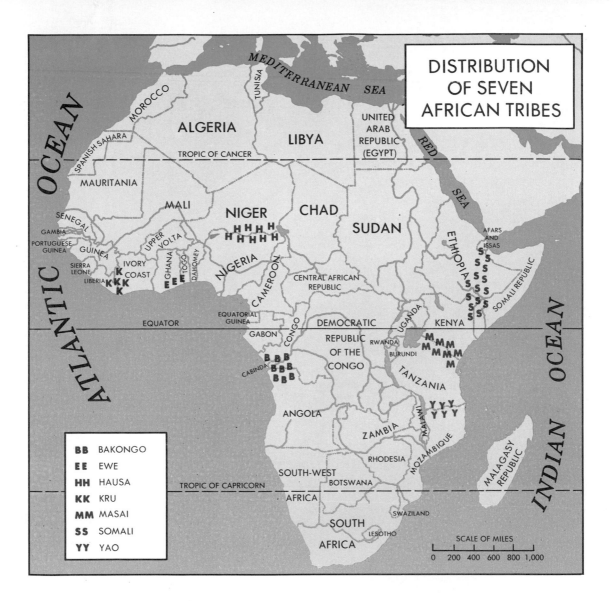

DISTRIBUTION OF SEVEN AFRICAN TRIBES

BB BAKONGO
EE EWE
HH HAUSA
KK KRU
MM MASAI
SS SOMALI
YY YAO

See #1 below.

They also predicted that the people of those countries would soon have better standards of living. The record shows that the economists' predictions were right.

Partly because of the success of the Common Market, nations in Africa and in South America have formed trade organizations. The trend seems to be toward more such organizations in the future.

Groups for political cooperation Most political scientists believe that nations can work together to solve international political problems. And some nations seem ready to give up some of their political rights in order to get the benefits of working together.

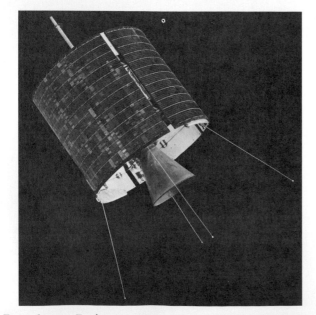

The 747
superjet
(710,000
pounds)

Everett, Washington

Political scientists have little reason to believe that nations will give up their rights to do things that are in their national self-interest. However, they do have evidence that great political changes are taking place in the world. Such changes are brought about partly because people are learning more about cultures other than their own. For example, planes like the Boeing 747 carry people to most of the world's major cities. Communication satellites, like the one below, enable us to learn of events in other countries as they happen. Movie films are exchanged among companies in different countries. All these things tend to affect the governments of countries. See if you can tell why.

One of the more important steps toward political cooperation was taken when the United Nations was formed in the 1940's. Although the stronger nations do not seem to trust the United Nations, its organization was a step toward a kind of world government. Political scientists believe that other steps must be taken in the near future and that they will be taken. Why?

Think for Yourself

Many nations fear any form of world government. Why? They feel that a world government might disregard the rights and special positions of the individual nations. Stress:

*1. How might improvements in communications benefit all mankind?

Intelsat I (communications satellite)

Things to Do

See page 356.

1. Write a paragraph or a short story telling how your life and the lives of some people on this earth might be different if three-fourths of the earth's surface were land instead of water.

See page 365.

2. Make a picture or model of an atomic power plant. Prepare a short statement to place under the picture or model that tells something about the power plant.

CLASS PROJECT—PART 2

Your model landscape of the map on page 354 should now be completed. A suggestion is to place the table on which you have constructed your model against a bulletin board so that you can use this space as a background area.

In developing plans to show the wise use of the land and water features on your model, consider the following possibilities for man-made things that you might be able to show.

1. Ways to prevent erosion of the land surface. What could you do to prevent gullies from developing further?
2. Industrial development. Could a hydroelectric power plant make good use of the water from the river?
3. Buildings that reflect wise use of the land area.
4. A good transportation system.
5. The development of a water system.

Continuing the class project, make plans to do the following: List the kinds of things you will need to place on your landscape. Develop a plan that will tell where to place the man-made things on the landscape. Begin to make or find models of things you will need.

People cooperating to clean up a slum

21. Challenges Facing Modern Man

For Teaching Helps, see page T114.

The young people shown here live in the central part of a big city. They have accepted the responsibility of helping to make it a good place in which to live. Why might these people and their families want to live in the central part of the city? Why might they want to move out?

Today more than one out of every three persons on earth lives in or near an industrial city. One out of every ten persons is now living in a city with a population of over 1,000,000. Social scientists tell us that the proportion of people living in cities is increasing. All these people need space in which to move around. They need decent housing, enough food, clean water, and fresh air. They also need other kinds of goods and services. Providing for the needs of its people presents every city—and nation—with many challenges. What some of these challenges are is the story told in this chapter.

S ↔

See #1 below.

See #2 below.

JUST FOR FUN

Refer to a newspaper or a news magazine, or watch a newscast on television. Discover one or more problems that face people of some country other than the United States.

Stress:

1. The proportion of people living in cities is continuing to grow.
2. Every city is challenged with the problems of meeting the needs of its people.
*3. What effects do challenges have on a society?

372

Stress: For Teaching Helps, see page T115.
1. Overcrowding can be detrimental to both mental and physical health.
2. There may be a direct relationship between overcrowding and crime.

SOCIAL AND PHYSICAL NEEDS

The need for space Throughout the world there are millions of people who have very little space which they can call their own. The following paragraphs were written by one of these people. Do you think that the writer enjoyed being crowded? How did you decide?

A pale grey light filters through the window, and somewhere an alarm goes off. You yawn and start to roll over, but your kid brother is in the way. You roll the other way, and bump smack into a wall. You slide down off the bed and look out the window, but you can't really tell what kind of day it is because the brick wall of the building just a few feet away blocks out all the sunlight anyway.

Downstairs, you bump and jostle your way through the crowded streets, then get into a bus with so many people already in it that it looks like a cartoon. But the squeezing and squashing aren't funny, and by the time you struggle your way to the door at your stop and shove your way through the throng of people waiting to get on, you feel so closed-in that you just want to scream. . . . *

In an attempt to find the effects of overcrowding, scientists have performed experiments with animals. They have discovered that the behavior of the animals changes for the worse as overcrowding increases.

*From "The Quest for Inner Space," by R. J. Lefkowitz in *Nature and Science*, March 31, 1969. Copyright © 1969 by *The Natural History Press*, a division of Doubleday and Company, Inc. Reprinted by permission.

The effects of overcrowding on people are probably different from the effects on animals, but social scientists believe that overcrowding is also bad for people. See #1 above. They believe that overcrowding may make people less healthy, both physically and mentally. They believe that there may be a relationship between overcrowding and crime and outbreaks See #2 above. of violence, such as riots.

Think for Yourself

Does crowding seem to make people happy or unhappy? What evidence can you give to show that your answer is right?

The need for housing The picture shown here was taken in one of the very old cities of the world—Saigon, Vietnam. Saigon is one of the most densely populated cities in the world, if not the most densely populated. The centers of Sai-

Saigon, South Vietnam

<u>Stress</u>:
1. Areas of overcrowded housing usually deteriorate into slums.

gon and many of the other older cities of Asia and Africa are thickly populated and overcrowded. Often the poor people of these cities live in very small houses along streets so narrow and clogged with traffic that people cannot get very far from their homes. Sometimes as many as twenty persons live in a single room. The population of such thickly populated parts of the very old cities increases as more children are born and as more and more people who are poor crowd into the cities.

S/G

S/P

As the parts of the city where poor people can afford to live become more and more crowded they become slums. In the newer cities of Asia, Africa, and South America, slums often develop just outside the city limits. Here people live in shacks or crude shelters which they build with whatever materials they can find. Millions of people live in such slums.

See #1 above.

S/E

No one knows exactly how many slum dwellers there are because it is almost impossible to count either the places used as houses or the people themselves. See if you can tell why.

In some cities of the world the governments are trying to get people to move out of the slum areas and into new housing units built for them, usually some distance away. Often the slum dwellers are unwilling to move from the slums. They do not want to be forced to live farther away from such jobs as they

S

S/P

have, and for good reason. In Rio de Janeiro, for example, workers may stand waiting in lines or on buses or trains for six hours a day to get from their homes to their jobs and back again.

Many slum dwellers refuse to leave the slums because they do not want to give up the traditions they have developed in their communities. Many of them do not want to move to places owned by the government. They fear that government officials, including police, will enter such homes without permission whenever they wish.

Because slum dwellers in many parts of the world do not want to be moved out of the slums, slum housing becomes even worse as populations increase throughout the world. Landlords who own buildings in slums often take advantage of the great demand for living quarters. They subdivide small apartments into even smaller ones. Often they refuse to make needed repairs.

Landlords have a responsibility to keep their buildings in good repair. But tenants also have a responsibility—to take care of the buildings where they live. When either landlords or tenants do not carry out their responsibilities, housing conditions become worse and worse.

Sometimes cities require slum landlords to spend money to repair their buildings. Then the landlord may lose money on his buildings and decide to

374

Stress:
1. At present, man is capable of producing enough food to feed all the
   people.

tear them down. What effect does tear-
ing down such buildings have on the
people who flock to cities looking for
jobs and places to live?

The need for food At the present
time man is able to produce larger
amounts of food than ever before in
history. Very likely he is producing
enough food, worldwide, for everyone to
have a good diet if everyone could get an
equal share of the food. This is not possible at the present time, and as a
result, great numbers of people suffer
from **malnutrition.** Malnutrition occurs
whenever people get the wrong amounts
or the wrong kinds of food over a long
period of time.

See #1
above.

See #2
below.

There are many reasons for malnutrition. One of the reasons is the uneven
distribution of population on the earth.
The demand for food in overcrowded
countries is greater than the supply.
Another reason why malnutrition is a
greater problem in some parts of the

G/E

SHARE OF FOOD DEFICIT

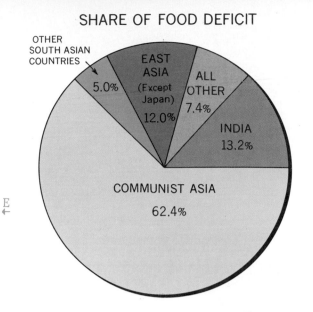

world than in others can be discovered
by studying the bar graph at the left
below. Which region has the least agricultural production per person? Which
region has the greatest agricultural production per person?

About two out of every three people
in the world live in parts of the world
where the diet is not adequate for good
nutrition. These places have a **food
deficit**—there is too little food or the
wrong kinds of food for good nutrition.
The circle graph shows some of the
places where the food deficit is greatest.
Are the places named on the circle graph
densely populated or not densely populated? Which place has the greatest
share of the food deficit?

The table on the next page will help
you see the great differences in the
amount and kind of food people in different places have. To understand the
table you need to know the meaning of

E/G

E

UNEVEN DISTRIBUTION OF WORLD'S POPULATION AND AGRICULTURAL PRODUCTION
(Per cent of world total by regions)

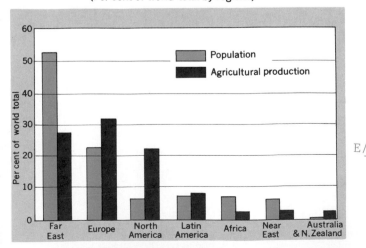

2. Problems are caused by the
   unequal distribution of the
   world's food.

375

FOOD CONSUMPTION		
Area	Calories per day	Grams of protein
North America, Oceania	3,200	100
Northwest Europe	3,000	80
Mediterranean	2,500	70
Japan	2,000	60
Southeast Asia, Africa	1,800	45

Asians harvesting rice (Indonesia)

calorie and the meaning of **protein.** A calorie is a unit of energy supplied by food. For example, an ounce of sugar produces about 100 calories. The word protein refers to a substance in food that is a necessary part of cells. Without sufficient protein, people do not grow properly.

Study the table. Do the people who get the most calories per day also get the most protein? Do the people who get the least number of calories also get the least protein? In which area would you expect malnutrition to be the greatest problem?

Tables like the one above show averages. Many people, especially the poor people in each area, get far fewer calories than the table shows. In some countries the people get far less protein than the table shows. People who get barely enough food when crops are good are in serious trouble when crops are bad. Then there are **famines,** or times of starving. Great numbers of people in India, Asia, and Africa die during famines that occur there during times of crop failure.

See #1 below.

See #2 below.

G/E →

E/G →

E/S ←

The picture shows people of Asia harvesting rice at the end of a growing season when rainfall was about normal. In such years most of the people have enough to eat. In some years, however, rains do not come at the right time. Then the crops fail and many people are unable to get food because they have little or no money to use in buying it. Getting more food and better food is one of the greatest challenges faced by people in much of Asia, Africa, and parts of South America.

Water The workers shown in the picture on the next page are helping lay a new pipeline to bring more water to the people of Los Angeles and southern California. Water for these people is piped in from northern California and from neighboring states. Plans are underway to pipe in water from as far away as Canada. Bringing water to the people of southern California is necessary because they are using far more water than falls as rain in that area.

Stress:
1. In some areas of the world, people suffer from protein deficiency.
2. In some areas of the world, crop failures cause famines.

Stress:
1. The surface of the earth has uneven rainfall.
2. Man sometimes transports the earth's water to wherever it is needed.
3. People often move to where there is an adequate supply of water.

Great amounts of water fall to the earth as rain each year. Geographers tell us that if all the land got the same amount of rain, that amount would be about thirty inches per year. However, the distribution of rainfall is very uneven.

See #1 above.

Man can do very little to control the distribution of rainfall. But man does not have to rely on local rainfall to meet his need for water. Instead, he can do one of two things. He can distribute water to where people are, as is being done for Los Angeles. Or he can shift populations, industry, or agriculture to places where the water is. Either of these things causes many problems which man is studying. What might some of these problems be?

See #2 above.

See #3 above.

As you study the graph about water use, notice that industry uses more than half of the water used in the United States. In Asia a smaller percentage of the water used is used for industry. Why?

Getting safe water Anyone who has tried to mix such things as sugar, salt, or ink with water knows that water holds many different kinds of materials in solution. Sewage, detergents, chemical fertilizers, insect-killing poisons, and thousands of other materials can be held in solution by water. When people drink water, they take into their body all the materials held in solution. Since earliest times, many of the waste products of human society have been dissolved in water, making the water unsafe for drinking. But man could almost always find other sources of water that were still safe to use. During recent decades, however, more and more waste materials have been dumped into our lakes and

Laying water pipe in Los Angeles

WATER USE IN THE UNITED STATES

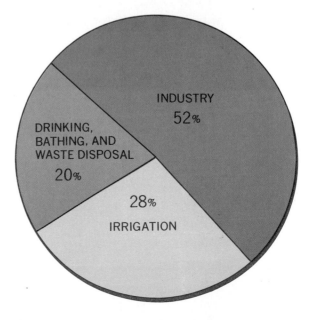

INDUSTRY 52%

DRINKING, BATHING, AND WASTE DISPOSAL 20%

28% IRRIGATION

streams. Man is finding it more and more difficult to find water that is safe for use. One of his greatest challenges today is how to get enough safe drinking water to the places where people must have it.

Air Scientists sometimes speak of an ocean of air. This ocean surrounds the earth even more completely than the oceans of water. Any sample of air is made up of gases such as oxygen and carbon dioxide, solids such as dust and bacteria, and liquids such as water.

Each day man adds large amounts of gases, solids, and liquids to the atmosphere. In fact in our country alone about 200,000,000 tons of gases, solids, and liquids are poured into the air each year. Almost half of this material comes from the exhaust pipes of automobiles. On a cold day you can see the exhaust from automobiles. Much of what you see is liquid in the form of water vapor. Things that you cannot see in the exhaust include carbon monoxide and even tiny particles of lead. Neither of these is good for people.

The factories and power-generating plants in our country throw about 50,000,000 tons of **fly ash**, very fine ash, into the air each year. They also send about 26,000,000 tons of sulfur oxides into the air. These things are not good for people, either.

Other countries of the world also are spoiling the air for their people. The

Tokyo school children wearing smog masks

picture you see here was taken in Japan. What is the purpose of the masks? The smokestack may help you decide.

The waste material man puts into the air mixes with the air to produce **smog.** This word was coined from two words, smoke and fog. Today the word smog is used to refer to any condition of the air that makes it harmful. Smog can kill animals. It often discolors paint on houses and automobiles. It kills pine trees as far as sixty miles away from some cities. Smog is also a danger to man's health—in fact, under certain conditions it can bring death.

Usually the waste materials man puts into the air rise as the sun heats the air. Then winds blow the smog away from places where the materials enter it. In some places on earth the warm air is at times prevented from rising. Then the gases, solids, and liquids forced into the

Stress:
1. The pollution of our air and water has become a very serious problem.

air by man are trapped near the surface of the earth. A condition of this kind is called an **inversion.** Have the newspapers ever reported an inversion in your community? If so, what was it like?

Man does not cause inversions. But he is responsible for making them dangerous to health.

Some scientists believe that one of

man's greatest challenges is that of keeping the air safe to breathe. See if you can think of a reason why the challenge is so great.

Think for Yourself

What can you do to help keep the air and the water cleaner than they are?

For Teaching Helps, see page T116.

THE NEED FOR MATERIALS

Coal The machine shown is an electric stripping machine. Its operator has moved soil and rock away, as you can see, to uncover great layers of coal formed during the period between about 350,000,000 and 270,000,000 years ago. Geologists believe that during this period many regions of the earth were

covered, from time to time, by vast, low-lying swamps. They believe that in these swamps the climate was moist and warm all year long and that large numbers of plants, the source of coal, grew well. Man knows how some of these plants looked because he sometimes finds fossils of them. One of these fossils is shown in the picture below. The patterning on the fossil gives evidence about the plants that were the source of coal. What plants are you reminded of as you observe the fossil?

Electric stripping machine
(Dipper: 180 cubic yard capacity)

Fossil fern

379

For a class activity, see #1 on page 389.

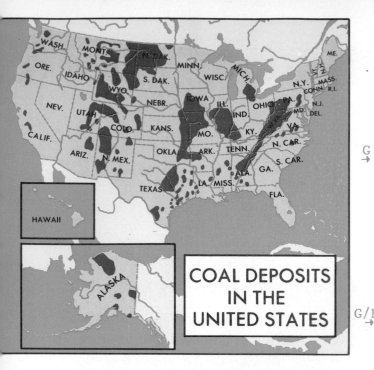

COAL DEPOSITS
IN THE
UNITED STATES

Study the map showing the location of some of the large coal deposits in the United States. Which of the states have very large deposits of coal? Which have little or no coal?

You may wish to find some of these same states on a **physical map** of the United States—a map showing the height of the land today. Would you say that the geography of our country has changed a great deal or very little since the time coal was formed? Why?

Coal is used to heat homes and in industrial plants. It is used to **smelt** iron ore—that is, to convert iron ore into iron. It is also used to convert iron into steel. Generators turned by steam produced by coal-fired boilers are a major source of electricity. Some of the clothes you are now wearing are probably made of fibers produced from coal. Much of the

See #1 below.

Stress:
1. Coal is very important in industry.
2. Coal deposits are not evenly distributed.

380

medicine used throughout the world is produced from coal.

Geologists believe that almost one-third of the coal deposits of the world are in the United States. They also believe that the United States has enough coal to last for centuries. However, when this coal is gone there will be no more.

See #2 below.

Europe and Asia have large deposits of coal, but Africa and South America have very little coal. And the coal deposits in North America, Europe, and Asia are unevenly distributed. How does this uneven distribution affect the economy of the nations of these continents?

See #2 below.

Think for Yourself

Do you think man will ever use up all the coal on earth? Why?

Petroleum and natural gas Deep in the earth below the water shown in the picture there are large deposits of petro-

Oil-drilling derrick

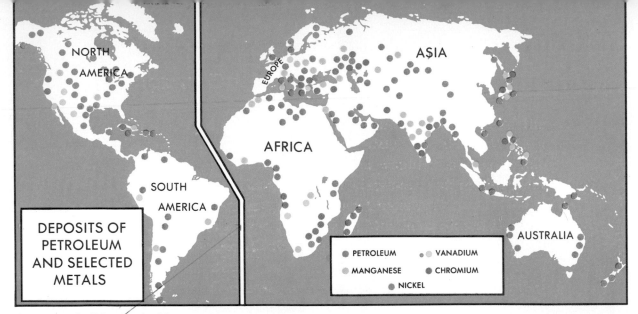

DEPOSITS OF
PETROLEUM
AND SELECTED
METALS

● PETROLEUM ● VANADIUM
● MANGANESE ● CHROMIUM
● NICKEL

Vertical lines indicate
deletion of ocean area.

leum, or oil. The tall derricks are required for the drilling operation needed
to reach the oil deposits. The men shown
in the picture are well drillers. Do you
think that their work is easy or hard?
Why?

See #1
below.

Petroleum and natural gas, which is
found in the same locations as petroleum, are trapped in layers of rock
formed a very long time ago. Some of
these layers of rock were formed at least
500,000,000 years ago. Even the most
recent layers of rock in which petroleum
and natural gas are found were formed
about 1,000,000 years ago. Most geologists believe that petroleum and natural
gas were formed from the remains of
plants and animals that lived—and died
—in shallow seas.

Study the map showing places where
petroleum is found. Would you say that
there are oil fields on all continents?
Would you say that the petroleum is

For Teaching Helps, see page T116.

evenly or unevenly distributed on the
various continents? How might a geographer explain the distribution of deposits of petroleum?

See #2
below.

Petroleum and natural gas are sources
of power, just as coal is. Petroleum is
also our most important lubricant. In
addition to its uses as a fuel and a lubricant, petroleum is widely used in building roads, manufacturing chemicals, and
in many other ways. See if you can tell
what one of these ways is.

Think for Yourself

*Do you think man will ever use up all the
petroleum and natural gas on earth? Why?*

See #3
below.

Iron ore and steel Man of today can
make better pots and pans, better tools,
longer bridges, and stronger wheels than
any of his ancestors of long ago. One
reason is that man knows how to produce metal from various ores. One of the

Stress:
1. Petroleum and natural gas deposits are millions of years old.
2. Besides its use as a source of power, petroleum has many other uses.
3. The discovery of how to produce metal from ore had important effects
   on the life of man.

381

Pouring pig iron into open-hearth furnace

Ore pit, Mesabi Range, Minnesota

most important metals is steel. The men shown in the first picture are producing steel. The basic raw material for steel is iron ore, which comes from ore deposits in the earth's crust. In the other G/E picture you see one of the great iron mines in the United States. What kinds of workers are probably needed to mine the ore and to get it to the steel mills?

The United States produces great amounts of iron and steel each year. In E fact, the national per capita production is about 2,200 pounds as compared, for example, with less than 200 pounds per person in Brazil. Why, do you think, does the United States produce so much more iron and steel per person than Brazil?

The Soviet Union claims to produce more iron ore than the United States, G/E but it is difficult to check the accuracy of economic information about the Soviet Union. Why?

The major countries of western Europe—including France, West Germany, Belgium, England, and Sweden—also have good supplies of iron ore and produce steel in quantity. In Asia, the Japanese produce low-priced steel of high quality. Japan is very short of iron ore, coal, and other materials used in steel production. The Japanese import these materials from Canada, the United States, Australia, and other parts of the world. China and India have large amounts of iron ore and coal. Until recently they have not produced much steel, but the picture in these countries is changing rapidly.

See #1 below.

See #2 below.

Iron is a part of the outer layer, or crust, of the earth. The average amount of iron in the earth's crust is about 5 per cent. But some iron-ore deposits are as much as 60 per cent iron. As man uses up the iron ore having a high percentage of iron, he must begin to use a lower

Stress:

382

1. Steel production is very important in Japan and in the major countries of western Europe.
2. Some countries with large deposits of iron ore are just beginning to produce steel in quantity.

See #1 above. grade of iron ore. Do you think that the change to a lower grade of iron ore would affect the cost of some kinds of goods? Why?

Other metals Although less plentiful than iron, a number of other metals are very important to man. Two of these are copper and aluminum. The United States gets much of its copper from mines in this country, although some is imported. Most of the aluminum comes from the ore, **bauxite** (bôk′sīt). The United States is short of bauxite, as are some of the other industrial nations. South America, Africa, and Jamaica have a surplus of bauxite. They export it to industrial nations, including the United States, Canada, Norway, and Japan, to be smelted. See if you can tell why.

Another metal used by industry is tin. The United States must depend upon other parts of the world for tin. Some tin comes from Bolivia, in South America. However, the largest tin deposits are in Asia. The Asian countries of Malaysia, Thailand, Indonesia, and China produce most of the world's supply of tin.

The map on page 381 shows the distribution of some of the other important metals. All these metals are used in producing steel. As you study the map, find out which continents produce all four metals. Which continent has none of them? Which continent has only two?

Think for Yourself

Would our economy be different if the deposits of metals and ores were evenly distributed on earth? Why? Yes. Our economy has always been bolstered by our huge share of the world's natural resources.

Forest products What three types of forest products do the pictures suggest to you? Which two of the types of forest products can be obtained without destroying the trees?

Felling tree (Washington state)   Tapping maple trees   Coconut palm (Tabago)

Two of the main products of forests are lumber and paper. What must be done to the trees in order to get these products?

The leading producers of forest products today are the Soviet Union, the United States, Brazil, and Canada. In some parts of Asia and Africa there are great forests which are still untouched by foresters. Do you think these will be used in the future? Why?

Think for Yourself

Is the earth more likely to run out of forest products or metals? What evidence can you give to support your answer? Metals. We can grow trees but we cannot replace ore.

For Teaching Helps, see page T117.

THE NEED FOR TRANSPORTATION

Transporting materials and goods The man who runs the big power shovel shown at the left is scooping up dry sulfur stored in a storage vat. Sulfur is one of the basic raw materials of the chemical industry. There are large deposits of sulfur in the United States, and others are found in Mexico, France, Canada, and the Soviet Union.

The ship shown in the picture was loaded with molten sulfur in Louisiana, in a city called Point Sulfur. The ship sailed in an easterly direction across the Gulf of Mexico to Tampa, Florida. There the sulfur will be stored in huge tanks. Two different forms of land transportation—truck and rail—will move the sulfur to fertilizer plants in Florida.

Many of the materials used in basic

Mining sulfur with power shovel

Unloading sulfur from a ship

Stress:
1. Industry depends heavily on both
   water and land transportation.

See #1 above.

industries like the chemical industry or the iron and steel industry are transported both by water and by land. See if you can name one or more materials of this type.

See #2 below.

Today there are very few, if any, nations that produce all the raw materials they need. Even the United States lacks a number of kinds of materials used by industry. At the same time, most nations have a surplus of some kinds of materials or crops for which they need a market.

Without suitable transportation the nations with a surplus of materials cannot get them to places that need them. Neither can the nations with shortages get the materials that they need.

The surplus materials within a nation may be far from the centers of population and not linked to them by transportation routes. For example, many of the major mineral resources of the Soviet Union are far from the places where they could be used or where a shortage exists. The Soviet Union, when making plans to obtain such minerals, had to face the challenge of developing a system of transportation. This proved to be difficult.

For one thing, great distances separated the resources from the populated areas. For another thing, much of the land across which transportation systems were to be built was underdeveloped. Building the transportation systems re-

Unloading foreign car at New York

quired a lot of time, large amounts of materials, and a great deal of money.

In Asia, Africa, and South America there are great surpluses of many kinds of materials. Will it be easy or hard to get these surplus materials to places where they are needed? Why?

In industrial nations such as the United States, Japan, Germany, and other countries of western Europe, surpluses of various kinds of goods are produced. Where can the manufacturers go to find markets for their surplus goods? How can they get the surplus goods to places where there are shortages? The picture on this page will help you to decide upon at least one way.

2. Since natural resources are unevenly distributed throughout the world, it is often necessary for a country to transport a consistent supply of raw materials from foreign countries.

385

A street scene in a seaport of East Java

A monorail in Japan

Transporting people The two pictures on this page show scenes in two cities of Asia. What types of transportation are illustrated in the first picture? What types are illustrated in the second picture? What other ways of taking people from where they are to where they want to go can you name?

In the United States and in other industrial nations great numbers of people own automobiles. The people demand good roads for the automobiles. As good roads are built, people can **commute,** or

travel to and from work, for longer distances and so suburbs develop. As G suburbs develop more people move to them and the roads become clogged with automobiles. Then there is a demand for new roads. Do you think that the demand for more roads will increase or decrease? Why?

Think for Yourself

What kinds of things can happen to public transportation systems when large numbers of people leave the cities for the suburbs?

Stress:
*1. What is significant in a society's demand for faster means of transportation?

POLITICAL CHALLENGES

For Teaching Helps, see page T118.

Settling disputes among nations Have you had a dispute with someone recently? What choices of ways to settle the dispute did you have? Nations, like people, often have disputes. And, like people, nations also have choices of ways A/S to settle disputes. One of these ways is suggested by the newspaper headlines shown on the next page. The first newspaper was printed in 1918 and the sec-

For a class activity, see #2 on page 389.
ond in 1945. What event led to each headline? Is warfare still carried on today?

Anthropologists and historians have much evidence to show that man has See #1 used warfare as a way of settling dis-below. putes for a very long time. According to sociologists and anthropologists, people usually act according to the traditions and views of their society. Thus, in effect, they act in the way they have

Stress:
1. Throughout history, man has often settled disputes by means of warfare.

Stress:

For Teaching Helps, see page T118.

1. Nations have relied on warfare to settle disputes.
2. Man must find other means besides warfare to settle disputes.

been taught to act. In certain situations, then, tradition and custom demand that men fight even at the risk of destroying themselves.

See #1 above.

Like people, nations have used warfare as a way of settling disputes for a very long time. Nations are accustomed to thinking of warfare as a method of getting things settled, and most nations, especially the stronger ones, seem unwilling to give up this method. Anthropologists explain that because people usually act as the traditions and views of their society demand, they find it hard to change, even when it is sensible to do so. Is the same thing true of nations? How do you know?

See #2 above.

Today the more powerful nations have enough weapons to destroy the earth. And if man is to continue to live on the earth, nations must find ways of settling disputes without destroying everyone.

Think for Yourself

Will it be easy or hard for nations to give up war as a way of settling disputes. Why?

Reducing crime Sociologists tell us that there is a relationship between urbanization and the number of people arrested for breaking the law. In making studies of this relationship, sociologists often make maps showing the location where each arrest is made within an area they are studying. Sociologists report that such maps show that arrests are made in high-income as well as in low-income parts of the area. Sociologists and anthropologists believe that crime is a product of a changing society—not merely a product of bad living conditions and poor jobs.

See #3 below.

According to our society's rules, a person who has been arrested for breaking the law must appear in court. If the court finds the arrested person guilty, he is classified as a **criminal.** No one knows how many criminals there are in the United States, but the number is very large. More than 300,000 people are in prisons at any given time.

In our society our governments are expected to reduce crime. Governments in other nations are also expected to

3. There is a relationship between urbanization and crime.

Stress:
1. There is a demand for legislation which would prevent pollution.
2. Reducing pollution will require the expenditure of time and money.

reduce crime. Thus, with the crime rates rising throughout the world, governments everywhere are faced with a very real challenge.

Reducing pollution Scientists tell us that various forms of transportation are responsible for about 60 per cent of our total air pollution problem. Automobiles and aircraft are, perhaps, the worst offenders. Some political scientists believe that government has the authority to stop the air pollution by automobiles in a very short time simply by stopping the sale of gasoline and motor oil. Would this be a wise or an unwise use of authority? Why? What would the citizens of our country probably do to political leaders who ordered the sale of gasoline and motor oil stopped? What might happen to our entire economy?

See #1 above.

There are, of course, other sources of air pollution besides automobiles and aircraft. Water pollution and land pollution are problems as serious as air pollution. What are some of the sources of water pollution? In what ways is the land sometimes polluted?

See #2 above.

The challenges faced by government in any attempt to reduce pollution are very great. Reducing pollution very much will require a great deal of planning and the spending of large sums of money. Study the graph on this page. In what year did the federal government begin to spend money to control pollution? How much money did the government plan to spend in 1970?

Pollution does not respect the boundaries man creates for the various nations. For example, the insect-killing poison, DDT, has spread all over the world. It is even found in Antarctica where man has never used it. Air currents carry smoke from city to city and from country to country. Fallout from atomic explosions is carried by air currents all around the earth.

The battle against pollution will require the cooperation of all governments. Someone once said at a meeting of people from many nations, "If we're going to make it, you'd better remember that the guy next to you is your brother." What do you suppose he meant?

Think for Yourself

What other challenges does our government face today?

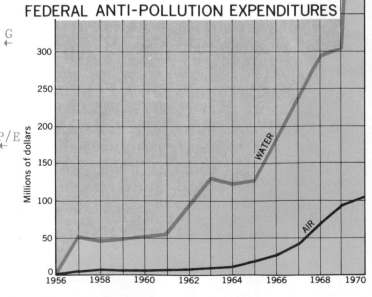

FEDERAL ANTI-POLLUTION EXPENDITURES

3. The nations of the world must battle pollution together.
*4. Why is it so difficult to persuade man to settle disputes through nonviolent means?

Things to Do

See page 380.

1. Collect pictures showing what you consider to be wise use of the land of the earth by man. Display your pictures with a statement under each telling why the picture shows good use of the land.

See page 386.

2. On a sheet of paper write the heading, "Challenges Facing Our Community." Decide what you will write under this heading. Tell your classmates about your work.

CLASS PROJECT—PART 3

Begin arranging your model according to the plan you developed while doing Part 2 of your class project.

You will want to give some attention to the development of the bulletin-board background of your model landscape. You might use this space to help tell some interesting information about your landscape. For example, if your model landscape includes a model of a hydroelectric plant, you could find or prepare a few statements telling something interesting about the hydroelectric plant. Place these statements on the bulletin board and run a piece of heavy, colored yarn from the statements on the bulletin board to the model on the landscape.

Continue your class project by doing the following:

1. Plan and carry out your bulletin-board display.
2. Review Chapters 20 and 21 and study Chapter 22 to find additional information about man's use of the surface of the earth. This information will give you further ideas for the development of both the model landscape and the bulletin board.

For Teaching Helps, see page T119.
Stress:
1. Man is in danger of exhausting the supply of some raw materials.

22. Meeting the Challenges

As you look around your classroom, you probably see a number of objects made of wood, of metal, of plastic, or of a combination of materials. The raw materials used in making these objects came from a number of sources. Most are either at the earth's surface or in a layer of the earth's crust that is about four miles deep. At his present rate of use, man is likely to run out of some kinds of raw materials, even during your lifetime. For this reason, and others, man is seeking new ways to make wise use of all natural resources. This wise use of natural resources is often called **conservation.** Like everyone on earth, you can do something about conservation. See if you can think right now of one thing that you might do.

See #1 above.

See #2 above.

Man faces the challenge of having a steady supply of lumber and forest products. What is one way of ensuring this supply? The picture will help you decide.

One way in which man can meet the challenge of getting such things as living space, food, air, and water is to practice conservation. Some of the other things he can do to meet these challenges is the story this chapter tells.

See #3 below.

A man planting a Douglas fir tree

JUST FOR FUN

Look around your community for examples of both good and poor conservation practices. Be ready to share your examples with your classmates.

3. Man faces many challenges concerning his supply of living space, food, air, and water.

390

*4. What are people in your community doing to conserve natural resources?

Stress:
1. Many people throughout the world today are moving from rural to urban places.
2. One challenge facing man today is how to provide people with living space without over-crowding.

MEETING SOCIAL AND PHYSICAL NEEDS

Conservation of space for housing

See #1 above.

Throughout the world, populations are moving from rural to **urban places**—to the cities and suburbs. Many of the newcomers to urban places must find places to live in apartment buildings built very close together with little or no space for lawns, shrubs, and trees.

See #2 above.

The crowding of people makes many of them very unhappy. Thus, one challenge man faces today is how to provide living space for people without over-crowding.

The picture at the right shows one group of buildings which the government of Hong Kong has built for poor families. Small, open areas are provided for each group of buildings. Why?

In some of the larger urban places in our country, builders of apartments are buying large land areas. They put tall buildings on as little as one-fifth of the land area. Some of the remaining land is

Government-built housing in Hong Kong

used for driveways, sidewalks, and parking lots, but much of it is used for lawns, shrubs, trees, and playgrounds. Some builders use more than one-fifth of the land area for the buildings, but then they provide for underground or rooftop parking. The land that is not required for parking may be used for recreation.

See #3 below.

One of man's attempts to make better use of existing space within a city resulted in the structure shown at the left. The structure, called "Habitat," was designed as an experimental community and was first displayed at a world fair in Montreal, Canada, in 1967. The community looks as though it were constructed of building blocks like those children sometimes use during their playtime.

Habitat—an experimental community structure

3. Some apartment buildings are now being built with open areas for lawns, shrubs, trees, and playgrounds.

391

See #1 above.

Unlike the playtime blocks, each of the blocks in Habitat consists of several rooms that together make an apartment for a family. Each of the apartments was constructed on the ground and then lifted into place with a crane. The apartments were fitted together in a way that gives each one a terrace. Do you think that Habitat shows a wise or an unwise use of space? Why?

Each of the apartments of Habitat can be considered a **molecule,** or small unit, of the Habitat community, just as playtime building blocks can be considered molecules of a structure made of those blocks. What kinds of things limit the size of a structure made of building blocks? What kinds of things might limit the size of Habitat?

See #2 below.

Conservation of land The idea of building large structures from molecules that are alike in size can be used in planning large urban places which are given the name **molecular metropolis.** A molecular metropolis will consist of both a central city where people go to earn money by working in industry and a group of surrounding cities where people make their homes. Most of the industrial places are to be underground in this molecular metropolis.

The planners of a molecular metropolis use many ideas gained by asking various social scientists to answer questions. For example, they might ask geographers questions such as these.

1. What are climatic conditions and weather likely to be at this site during various seasons of the year?
2. Is there enough land?
3. Is the land solid enough to support the weight of the buildings?
4. Can people easily reach the site?

What questions might the planners ask economists, sociologists, and political scientists to answer?

The surrounding cities of the molecular metropolis are planned for about 100,000 people each. When the population of each city reaches this number of people, other cities will be built nearby. There are advantages and disadvantages in this use of space for cities. See if you can tell what some of the advantages and disadvantages are.

Increasing the supply of food The problem of getting food for the hungry is a very old one. The author Jonathan Swift who wrote *Gulliver's Travels*, first published in the early 1700's, had a solution to the problem. Jonathan Swift had one of his story characters called the King make this statement.

See #3 below.

And he gave it for his opinion, that whoever could make two ears of corn or two blades of grass to grow upon a spot of ground where only one grew before, would deserve better of mankind, and do more essential service to his country than the whole race of politicians put together.

2. Well-planned central cities and surrounding communities may lead to the conservation of land.

392   3. Man has been facing the problem of feeding all the earth's people for a long time.

Observing a well-developed ear of corn

Scientists have learned to do what the King hoped could be done.

For example, the man shown in the picture is observing an ear of corn raised from seed that scientists have developed in recent years. Using this variety of corn seed makes it possible for farmers to produce far more corn per acre than ever before in history.

See #1 above.

Scientists have also developed a variety of wheat (a type of grass) that enables farmers to raise twice, and sometimes even three times, as much wheat per acre each year than could be raised in the past. And they have developed a variety of rice (another type of grass) that is ready to harvest in four months rather than in five or six months as required by older varieties of rice. At the same time, this new variety of rice yields far more grain per acre than older varieties of rice can yield.

In recent years farmers in less-developed countries are getting better farming tools. More and more farmers are

2. Scientists today are looking for new sources of food nutrients.

Stress:
1. Scientists are helping man produce more food per acre than in the past.

able to buy hand tractors like the one shown below. They use the tractors to pull their farming equipment. Do you think that using better farming equipment and tools will increase or decrease the amount of food man can produce? Why?

In addition to learning how to "make two ears of corn or two blades of grass [wheat or rice] to grow upon a spot of ground where only one grew before," scientists are looking for other sources of food nutrients such as protein. One promising source of protein is natural gas. The protein obtained is in the form of a white powder which can be added to foods that are low in protein.

See #2 below.

Social scientists, especially anthropologists and sociologists, point out that it is often very difficult to get people to change their ideas concerning food. For example, many of the people of India never saw corn before it was imported by their country. Consequently, they

Farmer in Japan using a hand tractor

Stress:
1. Many of the world's poorer farmers cannot afford fertilizers or new varieties
   of seeds, or they are unwilling to give up traditional farming practices.

had never tasted food made from corn. Some of these people, even though they were near starvation, would not eat food made of corn. How do you explain this fact?

See #1 above.

Economists point out that many of the poorer farmers of the world cannot afford new varieties of seeds. Neither can they afford to buy the fertilizer needed to make these seeds produce good crops. Many of the farmers are also unwilling to give up traditional farming practices that they have learned to follow. Why, do you think, are these things true?

Think for Yourself

What can the better-developed countries do to help people in less-developed countries secure adequate supplies of food?

Water Perhaps you have read these lines from the poem "The Rime of the Ancient Mariner" by Samuel Taylor Coleridge.

> Water, water, every where,
> Nor any drop to drink.

As you might have guessed from the title of the poem, the ancient mariner was at sea. Everyone on his ship, and until quite recently everyone on board any ship, had to get drinking water from supplies of water carried on the ship. When these supplies were gone, people could not survive, for the salt in seawater makes it unfit to drink.

In recent years man has learned to remove the salt and other impurities from seawater. Many ocean-going ships now have **desalinization equipment** that produces fresh water by removing various kinds of salt from seawater. The picture shows a desalinization plant on land. It can produce large amounts of fresh water from seawater. At present the cost of water produced in this way is rather high. Do you think that the cost of water produced in desalinization plants is likely to go up or down? Why?

See #2 below.

Some places that were once sparsely populated because of lack of fresh water became densely populated when fresh water became available. One of these

A desalinization plant (Key West, Florida)

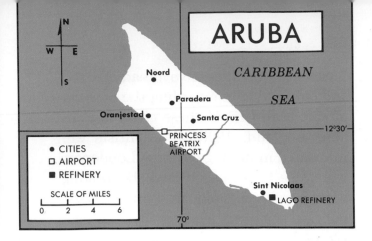

ARUBA

CARIBBEAN

SEA

- Noord
- Paradera
- Oranjestad
- Santa Cruz

PRINCESS
BEATRIX
AIRPORT

12°30'

- CITIES
- AIRPORT
- REFINERY

SCALE OF MILES
0   2   4   6

Sint Nicolaas

LAGO REFINERY

70°

Stress:
1. Aruba's fresh water is created
   mostly by desalinization of seawater.

Think for Yourself

Do you think that Aruba might again be sparsely populated if the supplies of either petroleum or fresh water disappeared? Why or why not?

Air The automobile you see in the picture is powered by electricity stored in batteries. As the electricity is used, the batteries run down. Then the batteries must be connected to a battery charger that gets electric current from a power line leading from a generating plant.

Automobiles powered by electricity do not pour gases, solids, or liquids into the air as gasoline-powered automobiles do. The widespread use of electric automobiles would greatly reduce air pollution.

See #2 below.

It seems, however, that man will need to depend on petroleum to provide energy for running engines for a long time. And he is working out ways to reduce the amounts of gases, solids, and liquids

places, Aruba, is shown on the map. What is the approximate latitude of Aruba? What kind of climate would you expect Aruba to have? Why?

A nearby country, Venezuela, is one of the world's great producers of petroleum. Much of this petroleum is transported to Aruba, where it is refined in a refinery built by an American oil company. Many people were needed to build the refinery, to run it, and to provide services. Both the people and the refinery required large amounts of fresh water, but Aruba has comparatively little rainfall. As a result, a huge desalinization plant was built to convert seawater into fresh water.

See #1 above.

Today Aruba is the home of many more people than in the past. In addition to its permanent residents, it has great numbers of tourists each year. And many social scientists believe that as the cost of desalinization is reduced, man can meet the increasing need for water in other parts of the world by turning to the oceans.

2. Man could greatly reduce air pollution by using automobiles powered by electricity instead of gasoline.

A battery-powered automobile

Stress: For a class activity, see #1 on page 406.
1. The use of lead-free gasolines could help reduce air pollution.
2. The use of low-sulfur coal could help reduce air pollution.

that the burning of petroleum products puts into the air. For example, the jet engines of planes have been redesigned to reduce pollution. Automobile manufacturers are also working on the problem of reducing pollution from automobile engines.

See #1 above.

One source of pollution from automobile engines is lead, which manufacturers of gasoline add to their product. The high-powered engines of many automobiles must use a gasoline containing lead. As the gasoline is burned, tiny bits of lead are poured into the air. Modern gasolines are being manufactured without adding lead to them, and modern engines are being built that will run properly on the lead-free gasolines.

See #2 above.

One of the important fuels used in heating homes, in producing electricity, and in providing heat needed in industry is coal. Some types of coal produce much larger amounts of sulfur than others. When such coal is burned, the sulfur is poured into the air as part of the smoke from smokestacks. Many communities are passing laws that require the use of low-sulfur coal in all furnaces. In what ways will these laws affect the producers of low-sulfur coal? Of other kinds of coal?

Great numbers of workers are affected by a changeover from one type of coal to another type. See if you can list some kinds of such workers and tell how they and their families might be affected.

Some major cities have already passed and enforced laws regarding the burning of soft coal. One of these cities is London, England. Political scientists are interested in finding out how Londoners were able to pass such laws. By talking with Londoners and studying history, political scientists learned that the people of London had burned soft coal in fireplaces and stoves for about six centuries. Many of the factories in and near London used soft coal, and no attempts were made to control the amount of smoke, soot, and ash that poured into the air from smokestacks. During all of the six centuries of unsupervised burning, London was regularly covered with dense fog, often called "pea soup." One of the worst of these fogs occurred in 1952. The smoke-laden fog lasted for four days, causing at least 12,000 deaths. Publicity resulting from these deaths made people anxious to take political action. As a result, laws were passed banning the burning of soft coal in homes and forcing factories to reduce smoke.

See #3 below.

The laws were strictly enforced. Now the pea soup of the past occurs on only three or four days in an entire year. Very few, if any, Londoners miss the fog and dirt of the past. And birds sing again in London's parks.

Think for Yourself

What can you do to help your community have cleaner air?

3. Political scientists have learned that laws restricting air pollution
   can be passed if people are made aware of the deadly results of pollution.
*4. What kind of buildings are being built in your community to conserve
   land and to prevent overcrowding?

Stress:
1. Modern equipment helps man produce many tons of coal a minute.

MEETING THE NEED FOR MATERIALS

See #1
above.

Coal The man shown in the picture is a coal miner working far underground in a mine in West Virginia. The machine he is using cuts the coal from a vein of coal. The loosened coal is picked up by a belt running through the center of the machine and is dumped onto a car that hauls it away. Machines like the one shown here can produce up to eight tons of coal a minute.

See #2
below.

The number of workers employed in the coal-mining industry declines almost every year, even though the amount of coal produced increases. Why, do you think, is this true? What effect might the loss of jobs have on miners?

Modern equipment used in mining of coal

See #3
below.

One problem in meeting the need for coal is the cost of getting the coal to the places where it will be used. Today much of the coal that man needs is used in producing electricity. As the generating plants use up nearby supplies of coal, they must turn to sources that are farther away. As a result, the cost of the coal they need increases. See if you can tell why.

See #4
below.

Sometimes, the producers and distributors of electricity, called **electric utilities,** build new plants near large supplies of coal. For example, one electric utility has built a huge generating plant close to coal fields about thirty miles from Springfield, Illinois. At this location the cost of transporting coal to the plant is very low. Why do you think this is true?

Most of the coal that is used is transported by either rail or water. Both methods of transportation are constantly being improved in an effort to reduce transportation costs. In addition new ways of transporting coal are being developed. One of these is to grind the coal into fine particles and mix it with water. This process produces a heavy black liquid that can be pumped through pipelines to electric utilities. Burners have been developed for burning the heavy black mixture of coal and water in much the same way that oil burners in furnaces burn oil.

2. Machinery increases production while it decreases the need for workers.
3. Much of the coal man uses today is for producing electricity.
4. A large part of the cost of coal is due to transportation costs.

397

Petroleum and natural gas The world production of petroleum is more than 12 trillion barrels a year and is increasing every year. See if you can tell how much 1 trillion is. Geologists are constantly searching for new oil fields. Some of these fields are as much as four miles below the earth's surface. Some are found under the sea. Recently new sources of petroleum and natural gas have been discovered in West Africa, South America, and Indonesia. In North America vast oil fields have been discovered in a region in the far north called the Arctic Slope. Oil companies have paid over 900,000,000 dollars for leases on land in the new oil fields.

See #1 above.

See #2 below.

E/G ←

The discovery of new oil fields sometimes makes people believe that there will never be a shortage of oil. However, material resources are limited. When the last oil field is found, no amount of genius or technology can create another.

See #3 below.

G ←

E ←

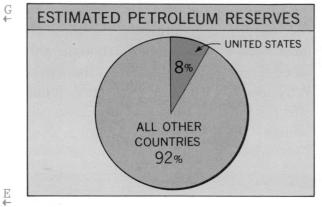

Study the two graphs above. Does the data make you think that the United States may soon be faced with a shortage of petroleum? Why?

Read the title of the bar graph. What were the per capita oil reserves in 1969? There are at least two reasons why the per capita oil reserves today are less than in 1969. See if you can tell what these reasons are.

G/E →

Much of the petroleum of the world is produced at great distances from the refineries. In most cases it is cheaper to transport the oil to refineries than it is

See #4 below.

G/E →

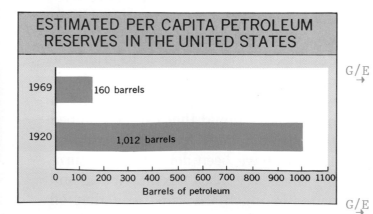

2. Because man uses much petroleum, geologists are searching for new sources.
3. The world's sources of petroleum are limited.
398 4. One cost factor in the production of petroleum is the distance separating oil fields and refineries.

Stress:
1. Scientists have found many ways of using petroleum by rearranging the molecules to produce new materials such as plastic.

to build refineries in the oil fields. The picture below illustrates one way of transporting petroleum and natural gas. What other ways can you name? Do you think that these methods of transportation ever cause pollution? How?

In some parts of the world the pipelines cross the boundary lines that separate countries. This fact sometimes causes political problems. Why? See if you can tell what one of these problems might be.

Scientists are constantly searching for new ways to use petroleum and natural gas without waste. Scientists believe that there are more than 1,000,000 different types of molecules in petroleum. They are learning to take out some of these molecules and rearrange them in various ways to produce new

Pipelines along the East Coast of the United States

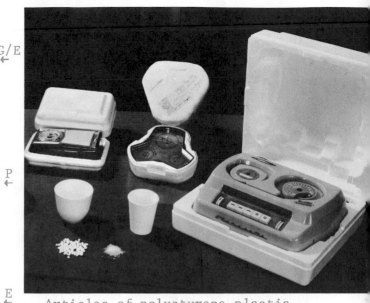

Articles of polystyrene plastic

materials man can use. One of these materials is **plastic.** The objects shown in the picture are made of plastic. Notice that plastic can be used in a variety of thicknesses. It can be molded into various shapes, sawed, drilled, and even glued. What are some advantages of plastic over older types of materials? What are some disadvantages?

Lumber One of the greatest needs of people is decent housing. Recognizing this need, Congress passed a Housing Act in the late 1960's. This Housing Act called for the building or rebuilding of 2,600,000 housing units each year for at least ten years. Great amounts of materials, especially lumber and plywood, are needed to provide this number of housing units each year. Much of the lumber and plywood is obtained from

Sec #1 above.

See #2 below.

2. Fulfilling man's housing needs requires much material from trees.

Fighting a forest fire with modern equipment

logs of **coniferous**, or cone-bearing trees. Examples of coniferous trees include pine, fir, and hemlock. The wood of these trees is often called softwood.

Federally managed forests contain almost two-thirds of all the softwood trees large enough to be cut for making lumber. The remainder of the softwood either comes from forests owned by industry or is imported.

Foresters are doing many kinds of things to help meet the coming demands for lumber. For example, they are developing better kinds of trees for forests. These trees grow fast. They also produce better lumber than older kinds of trees. Foresters are also thinning out forests. Because they have more room, the remaining trees grow faster and bigger. As shown in the picture, workers have good equipment to control forest fires.

E/G →

E/G ←

Lumbermen are searching for better ways to manage forests. They know that they must harvest trees before they become too old. Doing this gives the young trees a chance to grow. Lumbermen also know that they must cut the trees without leaving logging scars. Some of these are the result of logging roads. Building such roads, and hauling logs over them, often leads to erosion. Other scars are caused by leaving **logging slash,** limbs cut from fallen trees, behind. Methods of harvesting trees without building logging roads, without erosion, and without logging slash are being developed.

See #1 below.

Think for Yourself

What are some common materials used in building homes? Which of these materials are products of things that might someday be replaced by man-made materials?

Stress:
1. Many things are being done by man today to conserve the forests.
*2. Why is conservation of coal, petroleum, and forests important?

Stress:
For Teaching Helps, see page T122.
1. Today many people expect their government to help solve their problems.

GOVERNMENT AND SOCIAL CHANGE

Providing better living conditions

In many parts of the world, people are turning to their governments for help of various kinds. For example, many people believe that the government should help workers who live in slums or in overcrowded apartments find new homes in pleasant surroundings. Other people, especially those in industrial and commercial firms, believe that the government should help solve the problem of training enough of the right kinds of workers. Other people believe that the government should solve the problems created when thousands of workers must travel great distances to work.

See #1 above.

The British government is trying an experiment that should help solve all three of these problems and many others as well. In 1948 Parliament gave the national government power to develop towns wherever it chose. This power was very important. Without it the government would have been unable to deal with local governments that already controlled land and governed people living in places where new towns and cities were to be created.

See #2 below.

Parliament set aside a large amount of money to be loaned to corporations which the government organized. These corporations, called **developmental corporations,** were expected to use the money for such purposes as the following.

1. To build houses and apartments
2. To construct industrial buildings, offices, and shops
3. To construct roads and sewer systems
4. To provide all other essential services

The government gave the corporations a great deal of power, but it also required the corporations to meet certain requirements. For example, the corporations must see to it that there are jobs as well as homes for the people who come to the communities to live. Why is this important? What are some bad features about new towns or cities in which the people cannot find jobs?

The developmental corporations are building twenty-four towns in areas near London and other big cities of England. One of these towns is Harlow, which has a population of less than 100,000, about 100 industrial firms, and the offices of a number of other companies. The government has made strict laws concerning noise, smoke, and fumes. These laws are enforced, and Harlow is a clean place in which to live.

Sociologists who have studied Harlow report that the people who live in Harlow are proud of their community. They have formed many clubs and societies which the people enjoy. Sociologists report that the planners of Harlow made the mistake of planning the com-

401

Stress:
1. Runcorn is a new community that is different from Harlow.
2. The British devised a new method for financing new communities.

munity mostly for young workers or married couples. Very few older people moved to Harlow, and this created some kinds of social problems. See if you can tell what one or more of these problems might be.

The picture below shows a part of the city of Harlow. How would you describe the site on which this city is built? Does the city look crowded or uncrowded?

See #1 above. A still newer town being developed by a developmental corporation is Runcorn, just outside of Liverpool. Unlike Harlow and the older towns, Runcorn is being made attractive to older people as well as to young married couples. Do you think this is or is not a good idea? Why?

Economists study the ways in which money for building these new cities is obtained. They have discovered that the British government set aside about 2,000,000,000 dollars to be used in developing new towns. Instead of spending the money, the government loaned it to the developmental corporations. The developmental corporations were expected to repay the loans as soon as possible.

The developmental corporations encouraged business firms to build some of their own plants and office buildings as well as homes for sale. In Runcorn private builders will put up homes for sale. Economists believe that the methods used in getting money for the new towns are sound. The leaders of many countries seem to believe that the methods used in getting money for new towns in England may also work elsewhere. However, economists believe that money needed for building similar towns in the United States would have to come

See #2 above.

A view of a parking lot and factories in the community of Harlow near London, England

402

Stress:
1. Today automobile manufacturers are required by law to build automobiles that contain many safety features.

mostly from taxes paid to the federal government.

Political scientists point out some of the great difficulties of getting local governments to work together to create new towns. Each of the local governments, for example, would have to give up much of its authority to a stronger, regional authority. Do you think that local governments will be willing or unwilling to give up their authority? Why? What other political difficulties might there be?

Providing a safer environment When you compare the seats in newer automobiles with those in older ones you see a difference immediately. The backs of the seats are now much higher than they used to be. See if you can tell why. Other comparisons of the newer and older automobiles reveal other differences. For example, the newer automobiles have both seatbelts and shoulder harnesses, while many of the older automobiles have only seatbelts.

P/S ←

See #1 above.

Today's automobiles also have other safety devices that are less easily seen. For example, they have energy-absorbing steering columns that help prevent injuries to car drivers in case of accidents. In addition they have antismog devices to help prevent air pollution. Manufacturers of new automobiles are required by law to build all these safety features and many others into their products. Why are the people of our

E/P ←

country willing to obey such laws? How do these safety features affect the price of automobiles?

The government passes many other laws that help protect the consumer. For example, makers of cigarettes are now required to print this label on every package of cigarettes.

Warning: The Surgeon General Has Determined That Cigarette Smoking Is Dangerous to Your Health

P/E →

In many countries, governments are placing strict controls on chemicals used to kill insects. One of these chemicals, now known to be harmful to man, is called DDT. The Swedish government was the world's first government to completely ban the use of DDT. Many states in our country have passed laws concerning its use. Economists study the effects such laws have on our economy. What effects might such laws have on industry? On truck and railroad lines?

See #2 below.

In the 90th Congress at least 120 bills designed to improve our environment were introduced. Some of these bills were enacted into laws. Here is a list of some of the major laws which Congress has already passed.

P/S →

Air Quality Act
Clean Air Act
Water Pollution Control Act
Solid Waste Disposal Act
Federal Food, Drug and Cosmetic Act

2. The governments of many countries today are passing laws to protect consumers and to improve the environment.

Stress:
1. Both the President and the Congress of the United States have shown their concern for the quality of the environment in America.

The government employs a great many workers to check on the purity of both air and water. One of their jobs is to make chemical tests. The worker shown in the picture, for example, is testing water to find out how pure it is. His work is very important. Why?

See #1 above.

Richard M. Nixon, in his first year as President, felt that he needed advisers to help him reach decisions concerning ways to improve the environment. For that reason he formed a Council on Environmental Quality. Congress later passed a bill setting up a permanent three-member committee to help improve the quality of the environment. President Nixon signed that bill into law on New Year's Day, 1970. Now the President has two groups working to help improve the environment.

Cooperation among nations Perhaps you have a pen pal or know someone who has. If so, you have firsthand evidence that nations know how to cooperate in at least one way—through the postal services. People living in most countries can mail letters to people in other countries and be quite certain their letters will be delivered. The postal services provide evidence that nations generally respect one another's laws and that they can cooperate. The fact that telephone calls can be made between most of the world's nations is more evidence that nations can cooperate. See if you can think of other examples showing cooperation among nations.

The need for cooperation among nations in solving serious problems is greater today than ever before in his-

2. The nations of the world cooperate with one another in many ways.

A government chemist analyzing water for pollution

President Nixon in conference with Gerard Smith

tory. Several nations now have weapons that scientists believe can destroy all mankind. Two of these nations are the United States and the Soviet Union. Leaders of these nations sometimes meet to try to find ways of working together.

The picture on this page shows President Nixon meeting with Gerard Smith, the chief delegate to one of the early conferences on limiting the weapons of the United States and the Soviet Union. The first meetings on this conference were held in Helsinki, Finland. Do you think that it would be easy or hard for countries to decide how to limit their weapons? Why?

P/S →

P ←

The world leaders can help make the world a better place for people. But they can only do the kinds of things that the people of their homelands will let them do. The people—individuals, families, local communities—can do as much or more than their governments to help to make their world a safer, more satisfying place in which to live. Why is this true?

Think for Yourself

What can you do to improve your environment? Why is it important that you accept responsibilities for improving your environment?

Stress:
1. There is a great need for the nations of the world today to cooperate on serious problems such as weapons limitations.
*2. How can individuals promote cooperation among governments of the world?

Things to Do

See page 396.
1. Make a large, colorful cartoon or poster telling the value of having clean air.

See page 403.
2. Find a newspaper article telling about the work government officials are attempting to do to provide a safer environment. Place this article on the bulletin board and ask members of the class to study it. The display may lead to a class discussion of things you and your classmates could do to improve the environment.

CLASS PROJECT—PART 4

What remains to be done in completing work on the class project? The chart below may help you get started in evaluating your work.

SOME MAN-MADE THINGS OUR LANDSCAPE SHOWS				
	Yes	No	Models used	Additional work required
1. Good use of land				
2. Sources of power				
3. Transportation system				
4. Water system				
5.				
6.				

Each pupil could write this evaluation chart on a note card or piece of paper and mark it by himself. The individual pupil's results could be discussed by the entire class.

On the basis of your class evaluation, put the final touches on your display, making whatever changes are necessary.

You may wish to invite other classes to see your work. Plan to tell your visitors about your model landscape showing wise use of a land area.

Have the pupils find each of the review words in the unit. For each word, have them answer such questions as these:

Checkup Time

1. How was the word used in the book?
2. How might you use the word yourself?

For question 2 above, encourage the pupils to use each word in a social science context.

Review Words

calorie	famines	migrate
conservation	food deficit	molecular metropolis
corporations	Gross National Product (GNP)	physical map
desalinization	gully	protein
electric utilities	hydroelectric power	smog
erosion	malnutrition	Western culture

Review Questions

Typical answers only.

Social Science Facts

1. What are several ways that the land on the surface of the earth is being used by man today? (358) As pastureland, forest, and farmland.

2. What name do we give to the total amount of goods and services the people of a nation produce? (362) Gross National Product--GNP.

3. What are some sources of power used by man? (363, 364, 365) See bottom margin.

4. What are some basic social, physical, and economic needs of people? (372-378, 379-386) Good housing, food, water, air, and transportation.

5. What are two challenges that governments of all nations face? (387, 388) See bottom margin.

6. What do we call man's wise use of natural resources? (390) Conservation.

7. What are some new ways man is attempting to meet his needs for materials? (397, 399, 400) Using new methods and machinery.

8. What are some things man is doing to provide a safer environment? (403, 404) Making safer goods and passing laws regulating safety.

3. Wood, animals, wind, water, coal, petroleum, electricity, atoms, the sun, and so on.

5. Reducing crime and pollution.

Social Science Ideas

1. Why is it necessary for man to develop wise use of the land surface of the earth? Because it is limited.

2. Why does an economist, in studying a nation, want to know the amount of goods and services its people produce? See bottom margin.

3. Why do some people feel that man must find new sources of power? Present sources are limited.

4. Why does providing for the basic needs of its people present a challenge to every nation? Because resources are limited.

5. Why do crime and pollution present challenges to government officials? See bottom margin.

6. Why is it necessary for all of us to practice conservation of our resources? See bottom margin.

7. Why does man today need to create new ways to develop and use materials? To conserve them.

8. Why is man today seeking to work toward the establishment of a safer environment? To improve the quality of life.

2. To discover a nation's economic productivity.

5. Crime is increasing and pollution respects no political boundaries.

6. They are limited.

Test Yourself

On your own paper, write your answer to each question.

Test 1 Social Science Words

Which word or words in ( ) make each sentence below true?

1. A (metropolis, smog, gully) is a small, steep valley, or narrow gorge.

2. Another name for a time of starving is (malnutrition, famine, protein).

3. A map used in showing the height of a certain land area is called a (physical map, conservation map, political map).

4. A culture patterned after that of the Europeans is called a (Western culture, traditional culture, Eastern culture).

Which word or words are needed to make each sentence below correct?

conservation   migrate   calorie
corporations   protein   smog
          desalinization equipment

5. The wise use of natural resources is called __. conservation

6. A piece of equipment that is used to produce fresh water from seawater is called __. desalinization equipment

7. __ means to leave one's homeland for other lands. Migrate

8. __ refers to a substance in food that is a necessary part of cells. Protein

9. A __ is a unit of energy supplied by food. calorie

Test 2 Facts and Ideas

Which do you think is the best answer to each question below?

1. What social scientist would be most interested in studying the Gross National Product of a nation?
   a. anthropologist
   b. historian
   c. economist

2. What represents an attempt to establish political cooperation among nations?
   a. establishment of the United Nations organization
   b. establishment of several electric utilities
   c. establishment of rigid economic competition among nations

3. What is a major source of air pollution?
   a. desalinization equipment
   b. the exhaust of automobiles
   c. conservation practices

Which word in ( ) makes each sentence below true?

4. Man has (limited, unlimited) amounts of land and resources.

5. The problem of getting food for the hungry is a very (old, new) problem.

6. Man (doesn't need, needs) to be concerned with the wise use of natural resources.

HANDBOOK

Many of your questions about the work social scientists do, the tools they use, and the things they find out are answered for you in this Handbook. Form the habit of turning to it for reference and for review.

The Handbook is easy to use. Its six sections are arranged in alphabetical order. Each section is divided into four parts. The numerals in (   ) after the statements in the second part of each section tell the pages in the book that give more information about each of the statements.

ANTHROPOLOGISTS

Kinds of Questions Answered

1. How did the members of a society meet their basic needs for food, clothing, shelter, and recreation?

2. What were the cultural achievements of the people in such things as art, music, dancing, and literature?

3. What was the language of the people?

4. What kinds of materials did the people use in producing tools?

5. What do the tools of a society tell us about the people's level of technology?

6. What were some of the kinds of things the people of a society believed to be true?

7. How did the people of a society treat one another? How did they treat strangers or foreigners?

Kinds of Work

1. Analyzing skeletal bones. (10, 11, 13, 14, 44, 45, 93)

2. Classifying civilizations and groups. (47-48, 111)

3. Drawing conclusions from research. (9, 10-12, 13, 14, 44-46, 54-59, 60-74, 93-95, 188, 189-190)

4. Making diggings and explorations. (10, 11, 12, 13, 57, 68, 69, 70, 71, 73, 92, 93, 94, 188, 189)

5. Repairing and reconstructing artifacts. (9, 11)

6. Sharing information with other social scientists. (7, 17, 43, 363)

7. Studying artifacts. (9, 11, 12, 70, 111, 112, 189, 190)

8. Studying cave paintings, other paintings, and sculptures. (57, 73, 74, 97, 112, 189)

9. Studying traditions, customs, and habits and their effects on man. (386-387, 393-394)

Kinds of Tools

1. Calendars	7. Penknives
2. Cameras	8. Photographs
3. Dental picks	9. Reference books
4. Drills	10. Tape recorders
5. Films, slides, and tapes	11. Toothbrushes
6. Hoes	12. Vacuum hoses

Key Social Science Understandings

1. People everywhere are much more alike than they are different.

2. People from all races in all parts of the world and in every age have made contributions to progress.

3. All cultures provide some opportunities for the self-expression of their members through such things as music, dancing, art, and literature.

4. Man leaves evidence of his culture at places where he makes his home.

5. The meeting of two cultures introduces new ideas, customs, and habits into both cultures.

6. People who live in similar regions of the world often create very different kinds of cultures.

7. Unwillingness to accept new ideas often slows the process of invention.

8. Some of the institutions created by man result from his belief in a power greater than the power of man.

9. People in primitive cultures tend to be nomads who are hunters and food gatherers.

10. When early man became a farmer, he stopped being a nomad and built more permanent homes and villages in which to live.

11. The people of a strong culture often attempt to force their culture upon the people of a weaker, more primitive culture.

12. All cultures change, and each change creates new and challenging kinds of problems to be solved.

13. The style of life in many nations today is urban—even for people who actually live in rural areas.

14. The culture in which a person lives affects his thoughts, values, and actions.

15. The culture into which a person is born greatly affects his opportunities.

ECONOMISTS

Kinds of Questions Answered

1. What were some of the main needs and wants—for materials, goods, and services—of the people of a society?

2. What kinds of things did the people of a society do to conserve their raw materials and natural resources?

3. To what extent was division of labor important in a society?

4. What kinds and amounts of goods and services were produced?

5. By what methods were goods and services produced?

6. By what means were materials and goods distributed?

7. How did the people decide who should receive the goods and services that were produced?

8. To what extent did the government guide or control the economic system?

Kinds of Work

1. Advising governments on economic problems. (20, 28, 30)

2. Classifying civilizations by their technologies. (111, 112, 321-322)

3. Conducting market research. (21)

4. Describing or classifying types of economies. (321)

5. Sharing information with other social scientists. (7)

6. Studying economic growth. (321-322, 362-363)

7. Studying economic surpluses. (110-111)

8. Studying economic problems of less-developed countries. (394)

9. Studying trends such as the increased use of machines. (367)

10. Studying the use of human and natural resources. (20, 110, 321-322)

11. Taking part in city planning. (18-19, 30, 392, 402-403)

Kinds of Tools

1. Charts
2. Computers
3. Graphs
4. Maps
5. Market surveys
6. Questionnaires
7. Reference books
8. Reports of research
9. Statistics

Key Social Science Understandings

1. Societies that can meet their own needs for food, clothing, and shelter tend to change rather slowly.

2. Societies that trade with their neighbors tend to change because of the interchange of goods, ideas, and even peoples.

3. No society has enough resources to produce all the goods and services that all its people want.

4. In any society the people must make choices which determine the amount and the kinds of goods and services to produce.

5. Societies develop economic systems in order to make the best possible use of their limited resources.

6. Man's methods of getting the food he needs change as his environment changes.

7. Cultures that produce a surplus of goods tend to develop a trading economy.

8. Trading is affected by geographical, legislative, and cultural conditions.

9. As man learned to domesticate animals and to grow crops, he developed a better means of getting food than by food gathering.

10. Increased production of food made it possible for man to live in more stable communities.

11. Man can increase the production of goods by developing new tools and improving those previously used.

12. As a country places less emphasis upon farming and more emphasis upon trading, it tends to develop more and bigger towns and cities.

13. A country's resources, workers, and machines tend to determine the amount of goods it produces.

GEOGRAPHERS

Kinds of Questions Answered

1. What geographic factors affected the development of a society?

2. In what ways did the earth change man within a cultural area?

3. In what ways did the people of a culture area change the earth?

4. What was the population density of the place where a culture developed?

5. How did the population density affect the way the people used their natural resources to make a living?

6. How did the people use the earth's resources to make a living?

7. How completely were the people of a culture area able to get all the materials they needed from the place where they lived?

Kinds of Work

1. Estimating future needs for, and supplies of, coal. (380)

2. Helping to plan the wise use of natural resources. (23)

3. Making aerial surveys of land. (29-30)

4. Making maps. (22)

5. Searching for new sources of oil. (398)

6. Studying changes in the earth. (22, 23)

7. Studying climate, landforms, water, types of soil, and present land use. (30)

8. Studying the distribution of rainfall. (377)

9. Studying erosion and its effects on man. (358)

10. Studying the history of the earth. (48)

11. Taking part in city planning. (19, 29-30, 392)

Kinds of Tools

1. Cameras
2. Charts
3. Computers
4. Draftsmen's equipment
   a. Compasses
   b. Drawing boards
   c. Pencils, pens
5. Graphs
6. Maps
7. Measuring instruments
   a. Rain gauges
   b. Scales
   c. Tape measures
   d. Thermometers
8. Reference books
9. Reports of research

Key Social Science Understandings

1. The size and position of the continents have changed with the passage of time.

2. Climate affects the ways in which man meets his needs for food, clothing, shelter, and recreation.

3. The distance of any given place from the equator may greatly affect the climate of that place.

4. Man makes many changes in the places where he lives.

5. The geography of a region places certain limits on the way in which the people of a region live.

6. Man is able to live in a wide variety of geographical environments.

7. Man lives differently in different kinds of geographical environments.

8. The climate of places near oceans is affected by winds blowing over either warm or cold ocean currents.

9. The location of cultures was often determined by such things as climate, resources, and transportation routes.

10. As the population density of a place increases, the need for cooperation becomes greater.

11. A number of events over which man has no control—earthquakes, floods, droughts, diseases—affect the culture he develops.

12. Geographical changes in one part of the world often affect people's lives in other parts of the world.

13. Man's search for resources and his attempts to control places in which resources are found have accounted for many conflicts among nations.

14. The geographic features and the climate of a region change, but in most places the changes are gradual and take place over periods of hundreds of years.

15. People living on the same land at different times frequently develop different ways of using its resources.

16. As technological development increases, the relationships among the various cultures become more important and the need for cooperation among nations increases.

HISTORIANS

Kinds of Questions Answered

1. How was a specific event in a society affected by earlier events in that society? By earlier events in other societies?

2. What customs, traditions, values, and beliefs of the people of a society were affected by earlier customs, traditions, values, and beliefs of that society?

3. What were some of the causes of a historical event?

4. How did a historical event in one time or place—the downfall of an emperor, for example —affect events in other times and places?

5. In what ways did chance and accident influence the history of a culture?

6. What evidence is there to prove that certain events really happened?

7. What were some of the major changes that took place in a society?

8. How did the people try to keep their society from changing?

9. How was the history of a society affected by warfare and by invasions?

Kinds of Work

1. Choosing places and periods of time to study. (227)

2. Developing theories to explain events in the past. (12)

3. Drawing conclusions from research. (115)

4. Evaluating sources of information. (13-15)

5. Studying artifacts and remains of ancient civilizations. (115, 204)

6. Studying written records or fragments of written records. (13)

7. Tracing the spread of knowledge. (234)

8. Using primary and secondary sources of information about the past. (13)

9. Using information developed by other social scientists. (7, 13)

10. Working with other social scientists. (43)

Kinds of Tools

1. Artifacts such as ancient coins and seals
2. Calendars
3. Card catalogs
4. Encyclopedias
5. Government records
6. Historical atlases and dictionaries
7. Historical journals

8. Legends
9. Newspapers
10. Personal records
   a. Diaries
   b. Letters
   c. Mortgages
   d. Shopping lists
     of long ago
   e. Tax receipts
   f. Wills

Key Social Science Understandings

1. The first major civilizations developed in four great river valleys—the valley of the Tigris River and the Euphrates River, the valley of the Nile River, the Indus River Valley, and the Hwang Ho Valley.

2. The development of a written language made it possible for man to keep permanent records which are the foundation of history.

3. The events, movements, and institutions of the present have their roots in the past.

4. Each generation passes its customs, traditions, values, and beliefs to the succeeding generation.

5. Change is continuous, but occurs at different rates in different times and places.

6. In recent times the rate at which changes occur has increased.

7. Some changes result in progress, while other changes cause civilizations to go backward or even to disappear.

8. A civilization gets weaker and even disappears as its members fail in their attempts to solve problems that occur because of change.

9. Societies often record their past by preserving important places and by erecting statues and monuments in memory of special people and events.

10. Man needs an understanding of the past to help him understand things that are happening in the present.

11. The causes of historical events are often numerous and very complex.

12. The effects of historical events may influence the lives of great numbers of people in many parts of the world for long periods of time.

13. The same types of causes often produce similar results.

14. The same general pattern of development takes place in many civilizations.

15. Civilizations are more alike today than in the past because ideas are quickly spread to many countries by modern forms of communication.

POLITICAL SCIENTISTS

Kinds of Questions Answered

1. What rules and laws did the people make to enable them to live together in groups?

2. How did the government make laws? How did it enforce them?

3. Which of the various forms of government—democracy, communism, socialism, or fascism—did the people develop?

4. How did the leaders of the government obtain power and how did they use it?

5. What kinds of things did the government leaders do to keep themselves in power?

6. What rights did the government give to the people?

7. What were some of the duties of the people in relation to their government? What were some of their responsibilities?

8. In what ways did the nature of the government change with the passage of time?

Kinds of Work

1. Comparing types of governments. (24, 34)

2. Conducting and analyzing public opinion polls. (24)

3. Drawing conclusions from evidence. (73, 370)

4. Interviewing people. (24-396)

5. Studying history. (396)

6. Studying law enforcement. (73-396)

7. Studying political change in the world. (370)

8. Studying how governments face the problems of pollution. (388, 396)

9. Studying ways of solving political problems among nations. (369-370)

10. Taking part in city planning. (392, 403)

11. Using information developed by other social scientists. (7)

12. Working as aids to government officials. (24)

Kinds of Tools

1. Charts
2. Computers
3. Eyewitness reports
   a. Handwritten notes
   b. Letters
4. Government records and reports
5. Graphs
6. Legal papers
   a. Constitutions
   b. Court records
   c. Laws
7. Magazines
8. Maps
9. Newspapers
10. Questionnaires
11. Reference books
12. Reports of research

Key Social Science Understandings

1. When people live together in groups, some form of government is necessary for settling arguments and providing community services.

2. The main purpose of government is to make rules to enable people to live in groups.

3. All people have political and social rights and responsibilities.

4. Governments often limit the rights of an individual to ensure the rights of other individuals.

5. Man has developed a number of forms of government.

6. The chief difference among governments is the way in which the power to govern is obtained and used.

7. The forms of governments change to meet the changing conditions within a society.

8. Democracy is a form of government in which the people themselves have the power to govern.

9. In a democracy the authority of the state is limited by guarantees expressed in a constitution and by traditions.

10. Systems of government which do not meet the basic demands of the people are sometimes overthrown with great violence.

11. People who are used to political freedom usually will not accept a government that is too powerful.

12. In order to form a nation, the people must be willing to give up some of their freedom to a central government.

13. As technology improves, governments tend to become more complex.

14. Man has made laws and agreements for the control, development, and conservation of natural resources.

15. Nations sometimes organize with other nations to get certain kinds of jobs done.

SOCIOLOGISTS

Kinds of Questions Answered

1. What was the basic unit of a society?

2. What was the form of the family organization at different times within the same society?

3. Which of the social needs of man were met by the groups he formed?

4. Who accepted responsibility to teach the children the values, skills, and knowledge needed to live successfully within a society?

5. What institutions—schools, churches, clubs, and so on—did the people of a society form to make certain the culture would survive?

6. What groups did the people of a society form to encourage or discourage change?

7. What system of values did the people of a society develop?

Kinds of Work

1. Analyzing the effects of groups on man's behavior. (16)

2. Analyzing the effects of industrialization on family life. (294-295)

3. Specializing in the study of the social needs of people living in cities. (17, 18-19, 372-379, 401-402)

4. Studying crime. (387-388)

5. Studying man's customs, values, beliefs, and way of life. (19, 53, 125-139, 393-394)

6. Studying population concentration and movement. (19, 20, 372)

7. Taking part in city planning. (18, 19, 31, 35-36, 392)

8. Using information developed by other social scientists. (17)

Kinds of Tools

1. Charts	6. Population distribution maps
2. Computers	
3. Graphs	7. Questionnaires
4. Magazines	8. Reference books
5. Newspapers	9. Reports of research

Key Social Science Understandings

1. Human beings live in groups.

2. The family is the basic unit of human society.

3. The organization of the family has taken different forms in different societies at different historical periods.

4. Man organizes a wide variety of groups to meet his social needs.

5. Different members of a group are assigned different roles which may change as the needs of the group change.

6. People within societies usually classify one another into various groups based on such things as wealth, education, and job types. Then they rank these groups in order from the highest to the lowest.

7. Societies must have a system of written or unwritten rules and laws in order to survive.

8. A society can be altered by changing the beliefs, attitudes, and customs of its members and of its groups.

9. The welfare of an organized group depends upon the cooperation of the individuals within the group.

10. The physical, cultural, social, and economic environment helps determine the actions of a group.

11. Every society develops its own system of values.

12. Many individuals and groups—parents, schools, religious groups—are expected to teach children the values, skills, knowledge, and other things they must know in order to maintain their society in the future.

GLOSSARY OF SOCIAL SCIENCE WORDS

In this Glossary you will find short explanations of some of the social science words and terms used in this textbook. Most of the words are also defined or explained in the text.

The following system of indicating pronunciation, taken from the Thorndike-Barnhart Dictionary Series, is used in this Glossary.

a	hat	ėr	term	oi	oil	ch	child	ə	represents:
ā	age	i	it	ou	out	ng	long		a in about
ã	care	ī	ice	u	cup	th	thin		e in taken
ä	far	o	hot	ù	put	ᴛʜ	then		i in pencil
e	let	ō	open	ü	rule	zh	measure		o in lemon
ē	equal	ô	order	ū	use				u in circus

Anthropologist. A social scientist who is concerned with the study of man. He deals with the development, customs, races, and beliefs of man.

Aqueducts (ak′wə dukts). Channels or pipelines which were built by the ancient Romans to bring water into the cities.

Archaeologist. A social scientist who is concerned with the study of man in the past.

Artifacts. Objects such as tools or weapons made by man and left behind by him.

Balance of power. A balance of economic and military power among nations achieved through the joining of forces. The combined power of several weak nations, for example, might equal the power of a strong nation.

Barbarians (bär bãr′i ənz). Uncivilized people.

Barter. To carry on trade by the exchange of goods among countries. Bartering was used extensively to carry on foreign trade before money came into use.

Bauxite (bôk′sīt). The mineral which is the source of most aluminum.

Blade tools. Sharp pieces of flint which were used as tools during the Old Stone Age.

Calorie. A unit of energy supplied by food. An ounce of sugar, for example, produces about 100 calories.

Candangos. The first settlers and workers in Brasília. The Portuguese word for such pioneers is *candangos*.

Capitalism. An economic system in which private businesses operate for profit, with little or no government control. Such a system is also called a free enterprise system.

Capitalists. People whose money or property is used in a business or industry. Also, those people who have much money.

Carrying pole. A pole commonly used in China for transporting goods. The pole is balanced on a man's shoulders, with goods attached to each end of the pole.

Cartographers (kär tog′rə fərz). Persons who make maps or charts.

Cash crops. Crops grown to sell to others.

Caste. The particular class of society into which a Hindu is born.

Chain mail. A type of armor made of metal rings linked together.

Chief executive. The leader of a government, as in the United States and in Great Britain. The President is the chief executive of the United States and the prime minister is the chief executive of Great Britain and Northern Ireland.

Chivalry (shiv′əl ri). The code of behavior of the nobles in Europe during the Middle Ages. The code included bravery, loyalty, respect for women, and protection of the weak and the poor.

Cidade Livre (sē dä'dä lē'vrä). A community near Brasília where the workers lived while they were building Brasília. The community came to be called *Cidade Livre*, which means Free Town in Portuguese, because those living there while Brasília was being built did not pay taxes.

Citadel (sit'ə dəl). A fortress which probably housed the ruler and the priests of a city in the Indus civilization.

City-state. An independent city which also controlled a certain amount of the territory surrounding it.

Closed society. A type of society in which a person cannot rise out of the class into which he was born.

Cobblestone street. A street that is paved with stones.

Code of Hammurabi (ham ə räb'ē). The most complete ancient code of laws that has been found.

Codes of law. Written laws that are grouped together in such a way that they can be understood and used.

Collective farms. Government-owned and -operated farms in Russia which were worked by the people in groups. The products of the farms were given to the government and then distributed among the people.

Communism (kom'yə niz əm). A system of government based on the idea of public ownership of land and capital—a system in which the government has almost complete control over every phase of the economy.

Commute. To travel regularly between home and work by automobile, train, bus, or other means of transportation.

Coniferous. Bearing cones. Examples of coniferous, or cone-bearing, trees include pine, fir, and hemlock.

Conquistadors (kon kwis'tə dôrz). The Spanish conquerors, led by Hernando Cortes, who landed on the coast of Mexico in 1519.

Conservation. The protection and wise use of natural resources such as forests, soil, minerals, and water.

Consumer goods. Things such as radios, washing machines, and clothes bought and used by consumers.

Consumers. People who use goods and services.

Corporation. A group of persons who obtain a charter that gives them certain legal rights and privileges as a group that are different from those they have as individual members of the group. Corporations are widely used for organizing the business investments of many people.

Cowrie (kou'ri) **shells.** Shells made from small, snail-like animals with brightly colored shells.

Criminal. A person who has been found guilty of breaking a law.

Crusades (krü sādz'). Holy wars whose goals were to free Jerusalem from the control of the Muslims.

Cultural diffusion. The spread of new ways of living from centers where people have developed such new ways.

Cuneiform (kū'ne'ə fôrm) **writing.** Wedge-shaped writing of the ancient Sumerians.

Democracy. A government run by the people who live under it—a government that gets its powers from the people, either directly through meetings that all can attend or indirectly through representatives that the people choose.

Demography (di mog'rə fi). The study of population concentration and movement.

Dependent class. The people in Europe in the Middle Ages who did not work for profit, a wage, or a salary but for their food, clothing, and other needs. Servants, slaves, and apprentice craftsmen were included in this class.

Desalinization (dē sal'ə nə zā'shən) **equipment.** Equipment used to produce fresh water by the removal of salt from seawater.

Developmental corporations. Corporations financed by the British government to develop better living conditions for slum dwellers by providing housing, jobs, and services for those coming to the towns they build near large cities.

Dictator. A leader with absolute governing powers.

417

Direct democracy. A government which is run by meetings which all citizens may attend. The government of the city-state of Athens was a direct democracy. New England town meetings are a form of direct democracy.

Division of labor. A condition under which different workers perform different parts of a job. During the Neolithic period, for example, certain kinds of farm work were done by men and certain other kinds by women.

Dynasty (dī′nə sti). A series of rulers all from one family.

Economic surplus. The production by a society of more wealth than is needed for the survival of its people. This surplus can be used for economic purposes—it can be sold or traded for other goods.

Economic system. The way that a society produces, distributes, and uses goods and services.

Economist. A social scientist who is concerned with the study of how the people of a society produce, distribute, and use goods and services.

Ejidos (e hē′ᴛHōs). Lands in Mexico which were held in common by the people of a village and worked cooperatively by them.

Electric utilities companies. The producers and distributors of electricity.

Environment (en vī′rən mənt). The conditions and influences around man that affect him.

Erosion. The process by which rock or soil is removed from a given place by natural forces.

Exports. Goods sent out of a country for sale and use in another.

Extinct (ek stingkt′). Something, such as a type of plant or animal, that no longer exists.

Famines. Times when there is a lack of food; times of starvation.

Favelas. Shacks found in Rio de Janeiro's slum areas.

Favorable balance of trade. A condition in which the exports of a country are greater than its imports.

Feudalism (fū′də liz əm). The system in which political authority was held by the nobles who ruled over large pieces of land granted them by the king in exchange for their loyalty and military support.

Fiefs (fēfs). Under the feudal system, land granted in return for military support or other services. A lord, granted a fief by the king, pledged loyalty and support to the king. Lesser nobles, granted a part of a fief by the lord, gave services to him in return for his protection and for the use of the land.

Fly ash. The very fine ash which is found in the air. Ash is what remains of a thing after it has been thoroughly burned.

Food deficit. Too little food or the wrong kinds of foods that are needed for good nutrition.

Fossil fuels. Fuels such as coal, oil, and gas which have been formed from the hardened remains or traces of animals or plants of a former age.

Fragments. Parts of written records used by historians.

Free enterprise system. An economic system under which private businesses operate for profit, with little or no government control.

Geographer. A social scientist who is concerned with the study of how the places where man lives affect him and how man affects the places where he lives.

Gosplan. The Soviet central planning board which decides each year what will be produced, by whom, and when.

Gross National Product (GNP). The total amount of goods and services produced by the people of a country during a certain period.

Guilds. Cooperative groups for craftsmen or traders, such as those for pottery workers or metalworkers. The guilds set standards for products, preserved the traditions of the craft, and served as social groups.

Gully. A small, steep valley or narrow gorge.

Heavy industry. An industry such as one that produces machinery, machine tools, or ships.

418

Hereditary (hə red′ə ter′i). That which is passed on from one generation to another. The position of priest-king, for example, was passed from father to son in some ancient cultures.

Hieroglyphics (hī′ər ə glif′iks). A kind of picture writing developed by the ancient Egyptians.

Historian. A social scientist who is concerned with the written and other records of man produced over a long period.

Hydroelectric power. Power that is produced by using the energy of moving water.

Immortal. One who is believed to go on living after death. The Egyptians believed that their pharaohs were immortals.

Imports. Goods brought in from another country for sale and use.

Indentured servants. People bound by a contract to work for or serve another person for a specified period of time.

Indigo (in′də gō). A plant from which a blue dye can be obtained.

Industrialization. The use of power and machinery to produce goods.

Infantry. Soldiers trained to fight on foot.

Interrelated. Related to and dependent on one another.

Inversion. An unhealthful condition of the air in which gases, solids, and liquids are trapped near the surface of the earth.

Jasper stones. A variety of quartz that may be red, brown, green, or yellow.

Joint family. A family which includes not only the father, mother, and children but also other relatives such as aunts, uncles, cousins, and others, all living together.

Keep. Food, clothing, and shelter.

Knight (nīt). The lowest rank of a noble.

Kola nuts. The seeds of a kind of African tree. The juice of the kola is used in making many kinds of cola beverages.

Labor unions. Organizations of workers to promote the interests of the workingman through group action.

Laissez faire (les′ā fãr′) **period.** A time when the economy was largely allowed to run itself, with little interference from government.

Logging slash. Limbs cut from trees that have been felled and left lying on the ground.

Malnutrition. Poor nourishment resulting from eating the wrong amounts and kinds of foods over a long period of time.

Mandate. The right to rule.

Mandate of Heaven. The right of a Chinese emperor to rule—a right thought to be granted by heaven.

Manillas (mə nil′əz). Crescent-shaped rings of metal used as money by the people of Benin.

Manor. The land, owned by a noble in Europe during the Middle Ages, which contained the house where the noble lived, as well as a village for the common people and usually one or more churches.

Market research. A careful study of what makes people buy or not buy a product, and of other buying habits.

Martial law. Military law.

Mercantilism (mer′kən ti liz′əm). The economic system in which the resources and trade of the colonies were used for the benefit of the home countries rather than for the benefit of the colonies.

Migrated (mī′grāt əd). Moved from one place to settle in another.

Millet. Wheatlike grain which can be grown on many types of soil. Millet and rice are China's two major crops.

Minimum wage. The amount of money agreed upon or fixed by law as the lowest amount that may be paid to certain workers.

Ministers. People in Brazil who are selected by the President of Brazil to advise him on matters such as foreign affairs and finance.

Molecular metropolis. A model city consisting of a central city where people work and a group of surrounding cities where people make their homes.

Molecule. An apartment, or unit, of an experimental structure called a "habitat," which is designed to make better use of space.

Monarchs. Kings and queens who usually inherit their thrones.

Monasteries (mon′ə ster′iz). Religious communities.

Monsoons. Seasonal winds of the Indian Ocean and southern Asia. The southwest monsoons bring the rain that is essential to the farmers of India.

Mosque (mosk). A place of worship built by the Hindus and Muslims.

Nationalism. Patriotic feelings or devotion toward the interests of one's own country.

Naval stores. Things such as pitch, tar, rosin, and turpentine used in building and repairing wooden ships.

Nazi party. The fascist group in Germany led by Adolf Hitler.

Novacap. The name of a corporation which was set up to raise funds for the building of Brasília, the new capital of Brazil. *Novacap* is short for the Portuguese words for "new capital."

Opium (ō′pi əm). A powerful drug grown in India which the Indians traded with other countries.

Ostracism (os′trə siz əm). Exclusion of a person from a group and from its common privileges and activities by the general consent of that group.

Panchayats (pun chä′yətz). Village councils in India which were formed to solve local problems of government. The councils consisted of several villagers who were elected as councilmen.

Parlements (pär′lə mənts). The highest courts in France before the Revolution of 1789.

Parliament (pär′lə mənt). The national lawmaking body of Great Britain and Northern Ireland, made up of the House of Commons and the House of Lords. Also, the first representative assembly in England, which was the forerunner of the present lawmaking body.

Parliamentary system. The system of democratic government in Great Britain in which the chief executive, the prime minister, is elected by the members of Parliament and is himself a member of Parliament.

Patricians (pə trish′ənz). The highest-ranking social class in ancient Roman society. Government officials and military leaders were included in this class.

Pax Romana (Roman peace). The period of peace and growth which began under Emperor Augustus and lasted for two hundred years.

Pebble tools. Stones that were used as tools during the Old Stone Age. Early man either broke off one end of a stone and used the jagged edge or, later, chipped off pieces of stone for a sharper cutting edge.

Per capita GNP. The average amount per person of the Gross National Product, or the total value, in money, of all the goods and services produced in a nation during a certain period.

Physical map. A map which shows the physical features of a region of the earth, such as landforms, winds, or climate.

Pilgrimage. A religious journey to some sacred place. The Islams make pilgrimages to the Islamic holy city of Mecca.

Plebeians (pli bē′ənz). The class in ancient Rome which was made up of small farmers and craftsmen. This class was the next to the lowest in rank of the four social classes.

Politburo (pə lit′byûr′ō). The policy-making body of the Communist party in the Soviet Union, also called the Presidium. It sets up economic programs and controls foreign policy.

Political scientist. A social scientist who is concerned with the study of how the people of a society go about governing themselves and how they work out ways of getting along with other societies.

Pollution. A condition of uncleanness often caused in air and water by the amount of dirt, filth, and waste materials expelled into them.

Porcelain (pôr′sə lin). Very fine earthenware with superior whiteness and hardness to the outside finish. Vases, dishes, and other articles are made from porcelain.

Prehistoric period. The period before there was writing and written history. This period ended when writing was developed about 3400 B.C.

Presidential system. The system of democratic government in the United States, in which the chief executive, the President, is elected by the people.

Presidium (pri sid′i əm). The policy-making body of the Communist party in the Soviet Union, also called the Politburo. It sets up economic programs and controls foreign policy.

Primary sources. Firsthand sources of information about events. Examples include diaries, newspapers, or letters written by eyewitnesses of an event or by people living when the event took place.

Proletarian. A member of the working class in Europe.

Prosperity. An increase in business activity; the condition when the economy is healthy and growing.

Protein. A substance in food that is a necessary part of animals and plants.

Provinces. Territories in the Roman Empire, some of which were controlled by the Roman Senate and some by the emperor.

Pulses. Plants such as peas and beans which were grown in parts of India from 1500 to 1850.

Rajah (rä′jə). The king of an ancient independent state in India.

Raw materials. Such materials as lumber, fuels, and farm products that can be used in manufacturing or be prepared for sale and use.

Recodified. Reorganized. The laws of Spain were recodified by Philip II into a uniform system, thus making the same laws apply to people living in all parts of the country.

Regional cities. Communities planned to meet the social needs of the people. Linked to a large city, they have their own industries, trade, and social life, thus combining the advantages and opportunities of a large modern city with the friendliness of a small town.

Regional specialty. The specialized interest of a geographer in a particular region such as northern Europe or southeast Asia.

Reincarnation. The rebirth of a soul in a new human form.

Republic. A form of government in which the people elect representatives to carry on the work of government.

Rotate. To plant different crops from year to year on the same land.

Salaries (sal′ər iz). Payments made to persons usually by the week or month for regular work.

Savannas. Grasslands.

Secondary sources. Information about events that is not firsthand or original. An account of an event written by a historian after the event took place is an example of a secondary source.

Sedan chair. A chair in which one person may be carried. The chair is carried on poles by two people.

Serfs (serfz). Peasants under the control of the lords who owned the lands they farmed. Although a serf needed the permission of his lord to do such things as change jobs or marry, he was not, like a slave, owned by his lord and thus was considered semifree.

Shogun (shō′gun). The title for the commander in chief of the Japanese army. The shogun was the real ruler of Japan for centuries, beginning in 1192.

Slums. Crowded, dirty parts of a city or town with generally poor housing.

Smelt. To use heat to get the metal out of iron ore and to refine it by removing the impurities.

Smog. Air containing waste materials. Smog originally meant air containing smoke and fog, but today smog refers to air polluted by any substance.

Socialism. An economic and social system in which the government owns and runs the means of production such as farms, factories, and transportation systems for the benefit of all the people.

Social mobility. The freedom to move from one social class to another.

Social needs. The special needs of people living together in a group. Such needs include those for government, an educational system, and services provided by hospitals and the police.

Social scientist. One who studies people, their activities, and their customs in relationship to others.

Sociologist. A social scientist who is concerned with the study of man's relations to other men, especially when in groups.

Specialization of labor. Work of a specialized kind such as that performed by a carpenter or a metalworker.

Stockholders. People who invest their money in a business by purchasing shares of stock or pieces of paper telling how much money they have invested in the business.

Strike. A stopping of work in order to get certain demands met, such as those for more pay or shorter working hours.

Superblock. An arrangement of ten to sixteen apartment buildings in a residential area in Brasília.

Supreme Soviet. The legislative body of the Soviet Union.

Technology. The use of tools and machinery to supply man's needs. A society with only a few crude tools has a low level of technology. A society with many effective tools has a high level of technology.

Terracing. The technique of getting strips of level land on hillsides for farming. This technique is widely used in China.

Textiles. Cloth or woven materials.

Togas. Loose-flowing garments worn by the ancient Romans.

Topical specialty. A special interest in a particular topic. A geographer might be especially interested in a topic such as the climate or minerals of a particular region.

Tournaments (ter′nə məntz). Contests in which noblemen sharpened their skills in fighting.

Trading factories. English trading posts in India.

Traditional society. A society, such as that in India, which is based on the customs and traditions of the past.

Tribute. Money or something else of value paid for peace or protection.

Tsetse (tset′si) **fly.** A fly of Africa that causes sleeping sickness and other diseases.

Tyrants. Leaders of government in ancient Athens before the democratic form of government had developed.

Untouchables. A group of people in India who were forced to perform unpleasant jobs and were not permitted even to live within a community.

Urban. That which is of, or has the characteristics of, a city or large town.

Urbanization. The continuous growth and development of cities.

Urban places. Cities and suburbs.

Vassal (vas′əl). A noble who received a grant of land either from the king or from another noble. A vassal of the king, called a lord, granted parts of his land to lesser nobles, who then became his vassals.

Vizier (vi zir′). A government official appointed by the pharaohs of ancient Egypt.

Wastelands. Lands not suitable for agricultural purposes.

Wealth. All things that have money value.

Welfare state. A nation which provides for the economic security and basic welfare of its citizens, including provisions for old age and sickness, public housing, health services, education, and full employment.

Western culture. A type of culture patterned after that of the Europeans.

Ziggurats (zig′ù rats). Temples built by the Sumerians to please the gods whom they thought controlled the forces of nature.

INDEX

References in color indicate pages on which words or terms are defined. References marked *ill.* refer to an illustration, references marked *c.* refer to a chart, and references marked *m.* refer to a map.

428

Wealth *(continued)*
  in Sparta, 135
  in Sumer, 85
  surplus crops as, 110
  and trade, 132
  wars for seeking, 346
Weapons, 57, 61, 163, 164, 179, 180, 187, 190, 203, 204, 275, 344, 346, 405, *ill.* 164, 186, 203, 204
Weaving, 63, 65-66, 70, 163, 166, *ill.* 126, 131
Wei (wā) River, 159, *m.* 159
Welfare services and programs, 150, 302, 314, 317-318, 342, *ill.* 317
Welfare state, 316- 317, 318
Wheel, invention of, 82, 86
William and Mary of England, 276, *ill.* 276
William I, King of England, 203-204, *ill.* 204

Work and workers
  in Athens, 133, 164-165
  Aztec, 191-192, *ill.* 191
  for Brasília, 32-33
  in China, 163-164
  and communism, 299, 300
  in Egypt, 89, 90-91, *ill.* 89, 112
  in Europe during Middle Ages, 180-181
  in Greece and Roman Empire, 164-166, *ill.* 165, 166
  and guilds, 163, 254
  in India, 128, 162-163, *ill.* 162, 325
  and industrialization, 292, 295, 296, 297, 300-302
  in Japan, 186
  Mayan, 189, *ill.* 189
  in Mexico, 330, *ill.* 330
  in Neolithic period, 72, *ill.* 72
  and socialism, 316
  specialization of, 112-113

  in Sumer, 102, 113
  workweek of, 366-367, *ill.* 367
World maps, 227, 344, 355
World War I, 336, 344-345, 346, *ill.* 345, *m.* 345
World War II, 303, 308, 317, 337, 338, 343, 346-348, *ill.* 346, 347
Writing, 41, 82, 86, 88, 92, 95, 105, 118, 189, 190, *ill.* 95, 118
Wu-ti (wū′di′), 152

Yamato (yä′mä tō), 196-197, *m.* 197
Yoritomo (yō ri tō mō), 201-202, 205, *ill.* 194, 202

Ziggurats (zig′ů rats), 84, 100, 102, *ill.* 84
Zinjanthropus (zin′ jan thrō′ pəs), 10, *ill.* 10

THE SOCIAL STUDIES AND OUR WORLD

Concepts in Social Science

FREDERICK M. KING
Director of Instruction
Rochester, Minnesota

HERBERT C. RUDMAN
Professor of Education
Michigan State University
East Lansing, Michigan

HERBERT V. EPPERLY
Principal, Kellar West School
Peoria, Illinois

RALPH J. COOKE
Senior Editor
Laidlaw Social Science Program

LAIDLAW BROTHERS • PUBLISHERS
A Division of Doubleday & Company, Inc.
River Forest, Illinois

Palo Alto, California　　Dallas, Texas　　Atlanta, Georgia　　Toronto, Canada

CONTENTS

INTRODUCTION

Helping the child to be an effective human being in a rapidly changing world must be given a high priority in any list of educational goals. Through its unique plan for helping the child develop for himself concepts previously generated by social scientists, the *Laidlaw Social Science Program* enables the child to acquire the techniques essential to understanding an ever-changing environment and to living in it successfully both now and in the future.

Unlike the traditional program which, in effect, assumed that a child's sense of wonder and curiosity was largely limited to the part of the world he knew best—first his home, then his school, then his neighborhood, and so on—the *Laidlaw Social Science Program* utilizes the idea that psychological horizons are unlimited. For example, after a child has generated concepts about families he knows, he studies families in other parts of the world. He "sees" the homes where children in other parts of the world live, observing what they wear, what they eat, and how the parents provide for their families. He "sees," too, the surrounding communities and the schools as he makes his global psychological visits. As a result of these studies, the child generates concepts about families in general. As he becomes acquainted with other people in other environments, he develops empathy that extends to people of every ethnic group.

But the child develops even more than concepts, and understandings, and empathy. Equally important, he develops effective learning and thinking skills. And he develops, too, the values and beliefs essential to developing desirable attitudes toward himself, his family, other people and other families, and his government.

THE SOCIAL SCIENCE DISCIPLINES

In his unceasing search for knowledge of his physical environment, man considers, questions, explores, observes, makes tentative conclusions, tests, revises, restates, and tests again. His laboratory may be as simple or as complex as his ingenuity and resources permit. In addition to his search for knowledge of his physical environment, man searches, too, for knowledge about himself—about his past; about his societies; about various systems for providing himself with goods and services. He searches, too, for knowledge about customs and practices that man has developed to regulate relations among people constituting a society and among different societies. The scientists engaged in this search are called social scientists. Like physical scientists, they, too, have laboratories. Rarely, however, are their laboratories restricted by the walls of a building. Often their laboratories are places where people have lived or are now living. Like the physical scientists, the social scientists develop the tools and procedures essential to their investigations.

The concepts generated by the social scientists form the conceptual framework for the *Laidlaw Social Science Program*. For this reason, a brief description of the work of the various social scientists and a representative listing of concepts they generate are presented on the following pages.

Anthropology

In its broadest sense, anthropology is the study of man and his cultures. As is the case in so many sciences, anthropologists tend to specialize. Five of the main areas of specialization are these: archaeology, linguistics, physical anthropology, cultural anthropology, and social anthropology. Archaeologists collect evidence left behind by ancient man in cultures that have disappeared from the earth. They study the evidence in an attempt to find out what early man looked like and what he did. Linguists specialize in a study of language. Physical anthropologists specialize in studying the biological characteristics of ancient and modern man. Cultural anthropologists study human societies and the interrelationships between people and their environments. And social anthropologists study the way people live together in groups, giving special attention to the structure and dynamics of society.

Most interesting to children in the lower elementary grades is the work of the archaeologist. He is the specialist who has devised special tools to use in making excavations and who has developed special techniques for digging in the earth to uncover physical evidence of ancient man.

Anthropologists generate many concepts as they study man and his customs. The problem of separating the concepts generated by anthropologists and sociologists is such that they are treated together here. See the concepts under the heading *Sociology* for a representative list of such concepts.

Sociology

Sociologists study man and his culture, giving major emphasis to the study of modern man. The sociologist studies human groupings, their systems of relationships, and the behavioral patterns that evolve because of these groupings as he searches for the principles that govern the social behavior of man. The sociologist attempts to understand these principles or laws to help him better understand the workings of society.

Many of the concepts generated by anthropologists and sociologists overlap. Representative concepts from these two disciplines, concepts used in planning the framework of the first book in the program, PEOPLE AT HOME, follow.

1. People all over the world have similar problems and needs.
2. People in different cultures have their own ways of meeting their basic needs.
3. The family is the basic social and economic unit of life.
4. Human beings are more alike than different.
5. The culture in which a person lives influences his way of doing things.

This framework is equally adequate for all of the books in the program. Although it becomes more extensive in later grades, the framework itself requires no change.

Geography

A geographer specializes in a study of the earth. In this study, he does many of the things that anthropologists and sociologists do. The geographer, for example, makes a study of cultures. His studies reveal that people all over the earth view their physical surroundings differently. Because different men on earth see different values in their surroundings, they differ in their use of natural resources.

In his study of the earth, the geographer studies regions, giving particular attention to determining likenesses and differences on earth in such matters as topography, patterns of living, and the ways in which various parts of a region work together. Geographers, too, study areas and they study change—change in climate, in human behavior, in population movements, and in land forms.

Problems of special interest to geographers are those relative to the earth's population, the different shapes and kinds of land, the water on the earth, the climate of the earth, the resources of the earth, and the ways in which water, land, climate, and resources affect how people live.

Representative concepts of geography used in developing the conceptual framework for the second book in the program, FAMILIES AND SOCIAL NEEDS, follows.

1. The earth is very large.
2. Different parts of the earth have different land, climate, and resources.
3. There is a relationship between water, land, climate, and resources and man's activities.
4. Earth changes man and man changes earth.
5. Geographic factors play a significant role in the development of a country.
6. Maps and globes give a visual image of the earth and its parts, showing their spatial relationships.

Economics

Economics is the social science which is concerned with the system developed by a society to produce and distribute the goods and services used to satisfy the needs and desires of its members. Economists study various aspects of systems of production and distribution, as well as the ways in which goods and services are consumed or used. They study, too, other elements in the society that affect or are affected by the economic system.

Every economic system faces the basic fact of scarcity—the lack of enough productive resources to satisfy all the wants of its members. Given this fact of scarcity, all economic systems face the same basic problems which economists explore and attempt to solve. Representative concepts of economics used in developing the conceptual framework for the third book in the program, COMMUNITIES AND SOCIAL NEEDS, follow.

1. Human wants are always greater than the available resources.
2. Workers produce goods, services, or both.
3. Division of labor results in increased productivity.
4. People are interdependent for goods and services.
5. Communities are linked by transportation and communication.
6. All people must share the cost of governmental services.

History

History, at least in part, is the story of man's achievements and failures through the centuries. History is inseparable from man. This is because man, unlike other forms of life, can remember what happens to him and can tell other men about what has happened.

Historians supply much of the information essential to our understanding of ways in which people once lived. Historians collect and evaluate evidence recorded in such written materials as old newspapers, diaries, and other types of artifacts. Historians train themselves to reject those written and oral materials that are not authentic and to select from the authentic material that which makes sense or is believable. Finally, the historian organizes the reliable and authentic material into a meaningful story.

Like the other scientists, historians generate concepts. Representative concepts of history used in developing the conceptual framework for the fourth book in the program, REGIONS AND SOCIAL NEEDS, follow.

1. People often do things in the ways that are traditional for their culture.
2. Change is a constant in history.
3. Change may be good or bad.
4. Events in history have multiple causes.
5. Events in history have multiple effects.
6. Famous people have multiple effects.

Political Science

In one way or another, every society works out rules and regulations which define the kinds of behavior the society recognizes as acceptable or as unacceptable. These rules and regulations may be formally stated as laws; or they may be informally accepted as customs. In addition, every society provides some means of determining who in the society will enforce these rules and regulations.

Every society also provides some ways of settling disputes and disagreements when these rules and regulations are broken or when they need to be more clearly defined. The political scientist studies the ways and the means developed by a society to regulate relations between individuals and groups within the society and the relations the society has with other societies.

Representative concepts of political science used in developing the conceptual framework for USING THE SOCIAL STUDIES follow.

1. All people have rights and responsibilities.
2. The rights of each person are limited by the rights of others.
3. When people live together in groups, some form of government is necessary.
4. A society operates best when its rules and customs are understood and followed.
5. Every group formed by man needs leaders.
6. Citizens elect people to make laws that safeguard everyone's rights and property.
7. Leaders help people to help themselves get things they want and need.

AN INTERDISCIPLINARY PROGRAM

Concepts, thoughtfully selected from those generated by scientists specializing in the disciplines of anthropology, economics, geography, history, and sociology, provide the conceptual framework for the *Laidlaw Social Science Program.*

The diagram on page T7 illustrates how the disciplines and certain representative concepts generated by social scientists provide the conceptual framework for Unit 1 of PEOPLE AT HOME. Notice particularly how six disciplines are joined and how each discipline interacts with each other discipline *and* with the child. Observe too that, at the outer extremities of the diagram, a representative concept chosen from each of the disciplines is stated in language of elementary-school children. These statements are samples of the concepts the child will generate for himself as he explores purposeful questions, uses appropriate tools and materials of the scientists, makes observations, and does reflective thinking while studying the unit.

In reviewing the diagram, observe that concepts selected from all of the sciences contribute to the child's understanding of people and homes.

A similar diagram could be made for each unit in each book in the program. Because of this use of the interrelations among the sciences, the *Laidlaw Social Science Program* is truly an interdisciplinary program.

The interdisciplinary aspects of the program are highlighted in the pupils' text portion of the teacher's edition by such symbols as A, G, and A/G. A partial key to these symbols follows.

A—Anthropology   H—History
E—Economics   P—Political Science
G—Geography   S—Sociology
A/E—Anthropology and Economics

The symbols are used (1) to pinpoint paragraphs that develop concepts of each discipline other than the one presented in the unit being studied and (2) to pinpoint paragraphs that develop concepts resulting from the interplay of disciplines. An examination of any unit in the text reveals the fact that all the symbols appear in every unit, giving further evidence of the interdisciplinary nature of the *Laidlaw Social Science Program.*

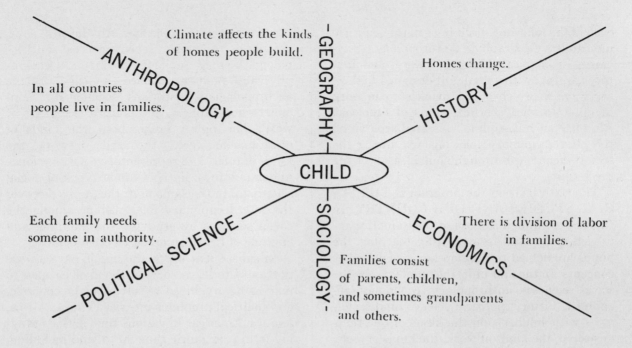

ANTHROPOLOGY
GEOGRAPHY
HISTORY
POLITICAL SCIENCE
SOCIOLOGY
ECONOMICS

CHILD

Climate affects the kinds of homes people build.

Homes change.

In all countries people live in families.

Each family needs someone in authority.

There is division of labor in families.

Families consist of parents, children, and sometimes grandparents and others.

AN OVERVIEW OF THE TEXTBOOKS

The first book in the *Laidlaw Social Science Program* is PEOPLE AT HOME. In this book the children study representative families in our country and in West Africa. They discover that the family is the basic unit of society in both countries, and that each family member must do certain kinds of work and must assume specific responsibilities. They discover, too, the economic role of the family both as a producer and as a consumer of goods unit.

The second book in the program, FAMILIES AND SOCIAL NEEDS, continues the work begun in PEOPLE AT HOME. In the second book the children make a more intensive study of families both in our country and in Japan, Switzerland, and India. Emphasis is given to the study of families of long ago (history and anthropology) and to factors that people consider when choosing a place to live (geography).

The third book in the program is COMMUNITIES AND SOCIAL NEEDS. In this book the children learn to think of communities in various countries as being political units designed to help people meet their needs. They also learn to better understand the economic life of a community as they explore topics related to the production and distribution of goods and services.

The fourth book in the program is REGIONS AND SOCIAL NEEDS in which much of the work is centered around finding out how people live in various regions of the earth and why they live as they do. Particular emphasis is given to anthropology and sociology and to the economic, social, and political structure of communities.

The fifth book in the program is USING THE SOCIAL STUDIES in which the content is centered around finding out how the various social scientists work to discover information about man and the societies he has created in the past and is in the process of creating today. The subject matter of USING THE SOCIAL STUDIES consists of a one-unit treatment of each of the following disciplines in the sequence indicated: Geography, Anthropology, Sociology, Economics, Political Science, and History together with a final unit designed to show the ways in which social scientists can work together to study certain kinds of problems. Although each discipline is treated separately, the interdisciplinary relationships among the social sciences are brought out in each of the seven units.

The sixth book in the program is THE SOCIAL STUDIES AND OUR COUNTRY. In this book, through the use of the inductive approach as opposed to expository teaching, the pupils are helped to develop key social studies concepts. In the first unit, the pupils review the social sciences—anthropology, economics, geography, history, political science, and sociology—with emphasis on the kinds of questions answered, the kinds of work, the kinds of tools, and representative social science understandings of the various types of social scientists. In the same unit, the pupils discover the interdisciplinary relationships among the social sciences as they study an early colonial industry. In the remainder of the book, the pupils learn about that part of the earth now called the United States and about the ways in which people living there at various times in history organized to solve social, economic, and political problems. Equally important, the pupils learn how social scientists acquire knowledge.

THE SOCIAL STUDIES AND OUR COUNTRY utilizes the findings of scientific research to help pupils develop the scientific base needed in discovering how any culture develops and in understanding *why* our culture is as it is. Through their study of THE SOCIAL STUDIES AND OUR COUNTRY, the pupils develop skills, knowledge, and values that will help them live as responsible citizens now and in the future.

The seventh book in the program is THE SOCIAL STUDIES AND OUR WORLD. In this book, as in previous books, the inductive approach is used in helping the pupils develop key social science concepts. In the first unit, the pupils review the social sciences—anthropology, history, sociology, economics, geography, and political science—as they observe anthropologists, historians, sociologists, economists, geographers, and political scientists at work. The pupils learn about the kinds of questions answered, the kinds of work, the kinds of tools, and representative social science understandings of the various types of social scientists. In the same unit, the pupils discover the interdisciplinary relationships among the social sciences by studying the planning and creating of Brazil's capital city, Brasília.

In subsequent units, the pupils have an opportunity to learn some of the choices open to man as he organized to solve social, economic, and political problems in Asia, Europe, Africa, and the Americas in various time periods ranging from prehistoric time up to, and including, the present. The pupils discover which of the many possible choices man made, and why he made different choices in different places at different times. The pupils are helped to realize that man today is still attempting to meet the same basic needs and to satisfy many of the same wants that man of earlier times had.

THE SOCIAL STUDIES AND OUR WORLD is interdisciplinary, utilizing the findings of scientific research to help pupils develop the base needed in discovering how any culture develops and *why* it develops as it does. Major emphasis is given to the question *why* and to the concepts that are generated in answering this question. Through their study of THE SOCIAL STUDIES AND OUR WORLD, the pupils develop skills, knowledge, and values that will help them live as responsible members of the world community now and in the future.

Each of the first four books has a unit on maps and globes. Each of these books, too, ends with a unit especially designed to help the child develop knowledge of our country and good attitudes toward it, its government, and the representatives of government.

THE CONTENT AND ORGANIZATION OF THE TEXTBOOKS

Book Titles	Unit Titles	Section Titles
PEOPLE AT HOME	People and Homes	Families, Houses, Streets
	Work and Play	Helping One Another, Family Money, Spending Money
	Maps and Globes	How the Earth Looks, Using a Globe, Using Maps
	People in West Africa	Families, How the People Live, Children
	Our Country	Holidays, The Flag
FAMILIES AND SOCIAL NEEDS	Families in Our Country	Families of Long Ago, Families of Today, What Families Need
	Where Families Live	Now and Long Ago, Choosing a Home, New Homes for Families
	Maps and Globes	Making Maps, Directions, Reading Maps and Globes
	Families in Other Lands	Families in Japan, Families in Switzerland, Families in India
	Houses in Other Lands	Houses in Japan, Houses in Switzerland, Houses in India
	Schools in Our Country	Schools of Long Ago, Schools of Today, Friends at School
	Schools in Other Lands	Schools in Japan, Schools in Switzerland, Schools in India
	Our Country	Our Country's Story, Our Government, Great Men of our Country
COMMUNITIES AND SOCIAL NEEDS	Communities	Communities of Today, People in Communities, Communities of Long Ago
	Kinds of Communities	Farm Communities, Towns and Small Cities, Big Cities
	Community Needs	Communities and Their People, Transportation and Communication, Community Government
	Maps and Globes	Maps and Their Symbols, Using a Globe, The Earth and the Sun
	Communities in Warm Lands	Hawaii, Mexico, Puerto Rico
	Communities in Cold Lands	Alaska, Norway
	Cities Around the World	Amsterdam, Tokyo, London
	Freedom in America	The Stars and Stripes, Being Good Citizens, Special Places in Our Country

Book Titles	Unit Titles	Section Titles
REGIONS AND SOCIAL NEEDS	The Earth We Live On	The Earth in Space, Maps and Globes, Land and Water
	Living in the Desert	American Deserts, The Sahara, The Gobi Desert, Australian Deserts
	Living in Western Coastal Lands	Northwest Coast of North America, Southwest Coast of South America, New Zealand, Northwest Europe
	Living in Tropical Rain Forests	The Amazon River Basin, The Congo River Basin, Malaya
	Living on Plains	Interior Plains of North America, The Pampa, Living Along the Hwang Ho, The Veld
	Living in Mountains	North America's Rocky Mountains, The Alps of Europe, The Andes of South America, Living in the Himalayas
	Man and His Resources	Man Needs Energy, Man Needs Materials, Governments
	Stories About Our Country	Great Events, Famous Americans, Historic Places
USING THE SOCIAL STUDIES	Concepts of Geography	The Science of Geography, People and Places, Geographers and Their Work
	Concepts of Anthropology	The Science of Anthropology, The Work of the Archaeologist, Changes in Cultures
	Concepts of Sociology	Families and the Sociologist, Community Groups, Living in Russia
	Concepts of Economics	Goods and Services, Producing Goods and Services, Distributing Goods and Services
	Concepts of Political Science	The Need for Government, Government in Our Country, Government and Change
	Concepts of History	Understanding Time, How History Is Made, How History Can Be Studied
	Studying a City	The Land and Its Use Long Ago, Early Days as a City, The City Today
THE SOCIAL STUDIES AND OUR COUNTRY	Reviewing the Social Sciences	The Social Sciences, Studying a Colonial Industry
	Indian Societies and Their Forerunners	The First People in America, Indians of More Recent Times, American Indians and Community Life
	Setting the Stage for Americans	Merchants and Explorers, Homelands in England, Settlers for American Colonies
	Societies in Early America	Families and Homes, Colonial Communities, Economic Life

Book Titles	Unit Titles	Section Titles
	Forming a New Nation	Land for a New Nation, Freedom and a Plan for Government, Making the New Government Work
	Growth of a New Nation	People and Land, The Nation Develops, A Changing America
	Our Country in the World Community	America Wins World Respect, America Faces Economic Challenges, America As a World Leader
THE SOCIAL STUDIES AND OUR WORLD	A Look at the Social Sciences	Social Scientists at Work, Planning a New City
	Man Before History	Early Man and His World, The Beginnings of Civilization
	Ancient Civilizations	Ancient Societies, Patterns of Ancient Governments, Ancient Economic Systems
	Eastern and Western Civilizations	Eastern and Western Societies, Eastern and Western Governments, Eastern and Western Economies
	Man in the Middle Ages	Social Development in the Middle Ages, Political Development in the Middle Ages, Economic Development in the Middle Ages
	The World of 1500 to 1850	How People Thought and Lived, Man's Ways of Getting Goods, Man's Political Activities
	The World Since 1850	Modern Societies, Solving Economic Problems, Governments of Modern Times
	Man in a Changing World	Recent Trends, Challenges Facing Modern Man, Meeting the Challenges

A CONCEPT-GENERATING PROGRAM

In the *Laidlaw Social Science Program* the learner's attention, by means of a unit title, is first directed to a major topic which social scientists explore. On pages T8-T10 under the heading THE CONTENT AND ORGANIZATION OF THE TEXTBOOKS all of these topics are indicated.

Upon having his attention directed to a topic, the learner investigates it in a series of separate lessons, each beginning with a question that can be resolved by accumulating pertinent data. "What things do families need?" which appears as the title of the lesson on page 6 of PEOPLE AT HOME is an example of this type of question. Like scientists, the children then accumulate data to use in finding appropriate answers to the question. In the first book, much of this accumulation of data results from observations of full-color photographs and through reflective thinking about personal experiences. In subsequent books, the learners still use photographs and other visual representations of reality to accumulate data, but they also use printed materials including maps, globes, and charts. They make greater use, too, of human contacts, of realia (things they can observe in their environment), of models, and of other multisensory materials as sources of data. Finally, after accumulating data pertinent to answering the lesson question, the children, like the scientists, generate their own concepts. These, having been generated on the basis of personal experience, take on meaning for the discoverer.

The principal steps in this concept-generating program are summarized below.

1. Begin with a concept or concepts chosen by teams of adults—child-development as well as subject-matter specialists.

2. Direct attention to a problem—a problem, which when solved, leads to the previously determined concept.

3. Present many examples in time and place —examples from which data essential in solving the problem can be accumulated.

4. Guide the learner's observation of the data.

5. Guide the child's verbalization of the concept—help him make it his own.

AN INDUCTIVE PROGRAM

In an inductive program, the learner focuses his attention on a specific problem or set of problems. He then collects data from a variety of sources, thinks reflectively about the evidence in terms of past or present experience, and finally arrives at a generalization or concept.

In textbooks of the *Laidlaw Social Science Program*, the unit and section introductions are designed to stimulate the learners to focus attention on specific topics. These introductions are followed by blocks of lessons. In the first four books of the program, the lessons are similar in structure. Each lesson in the first four books, for example, begins with a lesson question. It then presents data essential to answering the question. Finally, the lesson presents a question. This question is designed to stimulate reflective thinking about the evidence—thinking done against the background of the child's own experiences relating to the lesson question and the available data. The final stage of each lesson involves the verbalization of the concept or concepts the child has generated.

In summary the inductive-lesson plan entails these steps.

1. Presentation of problem (lesson title in question form).

2. Presentation of information (data), using one or more of the following.
   a. Full-color photographs or drawings
   b. Statements of fact
   c. Charts and graphs
   d. Maps

3. Analysis of available data and reflective thinking about it.

4. Reflective thinking about the lesson question in terms of past or present experience (concluding question of the lesson).

5. Verbalization of generalizations or concepts generated.

To give the later books of the *Laidlaw Social Science Program* a more mature look, the format of these books is unlike that of the earlier ones. For example, THE SOCIAL STUDIES AND OUR WORLD is divided into units and chapters, not units and sections.

Each unit begins with an introduction designed to focus attention on specific questions, and each chapter begins with an introduction designed to motivate interest in discovering the concepts presented in the chapter.

The chapters are divided into teaching units, each introduced by a centerhead, for example, "The Anthropologist at Work" on page 10 of THE SOCIAL STUDIES AND OUR WORLD. Centerheads may be considered as replacements of the introductory lesson questions used in the earlier books of the program. In most cases, teaching units end with a question in a special feature called "Think for Yourself." These questions are designed to stimulate reflective thinking about the implications of the evidence presented in the text. The "Think for Yourself" feature is also used within teaching units whenever appropriate.

Despite the more mature format of the later books of the program, the inductive nature of the texts is like that of the earlier books. In all the books of the program, the pupil is helped to generate concepts by utilizing the five steps of the inductive-lesson plan outlined above.

A PUPIL-INVOLVEMENT PROGRAM

As the child participates in the *Laidlaw Social Science Program*, he is guided in becoming personally involved in the learning process at each step along the way. Because the child can generate concepts for himself only as the result of reflective thinking in terms of available data, the inductive-type lessons are the main key to pupil involvement.

A few other examples illustrating pupil-involvement in the learning process follow.

Printed Matter—Pictorial Relationship

One tends to observe that to which his attention is directed. This idea is used extensively in the lessons of the various texts. An

example, chosen from page 199 of THE SOCIAL STUDIES AND OUR WORLD on which a diagram of feudal loyalties appears, follows.

The position of most men in the feudal system was that of both lord and vassal. Refer to the diagram on this page. Whose vassal was Count A? Whose lord was he? To whom did Duke D owe loyalty? What problems might this create for both vassals and lords?

Just For Fun

In each of the books of the program, the various section or chapter introductions conclude with an activity called "Just For Fun." These activities involve the pupil in certain tasks relating to the problems to be explored. An example of a "Just For Fun" activity, chosen from the chapter "Early Man and His World" in THE SOCIAL STUDIES AND OUR WORLD, follows.

"Make a time line covering one week. On the time line, show important events that happened to you during the period. How does this help you to understand how things change?"

Class Projects

All the later books of the *Laidlaw Social Science Program*, beginning with USING THE SOCIAL STUDIES, have a class project for each unit. The purpose of the class project is to provide activities for the pupils which are similar to the kinds of experiences which social scientists have. The pupils who complete the class projects in THE SOCIAL STUDIES AND OUR WORLD will have experience in using the techniques of the various types of social scientists in acquiring knowledge and in communicating this knowledge to members of their peer group and to others.

Things to Do

Except for the first two books, each section (or chapter) of a unit ends with a page having the title "Things to Do." Some of the activities suggested on these pages encourage the child to work on a problem all by himself. Other activities require him to engage in a group endeavor. In some cases the activity is one to be accomplished in school, while in other cases the activities are to be done at home or in the community. Each pupil is expected to participate in at least one activity.

Checkup Time

Each unit has one page with the title "Checkup Time." As its title suggests, this page enables the child to reexamine some of the concepts he has generated. The pages begin with a series of review words that serve as a nucleus for a cluster of social science ideas. The second part of each page presents review questions which the pupil is to answer to his own satisfaction. He is then expected to participate in a class discussion.

Test Yourself

The final page of each unit is entitled "Test Yourself." As the title suggests, these pages enable the child to evaluate his own understandings and concepts. As such, the pages are to be used only as self-evaluation tools, not as teacher-graded tests.

THE TEACHER'S EDITION

The teacher's edition is a self-contained teaching guide. It consists of the complete pupils' text, with all pages identical in size and color both in the teacher's edition and in the text which the pupils use. However, in the teacher's edition, the pupils' pages have annotations. In addition, the teacher's edition contains this manual.

A brief description of each of the parts of the teacher's edition follows.

The Manual

The manual presents a general overview of the entire program, giving some of the rationale of the program and general information concerning it. Except for PEOPLE AT HOME, the manual also presents independent tests and answers. For further information on these independent tests, see the next column.

The Annotations

In the *Laidlaw Social Science Program*, the child generates his own stock of social science concepts. The annotations on the pages reproduced from the pupils' text are designed to help teachers guide the child's reflective thinking that will lead him to concepts.

Most of the annotations are printed under a "Stress" heading. Many of these annotations identify elements common to several situations presented in the text. In many cases the last item under "Stress" is a question preceded by an asterisk. These questions, open-ended to the extent that many answers are possible, stimulate the child to do the reflective thinking necessary in generating his concepts.

On "Checkup Time" and "Test Yourself" pages, the annotations suggest teaching procedures and provide answers to test exercises.

The Independent Tests

The objective tests with answers that are printed at the end of the manual are intended to carry evaluation one step further than the self-evaluation tests included as part of each unit of the pupils' text. Teachers in school systems where the *Laidlaw Social Science Program* has been adopted as the basic social science text are granted permission to reproduce the tests in full or modified forms. Tests for the books of the program have also been published separately in booklet form and may be purchased from Laidlaw Brothers.

REFERENCES AND TEACHING AIDS

Professional Books

Bruner, Jerome S., *The Process of Education.* Cambridge, Mass.: Harvard University Press, 1960.

Clements, H. Millard, Fielder, William R., and Tabachnick, B. Robert. *Social Study: Inquiry in Elementary Classrooms.* Indianapolis: The Bobbs-Merrill Company, Inc., 1966.

Gibson, John S., *New Frontiers in the Social Studies: Goals for Students, Means for Teachers.* New York: Citation Press, 1967.

Michaelis, John U. and Johnston, A. M., editors, *The Social Sciences: Foundations of the Social Studies.* Boston: Allyn and Bacon, Inc., 1965.

Professional Periodicals

Social Education, published eight times yearly by the National Council for the Social Studies, 1201 16th Street, N.W., Washington, D.C. 20036.

The Social Studies, published eight times yearly by the McKinley Publishing Company, 112 S. New Broadway, Brooklawn, N.J. 08030.

Sources of Books for Children

Books to Build World Friendship. Available from Oceana Publications, Inc., 40 Cedar Street, Dobbs Ferry, New York 10522.

Children's Books to Enrich the Social Studies. Available from the National Council for the Social Studies, 1201 16th Street, N.W., Washington, D.C. 20036.

Children's Catalog, 11th ed., 1966. Available from the H. W. Wilson Company, 950 University Avenue, New York, New York 10052.

Reading Ladders for Human Relations, 4th ed., 1963. Available from Publications Division, American Council on Education, 1785 Massachusetts Avenue, N.W., Washington, D.C. 20036.

Widening Horizons, available from the Chicago Public Library, 78 East Washington Street, Chicago, Illinois 60602.

Sources of Films and Filmstrips

Coronet Films, Coronet Building, Chicago, Illinois 60601.

Encyclopaedia Britannica Films, Inc., 435 North Michigan Avenue, Chicago, Illinois 60611.

The Jam-Handy Organization, 2821 East Grand Boulevard, Detroit, Michigan 48211.

Society for Visual Education, Inc., 1345 Diversey Parkway, Chicago, Illinois 60614.

Text-Film Division of McGraw-Hill Book Company, 327 West 41st Street, New York, New York 10036.

Sources of Recordings

Decca Records, Inc., 445 Park Avenue, New York, New York 10022.

Folkways Records, 906 Sylvan Avenue, Englewood Cliffs, New Jersey 07630.

Vanguard Recording Society, Inc., 154 West 14th Street, New York, New York 10011.

TEACHER'S PREVIEW OF UNIT 1, pages 6-39

Unit 1 is divided into two chapters: 1. Social Scientists at Work, pages 9-25; and 2. Planning a New City, pages 26-37. Also included in this unit is a special feature, a three-part class project which is introduced on page 8 and continued on pages 25 and 37. The unit also has other suggested activities called *Things to Do* which appear on pages 25 and 37. Each of these activities is cross-referenced through annotations to the proper section within each chapter.

Unit 1 concludes with two pages of evaluation questions. *Checkup Time* is found on page 38 and *Test Yourself* is on page 39.

The basic goal of Unit 1 is to help the pupils learn the work, methods, and goals of the various types of social scientists. Chapter 1 discusses each of the six social sciences in detail and helps to explain how all of the social sciences are interrelated. In the second chapter the pupils can see how social scientists, with their special skills and knowledge, can help to improve man's way of life.

TEACHING HELPS—Unit Introduction, pages 6-8

CONCEPTS

1. All social scientists are involved in the study of man.
2. The social sciences are interrelated.

Recommended Procedure

Getting Started Before the pupils begin to study Unit 1, display pictures of several large cities which can be found in most magazines and newspapers. Have them compare these pictures and discuss some of the problems that are presented by life in cities. The pupils should be encouraged to discuss the similarities and differences they can find in the pictures they are studying.

Developing the Lesson Have the pupils turn to page 6 and study the picture of Hong Kong. Have the pupils compare the pictures you have gathered with the picture on page 6. The pupils should then classify their observations from the pictures under the headings of similarities and differences. From this material lead the pupils to the realization that *there are a number of similarities in the ways of life of city dwellers regardless of where the city is located.*

Before the pupils begin Chapter 1, ask them to study page 7 and list the various social sciences. Introduce the term *interrelated* and ask the pupils to explain what the term means. Have the pupils explain why knowledge gained by one social scientist, such as an economist, could be helpful to a political scientist.

Concluding the Lesson To conclude this lesson ask the class the open-ended question in the annotations on page 7. This question is marked with an asterisk (*). The answers to this question should help the pupils to realize the importance of the social sciences in their lives.

The work of social scientists and the value of this work can be emphasized through the class project which begins on page 8. Discuss Part 1 of the class project with the class and point out that this project will probably take several days or even weeks to complete.

Going Further Have the pupils discuss some things they think need to be improved in their community or neighborhood. Ask them to make a list of these improvements which should be considered as they investigate the area around their school. When they finish Part 1 of the class project, they may want to discuss how these improvements could be made. They should also discuss the reasons why these improvements might be difficult to accomplish.

TEACHER'S PREVIEW OF CHAPTER 1, pages 9-25

Chapter 1, "Social Scientists at Work," contains an introductory page and six teaching units:

The Anthropologist at Work (pages 10-12)
The Historian at Work (pages 12-15)
The Sociologist at Work (pages 16-20)

The Economist at Work (pages 20-21)
The Geographer at Work (pages 22-23)
The Political Scientist at Work (page 24)

This chapter is designed to help the pupils learn and understand what social scientists do to study and aid man. The chapter also explains how the social sciences are interrelated.

TEACHING HELPS—Chapter Introduction, page 9

CONCEPTS

1. Social scientists use different methods to gather and study information.
2. Social scientists try to gather accurate information.
3. Not all social scientists agree with one another.

Recommended Procedure

Getting Started Encourage the pupils to discuss various groups that exist in their community. One of these groups may include those people who are interested in a better government (a political group). Another group may be active in building better housing or fighting poverty (an economic and social group). Or other groups may be active in trying to end pollution, build parks, repair streets, and so on. Through a discussion of this sort, the pupils can realize that many people belong to, or are interested in, many different groups, and that these groups often cooperate to improve community life.

In the same way, it is possible to show that social scientists are also interested in different things—some political, some economic, and some social. But social scientists also cooperate and work to improve how we live, now and in the future.

Developing the Lesson Have the pupils study page 9. Point out that the picture shows an anthropologist reconstructing an artifact. Ask the pupils how artifacts tell us about ways of life of people in the past. Also ask the pupils to explain why they think a knowledge of the past is useful to people today. Mention that it is sometimes said that "The only thing we learn from history is that men don't." Have the pupils explain what is meant by this statement. Have the class discuss what can be learned from history.

Concluding the Lesson Have the pupils do the "Just For Fun" activity on page 9. Encourage the class to discuss how and why some of the artifacts could lead to different conclusions about the people who made them. Ask the pupils: Why is it difficult to understand about the way people live from artifacts alone?

Going Further Have the class make up a list of artifacts they think would help people from another country learn about their community. This activity may be more enjoyable if the pupils are not allowed to include any written records among their lists of artifacts.

To illustrate how different conclusions may be drawn by social scientists, try to find two opposing editorials on a subject dealing with your community. Read these editorials aloud and ask the pupils to explain why two different points of view may develop from the same facts. Have the pupils explain why social scientists may also disagree in their conclusions.

CONCEPTS

1. Anthropologists are interested in all aspects of man's life.
2. Many anthropologists are involved in the study of early man.
3. Anthropologists and archaeologists often base their conclusions upon the remains and artifacts of men.

Recommended Procedure

Getting Started Before the pupils begin this lesson, you may want to introduce these terms.

early man	culture
Zinjanthropus	educated guesses
Homo habilis	archaeological dig

Have the pupils turn to page 11 and study the two pictures. The picture at the upper left shows Dr. Leakey using a primitive stone chopper to skin and cut a ram. Point out that Dr. Leakey was able to do the entire job with his primitive tool in twenty minutes. The picture at the lower right shows archaeologists excavating some ancient ruins. Ask the pupils to explain how the activities shown in the two pictures help social scientists learn about man and his cultures of the past.

Developing the Lesson Have the pupils study pages 10, 11, and 12. On page 10, ask the pupils to answer the question that refers to the picture. Help the class to discuss how the physical features of *Zinjanthropus* and modern man are alike and different. Ask the class why they think *Zinjanthropus* may be considered to be a "near-man" rather than a "true man." (*Two telltale signs are the sloping forehead and the heavy brows.*)

As the pupils study pages 11 and 12, have them answer the questions in the material. Particular emphasis should be placed upon the questions on page 12 since these questions will help the class to understand how anthropologists and archaeologists use artifacts.

Concluding the Lesson Review the pupils' progress in Part 1 of the class project. Have the class answer and discuss the "Think for Yourself" question on page 12.

Going Further Ask the class to imagine themselves as anthropologists who are studying the way of life of the American Indians. Have them describe what artifacts they might find if they were digging for the remains of an Indian village. (*Some possible answers are: arrowheads, pots, buffalo bones, and knives.*) Ask the pupils to explain how each of the artifacts they described would help tell a social scientist something about the Indians' way of life. Ask the class: Why would this information be of value to the historian? Also discuss how this type of information might be of value to people who have contact with Indians today.

TEACHING HELPS—THE HISTORIAN AT WORK, pages 12–15

CONCEPTS

1. Historians study the events and actions of people of the past.
2. Historians use many different sources of information to learn about the past.
3. The historian must be careful to check the accuracy of his information.
4. Sources used by historians may be based on the same information but have different conclusions.

Recommended Procedure

Getting Started Select an important event that has occurred within the last day or so (for example, a space flight, an election, a tax increase, and so on). Have the pupils discuss the event. From this discussion have the pupils suggest answers to these questions: What happened? Where did it happen? How did it happen? and Why did it happen?

Several of the answers to "Why did it happen?" should be written on the chalkboard. The class should then discuss the reasons for the similarities and differences among their answers. Lead a discussion toward an understanding of how people may reach different conclusions even though they are dealing with the same facts. Ask the pupils: How can a historian reading these reports avoid reaching false conclusions? Also ask: Why might a historian's conclusions be influenced by his background or way of life?

Before the pupils begin the lesson you may want to introduce the following terms.

fragments	secondary sources
primary sources	Piltdown fraud

Developing the Lesson After the pupils have read the material on pages 12-14, have them answer and discuss the questions in the body of the text. Point out the difficulty faced by the historian in verifying the accuracy of his sources of information.

At this point turn to the activity which begins on page 15. After the pupils have read the selections on page 15, have them answer and discuss the questions that refer to the material. Have the pupils identify which of the selections are secondary sources and which is a primary source. Ask the class why an American source might differ from an English source. Have them explain their answers and to give any examples of how differences such as this occur today. The class may also want to vote on which source they believe is most accurate. The results can be tallied on the chalkboard.

Concluding the Lesson Following the discussion of the lesson, have the pupils turn to page 25 and complete the second item in "Things to Do." Also have the class answer "Think for Yourself" on page 14.

Going Further An interesting activity for the class might be to investigate how several different history books cover the same historical event. The class could be divided into committees and each assigned a specific event. Each committee could then gather data and report their findings to the class. Any differences they find in the reporting of these events should be analyzed, and the most accurate account should be identified and explained. Some of the historical events that may be studied include the Boston Massacre, the Boston Tea Party, the Battle of Bunker Hill, Benjamin Franklin's discovery of electricity, Washington's cutting down of the cherry tree, and so on.

TEACHING HELPS—THE SOCIOLOGIST AT WORK, pages 16-20

CONCEPTS

1. A society exists when people live together in cooperating groups.
2. Sociologists study man's environments.
3. Man's way of life differs in urban and rural environments.
4. Urbanization has created new problems for people throughout the world.
5. Sociologists, and other social scientists, are trying to find ways to meet man's social needs.

Recommended Procedure

Getting Started To begin this lesson you might ask the pupils to list on the chalkboard some of the groups that they belong to in their school. Ask the class to explain the functions of these groups and how these groups cooperate with one another. Explain that groups in every society cooperate to improve man's way of life.

Have the pupils read the first paragraph on page 16. Then ask them if the school groups they belong to affect their way of behaving. It may also be of interest to have each member of the class list the three most important things that influence his behavior. Listing the most common influences on the chalkboard will help the pupils to see a technique often used by sociologists to determine the things that influence group behavior.

Before the pupils begin to study the rest of this lesson, you may want to introduce the following terms.

society	regional cities
environment	demography
urban sociologists	demographic study
social needs	population density

Developing the Lesson Have the pupils read the material on pages 16 and 17. Lead the pupils into a discussion of why overcrowding and pollution are problems. See if they can discover why these conditions developed and why they are so difficult to solve. Ask the pupils to make a list of what they believe are additional social needs of people living in cities. A class discussion of how well these social needs are met in your community may be worthwhile.

After the pupils have studied the material on pages 18, 19, and 20, have them study the diagram of Columbia, Maryland, on page 19. Compare the aerial view of Columbia on page 18 with the diagram. See if the pupils can identify some of the items in the picture from the diagram. Emphasize the importance of the use of symbols on maps as aids to understanding maps.

Concluding the Lesson Call the pupils' attention to the map and questions on page 20. Have the pupils answer the questions and explain their answers. Try to lead the discussion around to the question of why some areas are more densely populated than are others. The pupils may also want to discuss the way population is distributed in their community. Reasons for this distribution might be classified into such categories as social, economic, or geographic.

Going Further Have the pupils turn to page 25 and do the first activity of "Things to Do." After they have completed this activity, have them save their drawings. After the pupils have completed Chapter 2, it may be interesting for them to compare their plans with those of Brasília which is discussed in detail in Chapter 2.

CONCEPTS

1. Economics is the study of how man uses limited resources to satisfy his unlimited wants.
2. Economists are interested in how people produce goods and services, and also how these goods and services are distributed.

Recommended Procedure

Getting Started Before you begin the lesson, you may want to introduce the following terms.

needs	resources
wants	market research

After these terms have been introduced, point out to the class that people throughout the world are constantly faced with the need to make economic decisions. They must decide how to use their limited resources to satisfy their needs and wants. To illustrate this point to the pupils, have them suggest a budget based on a certain amount of money, for example, $5.00 for a class party.

In their budget, the pupils are to decide how much money they would spend on certain items they want or need. As they make up their list of items, they will have to make choices of which items they want to buy with their limited resources ($5.00). As their money becomes less and less, choices become more difficult.

Discuss how a budget illustrates the principle of limited resources being used to bring about the greatest satisfaction. This is an economic problem that people, societies, and nations always face.

Ask the pupils: How could you satisfy all your wants? Lead a class discussion toward an understanding that the only way to supply everything that people want would require unlimited money and resources.

Developing the Lesson Have the class study the material on pages 20 and 21. Answer and discuss the questions on these pages. As the pupils study the picture at the upper left on page 21, have the pupils relate what they have learned from their budget to the picture.

Ask the pupils: What are some of the things that influence you to buy certain products? Make a list of the things that most often influence the pupils to buy certain goods. (*Possible answers are: advertising, other pupils, family, and so on.*) Have the class discuss why social scientists might be interested in what people in a society buy. Ask the question: In what ways do the things people buy reflect their values, customs, and beliefs?

Concluding the Lesson Direct the pupils' attention to the market research results on page 21. Have the pupils study the chart. Ask the pupils to give the reasons they think make people tend to buy the same make of car. Ask the pupils to explain why they think price is less important than style for many people when they buy a car. Have the pupils answer the questions: Why do you think sociologists would be interested in the answers to the market research study on page 21? Do the reasons people buy certain cars reflect the values, customs, and beliefs of our society? Discuss the answers to these questions with the class.

To complete the lesson, have the pupils answer the "Think for Yourself" question on page 21. Discuss their answers.

Going Further The class may enjoy conducting their own market research. To do this, have the pupils decide on an item(s) recently purchased by each of their families (food or clothing, for example). Each pupil can then ask his family what are the three most important factors that determine what the family buys. (*Common answers could be price, style, taste, or need.*) The results of the class poll can then be compiled and discussed. Have the pupils discuss how this type of information could help those who produce goods and services.

TEACHING HELPS—THE GEOGRAPHER AT WORK, pages 22-23

CONCEPTS

1. Geography is the study of man and the earth.
2. Man has, throughout history, adjusted to his geographic environment.
3. Today, man has developed ways to change his geographic environment to meet his needs and wants.
4. Maps are tools used by geographers and most other social scientists.

Recommended Procedure

Getting Started Have the pupils suggest what natural land features—such as plains, hills, rivers, and lakes—a cartographer would be likely to show on a map of their county. Ask them to suggest at least one place in their county where man has changed part of the natural features to meet his needs. Lead a class discussion of how, and why, these changes took place. Point out other examples of how man has changed the nature of the earth in your area.

You may then want to introduce several of the following terms.

    regional specialty   cartographers
    topical specialty   natural resources

Developing the Lesson After the class has studied the material on pages 22 and 23, have them explain the differences between *regional specialty* and *topical specialty*. Then have the pupils answer and explain their answers to the questions on page 22. Call their attention to the picture at the bottom of page 22, and have the pupils explain why they think man is better able today to change the nature of the earth. See if they can explain why early man had to adjust to his environment, while modern man is able to control his environment—at least to some extent.

The material on page 23 should open the way for a discussion of pollution. Have the pupils list on the chalkboard some of the ways man has polluted his environment. The class should discuss how geographers can aid in ending this pollution.

Concluding the Lesson To conclude this lesson, ask the question at the end of the lesson on page 23. Also have the class answer and discuss "Think for Yourself" on page 23. Discuss the importance of certain natural resources (for example, coal, gas, and oil) to our way of life.

Going Further It may be rewarding, and interesting, to bring in a speaker on the problems of pollution in your area. Prior to the presentation by the guest speaker, the pupils should investigate the air- and water-pollution problems in their community. You may want to form committees to make these investigations and report their findings to the class. Pictures and articles on pollution should be collected for a class display.

CONCEPTS

1. Man's control of his government is studied by the political scientist.
2. In some types of government, power is held by the people, while in other types of government, power is held by political leaders.
3. A government reflects the values, customs, and beliefs of the society.
4. Public opinion may influence the operation of governments.

Recommended Procedure

Getting Started Have the class suggest statements to be included in a letter the class might write to one of their state or national representatives requesting his views on a particular issue of interest to the group.

Lead a class discussion about why representatives in our system of government receive letters from people. Have the pupils explain why they think a representative in our political system is interested in receiving letters.

It may also be helpful to have the pupils discuss political systems in which people may not write to their leaders. Ask the pupils to explain how our political system reflects our society's belief in individual freedom.

At this point you may want to introduce the following terms.

king	congress
parliament	public opinion
president	sample

Developing the Lesson Have the pupils study the first two paragraphs on page 24 and answer the questions. Also have the pupils answer and discuss the question in the annotations shown by the asterisk at the bottom of page 24.

Next, direct the pupils' attention to the material on public opinion. Have them study this material and the results of the "Poll Questions." The questions at the end of the material on page 24 are designed to help the class understand something about public opinion polls. After the class has answered these questions, lead a discussion about why public opinion is so important in a democratic society and less important in a nondemocratic society. Ask the class to list on the chalkboard some of the various ways (including public opinion polls) that public opinion makes itself known in the United States.

Concluding the Lesson Have the pupils answer and discuss the "Think for Yourself" question on page 24.

Going Further Appoint, or have the class choose, several representatives. These representatives should visit city hall or a city council meeting and report their findings about how their city, town, or village government operates.

EVALUATION, CHAPTER 1

Ask the pupils to discuss the following questions.

1. Why are those people who study man called social scientists?
2. Do you think social scientists can improve man's way of life? Why?

TEACHER'S PREVIEW OF CHAPTER 2, pages 26-37

Chapter 2, "Planning a New City," includes an introductory page and three teaching units:

Brazil (pages 27-29)

Planning the New Capital (pages 29-32)

Building a New City (pages 32-36)

In Chapter 2 the pupils will study and learn about the population and resources of Brazil. They will also learn about Brazil. They will also learn about Brazil's need for a new capital city.

The last two teaching units in this chapter deal with the planning, construction, and nature of Brazil's new capital city—Brasília. From the study of these two teaching units the pupils will learn how social scientists can help to improve living conditions. The pupils will also learn about some of the problems faced in urban living, and how some of these problems can be solved.

TEACHING HELPS—Chapter Introduction, page 26

CONCEPTS

1. Social scientists may play a part in improving man's environment.
2. Unplanned cities of the past may create an unfavorable environment for man.
3. Planned cities may provide better living conditions in the future.

Recommended Procedure

Getting Started Ask the class to imagine they are planning a new neighborhood. Each pupil is to assume that he can decide what is needed in the neighborhood and where stores, houses, offices, and so on are to be located.

The first step is for each pupil to suggest the things he feels are needed by the people who will live in the neighborhood. A volunteer may make a list on the chalkboard of the things that are suggested. The list should include such things as houses or apartments, stores (tell what kind), and any other types of things a neighborhood might need.

After the lists are completed, have the pupils tell where they would locate the items on their list, assuming that they could actually construct such a new community. Ask each pupil to be ready to explain why he chose each location or site.

Developing the Lesson Have the pupils study the picture on page 26. Ask them to try to identify what these buildings are used for—the annotations on page 26 identify these buildings.

After the pupils have decided what the buildings are, ask them why the location of these buildings would be convenient for the people of the city.

Give the pupils an opportunity to study the text on page 26 to discover (1) an advantage of city planning, and (2) the name of the city shown in the picture. In the discussion, lead the pupils to an understanding of the many problems encountered by planners of a new city.

Concluding the Lesson Encourage the pupils to do the "Just For Fun" activity on page 26. Review the use of the scale of miles found on most maps. Pupils should also be introduced to the tables of distances between cities found in almost every atlas.

Going Further Have the pupils complete the third "Things to Do" activity on page 37. The pupils should turn to the map on page 33 and determine several of the possible ways Brasília could be reached from their community. Several pupils could also contact a travel agency and find out the cost of reaching Brasília by airplane, or by ship and train.

CONCEPTS

1. Social scientists use different types of maps to present different types of information.
2. Population distribution is often influenced by geography.
3. Increases in population frequently create new problems.
4. Urban planning can be used to solve urban problems.

Recommended Procedure

Getting Started Ask the pupils to turn to page 27 and study the maps on that page. Point out the fact that all of the maps at the top of the page are drawn to the same scale.

Then have the pupils study the last two maps on the page and challenge them to try to discover a relationship between resources and population distribution. Also lead a discussion about the influences of geography upon population.

Developing the Lesson Have your class study the material on pages 27, 28, and 29. Ask the class to answer and discuss the questions on these pages.

Direct the pupils' attention to the pictures on page 28. See if the class can suggest some of the problems faced by the people living in *favelas*. (*Overcrowding, poor housing, poor sanitation, limited water, and no parks or playgrounds are a few problems shown in the picture.*) Ask the class: Are the problems shown in the picture found in other cities? Why?

Have the class discuss some possible solutions to the problem of slums in the United States. Encourage the pupils to see why achieving these solutions are difficult.

Concluding the Lesson Have the pupils suggest one or more reasons why Brazil wanted a new capital. (*Some possible answers are overcrowding of Rio de Janeiro and a desire to develop the land of the interior.*) Have the pupils also suggest an argument for keeping the capital in Rio (*Cost*).

Challenge the pupils to think of ways in which objections to higher taxes and slum rebuilding might be overcome.

Going Further Ask: In what ways could cities in the United States raise money to rebuild slum areas? Why do you think some people would object to rebuilding slum areas?

Then have the class turn to page 37. Ask them to complete the first item of "Things to Do."

TEACHING HELPS—PLANNING THE NEW CAPITAL, pages 29–32

CONCEPTS

1. Geographers often are called upon to provide information and help for choosing sites.
2. City planning requires economic planning.
3. Urban sociologists study the social needs of cities and aid city planners.
4. Urban areas rely upon many types of transportation to move people and goods.

Recommended Procedure

Getting Started Ask the pupils to suggest a few questions that they believe planners of a new capital city would have to answer. As questions are suggested, you may want to list them on the chalkboard. Lead the pupils to suggest questions of interest to geographers, economists, and sociologists. Representative questions follow.

1. Where should we put the capital?
2. How will we link the capital to other cities?
3. What kinds of homes are needed?

Note that all of the questions should begin with either who, what, when, where, why, or how.

Developing the Lesson Have the pupils study the material on pages 29, 30, 31, and the top of page 32 to discover (1) which of the questions listed on the board had to be answered by the planners of Brasília, and (2) what additional questions the planners had to answer. In discussing the text, the pupils may be asked to tell how the various questions were answered. Direct attention to the plan of Brasília on page 31. Ask the pupils to identify the "wings" and the "body" of Brasília. Through a class discussion, lead the class toward an understanding of how the plans for Brasília were designed to avoid overcrowding and to meet the social and economic needs of the people. Ask the questions: Why are industries located where they are in the plan? Why are the government offices located between the "wings"?

Concluding the Lesson To complete this lesson, have the pupils review the problems faced by the developers of Brasília. Call the pupils' attention to the map of transportation routes on page 31. This map will help the class answer some of the questions on page 32.

In a class discussion try to help the class understand why President Kubitschek was anxious to have Brasília completed before he left office. Ask the pupils to discuss how policies and programs change with a new President in the United States.

As a final activity, have the pupils answer and discuss "Think for Yourself" on page 32.

Going Further Arrange for a member of your community's government (mayor, councilman, city manager, and so on) to be a guest speaker for your class. Have the pupils prepare a series of questions they would like the speaker to answer. Such questions might deal with the history and growth of your community. Other questions should cover some of the problems presently facing your community, and your community's plans for the future.

In most cases guest speakers appreciate a list of such questions in advance. Other questions may be prepared by the pupils for a question-and-answer period following the talk. Encourage the pupils to prepare honest and constructive questions about their community.

TEACHING HELPS—BUILDING A NEW CITY, pages 32-36

CONCEPTS

1. In a free society workers are attracted to new jobs through wages and benefits.
2. People in cities usually need goods that are produced in other areas (such as farm products).
3. Transportation is needed to supply city dwellers with the goods they need.
4. Educational facilities are needed in cities.
5. A well-planned city will attract people because it offers social and economic opportunities.

Recommended Procedure

Getting Started Take a poll of the class. Ask how many of the members of the class were not born in their present community. Make a class list of the reasons why the families of these pupils moved to your community. Arrange the reasons in categories such as social, economic, or other.

Ask the class to keep these reasons in mind as they study this lesson. At the end of the lesson, see if the class can compare their reasons for moving to their community with the reasons people moved to Brasília.

Developing the Lesson Have the class study the material on pages 32 and 33 up to "The superblocks," and to discuss (1) who built the city of Brasília, (2) where the workers formerly lived, and (3) where they lived while building Freetown. Ask the pupils to compare the map on page 33 with the map on page 31. Ask the class: What new transportation routes were built to serve Brasília? Why were the routes placed where they were?

The remaining material on pages 33 through 36 deals primarily with the nature of Brasília. As the pupils study this material, have them answer the questions in the text. In a class discussion try to lead the pupils to an understanding of how knowledge gained by social scientists helped determine the nature of Brasília.

Concluding the Lesson The "Think for Yourself" question will help conclude the lesson. It may also be helpful to have the class discuss why it may be undesirable for people to live in an extremely large city. See if the class can think of examples of how people can become isolated in a large, unplanned city. Have them answer this question: In what way was the feeling of "bigness" avoided in Brasília?

At this point, provide time to read and complete the third part of the class project on page 37.

EVALUATION, CHAPTER 2

Have the pupils answer these questions.
1. In what ways can Brazil expect to benefit from its new capital city?
2. Why were social scientists part of the team that planned Brasília?
3. What were the major problems that had to be overcome in the building of Brasília?

CONCLUDING THE UNIT

Discuss Part 3 of the class project. Ask the pupils what they have learned from the project.

"Checkup Time" and "Test Yourself" on pages 38 and 39 will complete the unit. See the annotations on those pages for suggestions pertaining to their use.

TEACHER'S PREVIEW OF UNIT 2, pages 40-77

This unit is divided into two chapters: 3. Early Man and His World, pages 43-58; and 4. The Beginnings of Civilization, pages 59-75. As in Unit 1, a three-part class project is introduced at the beginning of the unit on page 42. Other parts of the project are on pages 58 and 75. Additional suggested activities, called *Things to Do*, appear on pages 58 and 75. The unit ends with two pages of evaluation, *Checkup Time* (p. 76) and *Test Yourself* (p. 77).

The purpose of the unit is to provide the pupils with an understanding of how man has developed and adjusted to changing conditions. In Chapter 3 the pupil is introduced to the development of early man, his environment, and his early cultures. Chapter 4 continues the story of man's development, discussing the achievements that led to the growth of early civilizations.

While studying this unit, the pupils will discover how social scientists have cooperated to piece together the story of early man's progress. They will also discover how the history of man is a story of change, adjustment, and progress toward a better way of life.

TEACHING HELPS—Unit Introduction, pages 40-42

CONCEPTS

1. Throughout the past, man has had to use his skills to meet changing conditions.
2. Modern ways of life are built upon the achievements of earlier people.

Recommended Procedure

Getting Started Ask the pupils to turn to page 40 and study the two pictures on that page. Ask the pupils: What are the social scientists shown in the pictures doing? What type of social scientists are shown in the pictures? What do you think they are trying to find?

In a class discussion have the pupils suggest what type of climate exists in the areas shown in the pictures. Also have the pupils speculate about what materials were used to build the community being excavated. Ask the pupils to explain their answers.

Developing the Lesson Have the class study page 41. This material should lead the pupils to the discovery that (1) man adjusts to his environment; (2) man's prehistoric period ended about 5,500 years ago; and (3) early man produced tools, developed agriculture, and domesticated animals.

Ask the pupils to discuss the question: Why did early man have a more difficult time adjusting to his environment than man does today? Lead the discussion toward an awareness that today, modern tools, skills, and knowledge allow modern man to live in nearly every type of environment.

Concluding the Lesson To conclude this teaching unit, have the class discuss the importance of early man's achievements. Ask the pupils to suggest how their life would be different today if people did not know how to raise crops. Stress how important farming is to the growth of cities.

Read aloud the three questions at the end of the material on page 41. Have the class discuss these questions as a pretest of their knowledge about early man. Then have the pupils read Part 1 of the class project that appears on page 42.

Going Further Have the members of the class build dioramas showing how early man lived before the development of agriculture. The pupils should use boxes about the size of shoe boxes and draw the figures of early man. Pictures on pages 46, 52, and 53 should help the pupils design the figures and the scenes.

TEACHER'S PREVIEW OF CHAPTER 3, pages 43–58

Chapter 3, "Early Man and His World," includes the chapter introduction on page 43 and three teaching units:

The Development of Early Man (pages 44-48)
Early Man's Environment (pages 48-52)
Early Man and His Cultures (pages 52-57)
This chapter is designed to help the pupils understand how early man developed. Particular emphasis is given in the first two teaching units to the concept of change—both in man and in his environment.

The third teaching unit, "Early Man and His Cultures," concentrates upon how early man lived—his achievements, his migrations, and his abilities to adjust to new conditions. The pupils, as they study this teaching unit, should learn how early man began to produce the tools he needed to survive.

TEACHING HELPS—Chapter Introduction, page 43

CONCEPTS

1. The story of man's development covers a long period of time.
2. Social scientists have pieced together the story of man's development in very early times, but some knowledge is still missing.
3. Early man met many challenges and managed to adjust and survive.

Recommended Procedure

Getting Started Have the pupils study the time line on page 43, giving special attention to the pictures of early men shown above the time line. Ask the pupils to describe the physical changes they can observe that took place in the development of man. Ask the pupils, "What differences are there between the Java man and the Cro-Magnon man?"

A class discussion about why the pupils think early man changed will help to lay the foundation for the chapter.

Developing the Lesson After the pupils have studied the material on page 43, direct their attention to the time line. Have the pupils answer the three questions in the first paragraph on page 43. Lead a class discussion about how a time line can help a social scientist study a period of time. Ask the pupils: Why does a time line help us to compare developments within a certain period of time?

Take time to point out the way the time line on page 43 is divided. Help the pupils understand that these periods are only approximate and that two or more types of early man may have existed at the same time in some regions. The pupils should also be aware of the fact that evidence of still other types of man may be found in the future, and that social scientists will continue to learn more about man and his development.

Concluding the Lesson Encourage the class to do the "Just For Fun" activity on page 43. When the pupils have completed their time lines, have them explain how a time line could be helpful if they were to write a history of their lives. The pupils should also explain how a time line helps them to understand change.

Going Further From the illustrations on page 43, have each pupil trace the outline of the head of the Java man and then the head of the Cro-Magnon man. Have them do this on thin paper. After they have the outlines, have them darken the lines so they appear clearly. Placing one outline upon another, ask the pupils to describe how the physical features of early men differed and how they changed. (*The pupils should see the development of the forehead and chin and the decline of the heavy brow.*)

T30

CONCEPTS

1. The date when man first appeared, and where he first appeared, are unknown.
2. Changes in environment caused early man to migrate.
3. Many types of early man have not survived.
4. The races of man developed relatively late in the lengthy history of man.
5. All men are basically alike.
6. Every race has produced outstanding individuals.

Recommended Procedure

Getting Started Before the pupils begin this lesson, you may want to introduce these terms.

Homo erectus	Neanderthal man
Homo sapiens	Cro-Magnon man
Peking man	Negroid
Java man	Caucasoid
Swanscombe man	Mongoloid

Have the class turn to page 44 and study the map on that page. See if the class is able to identify which modern countries they would have to go to if they wanted to visit the locations of early man shown on the map. Let the class check their answers with a world map.

Developing the Lesson Have the class study the material on pages 44, 45, and 46. Ask the pupils to answer and discuss the questions in the body of the text.

Take a moment to compare the terms *Homo erectus* and *Homo sapiens*. Ask the pupils to define these two terms. Have them explain what these definitions indicate was an advantage a *Homo sapien* had over a *Homo erectus*. Encourage the pupils to refer back to the time line on page 43 to review the development of early man.

Stress the fact that early man, before he learned to farm, was dependent upon hunting and food gathering for survival. Have the pupils study the picture on page 46 and discuss how they think early food gatherers lived. Have the pupils study the material on pages 47 and 48. Ask the class to try to identify the three leaders shown in the pictures on page 47. Ask: Which race does each famous man represent? Encourage the class to discuss the racial characteristics shown in the pictures (for example, skin color, hair, and eyes). Also emphasize the similarities in facial features. Stress the fact that physical characteristics often differ within each race.

Concluding the Lesson Have the class answer and discuss these questions: (1) When did each of the races first emerge? and (2) What species do all men belong to? Then take time to have the pupils discuss the "Think for Yourself" questions on page 48.

Going Further Divide the class into three groups and assign each group a race to study (Negroid, Caucasoid, or Mongoloid). Ask the members of each group to develop a list of famous people from their assigned race. Each group should appoint a spokesman to give a class report about five famous people his group has picked to describe. Each report should tell something about each person that was chosen and what the person did to become famous.

CONCEPTS

1. Climate was an important factor in man's environment.
2. The continents of the world were once connected by land.
3. Environment affected plants, animals, and man.
4. Climate influenced early man's way of life.

Recommended Procedure

Getting Started Ask the class to turn to page 49 and study the map on that page to discover the extent of the Ice Age glaciers. Have the pupils compare the map on page 49 with the map on page 44. Ask them to identify which types of early man were most affected by the glaciers and which types were least affected by the glaciers. Lead a discussion about what adjustments those early men who were farthest from the equator probably had to make.

Before you begin the lesson, you may want to introduce these terms.

Recent Epoch	glaciers
Pleistocene Epoch	land bridges
Ice Age	extinct

Developing the Lesson Have the class study the material on pages 48, 49, and 50. Ask the pupils to answer and discuss the questions in the body of the material. During a discussion of the text, call the pupils' attention to these facts: (1) there were four glacial periods; (2) glaciers are still receding today; (3) glaciers exposed land bridges between continents; and (4) some types of animals, and perhaps some types of man, became extinct. Ask the class to study the map on page 50 and identify the continents joined by land bridges.

Next have the pupils study the material on pages 51 and 52. Ask the class to identify and discuss the three ways man adjusted to changing climates during the Ice Age.

Concluding the Lesson Call the pupils' attention to the picture on page 52. Have them explain how this picture shows how early man developed new skills which helped him to adjust to a new climate. Ask: In what way does the picture indicate that there was a change in climate? At this point, have the class answer and discuss "Think for Yourself" on page 52.

Going Further An interesting activity for the class is the second "Things to Do" activity on page 58. The picture on page 49 (and other pictures in an encyclopedia or other texts) can be used by the pupils.

Another interesting activity would be to have the class develop a time line showing the various epochs of the earth. The pupils can place the time line on the bulletin board and illustrate each period with drawings of the type of life (plant, animal, and human) that developed during the different epochs.

TEACHING HELPS—EARLY MAN AND HIS CULTURES, pages 52–57

CONCEPTS

1. A culture is a group's way of life.
2. Culture is learned, usually at an early age, from the family and the group.
3. Cultures differ from one group to another even in the same environment.
4. Different cultures are often similar in some ways.
5. New developments often cause cultures to change.

Recommended Procedure

Getting Started To begin this teaching unit, have the class suggest the way that basic needs (water, food, shelter, sleep, and physical comfort) are satisfied in their culture. Have a volunteer list what the class suggests are the accepted ways by which people in their culture satisfy these basic needs. Also have the class suggest what they think are the basic beliefs and attitudes of their culture. Lead a class discussion on how these beliefs and attitudes are learned.

Developing the Lesson After the class has discussed its culture, have the pupils study the material on pages 52 and 53. Call attention to the picture on the lower right-hand side of page 53. Ask the class to compare this picture with the picture of the igloo on page 51. Ask the class to then answer and discuss the two questions on page 53 just above the picture. Stress how similar environments may limit man's choices. Also stress that cultures will still vary from group to group in the same surroundings.

Next have the pupils study the remaining material on pages 54-57, answering the questions in the text as they study. Ask the pupils to try to identify the different tools shown on page 55. (*Each tool is identified in the annotations on page 55.*) Also ask the pupils to study the picture on page 56 and to suggest which method of toolmaking was used to make the tools on page 55.

Concluding the Lesson To conclude the lesson, discuss the cave painting on page 57. Stress how Cro-Magnon man demonstrated high artistic skills. Then have the class answer and discuss "Think for Yourself" on page 57.

Take time to review the progress that has been made on the class project presented on page 42. Then read and discuss what the pupils are to do in Part 2 of the class project on page 58.

Going Further An activity on page 58 is a useful addition to this lesson. This activity, the third one of the "Things to Do" activities on page 58, can aid the understanding of the pupils about early man and his environment. Another activity could be a display of stone tools made by the pupils using the methods shown on page 56.

EVALUATION, CHAPTER 3

Have each member of the class assume he is a member of a group of Neanderthals. Ask each pupil to write a brief description of how his way of life changed with: (1) the advance of glaciers; (2) the development of fire; (3) the development of sewing; (4) the production of sharper tools.

TEACHER'S PREVIEW OF CHAPTER 4, pages 59-75

Chapter 4, "The Beginnings of Civilization," contains a chapter introduction and four teaching units:

Man's Progress in the Stone Age (pages 60-62)
The Neolithic Revolution (pages 63-66)
Neolithic Communities (pages 66-70)
Neolithic Society (pages 70-74)
Chapter 4 helps the pupils to understand the remarkable changes that took place in man's way of life during the New Stone Age. The chapter is designed to help the pupils understand how the development of new skills laid the foundation for man's first true civilizations. Most of Chapter 4 focuses on the development of agriculture and the growth of man's early communities. Particular emphasis is placed upon how man's way of life changed from the older, nomadic way of life to that of a settled farmer working and cooperating with other members of his society.

TEACHING HELPS—Chapter Introduction, page 59

CONCEPTS

1. The story of man is a story of achievement.
2. The development of agriculture changed Stone Age man's way of life.

Recommended Procedure

Getting Started To begin this lesson, you may want to introduce the importance of agriculture in our modern way of life. Ask the pupils: How many of you come from families that raise all the food they eat? (*Only on an extremely rare occasion will any family produce all the food it consumes.*)

Then ask the class the following question: In what way is our way of life dependent upon others, such as farmers or industrial workers, who produce the goods we need?

Have the class discuss how town and city dwellers rely upon others to produce food. Try to lead the class toward an understanding that having a sufficient supply of food frees people to produce other goods or services which they can trade or sell. These goods or services, when sold or traded, enable people to buy the food they need to survive.

Developing the Lesson Have the class study the material on page 59. Ask the pupils to answer and discuss the questions at the end of the second paragraph. Stress the fact that the picture on page 59 shows a dramatic change in the way of life of man during the Stone Age. As a comparison of ways of life, suggest to the class that they turn back to the picture on page 46. Ask: In what ways did man's way of life change with the development of agriculture?

Concluding the Lesson Have the class complete and discuss the "Just For Fun" activity on page 59. Encourage the pupils to discuss how the achievements of early man have played a part in the way modern communities have developed.

Going Further Either supply the pupils with an outline map of their state, or ask the pupils to draw a map of their state showing where agricultural products are produced. Also have the pupils show on the map the location of the major cities in their state. Have the pupils use symbols similar to those used on the map on page 27. Using their maps as source material, encourage the class to discuss how agricultural products are transported to the major cities.

TEACHING HELPS—MAN'S PROGRESS IN THE STONE AGE,
pages 60-62

CONCEPTS

1. Social scientists establish periods of time (i.e., Paleolithic, Mesolithic, Neolithic) to help them study man.
2. Throughout the Stone Age, man continued to develop new tools, skills, and techniques.
3. Changes in climate stimulated early man's development.

Recommended Procedure

Getting Started Before you begin this teaching unit, call the pupils' attention to the time line on page 60. Have the pupils study the pictures above the time line. Ask them to describe the developments and changes that took place during the Stone Age. Have the pupils explain why they think these developments and changes occurred.

At this point you may want to introduce the following terms.

Paleolithic	pebble tools
Mesolithic	blade tools
Neolithic	Neolithic Revolution

Developing the Lesson Have the pupils study the material on pages 60, 61, and 62. In the discussion of the text, review the purpose of time lines and point out again how the time line on page 60 enables social scientists to show historical change visually. Have the pupils answer the questions at the end of the first and second paragraphs on page 60. Then ask the class: Do you see any connection between the developments shown on the time line during the Neolithic period? Why?

Next have the class turn to page 61 and discuss the pictures on that page. See if the pupils can identify in what way the pebble and blade tools were used and for what purposes. Have the pupils answer the questions in the body of the text on page 61. Stress that early man learned to use fire during the Old Stone Age.

Concluding the Lesson After the pupils have studied the picture on page 62, ask them to explain why social scientists—particularly anthropologists—study people living primitive lives today. Ask the class: Why are primitive cultures disappearing today? Lead a class discussion about some of the difficulties primitive people have as they try to adjust to new and more modern ways of life. Point out to the class that most primitive people have cultures based on the age-old traditions of their society. Have the class discuss the problems they would face if they had to change all their old habits, beliefs, and patterns of life.

Conclude the lesson with a discussion of the "Think for Yourself" question on page 62. Ask: Is our rapid progress today the result of developments in the past? Why?

Going Further Divide the class into several groups. Assign each group a specific topic (an industry) to research and discuss in class. For example, one group may be assigned the aircraft industry, another group may be assigned the automotive industry, and still another group may be assigned atomic energy.

Have the members of each group do research on the developments and changes that have occurred in each industry since 1900. Have each group serve as a panel to report and discuss the new developments in their industry. Suggest that each group prepare drawings or collect pictures to illustrate their report to the class.

Another interesting activity for the pupils is the first of the "Things to Do" activities on page 75.

TEACHING HELPS—THE NEOLITHIC REVOLUTION, pages 63-66

CONCEPTS

1. The Neolithic Revolution was based upon the development of agriculture and the domestication of certain animals.
2. New developments, such as agriculture, may occur in widely separated areas at about the same time.
3. Cultural diffusion aids the spread of knowledge.
4. Climatic and other geographic factors may influence the adoption of new ways of life.

Recommended Procedure

Getting Started Ask the class to study the pictures on page 63. Have the class identify each of the tools that are shown in the pictures. (The annotations on page 63 identify the tools.) After each of the tools has been identified, ask the pupils to suggest the various things each of these tools could be used for. Have a volunteer list these suggestions on the chalkboard under a heading for each tool. Have the class repeat the same process for the tools shown on page 61.

Have the pupils compare the uses they have listed for the Old Stone Age tools with the uses they have listed for the New Stone Age tools. Since the New Stone Age tools were designed primarily for building and harvesting, the class should be able to see how cultures differed in the two periods. Ask the pupils: In what way did New Stone Age cultures differ from Old Stone Age cultures? Why?

Developing the Lesson Ask the pupils to study the material on pages 63 and 64. Through a class discussion, stress the fact that the knowledge of agriculture spread rapidly. Have the pupils trace the spread of agriculture shown on the map on page 64, answering the four questions on page 64 which pertain to the map. Ask the pupils: Where do you think a cartographer would get the information he needs to draw a map such as the one on page 64? What other social scientists would be able to help the cartographer?

The pupils next should study the material on pages 65 and 66. After they have studied the material, have them answer and discuss the questions in the body of the material. Lead a class discussion about how social scientists are able to reach conclusions about cultures based on the artifacts (tools, pots, clothing, and so on) they find.

Concluding the Lesson To conclude this teaching unit, have the pupils answer and discuss the question in the annotations on page 66. This question is denoted by an asterisk. Also have the pupils answer and discuss the "Think for Yourself" questions on page 66.

Going Further Either give the pupils a map of a particular country or have them draw one. (These countries could be assigned to, or chosen by, each pupil.) The maps should show the agricultural regions in the country they have selected. Using map symbols, the pupils should also show which crops are usually raised in each region. Have each pupil present his map to the class and explain the geographic, climatic, or other factors that influence agriculture in the country they have chosen.

Also have the pupils complete the third "Things to Do" activity on page 75.

T36

TEACHING HELPS—NEOLITHIC COMMUNITIES, pages 66-70

CONCEPTS

1. Most Neolithic settlements were based upon agriculture and livestock.
2. A supply of fresh water was an important factor in determining the location of many early Neolithic settlements.
3. Life in Neolithic villages required cooperation among the people and respect for laws.

Recommended Procedure

Getting Started To introduce this teaching unit, have the pupils turn to page 67. Ask them to study the picture on that page and identify the geographic features shown in the picture. Ask the pupils to speculate about what type of climate the region in the picture has. Have the pupils suggest where this picture was taken— Africa, Asia, North America, South America, or Europe.

Through a class discussion, see if the pupils can explain how people are able to create a fertile area in the midst of less fertile land. See if the pupils can explain why the fertile area shown is so evenly arranged into square or rectangular patches of farmland. Ask: In what way are the fields separated?

Developing the Lesson Have the pupils study the material on pages 66, 67, and 68 up to "The first town." Ask the pupils to answer and discuss the questions in the body of the text. Direct their attention to the picture on page 68. Ask the pupils to explain what the men are doing and why.

Next have the pupils study the remaining material in this lesson beginning with "The first town" on page 68 and ending on page 70. Stress that remains of houses similar to the house shown on page 70 have helped social scientists piece together an understanding of the early culture of Jarmo. Have the pupils answer and discuss the question at the end of the second paragraph on page 70.

Concluding the Lesson End this lesson with a discussion of how the growth of communities changed early man's way of life. Have the pupils answer and discuss the "Think for Yourself" question on page 70.

Going Further Assign the second of the "Things to Do" activities on page 75. Before you assign this activity, you may want to establish certain geographic features of an area in which the pupils will set up their imaginary Neolithic settlement. Include such geographic features as a river valley, plains, mountains, deserts, forests, and so on. Try to arrange these geographic features in such a way that the pupils have several choices for their settlements.

In addition, you may also want to have the pupils complete and discuss the fourth of the "Things to Do" activities on page 75.

TEACHING HELPS—NEOLITHIC SOCIETY, pages 70-74

CONCEPTS

1. Not all Neolithic cultures were alike, nor did every Neolithic culture adopt all the new skills and techniques developed during Neolithic times.
2. The world's population grew rapidly during the Neolithic period.
3. New ways of life led to cultural changes during Neolithic times.

Recommended Procedure

Getting Started To begin this teaching unit, have a brief class discussion about the need for rules and regulations whenever there is a large group of people living or working together. To get the class started on the discussion of this topic, ask: What are some of the rules and regulations you obey while you are in school? Why do you think these rules and regulations are necessary? What are some other rules and regulations you obey in your community and why are these necessary?

As you lead the class discussion, try to bring out the idea that in small groups, such as a family, fewer and less strict rules are needed. Draw the parallel between a small food-gathering group in the Old Stone Age and a small family group today. (*Neither of these small groups needs elaborate rules.*)

Then point out that larger communities need rules to control behavior. Ask: Why would more rules and regulations be needed in Neolithic times than in Old Stone Age times?

Developing the Lesson Have the class study the material on pages 70, 71, and 72. Point out the value of bar graphs—such as the one on page 71—as a means used by social scientists to show change visually. After they have studied the graph, have the pupils answer the four questions in the material just above the graph. You may want to point out that the current population of the world is over 3,000,000,000— that is, over 34 times larger than it was less than 8,000 years ago.

Have the pupils next discuss the picture on page 72 and answer the questions in the body of the text. Stress the idea that division of labor increases as people develop new skills.

The material on pages 73 and 74 should be studied next by the pupils. Lead a class discussion about how the qualities desired in leaders change as the nature of a society changes.

Concluding the Lesson Use the "Think for Yourself" questions on page 74 to stress the idea that leaders are chosen on the basis of certain qualities they possess. Help the pupils realize that these qualities are important to the society and reflect the society's political attitudes, values, and beliefs.

EVALUATION, CHAPTER 4

Have the pupils discuss these questions.
1. In what ways have social scientists learned about the development of man in the Stone Age?
2. What can the study of Neolithic man tell us about the way we live?

CONCLUDING THE UNIT

Discuss Part 3 of the class project. Give the pupils ample time to complete their work on all parts of the class project. Perhaps it would be possible to arrange an area in the school where the pupils' display on early man can be seen by other classes. Parents may be invited to visit and view the display.

TEACHER'S PREVIEW OF UNIT 3, pages 78-121

Unit 3 is divided into three chapters: 5. Ancient Societies, pages 81-96; 6. Patterns of Ancient Governments, pages 97-108; and 7. Ancient Economic Systems, pages 109-119. A special feature is a class project which is introduced on page 80 and continued on pages 96, 108, and 119. Additional activities for the pupils, called *Things to Do*, are given on pages 96, 108, and 119. The unit concludes with two pages of evaluation, *Checkup Time* on page 120 and *Test Yourself* on page 121.

This unit introduces the pupils to the study of social, political, and economic systems of the past. Emphasis is placed upon the interrelatedness of these systems and upon the many different factors that influenced the development of these systems. An interdisciplinary approach is used to help the pupils understand how man developed his first civilizations.

As the pupils study this unit, they will develop an understanding of man's progress in ancient times. Emphasis is placed upon man's development in different areas of the world.

TEACHING HELPS—Unit Introduction, pages 78-80

CONCEPTS

1. Geographic, social, and historical factors influenced the development of man's first civilizations.
2. Civilization occurs when people live together in groups and develop social, political, and economic systems.
3. Writing and urbanization are characteristics of man's earliest civilizations.

Recommended Procedure

Getting Started Have the pupils turn to page 78 and study the picture on that page. The picture shows the pleasure boats of a royal prince. Ask the pupils to compare the upper and lower scenes in the picture. Have the pupils observe and explain how the two scenes differ. (*In the top scene the boat is sailing south with the prevailing wind. The lower scene shows the boat being rowed northward with the current.*) Have the pupils suggest some ways the development of the sailboat might have helped ancient man.

Developing the Lesson Ask the class to study the material on page 79. Ask the pupils: What are the characteristics of a *civilization*? Based on this definition, do you live in a civilized society?

Point out that man developed civilizations in several parts of the world. Stress the fact that this unit is designed to discuss three "typical" ancient civilizations as examples of how man progressed from his simple earlier, and less complex, way of life to a more complex civilized way of life. Have the pupils discuss why civilizations are found throughout the world today.

Concluding the Lesson Lead a class discussion about how contacts among people today lead to the development and growth of civilizations. Have the pupils suggest how ways of life in their country are affected by contacts with other civilizations from other places in the world.

Have the pupils turn to page 80. Introduce the class project and point out that it has three other parts on pages 96, 108, and 119.

Going Further Have the pupils obtain or draw a map of the world showing the continents. Using an encyclopedia for information, have each pupil locate and indicate on his map where civilizations first developed in Asia, Africa, and in the Americas. Ask the pupils to indicate on their maps the geographic feature the civilizations in Africa and Asia had in common. (*Pupils should show river valleys.*)

TEACHER'S PREVIEW OF CHAPTER 5, pages 81–96

Chapter 5, "Ancient Societies," has an introductory page and three teaching units:
The Sumerian Society (pages 82-86)
The Egyptian Society (pages 86-91)
The Indus Society (pages 91-95)
This chapter is designed to help the pupils understand the development of three river valley civilizations. It also will help the pupils understand how social classes developed and how urbanization changed man's way of life. The concepts developed in this chapter will enable the pupils to understand more fully the nature of societies in the past and in the present.

TEACHING HELPS—Chapter Introduction, page 81

CONCEPTS

1. A pattern of man's history has been the urbanization of societies.
2. Urbanization produces changes in man's way of life.

Recommended Procedure

Getting Started Ask the pupils to study the picture on page 81. Point out that the picture shows a town in Nigeria.

After the pupils have studied the picture, ask them to point out the examples of old and new ways of life that are shown in the picture. (The annotations on page 81 cover many of the old and new ways shown in the picture. You may want to expand upon these by including the way the people are dressed.)

Lead a class discussion about how old and new ways of life are blending together in your community. Have the pupils suggest reasons why they think this blending occurs.

Developing the Lesson Have the pupils study the material on page 81. Ask the class to suggest some of the reasons why the United States is becoming more and more urbanized. You may want to list these reasons under such headings as: *Social, Political, Economic.*

Next have the pupils answer the questions at the end of the second paragraph on page 81.
Concluding the Lesson End this lesson with a discussion of some of the new inventions that have influenced the way of life in America in the last twenty-five years. Then have the pupils do the "Just For Fun" activity at the bottom of page 81.
Going Further Divide the class into two groups to study about the growth of population and cities in their state. Have one group investigate how the population of their state has changed in the past fifty years. (Much of this information can be gathered from an encyclopedia.) Also encourage the members of this group to write to their state representatives for help and information.

The second group should investigate the growth and development of their state's largest city. Once again, the pupils should be encouraged to get their information from an encyclopedia and by writing to the government of the city.

Have both groups present their findings to the class for discussion as to why growth and change have taken place.

TEACHING HELPS—THE SUMERIAN SOCIETY, pages 82-86

CONCEPTS

1. The environment affects the development of a civilization.
2. Cultural diffusion can affect the development of a civilization.
3. Social classes often reflect the priorities of a society.
4. Social status may be reflected by the economic or political position of an individual.

Recommended Procedure

Getting Started Ask the class to turn to page 82 and study the map on that page. Ask the pupils to identify the two parts of Mesopotamia shown on the map. Also have the pupils identify the two rivers that are named on the map. Have the pupils explain the nature of the land shown on the map. Ask: Where were the desert areas? Where was the fertile land? Why was the land fertile?

Have the class suggest where they would establish cities if they lived in ancient Mesopotamia. Have the pupils explain the reasons for their site locations of the cities. (You may want to refer the pupils to the map on page 83 to check their suggestions with the actual locations selected over 5,000 years ago.)

Developing the Lesson Have the pupils study the material on pages 82 and 83. In a class discussion stress the importance of geographic conditions upon the development of the Su-

merian civilization. Ask the pupils: Are geographic conditions important in the choice of sites for cities today? Why?

Then have the pupils define the term *city-state*. Ask the class to study the reconstruction of the city-state of Ur shown in the picture at the top right-hand side of page 83. From what is shown in the picture, have the pupils suggest: (1) What type of climate the city of Ur enjoyed. (2) What the people used the large building in the background for.

Then have the pupils study the material on pages 84, 85, and 86 up to "The Egyptian Society." Have the pupils answer the questions in the body of the material. Discuss the answers to these questions with the class. Point out the contributions of the Sumerians discussed in the last paragraph of the material.

Concluding the Lesson Finish the lesson by asking: In what ways did the Sumerian society reflect the beliefs and attitudes of the Sumerian people? Do societies today also reflect the attitudes of their members? Have the pupils suggest ways that their society reflects the beliefs of the people. Then have the pupils answer the "Think for Yourself" questions on page 86. Lead a class discussion about why the ruler of a Sumerian city-state had so much power.

Going Further For a class activity have the class turn to page 96. Ask the pupils to complete the first of the "Things to Do" activities on that page. Mention to the class that the ruins of the ziggurat shown on page 84 can be a guide for their model or drawing.

TEACHING HELPS—THE EGYPTIAN SOCIETY, pages 86-91

CONCEPTS

1. Freedom from outside invasion may enable a civilization to develop.
2. Favorable geographic conditions helped the Egyptians to establish their civilization.
3. Isolation from outside influences may result in a slow-changing culture.
4. Religious beliefs influenced the nature of the Egyptian society.

Recommended Procedure

Getting Started Have the pupils compare the map of ancient Egypt on page 87 with the map of Mesopotamia on page 82. Ask the pupils to point out the geographic similarities (*fertile land and rivers*) between the two regions. Have them describe how the two areas differed. Ask the pupils: Why might the annual flood in Mesopotamia have been more difficult to control than the annual flood in Egypt? Lead a class discussion about how floods are controlled today. Ask: Is modern man better able to control his environment than ancient man was able to do 5,000 years ago? Why?

Developing the Lesson First have the pupils study the material on pages 86, 87, and 88 up to "A slow-changing culture." Have the pupils answer the questions in the body of the material. Discuss the answers with the class. Stress the fact that more favorable geographic conditions made everyday life easier and more enjoyable in Egypt than in Sumer. As a result, the Egyptians, generally, were a more cheerful and optimistic people than were the Sumerians. Also stress that the need for irrigation brought the people of Egypt together and increased cooperation within the society.

Next have the pupils study the remaining material on pages 88, 89, 90, and 91 up to the "Indus Society." Have the pupils answer and discuss the questions in the body of the text. Use the pictures, and their captions, on pages 89 and 90 as the basis for a class discussion about life in ancient Egypt.

Concluding the Lesson Lead a class discussion about the relationship of religion and social classes in Egypt. Have the pupils answer the "Think for Yourself" question on page 91. In the class discussion bring out the fact that much of the social, economic, and political power in Egypt was held by those who also had a religious position. Ask: Why was the control of the forces of nature so important to the Egyptian way of life? (*Egypt relied upon agriculture to maintain its civilized way of life.*) Stress the fact that the Egyptians believed that the forces of nature were controlled by the gods who were influenced by the religious leaders.

Going Further Divide the class into four groups. Have the pupils imagine that they are in ancient Egypt, and that they have just received payment for their labor in produce. The members of one group are to imagine that they have received five loaves of bread as their wages. The second group is to imagine they have each received a bushel of wheat as their wages. Each pupil in the next group is to imagine that he has been paid a bushel of rice. The members of the fourth group are to imagine that they have received ten pots.

Have the pupils attempt to trade some of their wages with other pupils to get the things they need. Explain that this is *barter* and that ancient people had to do this type of trading when they had no system of money. After the trading has ended, ask the pupils to discuss the difficulties they faced when they had to barter for goods. Ask: In what ways is a system of money better than a system of barter?

TEACHING HELPS—THE INDUS SOCIETY, pages 91–95

CONCEPTS

1. The population of India is made up of people of all the races of man.
2. The Indus River Valley offered favorable conditions for the development of a civilization.
3. The Indus civilization was remarkably static.

Recommended Procedure

Getting Started Have the class turn to page 92 and compare the maps on that page. Ask the pupils to notice where the cities of the Indus civilization were located. Then ask them to study the routes of migration shown on the map at the bottom of page 92. Ask the class: With what other civilization, or civilizations, do you think the people of the Indus Valley had contacts? Why?

Also lead a class discussion about the use of map symbols on the maps on page 92. In a class discussion point out how important map symbols are in showing information visually.

Developing the Lesson First have the pupils study the material on pages 91, 92, and 93 up to "Early Indus cities." Have them answer the questions in the body of the material. In a discussion stress the fact that social scientists assemble pieces of information and reach conclusions based on this information. Try to lead the pupils to an understanding of how geographers, anthropologists, and historians all rely upon each other for information about the Indus society.

Then have the pupils study the remaining material on pages 93, 94, and 95. As the pupils answer the questions in the text on these pages, discuss with them how bits of information are used to reach conclusions. (The material and the questions are arranged to show how social scientists investigate and assemble evidence about a civilization.) After the pupils have studied the material, lead a class discussion about what other conclusions could be drawn from the evidence found by social scientists. (*For example, the fact that Mohenjo-Daro and Harrapa were so much alike could have been a coincidence, although this is unlikely.*)

Concluding the Lesson End this lesson by having the pupils answer and discuss "Think for Yourself" on page 95.

Going Further You may want to have each pupil draw an original design of a seal similar to the ones shown in the pictures on page 95. Have the pupils show their designs to the class and explain why they chose the designs they pictured. You may also want to discuss with the class why it has been so difficult to understand the Indus writing. (*One reason has been the fact that so few samples have been found.*)

EVALUATION, CHAPTER 5

Ask the pupils to discuss the following questions.

1. In what ways were the ancient societies of Sumer, Egypt, and the Indus Valley similar?
2. Why did geographic factors and conditions influence the development of ancient societies?
3. Are geographic factors and conditions less important in influencing our civilization today than they were in the past? Why?

TEACHER'S PREVIEW OF CHAPTER 6, pages 97-108

Chapter 6, "Patterns of Ancient Governments," consists of one introductory page and three teaching units:

The Nature of Ancient Governments (pages 98-101)

The Operation of Ancient Governments (pages 102-104)

Law in Ancient Societies (pages 104-107)

The second chapter of this unit presents material which covers the organization, operation, and philosophy of governments in ancient Sumer, Egypt, and the Indus Valley. As they study this chapter, the pupils will develop an understanding of how and why ancient governments developed. They will also develop an understanding of how a government is directly related to the beliefs, customs, traditions, and attitudes of its society.

During their study of the material in Chapter 6, the pupils will discover how geographic, social, political, and economic factors influenced the development of ancient governments. The comparison of three ancient political systems will help the pupils to learn and understand how a number of interrelated factors influenced the development and growth of man's first civilizations in Africa and Asia.

TEACHING HELPS—Chapter Introduction, page 97

CONCEPTS

1. A political system usually reflects the beliefs and values of the society.
2. Ancient governments often performed the same basic functions even though the nature of ancient societies was different.

Recommended Procedure

Getting Started Have the pupils turn to page 97 and study the picture of the Great Sphinx on that page. Point out the pyramid in the background.

After the class has had an opportunity to study the picture, lead a class discussion about why societies build statues or monuments to honor their political leaders. Ask: In what ways do such statues or monuments tend to unify a country? Discuss the answer to this question.

Developing the Lesson Ask the pupils to study the material on page 97. After they have studied the material, lead a class discussion about what functions the pupils feel should be performed by a government. Have a pupil list some of the suggested functions of government on the chalkboard. Ask the pupils to keep these functions of government in mind as they study Chapter 6 to see if these functions were performed by ancient governments in Africa and Asia.

Concluding the Lesson Have the pupils complete the "Just For Fun" activity on page 97. Suggest that the class prepare a display of their models and invite another class or their parents in to view the display.

Going Further An interesting activity for the class would be to have each pupil collect pictures of statues and monuments honoring political or military leaders. Have them gather these from newspapers or magazines. Then have the class prepare a bulletin-board display of these pictures with captions explaining when the statues and monuments were built and in whose honor.

TEACHING HELPS—THE NATURE OF ANCIENT GOVERNMENTS, pages 98-101

CONCEPTS

1. People living in groups need a government.
2. Governments reflect their society.
3. Religious beliefs influenced the nature of ancient governments.
4. Powers of governments, and the government's control over the people, differ from one society to another.

Recommended Procedure

Getting Started Before you begin this lesson, have the pupils think about what control the government of the United States has over them. Have the pupils also consider what power American citizens have to control their national government. Lead a class discussion about *why* Americans are able to control their government. Also discuss some of the ways in which Americans control or change their government. In the discussion try to lead the pupils to an understanding of how the American belief that all men are created equal is reflected by their system of government. Ask the class: Could people have a democratic system of government if the leader of a country was believed to be a god? Why or why not?

At this point you may want to introduce the following terms.

hereditary   citadel

Developing the Lesson To develop the pupils' understanding of the need for government, first have them study the material on page 98 entitled: "The development of ancient governments." Have the pupils answer and discuss the questions in the body of the material. Then ask the class: Why do we have rules of behavior in our school? What might happen if we had no rules?

Next have the pupils study the remaining material on pages 98, 99, 100, and 101. Ask the pupils to study the map and pictures on page 99 and answer the questions in the text on that page that pertain to these illustrations. Pay particular attention to the question at the end of the second paragraph on page 99 about the use of slaves. In a class discussion try to have the class suggest ways in which Americans voluntarily work to aid their society as did the ancient Egyptians. Then have the pupils answer and discuss the questions in the body of the material on pages 100 and 101.

Concluding the Lesson Stress the fact that man's modern concept of political freedom was unknown in ancient societies. Have the class discuss why people in ancient societies were less interested in political freedom than we are today. Try to help the pupils understand that life in most ancient societies was less certain since man was at the mercy of his environment. In the discussion help the pupils to discover that ancient man's low level of technology prevented him from controlling his environment as man does today. As a result, ancient man was more concerned about maintaining peace with nature and the gods than in individual freedom.

Going Further As a class activity, have the pupils prepare a display showing how pyramids were built and what the finished pyramids looked like. Have part of the class investigate the methods, tools, and materials that ancient Egyptians used to build their pyramids. Have this group of pupils draw pictures and designs to show how the pyramids were built. (Information on these topics can be found in most encyclopedias.)

Have a second group of pupils build models of several pyramids. Combine the efforts of both groups into a display to be shown to other classes in your school.

Also have the pupils complete the first activity in "Things to Do" on page 108.

TEACHING HELPS—THE OPERATION OF ANCIENT GOVERNMENTS, pages 102–104

CONCEPTS

1. A government tends to perform functions needed by its society.
2. In most ancient political systems, governments controlled the economic activities within their societies.
3. Political power in a society may be controlled by one social class.

Recommended Procedure

Getting Started Review with the pupils the types of rulers in Sumer and Egypt. (*A god-king, called a pharaoh, ruled Egypt and a priest-king ruled Sumer.*) Also review, in a class discussion, the reasons why these rulers enjoyed such great power and why they were supported by the people. (*The people believed that if they did not support their kings they would anger the gods.*)

Developing the Lesson As they study the material in this lesson, suggest that the pupils compare how their government operates with the way governments of ancient societies operated. You may want them to make a list of differences for a discussion at the end of this lesson.

Ask the class to study the material on pages 102, 103, and 104. Have the pupils answer the questions at the end of the first paragraph on page 102. Use the annotations on that page as a basis for the discussion of these questions.

The list of Egyptian dynasties on page 103 can be used to help the pupils understand how internal struggles may cause governments to fall from power. The questions at the end of the material on page 103 deal with the list of dynasties. Have the pupils answer and discuss these questions. In the class discussion try to relate the rise and fall of Egyptian dynasties to *current* political events in some part of the world.

Concluding the Lesson Discuss how political scientists have used evidence gathered by other social scientists to determine what they think the Indus government was like. Ask the pupils to suggest some ways in which uniform systems (*such as weights, measures, and money*) indicate a strong national government in their country. Ask: Do you agree with the conclusion that the Indus civilization was ruled by a strong central government? Why?

Then have the pupils answer and discuss "Think for Yourself" on page 104.

Going Further Have the pupils draw a standard similar to the Standard of Ur on page 102. On their standard, have the pupils show some of the various functions of the President of the United States. They should include such things as chief executive officer, chief diplomat, commander in chief of the army, leader of the people, and so on. Display the completed standard on the bulletin board.

TEACHING HELPS—LAW IN ANCIENT SOCIETIES, pages 104–107

CONCEPTS

1. Rules of behavior are needed whenever people live in groups.
2. Every civilization develops laws to protect the welfare of the people.
3. Changing conditions produce new customs, traditions, and laws.

Recommended Procedure

Getting Started Read aloud to the class the first three excerpts from Hammurabi's Code on page 107. Ask the pupils if they would want to live in a society that had such laws. Discuss the reason a society might have harsh laws. (*People often hope that harsh laws will cause people to be afraid to break the law.*)

Lead a class discussion about why the vast majority of people obey laws. Try to help the class understand why obeying the law protects the welfare of the people within a society. Discuss the fact that in a free society the people have the power to change laws peacefully if they think the laws are unfair. Introduce the term *code of laws* to the class.

Developing the Lesson Introduce the idea that rules of behavior help people to live together in groups. Then have the class study the material on pages 104 and 105 up to the heading "Written laws." Have the pupils answer the questions in the body of the text. Then, through a class discussion, stress the point that customs and traditions are found whenever people live in groups. Point out that as groups of people began to form societies, customs and traditions gradually became laws.

Have the class then study the remaining material on pages 105, 106, and 107. Pay particular attention to the discussion of the Code of Hammurabi. Use the excerpts from Hammurabi's code to answer the questions on page 106 and as a springboard into a discussion about how the laws of a society reflect the values and attitudes of the people.

Concluding the Lesson Review briefly the ways laws were enforced in ancient societies. Emphasize the interrelation of religion and the laws governing a society. Conclude the lesson by having the pupils answer the "Think for Yourself" questions on page 107. Discuss the pupils' answers with the class.

Going Further Have the pupils compile a list of traffic laws that are in force in their community. List the laws on the chalkboard and have the pupils suggest reasons for each of these laws. In a class discussion bring out the fact that most laws are enforced because they benefit the people of the community.

Also have the pupils do the second "Things to Do" activity on page 108.

EVALUATION, CHAPTER 6

Have the pupils answer the following questions.

1. Why do governments tend to grow in size as a society becomes larger?
2. Why might it be difficult to control behavior in the United States through customs and traditions alone?
3. In what ways does Hammurabi's code of laws differ from the laws of the United States?

TEACHER'S PREVIEW OF CHAPTER 7, pages 109-119

Chapter 7, "Ancient Economic Systems," includes an introductory page and three teaching units:

Production (pages 110-113)
Economic Activity in Ancient Civilizations (pages 113-116)
Transportation and Communication (pages 116-118)

In this chapter the pupils are helped to understand the importance of surplus production as a basis for the growth and development of civilizations. The pupils will also discover how improvements in technology can lead to sur-

plus production, and that surplus production, in turn, can then lead to trade and an interdependence among people.

Chapter 7 is also designed to help the pupils discover and understand basic economic concepts. These concepts are explained within the context of ancient civilizations. The questions within the body of the material will enable the pupils to see and understand how these concepts were applied in the past and how these same concepts are applicable today. In this way the pupils will learn how to apply basic concepts in an analysis of a society's economic way of life.

TEACHING HELPS—Chapter Introduction, page 109

CONCEPTS

1. Every civilization must solve the basic economic questions of what will be produced, and in what way production will be distributed.
2. A society's economic system is the way in which a society goes about solving its basic economic questions.

Recommended Procedure

Getting Started Ask the pupils to imagine they were living back in the Old Stone Age. Have them describe how they would have gone about satisfying their basic need for food. Ask the pupils: In what way did the people in the Old Stone Age produce or obtain the food they needed? How do you think the food was distributed among the members of a group? Introduce the term *economic system*. Then point

out that even in the most primitive groups some type of economic system is established to meet the basic economic needs of the people.
Developing the Lesson Have the class turn to page 109 and study the picture and the material on that page. Ask the pupils to answer and discuss the questions in the body of the material. Discuss how modern man's improved technology has changed the way goods are produced and distributed.
Concluding the Lesson Bring this lesson to a close by having the pupils do the "Just For Fun" activity at the bottom of page 109.
Going Further Have the class find pictures showing how man's means of distributing goods have changed since 1900. These pictures should show the development and/or changes in railroads, trucks, airplanes, ships, pipelines, and other means used to transport and distribute the goods people produce.

TEACHING HELPS—PRODUCTION, pages 110-113

CONCEPTS

1. The surplus production of agricultural products was the basis for every ancient civilization.
2. Improved technology usually leads to increased production.
3. Surplus production often leads to trade among people.
4. Trade and increased production normally lead to increased specialization and interdependence.

Recommended Procedure

Getting Started Ask the class to imagine that they are the entire population of an ancient farming village. The pupils are to assume that for the last several years, each of them has been a farmer. The result of their labor has been a continually growing surplus of crops which they have stored. They are now faced with deciding what they will do in the future. They should suggest plans that will answer the following questions.

1. What should they do with their surplus crops they are unable to use?
2. Should all of the members of the community continue to work as farmers?
3. How should they obtain the additional goods—such as tools, pots, and so on—they need?

Discuss the suggestions put forward by the pupils. Ask them to keep their suggestions in mind as they study this lesson.

At this point you may want to introduce the following terms.

surplus	technology
wealth	interdependence
economic surplus	specialization

Developing the Lesson Have the pupils study the material on pages 110, 111, and 112 up to "Interdependence and the specialization of labor." Ask the pupils to answer the questions in the body of the material. Discuss these answers with the members of the class.

Then have the class read the remaining material in this lesson on pages 112 and 113. In a class discussion try to lead the pupils to an understanding of *interdependence* and *specialization*. Stress the point that people in most modern industrial societies rarely produce an entire item, but instead they usually produce only a part of a product. As a result, people today are highly specialized in their jobs and are also interdependent.

Concluding the Lesson Have the pupils answer the "Think for Yourself" question on page 113. In a class discussion challenge the class to suggest other ways in which man has managed to provide a better economic way of life for his society. (*Typical answers could include such things as improved technology which improves quality and lowers prices, labor-saving machines, better transportation facilities, the use of money, and so on.*)

Going Further Have a group of five pupils assemble five sheets of paper, print their school name on each sheet of paper, staple the five sheets together, and then stack the stapled sheets in one stack. Have each pupil do the entire job from beginning to end. Ask the class to time the operation.

Then ask the class to suggest faster ways of doing the job. One or more members will probably suggest that each pupil do only one of the tasks and in this way establish an assembly line where each pupil specializes in one job. Time the assembly-line operation—it should be faster. Discuss what specialization does for production.

TEACHING HELPS—ECONOMIC ACTIVITY IN ANCIENT CIVILIZATIONS, pages 113–116

CONCEPTS

1. A society's economic system may be influenced by geographic conditions.
2. Economic systems may be controlled by governments.
3. A stable government is needed for rapid economic growth.

Recommended Procedure

Getting Started For the purpose of a class discussion, ask the pupils to imagine that they have to set up an economic system for the imaginary country of Ore. The following conditions of their nation—which should be read aloud—are:

1. Limited fertile land, and a cool rainy climate.
2. Huge deposits of copper, gold, and iron ores.
3. A rapidly growing population which is in need of food.
4. Almost all the people are farmers.
5. The country has friendly relations with the nation of Pewter which produces surplus crops and has skilled metalworkers, but is short of natural resources.

Ask the pupils: (1) Do you recommend that the people of Ore specialize in certain jobs, and if so, what jobs? (2) Do you recommend that the people of Ore trade with the people of Pewter, and if so, what should they export? (3) What goods or products should Ore import, and why? (4) Why will trade between Ore and Pewter lead to an interdependence of the people and a better way of life for the people of the two countries? After the pupils have answered these questions, lead a class discussion about why trade can improve man's way of life. (*For example, trade can help man obtain needed goods, and trade and specialization can increase production.*)

Developing the Lesson Have the class study the material on pages 113, 114, 115, and the top of page 116. Stress how the Sumerians developed an economic system which helped them to adjust to their environment. (*They were short of natural resources but had surplus crops.*) Ask the pupils to explain how the Sumerian economic system was influenced by the social and political nature of the society.

In a class discussion try to lead the pupils to an understanding of why the Egyptian economic system developed as it did. (The annotations on page 103 will be helpful in guiding this discussion.) Then discuss the Indus economy with the pupils. Use the picture at the top of page 115 and the questions in the body of the material on page 115 as the bases for the discussion.

Concluding the Lesson Ask the class to answer the question in the annotations at the top of page 116 which is denoted by an asterisk. Discuss the pupils' answers. Conclude this lesson with "Think for Yourself" on page 116.

Going Further Have the pupils complete the first and the third "Things to Do" activities on page 119.

Another interesting class activity would be to have the pupils collect advertisements of items imported by this country. (Advertisements of imported automobiles can be easily found in many magazines.)

Analyze these advertisements in class. Discuss prices of imported products and what P.O.E. (*port of entry*) means. Ask: Why are prices of imported products lower at the *port of entry* than they are away from the port?

CONCEPTS

1. Cultural diffusion encourages the growth of civilizations.
2. Trade and communication among people increase cultural diffusion.
3. The acceptance, or use, of technological achievements may vary from society to society depending upon local conditions and the nature of the society.

Recommended Procedure

Getting Started Have the class turn to page 118 and study the picture showing Egyptian hieroglyphics at the lower left-hand corner of that page. Tell the class that the Egyptians used symbols for consonant sounds to form words. Ask the pupils to identify some of the symbols shown in the picture. (*Birds and snakes are easily identified*.) Other symbols are circled in your teacher's edition. For example, in the upper left corner of the picture, the symbol for face is circled. In ancient Egypt this symbol usually represented an *hr* sound. At the lower right corner of the picture, the symbol for mouth is circled. This symbol usually represented an *r* sound.

After the class has studied the picture of hieroglyphics, ask the pupils to suggest some of the difficulties this type of writing would cause. Lead a class discussion about how our writing differs from the Egyptian hieroglyphics.

Developing the Lesson Ask the pupils to study the material on pages 116, 117, and 118. Discuss the importance of the wheel to man's capability to transport goods. Ask the pupils: In what way could you get goods to your community if the wheel had not been invented?

Have the pupils study the picture at the bottom of page 116. Stress that the Sumerians made their wheels out of solid wood. In a class discussion help the class to understand how man has improved upon the first wheel.

Then have the class study the map on page 117. Ask them to answer the questions in the material entitled "Water transportation." Discuss the answers with the class. Stress how important water transportation was for hauling heavy loads.

Concluding the Lesson Ask the class to suggest some reasons why, when the idea of writing spread from the Sumerians to other people, the Sumerian style of writing was not adopted. Stress the fact that cultural diffusion does not mean that each society will adopt new ideas without modification. Ask the pupils if they can think of something that was first developed in the United States and later modified by other people. (*For example, our presidential system of government has been adopted and modified in some Latin-American countries to fit their beliefs, values, customs, and ideas.*)

End the lesson with the "Think for Yourself" question on page 118.

Going Further Have the pupils complete the second "Things to Do" activity on page 119.

EVALUATION, CHAPTER 7

Have the pupils list the achievements of man's first civilizations discussed in Chapter 7. Ask the pupils to speculate what life would be like if these achievements were unknown.

CONCLUDING THE UNIT

Discuss Part 4 of the class project on page 119. If necessary help the class to develop additional conclusions and concepts about ancient civilizations. Discuss how these conclusions and concepts could be applied to civilizations today. Ask the pupils: In what ways does a study of ancient civilizations help us to understand the way man lives today?

TEACHER'S PREVIEW OF UNIT 4, pages 122-173

This unit is divided into three chapters: 8. Eastern and Western Societies, pages 125-140; 9. Eastern and Western Governments, pages 141-156; and 10. Eastern and Western Economies, pages 157-171. A special feature is a four-part class project, introduced at the beginning of the unit on page 124. Suggestions for carrying out subsequent parts of the class project are given on pages 140, 156, and 171. Other activities called *Things to Do* are also given on pages 140, 156, and 171. The unit concludes with two pages of evaluation, *Checkup Time* (p. 172) and *Test Yourself* (p. 173).

This unit helps the pupils to understand the social, political, and economic developments that occurred in four societies that were flourishing between 1500 B.C. and A.D. 500. Two Eastern societies, those of India and China, will be studied along with two Western societies, those of Greece and Rome.

Unit 4 helps pupils to understand why these four societies developed in somewhat different ways and how the four societies were similar.

The pupils learn some of the factors that shaped the way people thought. The social structure that was established in each society depended on the people's views of what was important in their society.

Pupils also learn how the people of these societies developed governments that would enable them to better meet their needs and satisfy their wants. Pupils learn the economic systems that each society established, and why each was established.

TEACHING HELPS—Unit Introduction, pages 122-124

CONCEPTS

1. Geographical expressions may have different meanings for various social scientists.
2. Knowledge of other countries can come about through trade and exploration.

Recommended Procedure

Getting Started Ask the pupils how a country is able to learn more about another country in the world today. (*from newspapers, magazines, television, and so on*) Have them speculate as to how countries in one part of the world were able to learn about other countries before such developments as printing and television. (*exploration, trade*)

Developing the Lesson Have the pupils study the first two paragraphs on page 123 to find out some of the different meanings that can be applied to the terms East and West. Emphasize the fact that the terms Eastern civilization and Western civilization as used in this unit have the meanings ascribed to them by the Europeans of the time period between 1500 B.C. and A.D. 500.

Have the pupils study the third paragraph to discover how the meanings of the terms East, Eastern, West, and Western are used today.

Concluding the Lesson Review the use of the terms East and West, and how their meanings have changed. Take time to read the last two questions on page 123 aloud. Have the pupils speculate as to reasons why there were both similarities and differences among the civilizations.

Allow time for the pupils to read and begin Part 1 of the class project which appears on page 124.

Going Further Suggest that the pupils draw maps which show how much of the world was known in 500 B.C., A.D. 100, and A.D. 500. World history books and historical atlases can be used to obtain this information. These maps may be displayed on the bulletin board.

TEACHER'S PREVIEW OF CHAPTER 8, pages 125-140

Chapter 8, "Eastern and Western Societies," includes an introductory page and four teaching units:

The Closed Society of India (pages 126-128)

The Traditional Society of China (pages 129-131)

The Greek Way of Life (pages 132-136)

The Roman Way of Life (pages 136-139)

This chapter helps the pupils to understand some of the reasons why certain societies have changed very little over the years while other societies have changed greatly. Pupils learn of the beliefs and the ways of life that have shaped these societies.

The differences and similarities among selected societies of the East—India and China—and selected societies of the West—Greece and Rome—are explored.

TEACHING HELPS—Chapter Introduction, page 125

CONCEPTS

1. Societies develop and change at different rates of speed.
2. Some societies have shown very little change.

Recommended Procedure

Getting Started Show the class several historical pictures which include earlier modes of transportation, earlier styles of clothing, earlier types of homes, and so on. Ask the pupils how it would be possible to judge the date of each picture. Note that at this time the pupils are not being asked to give a date for each picture, but rather to decide what elements in each picture could be used to supply a date.

Have the pupils study the picture on page 125. Ask them to determine what elements in the picture could be used to indicate a date. Lead the pupils to the understanding that the style of clothing worn by the people and the type of oxcart in the background could indicate a scene from many years ago or a recent scene because the people in this society have not changed their way of living very much.

Developing the Lesson Have the pupils study page 125 to discover some of the questions social scientists might ask when studying societies that have remained relatively unchanged and those that have changed greatly.

After discussion have the pupils suggest answers to the questions that are on the page. Perhaps a list could be kept of the pupils' suggested answers. The list could be referred to and modified when the chapter has been completed.

Concluding the Lesson Encourage the class to do the "Just For Fun" activity. A display for the bulletin board can be made with the pictures that the pupils are able to find.

Going Further To expand upon the display for the bulletin board, have the pupils search for pictures that show the impact of the West upon the East and vice versa. For example, pupils may be able to find pictures of an Indian farmer with a modern tractor; or pictures of buildings in Europe or the United States which show an Oriental influence.

CONCEPTS

1. Societies that have a rigid social structure tend to develop obedient members.
2. Invasions produce many changes in societies.
3. When two groups live close together their cultures often blend and form a new culture.

Recommended Procedure

Getting Started Have the pupils speculate as to what happens to the culture of a group of people that is conquered by a stronger group of people. Ask such questions as these.

1. What ways might the conquerers use to keep the conquered people under control?
2. What might happen to the culture of the conquered people if the conquerors decided to rule very harshly?
3. What might happen if the conquerors allowed the conquered people to keep many of their own ways of life?

Lead the pupils to the understanding that both the conquerors and the conquered change their ways of life as a result of invasions.

You might introduce at this time the new terms that are used in this lesson.

caste	untouchables
closed society	ostracism
joint family	reincarnation

Developing the Lesson Have the pupils study "A closed society," answering the questions in the text as they study. Point out that a closed society develops certain techniques to keep itself "closed." For example, it closely regulates the activities of its members. Ask the pupils to tell why such regulations are an absolute necessity.

Have the pupils study "The Hindu family" to find out the meaning of the term *joint family*. Ask why a joint family was a good type of organization for a closed society. (*Family pressure could be applied to family members*.)

Have the pupils study "Invasion of India." Ask: Why did the Aryans not mingle with the Dravidians? After discussion have the pupils study "The caste system" to find out (1) why the caste system was established by the Aryans and (2) how people were limited by the caste system. Review the idea that one of the methods people use to keep a society from changing is to establish a caste system. Ask the pupils to speculate on the probable effects a breakdown in the caste system would have on a closed society. Ask the pupils to speculate as to why the order of importance of the classes shifted from warriors to priests. (*After the invasions, warriors were no longer the most important members of society*.)

Have the pupils study "Power of the caste" to discover how the caste was able to keep its members under control. Emphasize the idea that a closed society needs powerful methods to prevent the collapse of its caste system. After discussion have the pupils study "Growth of Hinduism" to learn of another method used by a closed society to maintain itself with relatively little change. Have the pupils speculate as to why Hinduism proved so effective in maintaining a closed society.

Concluding the Lesson Review with the pupils the factors that have maintained the closed society of India, (*joint family, caste system, and Hinduism*), and why each factor worked as effectively as it did.

Allow time for the pupils to answer the "Think for Yourself" question on page 128. Encourage the pupils to do the second activity of the "Things to Do" on page 140.

Going Further Divide the class into four groups. Have one group represent the Aryans, one group represent the Dravidians, one group represent a joint family, and one group represent the untouchables. Have the class make up questions to ask the members of these groups. Have a panel discussion in which members of these groups would answer the questions.

TEACHING HELPS—THE TRADITIONAL SOCIETY OF CHINA, pages 129-131

CONCEPTS

1. Traditional societies are based on customs and traditions of the past.
2. Strong family ties tend to maintain a traditional society.
3. Education which stresses earlier customs tends to maintain a traditional society.

Recommended Procedure

Getting Started To spark interest in the lesson, you might have the pupils discuss what the Chinese scholar Confucius meant by these excerpts from his writings.

If a man take no thought about what is distant, he will find sorrow near at hand.

Recompense injury with justice, and recompense kindness with kindness.

When we see men of worth, we should think of equaling them; when we see men of contrary character, we should turn inwards and examine ourselves.

Through the discussion lead pupils to the understanding that these ideas helped shape the customs and traditions of the Chinese people.

Developing the Lesson Have the pupils study "A traditional society" on page 129 to discover what a traditional society is. In discussion point out the fact that a traditional society operates as a closed society and needs specific methods to maintain itself. Have the pupils suggest some of these methods. A quick scanning of pages 129-131 will give them some ideas to present. (*strong family units, religion, social classes, education*)

Then have the pupils study "Family life" on pages 129 and 130. Have the pupils tell why that type of family organization was a good type for a society that wanted to maintain itself unchanged for a long period of time.

Have the pupils study the remaining paragraphs on page 130 to discover (1) why ancestor worship was so important to the Chinese and (2) why the social classes in Chinese society were not as rigid as in some other societies. In discussion review the kinds of things societies can do to teach their beliefs and customs to their members and what the societies can do to ensure that everyone observes the customs.

Have the pupils study page 131 and answer the questions on that page. Lead the pupils to the understanding that education which places its emphasis on the customs and traditions of the past will tend to produce people who act little differently from their ancestors. Also help the pupils realize that the teachings of Confucius on the five basic relationships, if followed, would tend to produce a very stable society.

Concluding the Lesson Review those factors which helped to maintain a traditional society in China. (*strong family ties, education based on customs of the past, and Confucianism*) Allow time for the pupils to discuss the "Think for Yourself" question on page 131.

Going Further The pupils might be interested in finding information on the Chinese in the United States. Pupils could prepare brief reports to share with the class on when the Chinese came to the United States, the reasons why they came, where they settled, and the role of the Chinese family associations.

TEACHING HELPS—THE GREEK WAY OF LIFE, pages 132-136

CONCEPTS

1. Different ways of life develop as cities isolate themselves.
2. Contradictions in a society often exist.
3. A militaristic state often stifles the creative instincts of its citizens.

Recommended Procedure

Getting Started Ask the pupils to speculate as to what would happen if each of the communities located around them were to set up its own social system, its own economic system, and an independent government. Have pupils point out the problems that would have to be solved by the planners of the systems. Ask the pupils to speculate as to what problems would arise as communities tried to expand beyond fixed borders. Lead them to the understanding that communities would eventually begin to work together. The alternative would be disastrous to one or more of the communities.

Developing the Lesson Have the pupils study page 132 to "Athens," answering the questions as they study. Point out the part geography plays in determining the size of communities.

Then have the pupils study "Athens" on page 132 and "Social classes" on pages 133 and 134, answering the questions as they study. Emphasize the idea that the people of Athens developed a very successful civilization. Have the pupils suggest some of the things the Athenians probably did to maintain their civilization. Ask the pupils how some Athenians felt they could justify slavery while promoting political freedom.

Next have the pupils study "Life in Athens" and "Greek art" on pages 134 and 135 to find answers to questions such as these.

1. What was the role of each member in an Athenian family? How were members prepared for their role?
2. How were the boys and the girls educated in Athens? Why were they educated as they were?
3. What artistic works of the Greeks are still enjoyed today? What do these works tell us about the success of the Athenian civilization?

Ask the pupils to compare education as it existed in India, in China, and in Athens. Then have them decide how American education is similar to and how it is different from Athenian education.

Have pupils study the rest of page 135 and page 136 to find out the methods used by the Spartans in maintaining their civilization. In discussion stress the idea that it was very important to the Spartans to train people to be warlike. Have the pupils review the kinds of things a society can do to help it be successful in war.

Concluding the Lesson Review with the pupils the social structure of Athens as compared with the social structure of Sparta. Discuss the differences in the educational systems that existed in the two city-states. Stress the idea that societies develop educational systems designed to train people to help maintain their society. Ask the pupils to suggest ways that our educational system does this.

Allow time for the pupils to discuss the "Think for Yourself" question on page 136.

Going Further The pupils might be interested in finding information on American citizenship. Brief reports could be shared with the class on such topics as how people become American citizens, the rights of naturalized Americans, and how citizenship can be lost.

TEACHING HELPS—THE ROMAN WAY OF LIFE, pages 136–139

CONCEPTS

1. When one country controls many different areas, the people of all areas learn from one another.
2. Governments often repress that which they feel poses a threat.
3. The greater the area that is controlled, the greater need there is for governmental services to be provided.

Recommended Procedure

Getting Started Ask the pupils what services have been provided for the people of their community by local, state, and federal governments. Among the services mentioned should be schools, parks, highways, sanitation facilities, and so on. Lead pupils to the understanding that the larger the area that is governed, the greater need there is for these services.

Developing the Lesson Have pupils study "A great empire" on pages 136 and 137 to discover the amount of land controlled by the Roman Empire at its peak. Have them answer the questions in the text as they study. Lead pupils to an understanding of the cultural exchange that took place among the people of Rome and the people of the conquered areas. Stress the idea that the Romans, as well as the people they conquered, changed as the people and the cultures interacted.

After discussion have the pupils study "Social classes" and "Family life," answering the questions in the text as they study. In discussion stress the idea that people in various social classes, especially those in the higher classes, often have status symbols that set them apart. Also emphasize the fact that family life in most societies is designed to help people fit well into their societies.

Have the pupils study "Religion in Rome" and "A new religion." Review the fact that religion plays an important role in helping produce people who want to maintain the beliefs and customs of their society. Challenge the pupils to offer reasons to explain why the early Romans worshiped as they did and why the Romans feared the spread of certain religions.

After discussion have the pupils study "Roman achievements" and "Breakdown of the empire" to find out what needed services the Roman Empire provided for its citizens and how they were provided. Ask pupils why the use of one language was so essential for the Roman Empire. Emphasize the fact that despite the breakdown of the Roman Empire, it greatly affected later civilizations.

Concluding the Lesson Review with the pupils the ways in which Roman society differed from other societies that have been studied. Stress the many achievements of the Roman Empire in providing a better life for its citizens. Also help the pupils realize that not everyone was well treated by the Romans, for example, the slaves, the Jews, and the Christians.

Allow time for the pupils to discuss the "Think for Yourself" question on page 139.

Going Further Encourage the pupils to work on the first activity of the "Things to Do" on page 140. The pupils may use the materials to find information on some aspect of Roman life that interests them. Some pupils may draw scenes depicting Roman life. Others may build models of aqueducts. Some pupils could find information on Roman gods and goddesses.

EVALUATION, CHAPTER 8

Have the pupils respond to questions such as the following.

1. What are some factors that can cause a society to change?
2. In what ways does education shape a society's views?
3. Why do societies establish social systems?

TEACHER'S PREVIEW OF CHAPTER 9, pages 141-156

Chapter 9, "Eastern and Western Governments," contains an introductory page and three teaching units:

Government and the People (pages 142-146)

Government and Strong Leaders (pages 146-149)

Government in Action (pages 150-155)

This chapter helps pupils understand the role people in the societies of India, China, Greece, and Rome played in their governments.

The role of citizens in their local governments is studied along with their participation in their country's government. Pupils learn the differences between a direct democracy and a republican form of government.

Pupils also learn how and why strong leaders were able to rise to power. The various types of central governments that were established in the four societies are studied. Pupils will learn how these societies handled the problem of ruling large areas. The role of government officials is also studied.

TEACHING HELPS—Chapter Introduction, page 141

CONCEPTS

1. Different societies allow differing amounts of power to the people.
2. Larger communities need more complex political systems than do smaller communities.

Recommended Procedure

Getting Started Ask the pupils how power is divided in their school. Have them determine who has the power to make major decisions for the school. If your school has a student council, have the pupils find out what role the council plays in the decisions made for the school.

If your school does not have a student council, it might be interesting to ask the pupils to decide how much power such a group should have.

Developing the Lesson Have the pupils study the first paragraph on page 141 to discover whether or not people in different societies held differing amounts of power. Point out to the

pupils that this was true during the period from 1500 B.C. to A.D. 500 and is equally true today. In some totalitarian societies people have little say in their government. Most decisions are made by the leaders.

After discussion have the pupils study the second paragraph to find out what happens to political systems as communities grow larger. Lead the pupils to the understanding that in many cases the basic form of government will remain the same but the powers and responsibilities will be shifted.

Concluding the Lesson Review with the pupils the idea that the amount of power held by the people differed in various societies. Review also the idea that more complex political systems developed as communities grew larger.

Going Further Encourage the class to do the "Just For Fun" activity. Pupils may be interested in finding further information on how their community was governed, who some of the early leaders were, and if any of the early government buildings are still being used. Have pupils share their findings with the class.

TEACHING HELPS—GOVERNMENT AND THE PEOPLE, pages 142-146

CONCEPTS

1. Small communities develop methods of handling their local problems.
2. In some societies citizens are directly involved in making the laws.
3. In some societies citizens are indirectly involved in making the laws.

Recommended Procedure

Getting Started Ask the pupils to speculate as to what could happen if the laws of their community were not written down and publicized. Lead pupils to the understanding that a code of laws to which all people have access is necessary as communities grow larger and the number of laws increases. To ensure justice, laws must be made known to all members of the community.

You might wish to introduce the new terms that are found in this teaching unit.

panchayat   direct democracy   republic

Developing the Lesson Have the pupils study pages 142 and 143 up to "Athens" and answer the questions in the text. Emphasize the idea that small communities found councils of citizens selected by the villagers to be effective for governing on a local level. Point out that the panchayat shown on page 143 has a woman presiding. In many societies women were long denied the political rights that men had. The villages of India were an exception.

Lead pupils to the understanding that the methods of selection of officials in Chinese villages would only work in small communities. Also point out that the closeness among the villagers made possible volunteer groups that carried out solutions to many of the problems of the village.

Then have the pupils study the remainder of page 143 and page 144 and answer the questions in the text. Emphasize the fact that the citizens of Athens had the right to take a direct part in their government. This right was limited to free, male citizens. Point out that all societies place limitations on who may participate in the political activity of the community. Emphasize the fact that societies develop methods to preserve their political systems. Banishment was used by the citizens of Athens. Have the pupils suggest other methods which a society could use.

Then have the pupils study page 145 and page 146 up to "Government and Strong Leaders" and answer the questions in the text. Emphasize the fact that some societies establish a political system which enables people to take an indirect part in their government by electing representatives. Point out that as the Roman Empire grew in size and population, it became more difficult to have citizen participation in the government. Point out that the laws were posted for all people to read. Ask pupils to decide why this was necessary.

Concluding the Lesson Review with the pupils the roles that citizens are able to play in their political systems. Discuss the difference between a direct democracy and a republic. Then have the pupils discuss the "Think for Yourself" questions on page 146.

Going Further Have the pupils work on the third activity of "Things to Do" on page 156. After the class has established and posted the rules, have the pupils elect several representatives to act as a panchayat for the class. Have the class suggest several possible new rules. Have one suggestion treated by the panchayat and another suggestion discussed and voted on by the entire class. Have the class decide what advantages and disadvantages there were in both methods.

TEACHING HELPS—GOVERNMENT AND STRONG LEADERS, pages 146–149

CONCEPTS

1. Powerful leaders may develop as societies become more complex.
2. As strong leaders gain control, the people may lose power.
3. The role of the leader varies from one society to another.

Recommended Procedure

Getting Started Have the pupils speculate as to the changes which might take place in a society if a strong leader gained control. Ask such questions as these.

1. What conditions might make it possible for a strong leader to rise to power in a country?
2. What effects might strong leaders have on the powers and rights of citizens?
3. What are some of the advantages and disadvantages of having a strong leader?

Developing the Lesson Have the pupils study pages 146 and 147 and answer the questions in the text. Emphasize the unity and strength that a powerful leader was able to bring to Indian society. Have the pupils study the excerpts from "Ramayana" on page 147 to discover how the people of India viewed the importance of having a strong leader. Point out to the pupils that this view indicates that the people felt that a strong leader was an absolute necessity to maintain a stable society.

Then have the pupils study page 148 up to "Athens" to discover how the people of another traditional society, that of China, viewed the role of the leader. Emphasize the fact that the teachings of Confucius which stressed loyalty and obedience would help to shape a stable society. Also point out that the idea of the Mandate of Heaven indicated the great respect that was due the leader. However, the idea of blaming the leader for natural calamities often led to many problems in the society.

Have the pupils study "Athens" and "Two Athenian leaders" to find out how the people of the more democratic society of Athens viewed the role of the leader. Then have the pupils study the remainder of page 149 to discover how strong leaders rose to power in Rome. Point out some of the ways that people lose power. Emphasize that as the Roman Empire increased in size, a new form of government was needed. The political system that was established worked well for the empire providing a 200-year period of relative peace.

Concluding the Lesson Review with the pupils the reasons for the development of strong leaders in a society, and the way the people of each of the four societies viewed the role of its leader.

Allow time for the class to discuss the "Think for Yourself" question on page 149. Encourage the pupils to do the second "Things to Do" activity on page 156.

Going Further The pupils might be interested in finding more information about how some of the leaders studied in this lesson managed to rise to power and to maintain their power. Brief reports could be prepared and given to the class.

TEACHING HELPS—GOVERNMENT IN ACTION, pages 150-155

CONCEPTS

1. Strong central governments often arose as countries increased in size.
2. Large governments need many people to do the work of government.
3. Many societies establish a written code of laws for themselves.

Recommended Procedure

Getting Started . Ask the pupils to suggest possible ways that government officials might get their jobs. (*by election, appointment, examination, or heredity*) Have pupils discuss the possible advantages and disadvantages of each method by which government officials receive their power.

Developing the Lesson Have the pupils study page 150 up to "China." Emphasize the fact that a large central government, if run efficiently, is able to provide many needed services for the people.

Then have the pupils study "China" and answer the questions in the text. Lead the pupils to the understanding that in order to govern a large area, many people are needed to carry out the work of government. This tends to produce a bureaucracy. Refer again to the discussion about the various ways by which officials can obtain jobs. Ask the pupils to decide which methods are likely to be better for selecting the most qualified people.

Have the pupils study "Han Dynasty" to discover how one society, China, selected its officials. Emphasize that the use of examinations based on the teachings of Confucius would tend to maintain a traditional society.

Have the pupils study pages 153 and 154 up to "Rome" and answer the questions in the text. Point out that a central government did not develop among the city-states of Greece until it was imposed on them by an outside force.

Point out the failure of Spartan rule of Athens. Have the pupils speculate as to how the Spartans would have reacted to Athenian rule. Ask: What problems would the Spartans have had changing from a government-controlled society to a democratic society?

Have the pupils study the remainder of page 154 and page 155 and answer the questions in the text. Emphasize the fact that if a larger area were to be controlled a more elaborate form of government had to be set up. Point out the emphasis that the people placed on a written code of laws.

Concluding the Lesson Review with the pupils the types of central governments that were established by the four societies. Compare and contrast the ways they operated.

Allow time for the pupils to discuss the "Think for Yourself" questions on page 155. Encourage the pupils to work on the first "Things to Do" activity on page 156. Provide time for the class to read and complete Part 3 of the class project.

Going Further Have the pupils find out if your school has a handbook of school rules or a "code of laws." If not, have the pupils work on developing one that will include the rules they know exist in their school. If your school has such a handbook, the pupils could develop a "code" that contains the rules that they follow in their classroom.

EVALUATION, CHAPTER 9

Have a class discussion of questions such as these.

1. How may the power of the people vary from one society to another?
2. What are some reasons why a strong leader may rise to power?
3. What are some of the advantages and disadvantages of a strong central government?

TEACHER'S PREVIEW OF CHAPTER 10, pages 157–171

Chapter 10, "Eastern and Western Economies," consists of an introductory page and three teaching units:

The Land and Its Use (pages 158-162)

Producers of Goods and Raw Materials (pages 162-166)

Trade and Commerce (pages 167-170)

In this chapter the pupils will learn how the land affected economic activity in Europe and Asia prior to A.D. 500. The material in the first teaching unit will help the pupils dis-cover how people in India, China, Greece, and Rome learned to develop ways to effectively produce goods they needed.

The next two teaching units of Chapter 10 help the pupils understand how goods were produced and how they were distributed among people within each society. Special emphasis is given to the development of new ways of life in Europe and Asia which will en-able the pupils to understand the importance of trade in the growth of man's way of life.

TEACHING HELPS—Chapter Introduction, page 157

CONCEPTS

1. Every society develops an economic system for the production and distri-bution of goods.
2. All societies must meet the economic needs of the people.

Recommended Procedure

Getting Started Have the pupils locate Israel on a map in the classroom. Ask the pupils to suggest the type of climate Israel probably has. (*The area is hot and dry.*) Have the pu-pils then study the picture on page 157. Point out that the picture shows an Israeli ship being loaded with goods for other coun-tries. See if the pupils can tell what is being loaded onto the ship. (*Oranges raised near Tel Aviv are being put aboard the ship.*) Dis-cuss why a nation such as Israel needs to trade with other nations. Ask: Why may trade with other nations benefit a society?

Developing the Lesson Have the pupils study the material on page 157. Ask the pupils to answer and discuss the questions in the body of the material. Stress that some trade exists in every society, and that as a society in-creases its production, trade with other so-cieties often increases.

Concluding the Lesson To help the pupils understand how many different economic ac-tivities may occur in a society, have them complete the "Just For Fun" activity on page 157.

Going Further Have the class use the list of economic activities prepared for the "Just For Fun" activity and try to determine (1) when the economic activity was initiated in their town and (2) who was responsible for initiat-ing the activity. You may wish to have the class divide into groups, assigning each group a different economic activity to research. En-courage the groups to find evidence to sub-stantiate their various findings. Give each group an opportunity to report to the class.

TEACHING HELPS—THE LAND AND ITS USE, pages 158–162

CONCEPTS

1. Geographic factors usually influence the economic activity of a people.
2. Technology helps man to meet the challenges of his environment.
3. Changes in economic activities and in economic conditions may cause social changes.

Recommended Procedure

Getting Started Have the pupils imagine that they are living in the nation of Yap. Write the following information about Yap on the chalkboard for the pupils to study.

1. Estimated population in 1970—about 750,000,000 people.
2. Land area—about 360,000 square miles.
3. Primary economic activity—farming for about 80 per cent of the people.

Inform the class that Yap has always faced a serious problem in providing enough food for the people since only about *11 per cent* of the land in Yap is suitable for farming. Also point out that the population of Yap is increasing by about 10,000,000 people a year.

Have the pupils suggest some of the problems facing Yap in the future. Also ask the pupils to suggest what the people of Yap might do to solve these problems. Then point out that the facts listed are for Communist China and that the figures illustrate the economic problems that China has faced for nearly 2,000 years.

Developing the Lesson Have the pupils study the material about land use in India and China on pages 158, 159, and 160. Stress the use of maps as a means of understanding how geography and economics are interrelated.

Have the pupils study the maps on pages 158 and 159. Ask them to answer and discuss the questions on pages 158 and 159 which pertain to the maps. Explain how mountain ranges tend to affect rainfall. Then ask the pupils to explain why age-old farming traditions may limit the production of surplus crops. (*Usually, people in traditional societies are reluctant to adopt new tools and techniques which would produce more crops.*)

Have the pupils study the remaining material on pages 160, 161, and 162 which discusses land use in Greece and Rome. In a class discussion have the class compare the geographic problems of India, China, Greece, and Rome. Then ask the pupils to explain how each country's solution to its problems was different. Ask: Why do nations tend to solve some of their problems in different ways? (*A typical answer might be that nations often have different values, beliefs, customs, and traditions.*)

Concluding the Lesson End this lesson with a discussion of the question in the annotations marked with an asterisk. Also have the pupils answer and discuss the "Think for Yourself" question on page 162.

Going Further The two activities in "Things to Do" on page 171 can be used with this lesson. Divide your class into two groups and assign one of the activities to each group.

TEACHING HELPS—PRODUCERS OF GOODS AND RAW MATERIALS,
pages 162–166

CONCEPTS

1. The use of metal led to the development of skilled craftsmen in many societies.
2. Political and economic activities of nations are often interrelated.
3. Specialization of labor occurred in many societies before A.D. 500.

Recommended Procedure

Getting Started Explain that craftsmen in India formed groups called *guilds*. Also explain that a guild established standards for the products made by the members of each guild. (For example, members of a potters' guild might be required to produce pots made with a certain quality of material and workmanship.)

Now ask the class to select a product that is produced in our country today. Have the pupils imagine they are members of a guild which establishes the standards for this product. Ask the class: What standards would you require each product to meet? Why?

List the suggestions on the chalkboard. Have the class discuss the practicality of the standards they have suggested.

Developing the Lesson Have the pupils study the material on pages 162, 163, and 164 up to the heading, "Workers of Greece and the Roman Empire." Ask the pupils to study the material about the production of goods in India and China and have them answer the questions in the body of the material. Stress the fact that some of the economic activity in both India and China operated under government control. Ask the pupils to identify the industries that were controlled by the government of India and to explain why the government decided to control these industries. Ask the same questions about the government's actions in China. Emphasize the effect a limited supply of silk had upon the price of silk. You may also want to explain at this point how supply and demand affect prices.

Then have the pupils study the remainder of the material in this lesson on pages 164, 165, and 166. Emphasize how social attitudes toward work in Greece resulted in the use of slaves. Ask: Why was slave labor not important, or used very much, in India and China?

Concluding the Lesson Have the pupils answer the "Think for Yourself" questions on page 166. Then ask the class the question in the annotations on page 166 which is marked with an asterisk. Through a class discussion explore the effects slavery has upon a society. Encourage the pupils to suggest reasons why slavery has been condemned by social scientists today.

Going Further You might have the class divide itself into groups of five or six pupils to do some role-playing. One group may role play a day in the life of some craftsmen in India. Another group may role play a day in the life of some Chinese craftsmen, and so on. Much of the information needed in acting out the parts can be obtained by studying the text, but encourage the pupils to do outside research in order to make their presentations more interesting.

TEACHING HELPS—TRADE AND COMMERCE, pages 167–170

CONCEPTS

1. To some extent, trade exists in every society.
2. An accepted medium of exchange— money—may allow trade between societies to operate more efficiently.
3. Trade may lead to territorial expansion.

Recommended Procedure

Getting Started Have the pupils turn to page 169 and study both of the maps on that page. Based on the two maps, ask the class to suggest what different groups of people had trade contacts with the Greeks through the Greek colonies. Also ask the pupils to suggest other areas they would have colonized if they were Greeks living 3,000 years ago. Have the pupils explain why they would locate additional Greek colonies where they have suggested. Then ask: Why do you think the Greeks did not establish colonies in other locations? (*Limited means of transportation and communication are possible answers.*)

Developing the Lesson Have the pupils study the material on pages 167, 168, 169, and 170 to discover how trade affected the people in various societies in the ancient world. Stress that some trade exists within every society. Also stress the idea that extensive trade within and among countries depends, to some extent, upon transportation and communication.

Review the nature of a barter system with the class. Then direct the pupils' attention to the pictures of ancient money on page 168. Have them compare the money in the pictures with the money used in our country. Ask: What improvements have been made in the nature of money since ancient times?

Next have the pupils study the maps on page 169. Discuss the questions in the body of the text on pages 168 and 169 that pertain to these maps.

Concluding the Lesson Lead a class discussion about how the Roman Empire was supported by the production of its provinces. Ask the class to suggest why very few nations today rely upon colonies or provinces to support their empires. (*Most former colonies are now free and independent nations, thus most modern nations must rely upon trade among themselves for goods they need.*)

End the lesson by having the class answer and discuss "Think for Yourself" on page 170.

Going Further Have the class gather pictures of various types of money that are used today and that were used in the past. These pictures should be arranged into a bulletin-board display to show how money is different from society to society today, as it was in the past.

EVALUATION, CHAPTER 10

Have the class discuss the following questions.

1. What were some of the economic problems facing India and China 2,000 years ago?
2. Why might people in some societies refuse to use new tools and machines?
3. Were the people of Greece and Rome better able to adopt new techniques and tools than were the people in India and China? Why or why not?

CONCLUDING THE UNIT

Discuss Part 4 of the class project and allow the pupils time to complete their work on the project. Have the class evaluate what they have learned by completing the class project for this unit.

TEACHER'S PREVIEW OF UNIT 5, pages 174–223

Unit 5 is divided into three chapters: 11. Social Development in the Middle Ages, pages 177-193; 12. Political Development in the Middle Ages, pages 194-208; and 13. Economic Development in the Middle Ages, pages 209-221. The unit also includes a special four-part class project which is introduced on page 176. The class project is continued on pages 193, 208, and 221. Additional suggested activities, called *Things to Do*, appear on pages 193, 208, and 221. Unit 6 concludes with two pages of evaluation, *Checkup Time* on page 222 and *Test Yourself* on page 223.

This unit helps the pupils to understand the nature of societies in Europe, Asia, and America during the period called the Middle Ages (A.D. 500-A.D. 1500). The basic unit objective is to show how civilization in Asia, Europe, and America developed in different ways. Particular emphasis is placed upon how civilizations in Asia reached a high level of development while European civilizations were in a period of confusion and decline. A study of this unit will help the pupils understand some of the factors that influenced the growth and development of civilizations in all parts of the world.

TEACHING HELPS—Unit Introduction, pages 174–176

CONCEPTS

1. Man and his societies change to meet new challenges and conditions.
2. Cultural diffusion can cause societies to change.
3. Different ways of life exist in different regions of the world.

Recommended Procedure

Getting Started In a class discussion encourage the pupils to suggest some of the challenges facing their society today. (*These challenges might include such things as poverty, air and water pollution, overcrowded schools, unemployment, and so on.*) Ask the class: How is the United States trying to meet these challenges? In what way would our ability to solve these problems be affected if the United States had a major war or was invaded?

Discuss these questions and help the pupils understand that a civilization's progress in meeting challenges can be affected adversely by an attack from the outside. Point out that during the Middle Ages, civilizations in Europe and Asia had to face such attacks and it affected their development.

Developing the Lesson Have the class study the material on page 175. Stress the point that the term *Middle Ages* is used in this unit to identify the historical period that covers the 1,000 years between A.D. 500 and A.D. 1500.

Concluding the Lesson Have the pupils turn to page 176. Tell them that the class project is designed to help them understand the social, political, and economic ways of life of people in several parts of the world. Stress the continuing nature of the class project.

Going Further Have the pupils study the picture on page 174. Based on this picture, and other information they can gather from encyclopedias and history books, have the pupils draw and display pictures of the types of ships used by Europeans in the eleventh century.

TEACHER'S PREVIEW OF CHAPTER 11, pages 177–193

Chapter 11, "Social Development in the Middle Ages," has an introductory page and three teaching units:

Social Order in Europe (pages 178-183)

Societies of Asia (pages 184-187)

Societies of Latin America (pages 188-192)

This chapter presents material covering the social systems that existed in parts of Europe, Asia, and Latin America in the Middle Ages. Each teaching unit is designed to help the pupils understand how various social systems helped man meet the challenges he faced in different areas of the world. Each teaching unit also helps the pupils understand how social systems change to meet new conditions as they arise.

TEACHING HELPS—Chapter Introduction, page 177

CONCEPTS

1. Invasions and warfare can change man's way of life.
2. New ways of life must be developed to meet new changes.

Recommended Procedure

Getting Started Tell the class to turn to page 177 and study the map on that page. Have the pupils identify the nine barbarian tribes, or groups, that moved about in Europe after A.D. 350. Based on the map, ask the pupils to suggest which barbarian tribe (*the Huns*) created the movement of other groups of barbarians. Have the pupils explain what technique was used by the cartographer to show how this barbarian tribe affected others.

Developing the Lesson Have the pupils study the material on page 177. After they have studied the material, ask them to define the term *barbarian*. In a class discussion have the pupils suggest some reasons why the Huns might have invaded Europe in the fourth century. (*Typical answers might include such things as a growing population, a drought that destroyed crops, decline in fertility of their land, desire for plunder, and so on.*)

Concluding the Lesson End this lesson by having the pupils complete the "Just For Fun" activity on page 177. As a guide for their time lines, suggest that the pupils refer to the time lines on pages 43 and 60. At this point you may want to discuss the difference between B.C. and A.D.

Going Further Divide the class into several groups. Have each group prepare a report on one of the barbarian groups shown on the map on page 177. This report should cover such topics as how each barbarian group did the following:

1. Made a living
2. Built communities
3. Organized their government
4. Fought battles

Have each group present its findings to the class and be prepared to answer and discuss questions.

TEACHING HELPS—SOCIAL ORDER IN EUROPE, pages, 178-183

CONCEPTS

1. The breakdown of a society may cause a change in the society's values.
2. During the Dark Ages, the people of Europe began to develop a new social system.
3. The breakdown of law and order in Europe caused most European societies to place a high priority upon man's fighting abilities.
4. The ruling class in Europe was largely made up of warriors.

Recommended Procedure

Getting Started Ask the pupils to turn to page 179 and study the picture on that page. Point out that the picture shows a teen-age lad of the Middle Ages who is training to be a knight. The target he is aiming at was called a *quintain*. Mention that in some instances, the *quintain* was built to spin around and hit the rider if he was not alert enough to avoid it. Ask the pupils: Why might a society train its young people to fight? Have the pupils suggest some reasons why, in our society, it is not necessary to train our youth to fight at an early age. Ask: In what ways are American citizens protected by their government? (*Answers should include the fact that we have police departments and armies provided by our government to protect our citizens.*)

At this point you may want to introduce the following terms.

Dark Ages	page
clergy	squire
knight	chivalry

Developing the Lesson Divide this lesson into two parts. First, have the pupils study the material on pages 178, 179, and 180 up to the heading "Life of the peasants." As they study the material, have the pupils answer the questions in the body of the text. Discuss these questions with the pupils when they complete their study of the material. Stress the point that many people in Europe were willing to trade their freedom for protection and security. Discuss whether people in the United States today would be willing to make a similar exchange. Ask the pupils for their opinions about this subject.

Next have the pupils study the remaining material on pages 180, 181, 182, and 183. Have the class define the term *serf* and explain why a serf was considered to be "semifree." Ask: In what way did religion influence the people of Europe in the Middle Ages? Why was religion so important to the people at that time?

Concluding the Lesson Lead a class discussion about the reasons for the Crusades. Also discuss with the pupils the effects of the Crusades. Ask the class to suggest why a new social class developed in Europe because of the increase of trade and commerce.

Conclude the lesson by having the pupils answer and discuss the "Think for Yourself" question on page 183.

Going Further As an interesting activity, have the pupils complete the first "Things to Do" activity on page 193. To help them understand one type of picture they might look for, have the pupils turn to page 105 and observe the picture on that page as an example.

TEACHING HELPS—SOCIETIES OF ASIA, pages 184-187

CONCEPTS

1. Peaceful conditions in India and China helped those countries to reach a high level of civilization before A.D. 1000.
2. Eastern societies did not suffer an early breakdown as did societies in Europe, thus traditional values and customs were maintained.

Recommended Procedure

Getting Started Have the pupils compare the three maps on pages 92, 127, and 184. Ask the pupils what the three maps have in common. Have the members of the class discuss the similarities between the Aryan invasion of India and the Muslim invasion of India. Also ask the class to speculate about what area, of what was once India, they think would be most strongly Muslim today. (*They should suggest the northwestern section of India since that was under Muslim control the longest.*) Ask the pupils: Which modern country is found in that area today? (*The country is Pakistan.*)

Developing the Lesson First, have the pupils study the material about India and China which is on pages 184 and 185. Have them answer the questions in the body of the text. Stress how both India and China were free from outside invasion for a period of time prior to A.D. 1000. Also stress that this enabled both societies to retain their old customs and ways of life without interruption. This freedom from invasion helped both countries to achieve a high level of civilization. Emphasize the fact that a very high level of civilization existed in Asia while Europe was still without a stable civilization.

Next have the pupils study the material about Japan on pages 185, 186, and 187. Emphasize that Japan, isolated as it was, developed a social system based upon earlier tribal systems. Through a class discussion, help the pupils to discover why the Japanese, who were free from invasion, developed a warrior class. (*One reason was the struggle against the Ainu for land.*) You may also want the class to discuss why America did not develop a warrior class.

Concluding the Lesson Draw the lesson to a close by having the class answer and discuss the "Think for Yourself" question on page 187. In the discussion try to help the pupils understand that European advances have largely occurred since the eleventh century A.D. during which time Europeans enjoyed relatively peaceful and stable civilizations. You may also want to point out that traditional patterns of life broke down in Europe earlier than they did in Asia, and thus European societies were more open to change than were Asiatic societies.

Going Further Have the pupils compare the code of *bushido* and the code of chivalry. Ask the pupils: Which code is more often reflected in the customs of your society? Why?

Have the pupils consult encyclopedias to discover some additional aspects of the code of *bushido*. Lead a class discussion about the way the code of *bushido*, as a code of behavior, differs from the code of behavior accepted by the American society.

CONCEPTS

1. Man developed elsewhere and migrated to the Americas.
2. Agriculture developed independently in Central America and then spread to North and South America.
3. The warlike society of the Aztecs was a result of its traditional religious beliefs.

Recommended Procedure

Getting Started Have the pupils study the map on page 188. Ask them to identify the three civilizations that first developed in America. Encourage the pupils to speculate about why the first civilizations developed where they did. Ask the pupils: What type of climate did these early civilizations enjoy? How can you tell from the map?

Also have the pupils suggest why the *main* route of man's migration was not along the West Coast of North America. Ask: What natural geographic features tended to cause the main migration route to be through the inland area of North America? (*For example, the Rocky Mountains and the plateaus helped to determine the route of migration.*)

Developing the Lesson Have the pupils study this lesson in two parts. First, ask the pupils to study the material on pages 188, 189, and 190 up to the heading "The Aztec civilization." In a class discussion ask the pupils to answer and discuss the questions in the body of the material. Stress what can be learned from the picture of the Mayan fishing village on page 189. (*For example, the pupils should discover the type of town, kinds of clothes, kinds of jobs, types of transportation used, and so on.*) Discuss how such artifacts aid social scientists in learning about early societies. Emphasize that human sacrifice did not play a large part in the Mayan society.

Then have the pupils study the remaining material on pages 190, 191, and 192. Ask the class to suggest in what ways the Aztec society differed from most societies in Asia and Europe at this time. (*For example, the Aztecs believed in human sacrifice, and they had a strong central government that controlled all aspects of their life.*)

Have the pupils answer and discuss the questions in the body of the material. Use the pictures on page 191 to illustrate some of the occupations of the Aztecs.

Concluding the Lesson Identify the picture of the Aztec god of death on page 192. Ask the pupils to speculate about how the Aztecs viewed their gods—i.e. were they kind or harsh? Finish the lesson by having the pupils answer "Think for Yourself" on page 192.

Going Further Divide the class into three groups. Have each group draw a time line on long sheets of paper at least ten inches wide. One time line should show the development of civilizations in Asia. The second should show the development of civilizations in Europe. The third time line should show the development of civilizations in Latin America.

Display the three time lines, one above another, on the bulletin board. Compare the developments in the three areas during certain periods of time. For example, have the pupils explain what was happening in Europe, Asia, and America between A.D. 500 and A.D. 800. Discuss why civilizations were different in their development at certain periods of history.

EVALUATION, CHAPTER 11

Have the pupils respond to these questions.
1. Why did civilizations develop differently during the Middle Ages in Europe, Asia, and Latin America?
2. Why is a stable social system desired by people in various societies?

TEACHER'S PREVIEW OF CHAPTER 12, pages 194–208

Chapter 12, "Political Development in the Middle Ages," has an introductory page and three teaching units:

Early Leaders of Government (pages 195-198)

Patterns of Government (pages 199-202)

Changing Governments for Changing Times (pages 203-207).

This chapter contains material dealing with the various political systems that developed in Europe, Asia, and Latin America during the Middle Ages. As the pupils study this material, they will develop an understanding of why the feudal system developed in Europe and in Japan. They will also discover how and why strong central governments developed in Latin America. The effects of these various political systems upon the people are emphasized, as is the manner in which these political systems changed with the passage of time.

TEACHING HELPS—Chapter Introduction, page 194

CONCEPTS

1. Governments provide services.
2. Complex societies need stable central governments.

Recommended Procedure

Getting Started To begin this lesson you may want to help the pupils understand how a political system reflects the beliefs and values of the people. One way to do this could be to help the pupils discover that the way a ruler dresses reflects some of the attitudes of the people.

First, have the pupils study the pictures on page 194. Ask the pupils to suggest some reasons why each political leader shown dressed as he did. (*For example, their dress included symbols of power, such as a crown. The leaders' dress also reflected, to some extent, their social class since other members of the upper class wore similar, but less distinctive dress.*)

Then have the class turn to page 342. Ask the pupils: In what way did Adolf Hitler's dress reflect the nature of the government and society in Nazi Germany? Then ask the pupils to study the picture of President Nixon on page 405. Have the pupils suggest how the way our political leaders dress (*much like any member of our society might dress on a semiformal occasion*) reflects the American democratic political system and society. Discuss the role of a leader in a democratic society as compared to the role of a leader in a dictatorial society.

Developing the Lesson After the pupils have studied the pictures on page 194, ask them to suggest which leader came from Europe, Japan, and Latin America. Then have the pupils study the material on page 194. Stress the fact that every government is established to meet the needs of the people and to provide services. If a government fails to do these things, it is usually changed. In a class discussion have the pupils suggest reasons why a central government helps a society remain stable. (*For example, a central government enforces laws, settles disputes, and protects its citizens.*) Emphasize that as they study Chapter 12, the pupils will discover ways in which political systems are alike and ways in which they are different.

Concluding the Lesson Ask the pupils to answer and discuss the question in the annotations on page 194 denoted by the asterisk. Then conclude the lesson by having the pupils complete "Just For Fun" on page 194.

Going Further Ask the pupils to speculate about the saying that a government that does not have the support of the people cannot remain in power.

TEACHING HELPS—EARLY LEADERS OF GOVERNMENT, pages 195–198

CONCEPTS

1. The breakdown of a society often leads to the development of new political systems.
2. A stable government helps to maintain a stable society.
3. In a decentralized political system, political authority is held by a number of people, and this decentralization often leads to conflicts.

Recommended Procedure

Getting Started Ask the pupils to study the map of Charlemagne's Empire on page 195. Have them try to name as many modern European nations they can think of that were part of Charlemagne's Empire. List their suggestions on the chalkboard. Then have the pupils check the suggestions with a modern map in the classroom. Have the pupils add to the list any nations they have overlooked. Ask the pupils: Why would it be difficult to unite these nations under one central government today? Discuss the cultural differences that exist among these various European countries and the problems these differences can cause when you try to unite people into one nation. You also may want to discuss how cultural differences in the United States cause difficulties today among different regions in our nation.

Developing the Lesson Divide this lesson into two parts. Have the pupils study the material on Europe on pages 195 and 196. Review the problems faced by Europeans after the collapse of the Roman Empire. Have the class suggest reasons why Charlemagne's Empire broke up when he died and weak rulers came to power. In a class discussion bring out how feudalism decentralizes political power and weakens a central government.

Next have the pupils study the material about Asia and Latin America on pages 196, 197, and 198. Have the class answer the questions in the body of the text. Then, in a class discussion, have the pupils compare and contrast the types of government found in Japan, and in Latin America, with feudalism. Have a pupil make lists of these similarities and differences on the chalkboard. Ask the pupils: Which system of government do you think was best? Why? Were any of these governments democratic? Why?

Concluding the Lesson Lead a class discussion about the differences between the Inca and the Aztec governments. Try to help the pupils understand why the Aztecs were not interested in having friendly relations with all the people they conquered. (*In a number of instances the Aztecs deliberately provoked or continued a war so that they could have a supply of human sacrifices.*)

Conclude the lesson by having the class answer and discuss the "Think for Yourself" question on page 198. Bring the discussion of the question up to modern times and explore how different modern nations treat people they have defeated and conquered.

Going Further As an interesting class activity, have the pupils complete the first "Things to Do" on page 208. You may want to expand this activity by having each pupil report to the class something about the way the leaders, of which he has found pictures, are chosen and how they rule. (*For example, the pupils can tell if the leader is elected or appointed, how long he holds his office, and whether he answers to the people or whether he has total power and does as he pleases.*)

CONCEPTS

1. People strive for security in an unstable society.
2. Living in groups requires people to give up some freedom in return for protection and the group's welfare.
3. Feudalism was a combination of political, social, and economic obligations and privileges.
4. Feudalism is a type of political decentralization.

Recommended Procedure

Getting Started Ask the pupils to carefully study the illustration on page 199. Explain that the illustration shows some of the loyalties that nobles might owe to other nobles in a feudal system. Then set up this hypothetical situation.

1. The king accuses Count B of treason.
2. Count B attacks the king.
3. Counts A and C go to the king's aid.
4. All the counts call on the various dukes and knights who owe them loyalty to come to help them fight.

Ask the pupils: What would Duke C do in this situation? Why? What would Duke D do in this situation? Why?

To point out other difficulties presented by feudal loyalties, have the pupils assume that Dukes D and F are brothers and have the pupils suggest what might happen. Ask the pupils to think of other things that might confuse feudal loyalties. Then ask the pupils to discuss: Why, in a feudal system, is the king at the mercy of his nobles?

Developing the Lesson To help the pupils compare the types of political systems covered in this lesson, first have them study the material on feudalism in Europe on pages 199 and 200 up to the heading "Beginnings of feudalism in Japan." Have the pupils define the terms, *fief*, *vassal*, *trial by combat*, and *trial by ordeal*. Stress the point that the feudal system in Europe was a contractual system based on mutual obligations of lord to vassal and vassal to lord. Have the class suggest what obligations the lord and the vassal had to each other. List these obligations on the chalkboard and discuss whether these were "fair" for both sides.

After the pupils have developed an understanding of feudalism as it developed in Europe, have them study the material about feudalism in Japan on pages 200, 201, and 202. Ask the class to compare and contrast European and Japanese feudalism.

Then have the pupils study the material about the government of the Aztecs on page 202. In a class discussion contrast the Aztec system of government with European and Japanese feudalism.

Concluding the Lesson Lead a class discussion about the drawbacks of a feudal system of government. Ask the class: In what ways is a political system with a strong central government more efficient than a political system based on feudalism? Also have the class speculate about some of the dangers, or drawbacks, of a strong central government such as the one established by the Aztecs.

Have the pupils answer and discuss "Think for Yourself" on page 202.

Going Further The second activity in "Things to Do" on page 208 can be of aid in helping the pupils understand how laws are enforced. It will also help the pupils discover how man's attitudes toward law and justice have changed since the early Middle Ages in Europe. Stress the fact that the idea of a trial by jury developed late in the Middle Ages, and has since become a legal custom in the United States.

TEACHING HELPS—CHANGING GOVERNMENTS
FOR CHANGING TIMES, pages 203–207

CONCEPTS

1. New conditions and developments led to the decline, and ultimate disappearance, of feudalism in Europe and Asia.
2. Technological changes may cause political changes.
3. Invasions led to a breakdown of society and a decline of civilizations in Asia and Latin America.

Recommended Procedure

Getting Started To begin this lesson, have the pupils study and compare two pictures. First, ask the pupils to turn to page 180 and notice how the European nobility (the knights) fought on horseback with lances and swords. Then have the pupils study the picture on page 203. Ask them to describe the new weapons being used in warfare. Encourage the pupils to explain how the new weapons (*the crossbow, and more particularly, the longbow*) would reduce the effectiveness of the noble on horseback. Ask the pupils: Are the men on foot, who are using bows and arrows, knights?

Through a class discussion lead the pupils to an understanding of how new weapons decreased the importance of the knight on horseback. Help the pupils understand how new weapons enabled the common man to defend himself. Ask: In what way would the common man's ability to defend himself affect the system of feudalism? Why?

Discuss the answers to these questions and lead the pupils toward an understanding of how, as the role of the fighting man on horseback declined, feudalism became outmoded.

Developing the Lesson Have the pupils study the material on pages 203, 204, and 205 up to "A new type of leadership in Japan." Have the pupils answer and discuss the questions in the body of the material. Stress how the rise of powerful kings led to strong central governments in Europe. Also stress the importance of the Magna Charta in limiting the power of the king of England. Ask: Are the rights listed on page 205 from the Magna Charta guaranteed to people in the United States? If so, by what?

Next have the pupils study the material about governments in Asia on pages 205 and 206 up to "Europeans invade America." Have the class answer and discuss the questions in the body of the material. Stress the fact that a divided country, as China was in the thirteenth century, is an easy victim to an invader.

Then have the class study the remaining material on pages 206 and 207. Ask the pupils to explain why such a small group of Europeans was able to conquer the powerful Aztec Empire. (*They had guns and cannons and the aid of other Latin Americans who hated the Aztecs.*)

Concluding the Lesson This lesson can be brought to a close by having the pupils answer the "Think for Yourself" questions on page 207. Discuss how, and why, people in a democratic society are better able to adjust to challenges and new conditions than are those people who have been strictly controlled in a dictatorial political system.

Going Further The third activity of "Things to Do" on page 208 will be an interesting and informative exercise for the pupils.

EVALUATION, CHAPTER 12

Ask the pupils to rate the political systems they have studied as *democratic, partially democratic,* or *not democratic at all.* Have the pupils explain the reasons for their ratings. As you listen to the responses of the pupils, evaluate their understanding of the relationship between a society and the nature of its political system.

TEACHER'S PREVIEW OF CHAPTER 13, pages 209-221

Chapter 13, "Economic Development in the Middle Ages," has an introductory page and three teaching units:

Agriculture (pages 210-214)
Trade and Commerce (pages 215-217)
Urbanization (pages 218-220)

The material in Chapter 13 covers the various economic developments in Europe, Asia, and Latin America during the period called the Middle Ages. The material is designed and organized to help the pupils understand the relationships among a society's social, political, and economic systems.

Emphasis in this chapter is placed upon why a society needs a stable social and political system if it is going to enjoy economic growth. Economic systems are described and related to each society's social system. The material is organized so that it will help the pupils take a truly interdisciplinary approach to the study of man's development.

TEACHING HELPS—Chapter Introduction, page 209

CONCEPTS

1. Europe's major economic activity was agriculture during the Middle Ages.
2. Peace and a stable society encourage economic growth.
3. Surplus crops can lead to the growth of civilizations.

Recommended Procedure

Getting Started To begin this lesson, point out that societies during the Middle Ages were pre-industrial societies, that is, they relied primarily upon agriculture. With this in mind have the pupils turn to page 209 and observe the picture on that page. Ask the pupils to suggest what area (Europe, Asia, or Latin America) is shown in the painting. Have them explain the reasons for their answers.

Then have the pupils answer and discuss the following questions.

1. Compared with American farmers today, were the farmers shown in the picture technologically advanced? Why?
2. Does the picture show a division of labor and specialization?

3. Who do you think owns the crops being harvested? Why?

Developing the Lesson Ask the pupils to study the material on page 209. Stress the important point that European economic development was limited by wars before A.D. 1000. Then review the need for surplus crops as the basis for the growth and development of cities.

In a class discussion have the pupils answer and explain the question at the end of the third paragraph on page 209.

Concluding the Lesson Finish this lesson by having the class answer and discuss the question denoted by an asterisk in the annotations on page 209. Also have the class do the "Just For Fun" activity on that page.

Going Further Have the class prepare a bulletin-board display with drawings and pictures that show how man has improved the tools he has used for the production of agricultural products. Have the pupils begin the display with drawings of the tools used during the Middle Ages. The display should then show the various changes these tools have undergone over the years. The illustrations on pages 212 and 215 will help the pupils get started.

TEACHING HELPS—AGRICULTURE, pages 210-214

CONCEPTS

1. All medieval civilizations depended primarily upon agricultural production.
2. When society broke down in Europe after the fall of the Roman Empire, the people developed a new economic system.
3. Medieval economic systems reflected the basic customs, values, attitudes, and needs of each society.

Recommended Procedure

Getting Started Ask the class to turn to page 211 and study the diagram of a manor in Europe. Ask the pupils to suggest how the meadow and the pasture were used by the people. (*They were used in common by all members of the village.*)

In a class discussion have the pupils suggest how farming and, particularly, how land ownership may have been different in the Middle Ages in Europe than they are in the United States today. After the discussion point out that this lesson will help the pupils understand some of the differences between agriculture in medieval times and agriculture in modern times.

At this point you may want to introduce the following terms.

three-field system   chinampa system

Developing the Lesson Divide this lesson into three sections. First, have the pupils study the material dealing with farming and the manor system in Europe on pages 210, 211, and 212 up to "The manor system in Japan." Stress the fact that in Europe, most agricultural practices were based on custom and tradition rather than upon scientific knowledge. Have the pupils use the diagram of the manor on page 211 to learn about the three-field system. Discuss the questions on page 210 that pertain to the diagram. Ask the pupils to discuss: Why did the peasants, or serfs, work for the lord of the manor?

Then have the pupils study about manors in Japan on pages 212 and 213. Have the pupils answer the questions in the body of the material. In a class discussion compare and contrast the Japanese manor system with the manor system in Europe.

To bring the material in this lesson together, have the pupils now study about Aztec farming on pages 213 and 214. Ask: In what ways did the Aztecs' methods of farming and rural life differ from that of the Europeans and the Japanese? Stress the fact that the Aztec society was strictly controlled by the central government and, as a result, so was the society's economic system. Therefore independent manors did not develop in the Aztec Empire.

Concluding the Lesson Ask the pupils to answer the "Think for Yourself" question on page 214. (*A typical answer might be that manors tend to decentralize political power by making the lords of the manors independent and powerful.*) Discuss what peculiar conditions (social and political) led to the manor system in Europe and Japan.

Going Further For a class discussion ask the class to imagine their society has just broken down, and that they no longer can produce anything but agricultural goods. Ask the class to discuss the following questions.

1. Would the people in your society be likely to develop a manor system similar to that developed in Europe? Why or why not?
2. Would cities in your society decline if a manor system was developed? Why?
3. Would education change if your society became almost entirely agricultural? How and why?

TEACHING HELPS—TRADE AND COMMERCE, pages 215-217

CONCEPTS

1. Economic growth and technological developments often lead to increased trade and commerce.
2. Trade leads to cultural diffusion.
3. Trade, to some extent, exists in every society.

Recommended Procedure

Getting Started Have the members of the class assume they were lords of manors in Europe when the following conditions occurred.

1. Production of crops increased so that there was a surplus.
2. People lived longer and the population began to grow rapidly.
3. Warfare and invasions had declined and roads became safe to travel.
4. Crusaders returned with new products from the East.
5. Cities began to develop not far from the manors.

Ask the class to suggest what steps they would take to improve life on their manors. Have them explain how they would adjust their economic systems to meet the new conditions. List the suggestions on the chalkboard and refer to them as you discuss the material in this lesson.

Developing the Lesson Ask the pupils to study the material on pages 215, 216, and 217. Have the class answer and discuss the questions in the body of the text. Use the pictures on page 215 for a discussion of medieval technology. Point out the nomadic way of life of the Mongols as is shown in the picture on page 216. Ask the pupils: Why would a civilized nation, conquered and ruled by the Mongols, suffer a decline in its way of life?

Then, in a class discussion, try to lead the class toward an understanding of how, and why, a government (such as the Aztec government) might control and use the society's economic system to further the aims of the government. Try to point out that today, communism is one type of a state- or government-controlled economic system. Ask the class to discuss the question: Can a free economic system exist in a society where the people are not free?

Concluding the Lesson Bring this lesson to a conclusion by having the pupils answer and discuss the "Think for Yourself" question on page 217. See if the class can point out modern examples of how war has reduced trade.

Going Further Have the class turn to page 221 and study the second activity of "Things to Do" on that page. Ask the pupils to complete the activity and display their models and artifacts in class.

TEACHING HELPS—URBANIZATION, pages 218-220

CONCEPTS

1. Cultural changes and economic changes are interrelated.
2. Social, political, and economic factors influence the nature of a society's urbanization.

Recommended Procedure

Getting Started Before discussing this lesson, you may want to develop the differences urbanization makes in the way people live. One way to do this is to ask the pupils how many of them have lived in small towns or cities of less than 100,000 people. (If your class is in a small town, ask how many pupils have lived in a large city with a population of more than 100,000 people.)

Ask the pupils to explain how their way of life has changed as a result of their move to a larger (or smaller) city. Lead a class discussion about why these differences exist. Be careful to avoid being critical of the ways of life found in either larger or smaller cities and towns.

Developing the Lesson Have the pupils study the material on pages 218 and 219 up to "Cities in Asia." Ask the pupils to answer and discuss the questions in the body of the material. Be sure to stress how the Dark Ages affected cities in Europe. (*It caused them to decline.*)

In a class discussion ask the pupils to analyze the social, political, and economic factors that led to the growth of medieval cities in Europe. Emphasize that the growth of cities helped to destroy serfdom in Europe. Ask the pupils to explain why this was true.

Next have the pupils study the remaining material on pages 219 and 220. Ask the pupils to suggest some reasons for the decline of the Aztec and Incan cities in Latin America after

the Spaniards arrived. Discuss how these earlier cities lost their basic functions after the Spanish conquest of Latin America. (*They were no longer needed as political centers of empires, and centers of trade grew up nearer the sea because the spaniards concentrated upon sending materials and goods back to Europe.*)

Concluding the Lesson Discuss the similarities of cities (*used as centers of trade and political power*) in Europe, Asia, and Latin America. Then conclude the lesson by having the pupils answer and discuss "Think for Yourself" on page 220.

Going Further To help the pupils understand the geographic and economic factors that influence the location of cities, have the class turn to page 221. Ask the pupils to study the first activity of "Things to Do" on that page.

Allow the pupils sufficient time to complete the activity and discuss their findings in class. Ask the pupils: Do you think the same factors influenced the location of cities in other states? Why?

EVALUATION, CHAPTER 13

Have the pupils answer and discuss the following questions.
1. In what way does a society's economic development affect urbanization?
2. Why may urbanization lead to further economic growth?
3. Why is urbanization occurring throughout the world today?

CONCLUDING THE UNIT

Review the pupils' progress on the class project. Discuss the final part of the class project on page 221. Have the class present its final panel discussion. Ask the class to evaluate the panel discussions that were presented.

Unit 6 is composed of three chapters: 14. How People Thought and Lived, pages 227-247; 15. Man's Ways of Getting Goods, pages 248-268; and 16. Man's Political Activities, pages 269-285. A special feature is a four-part class project which is introduced on page 226 and continued on pages 247, 268, and 285. Other suggested activities called *Things to Do* are also given on pages 247, 268, and 285. The unit concludes with two pages of evaluation, *Checkup Time* on page 286 and *Test Yourself* on page 287.

This unit covers the period from 1500 to 1850 during which time societies underwent some dramatic changes. The goal of this unit is to help the pupils understand why some societies began to industrialize while other societies developed differently.

Throughout Unit 6, special emphasis is placed upon man and how he lived, produced goods, and governed himself. Interrelationships among societies and their economic and political activities are stressed to help the pupils understand how, and why, changes occurred in social, economic, and political systems in various parts of the world. Important concepts are introduced, and societies in Europe, Asia, Africa, and America are analyzed through an interdisciplinary approach to the study of man and his societies.

TEACHING HELPS—Unit Introduction, pages 224-226

CONCEPTS

1. The breakdown of the older ways of life in Europe created conditions favorable to new developments and change.
2. Traditional societies in Asia and Africa tended to retain their older ways of life.

Recommended Procedure

Getting Started Ask the pupils to turn to page 224 and study the picture on that page. Point out that the picture shows Queen Elizabeth I of England who ruled from 1558 to 1603. Ask the pupils what social class is shown in the picture. (*Members of the upper class of England are shown.*) Point out that members of the upper class held political power in every European nation during the sixteenth and seventeenth centuries. Ask the class: Why does the middle class hold most of the power in Europe today? Have the class suggest some of the things they think must have happened to change societies in Europe.

Developing the Lesson Have the pupils study the material on page 225. Stress the fact that the way people think and their attitudes toward life can influence, or bring about, changes in social, political, and economic systems.

Concluding the Lesson Direct the pupils' attention to the four questions at the end of the material on page 225. Ask the pupils to suggest which social scientists would be most likely to ask these questions. Emphasize that the material in Unit 6 reflects the knowledge gathered by many different social scientists. Discuss with the pupils why it is necessary to study societies from the points of view of many social scientists (i.e. economists, sociologists, historians, political scientists, and so on) if one is to gain a full understanding of the way man lived in the past.

Going Further Ask each pupil to interview two adults who agree to being interviewed. Each pupil should ask the adults to name two social customs that exist today and that have not changed in the last twenty years. Have the pupils compare the lists of customs in class. Ask the pupils: Why have these social customs remained unchanged while others have changed?

TEACHER'S PREVIEW OF CHAPTER 14, pages 227-247

Chapter 14, "How People Thought and Lived," contains an introductory page and four teaching units:

The Social Order (pages 228-233)
Education and Learning (pages 234-237)
Religion (pages 238-241)
People and Communities (pages 242-246)

Chapter 14 helps the pupils understand the nature of the social systems in parts of Europe, Asia, Africa, and America after the Middle Ages. The chapter also helps the pupils to discover how, and why, some of these societies changed while other societies remained largely as they had been in the past. Previously learned concepts are applied throughout the chapter, and new concepts are developed.

TEACHING HELPS—Chapter Introduction, page 227

CONCEPTS

1. Societies in western Europe changed more rapidly after 1500 than did societies in Asia, Africa, and eastern Europe.
2. Changes in ways of life create new problems. Thus, change may not be welcomed by all the people in a society.

Recommended Procedure

Getting Started Have the pupils study the map on page 227. Ask them to locate England, France, and Spain on the map. Point out that the people of these three nations probably experienced more dramatic changes in their ways of life between 1500 and 1850 than did people of most other nations or areas in Europe. Based on what they can tell from the map, ask the pupils to suggest some reasons why England, France, and Spain experienced more change immediately after the Middle Ages than did eastern European nations such as Russia. (*The facts that they had access to the sea and that they were active in trade with other areas of the world are two possible suggestions.*)

Developing the Lesson Have the pupils study the material on page 227. Stress the point that the ways of life in various societies did not change at the same time. Review the concept of cultural diffusion and ask the pupils to sug-gest some examples of how cultural diffusion is bringing about social change today.

In a class discussion help the pupils to understand that many people often do not want to see their way of life change. Ask the pupils: Why might people in a traditional society be against changes in their way of life? Also ask the pupils to discuss some of the changes that are taking place in their way of life. Ask them to describe which changes they are opposed to and why.

Concluding the Lesson Ask the pupils to answer and discuss the questions at the end of the second paragraph on page 227. Then conclude this lesson by having the pupils complete the "Just For Fun" activity on page 227.

Going Further Social change is an important concept. To help the pupils understand how customs change, have them prepare a bulletin-board display showing how the way people dress has changed in the United States.

Ask the pupils to collect pictures from magazines and newspapers showing how people dressed in the past in the United States and how they are dressing today. Have the pupils prepare their display and have them date their pictures. The pictures should be arranged in chronological order.

In a class discussion, encourage the pupils to suggest some of the social changes that occurred that have affected the way Americans dressed in the past and are dressing today.

TEACHING HELPS—THE SOCIAL ORDER, pages 228-233

CONCEPTS

1. Social change may come as the result of economic activity.
2. Social mobility is usually restricted by custom and tradition in traditional societies.
3. A society's social system reflects the values and priorities established by the people.

Recommended Procedure

Getting Started Draw a triangle (pyramid) on the chalkboard. Label the drawing "social pyramid." Toward the top of the pyramid draw a line across the pyramid making a small section and write "upper class" in this section. Below this section, draw another line marking off a larger section and write in the space "middle class." The largest section at the bottom of the pyramid should be labeled "lower class." Then explain to the pupils that your social pyramid represents the type of social structure that developed in Europe after 1500.

Ask the pupils to study the drawing. Then have the class suggest some of the things a social pyramid can tell about a society. (*For example, which class is the largest, which class has the highest social position, and also the relative relationship of one class to another.*) You may want to ask the pupils to suggest what a social pyramid would look like if it were drawn of their society.

Developing the Lesson First have the pupils study the material about the social order in Europe on pages 228 and 229 up to "Social classes in the American colonies." Have the pupils answer and discuss the questions in the body of the text. Ask the pupils: Why might the middle-class people in Europe have been in favor of democracy? Why might the upper-class people in Europe have been opposed to democracy?

Next have the pupils study the material on pages 229, 230, and 231 about social classes in America. In a class discussion help the pupils to understand how the American social system was both similar to and different from the social system in Europe.

The pupils should then study the remaining material in this lesson on pages 231, 232, and 233. Through a class discussion bring out how social systems in Asia and Africa were alike and different. Then have the class compare all the social systems they have studied in this lesson. Have the pupils suggest the ways all these societies were alike and how they were different. Stress how traditional societies are less likely to change as rapidly as are less traditional societies.

Concluding the Lesson Discuss the relationship of social mobility to such things as economic growth (*social mobility encourages economic growth as a means of rising to a higher class*), political freedom (*democracy is based on the idea that men are equal before the law and not judged according to social class*), and acceptance of change (*fewer social restrictions to hinder change*).

Also have the pupils answer and discuss the "Think for Yourself" question on page 233.

Going Further Have the pupils turn to page 247 and study the first "Things to Do" activity on that page. Have the pupils complete this activity. You may also want to have a few pupils prepare reports on the way people live in the modern countries that are located in Africa where the kingdoms Benin and Kanem-Bornu once existed.

TEACHING HELPS—EDUCATION AND LEARNING, pages 234–237

CONCEPTS

1. Contacts between people of different civilizations may produce cultural changes.
2. Social changes may be reflected by an increase in education.
3. Education in traditional societies is usually strongly influenced by the customs of the past.

Recommended Procedure

Getting Started Have the pupils study the map on page 234. Then have them compare the map on page 234 with the map of ancient trade routes on page 169. Have the pupils answer the following questions.

1. What was Constantinople called in ancient times?
2. Why was Constantinople a trade center for goods from some Asian nations?
3. In what way were some European trade routes influenced by geographic conditions?
4. Why might an increased interest in education have first begun in Italy and then spread to the rest of Europe?

In a class discussion help the pupils to understand how trade can lead to the spread of knowledge and ideas.

Developing the Lesson First have the pupils study the material on pages 234, 235, and 236. Stress the point that education began to increase in Europe in the late Middle Ages as societies became more stable and warfare and invasions decreased or ended. Ask the pupils to explain why education and learning increase in stable societies but tend to decrease during times of warfare and confusion.

As the pupils study the material on pages 234, 235, and 236, have them answer and discuss the questions in the body of the material.

Through a discussion compare the educational systems of Europe and Asia. Ask the pupils to suggest how the goals of education differed in each society. (*Education in Europe was designed to lead to new ideas while education in China, for example, was used to maintain old ways of life.*) Have the pupils suggest reasons why education differed in some European countries from education in China.

Next, have the pupils study the remaining material on page 237. In a class discussion compare the type of education children in Benin and Kanem-Bornu had with the type of education pupils now receive in the United States. Ask: Why is modern education in most parts of the world different today than it was in Asia and Africa over 100 years ago?

Concluding the Lesson Ask the pupils to explain how a society's system of education reflects the nature of a society. (*For example, a hunting and food-gathering society will educate its young people in practical tasks needed to survive, while a society that produces surplus goods can afford to allow its young people to study many different subjects.*)

Conclude this lesson by having the class answer and discuss the "Think for Yourself" question on page 237.

Going Further Have the pupils ask their parents about what they studied when they were in school. Each pupil should list the things his parents studied and bring the list to class. Ask the pupils to compare their lists with the things they study today. Have the pupils list all the new things they study that were not taught when their parents were in school. Discuss with the class the reasons why many new things have been added in the schools today and how these changes in their curriculum reflect changes in our knowledge and our way of life.

TEACHING HELPS—RELIGION, pages 238-241

CONCEPTS

1. Social changes may produce changes in a society's religious practices and beliefs.
2. Religious changes led to the development of a national church in England.
3. In a traditional society, religion is so closely tied to the social structure that a change in religious beliefs would produce basic changes in the society.

Recommended Procedure

Getting Started Ask the class to study the picture of the cathedral (Roman Catholic) on page 238, the picture of the temple (Hindu) on page 240, and the picture of the mosque (Islamic) on page 241. After the pupils have studied the pictures, ask them to identify which religious faith uses each building. Also ask the class to suggest to which countries they would travel to see these buildings. (*The cathedral is in France, and the temple and the mosque are in India.*)

Next, ask the pupils to suggest how these religious buildings are similar. (*For example, each building shows that religion was important in each society because of its size and construction.*) Then have the class suggest how these religious structures differ from one another.

Point out to the class that the material in this lesson discusses the part each of these religions played from 1500 to 1850.

Developing the Lesson Begin this lesson by having the class first study the material on pages 238, 239, and 240 up to "The religious situation in India." Have the pupils answer and discuss the questions in the body of the material. Stress the fact that Martin Luther originally was trying to get the Roman Catholic Church to reform itself. For a class discussion ask the pupils to suggest some reasons why more than one Protestant religion developed after 1500.

Then ask the class to study the remaining material on pages 240 and 241. Review the basic beliefs of Hinduism and Islam. Ask: What changes in the social order might have occurred if the people of India had all become Muslims? (*The caste system in India was closely related to the basic beliefs of Hinduism, thus a change in religious beliefs might have led to a new social system.*)

Concluding the Lesson Have the pupils answer and discuss the "Think for Yourself" question on page 241. Then ask the pupils why the members of the upper class in China tended to follow Confucianism rather than Buddhism.

Going Further You may want to illustrate how widespread the major religions are today. To show this, have the pupils obtain or draw a large map of the world. Then have the pupils use encyclopedias to determine which countries in the world today are primarily Christian, Jewish, Hindu, Islamic, or Buddhist. Assign each major religion a color and have the pupils color the map to show the areas in which the majority of the people practice one of these religions. Display the map on the bulletin board and discuss the findings with the class.

TEACHING HELPS—PEOPLE AND COMMUNITIES, pages 242-246

CONCEPTS

1. A stable political system helps to maintain a stable social system.
2. Technological improvements can produce a higher standard of living.
3. Industrialization creates changes in a society's way of life.
4. People in traditional societies tend to dress and live as their ancestors did in the past.

Recommended Procedure

Getting Started To help the pupils understand how conditions affect the ways in which man lives, have the pupils study the pictures on page 242. Ask them to compare the pictures on page 242 with the pictures of dwellings on page 391. Have the pupils answer and discuss the following questions.

1. What conditions made castles necessary in Europe during the Middle Ages?
2. In what ways had conditions changed so that cottages, such as the one shown on page 242, were built shortly after the Middle Ages ended?
3. What new conditions make modern man build and live in dwellings such as those shown on page 391?

In a brief class discussion help the pupils compare man's way of life as is illustrated by the picture of the cottage on page 242 with the way of life experienced by people living in the apartments illustrated on page 391. Explain that some of the conditions that led to changes in the way people lived are discussed in this lesson.

Developing the Lesson To help the pupils understand how life differed in Europe, America, Asia, and Africa, have the pupils first study the material on pages 242, 243, and 244 up to "Life in India." Stress the fact that cities in Europe grew as people came to the cities in search of jobs. Also emphasize that a lack of city planning led to overcrowded and poor living conditions in many European cities. Ask: Given a choice today, would you prefer to live in a large city or a small, rural town? Why?

Next, have the pupils study the material about life in India and China on pages 244 and 245. In a class discussion encourage the pupils to suggest how life in Europe and Asia was similar and how it was different. Then have the pupils study the remaining material on pages 245 and 246. Ask the pupils to speculate about some of the problems that could arise from living in a village similar to the one shown on page 245. Ask: In what way are social problems solved in traditional societies?

Concluding the Lesson Ask the class: Of the societies you have studied in this lesson, which one is most similar to your society? Why is this so? Discuss the answers to these questions with the class.

Going Further Suggest that the pupils complete the third activity in "Things to Do" on page 247. After the pupils have compared the modes of dress in China in the 1600's with the way people in China dress today, ask the pupils to suggest why changes have occurred. See if the pupils can point out any examples of cultural diffusion in their pictures.

EVALUATION, CHAPTER 14

Have each pupil make up two questions about societies between 1500 and 1850. In a class discussion, the pupils may take turns asking their questions of the class. Evaluate the responses to these questions.

TEACHER'S PREVIEW OF CHAPTER 15, pages 248-268

Chapter 15, "Man's Ways of Getting Goods," contains an introductory page and four teaching units:

Agriculture (pages 249-253)

The Manufacturing of Goods (pages 254-258)

The Distribution of Goods (pages 258-264)

Transportation (pages 265-267)

This chapter helps the pupils to understand the nature and the operation of economic systems in Europe, America, Asia, and Africa prior to 1850. The chapter also emphasizes the conditions that led to industrialization in some societies and the conditions that led other societies to remain nonindustrialized.

The development of economic concepts in Chapter 15 will enable the pupils to understand more fully the economic system they live in today. And the interdisciplinary approach to other economic systems covered in this chapter will help the pupils grasp the various factors that influenced economic development in the past and are influencing economic growth today.

TEACHING HELPS—Chapter Introduction, page 248

CONCEPTS

1. Nations tend to produce the goods they can produce most efficiently.
2. Nations import and export goods with other nations.
3. Economic changes affect man's social and political ways of life.

Recommended Procedure

Getting Started Have the pupils study the picture on page 248 and then compare it with the picture of New York in 1900 on page 293. Ask the pupils to discuss the following questions.

1. How does the way goods are sold today differ from the way goods were sold in New York in 1900?
2. Why may the way goods are sold today in supermarkets be more efficient than the way goods were sold in the past?
3. In what ways have the new methods of merchandising (selling) goods improved life in the United States?

Explain that the material in this chapter will help the pupils understand how man developed some of the economic techniques from which he benefits today.

Developing the Lesson Ask the pupils to study the material on page 248, which will help them to begin to understand some of the economic changes that occurred between 1500 and 1850. Stress the fact that trade is one way that man goes about getting the goods he needs and wants. Emphasize that the more goods a person uses, the better his way of life may be.

Concluding the Lesson You may want to conclude this lesson by having the pupils do the "Just For Fun" activity on page 248. Ask the pupils to explain how goods from other countries may improve their way of life.

Going Further Suggest that the pupils design, for a bulletin-board display, a plan for a modern grocery store. Have the pupils visit a supermarket in their neighborhood and observe how the store is designed, stocked, and operated. Then have the pupils use this knowledge, and their imagination, to plan their designs.

TEACHING HELPS—AGRICULTURE, pages 249–253

CONCEPTS

1. The improved production of agricultural products in Europe after the Middle Ages led to the development of a new economic system.
2. Agricultural methods in many traditional societies sometimes are inefficient and based on outdated customs and traditions.
3. Geographic conditions varied in Africa and, as a result, so did agricultural methods and production.

Recommended Procedure

Getting Started Have the pupils turn to the diagram of a medieval European manor on page 211. Briefly review the way land was divided into strips on a manor. Ask the pupils to suggest some ways in which the land could have been used more efficiently. (*A typical answer would be to combine the land into larger sections rather than strips, and to plant different crops in each section.*)

Point out that changes in the manor system of Europe would have meant that fewer people were needed to farm the land. Ask the pupils to explain what the people who were not farmers would have had to do to make a living. (*They could have produced other goods for trade with other people.*)

Stress the fact that as social and political conditions changed, the manors tended to disappear in parts of Europe. Explain that this lesson will discuss how and why these conditions changed.

Developing the Lesson Divide the lesson into two parts. First, have the pupils study the material on pages 249, 250, and 251 up to "Farming in India." Review briefly the social changes that occurred in Europe after 1500. Point out that societies in Europe had become less traditional after 1500 and, therefore, more accustomed to change. Then ask the pupils to suggest some of the changes in agricultural production that occurred in Europe. List these changes on the chalkboard and discuss with the class how these changes altered the nature of the economic systems in western Europe.

Next have the pupils study the material about agricultural production in India, China, Benin, and Kanem-Bornu. This material is on pages 251, 252, and 253. Ask the pupils to explain some of the reasons why there were fewer changes in agriculture in these areas than there were in Europe. Stress the fact that geographic and social conditions may limit changes in the way a society produces goods.

Concluding the Lesson Compare the picture of the Indian farmer on page 251 with the picture of a farmer in India today on page 111. Ask: Do the pictures indicate a change in technology? Why might technological change occur more rapidly in some societies than in others?

End this lesson with a discussion of the "Think for Yourself" questions on page 253. Ask the pupils: Is it more difficult to maintain good farmland year after year in a traditional society than in a nontraditional society? Why?

Going Further Divide the class into three groups. Have one group prepare a large map showing the agricultural products produced in the various parts of the United States. Have the second group prepare a large map showing the physical features (landforms) of the United States. The third group should draw a large map showing climatic conditions in the United States. (Information and examples for these maps can be found in most encyclopedias.)

Have the pupils compare their maps and explain how different geographic and climatic conditions affect agricultural production in the United States.

TEACHING HELPS—THE MANUFACTURING OF GOODS,
pages 254-258

CONCEPTS

1. Technological improvements replaced muscle power with machine power.
2. Industrialization changed the nature of man's social and economic life.
3. Industrialization increased specialization and man's interdependence.

Recommended Procedure

Getting Started Explain to the pupils that the use of machines in manufacturing has dramatically changed man's way of life. Point out to the class that in the late eighteenth century ten men could produce about 48,000 needles a day. But by 1850, one girl could run four machines and produce as many as 600,000 needles. With these facts in mind, have the class discuss the following questions.

1. Does the use of machines increase production? Why?
2. In the case of the use of machines in the production of needles, what effect do you think the increase in production had upon the price of needles? Why?
3. In what ways can the use of machines to produce goods help workers? Why?

Developing the Lesson Ask the class to study the material which deals with the manufacturing of goods in Europe and America on pages 254, 255, 256, and 257 up to "Craft industries in India and China." Also have the pupils study the two pictures on page 254. Have the pupils answer and discuss the questions at the end of the third paragraph on page 254 that pertain to these pictures. Then have the pupils answer and discuss the remaining questions in the body of the material. Stress the point that resources—both human and natural—are needed for industrialization. Ask the pupils to suggest some of the reasons why the United States is so heavily industrialized today. (*The United States has many natural resources and well-trained workers.*)

Ask the pupils to study the remaining material in this lesson on pages 257 and 258. Have them compare the type of manufacturing used in Asia and Africa with the type of manufacturing that took place in Europe during this period of time (1500–1850). Ask the pupils to suggest some of the reasons why industrialization did not occur as quickly in Asia and Africa as it did in Europe. (*The nature of the traditional societies in Asia and Africa inhibited change.*)

Concluding the Lesson Bring this lesson to a close through a discussion of the "Think for Yourself" questions on page 258. Lead the pupils toward an understanding of how rising demand tends to encourage change in manufacturing and tends to encourage an increase in the production of goods.

Going Further To help the pupils understand the speed with which inventions were developed after 1750, have the pupils prepare a time line. Have them begin their time line at 1700 and end it at 1850. Ask the pupils to check encyclopedias and textbooks to discover the major inventions that occurred during this period. (*The inventions included such things as the steam engine, the flying shuttle, the spinning jenny, the power loom, the cotton gin, and so on.*) Have the pupils list the major inventions at the appropriate places on their time line.

Also have the pupils complete the first of the "Things to Do" activities on page 268.

CONCEPTS

1. An increase in demand for goods may lead to an increase in production and trade.
2. Colonialism was often the result of economic policies established by nations seeking economic growth.
3. Economic growth and a favorable balance of trade are usually interrelated.
4. Social and geographic factors may tend to limit a society's economic development.

Recommended Procedure

Getting Started Have the pupils turn to page 263 and study the pictures at the top of the page. Point out that the pictures show two types of articles once used as money in the kingdom of Benin. Ask the pupils to identify the two articles shown in the pictures. (*They are rings of metal and a cowrie shell.*) Then ask the pupils to answer and discuss these questions.

1. What makes money valuable? (*It is scarce, and it is accepted as valuable by the people in the society.*)
2. Why do you think the people of Benin used metal rings and cowrie shells as money?
3. How might metal rings and cowrie shells make buying and selling difficult? (*They had no set value, and it was impossible to make change.*)
4. Why might Benin's money have made it difficult for the people to trade with people from other countries? (*It had no common value—money might not be acceptable to others.*)

Developing the Lesson This lesson should be divided into two sections to help the pupils compare and contrast the way goods were distributed in various parts of the world. Begin the lesson by having the pupils study about Europe and America on pages 258, 259, 260, and 261 up to "The commercial activities of India." Ask the pupils to explain why trade grew and developed in some countries of Europe but not in others. Ask the pupils: Why were colonies valuable to their home countries? What was *mercantilism?* Why did people in the American colonies object to mercantilism? Discuss the answers to these questions with the class.

Next have the pupils study the remaining material about India, China, Benin, and Kanem-Bornu on pages 261, 262, 263, and 264. Ask the pupils to compare the commercial activities of India with those of China. Have the pupils suggest some reasons why Europeans found it easier to trade with India than with China. (*India was closer to Europe, and the Chinese did not want European goods, while many Indians did.*) Then, in a class discussion, ask the class to explain why Europeans carried on direct trade with Benin but only limited direct trade with Kanem-Bornu. Ask: Why did Kanem-Bornu prosper through trade while Benin did not?

Concluding the Lesson Ask the pupils to speculate about why today, the United States is able to maintain a favorable balance of trade. Have the pupils answer the "Think for Yourself" questions on page 264. Ask: Does its location help the United States maintain a favorable balance of trade? Why or why not?

Going Further Have the class turn to page 268 and study the second "Things to Do" activity on that page. Ask the pupils to complete the activity and to be prepared to participate in a class discussion about how trade helps Americans enjoy a comfortable way of life.

TEACHING HELPS—TRANSPORTATION, pages 265-267

CONCEPTS

1. Geographic conditions tend to encourage trade in some nations.
2. Trade and economic growth often lead to internal improvements.
3. Technological improvements in transportation foster economic growth.

Recommended Procedure

Getting Started On a map in the classroom, have the pupils locate the three largest cities in Asia—Tokyo, Japan; Shanghai, China; and Bombay, India. Ask the pupils to explain what each of these large cities has in common from a geographic point of view. Have the pupils suggest some reasons why the geographic locations of these cities may have led to their development and growth. You may want the pupils to suggest how important the geographic location of a city near water is as shown by the growth of some major cities in the United States. Ask: Why is being located near water an advantage for a city?

Developing the Lesson Have the pupils study the material dealing with transportation on pages 265, 266, and 267. Stress the fact that before roads were developed, rivers and canals served as the main highways for trade. Ask the pupils: Are rivers and lakes the main highways for trade in the United States today? What technological developments have changed man's means of transportation since 1800? (*Typical answers would include the steam locomotive, the internal-combustion engine for cars and trucks, the airplane, and so on.*)

Stress that in countries with large populations, such as China, human resources were used as a cheap means of transportation. Have the class discuss why a country with a huge population and very little industry might be inclined to continue to use "muscle power" rather than "machine power." Ask: Why might people in traditional societies be willing to accept a way of life that is based upon the use of human labor rather than on the use of machines? (*Often because this was the way things were done in the past.*)

Concluding the Lesson In a class discussion have the pupils compare transportation in Benin and Kanem-Bornu. Ask the pupils to suggest which of the two kingdoms might have developed more rapidly than the other. Ask them to explain their answers. Then have the pupils answer and discuss the "Think for Yourself" question on page 267.

Going Further Have the pupils gather pictures from newspapers and magazines showing the types of transportation used in different countries. Prepare a bulletin-board display of these pictures and ask the class to suggest reasons why means of transportation differ in some countries.

EVALUATION, CHAPTER 15

Have the pupils discuss the following questions.

1. What conditions might encourage one nation to remain agricultural and another nation to become industrialized?
2. Why can the use of machines—industrialization—improve man's way of life?
3. Why can every nation in the world find it to be possible and valuable to enter into trade with other nations?

TEACHER'S PREVIEW OF CHAPTER 16, pages 269-285

Chapter 16, "Man's Political Activities," includes an introductory page and three teaching units:

Strong Central Governments (pages 270-275)

Democratic Trends (pages 275-280)

Relations Among Countries (pages 281-284)

In this chapter the pupils will learn how powerful central governments developed in Europe. The pupils will also learn how the development of central governments in Europe affected people throughout the world.

The material in this chapter is designed to help the pupils discover how and why the desire for democracy began to develop. They will also discover how the desire for a democratic political system led to changes in the way people were governed.

In the final section of this chapter, the pupils will learn the ways in which the relations among nations affect the way people live.

TEACHING HELPS—Chapter Introduction, page 269

CONCEPTS

1. Political leaders affect political developments.
2. A strong central government can aid the economic growth of its country.

Recommended Procedure

Getting Started Have the pupils observe a political map of the world. Point out that, today, there are more than 125 nations in the world. Then ask the pupils to discuss the following questions.

1. Why do people prefer to live as members of independent nations?
2. What advantages are there in being a citizen of a strong, independent nation?
3. Would it be a good thing for people, in some cases, to unite several modern nations into one large nation? Why?

In a class discussion point out the fact that many countries first began to emerge as unified nations between 1500 and 1850. Explain that the material in Chapter 16 deals with some of these countries.

Developing the Lesson Ask the pupils to turn to page 269 and to study the material on that page. Stress that a strong leader tends to unify the people of a nation and that this unity can bring about a stable political system. Ask: Why may a stable political system help a country develop its economic system?

Concluding the Lesson It may be of interest to have the pupils discuss and express their opinions about whether powerful leaders make events happen or whether events happen and thus create powerful leaders. After this discussion have the pupils complete the "Just For Fun" activity on page 269.

Going Further Have the pupils refer to an atlas or an encyclopedia to determine what new nations have emerged in Africa since 1945. Then have the pupils draw a map showing the political boundaries of the various nations in Africa. Have the pupils show on the map the date each African nation achieved independence.

TEACHING HELPS—STRONG CENTRAL GOVERNMENTS, pages 270-275

CONCEPTS

1. Most European countries first developed as authoritarian governments ruled by a hereditary monarch.
2. Authoritarian political systems often have powerless legislatures.
3. India lacked a strong central government because the people were traditionally loyal to their caste and to their village.
4. The Chinese political system remained virtually unchanged prior to the twentieth century.

Recommended Procedure

Getting Started You may want to begin this lesson by asking the pupils what they think the term "strong central government" means. Ask: Do you live in a society with a strong central government? Have them explain their answers.

Through a class discussion have the pupils suggest some of the advantages and disadvantages of a strong central government. Avoid taking sides, but help the pupils understand that people disagree about this issue and that the disagreement often is the result of the person's idea of what functions a central government should perform.

Developing the Lesson Ask the pupils to study the material on pages 270, 271, 272, and 273 up to "Personal lines of rulers in India." Discuss the nature of the national government in Spain with the pupils. Ask the pupils to explain why Philip II appointed members of the middle class as government officials. (*They were wealthy, educated, and anxious to hold government office.*) Then turn the discussion to the political system in France. Ask: In what ways were the policies of Philip II of Spain and Louis XIV of France alike? In what ways were they different? How do you explain the differences?

Next discuss the type of government that developed in England. Have the pupils explain why Parliament's control of taxes limited the power of English kings.

Now have the pupils study the remaining material on pages 273, 274, and 275. In a class discussion have the pupils compare the political systems that developed in Asia and Africa. Ask the pupils what effect the absence of a strong middle class may have had on the political development of India and China.

Concluding the Lesson Stress the point that monarchs with absolute power developed in Asia, Africa, and Europe. Ask the pupils to discuss "Think for Yourself" on page 275.

Going Further For an interesting activity see the first of the "Things to Do" activities on page 285. You may want to encourage class discussion by having the pupils read their reports aloud to the class and discuss why they might act differently as a king or queen of various countries.

CONCEPTS

1. The belief in democracy is based upon the idea that man has the ability to direct his own political affairs.
2. Societies that do not have cultural traditions of democracy may have difficulty in maintaining a democratic political system.
3. In democratic nations, legislatures operate as a check upon the powers of the executive.

Recommended Procedure

Getting Started Ask the pupils what the executive and the legislative branches of the United States are called. Then ask the pupils to name some of the powers of our President. (*He is commander in chief of our armed forces. He is head of the federal executive branch. He executes our national laws.*) List the powers of the President on the chalkboard.

Then ask the pupils to suggest some of the powers Congress has. (*For example, Congress declares war, approves presidential appointments, passes laws, appropriates money, and so on.*) Ask the pupils to compare the powers they have suggested for the President and Congress and ask them to explain how the powers of the President and the powers of Congress serve to prevent either the executive branch or the legislative branch from gaining total control of our government.

Developing the Lesson Have the pupils study the material on pages 275, 276, and 277 up to "Thirteen colonies of England declare their independence." Review the important provisions of the Magna Charta (see pages 204-205).

Then ask the pupils what two other documents helped establish the rights of Englishmen. (*These were the Petition of Right and the Bill of Rights.*) Ask: What were some of the rights established by the Petition of Right? (*The king had to get Parliament's approval for certain taxes, and the king's power to quarter troops and declare martial law was restricted.*) What were some additional rights established by the Bill of Rights? (*The king could not set aside laws. Free speech was guaranteed in the Parliament. The Parliament had to consent to a peacetime standing army.*)

Have the pupils study the material on pages 277 and 278 up to "Attempts at gaining independence in Latin America." Ask the pupils: Do you think that being Englishmen, the American colonists were more likely to question the king's right to rule them? Why?

Ask the class to study the remaining material on pages 278, 279, and 280. Have them answer and discuss the questions in the body of the material. Ask the pupils to discuss the differences between the growth of democracy in England and the growth of democracy in France. Try to help them understand that England had a background of democratic development but that France did not.

Concluding the Lesson Ask the class to suggest some reasons why they think the first attempt to establish a democratic government in France failed. Then have the pupils discuss the "Think for Yourself" questions on page 280.

Going Further To help the pupils understand the nature of the struggle for independence in Latin America, have them complete the second activity in "Things to Do" on page 285.

CONCEPTS

1. Industrialization leads to international contacts and, possibly, to international competition.
2. The United States tried to isolate itself from most foreign disagreements during the nineteenth century.
3. The economic policies of some European nations led to wars in Asia.

Recommended Procedure

Getting Started Read aloud to the class the following excerpt from President George Washington's "Farewell Address" which he delivered in 1796.

"Observe good faith and justice towards all Nations. Cultivate peace and harmony with all . . .

" 'Tis our true policy to steer clear of permanent Alliances, with any portion of the foreign world . . ."

Ask the pupils: (1) What type of relations did Washington suggest we should have with foreign nations? (2) Why do you think he was opposed to permanent alliances? (3) Why might Washington's advice be hard to follow today?

Explain to the class that this lesson will help them understand some of the difficulties that can arise in international relations.

Developing the Lesson Have the pupils study the material on pages 281 and 282 up to "Early foreign policy of the United States." Ask the pupils to define *nationalism* and *balance of power*. Have the pupils give examples of nationalism and balance of power today. Ask: Why could either nationalism or balance of power lead to conflicts among nations?

Next have the pupils study the remaining material on pages 282, 283, and 284. Have the pupils compare the relations that the United States had with other nations with the relations India, China, Benin, and Kanem-Bornu had with other nations. In a class discussion have the class suggest reasons why the United States was not colonized or attacked as India and China were. Ask the class: How do you think the colonization of India and China affected the attitudes of the people of those countries? Why?

Concluding the Lesson Bring this lesson to a close with a discussion about how the geographic locations of Benin and Kanem-Bornu influenced their relations with other nations. Then have the pupils answer and discuss the "Think for Yourself" questions on page 284.

Going Further Have the pupils gather articles from newspapers regarding some major event in the relations of the United States with another nation. Have the pupils read their articles aloud to the class and describe what our nation's relations are with the other country. Then have the pupils prepare a bulletin-board display of their articles to show the extent of our nation's relations with other countries throughout the world.

EVALUATION, CHAPTER 16

Have each pupil prepare a list of the advantages and disadvantages of a strong central government. Ask several pupils to read their lists aloud to the class and explain the reasons for their listings. In a class discussion have the pupils analyze the advantages and disadvantages of a strong central government. Evaluate the responses.

CONCLUDING THE UNIT

Have the pupils complete Part 4 of the class project. Allow the pupils time to write the third act of their play and to present it. Have the pupils compare and contrast the political systems of the United States and Great Britain. Ask: Do you think a parliamentary system of government would work well in the United States? Why?

TEACHER'S PREVIEW OF UNIT 7, pages 288-351

This unit is divided into three chapters: 17. Modern Societies, pages 291-311; 18. Major Economic Systems, pages 312-331; and 19. Governments of Modern Times, pages 332-349. A special feature is a four-part class project, introduced on page 290 and continued on pages 311, 331, and 349. Other suggested activities, called *Things to Do*, are given on pages 311, 331, and 349. The unit concludes with two pages of evaluation, *Checkup Time* (p. 350) and *Test Yourself* (p. 351).

Unit 7 is a survey of some economic, political, and social changes which have greatly altered the societies of the modern world. The pupils will see how industrialization has been closely tied to many recent changes. For exam-

ple, industrialization caused millions of people in many societies to leave farms and find work in factories. This new working class has had profound social, economic, and political effects in some societies. Another result of industrialization was the growth of cities. Urban centers became very large in some industrialized societies. The cities have greatly changed the culture of many societies.

The pupils should learn after studying this unit, that social, economic, and political conditions are not permanent in any society. One theme of Unit 7 is that the world is constantly changing and that the social sciences are important tools for explaining and guiding changes.

TEACHING HELPS—Unit Introduction, pages 288-290

CONCEPTS

1. Increasingly rapid changes have characterized most societies of the world since the middle 1800's.
2. Today societies regularly borrow economic, political, and social ideas from one another.

Recommended Procedure

Getting Started Direct the pupils' attention to the two pictures on page 288. Establish for the class that the top picture shows one aspect of Indian society and that the bottom picture shows an aspect of Japanese society. Point out to the pupils that much of India's production of goods is still done by hand or with simple tools. Now have the same kind of discussion about Japan. You could encourage the pupils to offer some ideas on why these two societies have not progressed at the same rate.

Developing the Lesson Have the pupils carefully study the unit introduction on page 289 in order to find the answers to these questions: In what fields has great progress been made

over the last 100 years? (*science, business, industry*) What areas of the world were first to industrialize? (*England, Europe, Japan, North America*)

Discuss with the class the impact which the industrialized nations have had on other societies. (*jet airplanes, television, motion pictures*) Let the pupils consider other ways in which scientific and industrial progress has brought all parts of the world closer together.

Concluding the Lesson You might have the class study page 290. Tell the pupils that the class project will require them to act as social scientists. Also point out to them that it will probably take several days for them to complete Part 1 of the class project. Call attention to other parts of the class project on pages 311, 331, and 349.

Going Further Remind the class that movies and television are ways of spreading information and knowledge. American movies and television programs are seen by people in other societies. Ask: Does television seem to show life in America as it really is? Why or why not?

TEACHER'S PREVIEW OF CHAPTER 17, pages 291-311

Chapter 17, "Modern Societies," contains an introductory page and four teaching units:

Industrialization Changes Society (pages 292-296)

New Ideas About Society (pages 297-300)

Democracies and Social Change (pages 300-304)

Examples of Social Systems (pages 305-310)

The aim of this chapter is to show how societies have been changed by industrialization. The pupils will learn how societies were reorganized as industrialization was changing the ways in which people lived. A major concept of Chapter 17 is that societies responded differently to industrialization because of their different histories, cultures, governments, and economic conditions. This chapter gives some background and explanation of the major social systems which have evolved over the last century. After studying the chapter, the pupils should better understand why there are differences in the ways in which societies are organized. And they should become more familiar with sociological tools and concepts as they study Chapter 17.

TEACHING HELPS—Chapter Introduction, page 291

CONCEPTS

1. Machines have both simplified and complicated people's lives.
2. Industrialization has caused social changes in nearly every part of the world.

Recommended Procedure

Getting Started Discuss with the class the significance of social changes. Tell the pupils that social changes are changes in the organization of a society which affect the ways in which people live together. For example, wars can bring about drastic changes in a society. The Civil War in America had a most significant impact on American society. Ask: What were some ways in which American society was changed by the end of slavery?

Discuss with the class some conditions in America today that will probably change our society. You might use population statistics as an example. (*expanding population, increasing number of young people, increasing number of aged people, growing urban and suburban populations*) Let the pupils consider what possible social changes might result from these conditions.

Remind the class that social scientists today study conditions and attempt to explain social changes and their consequences. Ask: Why did most people of the 1800's not realize the kinds of social changes which industrialization would bring?

Developing the Lesson Have the pupils study page 291 to discover what has caused many of the social changes in the world's societies in the last 100 years. Discuss with the class the advantages of peaceful social changes. Ask: Why might rapid social changes be accompanied by violence?

Concluding the Lesson Once more remind the class that Chapter 17 will be largely about the changes in societies brought about by industrialization. Have the class examine the picture on page 291 to see some ways in which the daily lives of people in industrialized societies have been affected by machinery and scientific progress.

Going Further Let the pupils prepare reports on the "Just For Fun" activity on page 291. Discuss with the pupils the significance of their findings. Have them consider the reasons why people generally work far fewer hours today than they did forty or fifty years ago.

TEACHING HELPS—INDUSTRIALIZATION CHANGES SOCIETY, pages 292-296

CONCEPTS

1. New social classes were created and other social classes became more powerful as a result of industrialization.
2. Industrialization often was carried on without regard for its social consequences.

Recommended Procedure

Getting Started You might prepare the pupils for the lesson by presenting them with some additional information about the impact of industrialization on the skilled workers. Tell the class about the Luddites of early nineteenth century England. Organized groups of craftsmen, called Luddites, roamed through sections of England destroying textile machines. In many cases skilled craftsmen were being put out of work by the textile machines. Other craftsmen who kept their jobs had their wages lowered. Eventually the organization of the Luddites was broken up by the English government.

Point out to the pupils that people of that time actually feared the introduction of machinery into the society. Let the pupils express their ideas about the objections which the Luddites and others had about machinery. Ask: How might English manufacturers or the English government have prepared the population for industrialization?

Developing the Lesson Tell the pupils that this lesson will be about some of the ways in which groups or organizations within a society were affected by industrialization. Have the pupils study "Social classes" on page 292 to find out (1) which social class became more powerful and (2) what new social class came into existence. Discuss these social changes and the questions in the text with the class.

Have the pupils study "Increasing urbaniza-tion" on pages 292 and 293. Ask them to list the problems of the cities which they discover in their text. One pupil might read aloud the selection from Michael Gold's book on page 293 while the other pupils study the picture on that page. Ask: Would any of you have enjoyed the life described in the selection and in the picture? Discuss with the class whether there are similar neighborhoods now in big cities.

Direct the class to study the picture on page 294 and then study the text on that page to discover the significance of the action of the young man shown in the picture. Ask: How did the movement of people from the farms into the cities change society?

You might tell the pupils that the young man in the picture on page 294 will probably find work in a factory. He will quite likely be unhappy with his job. Suggest to the pupils that they study pages 295 and 296 to find out why industrial workers were unhappy. Remind the class to answer the questions in the text.

Concluding the Lesson Stress to the class that most working people of the early industrial era were trapped in misery. Allow the pupils to repeat some of the awful problems faced by these people. Emphasize the unsettling effect which social changes can have on people. Now encourage the pupils to answer the "Think for Yourself" question on page 296. Permit the class to discuss the ideas presented so that they might see the possible consequences of their proposed solutions.

Going Further You might ask the pupils to complete the first activity of "Things to Do" on page 311. Some pupils might be encouraged to do research on recent coal-mining tragedies in the United States. Ask: Why might such poor working conditions continue to exist in the coal-mining industry? What might be done to improve these conditions?

CONCEPTS

1. Some people hoped that socialism would correct the social evils caused by industrialization.
2. In many cases the social abuses were so extreme that some people believed that societies could only be changed by destroying the existing institutions.

Recommended Procedure

Getting Started To prepare the pupils for a better understanding of society as Robert Owen and other early socialists desired it to work, you might let them discuss how a committee functions in the classroom. Point out that the members of a committee are expected to play some of the same roles as those played by members of a socialistic society. To stimulate a discussion of these roles, place the following questions about committees on the board.

1. Is there usually a leader of a committee?
2. How is the leader chosen, and what does he do?
3. In order for a committee to work well, what must each member do?
4. How are the rewards of the committee, such as grades, divided among the members? In other words, who gets the rewards or the credit for the accomplishments of the committee?
5. What are the advantages of doing work in a committee?

After a discussion of the questions, ask: For what reasons might committees fail to work well? Guide the pupils' thinking so that they will reach an understanding of how necessary cooperation is to the proper functioning of a committee. Stress, too, the disadvantages of committee work. For example, only one or two people might take responsibility for the work, yet all the members receive equal credit for the results. Or, if cooperation breaks down entirely, then no work is done. Ask the pupils: Would you prefer to work on your own or in a group? Why?

Developing the Lesson Have the pupils study "Help for the workers" and "A model society" on pages 297 and 298 in order to discover how Robert Owen tried to create a better society. Ask the pupils why New Harmony, Indiana, was considered a socialistic society. Discuss the questions in the text with the class.

Direct the class to study from "The spread of socialism" on page 298 through the end of page 299 to determine some of the beliefs of the communists. In discussing these beliefs point out how they differed from the beliefs of the socialists.

Explain to the pupils that most socialists believed that society could be changed gradually and peacefully. The communists, on the other hand, had a pessimistic view about future changes in society. Ask the pupils to study "Marx and the working class" on page 300 to discover Karl Marx's predictions for industrialized societies. Discuss with the pupils why Marx's predictions might have been believed in the late 1800's.

Concluding the Lesson The "Think for Yourself" question on page 300 will serve as a review of some of the ideas presented in the lesson about societies under communism. You will have an opportunity to stress again to the pupils that communism, as well as socialism, was developed in an attempt to help solve the social problems caused by industrialization.

Going Further Encourage the pupils to imagine an ideal society. Ask them to jot down some ideas about the kind of society they might consider to be perfect. Let the pupils discuss their ideas, telling why they believe the society they have described is a good one. Ask: Do you believe that people could create a society like the one you described? How might it be accomplished?

TEACHING HELPS—DEMOCRACIES AND SOCIAL CHANGE, pages 300-304

CONCEPTS

1. As a society became more industrialized, the living conditions of the people improved.
2. Social legislation and concern for the workers came about gradually in most democratic societies.

Recommended Procedure

Getting Started Ask the pupils to examine the chart on page 301 to see how the average life span in the United States has increased. Discuss with the class the reasons the average life span has increased for Americans. (*decreased infant mortality rate, better medical care, progress in medical science, better diets*) Encourage the pupils to consider ways in which longer life spans affect society. (*greater problems of caring for the aged, greater demand for hospitals and colleges*) Tell them that in most Asian, African, and Latin-American countries infant mortality rates are still very high. In these areas today the average life span is about what the average life span in America was in 1850 or 1870. However, increasing birth rates and medical progress have caused the populations in Asia and Latin America to rise steadily. Lead the pupils to see how industrialization can have great social impact.

Developing the Lesson Tell the pupils that there was a lag between industrialization and the general improvement of people's living conditions. Instruct the class to study from "Threat of class war" on page 300 to "Education" on page 302 to discover why this gap was present and to learn some reasons why social changes began to take place in democratic societies. Also encourage the pupils to find out why the formation of labor unions was a significant move toward achieving a more equal distribution of the benefits of industrialization.

Remind the class to answer the questions in the text. Discuss with the pupils the roles which writers, social workers, and unions played in bringing about social changes in democratic societies.

You might discuss with the pupils some of the social progress made in the democratic societies during the late 1800's and the early 1900's. Have them study from "Education" on page 302 to "Think for Yourself" on page 304 to find out the kinds of changes that took place. Discuss with the pupils the importance of each of these changes. You might emphasize the significance which free public schooling has had in making opportunities more equal for people. Ask: Has free public schooling given every person in society the same chance for success? Why?

Remind the pupils to answer any questions in the text. Many of them might be used as questions for discussion.

Concluding the Lesson Challenge the pupils to supply some answers to the "Think for Yourself" question on page 304. The two pictures on page 304 should provide them with some ideas. Ask: Can you name one social problem which you believe requires the immediate attention of the American people? The pupils might discuss the problems presented, expressing their views on how each problem might be solved.

Going Further Have the pupils study the newspapers and watch television for a few days to learn whether there is a strike taking place. If so, they might find out the details of the strike. Discuss whether the strike has any social implications. Ask: Do you believe that every American worker, including a teacher or a doctor, has the right to strike? Encourage each pupil to explain his point of view. Again, stress that a strike can become a major social issue.

CONCEPTS

1. When societies are in a state of crisis and the people find the old institutions incapable of meeting their needs, a different social system might be tried.
2. When a society is creating a new social system, it often borrows ideas from another society which has a working social system.

Recommended Procedure

Getting Started You might provide the pupils with some additional information about the persecution of the Jews by the Nazis. Explain to the class that by the time World War II began in 1939, German Jews were no longer citizens. They could not attend public schools, engage in most businesses or professions, own land, visit parks, libraries, or museums, nor associate with non-Jews. Ask the class: How did the Nazis know who the Jews were? (*All Jews over age six wore yellow badges and only about 1 per cent of the German population was Jewish.*)

Discuss with the pupils why other nations did not rescue the European Jews. (*the major powers were fighting the fascist powers*)

Developing the Lesson Have the pupils study from "A communist society" on page 305 to "Another undemocratic social system" on page 307 to discover why communism won many followers in Russia and how Russian society has been changed by the communists. In discussing their discoveries with the pupils, stress the point that most Russians before 1917 were oppressed, illiterate, and poverty-stricken. Ask: Why does communism seem to appeal to people living in wretched conditions?

You might challenge the pupils to study from "Another undemocratic social system" on page 307 to the "Think for Yourself" question on page 308 in order to discover why fascism became popular in Germany and Italy. Discuss with the class the ways in which a fascist society is undemocratic. Then the class might discuss the questions in the text, especially the "Think for Yourself" question on page 308.

Have the pupils study from "A communist society in China" on page 308 through the first "Think for Yourself" question on page 310 to determine how Soviet ideas about society have influenced the Chinese. Discuss with the class how the communists are attempting to build a new society in China. Ask: What is happening to much of the traditional Chinese society? The first "Think for Yourself" question on page 310 might be discussed by the class.

Concluding the Lesson The material in "Spread of social systems" and the final "Think for Yourself" question on page 310 offer a review of some of the principal ideas of the lesson. Ask the pupils to study this section and discuss the questions with them. Stress to the class that each society changes a social system to suit its own needs.

Take time to check the progress on Part 1 of the class project. You might provide the class with some help in carrying out Part 2 of the class project on page 311.

Going Further The class might be interested in doing further research on Adolf Hitler. Have the pupils seek information in other texts, encyclopedias, and books about his rise to power in Germany. Allow the pupils to share their discoveries about Hitler and lead them to consider some possible reasons why he was able to so greatly affect German society.

EVALUATION, CHAPTER 17

Have the class discuss this question: Why have societies undergone so many changes in the last century? The responses of the pupils to this question will help you evaluate their understanding of Chapter 17.

TEACHER'S PREVIEW OF CHAPTER 18, pages 312-331

Chapter 18, "Solving Economic Problems," contains an introductory page and three teaching units:

Modern Economic Systems (pages 313-320)

Economic Development (pages 321-323)

Some Newly Developing Economies (pages 323-330)

This chapter presents a comparison of the world's major economic systems—capitalism, socialism, and communism. In their study of the chapter, the pupils should become aware of the significant differences among these systems. A brief history of the development of each economic system in selected societies is included in Chapter 18. This background material will help the pupils to understand why societies have chosen different ways to solve economic problems. Certain concepts about economic development will be studied by the pupils. Knowledge of these concepts should help them understand the kinds of economic problems facing most societies in Asia, Latin America, and Africa and some of the attempts being made to solve these problems.

TEACHING HELPS—Chapter Introduction, page 312

CONCEPTS

1. Each society develops a way of producing and distributing goods and services.
2. A society's economic system evolves and changes as the society changes.

Recommended Procedure

Getting Started Direct the pupils' attention to the three pictures on page 312. Give them an opportunity to identify the economic activity being performed by these people. (*production of goods*) Tell the pupils that the picture on the left is of a factory in India. The center picture shows villagers at work in Kenya. And the picture on the right was taken in a Swedish plant. Let the pupils decide which of these societies appears to have the least advanced economy. Point out to the pupils that although there are factories in India, much of India's production is still done by hand. Also tell the class that there are factories in Kenya. Ask the pupils: Why would it be difficult to use these pictures to describe the economies of these societies?

Developing the Lesson Have the pupils study page 312 in order to find out (1) why societies devise economic systems and (2) why societies develop somewhat different economic systems.

You might stress to the class that there are only a few basic ways of organizing an economy. Then lead the pupils to understand that the same economic system will vary from one society to another. Ask the pupils: Why is a society's economic system always changing?

Concluding the Lesson Remind the pupils that every society has an economy and some form of an economic system. Tell the class that this chapter will be about the major economic systems which evolved with industrialization. Suggest to the pupils that they carry out the "Just For Fun" activity.

Going Further You might have the pupils list some products which America imports from Britain, Japan, and West Germany. Also ask the class to list some products which Americans buy from Latin-American countries. After allowing the pupils some time to find this information by looking through a department store or in their own home, encourage them to discuss their findings. Lead the pupils to see that the imported products of the first group of countries are mostly manufactured goods. The goods imported from Latin America are usually agricultural products or raw materials for industrial use. Ask the class: What conclusions can you reach concerning the economies of Britain, Japan, West Germany, and most Latin-American countries?

TEACHING HELPS—MODERN ECONOMIC SYSTEMS, pages 313–320

CONCEPTS

1. The economic systems of most societies are a mixture of socialism and capitalism.
2. As societies become more industrialized, their governments tend to pass more social legislation.

Recommended Procedure

Getting Started You might explain to the pupils that a chief difference among major economic systems is the amount of government control of the economy. Tell the class that throughout history there have been many examples of governments' regulating business activities. For example, before the Industrial Revolution, the European mercantilists supported strict government regulation of business.

As the business class became more powerful in Europe, the power of governments to control businesses diminished. But immediately there were disagreements over what role the government should play in the economy. Three major opinions about this question emerged. You might write these opinions on the board: (1) The government should keep its hands off business. (2) The government should regulate business. (3) The government should own the means of production. Ask the pupils: Which views of the government's role in the economy do many people in our society have? Why? Tell the pupils that these different views help to explain how different economic systems developed.

Developing the Lesson Have the pupils study from "Free enterprise" on page 313 through the "Think for Yourself" questions on page 315, answering the questions as they study. Ask them to describe capitalism by listing some of its characteristics. (*profit motive, private property, individual choices*) Discuss with the class why American capitalism is now regulated by the government. Be sure that the

pupils have answered all questions in the text, giving special attention to the "Think for Yourself" questions on page 315.

Encourage the class to study from "Democratic societies with planned economies" on page 315 to "Think for Yourself" on page 317 to find out how Great Britain has answered the question: What should be the relationship of the government to the economy? Discuss the "Think for Yourself" questions on page 317 with the pupils.

After the pupils study "Other socialist economies" on pages 317 and 318, ask them: Why did many western European countries adopt socialistic practices? Then discuss the "Think for Yourself" question on page 318 with the class.

Instruct the class to find out about the economic system of the Soviet Union by studying from "Nondemocratic societies with government-owned economies" on page 318 to "Think for Yourself" on page 320. Lead the pupils into a discussion of how communism was used to make economic progress in the Soviet Union. Ask: What have been the disadvantages of the communist economic system for the Soviet people? Discuss with the class the "Think for Yourself" question on page 320.

Concluding the Lesson You might list the three major economic systems on the chalkboard. Mention some characteristics of different economic systems. (*private property, government ownership of the means of production, central planning, stockholder meetings*) Ask the pupils to identify the economic system or systems being described.

Going Further The economic depression of the 1930's is merely mentioned in the chapter. Have the pupils do some research on how this depression affected people's lives in America. Some pupils might be able to interview their parents or grandparents. They should ask them about job opportunities, wages, and prices during the 1930's.

TEACHING HELPS—ECONOMIC DEVELOPMENT, pages 321-323

CONCEPTS

1. All societies do not possess the same amounts of wealth.
2. A problem for all the world is to find ways to speed up economic progress in the poorer nations.

Recommended Procedure

Getting Started Prepare the pupils for the lesson by encouraging them to consider how great numbers of people in the world live. Ask them to imagine themselves as members of a poor family living in Asia. Then have the pupils answer questions such as these.

1. What would your diet probably be? (*rice*)
2. What kind of medical and dental attention would you receive? (*none*)
3. What would you do for a living? (*farming*)
4. How would you do the work? (*by hand*)
5. How much formal education would you have? (*none*)

Discuss with the pupils the idea that many people in Asia live in poverty. Point out to them that if the rice crops in Asia fail, millions of people might starve. Ask the pupils to consider some reasons why Asians and many other people are facing such overwhelming economic problems.

Developing the Lesson Have the pupils study page 321 to discover the names and descriptions of the three major stages of economic development. (*highly developed, partly developed, newly developing*) Discuss the terms with the pupils, asking them to give examples of countries in each of the three major stages. Ask the pupils to tell what stage of economic development the United States has reached.

The pupils might study "Importance of economic growth" on page 322, answering the questions in the text to their own satisfaction and then listing those countries and areas of the world which possess the most developed economies. Discuss the questions in the text with the class.

Instruct the class to study from "Barriers to economic growth" on page 322 through the "Think for Yourself" question on page 323. You might encourage the class to answer all questions in the text, including the "Think for Yourself" question. Stress to the pupils that there are no easy solutions to the economic problems facing the poorer societies of the world.

Concluding the Lesson Remind the pupils of the kinds of problems which plague the societies with newly developing economies. (*overpopulation, lack of food, illiteracy, lack of capital*) Ask the pupils: Could America's capitalistic system work successfully in India or China? Why? Point out to the pupils that while capitalism has worked well in the United States, it might not work well under the present social and economic conditions of China or India.

Going Further The pupils might be encouraged to debate a theory made popular by a man called Thomas Malthus who lived from 1766 to 1834. Malthus, an English economist, predicted that the population of the world would continue to increase until there would not be enough food to feed all the people. He warned that eventually starvation would strike the poorer people. Others believe that science and education will solve the problems of food supply. Suggest to the pupils that they express their ideas on these two viewpoints. They should be prepared to give some reasons for their opinions. Ask the class: Will the responsibility for raising living standards in the poorer societies rest with the richer societies or with the poorer societies? Why?

TEACHING HELPS—SOME NEWLY DEVELOPING ECONOMIES, pages 323–330

CONCEPTS

1. Most societies with newly developing economies are adopting largely socialistic economic systems.
2. India and China are trying to solve similar economic problems with opposing economic systems.

Recommended Procedure

Getting Started Prepare the pupils for this lesson by emphasizing to them the way that social and economic problems are often intertwined. For example, some people believe that India's economic problems cannot be solved until its social conditions are changed. Explain to the pupils that India's first prime minister, Jawaharlal Nehru, introduced a program which was designed to make important changes in the lives of the Indian villagers. Most Indians live in small and scattered farming villages. Nehru's program involved the supplying of money and equipment by the government to special teachers. These teachers were to travel to the villages, teaching scientific farming, carpentry, printing, and other trades.

Point out to the pupils that similar educational programs have been developed in many African and Asian nations. Encourage the pupils to suggest other changes that countries with newly developing economies can make to solve their economic problems.

Developing the Lesson Suggest to the pupils that they study from "India in its first years of independence" on page 323 through the "Think for Yourself" question on page 327 in order to find out how India and China are going about solving their very similar economic problems. Have the pupils identify the economic system which each of these nations has adopted. Remind them to answer all questions in the text.

Discuss with the class the problems which India and China have in common. (*large populations, insufficient agricultural production, illiteracy*) Ask the class: How have these two nations chosen different paths to achieving economic progress? The "Think for Yourself" question on page 327 might be discussed.

To discover some of the economic problems confronting Nigeria and Mexico, the pupils might study from "Nigeria" on page 327 to "Think for Yourself" on page 330. Encourage the class to discover what economic advantages these two societies have which India and China do not have. Remind the class to answer all questions in the text.

Concluding the Lesson Have the class discuss the "Think for Yourself" question on page 330. You might encourage the pupils to discuss possible economic programs for Nigeria, China, and India.

Have the pupils continue the class project by carrying out Part 3 on page 331. Remind the pupils to follow the procedures used in Part 2 of the class project.

Going Further Suggest to the pupils that they imagine themselves as powerful leaders in the American government. Suppose that they have decided that the American government should lend a large sum of money to India. Ask them to consider this question: How would you direct the Indian government to use this money in order to achieve social and economic progress in India? Have the class discuss the ideas presented.

EVALUATION, CHAPTER 18

Have the pupils imagine that they are visiting an unfamiliar country. Suggest that they make a list of questions to ask the people of that country in order to discover what kind of economic system they have. In this way, you can check the pupils' understanding of some of the economic concepts of Chapter 18.

TEACHER'S PREVIEW OF CHAPTER 19, pages 332-349

Chapter 19, "Governments of Modern Times," contains an introductory page and four teaching units:

Democratic Political Systems (pages 333-336)

Spread of Western Political Ideas (pages 336-339)

Undemocratic Political Systems (pages 340-343)

Conflicts Among Governments (pages 344-348)

In this chapter the pupils will study about the rise of modern political systems. They will see how democratic governments work in a few selected societies. The pupils should understand that although democratic governments are not all organized in the same way, they all govern with the consent of the people. Chapter 19 will also present a study of undemocratic governments. Again the pupils should gain insight into why a political system is undemocratic. They will see that undemocratic political systems are also organized differently in different societies. Finally, from their study of Chapter 19, the pupils will learn how the political ideas and political systems developed in Europe and North America have spread to many societies.

TEACHING HELPS—Chapter Introduction, page 332

CONCEPTS

1. Democratic political systems developed gradually in the Western world.
2. Many societies today do not have governments controlled by the people.

Recommended Procedure

Getting Started Suggest to the pupils that they examine the picture on page 332 in order to discover what the women are doing. Discuss briefly with the class the significance of the woman-suffrage movement. Tell the pupils that a small meeting in Seneca Falls, New York, has been considered the first woman-suffrage gathering in the United States. From this small beginning, a national campaign developed which was designed to give women the right to vote. Many women and some men joined the campaign. Finally an amendment to the Constitution in 1920 made the vote legal for women. Ask the pupils to think of examples of other groups in America today which are struggling to gain certain rights. Discuss the methods which these groups are using to attain their goals.

Developing the Lesson Have the class study page 332 in order to find answers to these questions: (1) What are the two basic kinds of political systems? (*democratic and undemocratic*) (2) Under a democratic political system where does the government get its power? (*from the people*) (3) Where did modern democratic governments develop? (*in Europe and North America*) Discuss these questions and the questions in the text with the class. You might have the pupils consider some reasons why modern democracy developed in Europe and North America rather than in Asia or in Africa.

Concluding the Lesson You might remind the class that all democratic political systems are not organized in the same way. Also point out to the pupils that undemocratic political systems can be different from one another. Ask the pupils: What is one way to determine whether a government is democratic or undemocratic? (*find out who has the governing power*)

Going Further Suggest to the pupils that they do the "Just For Fun" activity. They might ask members of their families for constitutions of organizations to which they are members. Let the pupils study the constitutions to discover who governs the organizations.

TEACHING HELPS—DEMOCRATIC POLITICAL SYSTEMS, pages 333–336

CONCEPTS

1. Democratic government was achieved gradually in North American and European societies.
2. Some societies achieved peaceful democratic reform while other societies underwent violent upheavals in their efforts to make their governments more democratic.

Recommended Procedure

Getting Started Suggest to the pupils that they examine the picture on page 333 and try to identify the woman seated at the right of the picture. (*Queen Elizabeth II of Great Britain*) You might explain to the pupils what functions the monarch of Great Britain performs today since the king or queen has only limited governing powers. Tell the pupils that the British monarch is the chief of state, performing many of the ceremonial functions of government. For example, Queen Elizabeth II of Great Britain represents the government by visiting the countries which were once British colonies. She tries to maintain good relations between Great Britain and its former colonies. Have the pupils imagine some reasons why this function of the queen is important to Great Britain's economy.

You might point out to the pupils that the queen performs many duties in place of the British prime minister. She attends charity functions, visits disaster areas, and is present at the openings of important buildings or highways. Ask the class: How does the queen help the British prime minister? You might tell the pupils that the President of the United States is the chief of state. Have the pupils discuss the kinds of ceremonial functions which he performs. (*attending the first baseball game of each season, visiting disaster areas, giving White House parties*)

Developing the Lesson Have the class study from "How the British government works" on page 333 to "How the American government works" on page 334 to find answers to these questions about the British political system: (1) Which group in Britain holds the governing power? (2) Who chooses the British prime minister? (3) How was the right to vote won by the British factory workers? Discuss these questions and the other questions in the text with the class.

The pupils might discover how the American political system differs from Great Britain's by studying from "How the American government works" on page 334 through "Slow growth of American democracy" on page 335. (*differences between a parliamentary and a presidential system of government*) Emphasize to the class that the American President exercises more executive power than the British prime minister.

The pupils might study "Democracy spreads through Europe" on page 335 through the "Think for Yourself" question on page 336 to find out how democracy was won in many nations in western Europe. (*by revolutions*) Remind the pupils to answer the questions in the text.

Concluding the Lesson Remind the pupils that democratic government was achieved gradually in most countries of the Western world. Have the pupils discuss how the United States is still working to ensure equal political rights for all its citizens. (*civil rights movement*) You might discuss the "Think for Yourself" question on page 336 with the class.

Going Further Suggest to the pupils that they clip articles and pictures from newspapers or magazines which report the President of the United States performing ceremonial functions. The class might make a bulletin-board display of these newspaper clippings under the heading, "The American President as Chief of State." Discuss with the class how the President might be relieved of some of these duties.

TEACHING HELPS—SPREAD OF WESTERN POLITICAL IDEAS, pages 336-339

CONCEPTS

1. Western political ideas were spread to Africa and Asia by European colonists.
2. Many new African and Asian nations are attempting to establish democratic political systems like those of the European countries.

Recommended Procedure

Getting Started You might provide the class with some additional information about Africa. The peculiar social and political conditions of Southern Africa (Angola, Mozambique, Rhodesia, South Africa) might be of interest to the pupils. The region of South Africa should be located on a map for the pupils. Then tell the class that you are going to describe the racial situation existing in the country of South Africa.

You could first explain to the pupils that there are about 3,500,000 whites out of a total population of about 18,000,000 in South Africa. Although the whites of South Africa have worked together with the blacks in economic activities, the blacks have little political power. Most blacks of South Africa live near white areas where they suffer severe political and social discrimination. White South Africans follow a policy of apartheid or separation of the races. Black South Africans are not permitted the representation in government which their larger numbers would require. Nor are they permitted to live among the whites. Have the pupils discuss possible reasons why the white South Africans have pursued this kind of policy toward the blacks. Ask: How might changes eventually come to South Africa?

Developing the Lesson Suggest that the pupils study from "Empire building in the 1800's" on page 336 to "Think for Yourself" on page 338 to determine ways in which some new nations in Africa and Asia have been affected by Western political ideas. (*India's parliamentary system, Japan's parliamentary government*) Discuss with the pupils all questions in the text including the "Think for Yourself" question on page 338.

Have the pupils examine other examples of new nations which have adopted Western political systems by studying from "Other new governments" on page 338 through the end of page 339. Remind the pupils to answer the questions in the text. Discuss the "Think for Yourself" question on page 339 with the class, emphasizing that most new nations face many problems in trying to establish stable governments.

Concluding the Lesson Instruct the class to look again at the pictures of government leaders on pages 337 and 339. Have the pupils identify each leader and the country which he or she represents. Remind the pupils that achieving stable government is a major political goal of most new nations. Ask the pupils: How can popular leaders help achieve political stability in new nations?

Going Further Encourage the pupils to do some research on the careers of some African leaders. These are men who have played, or who are playing, significant roles in the history of Africa's new nations: Tom Mboya of Kenya, Joseph Mobutu of the Congo, Kwame Nkrumah of Ghana, Sekou Touri of Guinea, and Julius Nyerere of Tanzania. Suggest that the pupils discover ways in which these men have affected Africa. Have the pupils discuss their findings with the class.

TEACHING HELPS—UNDEMOCRATIC POLITICAL SYSTEMS, pages 340-344

CONCEPTS

1. The Russian people have had little experience with democratic government.
2. Sometimes people will give up political freedoms in exchange for economic security.

Recommended Procedure

Getting Started Explain to the pupils that there is a great deal that the Americans and others of the world do not know about the political, social, and economic conditions of the Soviet Union. For example, write the following statements on the board and ask the pupils whether each is true or false.

1. All Russians are communists.
2. Religion does not exist in the Soviet Union.
3. No Russian can own any private property.

After a discussion of the pupils' answers, tell the class that all these statements are false. Ask the class: Why are there so many things which we do not know about the Soviet Union? (*Soviet and American propaganda, Soviet secrecy, limited contact between the Soviet Union and nations of the Western world*) Discuss with the pupils why this "wall" between the Soviet Union and the Western world might be a threat to world peace.

Developing the Lesson Suggest that the pupils discover how much democracy the Russian people have ever experienced by studying "Russia's long history of undemocratic government" on page 340. Stress to the class that the communists were not the first rulers in Russia to deny people any political rights.

Encourage the pupils to find out who holds the governing power in the Soviet Union today by studying "How government works in the Soviet Union" on pages 340 and 341. (*Communist party*) Remind the class to answer the questions in the text.

You might take time to discuss the chart on page 341 with the class. Emphasize to the pupils that the major difference between the Soviet government and democratic governments is that the Soviet government is not freely elected by the people. Discuss the "Think for Yourself" question on page 342 with the pupils.

Have the class study the remaining material through the "Think for Yourself" question at the top of page 344 and answer all questions in the text. Discuss with the pupils how the Nazi government in Germany was undemocratic. You might allow the pupils time to answer the "Think for Yourself" question on page 344.

Concluding the Lesson Emphasize to the pupils that many nations today which have undemocratic governments also have a long history of undemocratic governments. Ask the pupils: Do you think that people need to be educated in order to make a democratic government work in their country? Why?

Going Further Tell the class that Nikita Khrushchev, a former premier of the Soviet Union, once argued that the Soviet government was democratic. Khrushchev maintained that since the Communist party represented all the Soviet people, only one political party was necessary in the Soviet Union. Encourage the pupils to offer arguments against the one-party system. Allow them time to write their ideas on paper and present them to the class.

TEACHING HELPS—CONFLICTS AMONG GOVERNMENTS, pages 344-348

CONCEPTS

1. Because societies which hold conflicting political, economic, and social ideas have attempted to impose their ideas on other people, peace has been difficult to maintain in this century.
2. The threat of nuclear war makes it more necessary for nations to prevent wars.

Recommended Procedure

Getting Started You might prepare the pupils for this lesson by explaining to them that by 1914 Europe had come to dominate the world through colonialism. Tell the pupils that the colonial possessions of the European nations included a good portion of the world's population and land surface. You might write this statement on the board: "The sun never sets on the British Empire." Let the class interpret the meaning of the statement. Remind the class that the British Empire has now virtually disappeared. Encourage the pupils to think of reasons why acquiring colonies became so important to the European nations. (*power, prestige, raw materials, markets*) Stress to the class that competition among these nations for colonies was a major cause of World War I.

Developing the Lesson Suggest to the class that they find out other causes of World War I by studying from "A struggle for power" on page 344 through "European governments faced many problems" on page 345. Stress the extent of the war to the pupils by referring them to the map on page 345. Discuss the questions in the text with the class.

Ask the pupils: How did World War I cause serious economic and political problems for Europe? Encourage them to find answers to this question by studying from "European governments faced many problems" on page 345 to "The Second World War, 1939-1945" on page 346.

Have the class study from "The Second World War, 1939-1945" on page 346 to "Distrust among governments continues" on page 348 to discover in what way World War II was a struggle between conflicting political systems. Ask the class: Why did the Soviet Union fight on the side of the democratic nations? Remind the class to answer all questions in the text.

The pupils might complete this lesson by studying the remainder of page 348 to find out why World War II did not lead to permanent world peace.

Concluding the Lesson Allow the pupils some time to discuss the "Think for Yourself" questions on page 348. Remind the class that most of the conflicts in the world since 1945 have been between communist and noncommunist nations.

Going Further Ask the pupils to write a few paragraphs expressing their ideas on how world peace might be achieved. Allow time for the pupils to present their ideas to the rest of the class.

EVALUATION, CHAPTER 19

Have the pupils compare what life is like for the individual in a society with a democratic government, a communist government, and a fascist government. Remind them of such things as schooling, religion, and freedom of expression. The pupils' responses should help you evaluate their understanding of the major political concepts of this chapter.

CONCLUDING THE UNIT

Allow the pupils sufficient time to complete Part 4 of the class project on page 349. You might use the final questions in the class project as a review of the unit. To further evaluate the pupils' understanding of Unit 7, ask them: How will societies influence one another even more in the future?

TEACHER'S PREVIEW OF UNIT 8, pages 352-408

Unit 8 is divided into three chapters: 20. Recent Trends, pages 355-371; 21. Challenges Facing Modern Man, pages 372-389; and 22. Meeting the Challenges, pages 390-406. There is a four-part class project introduced on page 354 and continued on pages 371, 389, and 406. Other suggested activities, called *Things to Do*, are given on pages 371, 389, and 406. The unit concludes with two pages of evaluation, *Checkup Time* (p. 407) and *Test Yourself* (p. 408).

Unit 8 provides background material for the pupils to use to develop an understanding of some of the trends in the world and to help the pupils understand the social scientists' part in planning for the future. The unit begins, in Chapter 20, with the subject of land use and population trends. Some of the various kinds of geographic areas are discussed in terms of their ability to adequately support human life. Then the chapter goes into the subject of population growth and migration patterns and concludes with information on both economic and political trends. The unit continues, in Chapter 21, with a discussion of some of the challenges facing modern man. Then, in Chapter 22, there is an explanation of how man meets his challenges.

TEACHING HELPS—Unit Introduction, pages 352-354

CONCEPTS

1. The world is in a state of constant change.
2. Man attempts to shape his environment to enable him to live satisfactorily in it.

Recommended Procedure

Getting Started The pupils may wish to discuss their impressions of the pictures on page 352. Directing their attention to these pictures, have them discuss the answers to the following questions.

1. What obvious changes have taken place in the societies of which these people are a part?
2. Do some societies seem to resist change? If so, what reasons might social scientists give for this resistance? (*Examples: Geographer—The geography of a society might isolate it from other societies; Anthropologist—Tradition may bring some societies to resist change; Sociologist—In some societies, isolated village life may keep people out of touch with certain forces of change; Economist—Some societies are not far above a subsistence level. Their people are kept busy trying to satisfy basic needs.*)
3. Is change inevitable? Explain.

Developing the Lesson Have the pupils turn now to page 353 and study the lesson. Then lead them in a discussion of the meaning of the inset quotation and of how it applies to man's continuing problems. Explain that social scientists study day-to-day events in order to determine whether or not the events seem to be establishing a pattern. This pattern—or trend—helps the social scientists to help man plan for the future.

Concluding the Lesson Review the lesson, going over again, what trends are and why they are so significant to the social scientists.

Refer to the class project on page 354. Tell the pupils that Part 1 of the project will help them understand some of the decisions man must make in order to make wise use of his land. Point out that the project has other parts on pages 371, 389, and 406.

Going Further Have the pupils make a class list of problems posing great challenges to mankind. The pupils might keep these lists for reference and modification as they study the lessons in this chapter.

TEACHER'S PREVIEW OF CHAPTER 20, pages 355-371

Chapter 20, "Recent Trends," contains an introductory page and three teaching units:

Land Use and Population Trends (pages 356-361)

Economic Trends (pages 362-367)

Political Trends (pages 368-370)

The chapter helps the pupils understand the changes and trends in the world. Separate teaching units are devoted to population trends, economic trends, and political trends.

TEACHING HELPS—Chapter Introduction, page 355

CONCEPTS

1. Changes that have taken place in the past give some clues of the direction of changes in the future.
2. Man must try to anticipate his future needs.

Recommended Procedure

Getting Started Directing attention to the map on page 355, have the pupils tell the meaning of the map title. Help them to use the map key in determining the approximate population of each of the ten countries represented on the map. Also, discuss the cartographer's technique of using a somewhat vertical, double-ruled line to indicate that much of the ocean is not shown on this map.

Developing the Lesson Have the pupils study the lesson on page 355. You might wish to lead the pupils in a discussion of why man must be aware of trends and help them with the answers to the questions included in the text. Discuss the particular problems that would be caused by a high population density such as that in India. Then discuss the problems that might be caused by a low population density. (*inadequate labor supply; underdeveloped industries*)

Concluding the Lesson Review the lesson, giving the pupils an opportunity to share their answers to the questions in the second paragraph on page 355. Stress the importance of man's being aware of trends. Then ask the pupils to follow the suggestion in "Just For Fun."

Going Further You might have the pupils set up a little research study to help determine the trend in the average size of families. Perhaps the pupils could gather and record the following information.

1. The number of children in their family.
2. The number of children in the family of each of their grandparents.
3. The number of children in the family of each of their great grandparents.

Consolidate the data gathered by the class. Ask the class to determine whether or not a trend in family size is indicated. Discuss the data and its possible use by economists, sociologists, and any other social scientists who might be concerned.

TEACHING HELPS—LAND USE AND POPULATION TRENDS, pages 356–361

CONCEPTS

1. A relatively small portion of the earth's surface is suitable for human life.
2. The earth's surface is unevenly populated.

Recommended Procedure

Getting Started You might begin this lesson by pointing out that man is becoming increasingly concerned over the rapid growth in the world's population. Explain that man's fears are thoroughly justified in that, while the area of the land surface remains the same, the number of people on that surface is growing very rapidly. And, you might also explain that not all the land is suitable for human life. Perhaps you might involve the pupils in a discussion of the factors making some parts of the earth uninhabitable. Stress such things as climate (*excess or deficiency of heat and water*), topography (*too high, too low*), and location. You may wish to refer the pupils to physical maps and rainfall maps to discover places with unfavorable environments.

Developing the Lesson The lesson on pages 356–361 might best be presented by dividing the material into two discussion sections.

Section 1. "The earth's land and water"— "Land use"

Section 2. "A crowded planet"—"Migrations of people"

Before having the pupils study section 1, you may wish to give some help in reading the map on page 356. Help the pupils locate the North Pole. Encourage speculation as to why the cartographer chose the type of projection he used. You may wish to call attention to the continuous nature of the oceans and the proximity of the various continents to one another. Then have the pupils study the text material to "A crowded planet," on page 359. You might wish to help them in reading and interpreting the circle graph on page 358. Point out that the total amount of land on earth is represented by the circle. Discuss the possibility of increasing the amount of land under cultivation, the possible sources of this land, and the probable effects on the sources. (*Land taken from woodlands or forests spoils them for their original use.*) Then ask the pupils to discuss why social scientists are so concerned over the way man uses the land.

Next, have the pupils study section 2. Give special attention to the chart on page 360. On a world map, or on a globe, have the pupils locate the various parts of the earth named on the chart. Challenge them to make comparisons of the amount of available land in each of these places. Upon completing their study of section 2, the pupils may be asked to answer the questions in the text. Then, ask the pupils to think of ways social scientists might help man plan to make better use of the land and living space.

Concluding the Lesson Review the two discussion sections of this lesson, going over the land use and population trends. Ask the pupils to answer the questions in "Think for Yourself" on pages 359 and 361.

Going Further Have the pupils do some research on the ways man is trying to make wiser use of his land. Perhaps the pupils could do some research on a piece of land in their community. They might gather data to use in making a graph like the one on page 358, after establishing their own classifications. (*land for houses, land for other buildings, land for streets, and so on*)

CONCEPTS

1. The resources of the earth are unevenly distributed.
2. In many parts of the world, the rate of population growth exceeds the rate of increase of production of goods and services.

Recommended Procedure

Getting Started It is important that the pupils realize why man is concerned with economic trends. You might take some time to help them discover what economic trends are. For example, in a country where the population increases rapidly and the total production of goods and services is stable, the economic trend is toward poverty. Have the pupils conjecture as to the economic trend in their own state during the past ten years. (*toward poverty, toward greater affluence, or unchanged*)

You may wish to introduce the following terms now. Help your pupils with the pronunciation of each term in the list, and develop background for understanding its meaning when it appears in the lesson.

fossil fuels	hydroelectric power
Statistical Yearbook	nuclear power
per capita	uranium
Gross National Product	

Developing the Lesson This lesson might best be presented by dividing the material into three discussion sections.

Section 1. "More goods and services"—"Uneven economic growth"

Section 2. "Sources of power"—"Uneven production of electricity"

Section 3. "Number of workers and hours worked"

Before the pupils study section 1, ask them to use the map on page 355 in locating the countries named in the table on page 362. Then have the pupils conjecture as to the possible reasons for including these countries in the table. Discuss the possible reasons why economists often have to rely on statistics that are not truly correct (census figures cannot be up to date). As the pupils study section 1, encourage them to answer each question in the text to their own satisfaction.

When discussing section 1, stress the social implications of uneven economic growth—the dissatisfactions that arise among people who see the inequities caused by uneven growth.

After taking the time to help the pupils understand how to read the table on page 363, have them study section 2. As the pupils study, ask them to determine the relation between the sources of power used and the development of a country's economy. Discuss the answers to the questions in the body of the text. Again stress the fact that some parts of the world have a much greater share of the common sources of power than other parts have.

Finally, have the pupils study section 3 of the teaching unit, answering the questions included in the body of the text as they study. In discussing this part of the lesson point out that their are variations in the amount of time workers spend in doing productive labor. Point out some of the social consequences that result from these variations.

Concluding the Lesson Review the lesson, going over the GNP, per capita income, sources of power (energy), and employment trends. Stress the idea that there are definite limits on the resources—material as well as human—but there are no definite limits on man's wants. Also, stress the fact that man cannot have everything that he wants. However, he can come closer to meeting this goal in some parts of the earth than he can in other parts.

Going Further Ask the pupils to prepare to discuss the following question.

How might longer life spans and lower death rates affect economic trends?

TEACHING HELPS—POLITICAL TRENDS, pages 368-370

CONCEPTS

1. The people of the earth can better their living conditions through cooperation.
2. There must be improved means of communication among the people of the earth.

Recommended Procedure

Getting Started The point was made, in one of the earlier lessons, that while the area of the earth's surface remains the same, the number of people on that surface is growing rapidly. You might begin this lesson by reminding the pupils of this fact and then telling them that social scientists—and all mankind—are very much concerned with the special problems that are caused by the growing number of people. (*Man must find ways to increase food production; find ways of increasing production of goods and services; improve economic relations among countries; help underdeveloped nations; raise the world's standard of living; find ways to improve relations among all people.*) Point out that people often turn to their government to help in the solution of social and economic problems. In cases where governments cannot solve the problems, people sometimes create new forms of government. Have the pupils discuss some of the options open to people who want new forms of government. Point out that political trends might be toward a greater or lesser degree of world cooperation, a greater or lesser degree of isolationism, and so on.

Developing the Lesson Have the pupils turn now to page 368 and study the lesson on pages 368-370. Ask the pupils to answer the questions included in the body of the text and determine the answers to the following questions.

1. What significance can be found in the rapidly increasing number of small, independent nations? (*People want to determine their own future. They will not submit to being governed by others.*)

2. In what ways is the economic association of the European Economic Community similar to the economic association of the states of the United States? (*The member nations have furthered economic cooperation by reducing or removing tariff barriers within the association.*)
3. What significance is there to be found in the giant steps forward that have been taken in the field of communication? (*The people of the earth can learn the habits and customs of one another.*)

Point out that the African tribes developed on land that is relatively near the equator. Also point out the fact that the tribes are unevenly distributed—more tribes developed near the coasts than farther inland.

Concluding the Lesson Review the lesson, asking the pupils to supply evidence indicating a trend toward cooperation among the nations of the world. Stress the importance of improved transportation and communication. Then ask the pupils to answer the question in "Think for Yourself" on page 370.

Going Further Perhaps the pupils would be interested in comparing some pre-World War I maps of Europe and Africa with modern maps to collect data showing whether the political trend on those continents is toward more or fewer nations.

EVALUATION, CHAPTER 20

Have the class discuss these questions.
1. Why is it becoming more and more necessary that man make wise use of the earth's land and water?
2. Why is it that some of the nations with the largest populations have a relatively small Gross National Product?
3. What is significant about the growth of such institutions as the United Nations and the European Economic Community?

TEACHER'S PREVIEW OF CHAPTER 21, pages 372–389

Chapter 21, "Challenges Facing Modern Man," contains an introductory page and four teaching units:

Social and Physical Needs (pages 373-379)
The Need for Materials (pages 379-384)
The Need for Transportation (pages 384-386)
Political Challenges (pages 386-388)

The chapter helps the pupils understand the challenges and problems facing modern man. The pupils gain an insight into the problems of overcrowding, food scarcity, smog conditions, fuel and material shortages, and inadequate transportation facilities. They also are made aware of the political challenges facing man today.

TEACHING HELPS—Chapter Introduction, page 372

CONCEPTS

1. The cities of the world are increasing in size.
2. Some of the problems of man become more severe as a result of increasing concentrations of people.

Recommended Procedure

Getting Started To begin this lesson, direct the pupils' attention to the picture on page 372. Ask them to study the picture carefully to find specific details that might be of interest to social scientists. Then have the pupils answer such questions as the following: What conclusions might an economist and a sociologist come to concerning the people and the area pictured here? What problems are the people pictured here facing in their everyday life?

Developing the Lesson Have the pupils study the lesson on page 372 to discover something about recent population trends. Stress the fact that the world's population is becoming more and more concentrated in huge metropolitan areas. Ask the pupils to suggest some of the social, political, and economic reasons why people migrate to the cities and what problems are developing because of these migrations. You might develop the discussion further by asking the pupils to discuss the open-ended question in the annotations on page 372. Suggest to the pupils that the picture they have just studied will help them in their discussion.

Concluding the Lesson You might have the pupils suggest some of the challenges that people in their own community must face in meeting their needs for food, clothing, shelter, and recreation. Discuss how these challenges are like those of city dwellers everywhere. Then have the pupils do the "Just For Fun" activity on page 372.

Going Further Have the pupils prepare a chart indicating the problems that are created when the population of a community or city increases. They might use their own community for this project. Then, on the same chart, the pupils might make suggestions as to how the problems could be solved. Have a class discussion of the various problems and solutions that the pupils suggest.

CONCEPTS

1. The problems involved in satisfying man's needs increase as the population increases.
2. The resources that are required to satisfy man's needs are not evenly distributed throughout the world.
3. Many people of the world cannot meet their basic social and physical needs.

Recommended Procedure

Getting Started Have the pupils turn to page 373 and observe the picture of a marketplace in Saigon. Ask the pupils to note those details in which social scientists would be particularly interested. (*narrow, crowded streets; small, cluttered shops with wares piled in the street; people are not wearing shoes; people are simply and similarly dressed*) Then ask the pupils to draw conclusions from these details. Lead the pupils to the conclusion that the narrow, cluttered streets would certainly suggest a lack of living space.

Before going further, direct the pupils' attention to the bar graph and the circle graph on page 375 and the circle graph on page 377. Help the pupils to interpret these graphs during the development of the lesson.

Developing the Lesson This lesson might best be presented by dividing it into three discussion sections.

    Section 1. "The need for space"—"The need for housing"
    Section 2. "The need for food"
    Section 3. "Water"—"Air"

Before the pupils turn to section 1, write the following word pattern on the chalkboard. Tell the pupils that after they have studied section 1, they should be able to explain the meaning implicit in this word pattern. Have them explain the problems created when too many people are crowded into too little space.

overcrowding
↓
slums → unsanitary conditions
↓
violence
↓
crime

Then ask the pupils to study section 2, "The need for food" on pages 375-376, in order to discover the challenges man faces in his attempt to meet his needs for food and to have proper nutrition. Once again, direct the pupils' attention to the graphs on page 375 and to the table on page 376. Then you might ask such questions as the following.

1. What is the relation between overpopulation and malnutrition?
2. Is there sometimes a connection between the overcrowding of an area and the protein deficiency of the people in that area? Explain.

Next, ask the pupils to study section 3 beginning with "Water" on page 376 and ending on page 378, answering the questions as they study. Call special attention to the graph on page 377 which will help them realize the major uses man has for water. You might have the pupils answer the following question: Does man sometimes seem to be shortsighted in his use of the water and air? Explain.

Concluding the Lesson Go over, once again, man's social and physical needs and his use of air and water. Then ask the pupils to answer the questions in "Think for Yourself" on pages 373 and 379.

Going Further Have the pupils do some research on the problems caused by the pollution of our physical environment. Some of the pupils might be interested in preparing a chart which would indicate both the problems caused by pollution and the ways man is trying to reduce pollution.

TEACHING HELPS—THE NEED FOR MATERIALS, pages 379–384

CONCEPTS

1. The amount and distribution of natural resources are related to the well-being of man and nations.
2. The natural resources of the world are not evenly distributed.
3. Man has learned to use his natural resources to improve his life.

Recommended Procedure

Getting Started You might begin this lesson by emphasizing the need man has for materials. Have the pupils carefully examine the picture of the electric stripping shovel on page 379 and point out the vast difference in size between the automobiles at the base of the stripping machine, and the stripping machine itself. Carry out this comparison further by explaining that the weight of the shovel (27,000,-000 lbs.) is equal to the total weight of about 7,000 automobiles, and that it would be possible to put several automobiles into the dipper (180 cubic yard capacity) at the same time. Then, as the pupils consider these facts, have them think of possible answers to the following questions.

1. What is the purpose of constructing such a large machine?
2. What does the size of this machine indicate about man's need for materials?

Allow the pupils time to discuss their answers to these questions. Then lead them to the conclusion that the size of the shovel suggests a vast need for coal to satisfy man's expanding industries.

Developing the Lesson This lesson might best be presented by dividing it into two discussion sections.

Section 1. "Coal"—"Petroleum and natural gas"
Section 2. "Iron ore and steel"—"Forests"

Have the pupils study section 1 to discover some of the ways coal, petroleum, and natural gas are important to man. Then direct their attention to the map on page 380 and ask them the following question: What evidence can you give to prove that there is an uneven distribution of coal in the United States?

Discuss the answers to the questions in the text, giving particular attention to this question: How does the uneven distribution (of coal) affect the economy of the nations of these continents?

Then direct attention to the map on page 381. Point out that the cartographer has used parallel lines to indicate the deletion of much of the Atlantic Ocean area. After you have discussed the answers to the questions in the text, have the pupils answer the questions below.

1. What areas of the world are rich in both petroleum and metal deposits?
2. Why is petroleum so important to man?

Next, have the pupils study the material in section 2 beginning with "Iron ore and steel" on page 381 and ending on page 384. After discussing the answers to the questions in the text, lead the pupils in a discussion of why steel, probably more than any other metal, is important in a nation's economy.

Concluding the Lesson In reviewing the lesson, go over, briefly, man's need for materials. You might have the class suggest reasons why, and to what degree, a nation's economy depends on its access to the world's natural resources. Then have the class answer the questions in "Think for Yourself" on pages 380, 381, 383, and 384.

Going Further The pupils might be interested in preparing a large map (for display) showing the location of mineral deposits and other natural resources of the United States. Some of the pupils might like to prepare a report which would accompany the map and explain just what percentage of the world's most important natural resources are located within the United States.

TEACHING HELPS—THE NEED FOR TRANSPORTATION,
pages 384-386

CONCEPTS

1. A nation must have adequate transportation facilities.
2. Improvements in the systems of transportation must keep pace with the expansion of the economy.

Recommended Procedure

Getting Started In getting started, refer back to the teaching lesson *Economic Trends*, pages 362-367. It was in this particular lesson that the meaning of Gross National Product was explained. Take some time now to review the definition and meaning of GNP, and then you might remind the pupils that it is estimated (see "Uneven economic growth," page 363) that in the 1970's alone, the production of goods and services in the United States will almost double. With this estimate in mind, the pupils should discuss the answer to the following question: What would happen if transportation systems in the United States were not improved and expanded to keep pace with the expansion in industrial output?

Developing the Lesson Have the pupils study the lesson on pages 384-386 to discover the importance of an adequate system of transportation to economic advancement. The pupils should answer the questions included in the body of the text. Then you might ask the pupils this question: Why would a society with a subsistence economy be expected to have a backward system of transportation? After the pupils have discussed the answer to this question to their own satisfaction, draw the pupils' attention to the huge sulfur storage depot pictured on page 384. You might point out that the combined capacity of the tanks at this depot would probably be millions of gallons. To go further, you might add that the ship in the picture was designed to carry great amounts of sulfur, and probably it would be capable of making transoceanic voyages. Then ask the pupils the following question: What effect might the expansion of international, worldwide trade have on the size and number of ships needed? After discussing the answer to this question, the pupils might examine the pictures on page 386 and answer such questions as the following: What is significant in the contrast between the two forms of transportation pictured here?

Concluding the Lesson Review the lesson, going over the reasons why it is essential to develop transportation facilities. Perhaps the pupils can think of ways man is further improving his systems of transportation. Then have the pupils answer the question in "Think for Yourself" on page 386.

Going Further Have different pupils choose a specific food or article of clothing and try to list the possible forms of transportation involved in getting it from its source to the consumer. The pupils may wish to compare lists to see who has the longest one.

TEACHING HELPS—POLITICAL CHALLENGES, pages 386-388

CONCEPTS

1. Man needs to settle disputes peacefully.
2. Governments must find ways to reduce the crime rate.
3. Governments must find ways of winning the battle against pollution.

Recommended Procedure

Getting Started You might begin this lesson by leading the pupils to the conclusion that, of all the problems challenging the governments of the world, the following are among the most serious.

1. How to solve international disputes peacefully.
2. How to reduce the crime rate.
3. How to eliminate the pollution of the physical atmosphere.

Then, you might ask the following questions and take some time to discuss the answers.

1. Why is it becoming more and more necessary that people learn to settle things peacefully?
2. How does the rising crime rate endanger a nation's government and way of life?
3. How might a government's hasty efforts to eliminate pollution be detrimental to its economy?

Developing the Lesson You might divide this lesson into three discussion sections.

Section 1. "Settling disputes among nations"
Section 2. "Reducing crime"
Section 3. "Reducing pollution"

Have the pupils study section 1 "Settling disputes among nations" on pages 386-387 to discover why man has often chosen warfare as a way of settling disputes and why, if he is to survive, he must find ways to settle disputes peacefully. You might ask the pupils to discuss the following statement: The development of weapon systems has brought an urgent need for nations to avoid the use of force in settling their differences.

Next, have the pupils study section 2 "Reducing crime" on pages 387-388 to discover the ways the governments of the world are challenged by the increased crime rate. The class might speculate as to what changes in our society might have brought an increase in crime and what political changes society can make to reduce crime.

Then, ask the pupils to study section 3 "Reducing pollution" on page 388 to discover how the governments of the world are challenged by the pollution of the physical atmosphere. The class might then discuss the answer to the following question: Why is it necessary that nations work together in meeting the challenge of reducing pollution?

Concluding the Lesson Review the lesson, going over the political challenges facing man. Then ask the pupils to answer the questions in "Think for Yourself" on pages 387 and 388.

Going Further You might ask the class to think about the pollution problem as it affects their own community. Then have the class prepare a report on what could be done to reduce the pollution of their land, air, and water.

EVALUATION, CHAPTER 21

Have the class discuss these questions.

1. What is significant in the fact that the most densely populated areas of the world are also the areas where there is a great food deficit?
2. What relationship is there between the status of a country's economy and the status of the country's transportation system?
3. Why must man meet his political challenges as a joint effort among nations?

Chapter 22, "Meeting the Challenges," has an introductory page and three teaching units:

Meeting Social and Physical Needs (pages 391-396)

Meeting the Need for Materials (pages 397-400)

Government and Social Change (pages 401-405)

This chapter helps the pupils understand a number of man's social and economic needs and his problems in meeting them. It acquaints the pupils with many of the challenges facing man today as he attempts to adjust his living to the realities of a world of limited resources and to an environment that will not sustain life unless pollution diminishes, past abuses are corrected, and conservation is practiced. The pupils are also made aware of some of the ways that governments today are helping their people to have better living conditions.

TEACHING HELPS—Chapter Introduction, page 390

CONCEPTS

1. The natural resources and raw materials of the earth are limited.
2. Man's supply of natural resources and raw materials affects how he lives.

Recommended Procedure

Getting Started You might begin by having the pupils think about some of the earth's resources that they might help to conserve in their daily living and the ways by which they might do so. The pupils might suggest such things as conserving water by not letting it run longer than is necessary, saving electricity by turning off lights when they are not being used, and not wasting food by eating all the food on their plate.

You may have to guide the pupils' thinking when it comes to some areas of conservation. For example, the pupils may not immediately see that not burning trash in their yard and not throwing trash in streams, on highways, and elsewhere are ways by which they can help reduce air pollution and water pollution.

Developing the Lesson Ask the pupils to study page 390 to gain some general ideas about the earth's resources and why conservation of them is necessary. You might suggest that the pupils think about some of the conse-quences to man and the quality of life he will be able to have if he does not practice conservation of the earth's resources.

Concluding the Lesson Discuss the lesson on page 390 with the class. Emphasize the importance of the earth's environment to man's safety and health. Also stress the importance of the natural resources and raw materials of the earth in satisfying man's needs and wants. Remind the class to do the "Just For Fun" activity suggested at the bottom of page 390.

Going Further You might suggest that the pupils think about some of the different kinds of materials that are part of the articles that they use in their daily living. They might also attempt to identify the raw materials from which the articles they name have been processed or made. The pupils will probably have little difficulty identifying the raw materials of many articles made of wood, copper, tin, cotton, silk, wool, and leather. You might suggest that the pupils look in dictionaries, encyclopedias, or other books to discover the raw materials used in making articles of aluminum, glass, plastics, rayon, and so forth. A list of articles and the raw materials from which they are made might be placed on the chalkboard as the pupils discuss their suggestions and findings.

CONCEPTS

1. Conservation of space and land are important to man and the quality of his life.
2. A lack of fresh water or clean air can greatly limit man's life and activities.

Recommended Procedure

Getting Started You might have the pupils study the pictures on page 391 to see how the builders of such housing units made use of land and space. Then you might have the pupils compare such housing units with the kinds of housing that exist in their own community. Remind the pupils to stress both the similarities and differences between the way in which the housing in their community and in the pictures uses land and space for living purposes.

Developing the Lesson Have the pupils study page 391 and page 392 to "Increasing the supply of food" to find out about some attempts of man to meet the challenge of providing living space in today's cities without causing overcrowding. In a class discussion stress the fact that because more and more people are moving to cities the need to conserve living space and to use it wisely is constantly increasing.

Next have the pupils study the remainder of page 392, all of page 393, and page 394 to "Water" to learn how the findings of scientists are helping today's farmers raise more and better crops than ever before. Also ask the pupils to look for reasons why some of the world's farmers are not using the modern and scientific methods of farming. Discuss the material with the class, emphasizing the need for both economic aid and modern education for the people in some parts of today's world. Help the pupils to understand why change is a difficult thing for some people.

Finally, have the pupils study the remainder of page 394 and all of pages 395 and 396 to become aware of the challenges faced by man in getting a sufficient supply of fresh water and in securing a healthy environment of clean air. Discuss the problems man has today in maintaining a healthy environment. Point out the fact that man may have to change some of his ways of living in order to conserve his environment and to keep it safe and healthy.

Concluding the Lesson You might draw together all the material in this lesson on meeting man's social and physical needs in a class discussion. Emphasize the fact that man's needs for good housing, food, water, and air are interrelated. For example, you might point out that sometimes some people want to use an area of land for housing while others want to use the same land for raising food. Then two good purposes are competing for the use of the same land. Stress the fact that wise planning and cooperation are necessary to satisfy the needs of the greatest number of people with the limited resources of the earth that are available.

Encourage the pupils to answer the "Think for Yourself" questions on pages 394, 395, and 396. Also remind the pupils to carry out the first class activity suggested under "Things to Do" on page 406.

Going Further You might have the pupils discuss the problems of clean air and water in their community. If the pupils do not have any ideas on this subject, you might ask questions such as the following.

1. Are any buildings in your community blackened from smoke and soot?
2. Does smog ever darken the sky in your community?
3. Does being out in the air in your community ever make your eyes hurt or water?
4. Are there any signs posted by rivers or streams in your community giving a warning that the water is polluted or unsafe for swimming?

TEACHING HELPS—MEETING THE NEED FOR MATERIALS, pages 397-400

CONCEPTS

1. Man's uses of the earth's natural resources are increasing in both variety and amount.
2. Man is constantly looking for new sources of natural resources.
3. Today man is using many improved methods of processing the earth's resources in order to conserve them as long as possible.

Recommended Procedure

Getting Started You might begin by asking the pupils how their lives might be affected if the United States should run out of such materials as coal, petroleum, and wood. They may not at first think that their lives would be affected very much. You might get them to see the seriousness of such a situation by pointing out that much of the electricity used in people's homes and in business and industry is produced by using coal. You might mention that some substitutes for wood, such as plastics, are produced from petroleum. Certainly a lack of petroleum to use in the family automobile would probably be seen by the pupils as constituting a real catastrophe.

Developing the Lesson You might have the pupils study the material in "Coal," "Petroleum and natural gas," and "Lumber" separately. Begin by having the pupils study page 397 to learn about man's need for coal. In a class discussion stress (1) how coal is mined today, (2) how modern mining methods affect workers in the coal industry, and (3) how coal is transported long distances to where it is used.

The part of the lesson on "Petroleum and natural gas" covers page 398 and page 399 to "Lumber." Have the pupils study this material to discover (1) why man's supply of petroleum and natural gas is a problem and (2) what new uses man is making of petroleum today. Impress upon the pupils the importance of carefully studying the graphs on page 398 and answering the questions that are contained in the copy about them. Discuss pupils' answers to the questions in the copy. Emphasize the importance of wise use and conservation of man's sources of petroleum and natural gas.

The last part of the lesson is on "Lumber." Ask the pupils to study the remainder of page 399 and all of page 400 to find out (1) what one of man's major needs for lumber is, (2) what kind of trees produce much of man's lumber and plywood, and (3) what man is doing today to conserve his sources of lumber. Discuss these things with the class. You might point out that, unlike coal, petroleum, and natural gas, man can replenish his sources of lumber and plywood but that many years are required to do so.

Concluding the Lesson In a class discussion emphasize the fact that conservation of coal, petroleum, natural gas, and lumber is a matter that concerns all of us, not just conservation specialists. Point out how man's waste of these materials tends to place increased demands upon the supplies of them. Encourage the pupils to answer the "Think for Yourself" questions on page 400.

Going Further You might have the pupils look in newspapers, magazines, pamphlets, and books for information and pictures on coal, petroleum, natural gas, and lumber. You might suggest that they concentrate on (1) the known supply of these materials, (2) the methods of getting these materials, (3) the ways of transporting them, (4) some of the products made from them, and (5) the methods currently being employed in conserving them. If good pictures, charts, or graphs are found, they might be cut out and posted on a class bulletin board. If these things are in a book, perhaps they can be duplicated.

TEACHING HELPS—GOVERNMENT AND SOCIAL CHANGE, pages 401-405

CONCEPTS

1. Governments today are taking some responsibilities for providing their people with better living conditions.
2. Cooperation among the nations of the world is necessary for a safe and healthy environment.

Recommended Procedure

Getting Started You might begin by asking the pupils for their opinions on whether the local, state, and federal governments in our country should help people and why or why not. Encourage the pupils to offer specific examples of how the government might help.

Developing the Lesson Have the pupils study from the top of page 401 to "Cooperation among nations" on page 404 to discover some of the ways governments today are helping their people have better living conditions and a safer environment. In a discussion with the class, stress the fact that the governments of many countries are helping their people have better lives. Also stress the ways in which sociologists, economists, and political scientists are interested in government plans and projects for helping people.

Next have the pupils study the remainder of page 404 and all of page 405 to learn some of the ways that nations cooperate with one another and why it is vitally important that they learn to cooperate even more. In a class discussion emphasize the fact that in today's world —with many nuclear weapons—what one nation does may affect many other nations.

Concluding the Lesson In a class discussion you might help the pupils understand why nations sometimes act the way that they do. Point out the fact that, since nations are made up of people, they often behave like people. In other words, just as people sometimes get angry or become jealous of others, so, too, do na-

tions. And, as people sometimes cooperate, so do nations. Stress the fact that the people of our nation and all the world's nations need to work hard to remove the causes of anger and jealousy in the world and to promote ways of cooperating for the good of all mankind.

Have the pupils answer the "Think for Yourself" questions on page 405 and do the second class activity suggested under "Things to Do" on page 406.

Going Further You might have the class think of several ways that people in their community are helped by the local, state, or federal governments. The pupils have undoubtedly seen meat-inspection stamps and heard announcements on radio or television about the Federal Communications Commission. They probably know people receiving social security benefits. They may be aware of local laws controlling air and water pollution. You and the class working together might make a list on the chalkboard of all the ways suggested.

EVALUATION, CHAPTER 22

Have the pupils respond to the following statement: The ways men go about meeting the challenges of people's social and physical needs and of living in a cooperative world will greatly affect the quality, and probably the length, of their life. The responses that pupils make to the above statement will help you discover their level of understanding of Chapter 22.

CONCLUDING THE UNIT

Read and discuss with the pupils Part 4 of the class project on page 406. Make sure all the pupils have an opportunity to share the things they have learned by doing this project.

Pages 407 and 408 present material that can be used in reviewing the unit and in evaluating learnings. See the annotations on those pages for specific suggestions about their use.

Test 1—A Look at the Social Sciences

(Use as test for textbook pages 6-39.)

NAME _____

Match each word in the first column below with a statement in the second column. Do this by writing the correct letter in the blank at the left.

f 1. anthropologists

c 2. economists

d 3. geographers

e 4. historians

a 5. political scientists

b 6. sociologists

a. Social scientists who are especially interested in man's relationship to his government

b. Social scientists who ask questions about the ways in which various groups affect man

c. Social scientists who study how people and nations use their resources to satisfy their needs

d. Social scientists who ask questions concerning how the earth affects man and how man affects the earth

e. Social scientists who are especially involved in studying the record of past events

f. Social scientists who make excavations to try to find information about man's early ancestors

Which answer to each of the following questions is best? Write the letter of the answer you choose in the blank at the left.

b 7. Which sentence tells what some sociologists have discovered about the cities of the past?
   a. They were well planned.   **b.** They were hardly planned at all.
       c. They were so well planned that they became a problem.

c 8. Which city is the capital of Brazil today?
   a. Rio de Janeiro   **b.** Cidade Livre   **c.** Brasília

b 9. Which sentence describes the size of Brazil?
  a. It is the smallest country in South America.
  b. It is the largest country in South America.
  c. It is about the same size as most other South American countries.

c 10. Which of the following is a primary source for historians?
  a. a history book   b. a biographical movie   c. a diary

a 11. Which word describes the divisions of Brasília's residential areas?
  a. superblocks   b. candangos   c. *favelas*

a 12. With what kind of people did the city of Brasília begin?
  a. the young   b. the middle aged   c. the elderly

c 13. Which of the following words means the study of population concentration and movement?
  a. urban   b. poll   c. demography

Which of the following sentences are true? Write **T** in the blank at the left of the sentences you choose. Write **O** before the other sentences.

T 14. The social needs of people must become the most important part of city planning.

O 15. People and nations have unlimited resources.

O 16. Brasília has many large industries.

T 17. The earth is continually changing.

T 18. Environment means the surrounding conditions and influences that affect man.

T 19. Piltdown Man was a fraud.

T 20. Brazil's government is very much like that of the United States.

SCORE CHART

Number of Answers_____20

Number Right_____ _____

Score (Number Right × 5)_____ _____

Test 2—Man Before History
(Use as test for textbook pages 40-77.)

NAME ....

Which answer to each of the following questions is best? Write the letter of the answer you choose in the blank at the left.

C 1. Which of the following does *Homo sapiens* mean?
    a. erect man   **b.** handy man   **c.** thinking man

b 2. Which material did early man use to make most of his tools?
    a. clay   **b.** stone   **c.** steel

a 3. Which of the following is an example of man today having a highly primitive type of life?
    a. the Arunta   **b.** the Bedouin   **c.** the Cro-Magnon

C 4. During the New Stone Age, man began to develop a new way of life based upon which of the following?
    a. fishing   **b.** hunting   **c.** agriculture

a 5. Which sentence tells what happened to the population in most New Stone Age villages?
    a. It increased.   **b.** It decreased.   **c.** It remained unchanged.

a 6. With which of the following was man in the Old Stone Age most concerned?
    a. the stars   **b.** the seasons   **c.** the animals

a 7. Near which of the following were New Stone Age villages usually located?
    a. a supply of water   **b.** a trade route   **c.** a forest area

b 8. Which town below is the oldest known town?
    a. Jarmo   **b.** Jericho   **c.** Iraq

Which of the following sentences are true? Write **T** in the blank at the left of the sentences you choose. Write **O** before the other sentences.

T 9. All modern men are part of the species we call *Homo sapiens*.

T 10. As glaciers advanced and retreated, plant and animal life changed in many areas of the world.

T 11. Environment can limit man's choices.

O 12. All cultures in the same environment are the same.

O 13. Exactly how man first learned to plant and raise crops has been discovered by the social scientists.

T 14. Man in both the Old Stone Age and the New Stone Age worshiped spirits found in nature.

Match each group of words in the first column below with a statement in the second column. Do this by writing the correct letter in the blank at the left.

f 15. prehistoric period   a. The Old Stone Age

d 16. division of labor   b. The spread of knowledge of cultural achievements

b 17. cultural diffusion   c. The Middle Stone Age

c 18. Mesolithic period   d. Dividing work into different jobs

a 19. Paleolithic period   e. The New Stone Age

e 20. Neolithic period   f. The entire period of early man before writing and written history

SCORE CHART

Number of Answers _____ 20

Number Right _____ _____

Score (Number Right × 5) _____ _____

Test 3—Ancient Civilizations

(Use as test for textbook pages 78-121.)

NAME ....

One of the words in the box belongs in each sentence below. Write the proper word where it belongs.

| Cuneiform | Dynasty | Hieroglyphic | Pharoahs | Scribes | Technology |

1. *Pharoahs* .... were kings of ancient Egypt.

2. *Dynasty* .... means a series of rulers all from one family.

3. *Cuneiform* .... writing, which uses wedge-shaped characters, is considered to be the first writing developed by man.

4. *Scribes* .... were educated men who served as lesser officials in some ancient governments.

5. *Technology* .... refers to the tools that are developed by a group of people and the ways the people use these tools.

6. *Hieroglyphic* .... writing, which consists of pictures, was developed by the ancient Egyptians.

Which answer to each of the following questions is best? Write the letter of the answer you choose in the blank at the left.

b 7. Which statement gives the conditions that some social scientists believe helped in the development of man's first civilization?

    a. a good supply of fur-bearing animals and a cool climate
    b. an abundance of rich, fertile land and a warm climate
    c. a great supply of trees and other plants and a hot climate

b 8. To which social class did the largest number of Sumerians belong?

    a. the upper class   **b.** the middle class   **c.** the third class *a* 9. For which reason did ancient societies establish law courts?

    a. to handle disputes   **b.** to code laws   **c.** to make laws

b 10. For which purpose do the homes in the cities of Mohenjo-Daro and Harappa seem to have been built?

    a. for appearance   **b.** for use   **c.** for monuments

b 11. Which people invented the first wheeled vehicle?

    a. the Egyptians   **b.** the Sumerians   **c.** the people of the Indus Valley

c 12. Crimes against which of the following were considered the most serious crimes in both the Sumerian and the Egyptian societies?

    a. the family   **b.** the school   **c.** the government

b 13. A surplus of which of the following was the basis for each ancient civilization?

    a. workers   **b.** crops   **c.** ships

c 14. Which fraction is the estimate of the adult people in the world today who are farmers?

    a. one-fourth   **b.** one-third   **c.** one-half

Which of the following sentences are true? Write **T** in the blank at the left of the sentences you choose. Write **O** before the other sentences.

T 15. The world's first civilization developed in Sumer about 3400 B.C.

O 16. Because of the flooding of the Euphrates River, the Sumerians had no need for an irrigation system.

O 17. During the time that ancient Egypt was isolated, Egyptian culture changed very rapidly.

T 18. The Egyptians believed in life after death.

T 19. Religious beliefs played an important part in the development of governing structures in the Egyptian, Sumerian, and Indus societies.

T 20. As people in ancient societies specialized in certain jobs, production increased.

SCORE CHART

Number of Answers..20

Number Right.. _____

Score (Number Right × 5)................... _____

Test 4—*Eastern and Western Civilizations*

(Use as test for textbook pages 122-173.)

NAME ....

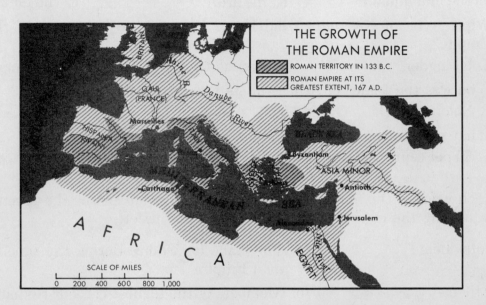

Use the map to decide which of the following sentences are true. Write **T** in the blank at the left of the sentences you choose. Write **O** before the other sentences.

O 1. The Roman Empire was larger in 133 B.C. than it was in 167 A.D.

T 2. During the time of the Roman Empire, Spain was known as Hispania.

T 3. Britain was part of the Roman Empire in 167 A.D.

T 4. The Roman Empire included all the countries located along the Mediterranean Sea.

O 5. The distance from Rome to Byzantium was about 600 miles.

Which answer to each of the following questions is best? Write the letter of the answer you choose in the blank at the left.

b 6. Which sentence describes the land of Greece?

    a. It is very flat.   **b.** It is very mountainous.   **c.** It is very sandy.

_a_ 7. Which of the following is the basic unit of Hindu society?

    a. the family   **b.** the individual   **c.** the government

_c_ 8. Which condition made a person a citizen of Athens?

    a. being born in Athens   **b.** paying a certain sum of money

            c. having parents who were Athenian citizens

_b_ 9. Which of the following was the most important unit in Spartan society?

    a. the individual   **b.** the army   **c.** the family

_b_ 10. Which type of government did Rome have at the beginning of the Roman Empire?

    a. a kingdom   **b.** a republic   **c.** a direct democracy

_c_ 11. Who was the leader of Athens at its highest point of democracy?

    a. Solon   **b.** Augustus   **c.** Pericles

_a_ 12. What per cent of the land in China is not good for agriculture?

    a. 70 per cent   **b.** 50 per cent   **c.** 30 per cent

Match each word in the first column below with a statement in the second column. Do this by writing the correct letter in the blank at the left.

_d_ 13. aqueducts

    a. The name for France during the time of the Roman Empire

_f_ 14. Athens

    b. Members of the highest class in Roman society

_h_ 15. bureaucracy

    c. A military Greek city-state

_g_ 16. caste

    d. Channels or pipelines built by the ancient Romans to bring water into the cities

_a_ 17. Gaul

    e. Members of the third class in Roman society

_b_ 18. patricians

    f. A democratic Greek city-state

_e_ 19. plebeians

    g. The class system of Hindu society

_c_ 20. Sparta

    h. A type of government in which much of the actual work is done by numerous officials

SCORE CHART

Number of Answers _____ 20

Number Right _____ _____

Score (Number Right × 5) _____ _____

Special Test—The Social Studies and Our World

(Use as test for textbook pages 6-173.)

NAME ....

One of the words in the box belongs in each sentence below. Write the proper word where it belongs.

| Demography | Glaciers | Guilds | Rajahs | Ziggurats |

1. *Guilds* were formed by craftsmen to set standards for the products they made.

2. *Ziggurats* were built by the Sumerians to please the gods of their city-states.

3. *Demography* is the study of population concentration and movement.

4. *Glaciers* covered large parts of the earth during the Pleistocene Epoch.

5. *Rajahs* became the kings or rulers of states created in India by joining villages together.

Which of the following sentences are true? Write **T** in the blank at the left of the sentences you choose. Write **O** before the other sentences.

O 6. Many of our natural resources such as coal, iron, and oil are unlimited.

O 7. The remains of man's earliest tools have been found in North America and South America.

T 8. Geography played a large part in determining where a New Stone Age settlement was located.

T 9. Revolts of the people against ancient governments were very rare.

T 10. The Roman Empire brought unity and stability to its part of the world.

Match each word or group of words in the first column below with a statement in the second column. Do this by writing the correct letter in the blank at the left.

e 11. civilization

a. A form of government in which the people elect representatives to carry on the work of the government

c 12. pebble tools

b. Accounts of events written after the events have taken place

d 13. primary sources

c. Smooth stones worn down by water that were used as tools by early man

a 14. republic

d. Accounts of events written by eyewitnesses

b 15. secondary sources

e. The culture of a people who build cities and have at least part of their population living in cities

Which answer to each of the following questions is best? Write the letter of the answer you choose in the blank at the left.

b 16. Which kind of climate does Brazil's new capital city have?
  a. hot   b. mild   c. cold

c 17. For which reason did early man usually have no permanent home?
  a. He was a fighter.   b. He was a thief.
              c. He was a hunter and a food gatherer.

c 18. To which class did the rulers, priests, and other governing officials in ancient civilizations belong?
  a. the lower class   b. the middle class   c. the upper class

a 19. Which of the following did each of the major ancient civilizations rely upon for making long trips with heavy loads?
  a. water transportation   b. wheeled vehicles   c. animals

a 20. Which language was the official language of the Romans?
  a. Latin   b. Greek   c. Italian

SCORE CHART

Number of Answers................................20

Number Right..................................... _____

Score (Number Right × 5)................. _____

Test 5—Man in the Middle Ages

(Use as test for textbook pages 174-223.)

NAME ....

One of the words in the box belongs in each sentence below. Write the proper word where it belongs.

| Chivalry | Huns | Manors | Serfs | Shoguns | Vassals |

1. *Chivalry* _____ was a code of behavior the nobles of Europe during the Middle Ages were expected to follow.

2. *Vassals* _____ received their land from some lord in return for pledging their loyalty to him.

3. *Shoguns* _____ ruled Japan with great military power during the 1200's.

4. *Serfs* _____ were semifree peasants who could not be sold to another lord.

5. *Manors* _____ in Europe during the Middle Ages included both the land and the buildings of a noble.

6. *Huns* _____ were barbarians who invaded Europe around A.D. 350.

Which answer to each of the following questions is best? Write the letter of the answer you choose in the blank at the left.

__a__ 7. On which of the following did a person's place in the social system of Europe during the Middle Ages usually depend?

    a. birth   **b.** education   **c.** job skills

__b__ 8. Which type of leader did the Incas have?

    a. a president   **b.** a king   **c.** a chief

__c__ 9. Which of the following did the Aztecs believe was necessary in order to be successful in war?

    a. soldiers on horses   **b.** large cannons   **c.** human sacrifices

b 10. By which way did the peasants help the cities of Europe to grow?

    a. by building many churches   **b.** by producing surplus crops

                  c. by organizing political groups

a 11. Which sentence gives one reason why European cities in the Middle Ages became overcrowded?

    a. They were built within walls.   **b.** They were overrun by factory workers.

             c. They were settled by many immigrants.

b 12. Which occupation did most people in Europe follow during the Middle Ages?

    a. trading   **b.** farming   **c.** tailoring

c 13. Which city named below is the largest city in the world today?

    a. Peking, China   **b.** London, England   **c.** Tokyo, Japan

Which of the following sentences are true? Write **T** in the blank at the left of the sentences you choose. Write **O** before the other sentences.

O 14. During the period of history known as the Dark Ages, the people in Europe had a strong central government.

T 15. The Roman Catholic Church became a powerful force in western Europe during the Middle Ages.

T 16. India's way of life changed very little during the Middle Ages.

T 17. As Europe was going through the Dark Ages, China began to develop a highly advanced civilization.

T 18. During the time that feudalism existed in Europe, the Japanese also developed a form of feudalism.

T 19. The increase of trade after the Crusades led to the growth of cities in Europe.

O 20. The Mayas, the Aztecs, and the Incas built no large cities.

SCORE CHART

Number of Answers..20

Number Right.. _____

Score (Number Right × 5).................. _____

Test 6—The World of 1500 to 1850

(Use as test for textbook pages 224-287.)

NAME ....

Match each word or group of words in the first column below with a statement in the second column. Do this by writing the correct letter in the blank at the left.

C 1. balance of power

a. Freedom to move from one social class to another

f 2. favorable balance of trade

b. Those materials suitable for manufacturing or processing

d 3. industrialization

c. A condition that exists when weaker countries join forces to protect themselves against a strong country

e 4. nationalism

d. The use of new sources of power and machinery to produce goods

b 5. raw materials

e. Patriotic feelings or devotion toward the interests of one's own country

a 6. social mobility

f. A condition that exists when a country's exports are greater than its imports

Which of the following sentences are true? Write **T** in the blank at the left of the sentences you choose. Write **O** before the other sentences.

T 7. People in the middle class were important in the development and spread of democratic ideas.

T 8. During the 1600's and 1700's, the Chinese were interested in preserving their ancient culture.

T 9. Most of the people of Kanem-Bornu were peasants.

O 10. The European merchants described Benin as a dirty and poorly kept city.

O 11. Explorers who got to India and China by sailing west discovered that a westerly route to the East was shorter than an easterly route.

_T_ 12. Bastille Day is celebrated as national independence day in France.

_O_ 13. China was finally successful in the 1800's in isolating itself from the rest of the world.

Which answer to each of the following questions is best? Write the letter of the answer you choose in the blank at the left.

_b_ 14. Of which class did the important merchants and shopkeepers become members?

    a. the upper class   **b.** the middle class   **c.** the lower class

_c_ 15. Which part of society was more important to the Chinese than any other part?

    a. the church   **b.** the government   **c.** the family

_a_ 16. Which country led Europe in industrialization?

    a. England   **b.** France   **c.** Spain

_b_ 17. Which country produced very fine articles of porcelain?

    a. India   **b.** China   **c.** Benin

_b_ 18. Which condition in India helped the European countries take over large parts of India?

    a. a very small population   **b.** a lack of political unity
                 c. a lack of economic resources

_a_ 19. Which kind of rulers did the people of Benin and of Kanem-Bornu have during the 1600's?

    a. kings   **b.** tribal chiefs   **c.** presidents

_a_ 20. Which leader named below is thought of as the "George Washington of Latin America"?

    a. Simón Bolívar   **b.** José de San Martín   **c.** Philip II

SCORE CHART

Number of Answers _____ 20

Number Right _____ _____

Score (Number Right × 5) _____ _____

Test 7—The World Since 1850

(Use as test for textbook pages 288-351.)

NAME ....

One of the words in the box belongs in each sentence below. Write the proper word where it belongs.

| Capitalists | Communes | Corporations | Czars | Proletarians | Radicals |

1. *Proletarians* are members of the working class as defined by Karl Marx.

2. *Corporations* are used for organizing the business investments of many people known as stockholders.

3. *Czars* ruled Russia until 1917.

4. *Capitalists* are people who own part of or all of a business or industry.

5. *Communes* were organized by the communists in China to control the lives and the economic productivity of peasant farmers.

6. *Radicals* are people who favor extreme social or other changes.

Which answer to each of the following questions is best? Write the letter of the answer you choose in the blank at the left.

a 7. For which reason did most factory workers move to the cities at the beginning of the Industrial Revolution?
  a. to be near their jobs **b.** to be near recreational facilities
  c. to be near schools and libraries

b 8. Which sentence tells what happened to the size of families as people moved to the cities?
  a. It increased. **b.** It decreased. **c.** It remained the same size.

a 9. In which country did women first win the right to vote?
  a. Australia **b.** Sweden **c.** the United States

C 10. Which of the following greatly influences what goods are produced by manufacturers in a free enterprise system?

    a. the government   **b.** the church   **c.** the consumers

a 11. Which statement gives the problems that are common to most of the world's economically poor countries?

    a. increasing population and lack of food
    b. decreasing population and a lack of consumers
    c. a stable population and a high rate of production

b 12. For which people was Israel created as a homeland in 1948?

    a. the Arabs   **b.** the Jews   **c.** the Nazis

C 13. Which organization has tried to keep peace in the world since World War II?

    a. the League of Nations   **b.** the Gosplan   **c.** the United Nations

Which of the following sentences are true? Write **T** in the blank at the left of the sentences you choose. Write **O** before the other sentences.

O 14. As a result of division of labor, many workers gained a feeling of satisfaction in their jobs.

T 15. People who believe in communism think that society can only be changed by the violent overthrow of existing governments.

O 16. Most Russian peasants have liked life on the collective farms.

O 17. The communists in China are strengthening family loyalties.

T 18. Private ownership of property is allowed in a socialistic economic system.

T 19. Communism in the Soviet Union has not equaled the performance of capitalism in the United States.

T 20. Most African nations are forming one-party governments with strong, popular leaders.

SCORE CHART

Number of Answers...........................20

Number Right......................... _____

Score (Number Right × 5)............ _____

Test 8—Man in a Changing World

(Use as test for textbook pages 352-408.)

NAME _____

Use the table to decide which answer to each of the following questions is best. Write the letter of the answer you choose in the blank at the left.

THE PEOPLE ON EARTH—MILLIONS					
Year	Asia	Africa	Europe incl. USSR	Western Hemisphere and Oceania	World
A.D.1	150	50	45	5	250
1650	300	100	90	10	500
1750	450	100	130	20	700
1850	660	100	290	50	1100
1900	900	120	380	200	1600
1950	1350	200	600	350	2500
2000*	3900	500	1000	900	6300

*A conservative estimate

_*a*_ 1. In which place is the population expected to increase the most between 1950 and the year 2000?

   a. Asia   **c.** Europe
          b. Africa

_*c*_ 2. Which fifty-year period shows the world population increasing the most?

   a. 1850 to 1900   **b.** 1900 to 1950   **c.** 1950 to 2000

_*a*_ 3. During the years from 1650 to 1850, what was the constant size of Africa's population?

   a. 100 million   **b.** 200 million   **c.** 500 million

_*c*_ 4. Which place had the smallest population in A.D. 1?

   a. Africa   **b.** Europe   **c.** the Western Hemisphere and Oceania

_*a*_ 5. Which place is expected to have the largest population by the year 2000?

   a. Asia   **b.** Africa   **c.** Europe

Which of the following sentences are true? Write **T** in the blank at the left of the sentences you choose. Write **O** before the other sentences.

_*T*_ 6. Today the rapidly increasing populations of the world must find places to live on their own continents rather than migrating to other continents.

_*T*_ 7. Increasing unemployment in a country generally leads to more poverty.

_T_ 8. Social scientists believe that overcrowding is bad for people.

_O_ 9. The distribution of rainfall in the world is very even.

_T_ 10. Many governments are helping people improve their living conditions.

_O_ 11. Low-sulfur coal produces much air pollution.

_O_ 12. Inversion is a process of removing soil from a place by natural forces.

_T_ 13. There is a world trend toward using machines to produce goods.

_T_ 14. Coal, oil, and gas are fossil fuels.

_T_ 15. Governments throughout the world are expected to reduce crime.

_T_ 16. Many people become unhappy because of overcrowding.

Which answer to each of the following questions is best? Write the letter of the answer you choose in the blank at the left.

_C_ 17. About what fraction of the earth's surface is covered by water?
   a. one-fourth   **b.** two-fourths   **c.** three-fourths

_C_ 18. Which country had the highest per capita Gross National Product in 1967?
   a. Japan   **b.** Brazil   **c.** the United States

_b_ 19. On which continent are many of the new nations of the world located?
   a. Antarctica   **b.** Africa   **c.** North America

_a_ 20. Which country gets fresh water mostly by desalinization of seawater?
   a. Aruba   **b.** Venezuela   **c.** India

SCORE CHART

Number of Answers _____ 20

Number Right _____ _____

Score (Number Right × 5) _____ _____

T140

Special Test—The Social Studies and Our World

(Use as test for textbook pages 174-408.)

NAME ....

One of the words in the box belongs in each sentence below. Write the proper word where it belongs.

Allah	Calories	Manillas	Shintoism	Socialists

1. *Manillas* were used as money by the people of Benin.

2. *Shintoism* is an early religion of Japan that is still practiced in that country today.

3. *Calories* are units of energy supplied by food.

4. *Socialists* expect the government to own the means of production.

5. *Allah* is worshiped by the Muslims or followers of Islam.

Which of the following sentences are true? Write **T** in the blank at the left of the sentences you choose. Write **O** before the other sentences.

T 6. Many peasant farmers during the Middle Ages in Europe were bound for life to the land which they farmed.

T 7. The University of Lima is the oldest university in the Americas.

O 8. Laws correcting poor social conditions were passed sooner in the United States than in any of the countries of Europe.

T 9. Countries with rapidly increasing populations have great difficulty in increasing their per capita Gross National Product.

T 10. Sociologists and anthropologists believe that much crime is a product of a changing society, such as the urbanization that has been occurring during the past twenty-five years.

Match each word in the first column below with a statement in the second column. Do this by writing the correct letter in the blank at the left.

d 11. barbarian

a. The protection and wise use of natural resources

e 12. capitalism

b. The political system in which authority was held by the nobles who ruled over large pieces of land in Europe during the Middle Ages

a 13. conservation

c. The economic system in which the resources and trade of colonies were used to benefit the home country

b 14. feudalism

d. A person who had not yet become civilized

c 15. mercantilism

e. An economic system in which manufacturers make goods they believe people will want to buy

Which answer to each of the following questions is best? Write the letter of the answer you choose in the blank at the left.

b 16. The need for which of the following helped to bring about the feudal system in Europe?

    a. foreign goods   **b.** protection   **c.** religious change

a 17. How did most of the people in villages in western Europe during the 1700's make their living?

    a. by farming   **b.** by trading   **c.** by working in factories

c 18. Which of the following did European countries expect to get from their colonies in America?

    a. manufactured goods   **b.** factory workers   **c.** raw materials

b 19. Which sentence tells the population problem which Nigeria has?

    a. It grows too slowly.   **b.** It grows too fast.

    c. It does not grow at all.

c 20. About which fraction of the earth's land area is too dry or too cold for raising crops?

    a. three-eighths   **b.** five-eighths   **c.** seven-eighths

SCORE CHART

Number of Answers _____20

Number Right _____ _____

Score (Number Right × 5) _____ _____

Final Test—The Social Studies and Our World

(Use as test for textbook pages 6-408.)

NAME ....

One of the words in the box belongs in each sentence below. Write the proper word where it belongs.

Athens	Brasília	Erosion	Inversion	Israel

1. *Israel* .... was created as a homeland for the Jews in 1948.

2. *Inversion* .... sometimes creates a situation that is very dangerous to man's health today because of air pollution.

3. *Athens* .... was a democratic Greek city-state.

4. *Erosion* .... of the earth's surface reduces the amount of land man has for raising food and for living space.

5. *Brasília* .... is the new capital of Brazil.

Which of the following sentences are true? Write **T** in the blank at the left of the sentences you choose. Write **O** before the other sentences.

T 6. People and nations have limited resources.

T 7. When man began building villages, he usually located them near a supply of water.

O 8. The first wheeled vehicle was invented by the Egyptians.

O 9. Most of the people of Europe during the Middle Ages were traders.

O 10. France led Europe into the Industrial Revolution.

Match each word in the first column below with a statement in the second column. Do this by writing the correct letter in the blank at the left.

d 11. chivalry

a. People who favor extreme social or other changes

c 12. plebeians

b. The tools that are developed by a group of people and the ways the people use these tools

a 13. radicals

c. People belonging to the third, or common, class in Roman society

b 14. technology

d. A code of behavior the nobles of Europe during the Middle Ages were expected to follow

e 15. vassals

e. People who received their land from some lord in return for pledging their loyalty to him

Which answer to each of the following questions is best? Write the letter of the answer you choose in the blank at the left.

c 16. To which species do all modern men belong?

    a. *Homo habilis*   **b.** *Zinjanthropus*   **c.** *Homo sapiens*

a 17. In which place did the world's first civilization develop?

    a. Sumer   **b.** Egypt   **c.** Indus

b 18. Which country celebrates Bastille Day as national independence day?

    a. Germany   **b.** France   **c.** China

b 19. The people of which social class were most important in the development and spread of democratic ideas?

    a. the upper class   **b.** the middle class   **c.** the lower class

c 20. Which sentence describes the distribution of rainfall in the world?

    a. It is very even.   **b.** It is very heavy.   **c.** It is very uneven.

SCORE CHART

Number of Answers _____ 20

Number Right _____ _____

Score (Number Right × 5) _____ _____

456789   098765